Visual Speech Recognition:
Lip Segmentation and Mapping

Alan Wee-Chung Liew
Griffith University, Australia

Shilin Wang
Shanghai Jiaotong University, China

Medical Information Science
REFERENCE

MEDICAL INFORMATION SCIENCE REFERENCE

Hershey · New York

Director of Editorial Content:	Kristin Klinger
Director of Production:	Jennifer Neidig
Managing Editor:	Jamie Snavely
Assistant Managing Editor:	Carole Coulson
Typesetter:	Amanda Appicello
Cover Design:	Lisa Tosheff
Printed at:	Yurchak Printing Inc.

Published in the United States of America by
Information Science Reference (an imprint of IGI Global)
701 E. Chocolate Avenue, Suite 200
Hershey PA 17033
Tel: 717-533-8845
Fax: 717-533-8661
E-mail: cust@igi-global.com
Web site: http://www.igi-global.com

and in the United Kingdom by
Information Science Reference (an imprint of IGI Global)
3 Henrietta Street
Covent Garden
London WC2E 8LU
Tel: 44 20 7240 0856
Fax: 44 20 7379 0609
Web site: http://www.eurospanbookstore.com

Library of Congress Cataloging-in-Publication Data

Liew, Alan Wee-Chung, 1968-

Visual speech recognition : lip segmentation and mapping / Alan Wee-Chung Liew and Shilin Wang, Editors.

p. cm.

Includes bibliographical references and index.

Summary: "This book introduces the readers to the various aspects of visual speech recognitions, including lip segmentation from video sequence, lip feature extraction and modeling, feature fusion and classifier design for visual speech recognition and speaker verification"-- Provided by publisher.

ISBN 978-1-60566-186-5 (hardcover) -- ISBN 978-1-60566-187-2 (ebook)

1. Automatic speech recognition. 2. Speech processing systems. I. Wang, Shilin. II. Title.

TK7895.S65L44 2009

006.4--dc22

2008037505

British Cataloguing in Publication Data
A Cataloguing in Publication record for this book is available from the British Library.

Editorial Advisory Board

List of Reviewers

Lynne E. Bernstein
House Ear Institute and University of Southern California, USA

Josef Bigun
Halmstad University, Sweden

Aggelos K. Katsaggelos
Northwestern University, USA

Costas Kotropoulos
University of Thessaloniki, Greece

Russell M. Mersereau
Georgia Institute of Technology, USA

Eric Petajan
CTO, VectorMAX Corporation, USA

Gerasimos Potamianos
IBM Thomas J. Watson Research Center, USA

Alice Caplier
GIPSA-lab, France

Sridha Sridharan
Queensland University of Technology, Australia

Say Wei Foo
Nanyang Technological University, Singapore

Patrice Delmas
University of Auckland, New Zealand

Hasan Ertan Cetingul
Johns Hopkins University, USA

Haibo Li
Umeå University, Sweden

Marc Lievin
SiCAT, Bonn, Germany

Jintao Jiang
House Ear Institute, USA

Thorsten Gernoth
Hamburg University of Technology, Germany

Alan Wee-Chung Liew
Griffith University. Australia

Shilin Wang
Shanghai Jiaotong University, China

Table of Contents

Section I
Introduction and Survey

Derek J. Shiell, Northwestern University, USA
Louis H. Terry, Northwestern University, USA
Petar S. Aleksic, Google Inc., USA
Aggelos K. Katsaggelos, Northwestern University, USA

Petar S. Aleksic, Google Inc., USA
Aggelos K. Katsaggelos, Northwestern University, USA

A. Caplier, GIPSA-lab/DIS, France
S. Stillittano, GIPSA-lab/DIS, France
C. Bouvier, GIPSA-lab/DIS, France
P. Y. Coulon, GIPSA-lab/DIS, France

Eric Petajan, VectorMAX Corporation, USA

Section II
Lip Modeling, Segmentation, and Feature Extraction

Section III
Visual Speech Recognition

Detailed Table of Contents

Section I
Introduction and Survey

Chapter I
> *Derek J. Shiell, Northwestern University, USA*
> *Louis H. Terry, Northwestern University, USA*
> *Petar S. Aleksic, Google Inc., USA*
> *Aggelos K. Katsaggelos, Northwestern University, USA*

The information imbedded in the visual dynamics of speech has the potential to improve the performance
of speech and speaker recognition systems. The information carried in the visual speech signal compliments the information in the acoustic speech signal, which is particularly beneficial in adverse acoustic
environments. Non-invasive methods using low-cost sensors can be used to obtain acoustic and visual
biometric signals, such as a person's voice and lip movement, with little user cooperation. These types
of unobtrusive biometric systems are warranted to promote widespread adoption of biometric technology in today's society. In this chapter, we describe the main components and theory of audio-visual and
visual-only speech and speaker recognition systems. Audio-visual corpora are described and a number
of speech and speaker recognition systems are reviewed. Finally, we discuss various open issues about
the system design and implementation, and present future research and development directions in this
area.

Chapter II
> *Petar S. Aleksic, Google Inc., USA*
> *Aggelos K. Katsaggelos, Northwestern University, USA*

There has been significant work on investigating the relationship between articulatory movements and vocal tract shape and speech acoustics (Fant, 1960; Flanagan, 1965; Narayanan & Alwan, 2000; Schroeter & Sondhi, 1994). It has been shown that there exists a strong correlation between face motion, and vocal tract shape and speech acoustics (Grant & Braida, 1991; Massaro & Stork, 1998; Summerfield, 1979, 1987, 1992; Williams & Katsaggelos, 2002; Yehia, Rubin, & Vatikiotis-Bateson, 1998). In particular, dynamic lip information conveys not only correlated but also complimentary information to the acoustic speech information. Its integration into an automatic speech recognition (ASR) system, resulting in an audio-visual (AV) system, can potentially increase the system's performance. Although visual speech information is usually used together with acoustic information, there are applications where visual-only (V-only) ASR systems can be employed achieving high recognition rates. Such include small vocabulary ASR (digits, small number of commands, etc.) and ASR in the presence of adverse acoustic conditions. The choice and accurate extraction of visual features strongly affect the performance of AV and V-only ASR systems. The establishment of lip features for speech recognition is a relatively new research topic. Although a number of approaches can be used for extracting and representing visual lip information, unfortunately, limited work exists in the literature in comparing the relative performance of different features. In this chapter, we will describe various approaches for extracting and representing important visual features, review existing systems, evaluate their relative performance in terms of speech and speaker recognition rates, and discuss future research and development directions in this area.

Lip segmentation is the first step of any audio-visual speech reading system. The accuracy of this segmentation has a major influence on the performances of the global system. But this is a very difficult task. First of all, lip shape can undergo strong deformations during a speech sequence. As many other image processing algorithms, the segmentation task is also influenced by the illumination conditions and by the orientation of the object to be segmented. In this chapter, we present an overview about lip modeling and lip segmentation (region-based and contour-based methods). We limit our study to the problem of lip segmentation in frontal faces. Section 1 gives an overview about the chrominance information that is used for lip segmentation and a comparison between different chrominance cues is proposed. Section 2 presents region-based approaches and training steps. Section 3 focuses on contour-based approaches and parametric lip models. Section 4 inventories methods for lip segmentation accuracy evaluation. Some specific applications are briefly presented in section 5.

Chapter IV

Automatic Speech Recognition (ASR) is the most natural input modality from humans to machines. When the hands are busy or a full keyboard is not available speech input is especially in demand. Since the most compelling application scenarios for ASR include noisy environments (mobile phones, public kiosks, cars), visual speech processing must be incorporated to provide robust performance. This chapter motivates and describes the MPEG-4 Face and Body Animation (FBA) standard for representing visual speech data as part of a whole virtual human specification. The super low bit-rate FBA codec included with the standard enables thin clients to access processing and communication services over any network including enhanced visual communication, animated entertainment, man-machine dialog, and audio/visual speech recognition.

Section II
Lip Modeling, Segmentation, and Feature Extraction

As the first step of many visual speech recognition and visual speaker authentication systems, robust and accurate lip region segmentation is of vital importance for lip image analysis. However, most of the current techniques break down when dealing with lip images with complex and inhomogeneous background region such as mustaches and beards. In order to solve this problem, a Multi-class, Shape-guided FCM (MS-FCM) clustering algorithm is proposed in this chapter. In the proposed approach, one cluster is set for the lip region and a combination of multiple clusters for the background which generally includes the skin region, lip shadow or beards. With the spatial distribution of the lip cluster, a spatial penalty term considering the spatial location information is introduced and incorporated into the objective function such that pixels having similar color but located in different regions can be differentiated. Experimental results show that the proposed algorithm provides accurate lip-background partition even for the images with complex background features.

An algorithm for lip contour extraction is presented in this chapter. A colour video sequence of a speaker's face is acquired under natural lighting conditions without any particular set-up, make-up, or markers. The first step is to perform a logarithmic colour transform from RGB to HI colour space. Next, a segmentation algorithm extracts the lip area by combining motion with red hue information into a spatio-temporal neighbourhood. The lip's region of interest, semantic information, and relevant boundaries points are then automatically extracted. A good estimate of mouth corners sets active contour initialisation close to the boundaries to extract. Finally, a set of adapted active contours use an open form with curvature discontinuities along the mouth corners for the outer lip contours, a line-type open active contour when the mouth is closed, and closed active contours with lip shape constrained pressure balloon forces when the mouth is open. They are initialised with the results of the pre-processing stage. An accurate lip shape with inner and outer borders is then obtained with reliable quality results for various speakers under different acquisition conditions.

Chapter VII

Alfonso Gastelum, The University of Auckland, New Zealand, & Image Analysis Visualization Laboratory, CCADET-UNAM, Mexico
Patrice Delmas, The University of Auckland, New Zealand
Jorge Marquez, Image Analysis Visualization Laboratory, CCADET-UNAM, Mexico
Alexander Woodward, The University of Auckland, New Zealand
Jason James, The University of Auckland, New Zealand
Marc Lievin, Avid Technology Inc., Canada
Georgy Gimel'farb, The University of Auckland, New Zealand

This chapter describes a new user-specific 2D to 3D lip animation technique. 2D lip contour position and corresponding motion information are provided from a 2D lip contour extraction algorithm. Static face measurements are obtained from 3D scanners or stereovision systems. The data is combined to generate an initial subject-dependent 3D lip surface. The 3D lips are then modelled as a set of particles whose dynamic behaviour is governed by Smooth Particles Hydrodynamics. A set of forces derived from ellipsoid muscle encircling the lips simulates the muscles controlling the lips motion. The 3D lip model is comprised of more than 300 surface voxels and more than 1300 internal particles. The advantage of the particle system is the possibility of creating a more complex system than previously introduced surface models.

Chapter VIII

Shafiq ur Réhman, Umeå University, Sweden
Li Liu, Umeå University, Sweden
Haibo Li, Umeå University, Sweden

The purpose of this chapter is not to describe any lip analysis algorithms but rather to discuss some of the issues involved in evaluating and calibrating labeled lip features from human operators. In the chapter we question the common practice in the field: using manual lip labels directly as the ground truth for the evaluation of lip analysis algorithms. Our empirical results using an Expectation-Maximization procedure show that subjective noise in manual labelers can be quite significant in terms of quantifying both human and algorithm extraction performance. To train and evaluate a lip analysis system one can measure the performance of human operators and infer the "ground truth" from the manual labelers, simultaneously.

Section III
Visual Speech Recognition

Chapter IX

Constantine Kotropoulos, Aristotle University of Thessaloniki, Greece
Ioannis Pitas, Aristotle University of Thessaloniki, Greece

This chapter addresses both low and high level problems in visual speech processing and recognition. In particular, mouth region segmentation and lip contour extraction are addressed first. Next, visual speech recognition with parallel support vector machines and temporal Viterbi lattices is demonstrated on a small vocabulary task.

Chapter X

Patrick Lucey, Queensland University of Technology, Australia
Gerasimos Potamianos, IBM T. J. Watson Research Center, USA
Sridha Sridharan, Queensland University of Technology, Australia

It is well known that visual speech information extracted from video of the speaker's mouth region can improve performance of automatic speech recognizers, especially their robustness to acoustic degradation. However, the vast majority of research in this area has focused on the use of frontal videos of the speaker's face, a clearly restrictive assumption that limits the applicability of audio-visual automatic speech recognition (AVASR) technology in realistic human-computer interaction. In this chapter, we advance beyond the single-camera, frontal-view AVASR paradigm, investigating various important aspects of the visual speech recognition problem across multiple camera views of the speaker, expanding on our recent work. We base our study on an audio-visual database that contains synchronous frontal and profile views of multiple speakers, uttering connected digit strings. We first develop an appearance-based visual front-end that extracts features for frontal and profile videos in a similar fashion. Subsequently, we focus on three key areas concerning speech recognition based on the extracted features: (a) Comparing frontal and profile visual speech recognition performance to quantify any degradation across views; (b) Fusing the available synchronous camera views for improved recognition in scenarios where multiple views can be used; and (c) Recognizing visual speech using a single pose-invariant statistical model, regardless of camera view. In particular, for the latter, a feature normalization approach between poses is investigated. Experiments on the available database are reported in all above areas. To our knowledge, the chapter constitutes the first comprehensive study on the subject of visual speech recognition across multiple views.

Chapter XI

Say Wei Foo, Nanyang Technological University, Singapore
Liang Dong, National University of Singapore, Singapore

Visual speech recognition is able to supplement the information of speech sound to improve the accuracy of speech recognition. A viseme, which describes the facial and oral movements that occur alongside the voicing of a particular phoneme, is a supposed basic unit of speech in the visual domain. As in phonemes, there are variations for the same viseme expressed by different persons or even by the same person. A classifier must be robust to this kind of variation. In this chapter, we describe the Adaptively Boosted (AdaBoost) Hidden Markov Model (HMM) technique (Foo, 2004; Foo, 2003; Dong, 2002). By applying the AdaBoost technique to HMM modeling, a multi-HMM classifier that improves the robustness of HMM is obtained. The method is applied to identify context-independent and context-dependent visual speech units. Experimental results indicate that higher recognition accuracy can be attained using the AdaBoost HMM than that using conventional HMM.

Chapter XII

Say Wei Foo, Nanyang Technological University, Singapore
Liang Dong, National University of Singapore, Singapore

The basic building blocks of visual speech are the visemes. Unlike phonemes, the visemes are, however, confusable and easily distorted by the contexts in which they appear. Classifiers capable of distinguishing the minute difference among the different categories are desirable. In this chapter, we describe two Hidden Markov Model based techniques using the discriminative approach to increase the accuracy of visual speech recognition. The approaches investigated include Maximum Separable Distance (MSD) training strategy (Dong, 2005) and Two-channel training approach (Dong, 2005; Foo, 2003; Foo, 2002) The MSD training strategy and the Two-channel training approach adopt a proposed criterion function called separable distance to improve the discriminative power of an HMM. The methods are applied to identify confusable visemes. Experimental results indicate that higher recognition accuracy can be attained using these approaches than that using conventional HMM.

Chapter XIII

Wai Chee Yau, RMIT University, Australia
Dinesh Kant Kumar, RMIT University, Australia
Hans Weghorn, BA University of Cooperative Education Stuttgart, Germany

The performance of a visual speech recognition technique is greatly influenced by the choice of visual speech features. Speech information in the visual domain can be generally categorized into static (mouth appearance) and motion (mouth movement) features. This chapter reviews a number of computer-based lip-reading approaches using motion features. The motion-based visual speech recognition techniques can be broadly categorized into two types of algorithms: optical-flow and image subtraction. Image subtraction techniques have been demonstrated to outperform optical-flow based methods in lip-reading. The problem with image subtraction-based method using difference of frames (DOF) is that these features capture the changes in the images over time but do not indicate the direction of the mouth movement. New motion features to overcome the limitation of the conventional image subtraction-based techniques in visual speech recognition are presented in this chapter. The proposed approach extracts features by applying motion segmentation on image sequences. Video data are represented in a 2-D space using grayscale images named as motion history images (MHI). MHIs are spatio-temporal templates that implicitly encode the temporal component of mouth movement. Zernike moments are computed from MHIs as image descriptors and classified using support vector machines (SVMs). Experimental results demonstrate that the proposed technique yield a high accuracy in a phoneme classification task. The results suggest that dynamic information is important for visual speech recognition.

  Marion Dohen, GIPSA-lab, France
  Hélène Lœvenbruck, GIPSA-lab, France
  Harold Hill, ATR Cognitive Information Science Labs, Japan, & University of
    Wollongong, Australia

The aim of this chapter is to examine the possibility of extracting prosodic information from lip features. We used two lip feature measurement techniques in order to evaluate the "lip pattern" of prosodic focus in French. Two corpora with Subject-Verb-Object (SVO) sentences were designed. Four focus conditions (S, V, O or neutral) were elicited in a natural dialogue situation. In the first set of experiments, we recorded two speakers of French with front and profile video cameras. The speakers wore blue lipstick and facial markers. In the second set we recorded five speakers with a 3D optical tracker. An analysis of the lip features showed that visible articulatory lip correlates of focus exist for all speakers. Two types of patterns were observed: absolute and differential. A potential outcome of this study is to provide criteria for automatic visual detection of prosodic focus from lip data.

  Lynne E. Bernstein, House Ear Institute, Los Angeles, USA
  Jintao Jiang, House Ear Institute, Los Angeles, USA

The information in optical speech signals is phonetically impoverished compared to the information in acoustic speech signals that are presented under good listening conditions. But high lipreading scores among prelingually deaf adults inform us that optical speech signals are in fact rich in phonetic information. Hearing lipreaders are not as accurate as deaf lipreaders, but they too demonstrate perception of detailed optical phonetic information. This chapter briefly sketches the historical context of and impediments to knowledge about optical phonetics and visual speech perception (lipreading). We review findings on deaf and hearing lipreaders. Then we review recent results on relationships between optical speech signals and visual speech perception. We extend the discussion of these relationships to the development of visual speech synthesis. We advocate for a close relationship between visual speech perception research and development of synthetic visible speech.

Section IV
Visual Speaker Recognition

    H. Ertan Çetingül, John Hopkins University, USA
    Engin Erzin, Koç University, Turkey
    Yücel Yemez, Koç University, Turkey
    A. Murat Tekalp, Koç University, Turkey

We present a multimodal speaker identification system that integrates audio, lip texture and lip motion modalities, and we propose to use the "explicit" lip motion information that best represent the modality for the given problem. Our work is presented in two stages: First, we consider several lip motion feature candidates such as dense motion features on the lip region, motion features on the outer lip contour, and lip shape features. Meanwhile, we introduce our main contribution, which is a novel two-stage, spatial-temporal discrimination analysis framework designed to obtain the best lip motion features. In speech recognition, the best lip motion features provide the highest phoneme/word/phrase recognition rate, whereas for speaker identification, they result in the highest discrimination among speakers. Next, we investigate the benefits of the inclusion of the best lip motion features for multimodal recognition. Audio, lip texture, and lip motion modalities are fused by the reliability weighted summation (RWS) decision rule, and hidden Markov model (HMM)-based modeling is performed for both unimodal and multimodal recognition. Experimental results indicate that discriminative grid-based lip motion features are proved to be more valuable and provide additional performance gains in speaker identification.

    Maycel Isaac Faraj, Halmstad University, Sweden
    Josef Bigun, Halmstad University, Sweden

The present chapter reports on the use of lip motion as a stand alone biometric modality as well as a modality integrated with audio speech for identity recognition using digit recognition as a support. First, we estimate motion vectors from images of lip movements. The motion is modeled as the distribution of apparent line velocities in the movement of brightness patterns in an image. Then, we construct compact lip-motion features from the regional statistics of the local velocities. These can be used as alone or merged with audio features to recognize identity or the uttered digit. We present person recognition results using the XM2VTS database representing the video and audio data of 295 people. Furthermore, we present results on digit recognition when it is used in a text prompted mode to verify the liveness of the user. Such user challenges have the intention to reduce replay attack risks of the audio system.

Foreword

It is my great pleasure to introduce this timely and comprehensive reference book for researchers interested in the emerging field of visual speech recognition.

It is well known from psychological studies that speech perception is multimodal - we use visual information from the lip of the speaker in addition to acoustic information for speech perception. As the technology matures, this physiological study of speech can find exciting real world applications such as audiovisual speech recognizers in moving vehicles or factory floors, mobile communication involving speech and video of the speakers, and even access control which makes use of the biometric information in both the acoustic and visual signal.

This book is a major edited monograph since the 1996 manuscript edited by Stork and Hennecke on "Speechreading by Humans and Machines: Models, Systems, and Applications". It represents a state-of-the-art coverage of research in the area of visual speech recognition. Contributors to this book include many renowned pioneers and active researchers in the field and their contributions collectively provide a comprehensive and up-to-date treatment of the discipline. In particular, the book contains chapters that treat lip modeling and segmentation, feature extraction, classifier design, training, validation, application in visual speech/speaker recognition, as well as chapters that deal with the emotional and phonetic/linguistic aspects of visual lipreading.

I am confident that this book will serve as an invaluable resource for all current researchers seeking further insight into the cutting edge advances on visual speech recognition. Furthermore, it should interest new comers to join in on this emerging and exciting field of research.

S.Y. Kung
Professor of Electrical Engineering
Princeton University

Preface

It has been widely accepted that speech perception is a multimodal process and involves information from more than one sensory modality. The famous McGurk effect [McGurk and MacDonald, Nature 264(5588): 746–748, 1976] shows that visual articulatory information is integrated into our perception of speech automatically and unconsciously. For example, a visual /ga/ combined with an auditory /ba/ is often heard as /da/. This effect is shown to be very robust and knowledge about it seems to have very little effect on one's perception of it.

Interest in machine lip reading starts to emerge in the mid-1980s (Petajan was probably the first to investigate the problem of machine lipreading (E.D. Petajan 1984), ,when it was shown that visual lip information extracted from the speaker's lip can enhance the performance of automatic speech recognition system, especially in noisy environment. Recently, it has also been shown that dynamics of the speaker's lip during speech articulation provides useful biometric information for speaker recognition.

Machine lip reading or visual speaker recognition, generally involves three major steps: lip segmentation, feature extraction, and classifier design. Although significant research effort and many technological advances have been made recently, machine lip reading is still far from practical deployment. Unlike the relatively mature field of automatic speech recognition, there are still many unsolved theoretical and algorithmic issues in machine lip reading. For example, the problems of lighting, shadow, pose, facial hair, camera resolution, and so forth, make reliable segmentation and extraction of lip feature a difficult task. The problem is further compounded by the difficult and variable environment visual speech recognition systems tend to operate in. There is also relatively little theoretical study on the amount of phonetic/ linguistic information that can be extracted from the speaker's lip for speech perception.

In this book, we introduce the readers to the various aspects of this fascinating research area, which include lip segmentation from video sequence, lip feature extraction and modeling, feature fusion, and classifier design for visual speech recognition and speaker verification. This book collects together recent state-of-the-art research in these areas. There are altogether 17 chapters, from 44 authors in 14 countries & regions (Australia, Canada, China, France, Germany, Greece, Hong Kong, Japan, Mexico, New Zealand, Singapore, Sweden, Turkey, and the United States). Many of the contributing authors are well-known researchers in the field. This book would be of great interest to researchers and graduate students working in the fields of audiovisual speech and speaker recognition.

The 17 chapters in the book are organized into four sections: *Section I: Introduction & Survey, Section II: Lip Modeling, Segmentation, and Feature Extraction, Section III: Visual Speech Recognition, and Section IV: Visual Speaker Recognition.* Section I contains four survey/tutorial type chapters (Chapter I to IV) that describe recent progress in the field. They serve to introduce readers to this emerging field of research and summarize the state-of-the-art techniques that are available today. Section II contains four chapters (chapter V to VIII), that deal with lip segmentation, modeling, and feature extraction. Section III (Chapter IX to XV) contains chapters that look at issues related specifically to visual speech recognition. For example, chapter X investigates the use of multiple views of the speaker for visual speech recognition, chapter XI and XII concentrates on classifier design and training, chapter XIV looks at the possibility of obtaining prosodic information from the lip, and chapter XV discusses perceptual studies that quantify the information content in visible speech. Section IV contains two chapters (chapter XVI and XVII) that describe the use of visual lip feature for biometric applications. Below we give a brief description of each chapter.

Chapter I, "Audio-Visual and Visual-only Speech and Speaker Recognition- issues about theory, system design, and implementation" provides a tutorial coverage of the research in audio-visual speech and speaker recognition. It describes the major research issues and techniques in feature extraction, feature fusion, classifier design, and performance evaluation, and lists the major audiovisual speech databases used for performance evaluation. The authors survey several current audiovisual speaker/speech recognition systems and discussed challenges and future research directions.

Chapter II, "Lip Feature Extraction and Feature Evaluation in the Context of Speech and Speaker Recognition" surveys the different dynamic lip features and their use in visual speech and speaker recognition. In this chapter, the focus is more on the approaches for detection and tracking of important visual lip features. Together, the two survey chapters serve to introduce readers to the exciting field of audiovisual speech and speaker recognition.

Chapter III, "Lip modeling and segmentation" is a detailed survey of state-of-the-art in lip modeling and segmentation. The authors discussed about the different color spaces that provide good separation of lip and non-lip region. They describe the two major approaches for lip segmentation, that is, contour-based and region-based. Within each category, they further categorize the methods as deterministic, statistical, supervised, or un-supervised. Different techniques to extract the lip, such as active shape model, snake, parametric model, deformable template, as well as their optimization, are discussed. The chapter further discusses different performance evaluation techniques and concludes by discussing some possible applications that would benefit from advances in lip segmentation.

Chapter IV "Visual Speech and Gesture Coding using the MPEG-4 Face and Body Animation Standard" introduces the MPEG-4 Face and Body Animation (FBA) standard for representing visual speech data as part of a whole virtual human specification. The super low bit-rate FBA codec included with the standard enables thin clients to access processing and communication services over any network including enhanced visual communication, animated entertainment, man-machine dialog, and audio/visual speech recognition. In the chapter, the author described the deployment of the MPEG-4 FBA standard in face animation, body animation, and visual speech processing. The computing architectures that support various applications are also outlined. This chapter would be of great interest to readers interested in the topic of Human Computer Interaction.

Chapter V "Lip Region Segmentation with Complex Background" describes a lip segmentation method that is able to handle complex non-lip region such as the presence of beard or shadow. The method employs a Multi-class, Shape-guided FCM (MS-FCM) clustering algorithm to separate the lip pixels from the non-lip pixels. A spatial penalty term, based on the lip shape information is introduced in the clustering algorithm, which boosts the lip membership for pixels inside the lip region while penalizes the value for pixels outside the lip region. With the spatial penalty term, lip and non-lip pixels with similar color but located in different regions can be differentiated.

Chapter VI "Lip Contour Extraction from Video Sequences under Natural Lighting Conditions" presents an algorithm for lip contour tracking under natural lighting conditions. The algorithm extracts the inner and outer lip borders from color video sequences. To extract the lip contour, the video images are processed in three steps. In step one the mouth area is segmented using color and movement information from the face skin. In step two, the mouth corners are detected. The mouth corners are used to initialize the active contours. Step three extracts the lip contour using active contours. The chapter gives detail description about the logarithmic hue-like color space transformation that are used to separate the lip and non-lip pixels, the hierarchical spatiotemporal color segmentation algorithm integrating hue and motion information, and finally, the theoretical derivation used in the optimization of the active contour. The algorithm has been successfully applied to several video sequences with no specific model of the speaker and variable illumination conditions.

Chapter VII "3D Lip Shape SPH Based Evolution Using Prior 2D Dynamic Lip Features Extraction and Static 3D Lip Measurements" describes a 3D lip modeling and animation technique whose dynamic behavior is governed by Smooth Particles Hydrodynamics. The 3D lip model is constructed from facial data acquired by a 3D scanner and 2D lip contours extracted from video-sequences of the subject. The influence of muscle contraction around the lip is considered in the model. The authors described in detail the 3D model construction and the derivation of the controlling forces that drive the model, and presented some simulation results to show the feasibility of their approach.

Chapter VIII "How to Use Manual Labelers in the Evaluation of Lip Analysis Systems?" examines the issues involved in evaluating and calibrating labeled lip features which serve as ground truth from human operators. The authors showed that subjective error in manual labeling can be quite significant, and this can adversely affect the validity of an algorithm's performance evaluation and comparative studies between algorithms. The chapter describes an iterative method based on Expectation-Maximization to statistically infer the ground truth from manually labeled data.

Chapter IX "Visual Speech Processing and Recognition" describes an algorithm that performs limited vocabulary recognition of the first four digits in English based on visual speech features. Three aspects of visual speech processing and recognition, namely, mouth region segmentation, lip contour extraction, and visual speech recognition are dealt with. For the mouth region segmentation, a modified Fuzzy C-means method with the addition of spatial constraints is introduced. For the lip contour extraction, the image gradient information is used to create a color map of edge magnitude and edge direction. Edge following is then applied on the color map to extract the lip contour. For the visual speech recognition, a SVM dynamic network is proposed. SVM classifiers are used to obtain the posterior probabilities and the SVMs are then integrated into a Viterbi decoding lattice for each visemic word. The authors showed that the SVM dynamic network has superior performance compared to some existing techniques.

Chapter X "Visual Speech Recognition across Multiple Views" investigates the use of multiple views of the speaker for visual speech recognition of connected digit strings. Most works on visual speech recognition assume that the speaker's face is captured in a frontal pose. However, in many applications, this assumption is not realistic. In this chapter, the authors considered the frontal and the profile views captured synchronously in a multi-camera setting. An appearance-based visual front-end that extracts features for frontal and profile videos is first developed. The extracted features then undergo normalization across views to achieve feature-space invariance. This normalization allows recognizing visual speech using a single pose-invariant statistical model, regardless of camera view.

Chapter XI "Hidden Markov Model Based Visemes Recognition. Part I: AdaBoost Approach" describes an AdaBoost-HMM classifier for visemes recognition. The authors applied AdaBoost technique to HMM modeling to construct a multi-HMM classifier that improves the recognition rate. Whereas conventional single HMM identifies the ideal samples with good accuracy but fail to handle the hard or outlier samples, Adaboosting allows new HMMs in a multi-HMM classifier to bias towards the hard samples, thus ensuring coverage of the hard samples with a more complex decision boundary. The method is applied to identify context-independent and context-dependent visual speech units. The technique was compared to conventional HMM for visemes recognition and has shown improved performance.

Chapter XII "Hidden Markov Model Based Visemes Recognition. Part II: Discriminative Approaches" describes an alternative approach to classifier training for visemes recognition. The focus is on emphasizing the minor differences between pairs of confusable training samples during HMM classifier training. The authors proposed two training approaches to maximize discrimination: Maximum Separable Distance (MSD) training and Two-channel HMM training. Both training approaches adopt a criterion function called separable distance to improve the discriminative power of an HMM classifier. The methods are applied to identify confusable visemes and their results indicate that higher recognition accuracy can be attained using these approaches than using conventional HMM.

Chapter XIII "Motion Features for Visual Speech Recognition" studies the motion features that are effective for visual speech recognition. A review of two motion feature extraction techniques, namely, optical flow method and image subtraction method is given. The authors then present their recent work on the motion history image (MHI) technique. The MHI method captures the lip dynamics through temporal integration of image sequence into a 2-D spatio-temporal template. Feature vectors based on DCT coefficients or Zernike moments are then computed from the MHI image and are used for visual speech recognition.

Chapter XIV "Recognizing Prosody from the Lips: Is it Possible to Extract Prosodic Focus from Lip Features?" This chapter investigates the feasibility of extracting prosodic information from visual lip features. Prosodic information plays a critical role in spoken communication, and reflects not only the emotional state of the speaker, but also carries crucial linguistic information, such as whether an utterance is a statement, a question, or a command, or whether there is an emphasis, contrast or focus. The authors used two lip feature measurement techniques to evaluate the lip pattern of prosodic focus in French. Lip opening and spreading and lip protrusion gestures are tracked and the lip features analyzed for prosodic focus in a natural dialogue situation.

Chapter XV "Visual Speech Perception, Optical Phonetics, and Synthetic Speech" reviews perceptual studies that quantify the information content in visible speech, demonstrating that visible speech is a rich and detailed source of phonetic information. The authors discussed the relations between optical phonetic signals and phonetic perception and demonstrated the existence of a strong second-order isomorphism between optical signals and visual perception. They further discussed how this second-order isomorphism of perceptual dissimilarities and optical dissimilarities can be exploited beneficially in the development of a visual speech synthesizer, and suggested that the perceptually relevant phonetic details in visible speech should be synthesized in order to create meaningful synthetic visual speech.

Chapter XVI "Multimodal Speaker Identification using Discriminative Lip Motion Features" describes a multimodal speaker identification system that integrates audio, lip texture, and lip motion modalities. The authors proposed a two-stage, spatial-temporal discrimination analysis framework that involves the spatial Bayesian feature selection and the temporal LDA to obtain the best lip motion feature representation for speaker identification. Two types of lip motion features, that is grid-based image motion features and lip shape features, are examined and compared. A multimodality recognition system involving audio, lip texture, and lip motion information is demonstrated to be feasible.

Chapter XVII "Lip Motion Features for Biometric Person Recognition" describes the use of lip motion as a single biometric modality as well as a modality integrated with audio speech for speaker identity recognition and digit recognition. The lip motion is modeled as the distribution of apparent line velocities in the movement of brightness patterns in an image. The authors described in detail how the lip motion features can be extracted reliably from a video sequence. Speaker recognition results based on single digit recognition using the XM2VTS database containing the video and audio data of 295 people are presented. They also described how the system can be used in a text prompted mode to verify the liveness of the user utilizing digit recognition.

Visual speech/speaker recognition is an emerging field of research that has many interesting applications in human computer interaction, security, and digital entertainment. This book provides a timely collection of latest research in this area. We believe that the chapters provide an extensive coverage of the field and would prove to be a valuable reference to current and future researchers working in this fascinating area.

Editors
Alan Wee-Chung LIEW
Shilin WANG

Acknowledgment

First, we would like to thank IGI Global for inviting us to embark on this book project. Special thanks go to the Development Editor of IGI Global, Julia Mosemann, for her help and patience in this book project. Without the help from Julia and all the editorial staffs from IGI Global, we would not be able to carry this project to its completion.

Secondly, we would like to thank Professor SY Kung of Princeton University for writing the Foreword. Special thanks also go to the seven Expert Editorial Advisory Board members for their valuable input and their help in reviewing submitted chapters, as well as all the authors that have contributed to the content of this book. Many of these authors also help with the review process.

Lastly, we would like to thank Griffith University, Australia, and Shanghai Jiaotong University, China, for providing us the needed resources and support during the entire duration of this project.

Alan Wee-Chung Liew
Griffith University, Australia

Shilin Wang
Shanghai Jiaotong University, China

Section I
Introduction and Survey

Chapter I
Audio–Visual and Visual–Only Speech and Speaker Recognition:
Issues about Theory, System Design, and Implementation

Derek J. Shiell
Northwestern University, USA

Louis H. Terry
Northwestern University, USA

Petar S. Aleksic
Google Inc., USA

Aggelos K. Katsaggelos
Northwestern University, USA

ABSTRACT

The information imbedded in the visual dynamics of speech has the potential to improve the performance of speech and speaker recognition systems. The information carried in the visual speech signal compliments the information in the acoustic speech signal, which is particularly beneficial in adverse acoustic environments. Non-invasive methods using low-cost sensors can be used to obtain acoustic and visual biometric signals, such as a person's voice and lip movement, with little user cooperation. These types of unobtrusive biometric systems are warranted to promote widespread adoption of biometric technology in today's society. In this chapter, the authors describe the main components and theory of audio-visual and visual-only speech and speaker recognition systems. Audio-visual corpora are described and a number of speech and speaker recognition systems are reviewed. Finally, various open issues about the system design and implementation, and present future research and development directions in this area are discussed.

INTRODUCTION TO AUDIO-VISUAL RECOGNITION SYSTEMS

Modern audio-only speech and speaker recognition systems lack the robustness needed for wide scale deployment. Among the factors negatively affecting such audio-only systems are variations in microphone sensitivity, acoustic environment, channel noise and the recognition scenario (i.e., limited vs. unlimited domains). Even at typical acoustic background signal-to-noise ratio (SNR) levels (-10dB to 15dB), their performance can significantly degrade. However, it has been well established in the literature that the incorporation of additional modalities, such as video, can improve system performance. The reader is directed to the suggested readings at the end of this chapter for comprehensive coverage of these multi-modal systems. It is well known that face visibility can improve speech perception because the visual signal is both correlated to the acoustic speech signal and contains complementary information to it (Aleksic & Katsaggelos, 2004; Barbosa & Yehia, 2001; Barker & Berthommier, 1999; Jiang, Alwan, Keating, E. T. Auer, & Bernstein, 2002; Yehia, Kuratatc, & Vatikiotis-Bateson, 1999; Yehia, Rubin, & Vatikiotis-Bateson, 1998). Although the potential for improvement in speech recognition is greater in poor acoustic conditions, multiple experiments have shown that modeling visual speech dynamics, can improve speech and speaker recognition performance even in noise-free environments (Aleksic & Katsaggelos, 2003a; Chaudhari, Ramaswamy, Potamianos, & Neti, 2003; Fox, Gross, de Chazal, Cohn, & Reilly, 2003).

The integration of information from audio and visual modalities is fundamental to the design of AV speech and speaker recognition systems. Fusion strategies must properly combine information from

Figure 1. Block diagram of an audio-visual speech and speaker recognition system

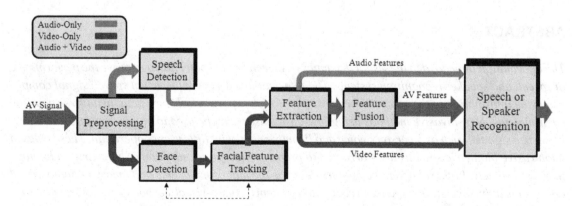

these modalities in such a way that it improves performance of the system in all settings. Additionally, the performance gains must be large enough to justify the complexity and cost of incorporating the visual modality into a person recognition system. Figure 1 shows the general process of performing AV recognition. While significant advances in AV and V-only speech and speaker recognition have been made over recent years, the fields of speech and speaker recognition still hold many exciting opportunities for future research and development. Many of these open issues on theory, design, and implementation and opportunities are described in the following.

Audio-visual and V-only speech and speaker recognition systems currently lack the resources to systematically evaluate performance across a wide range of recognition scenarios and conditions. One of the most important steps towards alleviating this problem is the creation of publicly available multi-modal corpora that better reflect realistic conditions, such as acoustic noise and shadows. A number of existing AV corpora are introduced and suggestions are given for the creation of new corpora to be used as reference points.

It is also important to remember statistical significance when reporting results. Statistics such as the mean and variance should to be used to compare the relative performance across recognition systems (Bengio & Mariethoz, 2004). The use of these statistical measures will be helpful in defining criteria for reporting system performance.

Continued advances in visual feature tracking robustness and feature representation such as 2.5D or 3D face information, will be essential to the eventual incorporation of speech and speaker recognition systems in everyday life (Blanz, Grother, Phillips, & Vetter, 2005; Bowyer, Chang, & Flynn, 2006; Sanderson, Bengio, & Gao, 2006). Development of improved AV integration algorithms with the ability to asynchronously model multiple modalities with stream confidence estimates will expedite this process. The most limiting factor to widespread adoption of recognition technology is the ability to perform robustly given the enormous variability found in the environment and recognition systems.

These issues are addressed throughout this chapter. The theory behind speech and speaker recognition along with system design is summarized and a selection of AV and V-only speech and speaker recognition implementations are described. Finally, we describe the design and implementation of our real-time visual-only speech and speaker recognition system and evaluate its performance, and describe future research and development directions.

AUDIO-VISUAL SPEECH PROCESSING METHODS AND THEORY

The Importance of Visual Information in Speech and Speaker Recognition

It has long been known that human perception of speech is not invariant to speaker head pose and lip articulation suggesting that visual information plays a significant role in speech recognition (Lippmann, 1997; Neely, 1956; Summerfield, 1992). However until recent years, automatic speech recognition systems (ASR) were limited to the acoustic modality. Consider the fact that hearing-impaired persons are able to demonstrate surprising understanding of speech despite their disability. This observation suggests a major motivation to include visual information in the ASR problem.

It is clear that visual information has the potential to augment audio-only ASR (A-ASR) especially in noisy acoustic situations. Visual and acoustic modalities contain correlated and complementary signals, but independent noise. For example, if an audio speech signal is corrupted by acoustic noise (i.e.

car engine, background speech, plane turbine, loud music, etc.) the corresponding visual information is likely to remain unaffected and consequently valuable for recognition. Similarly, noise in the visual domain is not likely to affect the audio speech signal. The next challenge is to optimally and dynamically combine the audio and visual information. This section will briefly review various methods of integrating audio and visual features and associated issues.

The following section describes typical speech and speaker recognition systems. Although the goals for speech and speaker recognition are not the same, the fundamental problem is very similar. The purpose of automatic speech recognition systems is to identify isolated or continuous words, whereas speaker recognition systems attempt to identify an individual.

Audio-Visual Speech and Speaker Recognition System Description

Audio-visual recognition systems consist of three main steps: *preprocessing, feature extraction, and AV fusion*. Figure 1 depicts a complete AV system highlighting these three parts. While the application may vary, speech and speaker recognition systems are, in general, component-wise identical. These systems are mainly differentiated by how they are trained as well as what features are chosen.

Preprocessing occurs in parallel for both the audio and visual streams. On the audio side, techniques such as signal enhancement and environment sniffing help prepare the incoming audio stream for the feature extraction step (Rabiner & Juang, 1993). Video preprocessing, which has traditionally been a major challenge, consists of face detection and tracking and, subsequently, the tracking of regions of interests (ROIs). In some cases, these ROIs will undergo further processing such as histogram equalization or photo-normalization. The specific techniques will vary from system to system and their choice is governed not only by properties of the expected inputs, but also by the choice of features to be extracted.

Audio feature extraction has been an active field of research for many years. Many results have been reported in the literature regarding the extraction of audio features for clean and noisy speech conditions (Rabiner & Juang, 1993). Mel-frequency cepstral coefficients (MFCCs) and linear prediction coefficients (LPCs) represent the most commonly used acoustic features. Additional research is ongoing in the field of noise robust acoustic features. After acoustic feature extraction, first and second derivatives of the data are usually concatenated with the original data to form the final feature vector. The original data is also known as the "static coefficients" while the first and second derivatives are also known as "delta" and "delta-delta" or "acceleration" coefficients.

Visual feature extraction is a relatively recent research topic, and many approaches to visual feature extraction and audio-visual feature fusion currently exist in the literature. Visual features can be grouped into three general categories: shape-based, appearance-based, and combinational approaches. All three types require the localization and tracking of ROIs, but when some shape-based features are used the method of localization and tracking during preprocessing may be chosen to directly output the shape-based features. Active Appearance Models (AAMs) and Active Shape Models (ASMs) are among the techniques that combine tracking and feature extraction (T. Cootes, Edwards, & Taylor, 1998, 2001; Gross, Matthews, & Baker, 2006; Matthews & Baker, 2004; Xiao, Baker, Matthews, & Kanade, 2004). For non-interdependent techniques, the features are extracted directly from the ROI and delta and delta-delta coefficients concatenated with the static coefficients to produce the final feature vector.

Shape-based visual features include the inner and outer lip contours, teeth and tongue information, and descriptions of other facial features such as the jaw (Aleksic & Katsaggelos, 2004). Shape information can be represented as a series of landmark points, parametrically as defined by some model, or in functional representations.

Appearance-based features are usually based off of transforms such as the discrete cosine transform (DCT), discrete wavelet transform (DWT), principal component analysis (PCA), and appearance modes from AAMs (Potamianos, Neti, Luettin, & Matthews, 2004). These transforms produce high dimensional data, but the transforms also compact the input signal's energy. This convenient property leads to the use of dimensionality reduction techniques such as PCA or linear discriminant analysis (LDA) to produce the static features.

Combinational approaches utilize both shape and appearance based features to create the final feature vector. The feature vector may be some concatenation of geometric and appearance based features, or, as in the case of AAMs, may be a parametric representation using a joint shape-appearance model.

Audio-visual fusion integrates acoustic and visual information to increase performance over single-modality systems. As shown in Figure 1, if fusion does not occur, audio-only or video-only systems result. However, fusing the audio and visual data results in more robust systems due to the diversity of the data acquisition. Various fusion techniques exist, as described later in this section. Some fusion techniques require equal audio and visual frame rates, but these rates are typically different. Acoustic frames are usually sampled at 100 Hz, while video frame rates are usually between 25 and 30 frames per second (50-60 interlaced fields per second). Normally, the video is up-sampled using interpolation to achieve equal frame rates.

Analysis of Visual Features

Choosing appropriate visual features remains an open research topic for audio-visual systems, and many considerations must go into the choice of features. While each feature extraction algorithm has its own positive and negative attributes, this section focuses on the general considerations that one must weigh such as robustness to video quality, robustness to visual environment, and computational complexity. Generally, visual feature extraction algorithms are divided into appearance-based and shape-based features, which then may be subdivided as shown in Figure 2.

Video quality affects the visual region of interest (ROI) localization and tracking as well as the extracted features themselves. Video artifacts, such as blocking and noise, along with poor video resolution may affect the localization and tracking algorithms and produce incorrect tracking results. Some techniques that use parametric models, such as facial animation parameters (FAPs), or statistical models, such as active appearance models (AAMs), may be more robust to these sorts of problems, while individual landmark tracking may be significantly affected. Other more robust approaches include the Viola and Jones object recognizer (Viola & Jones, 2001), the "bag of features" method (Yuan, Wu, & Yang, 2007), and other methods that focus on more global features or exploit the relationships between landmark points. Once the features are located, video artifacts can adversely affect the extracted features. Appearance-based features are especially susceptible to these corruptions as they perform operations directly on the pixel values. When using discrete cosine transform (DCT) based features, for example, blocking artifacts will significantly alter the DCT coefficients, but the DCT may not be as adversely affected by video noise. Shape-based feature extraction usually utilizes similar techniques to the ROI localization and tracking procedure, and has basically the same issues. In these ways, it is important to note the expected video quality and level of robustness needed when choosing visual front-end components.

Figure 2. Illustrating the shape-based feature extraction process in (Aleksic, Williams, Wu, & Katsaggelos, 2002)

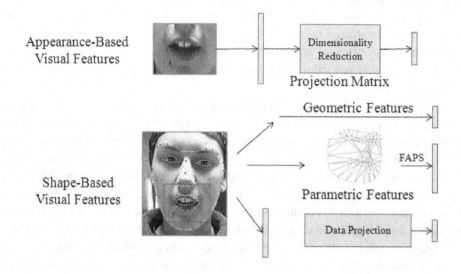

Visual environment plays a large role in accurate and useful feature extraction. In much the same way that video artifacts affect the visual front end, so do environmental factors such as lighting and the subject's distance from the camera. Appearance-based features are strongly altered by static lighting differences and dynamic lighting changes, such as shadows, while shape-based features can be robust to these problems if the underlying detection methods are also robust. Occlusions, however, present a major problem to both appearance and shape-based features. Appearance-based features provide almost no resiliency to occlusions, but certain levels of occlusions can be taken into account with model-based geometric feature extractors.

Computationally, appearance based feature extraction is naturally less expensive than shape-based methods due to the use of simple matrix-based transforms versus more complex techniques. Furthermore, appearance based features can perform at significantly faster speeds due to the availability of hardware digital signal processing (DSP) chips specifically designed to perform the DCT or other transforms. Additionally, shape-based feature extraction has yet to be offloaded directly onto hardware, but processing speed can be increased through the clever use of graphic processing units (GPUs). It should be said that this does not reduce the inherent complexity, nor does the speed rival DSP implementations of appearance-based extraction.

Audio-Visual Speech and Speaker Recognition Process

Speech Recognition

The goal of speech recognition systems is to correctly identify spoken language from features describing the speech production process. While acoustic features such as MFCCs or LPCs are good measures of the speech production process and may help achieve high recognition performance in some systems, there are non-ideal environments where there may be too much noise for these single modal systems to perform adequately. In these cases, multi-modal systems incorporating other measures of the spoken words can significantly improve recognition. We will not cover the details of A-ASR systems as they have been covered extensively in previous literature (J. P. Campbell, 1997). We discuss the process of AV-ASR and the integration of the audio and visual modalities. These bi-modal systems should ideally outperform their audio-only counterparts across all acoustic SNRs, especially for situations with high acoustic noise. Since hidden Markov models (HMMs) represent the standard tool for speech and speaker recognition, in the remaining part of this section we briefly describe the mathematical formulation of single- and multi-stream HMMs.

Hidden Markov models represent a doubly stochastic process in which one process, the "hidden", or unobservable process, progresses through a discrete state space while a second observable process takes on distinct stochastic properties dependent upon the hidden state. In this context, unobservable implies that the process itself does not emit any information that one may directly gather; therefore it is hidden from the observer. One, however, may infer information about this hidden process by gathering information produced by the directly observable process due to its dependence on the hidden process. This inference lies at the heart of HMMs.

Table 1 summarizes the notation used when working with hidden Markov models. The three primary issues facing HMMs are described in (Rabiner & Juang, 1993):

1. Evaluation - How does one evaluate the probability of an observed sequence given the model parameters?

Table 1. Notation reference for hidden markov models. Recreated from Aleksic 2003.

Notation	Representation
o_t	Vector of total observations at time t
o_t^a, o_t^v	Vectors of audio and video observations, respectively, at time t
Q	Time sequence of hidden states
π_{q_1}	Probability of starting in hidden state q_1
$a_{q_1 q_2}$	Probability of transitioning from hidden state q_1 to q_2
$b_j(o_t)$	Probability of state j emitting observation o_t
λ_i	Hidden Markov model parameters for model i, including state transition probabilities, state emission probabilities, and initial state probabilities

Figure 3. A diagram depicting a left-to-right single-stream HMM showing transition probabilities (a_{ij}), emission probabilities (b_j), and showing the observations mapped to states

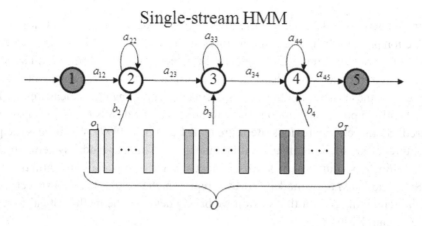

2. Hidden state recovery - How can the hidden state sequence be determined from an observation sequence given the model parameters?
3. Model updating - How can one determine the parameters of an HMM from multiple observations?

While we address HMMs in the context of speech recognition, they also find great use in a variety of disciplines including normality/abnormality detection, DNA sequencing, detection of ECG events, economics, and among many others.

If single stream HMMs are to be employed for speech recognition, audio and visual features must be combined into a single observation vector, o_t, consisting of the audio observation vector, o_t^v, concatenated with the visual observation vector, o_t^a, i.e.,

$$o_t = \begin{bmatrix} o_t^a \\ o_t^v \end{bmatrix}. \tag{1}$$

Most commonly, Gaussian mixture models (GMMs) are used to model the state emission probability distributions, which can be expressed as

$$b_j(o_t) = \sum_{m=1}^{M} c_{jm} N(o_t; u_{jm}, \Sigma_{jm}). \tag{2}$$

In Eqn. 2, b_j refers to the emission distribution for state j in a context-dependent HMM as in Figure 3. The Gaussian mixtures weights are denoted by c_{jm}, for all M Gaussion mixtures, and N stands for a multivariate Gaussian with mean, u_{jm}, and covariance matrix, Σ_{jm}. The sum of all mixtures weights, c_{jm}, should be 1. Now recognition occurs by summing the joint probability of a set of observations and state sequences over all possible state sequences for each model, that is,

$$\arg\max_{\lambda_i} P(O, Q \mid \lambda_i) = \arg\max_{\lambda_i} \sum_{\forall Q} P(O \mid Q, \lambda_i) P(Q \mid \lambda_i) \tag{3}$$

In Eqn. 3 λ_i stands for the ith word model, Q represents all combinations of state sequences, and we are summing over all possible state sequences for the given model. More specifically, given a series of observations $O = [o_1, o_2, \ldots o_T]$, state-transition likelihoods, $a_{q_{t-1}q_t}$, state-emission probabilities, $b_j(o_t)$ and the probability of starting in a state π_q for each model, the word with the highest probability of having generated O can be determined by summing over all possible state sequences, $Q = [q_1, q_2, \ldots q_T]$ as shown in Eqn. 4.

$$\sum_{\forall Q} P(O \mid Q, \lambda_i) P(Q \mid \lambda_i) = \sum_{q_1, q_2, \ldots q_T} \pi_{q_1} b_{q_1}(o_1) a_{q_1 q_2} b_{q_2}(o_2) \cdots a_{q_{T-1} q_T} b_{q_T}(o_T). \tag{4}$$

So the recognized word will have a certain state sequence with a higher probability of generating the observation vector, O, than any other word model. It is worth noting that the modeled objects could also be phonemes, visemes, or speakers. It is clear that the brute force method for computing probabilities for all models and combinations of state sequences becomes infeasible even for relatively small vocabularies. This has lead to more efficient algorithms for training model parameters and evaluating log-likelihoods such as Baum-Welch re-estimation, which relies on the expectation maximization (EM) algorithm, and the Viterbi algorithm which takes advantage of dynamic programming (Deller, Proakis, & Hansen, 1993; S. Young et al., 2005). For additional details on the theory of HMMs, the reader is encouraged to see Rabiner and Juang's introduction to HMMs (Rabiner & Juang, 1993). The Hidden Markov Modeling Tool Kit (HTK) and the Application Tool Kit for HTK (ATK) are excellent frameworks for HMM based modeling and evaluation, and are freely available online (see suggested readings).

When multiple modalities are present, multi-stream HMMs, stream weights are commonly used to integrate stream information as part of the evaluation process. The state-topology of a typical multi-stream HMM is shown in Figure 4. In the case of audio-visual speech or speaker recognition, audio and visual stream weights are applied as exponential factors to each modality in calculating the state emission probability, that is,

$$b_j(o_t) = \prod_{s \in \{a, v\}} \left[\sum_{m=1}^{M_s} c_{jsm} N(o_t^s; u_{jsm}, \Sigma_{jsm}) \right]^{\gamma_s}. \tag{5}$$

The index, s, indicates either the audio or visual modality, and the exponential weight, γ_s, reflects the importance of the audio or stream weight in the recognition process. It is often assumed that the

Figure 4. HMM state topology for a 3-state, multi- stream HMM. Shaded states are non-emitting

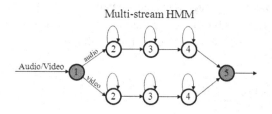

Figure 5. A product HMM with 9 states. Shaded states are non-emitting

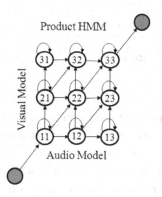

stream weights sum to one, $\gamma_a + \gamma_v = 1$. Multi-stream HMMs have been extensively applied to audio-visual speech and speaker recognition systems (Pitsikalis, Katsamanis, Papandreou, & Maragos, 2006; Potamianos, Neti, Gravier, Garg, & Senior, 2003; Tamura, Iwano, & Furui, 2005).

Product HMMs (PHMMs) are an extension to the standard and multi-stream HMMs, which have seen success in multi-modal speech and speaker recognition (Aleksic & Katsaggelos, 2003b; Movellan, 1995; Nefian, Liang, Pi, Liu, & Murphy, 2002). PHMMs have the advantage that they allow asynchrony between the audio and visual modalities within a phoneme during log-likelihood recombination (Nakamura, 2001; Neti et al., 2000). Figure 5 shows a diagram of the state-topology of a PHMM. The audio-visual emission probabilities for PHMMs are described in (Nakamura, 2001). In Figure 5, the PHMM audio stream emission probabilities are tied along the same column while visual stream emission distributions are tied in along the same row.

Other methods utilizing classifiers such as artificial neural networks (ANNs), genetic algorithms, and support vector machines (SVMs) have also been applied to the problem of speech and speaker recognition, however with less success than the HMM and its variants (Movellan, 1995; Nefian et al., 2002).

Speaker Verification and Identification

The speaker recognition process closely parallels the modeling approach to speech recognition, but instead of recognizing words or phonemes, the objective is to determine whether a person is part of an authorized group (verification) and possibly the identity of the person (identification). The acoustic and visual features used for speaker recognition are the same as in speech recognition. Similar statistical methods are used to model and evaluate a speaker's dynamic speech characteristics. During the recognition phase, speakers are identified by computing the posterior probability of each speaker generating the observations. The objective function for speaker recognition can be written similarly to Eqn. 3 as

$$\hat{c} = \arg\max_{c \in C} P\left(c \mid O_{s,t}\right), \qquad s \in \{a, v, f\}. \tag{6}$$

In Eqn. 6, $\hat{c}$ is the recognized class (speaker) from the set of all classes (speakers), C, and $P(c|O_{s,t})$ is the posterior probability of class, c, conditioned on the observations, $O_{s,t}$. In Eqn. 6, a static frontal face modality, f, representing static frontal face features is allowed in addition to the audio, a, and visual, v, modalities. Utilizing only the *maximum a posteriori* criterion across authorized users, classification will force a user outside the authorized users set to be identified as one of the possible enrolled persons.

A world class modeling arbitrary users outside the authorized client set is typically implemented to overcome this forced classification. In speaker verification systems there are two classes. One class corresponds to all enrolled or authorized users and the other class is the aforementioned general population, or world, model representing all other users (imposters). Authorization is determined by a similarity measure, D, which indicates whether biometric observations were more likely to come from the world (imposter) model or the authorized users model, that is,

$$D = \log P\left(c \mid O_{s,t}\right) - \log P\left(w \mid O_{s,t}\right). \tag{7}$$

In Eqn. 7, we have represented the world class as w. If the difference, D, is above or below some threshold the decision is made about whether the observations were generated by an authorized user or an imposter. The speaker identification, or recognition, process operates similarly to speech recognition. The speaker recognition problem is to determine the exact identity of the user from the set of authorized users and an imposter class. The maximum posterior probability is calculated for each class as it is for word models in speech recognition. One difference between speaker recognition and speech recognition is that the class priors are often modeled by GMMs, that is,

$$P\left(O_{s,t} \mid c_j\right) = \sum_{m=1}^{M} w_{jsm} N\left(O_t^s ; \mu_{jsm}, \Sigma_{sjm}\right). \tag{8}$$

In Eqn. 8, the conditional probability, $P(O_{s,t} \mid c_j)$, of seeing a set of observations, $O_{s,t}$, for the *jth* class, c_j, is expressed as a mixture of normal Gaussians with weights, w_{jsm}, similarly to Eqn. 2. This means that the GMM is being utilized to model the general speech dynamics over an entire utterance. However, speaker recognition may also use HMMs to capture the dynamics of speech in the exact same way as speech recognition. In either case, the experiments may be text-dependent or text-independent. Text-dependent experiments require all users to utter a specific phrase also used to train the recognition system. This type of biometrics system is vulnerable to imposters who may have a recording of the user saying the phrase. In order to overcome this limitation, text-independent systems have been proposed which attempt to capture general dynamic audio and visual speech characteristics of the authorized users, independent of the training data so that recognition systems can validate or identify the user based on a randomly chosen phrase.

Experiment Protocols and Analysis

Speech and speaker recognition experiments are most often characterized by their recognition rates and error rates or rank-N rates, meaning the correct result is in the top N recognition results. However, many times a deeper analysis of experimental results is desired. When the experiment is designed so that the result is binary, as in speaker verification systems, false-acceptance rates (FAR), false-rejection rates (FRR), and equal-error rates (EER) become important performance measures. In verification experiments, the FAR is defined as the number of imposter attacks accepted, I_a, over the total number of imposter attacks attempted, I. The FRR is defined as the number of authorized users incorrectly identified by the system as imposters, $\underline{C_R}$, divided by the total number of authorized user claims, C.

$$FAR = \frac{I_a}{I} \quad FRR = \frac{C_R}{C} \tag{9}$$

There is always a tradeoff between the FAR and FRR, and the rate at which they are equal is known as the EER. For instance, if security is of primary concern, it may be necessary to minimize the number of false acceptances at the expense of increasing the false rejections. Conversely, if ease of use is more important clients may not be willing to tolerate a large number of false rejections. Often, the receiver operator curve (ROC) or detection cost function (DCF) are generated to characterize the tradeoff between FAR and FRR for a system. More details are described in (Aleksic & Katsaggelos, 2006; Bengio, Mariethoz, & Keller, 2005).

The statistical significance of results should also be carefully analyzed. The mean and variance of the recognition rates over a number of trials should be considered when comparing recognition systems with the same setup. In order to exclude outlier effects (due to tracking errors, poor transcriptions, unusual or missing data, etc.), researchers should report the percent of speakers whose recognition rates were above a certain recognition threshold. For example, a researcher might report that the speech recognition rate was greater than 90% for 95% of the speakers. Standards for evaluating and comparing results could define testing configurations to provide statistically significant performance measures. For example, it is unfair to compare isolated digit recognition rates on a database of 10 subjects against rates obtained on a database consisting of 100 subjects. The design of performance measures should therefore take into account the size of the testing database. The statistical significance of results can also be improved using cross-validation or leave-one-out testing protocols. In these methods, a certain percentage of the speakers are used for training, while the remaining speakers are used for testing. The training and testing data sets can be shifted to obtain multiple recognition results which when averaged should give a better overall recognition rate than a single speaker independent result.

Audio-Visual Fusion Methods and Databases

In this section we review some of the most commonly used information fusion methods, and discuss various issues related to their use for the fusion of acoustic and visual information. We briefly review AV corpora commonly used for AV research and illustrate various desirable characteristics, such as, adequate number of subjects and size of vocabulary and utterances, realistic variability, and recommended experiment protocols.

Information fusion plays a vital role in audio-visual systems governing how the audio and visual data interact and affect recognition. Generally, information fusion techniques can be grouped into three categories indicating when the multi-modal integration takes place (Potamianos et al., 2003).

Early Integration implies the audio-visual data is combined before the information reaches the recognizer and, thus, the fusion takes place at either sensor (raw-data) level or at the feature level. A variety of methods exist performing the integration itself, including using a weighted summation of the data and simple data concatenation. While an intuitive fusion technique, data concatenation tends to introduce dimensionality related problems.

Intermediate Integration occurs during the recognition process and usually involves varying parameters of the recognizer itself. In the case of multi-Stream HMMs, for instance, a stream weight associated with each modality may be adjusted to increase or decrease the modality's influence. This technique allows for adjusting the modality's influence on a variety of time scales ranging from the state level to the phone level up to the word or sentence level. Unfortunately, the tradeoff for this level of control is that one becomes limited in the choice of the recognizer's HMM structure.

Late Integration combines the outputs of independent recognizers for each modality resulting in a single system output. This type of integration usually takes place at either the score-level or decision level. In decision fusion, methods for computing the final result include majority voting, N-best lists, and Boolean operations. Score-level fusion usually utilizes weighted summations/products or other machine learning classifiers. While late integration allows more freedom in information fusion methods, intermediate integration supports fusion at various time-scales.

In order to help the reader quickly peruse relevant AV databases we have summarized a number of popular AV speech corpora in Table 2. This table describes the number and breakdown of speakers, the audio-visual dialogue content, recording conditions, and audio-visual data acquisition characteristics for each database. Planning audio-visual speech experiments requires careful database selection to guarantee sufficient training and testing data for a given experiment, whether it is continuous AV-ASR, isolated visual-only digit recognition, text-dependent dynamic AV speaker recognition, or some other AV experiment.

Typically no single database is likely to contain all of the desired qualities for an AV speech corpus (number of speakers, audio or visual conditions, vocabulary, etc.), and a byproduct of this variability is that comparing AV speech or speaker recognition results on different databases becomes difficult. Consequently, there is an obvious need for new AV databases and standards on AV speech database

Table 2. A list of popular audio-visual speech corpora and short descriptions of each. All databases are publicly available (may require a fee) with the exception of the IBM ViaVoice database.

Audio-visual Speech Corpora			
Database	**Subjects**	**Description and environmental conditions**	**Recording characteristics**
AMP/CMU (Chen, 2001)	10 speakers • 7 male • 3 female	• 78 isolated words commonly used for time (i.e. days, months, time of day, etc.) are uttered 10 times per speaker. • High quality recording in a soundproof studio with a blue-screen background.	• Video was recorded with a Sony digital camcorder at 720x480 resolution. • Audio was recorded with a tie-clip microphone.
AVICAR (Lee et al., 2004)	100 speakers • 50 female • 50 male	• Speakers read a sequence of isolated digits and letters, phone numbers, and TIMIT sentences. • 60% of the speakers are native American English speakers. • Data was recorded in a car environment at 3 different speeds (idling, 35 mph, and 55mph) with windows rolled up and down.	• Four digital cameras are multiplexed into a single video stream with 4 views of the subject. • Audio was collected using an 8 microphone array mounted on the dashboard.
AV-TIMIT (Hazen, Saenko, La, & Glass, 2004)	223 speakers • 117 male • 106 female	• Primarily native English speakers utter 20 TIMIT sentences with the first being the same for all speakers. • Quiet office environment used with controlled lighting, background, and audio noise level.	• Digital video was recorded at 30 fps and 720x480 resolution. • Audio was recorded with video at 16 kHz.
BANCA (Popovici et al., 2003)	208 speakers • 104 male • 104 female	• Subjects repeat a random 12-digit number, and their name, address, and date of birth over 12 sessions spanning 3 months. • The database consists of 4 European languages and 3 scenarios; controlled, degraded, and adverse.	• A cheap analogue webcam and high quality digital camera were used. • Audio was recorded 16 bits and 12 bits at 32 kHz.
Bernstein (Bernstein, 1991)	2 speakers • 1 male • 1 female	• The script consists of 954 TIMIT sentences (474 female, 480 male). • The vocabulary is ~1000 words. • Video was recorded in a studio environment.	• Video was recorded at 30 fps and a spatial resolution of 320x240 with 24 bpp. • Audio was acquired at 16 kHz.
CUAVE (Patterson, Gurbuz, Tufekci, & Gowdy, 2002)	36 solo speakers • 17 female • 19 male 20 pairs of speakers	• Script is 7,000 utterances of connected and isolated digits. • The conditions include variable speaker backgrounds and multiple speakers. • Efforts were made to balance speakers for gender, skin tone, and accents.	• Video was recorded at 29.97 fps and 720x480 resolution using a 1-MP-CCD MiniDV camera. • Audio was recorded at 44 kHz with multiplexed 16 bit stereo.

content and acquisition to allow for fairer comparisons in AV speech and speaker recognition results across differing databases. AV speech corpora should better simulate realistic non-ideal conditions, and standardize evaluation protocols to avoid biased results. This requires speech corpora large enough and with enough variability to avoid database dependent results. For example, it is naïve to perform speaker independent speech recognition experiments on a database consisting of only 10 speakers, and then to make general claims about the system recognition performance on a general level. Even if the database is large, the results may be specific to the speakers in the database. Unfortunately, it is often extremely

Table 2. A list of popular audio-visual speech corpora and short descriptions of each. All databases are publicly available (may require a fee) with the exception of the IBM ViaVoice database. (continued)

Audio-visual Speech Corpora (continued)			
Database	**Subjects**	**Description and environmental conditions**	**Recording characteristics**
DAVID (Chibelushi, Gandon, Mason, Deravi, & Johnston, 1996)	100 speakers • 31 subjects recorded in 5 sessions	• Speakers utter a digit set, alphabet set, vowel-consonant-vowel syllables, and phrases recorded over 5 sessions. • The video contains variable background complexity and illumination conditions.	• Not reported in the literature.
IBM ViaVoice (Chaudhari & Ramaswamy, 2003)'	290 speakers	• Continuous speech was read consisting of a ~10,500-word vocabulary. • Approximately 50 hours of speech were recorded. • Recordings were done in an office environment (~19.5 dB)	• Video resolution is 704x480 interlaced at 30 fps. • Audio was collected at 16 kHz.
M2VTS (Pigeon & Vandendorpe, 1997)	37 speakers	• Subject utter digits 0 - 9 recorded over 5 sessions with at least one week between recording periods. • A head rotation shot was included for 3-D tracking purposes.	• An Hi8 video camera recorded video at 720x576 resolution at 50 Hz, interlaced. • Database images are 350x286 pixels and audio was digitally recorded at 48 kHz with 16 bit encoding.
VidTIMIT (Sanderson & Paliwal, 2003)	43 speakers • 19 female • 24 male	• Speakers recite continuous sentences from the NTIMIT corpus (Jankowski, Kalyanswamy, Basson, & Spitz, 1990). • Video was recorded in a noisy office environment. • All sentences are phonetically balanced. • The camera zoom factor was randomly perturbed between recordings. • Head rotation sequence is included.	• Database was stored as JPEG images at 512x384 resolution. • Audio was stored as 16 bit 32 kHz WAV files.
Tulips (Movellan, 1995)	12 speakers	• Speakers utter the first four digits in English. • Video was recorded in ideal conditions.	• Data was stored as 100x75 pixel 8 bit gray level PGM images.
VALID (Fox, O'Mullane, & Reilly, 2005)	106 speakers • 77 male • 29 female	• Subjects recite their names, a 10-digit string, and a 7-word sentence. • Speakers were recorded during 5 sessions, 4 in office environments and once in a studio environment. • A head rotation shot was included.	• A Canon 3CCD XM1 PAL digital camcorder was used to capture video at 25 fps and 720x576 resolution at 24 bpp. • Audio was recorded at 16 bits and 32 kHz.
XM2VTS (Messer, Matas, Kittler, Luettin, & Maitre, 1999)	295 speakers	• Subjects utter 2 specified ten-digit sequences, and a seven-word sentence. • There are two recordings of each phrase gathered over 4 sessions. • A head rotation shot was included for 3-D tracking purposes.	• A Sony VX1000E digital camcorder was used to capture 720x576 resolution video. • Audio was recorded at 16 bits and 32 kHz.

time consuming to collect large speech corpora (especially with video) due to the human element and database size considerations. As it becomes more feasible to store and transport large amounts of data, the database sizes should increase, however, database collection methods must also be considered to prevent artificial effects due to codec compression or other data processing artifacts. In a later section, we discuss challenges facing development of AV speech and speaker recognition systems.

A BRIEF SURVEY OF AUDIO-VISUAL RECOGNITION SYSTEMS

Many various AV speech recognition and biometrics systems have been reported in the literature. These systems are typically difficult to compare because each may use different visual features, AV databases, visual feature extraction methods, AV integration techniques, and evaluation procedures. Nonetheless, we present various AV and V-only dynamic speech and speaker recognition systems found in the literature, provide comparisons, and show experimental results.

Audio-Visual Biometrics Systems

In (Luettin, Thacker, & Beet, 1996), a dynamic visual-only speaker identification system was proposed, which focused solely on information present in the mouth region. They used the Tulips database (Movellan, 1995) to perform text-dependent (TD) and text-independent (TI) experiments utilizing HMMs for recognition. They reported TD speaker recognition rates of 72.9%, 89.6%, and 91.7% for shape-based, appearance-based, and hybrid (concatenated combination) visual features, respectively. They achieved TI recognition rates of 83.3%, 95.8%, and 97.9% utilizing the same shape-based, appearance-based, and joint visual features as in the TD experiments. Overall, they achieved better recognition rates using appearance-based over shape-based visual features, although the hybrid (shape and appearance) visual features showed further improvement.

Audio-visual speaker recognition systems utilizing static visual features have also been reported in the literature. In (Chibelushi, Deravi, & Mason, 1993), an audio-visual speaker identification system is proposed, which combines acoustic information with visual information obtained from speaker face profiles. Utilizing speech information, static visual information, and combined audio-visual information, they report EERs of 3.4%, 3.0%, and 1.5%, respectively, highlighting the usefulness of multiple modalities for recognition tasks.

In (Brunelli & Falavigna, 1995), the proposed, TI, AV biometrics system based on audio-only speaker identification and face recognition was able to identify speakers with recognition rates of 98%, 91%, and 88% utilizing integrated AV features, audio-only features and face recognition, respectively. In these experiments, the speech classifiers corresponded to static and dynamic acoustic features obtained from the short time spectral analysis of the audio signal. Audio-based speaker recognition was then determined using vector quantization (VQ). The face recognition used visual classifiers corresponding to image features extracted around the eyes, nose, and mouth. Again the integrated system's performance surpasses the audio-only speaker recognition and face recognition systems individually.

In another system (Ben-Yacoub, Abdeljaoued, & Mayoraz, 1999; Messer, Matas, Kittler, Luettin, & Maitre, 1999), TD and TI speaker verification experiments were performed on the XM2VTS database. This system made use of elastic graph matching to obtain face similarity scores. In the experiments, SVMs, Bayesian methods, Fisher's linear discriminant, decision trees, and multilayer perceptrons (MLP) were used for post-classification opinion fusion. They reported the highest verification rates utilizing SVM and Bayesian classifiers for fusion. In these cases, integrating information from multiple modalities outperformed single modality results.

The TI speaker verification system proposed in (Sanderson & Paliwal, 2004) utilized features of a person's speech and facial appearance. They used static visual features obtained by principle component analysis (PCA) on the face image area containing a speaker's eyes and nose. Mel frequency cepstral coefficients (MFCC) along with their delta and acceleration values were used as the audio features. Silence and background noise were removed using a voice-activity-detector (VAD), and Gaussian mixture models (GMM) were trained as experts to obtain opinions based on acoustic features. Sanderson and Paliwal performed an extensive investigation of non-adaptive and adaptive information fusion methods and analyzed the results in clean and noisy conditions. More specifically, they tested fusion techniques based on non-adaptive and adaptive weighted summation, SVMs, concatenation, piece-wise linear post-classifiers, and Bayesian classifiers. These fusion techniques were examined across a range of SNRs (12, 8, 4, 0, -4, -8 dB) on the VidTimit database. The best result achieved at 12 dB SNR had a total error rate (defined as the sum of FAR and FRR) near 5% using a Bayesian fusion method. The best total error rate achieved at -8 dB SNR was approximately 7% using a piece-wise linear post-classifier.

In (Jourlin, Luettin, Genoud, & Wassner, 1997), a TD AV speaker verification system was described utilizing dynamic audio and visual features. Acoustic features were LPC coefficients along with their first and second order derivatives. Visual features included lip shape parameters, intensity parameters, and the scale. In all, there were 39 acoustic features and 25 visual features, which were used to train HMMs for evaluation on the M2VTS database. The authors demonstrated an improved false acceptance rate (FAR) of 0.5%, utilizing a weighted combination of the audio and visual scores, over 2.3% realized by the audio-only system.

A speaker recognition and verification system utilizing multi-stream HMMs is presented in (Unknown, 1999; Wark, Sridharan, & Chandran, 1999, 2000). Acoustic features in this system were MFCCs, and visual features were found from the lip contours using PCA and LDA. Their integrated AV system showed significant improvement over the audio-only system at low SNRs, and even surpassed the visual-only systems in these noisy acoustic conditions while demonstrating competitive rates at high SNRs compared to the audio-only system.

In (Aleksic & Katsaggelos, 2003a, 2004) an AV speaker recognition system based on MFCCs (plus first and second order derivatives) and MPEG-4 compliant facial animation parameters (FAPs) was presented. FAPs are shape based visual features which represent the motion of facial components. In this work, PCA was performed on the FAPs corresponding to the outer-lip contour, and the three highest energy PCA projection coefficients, along with their first- and second-order derivatives, were used as visual features. In order to extract FAPs, a novel method based on curve fitting and snake contour fitting was developed to estimate the outer-lip contour from the video in the AMP/CMU database (Aleksic et

Table 3. Speaker recognition and verification results reported in (Aleksic & Katsaggelos, 2003a). Note the improvement of the integrated AV systems over the audio-only (AO) system at low audio SNRs (Adapted from Aleksic & Katsaggelos, 2003a).

	Identification Error (%)		Verification Error (EER%)	
SNR	AO	AV	AO	AV
30	5.13	5.13	2.56	1.71
20	19.51	7.69	3.99	2.28
10	38.03	10.26	4.99	2.71
0	53.1	12.82	8.26	3.13

al., 2002). Using these features and single stream HMMs, they performed speaker identification and verification experiments across audio SNRs of 0 to 30 dB. Their results are summarized in Table 3.

The AV speaker identification and verification system proposed in (Chaudhari & Ramaswamy, 2003), dynamically modeled the audio and visual information reliability with time-varying parameters dependent on the context created by local behavior of the AV data stream. Their system extracted 23 MFCC coefficients and 24 DCT coefficients from the normalized mouth region as the audio and visual parameters, respectively. GMMs were chosen to model the speakers and time-dependent parameters in order to estimate the stream reliability. System performance was evaluated on the IBM ViaVoice database, and EERs of 1.04%, 1.71%, 1.51%, and 1.22% were obtained for the adaptive integrated AV, audio-only, video-only, and static AV systems, respectively.

An Audio-Visual Dynamic Biometrics Implementation

In (Shiell et al., 2007) a dynamic video-only biometrics system was implemented with a robust and automatic method for tracking speakers' faces despite most of the adverse conditions mentioned previously. The overall system is shown in Figure 6 with the visual front-end expanded to show the sub-components of the visual feature extraction process. The system relied on Viola and Jones based face detection

Figure 6. Three examples of Haar features used to build classifiers in Viola and Jones face detection

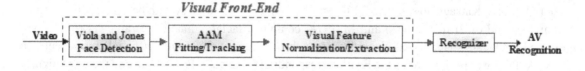

Figure 7. The automatic visual biometrics system proposed by (Shiell, Terry, Aleksic, & Katsaggelos, 2007). The visual front-end of the system consists of four main components: face detection, face tracking, visual feature normalization/extraction, and recognition.

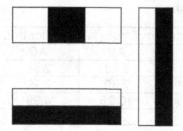

(Viola & Jones, 2001) for initialization, and active appearance models (AAMs) for face tracking and normalization as well as feature location. These visual detection and tracking methods represent robust and efficient algorithms, which allow the system to operate in real-time on a wide variety of speakers in most environments with little user cooperation required.

The AAM fitting algorithm used to track a speaker's face in this system was initialized near the speaker's face in the frame. The face region detected by the Viola and Jones face detection algorithm was used as the initial location for AAM fitting. Many variations on the Viola and Jones face detection algorithm exist, but in general these algorithms multiply simple (Haar) features, shown in Figure 7, over many positions and scales and across many training face images to train weak classifiers using Adaboost techniques. These weak classifiers can be cascaded to form a single strong face classifier. The filtering can be computed very quickly using the integral image, which reduces the simple feature multiplications to additions and subtractions. Aligning the weak classifiers in a cascade allows the filter to rapidly validate possible object locations by immediately discarding non-object locations in the early stages of classifier cascade. See (Barczak, 2004; Lienhart & Maydt, 2002) for more details and variations on the Viola and Jones face detection algorithm. The OpenCV C++ library was used in this system, and is freely available online (see suggested readings). The face detector implemented in (Shiell et al., 2007), detected only frontal faces; however, this is ideal for speaker recognition tasks since frontal views of the face and mouth are desired anyway. The result of the face detection was a bounding box containing the face region, which was consequently used to initialize the AAM location and scale as illustrated in Figure 8.

Face tracking was accomplished using an AAM tracker similar to (Potamianos et al., 2004). In general, AAMs attempt to solve the problem of aligning a generic object model to a novel object instance in an image. The end result is that the object location is defined by a number of control points, or landmarks, which can then be used to segment the object, such as lips or face, from the image. AAMs represent a

Figure 8. Example result of Viola and Jones face detection

Figure 9. Diagram illustrating the concept of AAM's. A linear combination of texture and shape modes form a novel model instance.

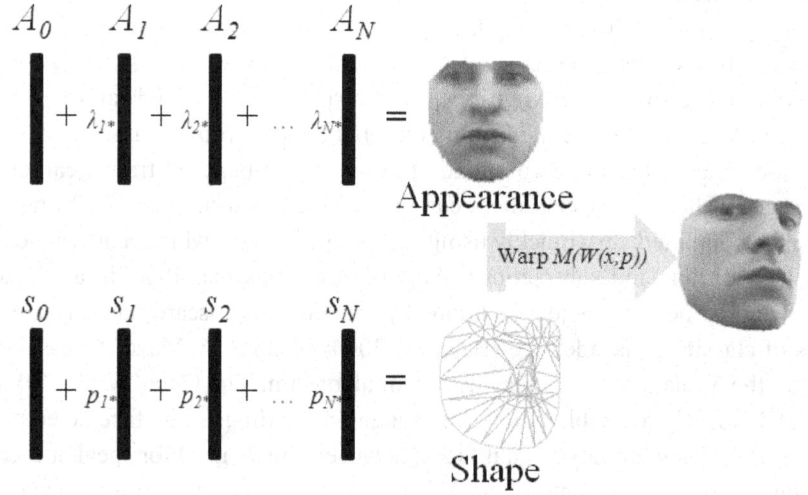

statistical model of shape and texture variation of a deformable object. Combining these shape and texture modes linearly, as in Figure 9, the AAM can then generate novel examples of the modeled object, $M(W(x,p))$, or can be fit to an existing object instance.

The process for training an AAM can be complex and many variations to the algorithm exist. Here we briefly discuss the steps involved and suggest additional sources for more detailed information regarding the theory of AAMs. The first step in training an AAM is to acquire landmark point data. Typically, specific points on the object to be modeled are marked by hand on many example images of the object. For example, in Figure 9, the vertices in the face mesh represent the landmark points. The landmark points are then aligned with respect to scale, in-plane rotation, and translation using a technique such as Procrustes analysis. The shape model is derived from performing PCA on the aligned landmarks and retaining the top few modes of variation, s_i. The texture model is obtained through a similar process. All pixels, x, in the image lying within the object mesh (defined by the control points) are warped by piecewise linear warp functions, $W(x,p)$, depending on the shape parameters, p, to the mean shape, s_o, to provide pixel correspondence across all the training images. This allows the mean texture, A_o, to be calculated, and the texture modes, A_i, to be determined by PCA of the rastered pixels. Fitting the AAM is then an optimization problem seeking to minimize the squared error between the model and the image textures with respect to the shape and texture parameters. For a more in depth discussion on implementing an AAM fitting algorithm see (Neti et al., 2000).

In this system, a frontal face AAM was trained by labeling 75 points on each of 300 training images, consisting of 24 different speakers under different lighting conditions, from the VALID database

(Fox, O'Mullane, & Reilly, 2005). In order to achieve a fast, stable algorithm speed and avoid model divergence, 5 model updates were computed for each frame. The system used a novel method using a least mean squares (LMS) adaptive filter to update the AAM appearance parameters at each iteration (Haykin, 2002). In the algorithm formulation proposed in (T. Cootes et al., 2001), the model update is estimated using multivariate linear regression. However, Matthews and Baker (2004) note that linear regression does not always lead to the correct parameter update. If the texture and shape models are kept independent, then an elegant analytical solution exists to determine the model update using the Hessian matrix and steepest descent images (Matthews & Baker, 2004). Using the inverse compositional optical flow framework, this algorithm is very efficient because it avoids recalculating the Hessian matrix at each iteration by optimizing the parameter update with respect to the average model texture instead of the extracted image texture which would require re-computing the Hessian every iteration. See (Baker, Gross, & Matthews, 2003a, 2003b; Baker & Matthews, 2004), for more information on the inverse compositional optical flow framework as well as other optical flow tracking methods. In addition, developers and researchers should be aware that Mikkel B. Stegmann and Tim Cootes have released AAM modeling tools that are publicly available online (see suggested readings).

An important and often overlooked real-time tracking issue is that of detecting tracking failure. The automated visual biometrics system described here used a simple reset mechanism based on the scale of the tracked face in the AAM rigid transform. The scale was found by calculating the norm of the scale factors in the AAM rigid transformation matrix. The system reinitialized at the face detection stage if the scale of the AAM is outside predefined bounds. In other words, if the AAM model became too small or too large the system reset. Generally, this reset mechanism worked since the AAM scale parameter typically exploded towards infinity or diminished to an extremely small scale very quickly in poor tracking conditions.

In the literature, AAMs are typically fitted iteratively until a convergence criterion is satisfied. This may be as simple as checking the fitted model error at the end of each model fitting, and resetting if the model does not converge after a certain number of iterations or converges with a large texture error. There is an opportunity here to improve tracking performance using outlier estimation to identify and correct for poor model fitting before the system tracking fails completely. The problem of visual feature extraction is greatly reduced given the results of the AAM fitting. The AAM explicitly defines landmarks on the face typically corresponding to important facial features, so extracting visual features only requires extracting the image region around some specified model landmarks. Shiell et al. extracted the center of the mouth region by determining the centroid of the mouth points. A region-of-interest (ROI) around the mouth was extracted using the scale and rotation information from the AAM rigid transform. The mouth region was rotated around the center of the mouth to match the average face shape. The extracted ROI was a square whose side length was chosen such that the ratio of the rigid transform scale to the ROI side length was equivalent to extracting a ROI with a side length of 40 pixels in the average face shape (scale = 1.0). In this way, scaling variation was reduced by consistently extracting a ROI of the same face scale to ROI side length ratio. Additionally, the in-plane rotation of the face was corrected for, by rotating the model back to horizontal utilizing the AAM rigid transformation matrix. This process is made clear in Figure 10.

After extracting and normalizing the ROI with respect to scale and in-plane rotation, Shiell et al. performed the 2D discrete cosine transform (DCT) keeping the first N DCT coefficients, taken in a zigzag pattern, for visual features, as in Figure 11.

Figure 10. Illustrating the process of visual feature extraction (Shiell et al., 2007) ©2007 IEEE. Used with permission.

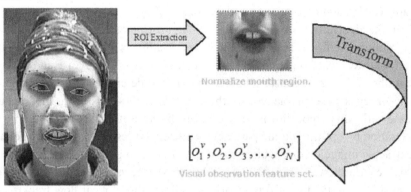

Figure 11. The pattern used to select DCT coefficients taken in a zigzag pattern

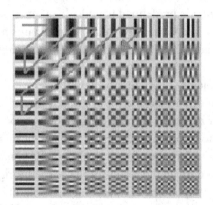

In order to test the effect of automated tracking on the speaker recognition task, Shiell et al. compared their automated visual-only biometrics system against the same system using visual features extracted using hand labeled landmarks. They performed speaker recognition experiments using the VALID database (Fox et al., 2005). A subset of 43 speakers was used in the speaker recognition experiments. For each script, every speaker was acoustically and visually recorded uttering the corresponding phrase in 5 different office environments, which varied widely in lighting conditions and background clutter. The reported speaker recognition experiments used the script "Joe took father's green shoe bench out,"

Figure 12. Extracted ROIs using manually labeled tracking showing the scale, rotation, and position variations due to interpolation. (Adapted from (Fox et al., 2005).

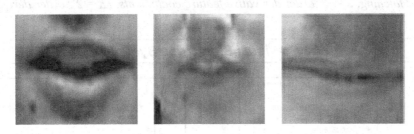

(though only the video was used) and the video sequences 2-5 because they were recorded in non-ideal environments. Experiments used shifted training and testing sets (i.e. train on videos 2,3,4 and test on video 5; train on videos 2,3,5 and test on video 4; etc.) and were done using 20, 40, 60, 80, and 100 zero-mean static DCT coefficients plus delta and acceleration coefficients. Left-to-right hidden Markov models (HMM) were tested with 1, 2, and 3 emitting states and 1, 2, 3, 4, and 5 Gaussian mixtures on the emission distributions.

Shiell et al. reported an optimal speaker recognition rate of 59.3% realized by the automatic visual biometrics system (60 DCT coefficients, 4 mixtures, 1 state) compared to an optimal recognition rate of 52.3% utilizing the manually labeled tracking data (100 DCT coefficients, 3 mixtures, 1 state). In both cases, the optimal number of HMM states was one, which reduces to a Gaussian mixture model (GMM). Surprisingly, the automatic biometrics system showed a 7% increase in speaker recognition rates, which the authors attributed to the interpolation required for the manually labeled tracking data. Interpolation was required to locate facial feature landmarks for the manually labeled data because the labeled data supplied with the database was done every tenth frame to make hand labeling feasible. It is easy to see the interpolated tracking positions may lag the actual scale, rotation, and/or position if a person moved quickly while speaking. This problem is illustrated in Figure 12, and exemplifies the need for automated tracking in visual or audio-visual speech experiments.

For convenience, the key characteristics of the AV and V-only biometrics systems reported in this section are summarized in Table 4.

Audio-Visual Speech Recognition Systems

Audio-Visual Automatic Speech Recognition (AV-ASR) and visual-only ASR (V-ASR) systems incorporate numerous parameter and design choices many of which are highly similar to AV speaker recognition and biometrics systems. Here we review several AV-and V-only ASR systems. As with AV biometrics systems, the primary design decisions include the choice of audio-visual features, pre-processing techniques, recognizer architecture, and fusion methods. Additionally, performance varies

Table 4. An overview of the visual features, fusion type, recognition methods, and databases used for the speaker recognition systems summarized. TD/TI = Text-Dependent/ Text-Independent, EGM = Elastic Graph Matching, Δ = 1ˢᵗ order derivative feature coefficients, ΔΔ = 2ⁿᵈ order derivative feature coefficients.

Audio-Visual Biometrics Systems					
System	Features	Integration	TD/TI	Recognition Methods	Database
Luettin, Thacker, & Beet (1996)	• PCA coeff. on lip shape. • PCA coeff. on grey level. profiles normal to the lip contours. • Concatentated shape and appearance parameters.	NA	TD/TI	• Speaker independent recognition performed using HMMs.	Tulips
Chibelushi, Deravi, & Mason (1993)	• Speaker face profile information.	Late	TI	• Weighted summation fusion used to evaluate speaker recognition rates.	-
Brunelli & Falavigna (1995)	• MFCCs + Δ • Static image templates corresponding to eyes, nose, and mouth.	Late	TI	• Speaker recognition performed by vector quantization on acoustic features combined with visual classifiers (template matching) of the eyes, nose, and mouth.	Private
Ben-Yacoub, Abdljaoued, & Mayoraz (1999)	• LPC coeff. • EGM similarity measure.	Late	TD/TI	• TI and TD speaker verification experiments were performed using a sphericity measure and HMMs, respectively, combined with an EGM similarity measure.	XM2VTS
Sanderson & Paliwal (2004)	• MFCCs + Δ + ΔΔ • PCA of intensity values surrounding eyes and nose.	Adaptive/ static late	TI	• Used GMMs for speaker verification and examined multiple late fusion methods.	VidTimit
Jourlin, Luettin, Genoud, & Wassner (1997)	• MFCC + Δ + ΔΔ coeffs. • LPC + Δ + ΔΔ coeffs.	Late	TD	• Utilized HMMs and a weighted combination of audio and visual scores.	M2VTS
Wark, Sridharan, & Chandran (1999, 2000)	• MFCCs. • PCA/LDA coeffs. on shape contours.	Late	TI	• Combine the audio and visual scores from a MSHMM using weighted summation approach for identification and verification.	-
Aleksic & Katsaggelos (2003a, 2004)	• MFCCs + Δ + ΔΔ coeffs. • PCA + Δ + ΔΔ coeffs. on FAPs.	Intermediate	TI	• HMMs were used for dynamic, independent, speaker recognition and verification.	AMP/CMU
Chaudhari, Ramaswamy, Potamianos, & Neti (2003)	• MFCC coeffs. • DCT coeffs. from mouth region.	Adaptive Intermediate	TI	• Used GMMs to dynamically modeled the audio and visual information reliability with time-varying parameters for identification and verification.	IBM ViaVoice
Shiell et al. (2007)	• DCT + Δ + ΔΔ coeffs. from mouth region.	Intermediate	TD	• MSHMMs were used for dynamic, independent, speaker recognition.	VALID

between databases and vocabularies, and experiments can be speaker dependent, speaker adaptive, or preferably, speaker independent.

Potamianos et al. reported results using both AV-ASR and V-ASR on the IBM ViaVoice™ database with a hidden Markov model (HMM) based recognizer (Potamianos et al., 2004). Audio features were chosen as MFCCs and remain constant throughout the reported experiments. By conducting V-ASR tests, the authors identified DCT based visual features as most promising for recognition tasks. These DCT based features outperform discrete wavelet transform (DWT), PCA, and AAM based features with word error rates (WER) of 58.1%, 58.8%, 59.4%, and 64.0%, for the aforementioned parameters respectively. The authors used DCT based visual features and MFCC based audio features in various fusion situations with babble-noise corrupted audio to analyze the performance of various audio-visual fusion techniques. Through these experiments, the authors showed that a multi-stream decision fusion technique performed as much as 7dB greater than audio alone for the large vocabulary continuous speech recognition (LVSCR) case, as shown in Figure 13 (left). In Figure 13 (right), the same systems were tested but in a continuous digits recognition case and the multi-stream decision fusion outperformed audio only by up to 7.5dB.

Aleksic and Katsaggelos developed an audio-visual ASR system that employed both shape- and appearance-based visual features, obtained by PCA performed on FAPs of the outer and inner lip contours or mouth appearance(Aleksic, Potamianos, & Katsaggelos, 2005; Aleksic et al., 2002). They utilized both early (EI) and late (LI) integration approaches and single- and multi-stream HMMs to integrate dynamic acoustic and visual information. Approximately 80% of the data was used for training, 18%

Figure 13. Speech recognition results reported in (Potamianos et al., 2004) over a range of SNRs for LVCSR (left) and digits (right) using various fusion techniques (Enhanced, Concat, HiLDA, MS-Joint). (© 2004, MIT Press. Used with permission.).

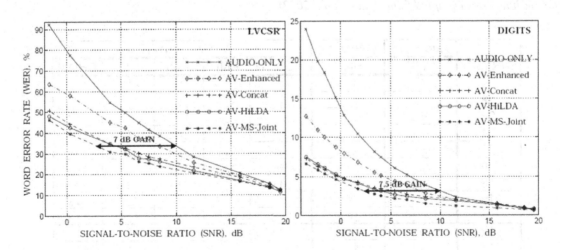

for testing, and 2% as a development set for obtaining roughly optimized stream weights, word insertion penalty and the grammar scale factor. A bi-gram language model was created based on the transcriptions of the training data set. Recognition was performed using the Viterbi decoding algorithm, with the bi-gram language model. Large vocabulary (~1000 words) audio-only ASR experiments were performed on the Bernstein lipreading corpus over a range of acoustic SNR conditions (~10 dB to 30dB), which were simulated by adding Gaussian noise (Bernstein, 1991). The audio-visual systems outperformed the audio-only system at all SNRs, but showed the most significant gains at ~10 dB with WERs around 54% compared to a NER of ~88% for the audio-only system. At 30 dB, the audio visual system showed 0-3% improvement in WER over the audio-only system.

In an extension to the work in (Biffiger, 2005), we demonstrated a 77.7% visual-only isolated digit recognition rate using zero mean DCT coefficients along with their delta and acceleration derivatives. Digits one through ten were uttered ten times for each of the ten speakers in the CMU database and visual-only, speaker-independent speech recognition experiments were done using the leave-one-out method. Optimal digit recognition results were obtained using 17 DCT coefficients, 10 HMM states (8 emitting states), and 3 Gaussian mixtures for the state emission probability distributions.

While most AV-ASR systems utilize the same HMM-based architecture, Nefian et al. explored a variety of HMM architectures (Nefian et al., 2002). Using DCT based visual features and MFCC based audio features for isolated digit recognition, the authors compared MSHMMs, independent stream HMMs (IHMMs), PHMMs, factorial HMMs (FHMMs), and coupled HMMs (CHMMs). Table 5 displays the authors' results reinforcing the advantages of the MSHMM and CHMM.

Marcheret et al. leveraged the multi-stream HMM in conjunction with audio and video reliability features to significantly improve AV-ASR performance for LVCSR by adapting the stream weights dynamically (Marcheret, Libal, & Potamianos, 2007). These results are shown in Figure 14. The authors showed that most of the increase in performance comes from the audio reliability measure. Dynamic Stream Weighting continues to be an active area of research and future research should continue to improve upon these results.

Table 5. Speech recognition rates at various SNR levels comparing the effect of various HMM recognition architectures (Adapted from Nefian et al., 2002)

SNR (dB)	Audio (%)	Visual (%)	Audio-Visual (%)				
	HMM	HMM	MSHMM	IHMM	PHMM	FHMM	CHMM
30	96.9	66.9	98.6	97.6	97.8	97.8	98.1
28	89.5	66.9	93.5	93.0	91.6	91.6	94.1
26	85.0	66.9	90.5	90.5	89.2	88.9	91.9
24	79.2	66.9	87.0	87.8	86.8	86.5	88.9
22	69.2	66.9	84.3	84.0	83.5	82.7	86.8
20	60.8	66.9	79.2	78.9	78.9	78.6	81.9
18	50.0	66.9	74.6	76.2	74.9	74.9	76.8
16	38.3	66.9	72.7	71.6	73.0	72.7	74.1
14	28.0	66.9	70.3	69.2	71.1	69.5	71.1
12	20.8	66.9	68.1	67.6	68.6	67.8	68.9
10	15.0	66.9	67.8	67.6	67.3	66.8	65.7

Figure 14. WER vs SNR using static and dynamic HMM stream weights for the LVCSR system proposed in (Marcheret et al., 2007). Dynamic stream weighting shows improvement over all SNRs.(© 2007, IEEE. Used with permission.)

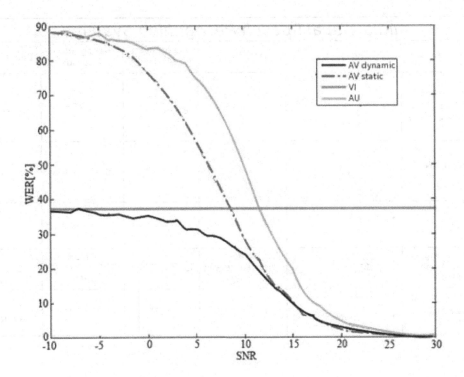

For convenience, the key characteristics of the AV and V-only ASR systems reported in this section are summarized in Table 6.

OPEN CHALLENGES IN AUDIO-VISUAL PROCESSING AND RECOGNITION

Despite the increasing interest and research on AV recognition systems, there are still many obstacles to the design, implementation, and evaluation of these systems. These issues include robust visual feature location and extraction, joint audio-visual processing, and real-time implementation issues in non-ideal environments. Additionally the lack of availability and conformity across AV speech databases makes it difficult to compare results of different AV recognition systems.

A fundamental obstacle in performing AV-ASR or V-ASR experiments is the extraction of visual features, especially under adverse conditions such as shadows, occlusions, speaker orientation, and speaker variability. Every AV recognition system requires some method of extracting visual features from a video sequence. In order to perform more meaningful experiments, large AV corpora should be used. However, it can be extremely time-consuming, if not totally infeasible, to manually label visual

Table 6. An overview of the audio-visual features, integration methods, recognition tasks, recognition methods, and databases used for the AV and V-only ASR recognition systems summarized. $\Delta = 1^{st}$ *order derivative feature coefficients,* $\Delta\Delta = 2^{nd}$ *order derivative feature coefficients.*

Audio-Visual Speech Recognition Systems					
System	Features	Integration	Recognition Tasks	Recognition Methods	Database
Potamianos, Neti, Luettin, & Matthews (2004)	• MFCCs + Δ + ΔΔ coeffs. • Compared DCT, PCA, DWT, and AAM features followed by LDA and MLLT	Compared early, intermediate, and late	LVCSR, Isolated Digits	HMM, MSHMM	IBM ViaVoice
Aleksic, Williams, Wu, & Katsaggelos (2002)	• MFCCs + Δ + ΔΔ coeffs. • PCA on FAPs + Δ + ΔΔ coeffs.	Compared early, intermediate, and late	LVCSR	HMM, MSHMM	Bernstein
Biffiger (2005)	• Zero-mean DCT + Δ + ΔΔ coeffs	N/A - Video Only	Isolated Digits	HMM	CMU
Nefian, Liang, Pi, Liu, & Murphy (2002)	• MFCCs + Δ + ΔΔ • DCT coeffs.	Compared early, intermediate, and late	Isolated Digits	HMM, MSHMM, PHMM, FHMM, CHMM	CMU
Marcheret, Libal, & Potamianos (2007)	• MFCCs + Δ + ΔΔ coeffs. • DCT features followed by LDA and MLLT.	Intermediate	LVCSR	MSHMM	IBM ViaVoice

features in each frame of a video for all video sequences in large AV corpora. Even labeling visual features every ten frames—less than half a second at 30 fps—can lead to interpolation errors, which can degrade overall performance. Furthermore, many automatic visual feature extraction systems described in the literature are tailored for the conditions in a specific database (size and position of speaker heads, colors, image quality, etc.) and may not function on a less ideal database. Additionally, virtually all AV recognition experiments reported in the literature train and test on the same database. Robust AV recognition systems should perform well on any audio-visual input.

Audio-visual feature integration also remains an open-ended problem. Now that AV speech and speaker recognition systems are maturing, more researchers are investigating methods to dynamically adapt the weight of the audio or visual features depending on real-time acoustic and visual feature reliability and consistency estimates. The AV system of Maracheret et al. described earlier reports encouraging results in this area. Other authors have reported similar results using various adaptive stream weights in MSHMMs (Marcheret et al., 2007; Pitsikalis et al., 2006), however, these systems typically rely primarily on audio reliability measures for adapting stream weights without incorporating the reliability of the visual modality.

Before AV speech and speaker recognition systems can become mainstream consumer applications there are significant challenges to overcome regarding real-time implementation. Firstly, the practicality of an AV recognition system depends on its processing time. The efficiency of the algorithm quickly becomes a priority for very large AV corpora consisting of millions of video frames or real-time operation. Second of all, the robustness of the visual feature tracking and extraction must be robust to all kinds of visual conditions. It is a considerable challenge to satisfy the robustness and efficiency criterion simultaneously. It can also be assumed that face tracking will fail eventually, and in these cases a robust system should be able to detect tracking failure and reset. Current AV recognition systems typically do not address these types of implementation issues.

SUMMARY

This chapter has discussed the primary components of audio-visual recognition systems: audio and visual feature tracking and extraction, audio-visual information fusion, and the evaluation process for speech and speaker recognition. Particular attention has been paid to the fusion problem and evaluation processes, and the implementation of a complete audio-visual system has been discussed. The overall system justifying the importance of the visual information to audio-visual recognition systems was introduced, and typical acoustic and visual features such as FAPs or DCT coefficients. Lip region tracking and feature extraction techniques were briefly reviewed followed by an analysis of the speech and speaker recognition process and evaluation. Early, intermediate, and late audio-visual integration techniques were described, and a detailed list of AV speech corpora was presented. A number of AV speech and speaker recognition systems found in the literature were surveyed to serve as a starting point for building AV recognition systems. Current issues in the field of AV speech recognition were addressed in order to identify possible areas of interest for aspiring researchers. The following section concludes with suggestions for future research in the area of audio-visual speech and speaker recognition, and points out general themes in the latest research related to AV recognition systems. Researchers are encouraged to look at the suggested readings section for helpful references related to audio-visual speech and speaker recognition.

FUTURE RESEARCH DIRECTION

Audio-visual and visual-only speech and speaker recognition is a field still in its relative infancy and has a bright and exciting future lies ahead for its research and applications. Current and future work needs to address such varied and multi-disciplinary issues as robust real-time visual tracking in real-world situations, optimal feature selection and extraction to capture linguistically salient attributes, audio-visual information fusion, system architectures to handle linguistic speech transforms such as accents and word reductions, among many other issues.

One of the first steps towards enabling the future research necessary is the compilation of relevant and complete audio-visual databases. Much work is taking place in identifying what attributes are needed in these databases, such as visual quality, environment, speech vocabulary, native-ness of the speakers, etc. Audio only corpora have addressed many of the linguistic issues and future audio-visual database collection must do so as well. The current trends in audio-visual corpora are converging on large databases recorded in real-world scenarios, such as office environments and automobiles that consist of native, as well as non-native, speakers. The content of these corpora are also advancing beyond the simple phonetically balanced TIMIT sentences to utterances that offer linguistic challenges such as those presented in conversational speech. It will be essential for emerging AV and V-only speech corpora to supply ground truth visual annotations of key facial features for evaluation benchmarking and experiment comparison. By having available databases with advanced content in real-world scenarios, improved audio-visual speech and speaker recognition systems can be researched and implemented.

As real-world audio-visual databases are produced, robust visual tracking methods are being developed. Unlike most traditional computer vision tracking applications, tracking for audio-visual speech and speaker recognition requires extreme levels of accuracy. To accomplish this, current research is turning towards 3D monocular methods that utilize motion to extract 3D parameters, as well as utilizing infrared cameras in conjunction with 2.5D methods. New facial representations have also been proposed including multi-linear models and even more advanced methods leveraging the power of tensor mathematics.

Coupled with the advancements in robust tracking, visual feature selection has moved into new areas such as 3D feature information. Currently used shape- and appearance-based features are also being combined in new and inventive ways. Much work is also beginning on selecting features that are inherently robust to rotation, translation, scale, lighting, speaker, and other physical parameters. Simultaneously, a focus is being put on designing and analyzing features that capture important linguistic information.

The fusion of audio and visual information continues to be a very active field with many new trends developing. As more research goes into current integration techniques, intermediate and late integration emerge as the best of the current breed. The focus has now turned to dynamically fusing the audio and visual information based on audio and visual environmental conditions. As important research is being undertaken on determining the modality's reliability, researchers must now learn how to best utilize this new information. Among the current approaches, two have recently come to the forefront. Firstly, statistical or functional mappings between reliability measures and fusion weights are being explored. Secondly, new hidden Markov model (HMM) based recognizer architectures are being explored. These new architectures attempt to implicitly include reliability information into the models and to allow for statistically based fusion techniques.

In order for automatic speech and speaker recognition systems to approach human capabilities, the ability to deal with speech variations must be factored in. Dealing with accented speech has led to advances in feature selection and speech modeling, but with limited overall benefit. Accounting for other linguistic affects such as the changes in speech in a conversational atmosphere have also been approached, but also with limited results. New efforts have begun in designing complete system architectures to handle these sorts of issues. Approaches include training multiple versions of system components under varied conditions in order to "switch" between system parts when certain conditions are detected and designing HMM systems with higher levels of abstraction to statistically incorporate more variation into the models.

ADDITIONAL READING

For the benefit of interested researchers we have compiled a list of suggested readings and resources in various areas related to audio-visual speech and speaker recognition.

Human Perception of Visual Speech - (R. Campbell, Dodd, & Burnham, 1998; Flanagan, 1965; Goldschen, Garcia, & Petajan, 1996; Lippmann, 1997; McGurk & MacDonald, 1976; Neely, 1956; Summerfield, 1979, 1987, 1992)

Feature Detection/Tracking/Extraction - (Baker et al., 2003a, 2003b; Baker & Matthews, 2004; Barczak, 2004; Chang, Bowyer, & Flynn, 2005; T. Cootes et al., 1998, 2001; Duda, Hart, & Stork, 2001; Gross, Matthews, & Baker, 2004; Gross et al., 2006; Hjelmas & Low, 2001; Hu et al., 2004; Hua & Y.Wu, 2006; Kass, Witkin, & Terzopoulos, 1988; Kaucic, Dalton, & Blake, 1996; Kong, Heo, Abidi, Paik, & Abidi, 2005; Koterba et al., 2005; Lienhart & Maydt, 2002; Matthews & Baker, 2004; Viola & Jones, 2001; Wu, Aleksic, & Katsaggelos, 2002, 2004; Xiao et al., 2004; Yang, Kriegman, & Ahuja, 2002; Yuille, Hallinan, & Cohen, 1992; Zhao, Chellappa, Phillips, & Rosenfeld, 2003)

Audio-Visual Speech Recognition - (Aleksic et al., 2005; Aleksic et al., 2002; Chen, 2001; Chibelushi, Deravi, & Mason, 2002; Dupont & Luettin, 2000; Gordan, Kotropoulos, & Pitas, 2002; Gravier, Potamianos, & Neti, 2002; Luettin, 1997; Movellan, 1995; Nefian et al., 2002; Neti et al., 2000; Petajan, 1985; Potamianos et al., 2003; Potamianos et al., 2004; Rabiner & Juang, 1993)

Audio-Visual Biometrics - (Aleksic & Katsaggelos, 2006; Ben-Yacoub et al., 1999; J. P. Campbell, 1997; Chang et al., 2005; Chibelushi, Deravi, & Mason, 1997; Jain, Ross, & Prabhakar, 2004; Luettin et al., 1996; Sanderson et al., 2006; Sanderson & Paliwal, 2003, 2004; Sargin, Erzin, Yemez, & Tekalp, 2006; Shiell et al., 2007)

Multimodal Information Integration - (Aleksic et al., 2005; Ben-Yacoub et al., 1999; Chibelushi et al., 1993, 1997; Gravier et al., 2002; Hong & Jain, 1998; Ross & Jain, 2003; Williams, Rutledge, Garstecki, & Katsaggelos, 1998)

Audio-Visual Speech Corpora - (Bernstein, 1991; Chaudhari & Ramaswamy, 2003; Chen, 2001; Chibelushi, Gandon, Mason, Deravi, & Johnston, 1996; Fox et al., 2005; Hazen, Saenko, La, & Glass, 2004; Lee et al., 2004; Messer et al., 1999; Movellan, 1995; Patterson, Gurbuz, Tufekci, & Gowdy, 2002; Pigeon & Vandendorpe, 1997; Popovici et al., 2003; Sanderson & Paliwal, 2003)

Speech and Face Modeling Tools - ("The AAM-API," 2008; Tim Cootes, 2008; "HTK Speech Recognition Toolkit," 2008; "Open Computer Vision Library," 2008; Steve Young, 2008)

REFERENCES

The AAM-API. (2008). Retrieved November, 2007, from http://www2.imm.dtu.dk/~aam/aamapi/

Aleksic, P. S., & Katsaggelos, A. K. (2003a, December). *An audio-visual person identification and verification system using FAPs as visual features.* Workshop on Multimedia User Authentication (MMUA), (pp. 80-84), Santa Barbara , CA.

Aleksic, P. S., & Katsaggelos, A. K. (2003b, July). *Product HMMs for Audio-Visual Continuous Speech Recognition Using Facial Animation Parameters.* In Proceedings of IEEE Int. Conf. on Multimedia & Expo (ICME),, Vol. 2, (pp. 481-484), Baltimore, MD.

Aleksic, P. S., & Katsaggelos, A. K. (2004). Speech-to-video synthesis using MPEG-4 compliant visual features. *IEEE Trans. CSVT, Special Issue Audio Video Analysis for Multimedia Interactive Services*, 682 - 692.

Aleksic, P. S., & Katsaggelos, A. K. (2006). Audio-Visual Biometrics. *IEEE Proceedings, 94*(11), 2025 - 2044.

Aleksic, P. S., Potamianos, G., & Katsaggelos, A. K. (2005). Exploiting visual information in automatic speech processing. In *Handbook of Image and Video Processing* (pp. 1263 - 1289): Academic Press.

Aleksic, P. S., Williams, J. J., Wu, Z., & Katsaggelos, A. K. (2002). Audio-visual speech recognition using mpeg-4 compliant visual features. *EURASIP Journal on Applied Signal Processing*, 1213 - 1227.

Baker, S., Gross, R., & Matthews, I. (2003a). *Lucas-kanade 20 years on: a unifying framework: Part 2*: Carnegie Mellon University Robotics Institute.

Baker, S., Gross, R., & Matthews, I. (2003b). *Lucas-kanade 20 years on: a unifying framework: Part 3*: Carnegie Mellon University Robotics Institute.

Baker, S., & Matthews, I. (2004). Lucas-kanade 20 years on: A unifying framework. *Int. J. Comput. Vision, 56*(3), 221 - 255.

Barbosa, A. V., & Yehia, H. C. (2001). *Measuring the relation between speech acoustics and 2-D facial motion.* Paper presented at the Int. Conf. Acoustics, Speech Signal Processing.

Barczak, A. L. C. (2004). Evaluation of a Boosted Cascade of Haar-Like Features in the Presence of Partial Occlusions and Shadows for Real Time Face Detection. In *PRICAI 2004: Trends in Artificial Intelligence*, 3157, 969-970. Berlin, Germany: Springer.

Barker, J. P., & Berthommier, F. (1999). *Estimation of speech acoustics from visual speech features: A comparison of linear and non-linear models.* Paper presented at the Int. Conf. Auditory Visual Speech Processing.

Ben-Yacoub, S., Abdeljaoued, Y., & Mayoraz, E. (1999). Fusion of face and speech data for person identity verification. *IEEE Trans. Neural Networks, 10*, 1065-1074.

Bengio, S., & Mariethoz, J. (2004). *A statistical significance test for person authentication.* Paper presented at the Speaker and Language Recognition Workshop (Odyssey).

Bengio, S., Mariethoz, J., & Keller, M. (2005). *The expected performance curve.* Paper presented at the Int. Conf. Machine Learning, Workshop ROC Analysis Machine Learning.

Bernstein, L. E. (1991). Lipreading Corpus V-VI: Disc 3. Gallaudet University, Washington, D.C.

Biffiger, R. (2005). *Audio-Visual Automatic Isolated Digits Recognition.* Northwestern University, Evanston.

Blanz, V., Grother, P., Phillips, P. J., & Vetter, T. (2005). *Face recognition based on frontal views generated from non-frontal images.* Paper presented at the Computer Vision Pattern Recognition.

Bowyer, K. W., Chang, K., & Flynn, P. (2006). A survey of approaches and challenges in 3-D and multimodal 3-D face recognition. *Computer Vision Image Understanding, 101*(1), 1-15.

Brunelli, R., & Falavigna, D. (1995). Person identification using multiple cues. *IEEE Trans. Pattern Anal. Machine Intell., 10*, 955-965.

Campbell, J. P. (1997). Speaker recognition: A tutorial. *Proceedings of the IEEE, 85*(9), 1437-1462.

Campbell, R., Dodd, B., & Burnham, D. (Eds.). (1998). *Hearing by Eye II: Advances in the Psychology of Speechreading and Auditory Visual Speech.* Hove, U.K.: Pyschology Press.

Chang, K. I., Bowyer, K. W., & Flynn, P. J. (2005). An evaluaion of multimodal 2D + 3D face biometrics. *IEEE Transactions on Pattern Analysis and Machine Intelligence, 27*(4), 619-6124.

Chaudhari, U. V., & Ramaswamy, G. N. (2003). *Information fusion and decision cascading for audio-visual speaker recognition based on time-varying stream reliability prediction.* Paper presented at the Int. Conf. Multimedia Expo.

Chaudhari, U. V., Ramaswamy, G. N., Potamianos, G., & Neti, C. (2003). *Audio-visual speaker recognition using time-varying stream reliability prediction.* Paper presented at the Int. Conf. Acoustics, Speech Signal Processing, Hong Kong, China.

Chen, T. (2001). Audiovisual speech processing. *IEEE Signal Processing Mag., 18,* 9-21.

Chibelushi, C. C., Deravi, F., & Mason, J. S. (1993). *Voice and facial image integration for speaker recognition.* Paper presented at the IEEE Int. Symp. Multimedia Technologies Future Appl., Southampton, U.K.

Chibelushi, C. C., Deravi, F., & Mason, J. S. (1997). *Audio-visual person recognition: An evaluation of data fusion strategies.* Paper presented at the Eur. Conf. Security Detection, London, U.K.

Chibelushi, C. C., Deravi, F., & Mason, J. S. (2002). A review of speech-based bimodal recognition. *IEEE Trans. Multimedia, 4*(1), 23-37.

Chibelushi, C. C., Gandon, S., Mason, J. S. D., Deravi, F., & Johnston, R. D. (1996). *Design issues for a digital audio-visual integrated database.* Paper presented at the Integrated Audio-Visual Processing for Recognition, Synthesis and Communication (Digest No: 1996/213), IEE Colloquium on.

Cootes, T. (2008). Modelling and Search Software. Retrieved November, 2007, from http://www.isbe. man.ac.uk/~bim/software/am_tools_doc/index.html

Cootes, T., Edwards, G., & Taylor, C. (1998). *A comparitive evaluation of active appearance models algorithms.* Paper presented at the British Machine Vision Conference.

Cootes, T., Edwards, G., & Taylor, C. (2001). Active appearance models. *IEEE Transactions on Pattern Analysis and Machine Intelligence, 23,* 681-685.

Deller, J. R., Jr., Proakis, J. G., & Hansen, J. H. L. (1993). *Discrete-Time Processing of Speech Signals.* Englewood Cliffs, NJ: Macmillan.

Duda, R. O., Hart, P. E., & Stork, D. G. (2001). *Pattern Classification.* Hoboken, NJ: Wiley.

Dupont, S., & Luettin, J. (2000). Audio-visual speech modeling for continuous speech recognition. *IEEE Trans. Multimedia, 2*(3), 141-151.

Flanagan, J. L. (1965). *Speech Analysis, Synthesis, and Perception.* Berlin, Germany: Springer-Verlag.

Fox, N. A., Gross, R., de Chazal, P., Cohn, J. F., & Reilly, R. B. (2003). *Person identification using automatic integration of speech, lip, and face experts.* Paper presented at the ACM SIGMM 2003 Multimedia Biometrics Methods and Applications Workshop (WBMA'03), Berkley, CA.

Fox, N. A., O'Mullane, B., & Reilly, R. B. (2005). *The realistic multi-modal VALID database and visual speaker identification comparison experiments.* Paper presented at the 5th International Conference on Audio- and Video-Based Biometric Person Authentication.

Goldschen, A. J., Garcia, O. N., & Petajan, E. D. (1996). Rationale for phoneme-viseme mapping and feature selection in visual speech recognition. In D. G. Stork & M. E. Hennecke (Eds.), *Speechreading by Humans and Machines* (pp. 505-515). Berlin, Germany: Springer.

Gordan, M., Kotropoulos, C., & Pitas, I. (2002). A support vector machine-based dynamic network for visual speech recognition applications. *EURASIP J. Appl. Signal Processing, 2002*(11), 1248 - 1259.

Gravier, G., Potamianos, G., & Neti, C. (2002). *Asynchrony modeling for audio-visual speech recognition.* Paper presented at the Human Language Techn. Conf.

Gross, R., Matthews, I., & Baker, S. (2004). *Constructing and fitting active appearance models with occlusion.* Paper presented at the IEEE Workshop on Face Processing in Video.

Gross, R., Matthews, I., & Baker, S. (2006). Active appearance models with occlusion. *Image and Vision Computing, 24*, 593-604.

Haykin, S. (2002). *Adaptive Filter Theory: 4th Edition.* Upper Saddle River, NJ: Prentice Hall.

Hazen, T. J., Saenko, K., La, C.-H., & Glass, J. (2004). *A segment-based audio-visual speech recognizer: Data collection, development and initial experiments.* Paper presented at the International Conference on Multimodal Interfaces.

Hjelmas, E., & Low, B. K. (2001). Face detection: A survey. *Computer Vision Image Understanding, 83*(3), 236-274.

Hong, L., & Jain, A. (1998). Integrating faces and fingerprints for personal identification. *IEEE Trans. Pattern Anal. Machine Intell., 20*, 1295-1307.

HTK Speech Recognition Toolkit. (2008). Retrieved November, 2007, from http://htk.eng.cam. ac.uk/

Hu, C., Xiao, J., Matthews, I., Baker, S., Cohn, J., & Kanade, T. (2004). *Fitting a single active appearance model simultaneously to multiple images.* Paper presented at the British Machine Vision Conference.

Hua, G., & Y.Wu. (2006). Sequential mean field variational analysis of structured deformable shapes. *Computer Vision and Image Understanding, 101*, 87-99.

Jain, A. K., Ross, A., & Prabhakar, S. (2004). An introduction to biometric recognition. *IEEE Trans. Circuits Systems Video Technol., 14*(1), 4-20.

Jankowski, C., Kalyanswamy, A., Basson, S., & Spitz, J. (1990). NTIMIT: A Phonetically Balanced Continuous Speech Telephone Bandwidth Speech Database. *IEEE Int. Conf. Acoustics, Speech and Signal Processing (ICASSP), 1*, 109-112.

Jiang, J., Alwan, A., Keating, P. A., E. T. Auer, J., & Bernstein, L. E. (2002). On the relationship be-tween face movements, tongue movements, and speech acoustics. *EURASIP J. Appl. Signal Processing, 2002*(11), 1174-1188.

Jourlin, P., Luettin, J., Genoud, D., & Wassner, H. (1997). *Integrating acoustic and labial information for speaker identification and verification.* Paper presented at the 5th Eur. Conf. Speech Communication Technology, Rhodes, Greece.

Kass, M., Witkin, A., & Terzopoulos, D. (1988). Snakes: Active contour models. *Int. J. Comput. Vision, 4*(4), 321-331.

Kaucic, R., Dalton, B., & Blake, A. (1996). *Real-time lip tracking for audio-visual speech recognition applications.* Paper presented at the European Conference on Computer Vision.

Kong, S. G., Heo, J., Abidi, B. R., Paik, J., & Abidi, M. A. (2005). Recent advances in visual and infrared face recognition - A review. *Computer Vision Image Understanding, 97*(1), 103-135.

Koterba, S., Baker, S., Matthews, I., Hu, C., Xiao, J., Cohn, J., et al. (2005). *Multi-view aam fitting and camera calibration.* Paper presented at the Tenth IEEE International Conference on Computer Vision

Lee, B., Hasegawa-Johnson, M., Goudeseune, C., Kamdar, S., Borys, S., Liu, M., et al. (2004). *AVICAR: Audio-visual speech corpus in a car environment.* Paper presented at the Conf. Spoken Language.

Lienhart, R., & Maydt, J. (2002). An Extended Set of Haar-like Features for Rapid Object Detection. *IEEE ICIP, 1*, 900-903.

Lippmann, R. (1997). Speech perception by humans and machines. *Speech Communication, 22*, 1-15.

Luettin, J. (1997). *Visual speech and speaker recognition.* Unpublished Ph.D. dissertation, University of Sheffield, Sheffield, U.K.

Luettin, J., Thacker, N., & Beet, S. (1996). *Speaker identification by lipreading.* Paper presented at the Int. Conf. Speech and Language Processing.

Marcheret, E., Libal, V., & Potamianos, G. (2007). *Dynamic stream weight modeling for audio-visual speech recognition.* Paper presented at the Int. Conf. Acoust. Speech Signal Process.

Matthews, I., & Baker, S. (2004). Active appearance models revisited. *Int. J. Comput. Vision, 60*(2), 135-164.

McGurk, H., & MacDonald, J. (1976). Hearing lips and seeing voices. *Nature, 264*, 746-748.

Messer, K., Matas, J., Kittler, J., Luettin, J., & Maitre, G. (1999). *XM2VTSDB: The extended M2VTS database.* Paper presented at the 2nd Int. Conf. Audio- and Video-Based Biometric Person Authentica-tion.

Movellan, J. R. (1995). Visual speech recognition with stochastic networks. In G. Tesauro, D. Toruetzky & T. Leen (Eds.), *Advances in Neural Information Processing Systems* (Vol. 7). Cambridge, MA: MIT Press.

Nakamura, S. (2001). *Fusion of Audio-Visual Information for Integrated Speech Processing.* Paper presented at the Audio- and Video-Based Biometric Person Authentication (AVBPA).

Neely, K. K. (1956). Effect of visual factors on the intelligibility of speech. *J. Acoustic. Soc. Amer., 28,* 1275.

Nefian, A., Liang, L., Pi, X., Liu, X., & Murphy, K. (2002). Dynamic bayesian networks for audio-visual speech recognition. *EURASIP J. Appl. Signal Processing, 11,* 1274-1288.

Neti, C., Potamianos, G., Luettin, J., Matthews, I., Glotin, H., Vergyri, D., et al. (2000). Audio-visual speech recognition, *Technical Report.* Johns Hopkins Univesity, Baltimore.

Open Computer Vision Library. (2008). Retrieved November, 2007, from http://sourceforge.net/projects/opencvlibrary/

Patterson, E. K., Gurbuz, S., Tufekci, Z., & Gowdy, J. N. (2002). *CUAVE: A new audio-visual database for multimodal human-computer interface research.* Paper presented at the Int. Conf. Acoustics, Speech and Signal Processing.

Petajan, E. (1985). *Automatic lipreading to enhance speech recognition.* Paper presented at the IEEE Conference on CVPR.

Pigeon, S., & Vandendorpe, L. (1997). *The M2VTS multimodal face database (release 1.00).* Paper presented at the 1st Int. Conf. Audio- and Video-Based Biometric Person Authentication.

Pitsikalis, V., Katsamanis, A., Papandreou, G., & Maragos, P. (2006). *Adaptive Multimodal Fusion by Uncertainty Compensation.* Paper presented at the INTERSPEECH 2006.

Popovici, V., Thiran, J., Bailly-Bailliere, E., Bengio, S., Bimbot, F., Hamouz, M., et al. (2003). *The BANCA Database and Evaluation Protocol.* Paper presented at the 4th International Conference on Audio- and Video-Based Biometric Person Authentication.

Potamianos, G., Neti, C., Gravier, G., Garg, A., & Senior, A. W. (2003). Recent advances in the automatic recognition of audio-visual speech. *Proceedings of the IEEE, 91,* 1306-12326.

Potamianos, G., Neti, C., Luettin, J., & Matthews, I. (2004). Audio-visual automatic speech recognition: An overview. In G. Bailly, E. Vatikiotis-Bateson & P. Perrier (Eds.), *Issues in Visual and Audio-Visual Speech Processing*: MIT Press.

Rabiner, L., & Juang, B.-H. (1993). *Fundamentals of Speech Recognition.* Englewood Cliffs: Prentice Hall.

Ross, A., & Jain, A. (2003). Information fusion in biometrics. *Pattern Recogn. Lett., 24,* 2215-2125.

Sanderson, C., Bengio, S., & Gao, Y. (2006). On transforming statistical models for non-frontal face verification. *Pattern Recognition, 29*(2), 288-302.

Sanderson, C., & Paliwal, K. K. (2003). Noise compensation in a person verification system using face and multiple speech features. *Pattern Recognition, 36*(2), 293-302.

Sanderson, C., & Paliwal, K. K. (2004). Identity verification using speech and face information. *Digital Signal Processing, 14*(5), 449-480.

Sargin, M. E., Erzin, E., Yemez, Y., & Tekalp, A. M. (2006, May). *Multimodal speaker identification using canonical correlation analysis.* Paper presented at the Int. Conf. Acoustics, Speech Signal Processing, Toulouse, France.

Shiell, D. J., Terry, L. H., Aleksic, P. S., & Katsaggelos, A. K. (2007, September). *An Automated System for Visual Biometrics.* Paper presented at the Forty-Fifth Annual Allerton Conference on Communication, Control, and Computing, Urbana-Champaign, IL.

Summerfield, Q. (1979). Use of visual information in phonetic perception. *Phonetica, 36*, 314-331.

Summerfield, Q. (1987). Some preliminaries to a comprehensive account of audio-visual speech perception. In R. Campbell & B. Dodd (Eds.), *Hearing by Eye: The Psychology of Lip-Reading* (pp. 3-51). London, U.K.: Lawrence Erlbaum.

Summerfield, Q. (1992). Lipreading and audio-visual speech perception. *Philosophical Transactions: Biological Sciences, 335*(1273), 71-78.

Tamura, S., Iwano, K., & Furui, S. (2005). A Stream-Weight Optimization Method for Multi--Stream HMMs Based on Likelihood Value Normalization. *Int. Conf. Acoustics, Speech and Signal Processing (ICASSP '05), 1*, 469-472.

Unknown. (1999). *Robust speaker verification via asynchronous fusion of speech and lip information.* Paper presented at the 2nd Int. Conf. Audio- and Video-Based Biometric Person Authentication, Washington, D. C.

Viola, P., & Jones, M. (2001). *Rapid object detection using a boosted cascade of simple features.* Paper presented at the IEEE Conf. on Computer Vision and Pattern Recognition.

Wark, T., Sridharan, S., & Chandran, V. (1999). *Robust speaker verification via asynchronous fusion of speech and lip information.* Paper presented at the 2nd Int. Conf. Audio- and Video-Based Biometric Person Authentication, Washington, D. C.

Wark, T., Sridharan, S., & Chandran, V. (2000). *The use of temporal speech and lip information for multi-modal speaker identification via multi-stream HMMs.* Paper presented at the Int. Conf. Acoustics, Speech Signal Processing, Istanbul, Turkey.

Williams, J. J., Rutledge, J. C., Garstecki, D. C., & Katsaggelos, A. K. (1998). Frame rate and viseme analysis for multimedia applications. *VLSI Signal Processing Systems, 23*(1/2), 7-23.

Wu, Z., Aleksic, P. S., & Katsaggelos, A. K. (2002, October). *Lip tracking for MPEG-4 facial animation.* Paper presented at the Int. Conf. on Multimodal Interfaces, Pittsburgh, PA.

Wu, Z., Aleksic, P. S., & Katsaggelos, A. K. (2004, May). *Inner lip feature extraction for MPEG-4 facial animation.* Paper presented at the Int. Conf. Acoust., Speech, Signal Processing, Montreal, Canada.

Xiao, J., Baker, S., Matthews, I., & Kanade, T. (2004). *Real-time combined 2D+3D active appearance models.* Paper presented at the IEEE Conference on Computer Vision and Pattern Recognition.

Yang, M.-H., Kriegman, D., & Ahuja, N. (2002). Detecting faces in images: A survey. *IEEE Trans. Pattern Anal. Machine Intell., 24*(1), 34-58.

Yehia, H. C., Kuratate, T., & Vatikiotis-Bateson, E. (1999). *Using speech acoustics to drive facial motion*. Paper presented at the 14th Int. Congr. Phonetic Sciences.

Yehia, H. C., Rubin, P., & Vatikiotis-Bateson, E. (1998). Quantitative association of vocal-tract and facial behavior. *Speech Communication, 26*(1-2), 23-43.

Young, S. (2008). The ATK Real-Time API for HTK. Retrieved November, 2007, from http://mi.eng. cam.ac.uk/research/dialogue/atk_home

Young, S., Evermann, G., Hain, T., Kershaw, D., Moore, G., Odell, J., et al. (2005). *The HTK Book*. London, U.K.: Entropic.

Yuan, J., Wu, Y., & Yang, M. (2007). *Discovery of Collocation Patterns: from Visual Words to Visual Phrases*. Paper presented at the IEEE Conf. on Computer Vision and Pattern Recognition.

Yuille, A. L., Hallinan, P. W., & Cohen, D. S. (1992). Feature extraction from faces using deformable templates. *Int. J. Comput. Vision, 8*(2), 99-111.

Zhao, W.-Y., Chellappa, R., Phillips, P. J., & Rosenfeld, A. (2003). Face recognition: A literature survey. *ACM Computing Survey, 35*(4), 399-458.

Chapter II
Lip Feature Extraction and Feature Evaluation in the Context of Speech and Speaker Recognition

Petar S. Aleksic
Google Inc., USA

Aggelos K. Katsaggelos
Northwestern University, USA

ABSTRACT

There has been significant work on investigating the relationship between articulatory movements and vocal tract shape and speech acoustics (Fant, 1960; Flanagan, 1965; Narayanan & Alwan, 2000; Schroeter & Sondhi, 1994). It has been shown that there exists a strong correlation between face motion, and vocal tract shape and speech acoustics (Grant & Braida, 1991; Massaro & Stork, 1998; Summerfield, 1979, 1987, 1992; Williams & Katsaggelos, 2002; Yehia, Rubin, & Vatikiotis-Bateson, 1998). In particular, dynamic lip information conveys not only correlated but also complimentary information to the acoustic speech information. Its integration into an automatic speech recognition (ASR) system, resulting in an audio-visual (AV) system, can potentially increase the system's performance. Although visual speech information is usually used together with acoustic information, there are applications where visual-only (V-only) ASR systems can be employed achieving high recognition rates. Such include small vocabulary ASR (digits, small number of commands, etc.) and ASR in the presence of adverse acoustic conditions. The choice and accurate extraction of visual features strongly affect the performance of AV and V-only ASR systems. The establishment of lip features for speech recognition is a relatively new research topic. Although a number of approaches can be used for extracting and representing visual lip information, unfortunately, limited work exists in the literature in comparing the relative performance of different features. In this chapter, the authors describe various approaches for extracting and representing important visual features, review existing systems, evaluate their relative performance in terms of speech and speaker recognition rates, and discuss future research and development directions in this area.

INTRODUCTION

Significant interest and effort has been focused over the past decades on exploiting the visual modality in order to improve human-computer interaction (HCI), but also on the automatic recognition of visual speech (video sequences of the face or mouth area), also known as automatic lipreading, and its integration with traditional audio-only systems, giving rise to AV ASR (Aleksic, Potamianos, & Katsaggelos, 2005; Aleksic, Williams, Wu, & Katsaggelos, 2002; Chen, 2001; Chen & Rao, 1998; Chibelushi, Deravi, & Mason, 2002; Dupont & Luettin, 2000; Oviatt, et al., 2000; Petajan, 1985; Potamianos, Neti, Gravier, Garg, & Senior, 2003; Potamianos, Neti, Luettin, & Matthews, 2004; Schroeter, et al., 2000; Stork & Hennecke, 1996). The successes in these areas form another basis for exploiting the visual information in the speaker recognition problem (J. P. Campbell, 1997; Jain, Ross, & Prabhakar, 2004; Jain & Uludag, 2003; Ratha, Senior, & Bolle, 2001; Unknown, 2005), thus giving rise to AV speaker recognition (Abdeljaoued, 1999; Aleksic & Katsaggelos, 2003, 2006; Basu, et al., 1999; Ben-Yacoub, Abdeljaoued, & Mayoraz, 1999; Bengio, 2003, 2004; Bigun, Bigun, Duc, & Fisher, 1997; Brunelli & Falavigna, 1995; Brunelli, Falavigna, Poggio, & Stringa, 1995; Chaudhari & Ramaswamy, 2003; Chaudhari, Ramaswamy, Potamianos, & Neti, 2003; Chibelushi, Deravi, & Mason, 1993, 1997; Dieckmann, Plankensteiner, & Wagner, 1997; Erzin, Yemez, & Tekalp, 2005; Fox, Gross, Cohn, & Reilly, 2005; Fox, Gross, de Chazal, Cohn, & Reilly, 2003; Fox & Reilly, 2003; Frischolz & Dieckmann, 2000; T. J. Hazen, Weinstein, Kabir, Park, & Heisele, 2003; Hong & Jain, 1998; Jourlin, Luettin, Genoud, & Wassner, 1997a, 1997b; Kanak, Erzin, Yemez, & Tekalp, 2003; Kittler, Hatef, Duin, & Matas, 1998; Kittler, Matas, Johnsson, & Ramos-Sanchez, 1997; Kittler & Messer, 2002; Luettin, 1997; Radova & Psutka, 1997; Ross & Jain, 2003; Sanderson & Paliwal, 2003, 2004; Sargin, Erzin, Yemez, & Tekalp, 2006; Wark, Sridharan, & Chandran, 1999a, 1999b, 2000; Yemez, Kanak, Erzin, & Tekalp, 2003). Humans easily accomplish complex communication tasks by utilizing additional sources of information whenever required, especially visual information (Lippmann, 1997). Face visibility benefits speech perception due to the fact that the visual signal is both correlated to the produced audio signal (Aleksic & Katsaggelos, 2004b; Barbosa & Yehia, 2001; Barker & Berthommier, 1999; Jiang, Alwan, Keating, E. T. Auer, & Bernstein, 2002; Yehia, Kuratate, & Vatikiotis-Bateson, 1999; Yehia, et al., 1998) and also contains complementary information to it (Grant & Braida, 1991; Massaro & Stork, 1998; Summerfield, 1979, 1987, 1992; Williams & Katsaggelos, 2002; Yehia, et al., 1998). Hearing impaired individuals utilize lipreading in order to improve their speech perception. In addition, normal hearing persons also use lipreading (Grant & Braida, 1991; Massaro & Stork, 1998; Summerfield, 1979, 1987, 1992; Williams & Katsaggelos, 2002; Yehia, et al., 1998) to a certain extent, especially in acoustically noisy environments. With respect to the type of information they use, ASR systems can be classified into audio-only, visual-only, and audio-visual. In AV ASR systems, acoustic information is utilized together with visual speech information in order to improve recognition performance (see Fig. 1). Visual-only, and audio-visual systems utilize dynamics of temporal changes of visual features, especially the features extracted from the mouth region. Although AV-ASR systems are usually used, there are applications where V-only ASR systems can be employed achieving high recognition rates. Such include small vocabulary ASR (digits, small number of commands, etc.) and ASR in the presence of adverse acoustic conditions.

Audio-only ASR systems are sensitive to microphone types (headset, desktop, telephone, etc.), acoustic environment (car, plane, factory, babble, etc.), channel noise (telephone lines, VoIP, etc.), or complexity of the scenario (speech under stress, Lombard speech, whispered speech). Audio-only ASR systems can perform poorly even at typical acoustic background SNR levels (-10dB to 15dB). It has been well established in the literature (Aleksic & Katsaggelos, 2006) that the incorporation of additional modalities can alleviate problems characteristic of a single modality and improve system performance. The use of visual information in addition to audio, improves ASR performance even in noise-free environments (Aleksic & Katsaggelos, 2003; Chaudhari, et al., 2003; Fox, et al., 2003). The potential for such improvements is greater in acoustically noisy environments, since visual speech information is typically much less affected by acoustic noise than the acoustic speech information. It is true, however, that there is an equivalent to the acoustic Lombard effect in the visual domain, although it has been shown that it does not affect the visual speech recognition as much as the acoustic Lombard effect affects acoustic speech recognition (Huang & Chen, 2001).

Speaker recognition can also benefit from visual modality, by utilizing static (visual features obtained from a single face image) or dynamic visual information in addition to acoustic information (see Fig. 1). Utilizing dynamic visual information also significantly reduces chances of impostor attacks (spoofing). Audio-only and static-image-based (face recognition) speaker recognition systems are susceptible to impostor attacks if the impostor possesses a photograph and/or speech recordings of the client. It is considerably more difficult for an impostor to impersonate both acoustic and dynamical visual information simultaneously. Audio-visual speaker recognition holds promise for wider adoption due to the low cost of audio and video sensors and the ease of acquiring audio and video signals (even without assistance from the client) (Woodward, 1997).

The performance of both speech and speaker recognition systems strongly depends on the choice and accurate extraction of the visual features. Visual features are usually extracted from 2D or 3D images, in the visible or infrared part of the spectrum. The various sets of visual facial features proposed in the literature are generally grouped into three categories (Hennecke, Stork, & Prasad, 1996): *appearance-*

Figure 1. Audio-visual recognition system

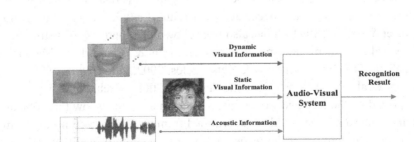

based features, such as transformed vectors of the face or mouth region pixel intensities; *shape-based features*, such as geometric or model-based representations of the face or lip contours; and features that are a combination of both appearance and shape features.

With shape-based features it is assumed that most of the information is contained in face contours or the shape of the speaker's lips. Therefore, such features achieve a compact representation of facial images and visual speech using low-dimensional vectors, and are invariant to head pose and lighting. However, their extraction requires robust algorithms, which is often difficult and computationally intensive in realistic scenarios. The advantage of the appearance-based features is that they, unlike shape-based features, do not require sophisticated extraction methods. In addition, appearance-based visual features contain information that cannot be captured by shape-based visual features. Their disadvantage is that they are generally sensitive to lighting and rotation changes. The dimensionality of the appearance-based visual features is also usually much higher than that of the shape-based visual features, which affects reliable training.

In summary, a number of approaches can be used for extracting and representing visual information utilized for speech and speaker recognition. Unfortunately, limited work exists in the literature in comparing the relative performance of visual speech features. Thus, the question of what are the most appropriate and robust visual speech features remains to a large extent unresolved. Clearly, the characteristics of the particular application and factors such as computational requirements, video quality, and the visual environment, have to be considered in addressing this question.

The remainder of the chapter is organized as follows: The importance of dynamic lip features for speech and speaker recognition is first described. Then, the structure of a speech and speaker recognition systems is presented. In the following section, classification and various approaches for detection and tracking of important visual features are reviewed. Subsequently, lip feature extraction methods are reviewed, and a description of some of the speech and speaker recognition systems, utilizing dynamic visual information, that appeared in the literature is provided. Finally, the chapter is concluded with an assessment of the topic, and description of some of the open problems.

THE IMPORTANCE OF DYNAMIC LIP FEATURES FOR SPEECH AND SPEAKER RECOGNITION

Face visibility benefits speech perception due to the fact that the visual signal is both correlated to the produced audio signal (Aleksic & Katsaggelos, 2004b; Barbosa & Yehia, 2001; Barker & Berthommier, 1999; Jiang, et al., 2002; Yehia, et al., 1998) and also contains complementary information to it (Grant & Braida, 1991; Massaro & Stork, 1998; Summerfield, 1979, 1987, 1992; Williams & Katsaggelos, 2002; Yehia, et al., 1998). There has been significant work on investigating the relationship between articulatory movements and vocal tract shape and speech acoustics (Fant, 1960; Flanagan, 1965; Narayanan & Alwan, 2000; Schroeter & Sondhi, 1994). It has also been shown that there exists a strong correlation among face motion, vocal tract shape, and speech acoustics (Grant & Braida, 1991; Massaro & Stork, 1998; Summerfield, 1979, 1987, 1992; Williams & Katsaggelos, 2002; Yehia, et al., 1998).

Yehia *et al.* (Yehia, et al., 1998) investigated the degrees of this correlation. They measured the motion of markers, placed on the face and in the vocal-tract. Their results show that 91% of the total variance observed in the facial motion could be determined from the vocal tract motion, using simple linear estimators. In addition, looking at the reverse problem, they determined that 80% of the total variance observed in the vocal tract can be estimated from face motion. Regarding speech acoustics, linear estimators were sufficient to determine between 72% and 85% (depending on subject and utterance) of the variance observed in the root mean squared amplitude and line-spectrum pair parametric representation of the spectral envelope from face motion. They also showed that even the tongue motion can be reasonably well recovered from the face motion, since it frequently displays similar motion as the jaw during speech articualtion.

The correlation among external face movements, tongue movements, and speech acoustics for consonant-vowel (CV) syllables and sentences, was also investigated by Jiang *et al.* (Jiang, et al., 2002). They used multilinear regression to predict face movements from speech acoustics for short speech segments, such as CV syllables. The prediction was the best for chin movements, followed by lips and cheeks movements. They also showed, like the authors of (Yehia, et al., 1998), that there is high correlation between tongue and face movements.

It is well known that hearing impaired individuals utilize lipreading and speechreading in order to improve their speech perception. In addition, normal hearing persons also use lipreading and speechreading to a certain extent, especially in acoustically noisy environments (Grant & Braida, 1991; Massaro & Stork, 1998; Summerfield, 1979, 1987, 1992; Williams & Katsaggelos, 2002; Yehia, et al., 1998). Lipreading represents the perception of speech based only on talker's articulatory gestures, while speechreading represents understanding of speech by observing the talker's articulation, facial and manual gestures, and audition (Summerfield, 1979). Summerfield's (Summerfield, 1992) experiments showed that sentence recognition accuracy in noisy conditions can improve by 43% by speechreading and 31% by audio-visual speech perception compared to audio-only scenario. It has also been shown in (Grant & Braida, 1991) that most hearing impaired listeners achieve higher level of speech recognition when the acoustic information is augmented by visual information, such as mouth shapes. The bimodal integration of audio and visual information in perceiving speech has been demonstrated by the McGurk effect (McGurk & MacDonald, 1976). According to it, when, for example, the video of a person uttering the sound /ba/ is dubbed with a sound recording of a person uttering the sound /ga/, most people perceive the sound /da/ as being uttered.

Dynamic lip features can also be used to improve speaker recognition performance, when utilized in addition to acoustic information (Aleksic & Katsaggelos, 2003; Chaudhari & Ramaswamy, 2003; Dieckmann, et al., 1997; Jourlin, et al., 1997b; Wark, et al., 1999a, 1999b, 2000). Exploiting dynamic visual information for speaker recognition significantly reduces chances of impostor attacks (spoofing). Audio-only and audio-visual systems that utilize only a single video frame (face recognition) are susceptible to impostor attacks, if the impostor possesses a photograph and/or speech recordings of the client. It is considerably more difficult for an impostor to impersonate both acoustic and dynamical visual information simultaneously.

Acoustic and Visual Speech

The *phoneme* represents the basic acoustically distinguishably unit that describes how speech conveys linguistic information. The number of phonemes varies for different languages. For American English, there exist approximately 42 phonemes (Deller, Proakis, & Hansen, 1993), generated by specific positions or movements of the vocal tract articulators. Similarly, the *viseme* represents the basic visually distinguishably unit (R. Campbell, Dodd, & Burnham, 1998; Massaro & Stork, 1998; Stork & Hennecke, 1996). The number of visemes is much smaller than that of phonemes. Phonemes capture the *manner*

Figure 2. Block diagram of a speech/speaker recognition system

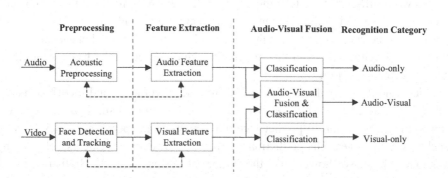

of articulation, while visemes capture the *place of articulation* (Massaro & Stork, 1998; Summerfield, 1987), i.e., they describe where the constriction occurs in the mouth, and how mouth parts, such as the lips, teeth, tongue, and palate, move during speech articulation. Many consonant phonemes with identical manner of articulation, which are difficult to distinguish based on acoustic information alone, may have different place of articulation, and therefore, are easier to distinguish visually than acoustically. For example, the two nasals /m/ (a bilabial) and /n/ (an alveolar). In contrast, certain phonemes are easier to perceive acoustically than visually, since they have identical place of articulation, but differ in the manner of articulation (e.g. the bilabials /m/ and /p/). Various mappings between phonemes and visemes have been described in the literature (Young, et al., 2005). They are usually derived by human speechreading studies, but they can also be generated using statistical clustering techniques (Goldschen, Garcia, & Petajan, 1996). There is no general agreement about the exact grouping of phonemes into visemes, however, some clusters are well-defined. For example, phonemes /p/, /b/, and /m/ (bilabial group) are articulated at the same place (lips), thus appearing visually the same.

AUDIO-VISUAL SPEECH AND SPEAKER RECOGNITION SYSTEM

The block diagram of a speech/speaker recognition system is shown in Fig. 2. It consists of *preprocessing, feature extraction, and AV fusion* blocks. Preprocessing and feature extraction are performed in parallel for the two modalities. The preprocessing of the audio signal under noisy conditions includes signal enhancement, tracking environmental and channel noise, feature estimation, and smoothing (Rabiner & Juang, 1993). The pre-processing of the video signal typically consists of the challenging problems of detecting and tracking of the face and the important facial features.

The preprocessing is usually coupled with the choice and extraction of acoustic and visual features as depicted by the dashed lines in Fig. 2. Acoustic features are chosen based on their robustness to channel and background noise (Akbacak & Hansen, 2003; Kim, Lee, & Kil, 1999; Paliwal, 1998). The

Figure 3. Mouth appearance and shape tracking for visual feature extraction: (a) Commonly detected facial features; (b) Two corresponding mouth ROIs of different sizes; (c) Lip contour estimation using a gradient vector field snake (upper: the snake's external force field is depicted) and two parabolas (lower) (Aleksic, et al., 2002)

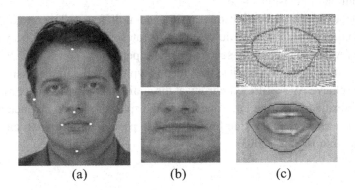

(a)   (b)   (c)

most commonly utilized acoustic features are mel-frequency cepstral coefficients (MFCCs) and linear prediction coefficients (LPCs). Acoustic features are usually augmented by their first- and second-order derivatives (delta and delta-delta coefficients) (Rabiner & Juang, 1993). The extraction of visual features for speaker recognition is a relatively newer research topic. Various face detection and tracking and facial feature extraction approaches (Hjelmas & Low, 2001; Rowley, Baluja, & Kanade, 1998; Senior, 1999; Sung & Poggio, 1998; Yang, Kriegman, & Ahuja, 2002; Zhao, Chellappa, Phillips, & Rosenfeld, 2003) that have been proposed in the literature will be discussed in more detail in the following sections. The dynamics of the visual speech are captured, similarly to acoustic features, by augmenting the "static" (frame-based) visual feature vector by its first- and second-order time derivatives, which are computed over a short temporal window centered at the current video frame (Young, et al., 2005). Mean normalization of the visual feature vectors can also be utilized to reduce variability due to illumination (Potamianos, Graf, & Cosatto, 1998).

The choice of classifiers and audio-visual fusion algorithms are clearly central to the design of a system. Statistical approaches, such as hidden Markov models (HMMs), Gaussian mixture models (GMMs), support vector machines (SVMs) (Gordan, Kotropoulos, & Pitas, 2002), artificial neural networks (ANNs), etc., are commonly used as classifiers. In order to achieve higher performance than both audio-only and visual-only systems, audio-visual fusion is utilized. If no fusion of the acoustic and visual information takes place, then audio-only and visual-only ASR systems result (see Fig. 2). There exist various fusion approaches, which weight the contribution of different modalities based on their discrimination ability and reliability. Fusion approaches are usually classified into three categories, *pre-mapping fusion*, *midst-mapping fusion*, and *post-mapping fusion* (Aleksic & Katsaggelos, 2006; Hall & Llinas, 2001; Ho, Hull, & Srihari, 1994; Luo & Kay, 1995; Sanderson & Paliwal, 2004). These are also referred to in the literature as *early integration*, *intermediate integration*, and *late integration*, respectively (Potamianos, et al., 2003). In the pre-mapping fusion audio and visual information are combined before the classification process. In the midst-mapping fusion, audio and visual information are combined during the mapping from sensor data or feature space into opinion or decision space. Finally, in the post-mapping fusion, information is combined after the mapping from sensor data or feature space into opinion or decision space.

The rates of the acoustic and visual features are in general different. The rate of acoustic features is usually 100 Hz (Young, et al., 2005), while video frame rates can be up to 25 frames per second (50 fields per second) for PAL or 30 frames per second (60 fields per second) for NTSC. For fusion methods that require the same rate for both modalities, the video is typically up-sampled using an interpolation technique in order to achieve AV feature synchrony at the audio rate. Finally, adaptation of the person's models is usually performed when the environment or the speaker's voice characteristics change, or when the person's appearance changes, due for example, to pose or illumination changes, facial hair, glasses or aging (Potamianos, et al., 2003).

CLASSIFICATION, DETECTION, AND TRACKING OF VISUAL FEATURES

Visual features are usually extracted from 2D or 3D images (Blanz, Grother, Phillips, & Vetter, 2005; Bowyer, Chang, & Flynn, 2006; Sanderson, Bengio, & Gao, 2006), in the visible or infrared part of the spectrum (Kong, Heo, Abidi, Paik, & Abidi, 2005). Facial visual features can be classified into *global* or *local*, depending on whether the face is represented by only one or multiple feature vectors. Each local feature vector represents information contained in small image patches of the face or specific regions of the face (e.g., eyes, nose, mouth, etc.). Visual features can also be either *static* (a single face image is used) or *dynamic* (a video sequence of only the mouth region, the visual-labial features, or the whole face is used). Static visual features are commonly used for face recognition (Belhumeur, Hespanha, & Kriegman, 1997; Hjelmas & Low, 2001; Kirby & Sirovich, 1990; Rowley, et al., 1998; Senior, 1999; Sung & Poggio, 1998; Turk & Pentland, 1991; Yang, et al., 2002; Zhao, et al., 2003), and dynamic visual features for speaker recognition, since they contain additional important temporal information that captures the dynamics of facial feature changes, especially the changes in the mouth region (visual speech). The various sets of visual facial features proposed in the literature are generally grouped into three categories (Hennecke, et al., 1996): (a): *appearance-based features*, such as transformed vectors of the face or mouth region pixel intensities using, for example, image compression techniques (Aleksic & Katsaggelos, 2004a; Aleksic, et al., 2005; Chaudhari, et al., 2003; Chen, 2001; Dupont & Luettin, 2000; Potamianos, et al., 2003; Potamianos, et al., 2004); (b): *shape-based features*, such as geometric or model-based representations of the face or lip contours (Aleksic, et al., 2005; Aleksic, et al., 2002; Chen, 2001; Dupont & Luettin, 2000; Potamianos, et al., 2003; Potamianos, et al., 2004); and (c): features that are a combination of both appearance and shape features in (a) and (b) (Dupont & Luettin, 2000; Matthews, Potamianos, Neti, & Luettin, 2001; Potamianos, et al., 2003; Potamianos, et al., 2004).

The algorithms utilized for detecting and tracking the face, mouth, or lips are chosen based on the visual features that will be used for recognition, quality of the video data, and the resource constraints. Only a rough detection of the face or mouth region is needed to obtain appearance-based visual features, requiring only the tracking of the face and the two mouth corners. In contrast, a computationally more expensive lip extraction and tracking algorithm is required for obtaining shape-based features.

Detection, and Tracking of Visual Features

In general, face detection constitutes a difficult problem, especially in cases where the background, head pose, and lighting are varying. There have been a number of systems reported in the literature (Graf, Cosatto, & Potamianos, 1997; Hjelmas & Low, 2001; Rowley, et al., 1998; Senior, 1999; Sung & Poggio, 1998; Viola & Jones, 2001; Yang, et al., 2002). Some systems use traditional image processing techniques, such as edge detection, image thresholding, template matching, color segmentation, or motion information in image sequences (Graf, et al., 1997), taking advantage of the fact that many local facial sub-features contain strong edges and are approximately rigid. Nevertheless, the most widely used techniques follow a statistical modeling of the face appearance to obtain a classification of image regions into face and non-face classes. Such regions are typically represented as vectors of grayscale or color image pixel intensities over normalized rectangles of a pre-determined size. They are often projected onto lower dimensional spaces, and are defined over a "pyramid" of possible locations, scales, and orientations in the image (Senior, 1999). These regions are usually classified, using one or more techniques, such as neural networks, clustering algorithms along with distance metrics from the face or non-face spaces, simple linear discriminants, support vector machines (SVMs) (Gordan, et al., 2002), and Gaussian mixture models (GMMs) (Rowley, et al., 1998; Senior, 1999; Sung & Poggio, 1998). An alternative popular approach uses a cascade of weak classifiers instead, that are trained using the AdaBoost technique and operate on local appearance features within these regions (Viola & Jones, 2001). If color information is available, image regions that do not contain sufficient number of skin-tone like pixels can be determined (for example, utilizing hue and saturation) (Chan, Zhang, & Huang, 1998; Chetty & Wagner, 2004; Summerfield, 1979) and eliminated from the search. Typically face detection is coupled with tracking in which the temporal correlation is taken into account (tracking can be performed at the face or facial feature level).

Figure 4. Various visual speech feature representation approaches discussed in this section: appearance-based (upper) and shape-based features (lower) that may utilize lip geometry, parametric, or statistical lip models (Bernstein, 1991)

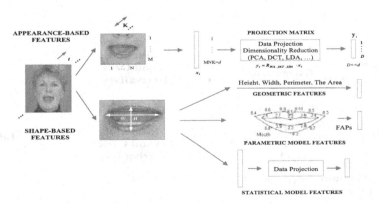

Following successful face detection, an appearance-based representation of the face can be obtained from the face image. Additional techniques can be used at this point to detect mouth corners, eyes, nostrils, and chin, by utilizing prior knowledge of their relative position on the face in order to simplify the search. In addition, if color information is available, hue and saturation information can be utilized in order to directly detect and extract certain facial features (especially lips) or constrain the search area and enable more accurate feature extraction (Chan, et al., 1998; Chetty & Wagner, 2004). These features can be used to extract and normalize the mouth region-of-interest (ROI), containing useful visual speech information. The normalization is usually performed with respect to head-pose information and lighting (Figs. 3a and 3b). The appearance-based features are extracted from the ROI using image transforms.

Shape-based visual mouth features (divided into *geometric*, *parametric*, and *statistical*, as in Fig. 4) are extracted from the ROI utilizing techniques such as, snakes (Kass, Witkin, & Terzopoulos, 1988), templates (Yuille, Hallinan, & Cohen, 1992), and active shape and appearance models (Cootes, Edwards, & Taylor, 1998). A snake is an elastic curve represented by a set of control points, and it is used to detect important visual features, such as lines, edges, or contours. The snake control point coordinates are iteratively updated, converging towards a minimum of the energy function, defined on the basis of curve smoothness constraints and a matching criterion to desired features of the image (Kass, et al., 1988). Templates are parametric curves that are fitted to the desired shape by minimizing an energy function, defined similarly to snakes. Examples of lip contour estimation using a gradient vector field (GVF) snake and two parabolic templates are depicted in Fig. 3c (Aleksic, et al., 2002). Examples of statistical models are active shape models (ASMs) and active appearance models (AAMs) (Cootes, Edwards, & Taylor, 2001). The former are obtained by applying principal component analysis (PCA) (Duda, Hart, & Stork, 2001) to training vectors containing the coordinates of a set of points that lie on the shapes of interest, such as the lip inner and outer contours. These vectors are projected onto

Figure 5. The shape-based visual feature extraction system of (Aleksic, et al., 2002), depicted schematically in parallel with the audio front end, as used for audio-visual speaker and speech recognition experiments (Aleksic & Katsaggelos, 2003, 2006)

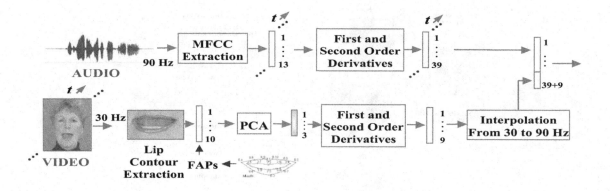

a lower dimensional space defined by the eigenvectors corresponding to the largest PCA eigenvalues, representing the axes of shape variation. The latter are extensions of ASMs that, in addition, capture the appearance variation of the region around the desired shape. AAMs remove the redundancy due to shape and appearance correlation, and create a single model that describes both shape and the corresponding appearance deformation.

LIP FEATURES EXTRACTION

In appearance-based approaches to visual feature representation, the pixel-values of the face or mouth ROI are utilized. The extracted ROI is typically a rectangle containing the mouth, possibly including larger parts of the lower face, such as the jaw and cheeks (Potamianos, et al., 2003) or could even be the entire face (Matthews, et al., 2001) (see Figs. 3b and 4). It can also be extended into a three-dimensional rectangle, containing adjacent frame ROIs, thus capturing dynamic visual speech information. Alternatively, the mouth ROI can be obtained from a number of image profiles vertical to the estimated lip contour as in (Dupont & Luettin, 2000), or from a disc around the mouth center (Maison, Neti, & Senior, 1999). A feature vector x_t (see Fig. 4) is created by ordering the grayscale pixel values inside the ROI. The dimension d of this vector typically becomes prohibitively large for successful statistical modeling of the classes of interest, and thus a lower-dimensional transformation of it is used instead. It is obtained utilizing a $D \times d$ dimensional linear transform matrix R, such that the transformed data vector $y_t = R \cdot x_t$ contains most speechreading information in its $D < d$ elements (see Fig. 4). Matrix R is often obtained based on a number of training ROI grayscale pixel value vectors utilizing transforms such as, PCA, generating "eigenlips" (or "eigenfaces" if applied to face images for face recognition) (Chan, et al., 1998; Chetty & Wagner, 2004; Summerfield, 1979), the discrete cosine transform (DCT) (Duchnowski, Meier, & Waibel, 1994; Potamianos, et al., 1998), the discrete wavelet transform (DWT) (Duchnowski, et al., 1994; Potamianos, et al., 1998), linear discriminant analysis (LDA) (Aleksic, et al., 2005; Potamianos, et al., 2003; Wark, et al., 1999b), Fisher linear discriminant (FLD), and the maximum likelihood linear transform (MLLT) (Chaudhari, et al., 2003; Potamianos, et al., 2003). PCA provides low-dimensional representation optimal in the mean-squared error sense, while LDA and FLD provide most discriminant features, that is, features that offer a clear separation between the pattern classes. Often, these transforms are applied in series (Potamianos, et al., 2003; Wark, et al., 1999b) in order to cope with the "curse of dimensionality" problem.

With shape-based features it is assumed that most of the information is contained in face contours or the shape of the speaker's lips (Aleksic & Katsaggelos, 2004a, 2005; Aleksic, et al., 2005; Matthews, et al., 2001; Williams & Katsaggelos, 2002). Such features achieve a compact representation of facial images and visual speech using low-dimensional vectors, and are invariant to head pose and lighting. However, their extraction requires robust algorithms, which is often difficult and computationally intensive in realistic scenarios. Geometric features, such as the height, width, perimeter of the mouth, etc., are meaningful to humans and can be readily extracted from the mouth images. Geometric mouth features have been used for visual speech recognition (Goldschen, et al., 1996; Zhang, Broun, Mersereau, & Clements, 2002) and speaker recognition (Zhang, et al., 2002). Alternatively, model-based visual features are typically obtained in conjunction with a parametric or statistical facial feature extraction algorithm. With model-based approaches the model parameters are directly used as visual speech features (Aleksic, et al., 2002; Cootes, et al., 2001; Dupont & Luettin, 2000).

An example of model based visual features is represented by the facial animation parameters (FAPs) of the outer- and inner-lip contours (Aleksic & Katsaggelos, 2003, 2004a; Aleksic, et al., 2002; Chibelushi, Deravi, & Mason, 1996). FAPs describe facial movement, and are used in the MPEG-4 audio-visual object-based video representation standard to control facial animation, together with the so-called facial definition parameters (FDPs) that describe the shape of the face. The FAPs extraction system described in (Aleksic, et al., 2002) is shown in Fig. 5. The system first employs a template matching algorithm to locate the person's nostrils by searching the central area of the face in the first frame of each sequence. Tracking is performed by centering the search area in the next frame at the location of the nostrils in the previous frame. The nostril location is used to determine the approximate mouth location. Subsequently, the outer lip contour is determined by using a combination of a GVF snake and a parabolic template (see also Fig. 3c). Following the outer lip contour detection and tracking, ten FAPs describing the outer-lip shape ("group 8" FAPs (Aleksic, et al., 2002)) are extracted from the resulting lip contour (see also Figs. 3 and 4). These are placed into a feature vector, which is subsequently projected by means of PCA onto a 3-dimensional space (Aleksic, et al., 2002), since the first three eigenvectors described 86% of the variance described by all 10 eigenvectors. The resulting visual features (eigenFAPs) are augmented by their first- and second-order derivatives providing a 9-dimensional dynamic visual speech vector.

Since appearance- and shape-based visual features contain respectively low- and high-level information about the person's face and lip movements, their combination has been utilized in the expectation of improving the performance of the recognition system. Features of each type are usually just concatenated (Dupont & Luettin, 2000), or a single model of face shape and appearance is created (Cootes, et al., 2001; Matthews, et al., 2001). For example, PCA appearance features are combined with snake-based features or ASMs, or a single model of face shape and appearance is created using AAMs (Cootes, et al., 2001). PCA can further be applied to this single model vector (Matthews, et al., 2001).

As discussed above, a number of approaches can be used for extracting and representing visual information utilized for speech and speaker recognition. However, limited work exists in the literature in comparing the relative performance of visual speech features. The advantage of the appearance-based features is that they, unlike shape-based features, do not require sophisticated extraction methods. In addition, they contain information that cannot be captured by shape-based visual features. Their disadvantage is sensitivity to lighting and rotation changes. Their dimensionality is also usually much higher than that of the shape-based visual features, therefore requiring much larger amount of data for reliable training. Hence, in applications in which the amount of training data is limited, or there are significant lighting and rotation changes, shape-based approaches should be used, provided that lip features can be accurately extracted. Most comparisons of visual features are made for features within the same category (appearance- or shape-based) in the context of AV or V-only speech or speaker recognition (Aleksic & Katsaggelos, 2005; Duchnowski, et al., 1994; Matthews, et al., 2001; Potamianos, et al., 1998). Features across categories have also been compared, but in most cases with inconclusive results (Aleksic & Katsaggelos, 2004a; Duchnowski, et al., 1994; Matthews, et al., 2001) (see also Fig. 6). In conclusion, the choice of the most appropriate and robust visual speech features depends on the particular application and factors such as computational requirements, video quality, and the visual environment.

In order to evaluate visual features with respect to speech and speaker recognition systems performance, we need to first evaluate the quality of feature extraction algorithms, and then evaluate the performances of recognition systems that utilize these visual features. For the first task, the *ground truth* visual features need to be provided through labeling of the evaluation data set, and compared to the extracted features. In case of shape-based features the measurement of the quality of the feature extraction algorithms can be the percentage of the overlapping area of the *ground truth* and extracted lip contours. Similarly, for appearance-based approaches, the percentage of the overlapping area of ROIs can be used as a measure. Labeling process is time intensive and costly and a large amount of labeled data is needed in order to evaluate quality of a particular feature extraction approach. In addition, for applications such as speech and speaker recognition, it is arguably more important to preserve dynamics of the visual features, rather than their absolute values. Therefore, the ultimate evaluation of visual features is performed by evaluating their effect on performance of speech and speaker recognition systems. We present various such systems in the following section.

AV AND V-ONLY SPEECH AND SPEAKER RECOGNITION SYSTEMS

In this section, we review evaluation measures, and databases commonly used for AV speech and speaker recognition and present examples of specific systems found in the literature and their performance.

Performance Evaluation Measures

The performance of speech recognition systems is usually measured in terms of word error rate (WER), or recognition accuracy. Speaker recognition systems can be classified into speaker identification and speaker verification (authentication) systems. Speaker identification is the problem of determining the identity of a speaker from a closed set of candidates, while speaker verification refers to the problem of determining whether a speaker is who s/he claims to be. Speaker recognition systems can also be classified into *text-dependent* and *text-independent*, based on the text used in the testing phase. The identification error or rank-N correct identification rate is usually used to report the performance of identification systems. It is defined as the probability that the correct match of the unknown person's biometric data is in the top N similarity scores (this scenario corresponds to the identification system which is not fully automated, needing human intervention or additional identification systems applied in cascade).

Two commonly used error measures for verification performance are the false acceptance rate (FAR) -- an impostor is accepted -- and the false rejection rate (FRR) -- a client is rejected. They are defined by

$$\text{FAR} = \frac{I_A}{I} \times 100\% \quad \text{FRR} = \frac{C_R}{C} \times 100\%,$$ (1)

where I_A denotes the number of accepted impostors, I the number of impostor claims, C_R the number of rejected clients, and C the number of client claims. There is a trade-off between FAR and FRR, which is controlled by an *a priori* chosen verification threshold. The receiver operator curve (ROC) or the detection error trade-off (DET) curve can be used to graphically represent the trade-off between FAR and FRR (Cardinaux, Sanderson, & Bengio, 2006). DET and ROC depict FRR as a function of FAR in a log, and linear scale, respectively. The detection cost function (DCF) is a measure derived from FAR and FRR according to

$$\text{DCF} = Cost(FR) \cdot P(client) \cdot \text{FRR} + Cost(FA) \cdot P(impostor) \cdot \text{FAR}$$ (2)

where *P(client)* and *P(impostor)* are the prior probabilities that a client or an impostor will use the system, respectively, while *Cost(FA)* and *Cost(FR)* represent respectively the costs of false acceptance and false rejection. Half total error rate (HTER) (Cardinaux, et al., 2006; Doddington, Przybycki, Martin, & Reynolds, 2000) is a special case of DCF when the prior probabilities are equal to 0.5 and the costs equal to 1, resulting in

$$ \text{HTER} = \frac{1}{2}(\text{FRR} + \text{FAR}) $$.

Verification system performance is often reported using a single measure either by choosing the threshold for which FAR and FRR are equal, resulting in the equal error rate (EER), or by choosing the threshold that minimizes DCF (or HTER). The appropriate threshold can be found either using the test set (providing biased results) or a separate validation set (Bengio, Mariethoz, & Keller, 2005). Expected performance curves (EPCs) are proposed as a verification measure in (Bengio & Mariethoz, 2004a; Bengio, et al., 2005). They provide unbiased expected system performance analysis using a validation set to compute thresholds corresponding to various criteria related to real-life applications.

Audio-Visual Databases

Although there is abundance of audio-only databases, there exist only a small number of databases suitable for audio-visual speech and speaker recognition research. This is due to the field being relatively young, but also to the fact that AV corpora pose additional challenges concerning database collection, storage, distribution, and privacy. Commonly used audio-visual databases in the literature were collected with limited resources, usually contain a small number of subjects, and have relatively short duration. They usually vary greatly in the number of speakers, vocabulary size, number of sessions, non-ideal acoustic and visual conditions, and evaluation measures. This makes the comparison of different visual features and fusion methods, with respect to the overall performance of an AV system difficult. Some of the currently publicly available AV databases which have been used in the published literature are the M2VTS (multi modal verification for teleservices and security applications) (Pigeon & Vandendorpe, 1997) and XM2VTS (extended M2VTS) (Messer, Matas, Kittler, Luettin, & Maitre, 1999), BANCA (biometric access control for networked and e-commerce applications) (Bailly-Bailliere, et al., 2003), VidTIMIT (Sanderson & Paliwal, 2003) (video recordings of people reciting sentences from the TIMIT corpus), DAVID (Chibelushi, et al., 1996), VALID (Fox, O'Mullane, & Reilly, 2005), and AVICAR (audio-visual speech corpus in a car environment) (Lee, et al., 2004) databases. We provide next a short description for each of them.

The M2VTS (Pigeon & Vandendorpe, 1997) database consists of audio recordings and video sequences of 37 subjects uttering digits 0 through 9 in five sessions spaced apart by at least one week. The subjects were also asked to rotate their heads to the left and then to the right in each session in order to obtain a head rotation sequence that can provide 3-D face features to be used for face recognition purposes. The main drawbacks of this database are its small size and limited vocabulary. The extended M2VTS database (Messer, et al., 1999) consists of audio recordings and video sequences of 295 subjects uttering three fixed phrases, two 10-digit sequences and one 7-word sentence, with two utterances of each phrase, in four sessions. The main drawback of this database is its limitation to the development of text-dependent systems. Both M2VTS and XM2VTS databases have been frequently used in the literature (see Table 2).

The BANCA database consists of audio recordings and video sequences of 208 subjects (104 male, 104 female) recorded in three different scenarios, controlled, degraded and adverse, over 12 different sessions spanning three months. The subjects were asked to say a random 12-digit number, their name, their address and date of birth, during each of the recordings. The BANCA database was captured in four European languages. Both high- and low-quality microphones and cameras were used for recording. This database provides realistic and challenging conditions and allows for comparison of different systems with respect to their robustness.

The VidTIMIT database consists of audio recordings and video sequences of 43 subjects (19 female and 24 male), reciting short sentences from the test section of the NTIMIT corpus (Sanderson & Paliwal, 2003) in 3 sessions with average delay of a week between sessions, allowing for appearance and mood changes. Each person utters 10 sentences. The first two sentences are the same for all subjects, while the remaining eight are generally different for each person. All sessions contain phonetically balanced sentences. In addition to the sentences, the subjects were asked to move their heads left, right, up, then down, in order to obtain head rotation sequence. The AV biometric systems that utilize the VidTIMIT corpora are described in (Sanderson & Paliwal, 2004).

The DAVID database consists of audio and video recordings (frontal and profile views) of more than 100 speakers including 30 subjects recorded in five sessions over a period of several months. The utterances include digit set, alphabet set, vowel-consonant-vowel syllables, and phrases. The challenging visual conditions include illumination changes and variable scene background complexity.

The VALID database consists of five recordings of 106 subjects (77 male, 29 female) over a period of one month. Four of the sessions were recorded in office environment in the presence of visual noise (illumination changes) and acoustic noise (background noise). In addition, one session was recorded in the studio environment containing a head rotation sequence, where the subjects were asked to face four targets, placed above, below, left and right of the camera. The database consists of recordings of the same utterances as those recorded in the XM2VTS database, therefore enabling comparison of the performance of different systems and investigation of the effect of challenging visual environments on the performance of algorithms developed with the XM2VTS database.

The AVICAR database (Lee, et al., 2004) consists of audio recordings and video sequences of 100 speakers (50 male and 50 female) uttering isolated digits, isolated letters, phone numbers, and TIMIT sentences with various language backgrounds (60% native American English speakers) inside a car. Audio recordings are obtained using a visor-mounted array composed of eight microphones under 5 different car noise conditions (car idle, 35 and 55mph with all windows rolled up or just front windows rolled down). Video sequences are obtained using dashboard-mounted array of four video cameras. This database provides different challenges for tracking and extraction of visual features and can be utilized for analysis of the effect of non-ideal acoustic and visual conditions on AV speaker recognition performance.

Additional databases for AV research are the CUAVE (Clemson University AV Experiments) corpus containing connected digit strings (Patterson, Gurbuz, Tufekci, & Gowdy, 2002), the AMP/CMU database of 78 isolated words (Chen, 2001), the Tulips1 set of four isolated digits (Movellan, 1995), the IBM AV database (Chaudhari & Ramaswamy, 2003), and the AV-TIMIT audio-visual corpus (Timothy J. Hazen, Saenko, La, & Glass, 2004).

The existing AV databases do not have all desirable characteristics, such as, adequate number of subjects and size of vocabulary and utterances, realistic variability (representing for example speaker identification on a mobile hand-held device, or taking into account other non-ideal acoustic and visual conditions), recommended experiment protocols, and ability to utilize them for text-independent as well as text-dependent verification systems. Hence, there is a great need for new, standardized databases that would enable fair comparison of different systems and represent realistic non-ideal conditions. Experiment protocols should also be defined in a way that avoids biased results and allows for fair comparison of different speaker recognition systems.

Audio-Visual Speech and Speaker Recognition Systems

Although, as mentioned above, AV speaker recognition systems can combine acoustic and only visual static (face recognition) information (Ben-Yacoub, et al., 1999; Brunelli & Falavigna, 1995; Chibelushi, et al., 1993; Timothy J. Hazen, et al., 2004; Sanderson & Paliwal, 2004) we focus here on speech and speaker recognition systems utilizing dynamic visual information.

The choice and accurate extraction of the acoustic and visual features, and the AV fusion approach utilized, strongly affect the performance of AV systems. A number of researchers have developed audio-visual systems (Abdeljaoued, 1999; Aleksic & Katsaggelos, 2003, 2006; Basu, et al., 1999; Ben-Yacoub, et al., 1999; Bengio, 2003, 2004; Bigun, et al., 1997; Brunelli & Falavigna, 1995; Brunelli, et al., 1995; Chaudhari & Ramaswamy, 2003; Chaudhari, et al., 2003; Chibelushi, et al., 1993, 1997; Dieckmann, et al., 1997; Erzin, et al., 2005; Fox, Gross, et al., 2005; Fox, et al., 2003; Fox & Reilly, 2003; Frischolz & Dieckmann, 2000; T. J. Hazen, et al., 2003; Hong & Jain, 1998; Jourlin, et al., 1997a, 1997b; Kanak, et al., 2003; Kittler, et al., 1998; Kittler, et al., 1997; Kittler & Messer, 2002; Luettin, 1997; Radova & Psutka, 1997; Ross & Jain, 2003; Sanderson & Paliwal, 2003, 2004; Sargin, et al., 2006; Wark, et al., 1999a, 1999b, 2000; Yemez, et al., 2003). These systems differ in visual features, fusion methods, AV databases, and evaluation procedures. Because of these differences, it is usually very difficult to compare systems. In this section, we present various visual-only, audio-visual- systems and provide some comparisons. An overview of various AV systems found in the literature is shown in Table 2. Several of those systems are discussed in more detail in the remainder of this section.

Table 1. Speaker recognition performance obtained for various SNRs utilizing the audio-only and the audio-visual systems in (Aleksic & Katsaggelos, 2003) tested on the AMP/CMU database (Chen, 2001)

SNR	Identification Error [%]		Verification Error (EER) [%]	
	AU	AV	AU	AV
30	5.13	5.13	2.56	1.71
20	19.51	7.69	3.99	2.28
10	38.03	10.26	4.99	2.71
0	53.10	12.82	8.26	3.13

Speaker Recognition Systems

Luettin *et al.* (Luettin, Thacker, & Beet, 1996) developed a visual-only speaker identification system by utilizing only the dynamic visual information present in the video recordings of the mouth area. They utilized the Tulips1 database (Movellan, 1995), consisting of recordings of 12 speakers uttering first four English digits. They performed both text-dependent and text-independent experiments utilizing shape- and appearance- based visual features. In text-dependent experiments, their person identification system, based on HMMs, achieved 72.9%, 89.6%, and 91.7% recognition rates when shape-based, appearance-based, and joint (concatenation fusion) visual features were utilized, respectively. In text-independent experiments, their system achieved 83.3%, 95.8%, and 97.9% recognition rates when shape, in text-dependent experiments -based, appearance-based, and joint (concatenation) visual features were utilized, respectively. In summary, they achieved better results with appearance-based, than with shape-based visual features, and the identification performance improved further when joint features were utilized.

Wark *et al.* (Maison, et al., 1999; Wark, et al., 1999a, 1999b, 2000) developed a text-independent AV speaker verification and identification systems, utilizing multi-stream HMMs, and tested it on the M2VTS database. The MFCCs were used as acoustic features and lip contour information obtained after applying PCA and LDA, as visual features. The system was trained in clean conditions and tested in degraded acoustic conditions. At low SNRs, the AV system achieved significant performance improvement over the audio-only system and also outperformed the visual-only system, while at high SNRs the performance was similar to the performance of the audio-only system.

Jourlin *et al.* (Jourlin, et al., 1997b; Wu, Aleksic, & Katsaggelos, 2004) developed a text-dependent AV speaker verification system that utilizes both acoustic and visual dynamic information, and tested it on the M2VTS database. Their 39-dimensional acoustic features consist of LPC coefficients and their first and second order derivatives. They use 14 lip shape parameters, 10 intensity parameters and the scale as visual features, resulting in a 25-dimensional visual feature vector. They utilize HMMs to perform audio-only, visual-only, and audio-visual experiments. The audio-visual score is computed as a weighted sum of the audio and visual scores. Their results demonstrate a reduction of FAR from 2.3% when the audio-only system is used to 0.5% when the multimodal system is used.

Aleksic and Katsaggelos (Aleksic & Katsaggelos, 2003) developed an AV speaker recognition system with the AMP/CMU database (Chen, 2001) utilizing 13 MFCC coefficients and their first and second order derivatives as acoustic features (Aleksic & Katsaggelos, 2003). A visual shape-based feature vector consisting of ten FAPs, which describe the movement of the outer-lip contour (Aleksic, et al., 2002), extracted using the systems discussed in previous sections, was projected by means of PCA onto a three-dimensional space (see Fig 5). The resulting visual features were augmented with first and second order derivatives providing nine-dimensional dynamic visual feature vectors. Feature fusion integration approach and single-stream HMMs were used to integrate dynamic acoustic and visual information. Speaker verification and identification experiments were performed using audio-only and audio-visual information, under both clean and noisy audio conditions at SNRs ranging from 0 dB to 30 dB. The data, consisting of each speaker uttering the same digit sequence 10 times, is divided into training, evaluation and testing part. The first six utterances of each speaker were used for training, one for evaluation, and the remaining three for testing. The same training, and testing procedures were used for both audio-only and audio-visual experiments. The obtained results for both speaker identification and verification experiments, expressed in terms of the identification error and EER, are shown in Table

Table 2. Sample audio-visual speaker and speech recognition systems

System	Features		Database	Non-ideal Conditions	Expert	AV Fusion Method	Recognition Mode*
	Acoustic	Visual					
Automatic Speaker Recognition Systems							
(Luettin, et al., 1996)	none	shape- and appearance-based, and joint (concatenation)	Tulips1	none	HMMs GMMs	none	TD+TI/ID
(Koterba, et al., 2005; Wark, et al., 1999a, 1999b, 2000)	MFCCs	shape-based (PCA and LDA)	M2VTS	white noise at different SNRs	GMMs	late integration	TI/ID+VER
(Jourlin, et al., 1997b)	LPCs+Δ+ΔΔ	appearance- and shape-based features	M2VTS	none	HMMs	late integration	TD/VER
(Aleksic & Katsaggelos, 2003)	MFCCs+Δ+ΔΔ	shape-based (PCA applied on lip-contours)	AMP/CMU	white noise at different SNRs	HMMs	early integration	TD/ID+VER
(Chaudhari & Ramaswamy, 2003)	MFCCs	appearance-based (DCT applied on ROI)	IBM	none	GMMs	early and late integration	TI/ID+VER
(Bengio, 2003, 2004)	MFCCs+Δ	shape-based and appearance-based	M2VTS	white noise at different SNRs	asynchronous HMMs	intermediate integration	TD /VER
(Fox, et al., 2003; Fox & Reilly, 2003)	MFCCs+ Δ	appearance-based (DCT)	XM2VTS	white noise at different SNRs	HMMs	early and late integration	TD/ID
(Nefian, Liang, Fu, & Liu, 2003)	MFCCs+Δ+ΔΔ	appearance-based (PCA+LDA)	XM2VTS	white noise at different SNRs	coupled HMMs embedded HMMs	intemediate and late integration	TD/ID
(Kanak, et al., 2003)	MFCCs+Δ+ΔΔ	appearance-based (PCA)	38 speakers (Kanak, et al., 2003)	white noise at different SNRs	HMMs	early and late integration	TD/ID
Automatic Speech Recognition Systems							
(Petajan, 1985)	none	shape-based	4 speakers letter and digit recognition (Petajan, 1985)	none	dynamic time warping	none	
(Aleksic, et al., 2005; Aleksic, et al., 2002)	MFCCs+Δ+ΔΔ	shape- and appearance-based (PCA applied on lip-contours and mouth images)	(Bernstein, 1991)	white noise at different SNRs	HMMs	early and late integration	
(Aleksic, et al., 2005; Potamianos, et al., 2003)	MFCCs + LDA	appearance-based (DCT and LDA)	IBM (Potamianos, et al., 2003)	white noise	HMMs	early and late integration, hybrid fusion	
(Dupont & Luettin, 2000)	PLP (RASTA-PLP)+Δ+ΔΔ	shape- and appearance-based	M2VTS	white noise	HMMs	early and late integration	

* *TD: text-dependent; TI: text-independent, VER: verification; ID: identification;* ** *Δ – first derivative, ΔΔ – second derivative*

1. Significant improvement in performance over the audio-only (AU) speaker recognition system was achieved, especially under noisy acoustic conditions. For instance, the identification error was reduced from 53.1%, when audio-only information was utilized, to 12.82%, when AV information was employed at 0 dB SNR.

Chaudhari *et al.* (Chaudhari & Ramaswamy, 2003) developed an AV speaker identification and verification system which modeled the reliability of the audio and video information streams with time-varying and context dependent parameters. The acoustic features consisted of 23 MFCC coefficients, while the visual features consisted of 24 DCT coefficients from the transformed ROI. They utilized GMMs to model speakers, and parameters that depended on time, modality, and speaker to model stream reliability. The system was tested on the IBM database (Chaudhari & Ramaswamy, 2003) achieving an EER of 1.04%, compared to 1.71%, 1.51%, and 1.22%, of the audio-only, video-only, and AV (feature fusion) systems, respectively.

Dieckmann *et al.* (Dieckmann, et al., 1997) developed a system which used visual features obtained from all three modalities, face, voice, and lip movement. Their fusion scheme utilized majority voting and opinion fusion. Two of the three experts had to agree on the opinion, and the combined opinion had to exceed the predefined threshold. The identification error decreased to 7% when all three modalities were used, compared to 10.4%, 11%, and 18.7%, when voice, lip movements, and face visual features were used individually.

Speech Recognition Systems

Petajan (Petajan, 1985) developed the first audio-visual automatic speech recognition system. He used image thresholding to obtain binary mouth images from the input video. They were analyzed to derive mouth height, width, perimeter, and area, which were used as visual features in speech recognition experiments. He reported visual-only speech recognition results performing isolated word speech recognition on a 100-word vocabulary, using dynamic time warping. He combined in serial fashion acoustic and visual speech recognizers. The visual speech recognition system is used to rescore several first choice words, obtained by the audio speech recognition system, and make a final decision.

Aleksic and Katsaggelos (Aleksic, et al., 2005; Aleksic, et al., 2002) developed an audio-visual ASR system that employs both shape- and appearance-based visual features, obtained by PCA performed on FAPs of the outer and inner lip contours (Aleksic, et al., 2005; Aleksic, et al., 2002), or mouth images (eigenlips). They utilized both early (EI) and late (LI) integration approaches and single- and multi-stream HMMs to integrate dynamic acoustic and visual information. Approximately 80% of the data was used for training, 18% for testing, and 2% as a development set for obtaining roughly optimized stream weights, word insertion penalty and the grammar scale factor. A bi-gram language model was created based on the transcriptions of the training data set. Recognition was performed using the Viterbi decoding algorithm, with the bi-gram language model. The same training and testing procedure was used for both audio-only and audio-visual ASR experiments. A summary of large-vocabulary (1k words) recognition experiments using the Bernstein lipreading corpus (Bernstein, 1991) is depicted in Fig. 6. There, audio-only WER is compared to audio-visual ASR performance over a wide range of acoustic SNR conditions (-10 – 30 dB), obtained by corrupting the original signal with white Gaussian noise. It can be clearly seen in Fig. 6 that considerable ASR improvement is achieved, compared to the audio-only performance, for all noise levels tested when visual speech information is utilized.

Figure 6. Audio-visual speech recognition system described in (Aleksic, et al., 2005). The results correspond to early (EI) and late integration (LI) information fusion approaches utilizing shape-based (FAPs) or appearance-based (eigenlips) visual features

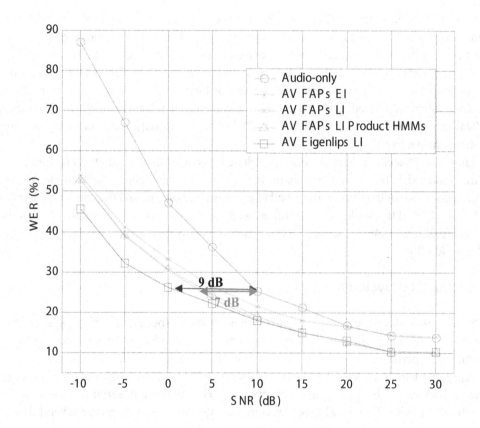

Potamianos *et al.* (Potamianos, et al., 2003) developed an AV ASR system that utilizes appearance-based visual features. They obtain a 41-dimensional visual feature vector by performing DCT and LDA on a normalized 64x64-pixel greyscale ROI centered at the mouth area. The visual features are synchronized with 60-dimensional MFCC-based acoustic features. They performed experiments on a speaker-independent, large vocabulary (10k words) continuous speech audio-visual database (Potamianos, et al., 2003). They used three fusion techniques for audio-visual ASR over a wide range of acoustic SNR conditions. They used early integration, late integration, as well as hybrid fusion approach which combines audio features with fused audio-visual discriminant features The hybrid fusion approach produced the best performance achieving, for example, an 8 dB "effective SNR" performance gain at 10 dB (Aleksic, et al., 2005; Potamianos, et al., 2003).

Dupont and Luettin (Dupont & Luettin, 2000) developed an AV ASR system utilizing a large multi-speaker database of continuously spoken digits (M2VTS). They use both appearance- and shape-based visual features. Lip contour information and grey-level information of the mouth area are used as visual features. Acoustic features are obtained utilizing perceptual linear prediction (PLP) or the noise-robust RASTA-PLP (relative spectra) methods. They employed HMMs in both early and late integration approaches for the fusion of acoustic and visual information. The experiments are performed under various acoustic SNRs (5-30dB) obtained by corrupting original signal by stationary Gaussian white noise. For example, at 15dB SNR their audio-only system using PLP or J-RASTA-PLP features, achieves 56.3% and 7.2% WER, respectively, while their audio-visual system that also utilizes lip features in addition achieves 2.5% WER.

DISCUSSION/CONCLUSIONS

This chapter describes various methods for extraction of visual features, generated by a talking person. These features can provide valuable information that benefits AV speech and speaker recognition applications. We first describe visual signals and various ways of representing and extracting information available in them. Several speech and speaker recognition systems that have appeared in the literature are reviewed and some experimental results presented. The results demonstrated the importance of utilizing visual information for speech and speaker recognition, especially in the presence of acoustic noise.

Although there are already a number of accomplishments in the field of AV and V-only speech and speaker recognition, there exist exciting opportunities for further research and development. Some of these open issues and opportunities are the following:

There is a need for publicly available multi-modal databases that better reflect realistic conditions, such as acoustic noise and lighting changes that would help in investigating robustness of AV and V-only systems. They can serve as a reference point for development, as well as, evaluation and comparison of various systems. Baseline algorithms and systems could also be designed and made available in order to facilitate separate investigation of the effects that various factors, such as, the choice of visual features, the information fusion approach, or the classification algorithms, have on system performance.

Employing 2.5D or 3D face information (Blanz, et al., 2005; Bowyer, et al., 2006; Sanderson, et al., 2006) in order to design a truly high-performing visual feature representation system with improved robustness to the visual environment needs to be further investigated.

The development of improved AV integration algorithms that will allow unconstrained AV asynchrony modeling and robust, localized reliability estimation of the signal information content, due for example, to occlusion, illumination change, or pose, are also needed.

Finally, the statistical significance of the results needs to be determined (Bengio & Mariethoz, 2004b; Rowley, et al., 1998) when speaker recognition systems are evaluated and compared. It is not sufficient to simply report that one system achieved a lower error rate than another one (and therefore it is better than the other one) using the same experiment setup. The mean and the variance of a particular error measure can assist in determining the relative performance of systems. In addition, standard experiment protocols and evaluation procedures should be defined in order to enable fair comparison of different systems. Experiment protocols could include a number of different configurations in which available subjects are randomly divided into enrolled subjects and impostors, therefore providing performance measures obtained for each of the configurations. These measures can be used to determine statistical significance of the results.

Robustness represents the biggest challenge in the practical deployment of the AV technology. However, there are few applications where the environment and the data acquisition mechanism can be carefully controlled enabling employment of current AV systems. For example, in the case of AV speaker recognition, the technology is already available for most day-to-day applications that have the following characteristics (Poh & Korczak, 2003):

1. Low security and highly user friendly, e.g., access to desktop using AV speaker recognition log-in

2. High security but user can tolerate the inconvenience of being falsely rejected, e.g., access to military, police property; a user, if rejected, would then be processed in series with another, more accurate and less user friendly biometric system

3. Low security and convenience is the prime factor (more than any other factors such as cost), e.g., time-stamping in a factory setting

The widespread use of the AV technology requires methods for handling variability in the visual environment, data acquisition devices, and degradations due to data and channel encoding. The technology is not yet available for robust, highly user-friendly and highly secured applications (such as banking). Further research and development is therefore required for AV speech and speaker recognition systems to become widespread in practice.

REFERENCES

Abdeljaoued, Y. (1999). *Fusion of person authentication probabilities by Bayesian statistics.* Paper presented at the 2nd Int. Conf. Audio- and Video-Based Biometric Person Authentication, Washington, DC.

Akbacak, M., & Hansen, J. H. L. (2003). *Environmental sniffing: Noise knowledge estimation for robust speech systems.* Paper presented at the IEEE Proc. of Int. Conf. Acoustics, Speech and Signal Processing.

Aleksic, P. S., & Katsaggelos, A. K. (2003). *An audio-visual person identification and verification system using FAPs as visual features.* Paper presented at the Works. Multimedia User Authentication, Santa Barbara, CA.

Aleksic, P. S., & Katsaggelos, A. K. (2004a). *Comparison of low- and high-level visual features for audio-visual continuous automatic speech recognition.* Paper presented at the IEEE Proc. of Int. Conf. Acoustics, Speech and Signal Processing.

Aleksic, P. S., & Katsaggelos, A. K. (2004b). Speech-to-video synthesis using MPEG-4 compliant visual features. *IEEE Trans. CSVT, Special Issue Audio Video Analysis for Multimedia Interactive Services,* 682 - 692.

Aleksic, P. S., & Katsaggelos, A. K. (2005). *Comparison of MPEG-4 facial animation parameter groups with respect to audio-visual speech recognition performance.* Paper presented at the Proc. of Int. Conf. on Image Processing.

Aleksic, P. S., & Katsaggelos, A. K. (2006). Audio-Visual Biometrics. *IEEE Proceedings, 94*(11), 2025 - 2044.

Aleksic, P. S., Potamianos, G., & Katsaggelos, A. K. (2005). Exploiting visual information in automatic speech processing *Handbook of Image and Video Processing* (pp. 1263 - 1289): Academic Press.

Aleksic, P. S., Williams, J. J., Wu, Z., & Katsaggelos, A. K. (2002). Audio-visual speech recognition using mpeg-4 compliant visual features. *EURASIP Journal on Applied Signal Processing*, 1213 - 1227.

Bailly-Bailliere, E., Bengio, S., Bimbot, F., Hamouz, M., Kittler, J., Mariethoz, J., et al. (2003). *The BANCA database and evaluation protocol.* Paper presented at the Proc. Audio- and Video-Based Biometric Person Authentication.

Barbosa, A. V., & Yehia, H. C. (2001). *Measuring the relation between speech acoustics and 2-D facial motion.* Paper presented at the Int. Conf. Acoustics, Speech Signal Processing.

Barker, J. P., & Berthommier, F. (1999). *Estimation of speech acoustics from visual speech features: A comparison of linear and non-linear models.* Paper presented at the Int. Conf. Auditory Visual Speech Processing.

Basu, S., Beigi, H. S. M., Maes, S. H., Ghislain, M., Benoit, E., Neti, C., et al. (1999). U. S. P. 6219640.

Belhumeur, P. N., Hespanha, J. P., & Kriegman, D. J. (1997). Eigenfaces vs. fisherfaces: recognition using class specific linear projection. *IEEE Trans. Patt. Anal. Mach. Intell., 19*, 711-720.

Ben-Yacoub, S., Abdeljaoued, Y., & Mayoraz, E. (1999). Fusion of face and speech data for person identity verification. *IEEE Trans. Neural Networks, 10*, 1065-1074.

Bengio, S. (2003). *Multimodal authentication using asynchronous HMMs.* Paper presented at the 4th Int. Conf. Audio- and Video-Based Biometric Person Authentication, Guildford, U.K.

Bengio, S. (2004). Multimodal speech processing using asynchronous hidden Markov models. *Information Fusion, 5*, 81-89.

Bengio, S., & Mariethoz, J. (2004a). *The expected performance curve: a new assessment measure for person authentication.* Paper presented at the Proc. of Speaker and Language Recognition Works. (Odyssey).

Bengio, S., & Mariethoz, J. (2004b). *A statistical significance test for person authentication.* Paper presented at the Speaker and Language Recognition Workshop (Odyssey).

Bengio, S., Mariethoz, J., & Keller, M. (2005). *The expected performance curve.* Paper presented at the Int. Conf. on Machine Learning, Workshop on ROC Analysis in Machine Learning.

Bernstein, L. E. (1991). Lipreading Corpus V-VI: Disc 3. Gallaudet University, Washington, D.C.

Bigun, E. S., Bigun, J., Duc, B., & Fisher, S. (1997, March). *Expert conciliation for multimodal person authentication systems by Bayesian statistics.* Paper presented at the 1st Int. Conf. Audio- and Video-Based Biometric Person Authentication, Crans-Montana, Switzerland.

Blanz, V., Grother, P., Phillips, P. J., & Vetter, T. (2005). *Face recognition based on frontal views generated from non-frontal images.* Paper presented at the Computer Vision Pattern Recognition.

Bowyer, K. W., Chang, K., & Flynn, P. (2006). A survey of approaches and challenges in 3-D and multimodal 3-D face recognition. *Computer Vision Image Understanding, 101*(1), 1-15.

Brunelli, R., & Falavigna, D. (1995). Person identification using multiple cues. *IEEE Trans. Pattern Anal. Machine Intell., 10*, 955-965.

Brunelli, R., Falavigna, D., Poggio, T., & Stringa, L. (1995). Automatic person recognition using acoustic and geometric features. *Machine Vision Appl., 8*, 317-325.

Campbell, J. P. (1997). Speaker recognition: A tutorial. *Proceedings of the IEEE, 85*(9), 1437 - 1462.

Campbell, R., Dodd, B., & Burnham, D. (Eds.). (1998). *Hearing by Eye II: Advances in the Psychology of Speechreading and Auditory Visual Speech.* Hove, U.K.: Pyschology Press.

Cardinaux, F., Sanderson, C., & Bengio, S. (2006). User authentication via adapted statistical models of face images. *IEEE Trans. on Signal Processing, 54*, 361-373.

Chan, M. T., Zhang, Y., & Huang, T. S. (1998). *Real-time lip tracking and bimodal continuous speech recognition.* Paper presented at the Proc. of Workshop on Multimedia Signal Processing.

Chaudhari, U. V., & Ramaswamy, G. N. (2003). *Information fusion and decision cascading for audio-visual speaker recognition based on time-varying stream reliability prediction.* Paper presented at the Int. Conf. Multimedia Expo.

Chaudhari, U. V., Ramaswamy, G. N., Potamianos, G., & Neti, C. (2003). *Audio-visual speaker recognition using time-varying stream reliability prediction.* Paper presented at the Int. Conf. Acoustics, Speech Signal Processing, Hong Kong, China.

Chen, T. (2001). Audiovisual speech processing. *IEEE Signal Processing Mag.,, 18*, 9-21.

Chen, T., & Rao, R. R. (1998). Audio-visual integration in multimodal communication. *Proc. IEEE, 86*(5), 837-852.

Chetty, G., & Wagner, M. (2004). *Liveness' verification in audio-video authentication.* Paper presented at the Proc. Int. Conf. on Spoken Language Processing.

Chibelushi, C. C., Deravi, F., & Mason, J. S. (1993). *Voice and facial image integration for speaker recognition.* Paper presented at the IEEE Int. Symp. Multimedia Technologies Future Appl., Southampton, U.K.

Chibelushi, C. C., Deravi, F., & Mason, J. S. (1996). *BT DAVID Database - Internal Report*: Speech and Image Processing Research Group, Dept. of Electrical and Electronic Engineering, University of Wales Swansea.

Chibelushi, C. C., Deravi, F., & Mason, J. S. (1997). *Audio-visual person recognition: An evaluation of data fusion strategies.* Paper presented at the Eur. Conf. Security Detection, London, U.K.

Chibelushi, C. C., Deravi, F., & Mason, J. S. (2002). A review of speech-based bimodal recognition. *IEEE Trans. Multimedia, 4*(1), 23-37.

Cootes, T., Edwards, G., & Taylor, C. (1998). *A comparitive evaluation of active appearance models algorithms.* Paper presented at the British Machine Vision Conference.

Cootes, T., Edwards, G., & Taylor, C. (2001). Active appearance models. *IEEE Transactions on Pattern Analysis and Machine Intelligence, 23*, 681 - 685.

Deller, J. R., Jr., Proakis, J. G., & Hansen, J. H. L. (1993). *Discrete-Time Processing of Speech Signals.* Englewood Cliffs, NJ: Macmillan.

Dieckmann, U., Plankensteiner, P., & Wagner, T. (1997). SESAM: A biometric person identification system using sensor fusion. *Pattern Recogn. Lett., 18*, 827-833.

Doddington, G. R., Przybycki, M. A., Martin, A. F., & Reynolds, D. A. (2000). The NIST speaker recognition evaluation - Overview, methodology, systems, results, perspective. *Speech Commun., 31*(2-3), 225-254.

Duchnowski, P., Meier, U., & Waibel, A. (1994). *See me, hear me: Integrating automatic speech recognition and lip-reading.* Paper presented at the Proc. Int. Conf. Spoken Lang. Processing.

Duda, R. O., Hart, P. E., & Stork, D. G. (2001). *Pattern Classification.* Hoboken, NJ: Wiley.

Dupont, S., & Luettin, J. (2000). Audio-visual speech modeling for continuous speech recognition. *IEEE Trans. Multimedia, 2*(3), 141 - 151.

Erzin, E., Yemez, Y., & Tekalp, A. M. (2005). Multimodal speaker identification using an adaptive classifier cascade based on modality reliability. *IEEE Trans. Multimedia, 7*(5), 840-852.

Fant, G. (1960). *Acoustic Theory of Speech Production.* Mouton, The Netherlands: S-Gravenhage.

Flanagan, J. L. (1965). *Speech Analysis, Synthesis, and Perception.* Berlin, Germany: Springer-Verlag.

Fox, N. A., Gross, R., Cohn, J. F., & Reilly, R. B. (2005, October). *Robust automatic human identification using face, mouth, and acoustic information.* Paper presented at the Int. Workshop Analysis Modeling of Faces and Gestures, Beijing, China.

Fox, N. A., Gross, R., de Chazal, P., Cohn, J. F., & Reilly, R. B. (2003). *Person identification using automatic integration of speech, lip, and face experts.* Paper presented at the ACM SIGMM 2003 Multimedia Biometrics Methods and Applications Workshop (WBMA'03), Berkley, CA.

Fox, N. A., O'Mullane, B., & Reilly, R. B. (2005). *The realistic multi-modal VALID database and visual speaker identification comparison experiments.* Paper presented at the 5th International Conference on Audio- and Video-Based Biometric Person Authentication.

Fox, N. A., & Reilly, R. B. (2003). *Audio-visual speaker identification based on the use of dynamic audio and visual features.* Paper presented at the 4th Int. Conf. Audio- and Video-Based Biometric Person Authentication, Guildford, U.K.

Frischolz, R. W., & Dieckmann, U. (2000). BioID: A multimodal biometric identification system. *Computer, 33*, 64-68.

Goldschen, A. J., Garcia, O. N., & Petajan, E. D. (1996). Rationale for phoneme-viseme mapping and feature selection in visual speech recognition. In D. G. Stork & M. E. Hennecke (Eds.), *Speechreading by Humans and Machines* (pp. 505-515). Berlin, Germany: Springer.

Gordan, M., Kotropoulos, C., & Pitas, I. (2002). A support vector machine-based dynamic network for visual speech recognition applications. *EURASIP J. Appl. Signal Processing, 2002*(11), 1248 - 1259.

Graf, H. P., Cosatto, E., & Potamianos, G. (1997). *Robust recognition of faces and facial features with a multi-modal system.* Paper presented at the Proc. Int. Conf. Systems, Man, Cybernetics.

Grant, K. W., & Braida, L. D. (1991). Evaluating the articulation index for auditory-visual input. *Journal of the Acoustical Society of America, 89*, 2950-2960.

Hall, D. L., & Llinas, J. (2001). Multisensor data fusion *Handbook of Multisensor data fusion* (pp. 1-10): CRC Press.

Hazen, T. J., Saenko, K., La, C.-H., & Glass, J. (2004). *A segment-based audio-visual speech recognizer: Data collection, development and initial experiments.* Paper presented at the International Conference on Multimodal Interfaces.

Hazen, T. J., Weinstein, E., Kabir, R., Park, A., & Heisele, B. (2003). *Multi-modal face and speake identification on a handheld device.* Paper presented at the Works, Multimodal User Authentication.

Hennecke, M. E., Stork, D. G., & Prasad, K. V. (1996). Visionary speech: Looking ahead to practical speechreading systems *Speechreading by Humans and Machines* (pp. 331-349). Berlin, Germany: Springer.

Hjelmas, E., & Low, B. K. (2001). Face detection: A survey. *Computer Vision Image Understanding, 83*(3), 236-274.

Ho, T. K., Hull, J. J., & Srihari, S. N. (1994). Decision combination in multiple classifier systems. *IEEE Trans. on Pattern Anal. Machine Intell., 16*, 66-75.

Hong, L., & Jain, A. (1998). Integrating faces and fingerprints for personal identification. *IEEE Trans. Pattern Anal. Machine Intell., 20*, 1295-1307.

Huang, F. J., & Chen, T. (2001). *Consideration of Lombard effect for speechreading.* Paper presented at the Proc. Works. Multimedia Signal Process.

Jain, A. K., Ross, A., & Prabhakar, S. (2004). An introduction to biometric recognition. *IEEE Trans. Circuits Systems Video Technol., 14*(1), 4-20.

Jain, A. K., & Uludag, U. (2003). Hiding biometric data. *IEEE Trans. on Pattern Analysis and Machine Intelligence, 25*(11), 1494-1498.

Jiang, J., Alwan, A., Keating, P. A., E. T. Auer, J., & Bernstein, L. E. (2002). On the relationship between face movements, tongue movements, and speech acoustics. *EURASIP J. Appl. Signal Processing, 2002*(11), 1174 - 1188.

Jourlin, P., Luettin, J., Genoud, D., & Wassner, H. (1997a). Acoustic-labial speaker verification. *Pattern Recogn. Lett., 18*, 853-858.

Jourlin, P., Luettin, J., Genoud, D., & Wassner, H. (1997b). *Integrating acoustic and labial information for speaker identification and verification.* Paper presented at the 5th Eur. Conf. Speech Communication Technology, Rhodes, Greece.

Kanak, A., Erzin, E., Yemez, Y., & Tekalp, A. M. (2003). *Joint audio-video processing for biometric speaker identification.* Paper presented at the Int. Conf. Acoustic, Speech Signal Processing, Hong Kong, China.

Kass, M., Witkin, A., & Terzopoulos, D. (1988). Snakes: Active contour models. *Int. J. Comput. Vision, 4*(4), 321-331.

Kim, D.-S., Lee, S.-Y., & Kil, R. M. (1999). Auditory processing of speech signals for robust speech recognition in real-world noisy environments. *IEEE Trans. on Speech and Audio Processing, 7*, 55-69.

Kirby, M., & Sirovich, L. (1990). Application of the Karhunen-Loeve procedure for the characterization of human faces. *IEEE Trans. Patt. Anal. Mach. Intell., 12*, 103-108.

Kittler, J., Hatef, M., Duin, P. W., & Matas, J. (1998). On combining classifiers. *IEEE Trans. Pattern Anal. Machine Intell., 20*, 226-239.

Kittler, J., Matas, J., Johnsson, K., & Ramos-Sanchez (1997). Combining evidence in personal identity verification systems. *Pattern Recogn. Lett., 18*, 845-852.

Kittler, J., & Messer, K. (2002). *Fusion of multiple experts in multimodal biometric personal identity verification systems.* Paper presented at the 12th IEEE Workshop Neural Networks Sig. Processing, Switzerland.

Kong, S. G., Heo, J., Abidi, B. R., Paik, J., & Abidi, M. A. (2005). Recent advances in visual and infrared face recognition - A review. *Computer Vision Image Understanding, 97*(1), 103-135.

Koterba, S., Baker, S., Matthews, I., Hu, C., Xiao, J., Cohn, J., et al. (2005). *Multi-view aam fitting and camera calibration.* Paper presented at the Tenth IEEE International Conference on Computer Vision

Lee, B., Hasegawa-Johnson, M., Goudeseune, C., Kamdar, S., Borys, S., Liu, M., et al. (2004). *AVICAR: Audio-visual speech corpus in a car environment.* Paper presented at the Conf. Spoken Language.

Lippmann, R. (1997). Speech recognition by humans and machines. *Speech Communication, 22*, 1-15.

Luettin, J. (1997). *Visual speech and speaker recognition.* Unpublished Ph.D. dissertation, University of Sheffield, Sheffield, U.K.

Luettin, J., Thacker, N., & Beet, S. (1996). *Speaker identification by lipreading.* Paper presented at the Int. Conf. Speech and Language Processing.

Luo, R. C., & Kay, M. G. (1995). Introduction. In R. C. Luo & M. G. Kay (Eds.), *Multisensor integration and fusion for intelligent machines and systems* (pp. 1-26). Norwood, NJ.

Maison, B., Neti, C., & Senior, A. (1999). *Audio-visual speaker recognition for broadcast news: some fusion techniques.* Paper presented at the Proc. Works. Multimedia Signal Processing.

Massaro, D. W., & Stork, D. G. (1998). Speech recognition and sensory integration. *American Scientist, 86*(3), 236-244.

Matthews, I., Potamianos, G., Neti, C., & Luettin, J. (2001). *A comparison of model and transform-based visual features for audio-visual LVCSR.* Paper presented at the Proc. Int. Conf. Multimedia Expo.

McGurk, H., & MacDonald, J. (1976). Hearing lips and seeing voices. *Nature, 264,* 746-748.

Messer, K., Matas, J., Kittler, J., Luettin, J., & Maitre, G. (1999). *XM2VTSDB: The extended M2VTS database.* Paper presented at the 2nd Int. Conf. Audio- and Video-Based Biometric Person Authentication.

Movellan, J. R. (1995). Visual speech recognition with stochastic networks. In G. Tesauro, D. Toruetzky & T. Leen (Eds.), *Advances in Neural Information Processing Systems* (Vol. 7). Cambridge, MA: MIT Press.

Narayanan, S., & Alwan, A. (2000). Articulatory-acoustic models for fricative consonants. *IEEE Trans. on Speech and Audio Processing, 8*(3), 328-344.

Nefian, A. V., Liang, L. H., Fu, T., & Liu, X. X. (2003). *A Bayesian approach to audio-visual speaker identification.* Paper presented at the Int. Conf. Image Processing, Barcelona, Spain.

Oviatt, S., Cohen, P., Wu, L., Vergo, J., Duncan, L., Suhm, B., et al. (2000). Designing the user interface for multimodal speech and pen-based gesture applications: State-of-the-art systems and research directions. *Human-Computer Interaction, 15*(4), 263-322.

Paliwal, K. K. (1998). *Spectral subband centroids features for speech recognition.* Paper presented at the Proc. Int. Conf. Acoustics, Speech and Signal Processing.

Patterson, E. K., Gurbuz, S., Tufekci, Z., & Gowdy, J. N. (2002). *CUAVE: A new audio-visual database for multimodal human-computer interface research.* Paper presented at the Int. Conf. Acoustics, Speech and Signal Processing.

Petajan, E. (1985). *Automatic lipreading to enhance speech recognition.* Paper presented at the IEEE Conference on CVPR.

Pigeon, S., & Vandendorpe, L. (1997). *The M2VTS multimodal face database (release 1.00).* Paper presented at the 1st Int. Conf. Audio- and Video-Based Biometric Person Authentication.

Poh, N., & Korczak, J. (2003). Automated authentication using hybrid biometric system. In P. D. Zhang (Ed.), *Biometric Authentication in the e-World:* Kluwer Academic Publishers.

Potamianos, G., Graf, H. P., & Cosatto, E. (1998). *An image transform approach for HMM based automatic lipreading*. Paper presented at the Proc. Int. Conf. Image Processing.

Potamianos, G., Neti, C., Gravier, G., Garg, A., & Senior, A. W. (2003). Recent advances in the automatic recognition of audio-visual speech. *Proceedings of the IEEE, 91*, 1306 - 12326.

Potamianos, G., Neti, C., Luettin, J., & Matthews, I. (2004). Audio-visual automatic speech recognition: An overview. In G. Bailly, E. Vatikiotis-Bateson & P. Perrier (Eds.), *Issues in Visual and Audio-Visual Speech Processing*: MIT Press.

Rabiner, L., & Juang, B.-H. (1993). *Fundamentals of Speech Recognition*. Englewood Cliffs: Prentice Hall.

Radova, V., & Psutka, J. (1997). *An approach to speaker identification using multiple classifiers*. Paper presented at the IEEE Conf. Acoustics, Speech Signal Processing, Munich, Germany.

Ratha, N. K., Senior, A. W., & Bolle, R. M. (2001). Automated biometrics. *Int. Conf. on Advances in Pattern Recognition*, 445-474.

Ross, A., & Jain, A. (2003). Information fusion in biometrics. *Pattern Recogn. Lett., 24*, 2215-2125.

Rowley, H. A., Baluja, S., & Kanade, T. (1998). Neutral networks-based face detection. *IEEE Trans. Pattern Anal. Machine Intell., 20*(1), 23-38.

Sanderson, C., Bengio, S., & Gao, Y. (2006). On transforming statistical models for non-frontal face verification. *Pattern Recognition, 29*(2), 288 - 302.

Sanderson, C., & Paliwal, K. K. (2003). Noise compensation in a person verification system using face and multiple speech features. *Pattern Recognition, 36*(2), 293-302.

Sanderson, C., & Paliwal, K. K. (2004). Identity verification using speech and face information. *Digital Signal Processing, 14*(5), 449-480.

Sargin, M. E., Erzin, E., Yemez, Y., & Tekalp, A. M. (2006, May). *Multimodal speaker identification using canonical correlation analysis*. Paper presented at the Int. Conf. Acoustics, Speech Signal Processing, Toulouse, France.

Schroeter, J., Ostermann, J., Graf, H. P., Beutnagel, M., Cosatto, E., Syrdal, A., et al. (2000). *Multimodal speech synthesis*. Paper presented at the Proc. Int. Conf. Multimedia Expo.

Schroeter, J., & Sondhi, M. (1994). Techniques for estimating vocal-tract shapes from the speech signal. *IEEE Transactions on Speech and Audio Processing, 2*(1), 133-150.

Senior, A. W. (1999). *Face and feature finding for a face recognition system*. Paper presented at the Proc. Int. Conf. Audio Video-based Biometric Person Authentication.

Stork, D. G., & Hennecke, M. E. (1996). Speechreading by Humans and Machines. Germany: Springer.

Summerfield, Q. (1979). Use of visual information in phonetic perception. *Phonetica, 36*, 314-331.

Summerfield, Q. (1987). Some preliminaries to a comprehensive account of audio-visual speech perception. In R. Campbell & B. Dodd (Eds.), *Hearing by Eye: The Psychology of Lip-Reading* (pp. 3-51). London, U.K.: Lawrence Erlbaum.

Summerfield, Q. (1992). Lipreading and audio-visual speech perception. *Philosophical Transactions: Biological Sciences, 335*(1273), 71-78.

Sung, K., & Poggio, T. (1998). Example-based learning for view-based human face detection. *IEEE Trans. Pattern Anal. Machine Intell., 20*(1), 39-51.

Turk, M. A., & Pentland, A. P. (1991). Eigenfaces for recognition. *Journal of Cognitive Neuroscience, 3*(1), 71-86.

Unknown (2005). *Financial crimes report to the public*: Federal Bureau of Investigation, Financial Crimes Section, Criminal Investigation Division.

Viola, P., & Jones, M. (2001). *Rapid object detection using a boosted cascade of simple features*. Paper presented at the IEEE Conf. on Computer Vision and Pattern Recognition.

Wark, T., Sridharan, S., & Chandran, V. (1999a). *Robust speaker verification via asynchronous fusion of speech and lip information*. Paper presented at the 2nd Int. Conf. Audio- and Video-Based Biometric Person Authentication, Washington, D. C.

Wark, T., Sridharan, S., & Chandran, V. (1999b). *Robust speaker verification via fusion of speech and lip modalities*. Paper presented at the Int. Conf. Acoustics, Speech and Signal Processing, Phoenix, Arizona.

Wark, T., Sridharan, S., & Chandran, V. (2000). *The use of temporal speech and lip information for multi-modal speaker identification via multi-stream HMMs*. Paper presented at the Int. Conf. Acoustics, Speech Signal Processing, Istanbul, Turkey.

Williams, J. J., & Katsaggelos, A. K. (2002). An HMM-based speech-to-video synthesizer. *IEEE Trans. on Neural Networks, Special Issue on Intelligent Multimedia, 13*(4), 900-915.

Woodward, J. D. (1997). Biometrics: privacy's foe or privacy's friend? *Proc. IEEE, 85*, 1480-1492.

Wu, Z., Aleksic, P. S., & Katsaggelos, A. K. (2004, May). *Inner lip feature extraction for MPEG-4 facial animation*. Paper presented at the Int. Conf. Acoust., Speech, Signal Processing, Montreal, Canada.

Yang, M.-H., Kriegman, D., & Ahuja, N. (2002). Detecting faces in images: A survey. *IEEE Trans. Pattern Anal. Machine Intell., 24*(1), 34-58.

Yehia, H. C., Kuratate, T., & Vatikiotis-Bateson, E. (1999). *Using speech acoustics to drive facial motion*. Paper presented at the 14th Int. Congr. Phonetic Sciences.

Yehia, H. C., Rubin, P., & Vatikiotis-Bateson, E. (1998). Quantitative association of vocal-tract and facial behavior. *Speech Communication, 26*(1-2), 23-43.

Yemez, Y., Kanak, A., Erzin, E., & Tekalp, A. M. (2003). *Multimodal speaker identification with audio-video processing*. Paper presented at the Int. Conf. Image Processing, Barcelona, Spain.

Young, S., Evermann, G., Hain, T., Kershaw, D., Moore, G., Odell, J., et al. (2005). *The HTK Book*. London, U.K.: Entropic.

Yuille, A. L., Hallinan, P. W., & Cohen, D. S. (1992). Feature extraction from faces using deformable templates. *Int. J. Comput. Vision, 8*(2), 99-111.

Zhang, X., Broun, C. C., Mersereau, R. M., & Clements, M. (2002). Automatic speechreading with applications to human-computer interfaces. *EURASIP J. Appl. Signal Processing, 2002*, 1228-1247.

Zhao, W.-Y., Chellappa, R., Phillips, P. J., & Rosenfeld, A. (2003). Face recognition: A literature survey. *ACM Computing Survey, 35*(4), 399-458.

Chapter III
Lip Modelling and Segmentation

A. Caplier
GIPSA-lab/DIS, France

S. Stillittano
GIPSA-lab/DIS, France

C. Bouvier
GIPSA-lab/DIS, France

P. Y. Coulon
GIPSA-lab/DIS, France

ABSTRACT

Lip segmentation is the first step of any audio-visual speech reading system. The accuracy of this segmentation has a major influence on the performances of the global system. But this is a very difficult task. First of all, lip shape can undergo strong deformations during a speech sequence. As many other image processing algorithms, the segmentation task is also influenced by the illumination conditions and by the orientation of the object to be segmented. In this chapter, we present an overview about lip modeling and lip segmentation (region-based and contour-based methods). We limit our study to the problem of lip segmentation in frontal faces. Section I gives an overview about the chrominance information that is used for lip segmentation and a comparison between different chrominance cues is proposed. Section II presents region-based approaches and training steps. Section III focuses on contour-based approaches and parametric lip models. Section IV inventories methods for lip segmentation accuracy evaluation. Some specific applications are briefly presented in section V.

WHICH IS THE BEST COLOR SPACE?

The main issue is to determine the most appropriate color space to make the difference between skin pixels and lip pixels. The problem of skin or non skin pixels characterization has been extensively studied in the context of face detection. But the point here is to be able to distinguish skin pixels from lip pixels (all these pixels belonging to a face). Concerning region based lip segmentation algorithms, the optimal color space is the one in which skin pixels and lip pixels are represented by two compact and distinct groups of pixels (low intra-class variances and high inter class variance). Regarding contour based lip segmentation algorithms, the optimal color space is a space in which the gradient information between lip and skin pixels is accentuated.

We propose a summary of the different color spaces that have been used for lip and skin pixels separation. We first focus on current color spaces such as RGB, HSV, and YCbCr which appear not completely efficient. Then we describe some specific color information that has been specially introduced in order to increase the difference between skin and lip pixels. We try to demonstrate the discriminative power of each considered color space by comparing the repartition of some skin pixel samples and some lip pixel samples. A specific database of skin and lip pixel samples has been built. All these samples have been manually extracted from a database of 150 frames representing 20 subjects acquired with the same camera and with the same conditions of illumination. For the purpose of comparison the dynamic of all the chromatic measures has been normalized to the range [0, 1] and the intra-class and inter-class variances have been computed.

In a second step, we present a set of specific luminance and/or chrominance cues that have been developed in order to accentuate lip boundaries gradient.

Current Color Spaces

RGB Color Space

We propose to study the *RGB* color space relevance for lip segmentation using our database of skin and lip pixel samples. In Figure 1, we give the histograms of the lip and skin pixel samples for the 3 color components R, G and B and the pixels repartition in the subspaces (R,G), (G,B) and (R,B). The intra-class and inter-class variances are also given in Table 1.

It is obvious that the color distributions of skin and lip pixel samples overlap each other for each R, G and B color component. We can also see the overlapping of the pixel repartition in the *RGB* subspaces. On Table 1, the inter-class variances are particularly low which also displays a strong overlapping.

We show in Figure 2 an example of the *RGB* components for a given mouth image. Visually it is very difficult to interpret the image. On the input image the lips seem to have more red color than the skin, but on the R component the values corresponding to the skin seem higher than those for the lips. Despite the fact that the *RGB* color space is very often used for displaying images and for computer graphics applications, it is not easy to interpret how the chromatic and luminance information is mixed in the *RGB* components. As we can see R, G, B channels cannot be used directly for lip segmentation because of the strong correlation between light and color information.

Figure 1. Lip and skin pixel histograms and projections in RGB. *The first row gives the histograms of the lip (dashed line) and skin (solid line) pixel distribution for the 3 colors components. The second row gives the pixel repartition in the (R, G), (G,B) and (R,B) subspaces respectively (area surrounds by dashed line corresponds to lip pixels and area surrounds by solid line to skin pixels)*

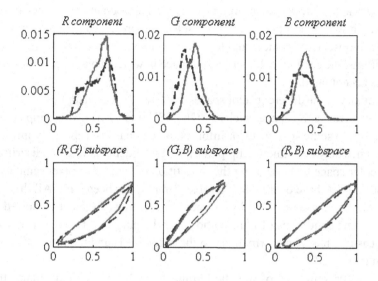

Table 1. Intra-class and inter-class variances of lip and skin pixel samples

	Lip pixels variance	Skin pixels variance	Inter-class variance
R component	0.026	0.016	6.10^{-4}
G component	0.01	0.01	$3.8.10^{-3}$
B component	0.016	0.01	4.10^{-4}

YCbCr Color Space

The *YCbCr* color space is derived from the *RGB* space (Ford, 1998) and resolves one of the main drawbacks of the *RGB* by decoupling the chromatic channels from the luminance one. The advantage of the *YCbCr* color space is that it is a linear and bijective transformation from the *RGB* space.

Figure 2. First line: a) R channel b) G channel c) B channel. Second line: d) Y channel, e) Cb channel, f) Cr channel

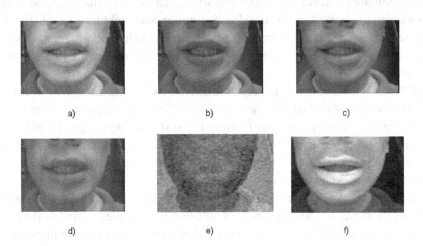

a)   b)   c)

d)   e)   f)

Table 2. Intra-class and inter-class variances of the lips and skin pixels for Cb and Cr components

	Lips pixel variance	Skin pixel variance	Inter-class variance
Cb component	2 10^{-4}	2 10^{-4}	1 10^{-4}
Cr component	1.3 10^{-3}	5 10^{-4}	3 10^{-4}

We can see in Figure 2e that the *Cb* channel is absolutely not distinguishing for lip description. It is very noisy and uniform for the entire face. The *Cr* channel (see Figure 2f) seems more suitable. In Figure 3 we present the histograms of the *Cb* and *Cr* components and the projection in the (*Cb, Cr*) subspace of the lip and skin pixels of our database. A strong overlapping between both pixels distributions can be noticed. The analysis of Table 2 confirms the overlapping between both classes but the intra-class variance for each distribution is lower than for the *RGB* components. The conclusion of our study is that the *YCbCr* color space is not very suitable for lip segmentation when dealing with different subjects.

HSI, HSV, HSL Color Spaces

Color spaces with luminance and chrominance separation such as *HSV* (Hue, Saturation and Value), *HSI* (Hue, Saturation and Intensity), and *HSL* (Hue, Saturation and Lightness) (Ford, 1998) have also been used for lip segmentation especially in order to work with the hue information. Despite the fact that the transformation formulas are different for every space, the different chromatic components describe similar information.

In (Zhang, 2000) the authors compare the discriminative power of the *RGB*, *HSV* and *YCbCr* color spaces for lip segmentation. After studying the histograms of various video sequences with different test conditions, Zhang et al. (2000) state that *H*, from the *HSV* color space gives a better separation between lip and skin pixels. (Coianiz, 1996) also uses the *H* information. The authors state that the hue is enough robust to light variations and that the contours of the lips are well defined in *H* space but the study with our database gives slightly different results.

We compute the normalized histograms of the *H* component using our database of skin and lip pixels (Figure 4-left). Since *H* values are homogenous to angle and since values related to the red color are located near the 2π value, the histogram has been shifted in order to have red hue in the middle of the

Figure 3. On the first row the Cb *and* Cr *lip (dashed line) and skin pixels (solid line) histograms are given. On the second row skin and lip pixels are projected in the (*Cb, Cr*) subspace. Area surrounds by the dashed line represents the lips pixel cloud, the area surrounds by the solid line represents the skin pixels cloud.*

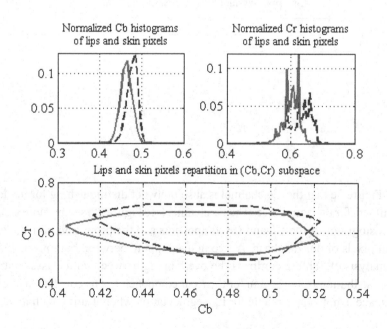

Figure 4. From left to right: H histogram; pseudo-hue histogram; Û Histogram

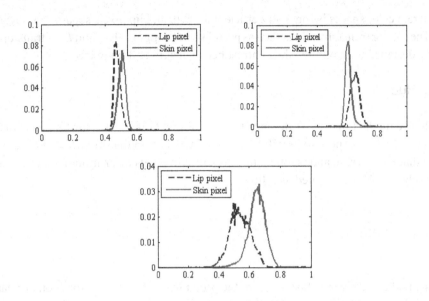

Figure 5. a) H channel, b) pseudo-hue channel, c) Û channel

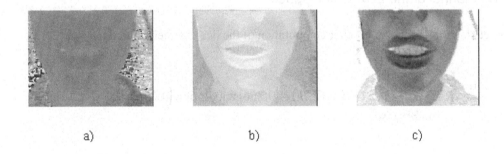

a)   b)   c)

window. We can see that the repartition of lip pixels on the one hand and of skin pixels on the other hand is compact so that the hue is almost uniform for each distribution (the intra class variance is 4×10^{-4} for lip pixels and is 5×10^{-4} for skin pixels). But the problem is that both distributions overlap (the inter-class variance is 5×10^{-4}). In Figure 5a we give an illustration of the H channel on a mouth image.

Specific Color Information for Lip Pixels Segmentation

None of the current color spaces being really efficient for skin and lip pixels separation, several authors have proposed new color transformations such as pseudo-hue (Poggio, 1998) and *LUX* transform (Liévin, 2004) specially designed to maximize the contrast between skin and lip pixels.

The Pseudo-Hue $\hat{H}$

$\hat{H}$ tends to enhance the fact that the difference between R and G is greater for lip pixels than for skin pixels. Eveno et al. (2003) propose to use $\hat{H}$ to separate the lips from the skin. Indeed $\hat{H}$ has higher values for the lips than for the skin and is robust for lips and skin pixels discrimination even when dealing with different subjects. $\hat{H}$ is computed as follows:

$$\hat{H} = \frac{R}{R+G} \tag{1}$$

In Figure 4-middle, we give the histogram of the pseudo-hue. The results for $\hat{H}$ on our database are similar to those obtained with the hue. $\hat{H}$ is almost uniform for both classes (the intra-class variance is 8×10^{-4} for lip pixels and is 5×10^{-4} for skin pixels) but the overlapping is less important (the inter-class variance is 1.2×10^{-3}). $\hat{H}$ shows also a lower noise level in the dark areas (Figure 5b). This is an important property in case of open mouth segmentation where pixels inside the mouth can have small luminance values. As a conclusion, the pseudo-hue achieves good results for lip and skin separation.

The $\hat{U}$ Channel of the LUX Color Space

Liévin et al. (2004) proposes another computation of the hue channel defined by:

$$\hat{U} = \begin{cases} 256 \times \dfrac{G}{R} & if \ R > G \\ 255 & otherwise \end{cases} \quad (R, G, B) \in [0,256[\times [0,256[\times [0,256[\tag{2}$$

This transformation is a simplification of the *LUX* color space introduced in (Liévin, 2004). This formulation has been inspired by biological considerations and logarithmic image processing (*LIP*) (Deng, 1993) in order to maximize the contrast for face analysis problems. In Figure 4-right, we give the $\hat{U}$ histograms for our pixels samples. The intra-class variance for the lip pixels class is 4.6×10^{-3} and is 3.2×10^{-3} for skin pixels class with inter-class variance of 7.5×10^{-3}. We can see that the color distributions are well separated using $\hat{U}$. We can also see on (Figure 5c) that it gives better result for dark areas: the area inside the mouth (the teeth) which has a similar hue than the skin on $\hat{H}$ has different hue on $\hat{U}$. Consequently $\hat{U}$ seems to be very suitable for lip color characterization.

We can also mention the $Q=R/G$ channel used by Chiou (1997) to locate the mouth. Q gives similar results as the $\hat{U}$ channel except that there is no condition on the ratio R/G when $G=0$. With $\hat{U}$ the ratio is only computed when $R>G$. Hsu et al. (2002) also propose a color transformation: The C_r/C_b-C_r^2 color information is computed in order to maximize the difference between lip and skin pixels. The authors claim that mouth region contains strong red component and weak blue component.

Lip Boundaries Enhancement

When dealing with the problem of lip contour extraction, the main issue is the enhancement of a gradient's information between lips and the other face features such as skin and the interior of the mouth. In order to have a strong gradient, the representation space of the image information has to give high variation values between skin and lip regions.

Intensity-Based Gradient

The most extensively used gradient for lip contour extraction is the intensity gradient (Hennecke, 1994; Radeva, 1995; Pardas, 2001; Delmas, 2002; Seyedarabi, 2006; Werda, 2007). Indeed, in the case of outer lip contour detection, the mouth area is characterized by illumination changes between skin and lips. For example, if the light source comes from above, the upper boundary of the upper lip is in a bright area whereas the upper lip itself is in a dark area. In the same manner, the lower boundary of the lower lip is in a dark area whereas the lower lip itself is in a bright area. The intensity gradient also allows the inner lip edges to be highlighted in the case of closed mouths (because this boundary is a dark line) and in the case of open mouths because the interior of the mouth is composed of bright areas (teeth) and dark areas (oral cavity).

The gradient information is composed of horizontal and vertical components, but frequently, only the vertical component is processed because mouth contours are predominantly horizontal (Hennecke, 1994). In addition, according to the sign of the gradient, the highlighted contour is either for a bright area above a dark area or a bright area below a dark area (see Figure 6b and c).

The intensity gradient emphasizes the outer and inner lip contours, but other non desired contours could be exhibited too. The problem concerns essentially the lower lip which can present shadow and over-exposed areas. In Figure 6, a shadow on the lower lip due to the upper lip gives a high gradient (see

Figure 6. a) intensity image b) positive vertical gradient c) negative vertical gradient

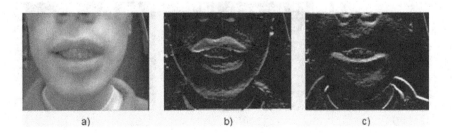

a)   b)   c)

Figure 6c). Another point noted in (Radeva, 1995) is the fact that, generally, the lower outer lip contour has a weaker gradient and is more difficult to extract.

Regarding the interior of the mouth, the visibility of teeth, oral cavity, gum or tongue may create strong intensity gradients on their boundaries in addition to the intensity gradient coming from the inner lip contours. The extraction algorithm must be able to choose the right contours among all the possibilities.

Color-Based Gradients

Eveno et al. (2004) propose two specific color gradients for the outer lip contour extraction. The gradient R_{top} is used for characterizing the upper boundary and the gradient R_{bottom} is used for the lower one (Figure 7b and c). They are computed as follows where I is the luminance:

$$R_{top}(x,y) = \nabla\left(\frac{R}{G}(x,y) - I(x,y)\right)$$

$$R_{bottom}(x,y) = \nabla\left(\frac{R}{G}(x,y)\right)$$

(3)

The ratio R/G (Chiou, 1997) increases the difference of contrast between the skin and the lips (see Figure 7a). The gradients have been built with the hypotheses that lip pixels have a higher ratio R/G than skin pixels and skin pixels above the upper lip have a higher luminance.

In the same way, Beaumesnil et al. (2006) define a color gradient as a combination of the color information $\hat{U}$ (see equation (1)) and the luminance (but the gradient expression is not specified in the article).

In (Stillittano, 2008), two gradients are proposed for the inner lip contour extraction. The gradient G_1 is used for characterizing the upper inner boundary and the gradient G_2 for the lower one. They are computed as follows, where R is the red component of the RGB color space, I is the luminance $\hat{H}$ is the pseudo-hue (see equation (3)) and u is a component of the color space CIELuv:

Figure 7. a) R/G image b) R_{top} c) R_{bottom}

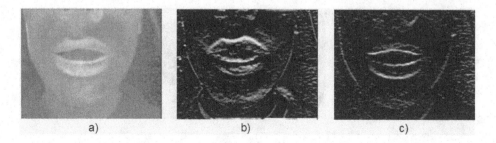

a)   b)   c)

Figure 8. a) G_1 b) G_2

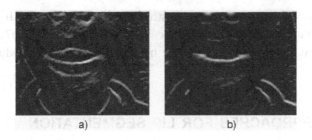

a)   b)

$$G_1(x,y) = \nabla\left(R(x,y) - u(x,y) - \hat{H}(x,y)\right)$$
$$G_2(x,y) = \nabla\left(I(x,y) + u(x,y) + \hat{H}(x,y)\right) \tag{4}$$

These 2 gradients have been considered for the following reasons:

- I and $\hat{H}$ are generally higher for the lips than for the pixels inside the mouth (in particular for the pixels of the oral cavity, where I and $\hat{H}$ are close to zero),
- u is higher for the lip pixels than for teeth pixels (indeed u is close to zero for teeth pixels)
- In other cases, R can be lower for lip pixels than for pixels inside the mouth.

Figure 8a gives an illustration of the gradient G_1 which truly highlights the upper inner boundary. Figure 8b gives an illustration of the gradient G_2 which truly enhances the lower inner contour.

Gradients Computed from a Probability Map

In (Vogt, 1996; Liévin, 2004), mouth edges are extracted by a contour detector applied on a probability map which shows the probability of a pixel to belong to the lips. In (Vogt, 1996) the probability map is computed by a 2D look up table algorithm applied on the H and S components of the *HIS* color space. The resulting image gives higher values for the pixels having a high probability to be a lip pixel. Liévin et al. (2004) build the probability map with a Markov Random Field model combining $\hat{U}$ and motion information. The MRF model gives a labeled image map with gray levels coding the hue clusters, where the lips represent a particular cluster.

Consequently, the contrast between lip and skin is improved by computing the probability of a pixel to be a lip pixel (Vogt, 1996) or to belong to a pixel cluster (Liévin, 2004). The edge extraction depends on the probability computational efficiency.

Gradients Computed from a Binary Image

In order to prevent the possibility to have parasitic strong gradients around the lip contours, the gradient is computed on a mouth binary image in (Wark, 1998 and Yokogawa, 2007). Therefore, only the contours belonging to the lips are detected but the major difficulty is the production of an accurate binary mouth area.

REGION-BASED APPROACHES FOR LIP SEGMENTATION

Three main categories can be proposed for lip region-based segmentation methods: the deterministic approaches based on color distribution modeling and thresholding operations, the supervised or non-supervised classification methods which consider lip segmentation as a pixel classification problem (generally classification between skin pixels and lip pixels) and the statistical methods based on the learning of mouth shape and appearance. As all these methods are region-based, a high accuracy of lip segmentation around the lip contours is not always guaranteed.

Deterministic Approaches

These methods regroup low level region based algorithms with no prior knowledge and no prior models about the statistics of the lip and skin color distributions. Lip segmentation mainly results from a thresholding step on luminance or particular chromatic component.

The simplest and most efficient segmentation method based on thresholding uses chroma keying. The lips are made up with blue lipstick which color is high contrasted with skin color. The lips are then easily segmented by applying a threshold on H (Chibelushi, 1997; Brandt, 2001). This leads to very accurate lip segmentation but such artifices are absolutely not compatible with current life applications for obvious ergonomic reasons.

Chiou (1997) proposes the thresholding of the Q ratio to segment the lips. Given an image focused on the mouth area, the idea is to compute a binary mask by thresholding pixels with high red values and with Q values in a given range. Wark et al. (1998) use the same approach for a corpus with different speakers with empirically chosen values for the upper and lower thresholds on Q. Coianiz et al. (1996) use a fixed threshold on H to segment the lips. In (Zhang, 2000) the authors apply fixed thresholds on H and S for all subjects to extract a binary mask of the lips.

The major limitation of these techniques is the automatic computation of robust thresholds. Fixed thresholds cannot be generalized as a slight change in environment conditions or with the subject imposes to reset the values. As a consequence, thresholds are generally set in an ad-hoc way by a human expert.

Classification Methods

If we make the hypothesis that the input image is focused on the lip area, the problem of lip region segmentation can be seen as a classification problem with two classes: the lip class and the skin class. When considering a classification problem, we have to define the considered classes, the attributes characterizing each class and the classification method. Classification techniques or clustering techniques are widely used in face analysis for various problems including lip modeling and segmentation. The problem is to regroup pixels in homogenous sets with specific properties. We can distinguish mainly 2 kinds of approach, the supervised classification approaches and the unsupervised classification approaches. The most frequently used methods for classification in face analysis are based on statistical techniques (Estimation theory, Bayesian decision theory, Markov random field), neural networks, support vector machine (SVM), C-means, and more recently fuzzy C-means. In the following paragraphs we will introduce some representative works about classification algorithms used for lip segmentation.

Supervised Methods

The supervised methods imply that prior knowledge is available on the different classes. The idea is to use knowledge learned from a set of samples and to generalize it in order to classify the pixels. The first step of a supervised classification algorithm is the compiling of a database. The database must cover a wide range of cases and environmental conditions. The construction of the database is a critical step.

Figure 9. Manually segmented lips from (Gacon, 2005)

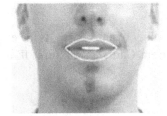

Figure 10. Lip segmentation example from (Gacon, 2005), from left to right, input image, classified pixels, classified pixels after noise reduction

Statistical Approaches

A current scheme for statistical classification approach is to estimate the distribution of the lip and skin pixels from the learning database.

Gacon et al. (2005) use a Gaussian mixture model of the lips trained on a database of manually segmented mouth images (Figure 9). $\hat{H}$ is computed (cf. equation (3)). A Gaussian mixture model which corresponds to the color distribution is then estimated by *EM*, Expectation Maximization. The optimum number of Gaussians for each class is given by the *MDL* Minimum Description Length principle (1 Gaussian distribution for every class in the case of Gacon's database). The $\hat{H}$ values of an unknown image are classified by finding the cluster c_i that maximizes the belonging probability $p(\hat{H}| c_i)$ (Figure 10). To be classified the probability of a pixel is constrained, $p(\hat{H}| c_i)>p_0$, p_0 corresponds to the minimum value of $p(\hat{H}| c_i)$ to be classified and is fixed empirically. Morphological closing and opening are then performed to reduce errors of classification.

In (Sadeghi, 2002) the approach also estimates the Gaussian mixture of areas included in the mouth bounding box to classify lip pixels and non-lip pixels. The authors work with normalized *RGB* components. The Gaussian distributions of lip and non-lip pixels are estimated on a semi-automatically segmented database in order to have prior knowledge about both classes of pixels. Then for an unknown mouth image the goal is to estimate the Gaussian mixture with an optimal number of Gaussians to describe the color of the mouth area. The two normalized chromatic channels (r,g) are then considered for the data mixture estimation. To find the optimal number of Gaussians, the authors compute 2 probabilities:

$$p_{emp}(x) = \frac{k(W)}{N} \quad and \quad p_{pred}(x) = \int_W p(x)dx \tag{5}$$

x is a vector of the (r,g) values of a pixel, p_{emp} is the empirical probability, p_{pred} the predicted probability computed using the current Gaussian mixture, W is a randomly generated window and $k(W)$ is the

Figure 11. Lips segmentation from (Patterson, 2002) a) Estimated distributions of non-face, face, lips pixels in RGB *space b) Example of lip segmentation*

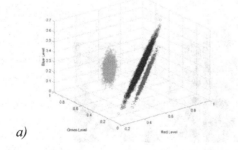

a)   *b)*

number of data points in the window and N is the total number of pixels of the mouth area. The optimal number of Gaussians is found by an optimization procedure. Randomly generated windows W are computed and the initial number of Gaussians in the mixture is set to 1. Gaussians are added until the least square error between p_{emp} and p_{pred} over the window W is minimized.

As the number of Gaussians in the estimated mixture cannot be predicted, a merging step is done using the distributions of the lip and non-lip pixels computed from the training database. The errors between the mean of the Gaussians from the unknown image and the mean of the classes given by the prior model are computed to classify the unknown Gaussians as lip or non-lip model. The pixel classification is done using a Bayes classifier. In (Lucey, 2002) the approach is similar.

(Patterson, 2002) also uses manually segmented images to estimate the Gaussians distribution for the non-face, face and lip pixels in the *RGB* color space (see Figure 11a). In this work, the authors use images from the *CUAVE* database (Cuavebase) where the image's speakers include the shoulders. The classification is done using Bayesian decision rule (see Figure 11b).

Instead of estimating a model of the color distributions of lip and skin pixels, some authors try to use the statistics computed on the lip and skin samples to estimate a transformation that will maximize the inter-class variance between both classes and minimize the intra-class variances. In (Chan, 1998) the authors train a linear model to maximize the contrast between lips and skin using manually segmented images. The optimal parameters α, β, δ are used to compute a composite channel $C=\alpha R+\beta G+\delta B$ using the *RGB* components. Finally the authors apply a threshold on C to classify the skin and lip pixels. Nefian (2002) uses a similar approach. Linear discriminant analysis (*LDA*) is run on the learning data in order to find the optimal transformation from *RGB* color space to a one dimension space where the contrast is maximized between lip and skin pixels. The classification is performed by thresholding the component computed by *LDA* to compute a binary mask of the lips.

We can also mention the work of Seyedarabi (2006). In this study a knowledge based system trained on several examples is used to estimate the initial mouth position with a bounding box.

Neural Networks Approach

Neural network have also been used for supervised classification of lip and skin pixels. The feed forward network can be used for that purpose. A multi-layer perceptron applies decision boundary in the input data space. This can be applied to separate lip and skin pixels. In (Wojdel, 2001) the authors develop a lip segmentation algorithm with a learning step. At the first image the speaker is asked to manually segment his/her lips in order to train a multi-layer perceptron to distinguish lip and skin pixels. The network is composed of 3 layers, with 3 neurons on the first layer, 5 on the second layer and 1 on the third layer. The 3 inputs of the neural network are the *RGB* values of the pixels. The output is set to 0 for lip pixels and 1 for skin pixels.

Daubias et al. (2002) have also study multi-layer perceptrons in order to classify lips pixel, skin pixels and pixels inside the mouth. The general architecture is a network with 3 layers with 3 neurons on the last layer, one output for the lips pixels, one for the skin pixels and one for the pixels inside the mouth. To classify a pixel, an nxn neighborhood is considered. Thus the input layer has $3n^2$ nodes, 1 node for the *RGB* components of each pixel in the neighborhood. The blocs are computed from a manually segmented database.

SVM Approach

The approach using the *SVM* also consists in computing decision boundaries between the lip pixels class and the skin pixels class. Castañeda et al. (2005) use SVM to detect face and lips in face images. A database of 10x20 images of the features of interest (lips, eyes, eyebrows,...) from 13 subjects has been built. A classifier is designed specifically for lips detection. After the training step, the number of support vectors is 2261 for the lips. The authors then perform an optimization procedure to reduce the number of support vectors.

Unsupervised Methods

We mentioned in the previous part that the building of the learning database for supervised methods is a critical step. In (Yang, 1996) the authors study color rendering of camera in controlled conditions. They show that a camera change introduces strong differences in color rendering. This underlines the challenge in compiling a database. In case of uncontrolled environments the model trained has to deal with unpredictable conditions such as lighting variations, different scales, different subjects, with different characteristics and different acquisition systems (for example mono CCD camera, 3-CCD camera ...). This leads to the development of unsupervised classification methods in order to avoid the difficult problem of building a learning database.

Unsupervised classification techniques do not require any training step. This means that no prior knowledge about skin and lip pixel statistics is taken into account.

Statistical Approaches

In (Bouvier, 2007) a mixed color-gradient approach is developed to perform unsupervised lip segmentation. The hypothesis is that the color distribution of mouth area can be approximated by a Gaussian mixture model. First $\hat{U}$ is computed (cf. equation (2)). Using Expectation maximization the Gaussian mixture describing the mouth hue area is estimated. The Gaussian with the highest weight is associated

Figure 12. Lip segmentation from (Bouvier, 2007) a) Input image, b) Membership map, c) Segmented lips

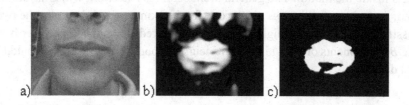

to the skin. It is supposed that most of the considered pixels belong to the skin class as the image is focused on the lower half of the face. A lip membership map M is computed as follows (Figure 12b):

$$MAP(x,y) = 1 - \exp\left(-\left(\hat{U}(x,y) - \mu_{skin}\right)^2 / 2\sigma_{skin}^2\right)$$

(6)

A threshold must be computed on the membership map to segment the lips. The gradient information used for that purpose is R_{top} and R_{bottom} (cf. equation (3)). The threshold and the lip binary mask are found at the same time by maximizing the mean gradient flows R_{top} and R_{bottom} through the contour of the binary mask (Figure 12c). Tian et al. (2000) use as well a Gaussian mixture model giving the lip color distribution and therefore, the mouth area.

(Liévin, 2004) proposes an unsupervised hierarchical algorithm to segment $n=N$ clusters based on a Markov Random Field approach. The idea in this work is to combine the color information extracted from the simplified $\hat{U}$ channel of the *LUX* color space and movement information. For example, lip motion can be used to improve the color segmentation in video sequence. The algorithm starts with $n=1$ cluster and computes the $\hat{U}$ channel and the frame difference $fd(x,y)=|I_t(x,y)-I_{t-1}(x,y)|$. The algorithm then performs the classification. If it remains unclassified pixels, a cluster is added and a new classification is run.

At pass n the first step is to estimate the mean μ_n and the standard deviation σ_n of the main mode on the hue $\hat{U}$ histogram of the unclassified pixels. The first and second derivatives of the histogram are used to find those parameters. Using the estimated mean and standard deviation (μ_n, σ_n) of the hue cluster and $fd(x,y)$, an initial label set $L(x,y) = (n,k)$ is computed by thresholding. Initial pixels associated to the cluster n are computed by thresholding the filtered hue channel $h_n(x,y)$.

$$h_n(x,y) = \left[256 - \left(\frac{\hat{U}(x,y) - \mu_n}{\sigma_n}\right)^2\right]$$

$$With \left|\hat{U}(x,y) - \mu_n\right| \leq 16\sigma_n$$

(7)

Figure 13. Lip segmentation results from (Liévin, 2004)

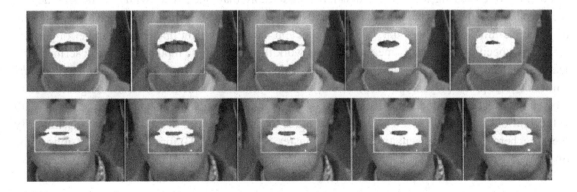

Figure 14. Lips segmentation from (Liew, 2003). From upper left to lower right, input image, lip membership map, map after morphological operations, map after symmetry-luminance-shape processing, map after Gaussian filtering and final segmentation

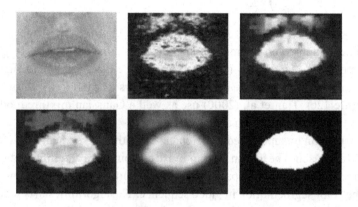

x and y are spatial coordinates, $n \in [0...N]$ corresponds to a hue cluster and $k \in [0,1]$ corresponds to a moving region.

For moving pixels k is set to 1 (0 if static). Those states are obtained by entropic thresholding on *fd*. A Markov random fields (*MRF*) approach is then used for label field optimization. For lip segmentation N is set to 2, there is one class for the lip pixels and one class for the skin pixels. The first pass corresponds to the skin segmentation as the considered images are focused on the lower part of the face. The second pass then segments the lips with the constraint that $\mu_2 < \mu_1$. Segmentation results are proposed in (Figure 13).

K-Means and Fuzzy C-Means Approaches

K-means and fuzzy C-means (or fuzzy K-means) are also well used algorithms for classification problem. In (Liew, 2003) a Fuzzy C-means based algorithm is used in order to segment the lips. Fuzzy C-means is a method of clustering where the data can belong to more than one cluster with membership degree included in [0, 1] instead of being a binary state (0 or 1). The fuzzy C-partition is obtained by minimizing an objective function. Liew et al. (2003) used that approach to segment lips with a number of clusters $K=2$ and a specific dissimilarity measure. In this work the pixels of the input image are described by a feature vector $x_{r,s}$ (with r,s the spatial coordinates) which corresponds to the CIE $L^*u^*v^*$ and CIE $L^*a^*b^*$ values of those pixels (Wyszecki, 1982). The dissimilarity measure is defined on a 3x3 neighborhood of a pixel. Its effect is to smooth the distance $\|x_{r,s} - v_i\|_2$ with the 8 neighbors distances $\|x_{r+l1,s+l2} - v_i\|_2$, with v_i the centroid of cluster i and $(l1,l2) \in [-1,1]$ in order to include spatial constraint in the dissimilarity measure, here spatial homogeneity of the pixel cluster. See (Liew, 2003) for detailed expressions of the dissimilarity measure and the expression of the optimization loop. After Fuzzy C-mean clustering the authors perform several post processing treatments in order to prevent false classification (morphological opening and closing, symmetry constraint, Gaussian filtering). A fixed threshold is applied on the filtered partition to segment the lips (Figure 14).

In classical Fuzzy C-means algorithm the dissimilarity measure is often the l_2 distance. The idea in (Liew, 2003) was to add spatial constraints on the clustering. This lead to a dissimilarity measure that smoothes the distance of the current pixel feature vector to the cluster centroid with the neighbors distances to the cluster centroïd.

In (Leung, 2004) a similar approach is used to classify lip pixels and skin-pixels by adding spatial constraints on the dissimilarity measure $D_{i,r,s}$. The hypothesis is that the spatial distribution of the lip pixels is approximately elliptic. Wang et al. (2007) also propose a Fuzzy C-means algorithm with spatial constraint added to the dissimilarity measure $D_{i,r,s}$. the constraint here is that the spatial distribution of the lips pixel is supposed to be elliptical.

K-means algorithm has also been used in order to find to mouth area. In (Beaumesnil, 2006), a K-means classification algorithm based on $\hat{U}$ is used to obtain three classes (lip, face and background). Then, a mouth boundary box is extracted by a simple scan of the connected component lip-hue area.

Statistical Shape Models

Statistical methods are supervised techniques: a learning database must be compiled. The difference with supervised classification methods is that the models are trained to describe lip main shape or appearance variation axes and not to estimate lip color distributions. The goal is to use this prior knowledge for lip segmentation in an unknown image. Active Shape Models *ASM* were first introduced for lip shape variations study. Active Appearance Models *AAM* have been thereafter introduced to add texture or appearance information.

Figure 15. Left, example of mouth shape model. (1,2) Outer lip contours, (3,4) Inner lip contours, (5,6) Teeth contours. Right, 4 main variation modes of a mouth ASM

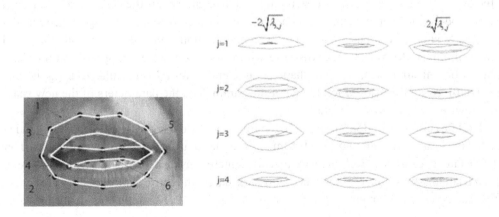

Active Shape Model

ASM are derived from the Point Distribution Model *PDM* introduced in (Cootes, 1992; Cootes, 1995). The *PDM* is built using a training set of manually annotated examples (see Figure 15-Left). This gives a vector x_i of the N contour points coordinates for each image in the database. A Principal Component Analysis *(PCA)* is performed on $X=[x_1,x_2,...x_M]$ (*M* the number of annotated images) to compute the variation modes. Given the matrix $P_s=[p_1,p_2,...,p_t]$ of the orthogonal variation modes and a vector $b_s=[b_1,b_2,...,b_t]^T$ of parameters, any shape x can be described by the following relation $x = \bar{x} + P_s b_s$ with $\bar{x}$ the mean shape (see Figure 15-Right). Usually 95% of the total variance of data is kept. This leads to an important dimensionality reduction. A shape can then be described by a smaller set of parameters. In order to segment lips in an unknown image, the parameters b_s which minimize a cost function is estimated. The goal of the cost function is to quantify the distance between the shape given by the statistical model and the unknown shape.

In (Cootes, 2004) the author proposes a coarse-to-fine method to fit a face shape model, the approach being the same with an image focused on the lips. For each image in the database, a Gaussian pyramid is built and for each point of the annotated contour at each level in the pyramid, the gradient distributions along the normal to the contour are estimated. The number of pixels in the profiles is the same at each scale. The fitting procedure starts at the coarsest level with the mean model. Then it searches the best position of each point of the contour using the gradient profile models. The new shape parameters b_s' are computed from the new positions of contour points

$$x': b' = P_s^{-1}(x'-\bar{x})$$

(8)

The procedure is repeated until convergence. When convergence is achieved at level L, the shape model fitting is restarted at level L-1 with the shape parameters found at level L until L=0, L=0 corresponds to the full resolution.

(Zhang, 2003) uses a similar algorithm with a constraint shape model for the face, the eyes and the mouth. The difference is that for the contour points, the response of 40 Gabor filters for different scales and orientations are used instead of some gray level profiles.

In (Jang, 2006) the algorithm uses an *ASM* to extract the inner and outer lips contour from mouth image. Using manually annotated mouth images, a mouth statistical shape model is trained. Models of normalized gray level profiles are also trained for each landmark. The shape parameters for all the images of the database are computed. The distribution of the parameters is then estimated using a Gaussian mixture model with 2 components. At each step of the fitting procedure, a shape is generated using the *ASM*. New landmark positions are found by searching for points in a neighborhood with gray level profiles that minimize the Mahalanobis distance with respect to the learned gray level profile. After the landmark optimization step, the new shape parameters vector b_s' is calculated using the formula of equation (10). Using the distribution model of the parameters, the parameters of the new shape are rescaled if their probabilities are too small.

Li et al. (2006) also use an *ASM* to segment the lips. The difference with (Cootes, 2004) and (Jang, 2006) is that the local texture around each landmark is modeled using Adaboost classifier based on 2-D Haar-like rectangle features. 24x24 intensity patches centered inside a 3x3 region with its center at the ground-truth landmark are collected for every landmark and for the entire database. They are considered as positive examples. 24x24 intensity patches centered inside a 12x12 region outside the previous 3x3 neighborhood with its center at the ground-truth landmark are collected for every landmark and for the entire database. They are considered as negative examples. The Real AdaBoost classifier is trained on those data. When searching for the new position of a landmark, the position that gives the strongest confidence is selected.

Active Appearance Model

The Active Appearance Models *AAM* have also been proposed by (Cootes, 1998; Cootes, 2000; Cootes, 2001) to describe the appearance of the lips. The goal is to compute a Statistical Shape Model and the associate Statistical Appearance Model and to combine both as appearance and shape variations are somehow correlated. Using some annotated lip images, the gray-level texture of each example is warped so that the contour points match the mean shape and the texture is sampled (see Figure 16-Left). The vector containing the texture samples for each example is normalized to cancel light variations. A *PCA* is run to compute the main variation modes of the appearance. The appearance g of any lip image can then be approached by a linear transformation $g = \bar{g} + P_g b_g$ where $\bar{g}$ is the mean appearance model, P_g is the matrix of the orthogonal appearance variation modes and b_g is the vector of the appearance parameters (Figure 16-Right):

The shape x and the appearance g of a feature can be described by a vector d:

$$d = \begin{bmatrix} W_s P_s^T (x - \bar{x}) \\ P_g^T (g - \bar{g}) \end{bmatrix}$$

(9)

Figure 16. Left, *example of mesh generated from a mouth* ASM *to sample the texture;* Right, *examples of the 6 main variation modes of the mouth* AAM *(Gacon, 2006)*

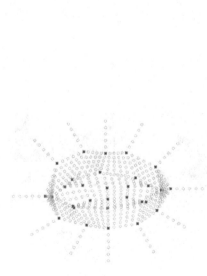
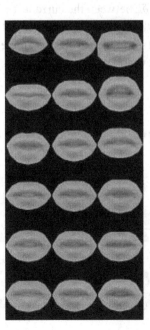

Where W_s is a diagonal matrix composed of unit normalization coefficients. By applying another *PCA* on the vectors *d* for each example, a model combining appearance and shape is computed:

$$d = Qc \tag{10}$$

Q is the matrix with the main variation modes given by the *PCA* of the combined parameters; *c* is a vector of parameters which controls the shape and the appearance. Detailed presentation of the *AAM* is available in (Cootes, 2004).

The fitting procedure to find the optimal parameters of the *AAM* for an unknown image is similar as the fitting procedure to find the optimal parameters of the *ASM*. It is treated as an optimization process where the algorithm has to minimize the distance between the generated appearance and the input image.

Gacon et al. (2005) develop a multi-speaker *AAM* for mouth segmentation. In this work the database is composed of *YCbCr* mouth pictures from various subjects. First the authors compute the *ASM* of the mouth and associate to the contour points the 9 responses of the filters G, G_x and G_y for the 3 components of *YCbCr*. G is a Gaussian filter; G_x and G_y are respectively the horizontal and vertical gradients of the filtered image. Then an *AAM* is computed. Figure 17 gives examples of lip segmentation results.

In (Matthews, 1998) *AAM* has also been applied to segment the lips but with a different fitting procedure. During the training of the statistical model of appearance, the appearance parameters are computed for the entire database. The procedure to find the optimal *AAM* parameters for an unknown image is treated as an optimization process. The goal is to minimize the error δE between the appearance of the input image and the appearance generated by the statistical model. Given the parameters *c* for all the images in the database, a linear transformation *A* between the error δE and the error δc on the model parameter is estimated. Random errors are added to the vector *c* and the transformation matrix is approximated by linear regression. Given *A*, the optimization loop is:

- Compute error δE between the current *AAM* and the input image
- Then compute the error δc using $A : \delta c = A \, \delta E$
- Subtracts the error to the current parameter $c' = c - \delta c$
- Compute the new appearance with c'

Figure 17. Examples of lip segmentation (Gacon, 2005)

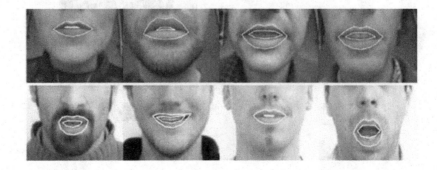

- Repeat until the error is below a desired threshold.

In (Matthews, 2003) the authors propose a gradient descent algorithm for fitting *AAM* based on the inverse compositional algorithm applied on independent *AAM* and *ASM* in order to resolve the non-linear optimization problem whereas in (Matthews, 1998) the hypothesis is that there is a constant linear relationship between δE and δc. In this work the shape and appearance parameters are not combined by a PCA. With this hypothesis, the authors apply the inverse compositional to fit first the shape and then to compute directly the optimal values of the appearance parameters.

The main advantage of lip segmentation methods based on *ASM* and *AAM* is that they always give a coherent result as the shape and appearance have been learned on real examples. However, like supervised methods, the difficulty is the definition of a representative database. This means that one has to manually put landmarks on hundreds of images. And as stated in (Yang, 1996), any camera change even in controlled environment, can introduce important variations on the image properties (*PSNR*, color rendering). Another problem is that the cost functions used for the fitting step often consider the problem to be linear, which is definitely not the case. For example, except in (Gacon, 2005), the link between shape and appearance parameters is supposed to be modeled with a linear transformation which is not obvious. Thus convergence to a global minimum of cost functions or to the optimum parameters is not guaranteed. The performances of the algorithm depend on the distance between the initialization and the desired result.

CONTOUR-BASED APPROACHES FOR LIP SEGMENTATION

In the context of contour-based approaches, algorithms are mainly based on deformable models. A deformable model consists in choosing and placing an appropriate mathematical model of the contour (a spline or a parametric curve for example) into the data space and in deforming it to lock onto the edges of the object of interest. The deformation of the initial contour is obtained by minimizing a model energy composed of an internal term, related to the curve geometric properties, and an external term, computed from the image data. The deformable models are divided into two main categories: active contours and parametric models. Active contours extract edges from an initial chained contour by modifying one by one the position of the model points. They are free-form algorithms: no *a priori* information about the global shape of the object to be extracted is taken into account. Parametric models define a parameterized description of the object of interest by integrating *a priori* knowledge about its global shape and reach an admissible form by modifying the model parameters.

Active Contours or Snakes

Active contours, first introduced by Kass et al. (1987), are usually called snakes because of the way the contours slither like a snake during deformations. Snake models are composed of a set of moving points located on a 2D curve. According to the application, the curve can be closed or not, with fixed extremities or not. Snakes evolve iteratively from an initial position up to a final position which is related to the closest local minimum of an energy function. The energy-minimizing algorithm is guided by different constraints and is controlled by the image data.

In the context of lip segmentation, the active contours are often used because they can provide high deformability with a final representation of the lip contours which seems natural. They also offer a simple implementation and fast convergence that could be very interesting in lip tracking application.

Snake Definition and Properties

A snake is parametrically represented by a curve v (where $v(s)=(x(s), y(s))$ and s is the curvilinear abscissa) and its energy functional is defined by the following equation:

$$\phi(v) = \int \left(E_{int}(v(s)) + E_{ext}(v(s)) \right) ds \tag{11}$$

The internal energy E_{int} corresponds to the curve mechanical properties and allows regularization during the deformations. The internal forces of the snake impose relatively weak constraints on the global shape obtained after convergence, because they act locally around each point. The external energy E_{ext} is linked to the data and deforms the curve according to the salient image features, such as lines or edges.

- Because of the high flexibility of the free-form models, the internal constraints have to be strong. In the case of active contours, the internal energy is globally defined as:

$$E_{int}(v) = \frac{1}{2} \int \left(\alpha(s)|v'(s)|^2 + \beta(s)|v''(s)|^2 \right) ds \tag{12}$$

  where $v'(s)$ et $v''(s)$ denote the first and second derivatives of $v(s)$. $\alpha(s)$ is the elasticity coefficient and represents the tension. It has an influence on the length of the curve. A high value of α leads to large tension constraints, whereas the curve can have discontinuities when $\alpha = 0$. $\beta(s)$ is the rigidity coefficient and represents the curvature. When $\beta=0$, the curve can present a high convexity, whereas the curve is smooth when β is high.
- The external energy of the snake is computed from the image features. Generally, the external energy rests on gradient information (for edges) and intensity image (for bright and dark areas).

The initial curve is iteratively deformed in order to minimize the energy function. This is an optimization issue of a functional with several variables, which are the snake points.

Active contours are largely used for contour extraction applications because of their capacity to integrate the two steps of edge extraction and chining in a single operation. Moreover, snakes can be used as well to detect open contours, as closed contours or contours with fixed extremities. Active contours are fast and simple to implement in 2D and transform a complex problem of minimization in the iteration of a linear matrix system. Another asset is the numerical stability facing internal constraints.

However the use of active contours presents several drawbacks. The initialization is the main difficulty and could lead to bad convergence. Indeed, the snake is a free-form algorithm and is blindly attracted by the closest local minimum of the energy function. Moreover, the parameters of the snake are difficult to tune and are often heuristically chosen. Three additional problems can be cited: the difficulty to converge to boundary concavities, the instability facing external constraints (the snake can cross the contour if the snake parameters are too large) and the fact that topology changes of an object are not managed. Many studies have been proposed to overcome these drawbacks, we can notably cite the balloon snake approach (Cohen, 1991), the Gradient Vector Flow (Xu, 1998) and genetic snakes (Ballerini, 1999).

Active contours have been extensively used for the extraction of lips. The process is always the same involving the extraction of a local minimum with successive displacements of an initial curve. We give here a summary of the works developed in that field. They are classified according to the type of active contour, the proposed method for snake's initialization and the considered internal and external constraints.

Different Kinds of Active Contour for Lip Segmentation

Since the introduction of active contours (Kass, 1987), different modified snake models have been proposed to reduce the initialization dependence or to improve the convergence force.

Wu et al. (2002) introduce a GVF snake using the Gradient Vector Flow (Xu, 1998). GVF is computed as a diffusion of the gradient vectors of a grey-level or binary edge map derived from the image. The resultant field allows the snake to be initialized far away from the object and can attract the snake to move into concave regions. But the diffusion process time is important and can be too penalizing for real-time applications.

Seguier et al. (2003) use genetic snakes. They associate genetic algorithms with active contours to overcome initialization difficulty and to prevent being trapped by a non-desired local minimum. The genetic algorithm finds the optimal snake among a population of several snakes.

Shinchi et al. (1998) propose a Sampled Active Contour Model (SACM) to extract the outer lip contour. The classical active contour converges with an energy-minimizing algorithm, whereas the SACM is operated by forces that are applied on the contour points. This modified snake makes the extraction of the lip contour faster.

In addition, realization of snakes using B-splines was developed in (Blake, 1995). B-snakes use B-splines which are closed curves defined by several control points. They are able to represent a large variety of curves and have interesting continuity properties. Indeed, the B-snake points are linked by polynomial functions including intrinsically regularity properties. As a consequence it is possible to only consider the external forces for the curve deformation. Moreover, they have a lower computational cost than classical snakes. B-snakes are used for lip contour extraction in (Wakasugi, 2004) and (Kaucic, 1998).

Active Contour Initialization and Snake Initial Model

In order to prevent the snake locking onto a non-desired local minimum, the curve has to be initialized close to the mouth contours. Since the snake tends naturally to shrink, it has to be initialized outside the mouth. The parameters of the snake result from a compromise: not too small to be able to pass through parasite contours but not too large to avoid jumping over the searched contour. Several approaches have been proposed for the snake initialization in case of lip segmentation, which are based on finding the mouth area and on choosing and positioning the initial snake curve.

Figure 18. Localization of the mouth by vertical projections in (Delmas, 1999)

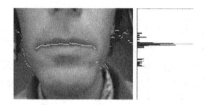 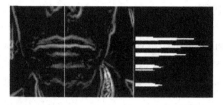

a) vertical accumulation of the darkest pixels　　　b) vertical projection of the intensity gradient

Mouth Region of Interest (ROI) Extraction

At this stage, the goal is to obtain a mouth bounding box in order to initialize the snake. Two mouth localization methods are presented: some methods are based on intensity or gradient intensity projections and some methods are based on color information analysis.

In (Radeva, 1995; Delmas 1999; Delmas, 2002; Kuo, 2005), projections of the image gradients or the intensity image are used to locate the mouth. Indeed, lips are characterized by a strong projection value of the derivatives along the normal to their edges. In (Radeva, 1995), the mouth position is found by analyzing the horizontal and vertical projections of the intensity image with some symmetrical constraints. In the same way, in (Delmas, 1999; Delmas, 2002; Kuo, 2005), the vertical mouth position is found by a vertical accumulation of the darkest pixels of each image column (Figure 18a). Then, the lip corners are extracted by making a chaining of the pixels with minimum luminance starting from the mouth center and by detecting the first jump of the chain. The vertical projection of the intensity gradient gives the top and low bounds of the mouth (Figure 18b).

The region-based approaches are also widely used to initiate snakes. For example, the lips area can be found by computing a lip mask or using statistical methods in order to estimate the position of the mouth. The mask contour or the mouth position can then be used for the snake initialization. See Section 2) for a detailed presentation of region-based techniques.

Snake Initial Model

When the mouth region is localized, the snake initial curves are placed close to the lip contours. The positions are chosen using the mouth boundary box, the mouth ROI or mouth key points. Different methods have been developed and differ whether the process is done on one single image (static methods) or on video sequences (dynamic methods and lip tracking).

In the case of static algorithms, the initial active contour is placed directly on the mouth bounding box in (Seo, 2003; Kuo, 2005). In (Delmas, 1999), the initial snake point positions for the inner and outer contour detection lie on the mouth edges. They are found with the lip corners positions and by reducing the number of edges of the mouth ROI.

However, to be near the searched contour, the initialization can use a model composed of curves located with respect to the mouth area characteristics, like in (Chiou, 1997; Delmas, 2002). Chiou et al. (1997) place a small circle at the centroïd of the mouth region. Several points are regularly spaced on the circle and their positions evolve by varying the lengths of radial vectors. In (Delmas, 2002), the preliminary extraction of mouth vertical extrema points and mouth corners allows the positioning of an initial model composed of quartics, which is sampled to give the snake points.

Some studies extract the inner and outer lip contours and use the position of the outer snake to initialize the inner snake (Beaumesnil, 2006; Seyedarabi, 2006). In (Beaumesnil, 2006), the outer snake is initialized on two cubic curves computed from the mouth bounding box and from the lip corner position, whereas the initial inner active contour is found shrinking the convergence result of a first snake by a non isotropic scaling with regard to the mouth center and taking into account the actual thickness of lips. In the same way, an oval shape around the lip area is used as initial outer snake and the initial inner snake is given by the convergence of the first active contour in (Seyedarabi, 2006).

When the main goal is lip contour tracking, the initialization of the snake in the current image is done by using information about the lip shape in the previous image. The position of the active contour on the previous frame is directly used as initialization in (Seyedarabi, 2006) whereas a dilation of 20% is done in (Kuo, 2005).

In addition, the initial active contour is found by the tracking of some key points from frame to frame (Delmas, 2002; Beaumesnil, 2006), or by template matching (Barnard, 2002; Wu, 2002; Seo, 2003).

In the first image of the sequence, either the contours are assumed to be known (Pardas, 2001) or the mouth is considered to be closed (Beaumesnil, 2006; Seyedarabi, 2006) to assure a good initialization for the first image.

Active Contour Energy Constraints

Once the position of the initial snake is given, the energy-minimization algorithm allows deforming the snake points to lock onto the lip contours. The convergence is achieved when the snake energy is minimal. The choice of the total energy is an essential feature of the active contour and different definitions have been proposed in the specific case of lip segmentation. Besides the E_{int} and E_{ext}, additional forces linked to the application or to the choice of the snake model can complete the active contour energy definition.

Regularization Constraints and Internal Energy

As described in the theory, the internal energy acts on the local constraints of the curve and controls the snake smoothness by two terms; α adjusts the tension and β controls the curvature. α and β are constant and fixed heuristically.

Active contours are free-form algorithms so that they have little information on the possible shape of the object. In the case of lips, it is possible to take into account the specificities of lip shape to define internal constraints. For example, a difficulty highlighted in several studies concerns the snake convergence around the lip corners. Lip corners are in blurred areas with weak gradients and they are located on concave edges. Since the limitations of active contour convergence to high curvature corners have been demonstrated, specific expressions of the internal energy have been proposed and suggest modifying the spacing of snake points or the value of α and β along the curve with different values near the mouth corners.

In (Seyedarabi, 2006), the initial snake points are equally spaced except around the lip corners. The same aspect is developed in (Delmas, 1999) where the snake points are reorganized to be equally spaced during the deformation phase and after a certain number of iterations. Pardas et al. (2001) introduce a term in the internal energy definition which forces the snake nodes to preserve the distance between them from one frame to the next one; the energy increases proportionally when the distance is altered.

In (Delmas, 1999; Pardas, 2001; Seguier, 2003), the rigidity coefficient β is not constant along the curve. It is higher in the middle of the mouth and is null on the points corresponding to the mouth corners. This choice is motivated by the fact that the curvature is minimal at the middle of the mouth and maximal around the lip corners. The same idea is exploited in (Kuo, 2005), where α and β are reduced near the corners.

Radeva et al. (1995) impose symmetrical constraints with respect to the vertical line passing through the middle of the mouth during the deformations.

To compensate the blind convergence of active contours and to reduce the influence of α and β, some studies use lip templates to regularize the curve. Wu et al. (2002) propose to use a template composed of two parabolas placed on the edges found by a Canny's detector. The two parabolas fitting result is blurred and an additional constraint is obtained by a gradient operator. In the same manner, the use of a curve model based on B-splines avoids the use of any internal energy in (Kaucic, 1998; Wakasugi, 2004).

Data Image and External Energy

The image forces, which are the external energy linked to the data, lead the snake towards interesting image features respecting contour extraction. Classical features are the lines and edges of the image. The simplest energy definition for the lines is the intensity image, which forces the snake to align on the darkest or lightest nearby contour depending on the sign of the energy functional. Whereas the intensity gradient attracts the snake towards strong or weak edges depending on the sign of the expression, Seyedarabi et al. (2006) define the external energy as the sum of the intensity image and the intensity gradient.

In current schemes the intensity gradient is generally used in the expression of the external energy, but certain parts of the lip contours sometimes have no particularly strong intensity gradient or parasitic intensity gradient block the convergence. For example in (Radeva, 1995), it is shown that the snake convergence for the lower lip contour is more difficult because, depending of the illumination conditions, the lower lip may be seen as a dark area, a bright area or composed of both dark and bright areas. To solve the problem, three snakes are defined with three different intensity gradients corresponding to the three cases (no further information is specified in the article) and the snake associated to the lowest energy estimation after convergence is chosen as the right snake for the lower lip contour. In (Wu, 2002), the external force is a GVF, increasing the capture range of the active contour. However to compensate this weakness, a weight coefficient is often assigned to the intensity gradient term and a second term is added to the expression of the external constraints. In (Pardas, 2001), the second term considers the compensation error obtained in a motion estimation process using block matching technique. Therefore, the external energy is low when the texture is similar to the one around the snake point position found in the previous image.

Otherwise, instead of using the intensity gradient, an edge map could be computed from a color space. Beaumesnil et al. (2006) propose to compute the gradient from a combination of hue and luminance, which is a much more appropriated space describing the lip contours than the intensity component.

The use of color information is also a usual way to formulate the external energy functional. In Seo et al. (2003), each snake node has "inside" and "outside" color patches. The patches are described by Gaussian distributions using red and green components in the case of skin pixels. In the case of mouth pixels, the "inside" component is the lip color and the "outside" component is the skin color (but the colors definition is not specified in the study). The nodes evolve with an external force which takes into account the difference between the patches and the original image. Kaucic et al. (1998) highlight the contrast between skin and lips by the projection of the color intensity onto an axis determined by Fisher discriminant analysis. This method is more effective for lips enhancement than transformation onto the hue.

Different higher level external energy functions have been developed in the case of mouth contour detection. For example, several studies propose different methods operating on binary images. Chiou et al. (1997) use a binary image obtained by thresholding the ratio R/G. The main external energy is computed on each pixel of the binary image using a block of neighboring binary pixels. The value of a pixel's energy depends on how many binary pixels are close to the current pixel. Seguier et al. (2003) define two external forces from binary images of both inside mouth and lips. The first term considers the number of pixels N belonging to the interior of the mouth (first binary image) and is computed as the ratio $1/N$. The second term takes into account the sum of the intensity values of the pixels belonging to the lips and its complement (the sum for non lip pixels). This term allows the two snakes surrounding the lips.

In (Shinchi, 1998), the external constraints are composed of three forces. A pressure force and an attraction force make the snake contracting and guiding each snake point towards the contour. When a point meets the lip contour, a repulsion force acts on the opposite direction of the two precedent forces to counterbalance their effect and to extract the edges (Figure 19). Finally, to help the snake to escape from noise, a vibration factor is added. This factor works perpendicularly to the force attracting the snake to

Figure 19. The three external forces used in (Shinchi, 1998)

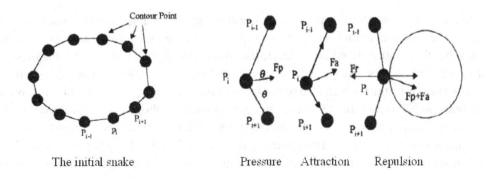

The initial snake   Pressure   Attraction   Repulsion

the contour. The direction of the vibration force reverses at each iteration and this zigzag move improves the ability to overpass the noise. In (Barnard, 2002), a combination of an active contour model and a 2D template matching technique is used to extract the outer mouth edges. The energy minimization of the snake is driven by a pattern matching which defines the external energy as the 2D correlation between patches taken from the image and the expected template for the specified snake point.

Additional External Forces

The previous external energy is defined to push the snake towards salient features of the image, but different local minima can be emphasized. In consequence, additional external constraints taking into account the application can be used to put the snake on the desired local minimum.

For example, in case of contour lip extraction, the mouth corners area is a weak gradient region and an active contour can be attracted away from their positions. Some studies propose to detect the lip corners before the snake convergence and then, other forces are added to guide the snake towards the corners during the deformation, or the lip corners are considered as fixed snake points (Liévin, 2004; Kuo, 2005).

Due to the shape configuration of the mouth, outer lip contour and inner lip contour, when the mouth is open, are initialized with a closed curve. Therefore, the balloon force introduced by (Cohen, 1991) is often added in the total energy definition. The balloon force inflates or deflates a closed curve like a balloon; this operation allows going through non-desired local minimum. The classical definition is used to inflate an initial active contour located inside the mouth in (Chiou, 1997) or compensate the snake tendency to shrink in (Delmas, 1999). Seyedarabi et al. (2006) use balloon energy for contour deflation in order to obtain the upper lip boundary from an initial active contour placed around the mouth. Then only the lower part of the previous active contour estimation evolves and locks onto the lower lip boundary by using balloon energy for inflation. In (Kuo, 2005), a modified balloon force is proposed using a pressure equation depending on color similarity. The parameters of an adaptive Gaussian color model are adjusted by analyzing the hue profile on the vertical passing through the middle of the mouth. In the expression of the balloon force, a coefficient controls the inflation or deflation power using the color similarity based on the Gaussian model. In other words, the hue regions which are statistically similar give positive pressure while the other regions give negative pressure. Finally, the additional force allows the deflation of an initial contour placed on a mouth bounding box. In (Beaumesnil, 2006), the active contour is forced to deflate and to converge towards the gravity center of the mouth area.

Discussion

The main difficulty of active contours is the initialization step. Concerning lip extraction applications, this problem is the most important because the configuration of the mouth can create several gradient extremums. When the mouth is closed, according to the origin of the illumination source, shadows around the lips or bright areas on lips give parasitic intensity gradients. In addition, a moustache, a beard or wrinkles are particular features which lead to the same result. Generally, the lower outer lip contour is the most difficult boundary to extract because the light comes from above in most of the cases.

It has to be noticed that the extraction of the outer contour has been studied more intensively than those of the inner one. Indeed, inner lip segmentation is a much more difficult task due to the non-linear appearance variations inside the mouth. When the mouth is open, the area between lips could take different configurations. The apparition of teeth, oral cavity, gum or tongue creates many gradient extremums.

Another drawback linked to the specificity of the mouth shape is the convergence around the lip corners. The lip corners are concave regions associated to weak gradient areas. Consequently, the external forces of the snake are, in general, too weak to compensate the elasticity of the active contour. The final contour could be too round around the mouth sides and does not exactly coincide with the lip corners.

However, active contours can be a good solution to cope with the high deformability of lip shape because of their large deformation freedom. Moreover, snake implementation is simple and fast, which is interesting for lip tracking in video sequences.

Parametric Models

Parametric models have some similarities with snakes; these models are deformed and fitted to the contours of the object by an energy-minimizing algorithm. The energy is the sum of an internal term and an external term. But the main difference is that an explicit assumption about the global shape of the contour to be extracted is made.

Description and Properties

Parametric models, introduced by Yuille et al. (1992), describe a shape with parameterized templates, generally composed of a set of different curves (circles, ellipses, parabolas, cubic curves...). The template interacts dynamically with the data through an energy cost function. The convergence is obtained when the position and the deformations of the model reach the best fit, which corresponds to the minimum of the energy function. Such as active contours, the cost function of the parametric models is the sum of an internal energy, representing the geometrical constraints of the model (distances, symmetry...) and an external energy, which is defined from the image data. The internal energy of a snake imposes local constraints only whereas the internal energy of the parametric models explicitly limits the possible deformations of the template by integrating global information about the expected shape of the object. The freedom of the model deformation is limited because the energy is not minimized in relation to the points of the model, as done with the snakes, but in relation with the parameter vector. This global parameterization allows being robust to partial occlusions.

Specifying a parametric model requires the definition of a template associated to some specific constraints with respect to the shape of the object of interest. The choice of a model is a compromise between the deformability and the algorithmic complexity.

The main advantage of parametric models is the geometric constraint which imposes a set of possible shapes for the segmentation result. This prevents from erratic deformations and the contour obtained after convergence is consistent with the predefined template. However, the limited deformability can make the model too rigid and not adequate to high deformable features. As the snakes, parametric models require good initialization because of the energy minimization step (the energy function is not necessarily convex).

Parametric model-based algorithms for lip segmentation require the definition of three main steps: the choice of the best template model for lip *a priori* description, the model initialization and the model optimization with the minimization of an energy function taking into account appropriate information

Figure 20. Different deformations of the mouth shape. The images come from the AR Database (Martinez, 1998)

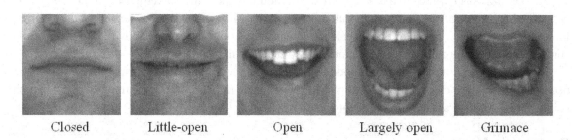

| Closed | Little-open | Open | Largely open | Grimace |

coming from the image. In the following sections, several works are discussed according to these three steps.

Mouth's Shape Modeling

The mouth is a high deformable feature and the first step is to define the right model for lip contour description. Lips can take several configurations with very different shapes (a closed mouth or a largely open mouth, a grimace … see Figure 20). The chosen model should fit the global shape of mouth, but has also to be flexible enough to allow important variations.

Several lip models have been proposed since the first study of Yuille et al. (1992). They are generally composed of parabolas (second order polynomial with three parameters), cubics (third order polynomial with four parameters) or quartics (fourth order polynomial with five parameters) depending on the desired result accuracy or the desired model complexity. The curve or set of curves is not necessarily the same for the upper boundary and the lower one. Indeed, the model of the upper contour can be more complex because of the presence of the Cupidon's bow (the "V" form located on the middle of the upper lip). Moreover, the goal of a mouth contour detection algorithm can be the outer lip segmentation, the inner lip segmentation or both the inner and outer boundaries detection. The models can be different according to the mouth state (closed or open) (Zhang, 1997; Yin, 2002; Stillittano, 2008) or according to the mouth shape (for example, "open", "relatively closed" and "tightly closed" (Tian, 2000)). Consequently, we firstly present some models representing the inner lip contour and secondly different models for outer lip contour.

Inner Lip Models

Two aspects have to be considered: can a same model be used to describe open and closed mouths? Has the chosen model to go up to the mouth corners (which could be linking points to an outer model for example) or does the inner model end to what we could call "inner" mouth corners?

The most used inner lip model is made of parabolas. The coordinates (x, y) of a parabola could be computed by the equation (11), where h is the height of the curve and w is the width.

Figure 21. a) Two-parabolas inner lip model b) and c) with the use of lip corners d) and e) with the use or "inner" lip corners

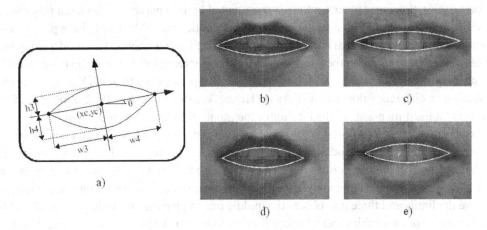

Figure 22. a) One-parabola inner lip model b) and c) examples of the model convergence

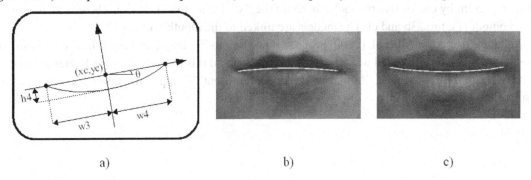

$$y = h(1 - \frac{x^2}{w^2})$$ (13)

In (Yuille, 1992), the model links the two mouth corners with two parabolas which are joined if the mouth is closed (Figure 21). This model imposes a vertical symmetrical constraint which is not always verified (Figure 21c). There are 5 parameters to tune, which are the coordinates (xc, yc) of the center, the inclination angle θ, the mouth width $w3+w4$ (with $w3 = w4$), the upper inner contour height $h3$ and the lower inner contour height $h4$. The same inner model is also used in (Hennecke, 1994; Coianiz, 1996; Zhiming, 2002) but the outer and inner lip contours are not linked by the mouth corners (Figure 21d and e)). In (Zhang, 1997; Yin, 2002), a closed-model with a single parabola (Figure 22) and an open-model with two parabolas, the same as in (Yuille, 1992) are proposed. In (Wu, 2002), the authors propose for inner lip modeling a two parabolas model controlled by four parameters, which are the left, right, top and bottom distances between the outer and inner contours.

In (Chen, 2006), the upper inner contour is represented by two parabolas (giving a possible asymmetric form) and the lower one by a single one, whereas Pantic et al. (2001) add also a parabola for the lower contour, which makes the final inner model composed of four parabolas. This model is asymmetric because each side of the mouth is processed separately to better represent the inner lip boundaries, while keeping the simplicity (6 parameters which are the same five parameters than in (Yuille, 1992) plus the width $w4$, taking a different value than $w3$). As in (Hennecke, 1994; Coianiz, 1996; Zhiming, 2002), $w3$ and $w4$ represent the dimensions of the interior of the mouth (model linked to the "inner" lip corners).

Cubic curves are used in (Stillittano, 2008) where two inner lip models for open and closed mouth are proposed. The open mouth model is composed of four cubics linking the mouth corners (Figure 22a). Each curve needs 5 point positions to be computed with the least squares approximation method, one of the two corners and a middle mouth point (one on the inner upper edge or one on the inner lower edge) to give the limits and three points near the middle one to give the curve shape. The closed mouth model is composed of two cubics and a broken line (Figure 22a). The two cubics have the same complexity as for the open mouth model, but they are linked with a new point and a broken line to describe the distortion due to the Cupidon's bow. Indeed, the authors show that some closed mouth shapes can not be represent by one or two parabolas because the "V" form of the Cupidon's bow is visible on the inner contour (Figure 23b and c). The models are linked to the mouth corners.

Vogt (1996) and Malciu et al. (2000) propose inner lip models based on nodes. In (Vogt, 1996), the inner contour is only computed when the mouth is closed and it is described with a Bezier curve composed of six points. In (Malciu, 2000), two B-splines represent the upper and lower contours and each B-spline has 5 nodes.

Figure 23. a) Closed-mouth and open-mouth inner lip models used in (Stillittano, 2008) b) and c) examples of the closed-mouth model convergence d) and e) examples of the open-mouth model convergence

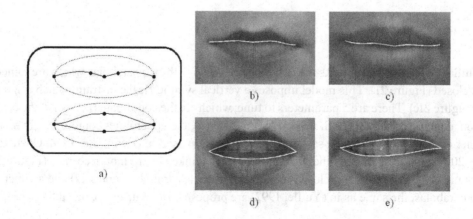

Outer Lip Contour Models

With regard to the outer lip contour extraction, the model has to be different between the upper and lower contours, due to the presence of the Cupidon's bow.

The first parametric model was proposed by Yuille et al. (1992). The coordinates (x, y) of a quartic could be computed by the equation (12), where h is the height of the curve, w is the width and the parameter q determines how far the quartic deviates from a parabola.

$$y = h(1 - \frac{x^2}{w^2}) + 4q(\frac{x^4}{w^4} - \frac{x^2}{w^2})$$

(14)

This template is made of three quartics with a symmetrical constraint (Figure 24). There are 8 parameters to tune, which are the coordinates (xc, yc) of the center, the inclination angle θ, the mouth width $w1+w2$ (with $w1 = w2 =$ the same value as $w3$ of the inner model), the upper outer contour height $h1$, the lower outer contour height $h2$, the offset a_off of the quartics center and the parameter q of the equation (12). The complete model (inner and outer contours) has 11 parameters. As in the case of inner contour, a symmetrical model is not recommended for outer lip modeling (Figure 24c). This model is also used in (Hennecke, 1994; Zhiming, 2002) (with different values between the outer mouth width ($2*w1$) and the inner mouth width ($2*w3$), which gives 12 parameters for the complete model (inner and outer contours)), and slightly modified in (Yokogawa, 2007) by using two quartics for the lower outer contour.

Many studies use parabolas for *a priori* outer lip modeling (Rao, 1995; Zhang, 1997; Tian, 2000; Yin, 2002) (Figure 25a). There are 6 parameters to estimate, which are the coordinates (xc, yc) of the center, the inclination angle θ, the mouth width $w1+w2$ (with $w1 = w2$), the upper outer contour height $h1$ and the lower outer contour height $h2$. Figure 25c shows that the model symmetry can give a rough outer contour extraction.

Figure 24. a) Three-quartics outer lip model; b) and c) examples of the model convergence

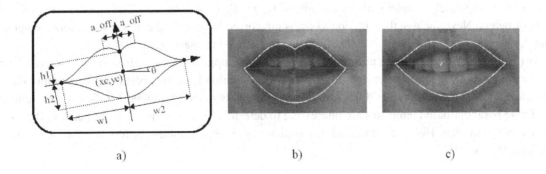

a)   b)   c)

Figure 25. a) Two-parabolas outer lip model b) and c) examples of the model convergence

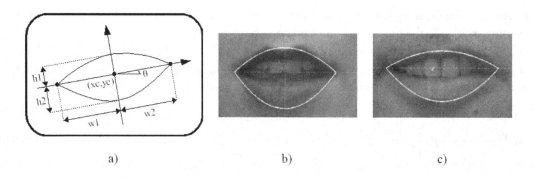

Figure 26. Three parabolas outer lip model; b) and c) examples of the model convergence

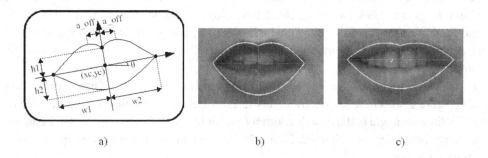

In (Liew, 2000; Werda, 2007) the two parabola models are improved by applying two transformations, a global torsion and a flattening, which make the model more accurate. In (Pantic 2001), four parabolas describe the outer mouth contours. This model is asymmetric because each side of the mouth is processed separately (model with 7 parameters: *xc, yc, θ, w1, w2, h1, h2*). The complete model has 11 parameters. Nevertheless, the Cupidon's bow is not correctly described because the authors suppose that the points, where the parabola derivatives are null, are on the same axis.

In (Coianiz, 1996), the authors propose also to describe the upper contour with two parabolas, but their center are offset by the parameter *aoff* (Figure 26). This solution leads to a better representation of the Cupidon's bow. Yokogawa et al. (2007) use the same model with two parabolas for the lower contour.

These parabola-based templates are interesting to determine some mouth features because the simplicity of the models. However, this kind of templates is either symmetric or too rough to accurately segment the mouth.

Figure 27. a) The outer model proposed in (Eveno, 2004) b) and c) examples of the model convergence

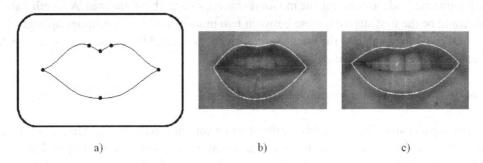

a)   b)   c)

Figure 28. a) Bezier curves model (© 1996 Stork. Used with permission.) b) B-splines model (Malciu, 2000)

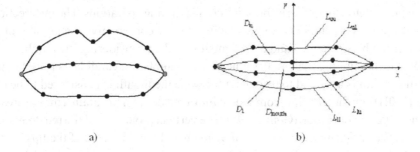

a)   b)

In (Eveno 2004), the authors use four cubic curves and one broken line linking five key points to represent the outer lip contour (Figure 27). Each cubic needs five point positions to be computed with the least squares approximation method, one of the two corners and a middle mouth point (one on the outer upper edge or one on the outer lower edge) to give the limits and three points near the middle one to give the curve shape. The model is flexible enough to describe a high variability of mouth shapes and the broken line is chosen to correctly follow the Cupidon's bow.

Bouvier et al. (2007) use the same model, excepted for the lower contour for which the two cubic curves are replaced by two Bezier curves.

The outer lip contour is described with two Bezier curves, composed of seven points for the upper lip and six points for the lower lip in (Vogt, 1996) and by B-splines in (Malciu, 2000) (Figure 28).

Model Initialization

Once the parametric model describing the mouth is chosen, it has to be initialized. A mouth state detection stage could be the first step to choose between two models in the case of inner lip segmentation. Then, the model has to be put into the image (initial localization) and the curves have to evolve to lock onto the contours (model optimization).

Open Mouth or Closed Mouth Model Selection

Some studies exploit two different models for the inner lip contours extraction (Zhang, 1997; Yin, 2002; Stillittano, 2008). A first model is built to deal with closed mouths and a second one to deal with open mouths. Consequently, during the initialization, a mouth state detection is necessary to decide which model is adequate.

The state "open or closed" of the mouth can be find with different techniques consisting in intensity gradient analysis (Zhang, 1997), integral projections (Pantic, 2001; Yin, 2002), color treatments (Chen, 2004) or classification method (Vogt, 1996).

In (Zhang, 1997), a mouth region of interest is extracted from the distance between the mouth corners. The contours within the mouth area are extracted on the Y component (from $YCbCr$ space) by a morphological edge detector, following by binarizing and thinning operations. The intersections between these contours and a line perpendicular to the one linking the corners give the number of possible lip contours. The decision between open and closed mouth is taken considering the number of candidates above and below the line linking the mouth corners. If the number of candidates is higher than two for each category, the mouth is assumed to be open, otherwise the mouth is considered to be closed.

Pantic et al. (2001) transform the hue component into a red domain to obtain a mouth area. The transformation is a hue filtering operation (Gong, 1995). The vertical projection of the red domain component applied on two vertical strips gives the state of the mouth and the thickness of the lips.

In (Yin, 2002), the integral projection of the hue component inside a strip passing through the middle of the mouth gives a profile with two peaks. If the width of the valley is beyond two pixels, the mouth is assumed to be open, otherwise the mouth is closed.

Chen et al. (2004) carry out multiple threshold operations on the RGB color space taking into account the skin color range and the dark range. The result is a binary image of the dark-black area located between the upper and the lower lips. Morphological treatments (erosion) allow the dark-black area contours inside the mouth to be detected. Finally, three lines crossing the mouth (a vertical and two diagonal lines) give six points, which are the intersections between the lines and the dark-black area contours. Comparing the values of the distances between the points with threshold values, it is possible to decide if the mouth is open or closed.

In (Vogt, 96), a neural network is trained with hue and intensity reference values to discriminate five classes, which are closed mouth, open mouth (without teeth), open mouth with only teeth inside the mouth, open mouth with upper and lower teeth separated by a dark area and open mouth with only the upper teeth.

Initial Model Parameter Estimation

The model convergence is made in two steps. Before the optimization and the extraction of the contour, the template has to be approximately placed into the image. This initial position can be found by detecting a mouth region of interest or by extracting some key points.

For mouth ROI detection, the most popular technique to find the mouth area is thresholding and morphological treatments (See section 2.1.). In addition, high-level methods could be used to segment the mouth ROI. In (Rao, 1995), lips and non-lips regions are found with an Hidden Markov Model in a mouth bounding box, manually placed in the first frame. Zhiming et al. (2002) detect a bounding box around the mouth from the previous frame and the mouth contours are highlighted by computing the Fisher transfer in the mouth area.

In (Coianiz, 1996), six features points are extracted from the mouth area, two points where the lower and upper external boundaries of the mouth meet (the mouth corners) and four points where the vertical symmetry axis of the mouth intersects the external and internal boundaries of the upper and lower lip. The two feature points are detected with color analysis and the four points are found by using luminance information. The initial amplitudes and positions of the parabolas of the parametric model are initialized from these six points. In (Pantic, 2001), a curve fitting algorithm is used to extract the outer mouth contours. The lowest mouth area pixel is chosen as the starting point algorithm and the contours are found by adding points with a chaining algorithm. The mouth corners are detected when the contour points change their directions. Four other key points (the vertical extrema) are initialized by integral vertical projections. Zhiming et al. (2002) use horizontal and vertical projections of the mouth area to extract the lip corners positions and a mouth bounding box very close to the lip contours to initialize the lip templates (Figure 29). In (Werda, 2007), in a mouth bounding box, projections of the saturation component allows the mouth corners to be detected.

As we have seen, Zhang et al. (1997) estimate several candidates on a vertical middle mouth line. Then, the mouth corners are detected with a template matching technique. Each candidate is a key point used to initialize the possible parabolas linking these points and the lip corners. For each parabola, three points are available.

Figure 29. (Zhiming, 2002) a) Horizontal and vertical projections on the mouth area b) Key point and mouth bounding box detection

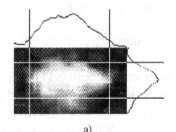 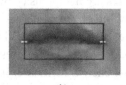

a)   b)

Some works use an active contour model to initialize the parametric model. The deformable template, by using some key points of the snake, smoothes the active contour result and, if the model is carefully chosen, extracts a large range of different shapes. Finally, active contours help to overcome the main drawback of the deformable template method which is the limited freedom of deformations.

In (Eveno, 2004), a set of points on the upper lip contour and three key points are extracted by the convergence of a "jumping snake". Unlike classic snakes, jumping snake can be initialized relatively far from the final contour and the adjustment of the parameters is easy and intuitive.

Model Parameter Optimization

We give some examples illustrating the possible optimizations used for parametric models in the context of lip segmentation. Like active contours, the parameters of the parametric models evolve iteratively by minimizing a cost function with 2 energy terms.

Internal Energy for the Model Regularization

The internal energy sets *a priori* constraints on the variability of the template model. In (Yuille, 1992), the internal energy gives preferential treatments to certain properties such as the upper lip symmetry, the centering of the mouth between the lip corners, a constant proportional coefficient between the thickness of the upper and lower lips and a cohesion by preventing too large vertical movements of the upper lip. Hennecke et al. (1994) simplify the internal energy proposed in (Yuille, 1992) by integrating the notions of symmetry and centering directly into the construction of the model. A temporal continuity constraint on the thickness of the lips is also introduced in the internal energy expression. In the same way, Coianiz et al. (1996) define penalty constraints which embody the admissible lip shapes, like forcing the outer lip width and height to have higher values than the inner ones. In (Mirhosseini, 1997), a potential is defined to control the mouth shape model by measuring differences between some lip distances. Vogt (1996) proposes internal energies which stabilize the distance between three connected nodes model and control the tensions between two connected nodes model. In the same manner, in (Malciu, 2000), the internal energy is a combination of elastic and symmetry local constraints, like stabilizing the distance between the model points for example.

External Energy Computed from the Image Data

In many studies using deformable templates, the geometric constraints given by the model curves are sufficient and the model parameters evolve with the external energy only. The external energy establishes interaction constraints in order to maintain the consistency between the model geometry and salient image features. The image information used in the expression of the external energy could take different forms.

The simplest features are the intensity image and the intensity gradients. In (Yuille, 1992), the external energy is composed of three energetic fields, the contour field obtained by a gradient operator on the intensity image, the valley field of the dark areas and the peak field of the bright areas. These three fields correspond to the image features: dark, bright and transition areas and the field's combination define the external energy. Mirhosseini et al. (1997) define a valley energy term and an intensity gradient term. The same information is exploited in (Malciu, 2000). The peak and valley information is incorporated in a single potential function by applying the connection cost operator to the original and negated image. The intensity gradient enhances the mouth outer boundaries and the valley-peak potential highlights the inner mouth composed of dark areas (valley potential) and bright areas (peak potential). Hennecke et al. (1994) use only the vertical component of the intensity gradient, because the mouth contours are predominantly horizontal. The Prewitt algorithm gives "positive" and "negative" gradient if the intensity is higher above or below the edge. The adequate gradient is applied according to the four lip edge (the two upper inner and outer contours and the two lower inner and outer contours). The gradient image is also used in (Werda, 2007).

The intensity gradient is essentially used for the outer lip detection, but it can be weak on certain mouth areas (the lower lip boundary for example) and it can depend on the illumination conditions. The use of color gradient can be a good information. In (Bouvier, 2007), the gradient is a combination of the pseudo-hue and the luminance component for the upper outer lip contour and the gradient of the pseudo-hue for the lower one. Stillittano et al. (2008) propose two different gradients to highlight the upper and lower inner lip contour. These gradients are a combination of color spaces that give different values for the inner mouth (teeth, tongue, oral cavity) and the lips (see section 1.).

In (Vogt, 1996), the gradient is computed on a probability map which enhances the lips. The map is found with a 2D look up table algorithm applied on the hue and saturation (from *HSI* color space). This gradient is used in the case of open mouth. Otherwise it is replaced by an intensity gradient for the inner lip contours detection. Yokogawa et al. (2007) use the mouth area found with hue thresholding to compute a value threshold (from *HSV* color space). A second area is obtained by value thresholding and a binary image is created by an AND operation between the two areas. Then, a differential operator gives the edge map. The external energy is a measure of the difference between the template model and the contour pixels of the edge map.

The lip model allows different regions, like the skin, the lips and the inner mouth to be separated. Different criteria based on color information have been created to be minimal when the regions are well separated and to guide the model curves displacements (Coianiz, 1996; Zhang, 1997; Pantic, 2001; Yin, 2002; Wu, 2002). In (Coianiz, 1996), three areas are defined, the interior of the mouth, the lips and an area of constant thickness surrounding the outer lip model. The external energy takes into account a measure of the red chrominance information in the three regions and the maximization (or minimization depending on the sign of the energy functional) of the energy allows the red regions of the image to be restricted to the lip area. The same kind of method with the same color information is used in (Pantic, 2001). In (Zhang, 1997), two cost functions are proposed, one for the closed model and one for the open model. They are defined with the intensity gradient image and weighted by the means and the variances of the *Cr* component from *YCbCr* space of the areas defined by the model (the upper lip, the lower lip and if the mouth is open, the interior of the mouth). The same models and regions are used in (Yin, 2002), but the criterion is built from the hue component by considering the fact that small intra-variance and large inter-variance of hue exist between the three regions (the criterion is the sum of mean and standard-deviation of the hue in each area). In (Wu, 2002), the outer lip contour is known after the convergence of an active contour and the inner lip contour has to be extracted with a model template. Therefore, two regions have to be distinguished, the lips and the interior of the mouth. The histogram of lip and of the inside mouth areas are learnt with a database. Then, a function estimates the similarity of a region *Reg* with the lip and inside mouth reference areas based on the value of the histogram of the region *Reg*.

Others methods use the color information to build probability map of the lip color (which is an image representing the probability for each pixel of the image to be a lip pixel) (Rao, 1995; Liew 2000). The criterion has a high value when the region enclosed by the lip model has the highest possible probability. The criterion has a small value for the region outside. In (Liew 2000), assuming that the probability associated with each pixel is independent of the probability of other pixels the optimum partition is found when the joint probability of the lip and non-lip region is maximized.

Optimization Method

The classical energy-minimizing algorithm is the downhill simplex (Yuille, 1992; Hennecke, 1994; Malciu, 2000). The downhill simplex is an algorithm which starts with an initial position of the model and makes iteratively move this position towards a local minimum by following the strongest slope. The slope of the function of several variables is the gradient. The main drawbacks of this method are the convergence time which increases rapidly with the number of the function variables (in our case, each new internal or external constraint brings a new variable) and the fact that the solution is not necessarily a global minimum, depending on the model initialization. Yuille et al. (1992) combine the downhill simplex with a sequential and looped "coarse to fine" optimization algorithm. Firstly the general position of the model (centering of the mouth, computation of the width and the orientation) is adjusted. Secondly, the downhill gradient gives a finer position of the mouth boundaries. This two-step process is done until the convergence.

In (Vogt, 1996), a point-based model is used and the nodes move into a randomly proposed direction at each optimization iteration. If the new position gives a better solution (only the model parts affected by the current nodes are taken into account) it is conserved, otherwise it is rejected.

A non-deterministic minimization algorithm is used in (Coianiz, 1996) and the conjugate gradient, which is a faster iterative algorithm than the downhill simplex, is chosen in (Liew, 2000).

Another technique is to compute different possible positions and to choose the best with an optimal criterion. In (Zhang, 1997), the parabolas for each lip contour candidate are computed and the adequate cost function allows the best solution (see previous part "External energy computed from the image data") to be determined. In (Wu, 2002), the variations of four distances between the known outer lip contour and the searched inner contour allow different positions of two parabolas to be computed. The best position is chosen with the criterion presented in the previous part "External energy computed from the image data".

In (Eveno, 2004; Bouvier, 2007), the curves fitting and the mouth corners detection are done at the same time. For each side of the mouth, a finite-number of possible lip corner positions is tested. Several curves are computed with the considered corner position and several points are found on the outer lip contour by a snake. The best solution is found by maximizing the gradient mean flow along the curves. In (Werda, 2007), all the possible model positions in the mouth bounding box are computed and the maximization of the gradient mean flow allows to choose the best position.

Some studies use directly the position of several key points to obtain the final lip contours. The main advantage is the faster convergence, because these algorithms are not iterative. The least square approximation algorithm used in (Wark, 1998; Stillittano, 2008) is the most current technique. In (Wark, 1998), the contours of the mouth ROI are found with a standard-edge detector and are sampled to give several points on the outer lip boundary. The least squares approximation algorithm is used to fit the model. In (Stillittano, 2008), several points on the upper and lower inner contours and the position of the mouth corners allow the inner lip model to be optimized.

Tian et al. (2000) track the position of four key points (the two mouth corners and the two vertical outer extrema) with the Lucas-Kanade algorithm (Tomasi, 1991). With the three extrema points on the upper lip contour and the three others on the lower contour, the two parabolas of the model are completely defined. Chen et al. (2006) detect the edges of the mouth ROI with the Laplacian of Gaussian algorithm, which extracts contour by finding the zero-crossings in the second derivatives gray image. Finally, several points on the inner contours are detected and a curve fitting algorithm, called Nearest-Neighbour Interpolation, is applied on the edge map and places the model composed of three parabolas on the inner edges.

Discussion

As for the snakes, the main difficulty of the parametric models convergence is the possibility to lock onto a local minimum. As a consequence, the initialization is very important and often dependent of the accurate mouth area or key point extraction.

In addition, the model choice has to make a compromise between low complexity, which gives a fast convergence but appreciative contours, and a high complexity, which gives accurate contours but a long optimization time. To give a realistic result, the upper outer model has to be composed of high order curves or by a set of several different curves, because of the presence of the Cupidon's bow. It is also important to propose a possible non symmetric model. In general, the inner model is simpler and the hypothesis of linking the outer and inner models with the lip corners is often made. Consequently, the inner contour result can be appreciative around the corners, especially when the mouth is partially closed.

Contrary to the active contours, the parametric models introduce a notion of *a priori* knowledge about the global lip shape. Therefore, the final contour obtained after the optimization is an expected form. The influence of local perturbations is reduced by the minimization of a global energy. Thus, a parametric model can be used to smooth the contours found with a snake convergence and the most efficient algorithms often mix active contours for coarse estimation and parametric models for refining and regularization.

SEGMENTATION RESULTS EVALUATION

The number of algorithms that have been proposed for lip area segmentation or for lip contour extraction is very significant. Each author a priori claims that his/her algorithm is the best but it is very difficult to appreciate without a defined benchmark of test images and without a unified protocol for quantitative results evaluation. In this section, we describe first the databases that have been commonly used and then we make a list of the methods used for lip segmentation results evaluation.

Lip Image Databases

To our knowledge, only two databases have been built for the purpose of lip segmentation and lip reading methods evaluation:

- The CUAVE (Cuavebase) database has been developed for audio-visual speech processing. It contains audio video sequences from 36 individuals (17 female and 19 male speakers). For information on obtaining CUAVE visit the webpage http://ece.clemson.edu/speech.
- The LIUM database (Daubias, 2003) was recorded without artificial lighting. It contains sequences with both natural and blue lips. The fact is that this database is almost never used by authors in order to test and evaluate their lip segmentation algorithm. The LIUM database is available freely for academic organizations at http://www-lium.univ-lemans.fr/lium/avs-database/.

We can also mention the following databases that have been used for lip segmentation algorithm evaluation though they have been initially developed for face identification algorithms:

- The FERET database (Philipps, 2000; Feret) contains a huge number of face images of frontal faces, quarter left or right faces, faces with different illumination, faces with different expressions... More precisely, the database contains 1564 sets of images for a total of 14,126 images that includes 1199 individuals. As a result, only a subset of the Feret database is used for lip segmentation evaluation. As an example, this database has been used in (Xin, 2005). The FERET database is not freely distributed. To obtain the FERET database visit the webpage http://face.nist.gov/colorferet/.
- The AR database (Martinez, 1998; ARbase) contains over 4,000 color images corresponding to 126 people's faces (70 men and 56 women). Images feature frontal view faces with different facial expressions, illumination conditions, and occlusions (sun glasses and scarf). This database has been used for lip contour segmentation evaluation in (Liew, 2003; Stillittano, 2008; Xin, 2005). The AR face database is publicly available and free for researchers for algorithm evaluation. It can be obtained at http://cobweb.ecn.purdue.edu/~aleix/aleix_face_DB.html.
- The M2VTS database (Pigeon 1997; M2VTS base) is made up from 37 different faces and provides 5 shots for each person. These shots were taken at one week intervals or when drastic face changes occurred in the meantime. This database has been used for lip segmentation evaluation in (Lucey 2000; Gordan 2001; Pardas 2001; Seguier, 2003; Wark, 1998). The M2VTS database is publicly available for non-commercial purpose. For information on obtaining the database visit http://www.tele.ucl.ac.be/PROJECTS/M2VTS/m2fdb.html.
- The XM2VTS database is an extension of the previous database (XM2VTS base; Messer, 1999). It has been used for lip segmentation evaluation in (Kuo, 2005; Liew, 2003; Sadeghi 2002). This database is not free. More information can be found at http://www.ee.surrey.ac.uk/CVSSP/xm-2vtsdb/.
- The Cohn-Kanade AU Coded-Facial Expression Database (Kanade, 2000) consists in approximately 500 image sequences from 100 subjects. Accompanying meta-data include annotation of FACS action units and emotion-specified expression. Initially built for the purpose of facial expressions recognition, this database has been also used for lip segmentation evaluation in (Pardas, 2001; Seyedarabi, 2006; Tian, 2000). This database is publicly available for free. More information regarding the procedure to obtain the database can be found at http://vasc.ri.cmu.edu/idb/html/face/facial_expression/index.html.

To sum up, it is obvious that there is no consensus about the database to be used for lip segmentation performances evaluation. That is the reason why many authors also use their own database for the evaluation purpose. For example, in (Wu, 2002), a sequence of 126 frames of the Bernstein Lip-reading

Corpus is used; in (Wakasugi, 2004), 200 color images of 10 persons that have been collected by the authors; in (Barnard, 2002), the image database consists in 6 sequences of 6 persons, which pronounced the sequence of numerals from "one" to "ten" without any pause between the numerals. Each sequence has over 200 images that have been acquired by the authors...

Performance Evaluations

The evaluation and the comparison of lip segmentation algorithms are two very difficult tasks. Concerning performances evaluation, three kinds of methods have been proposed: subjective evaluation, quantitative evaluation and evaluation with respect to a given application. The purpose of algorithms comparison has not been really broached. In our opinion, several reasons are responsible for this lack of algorithms comparison. No reference database has been exhibited for lip segmentation purpose. And no accurate and approved protocol for the comparison has been proposed for the moment.

Subjective Evaluation

The first common way to evaluate the performances of lip segmentation algorithm is a subjective evaluation where a human expert visually determines if the segmentation is good or not. For example, in (Barnard, 2002; Liévin, 2004; Liew, 2003; Zhang, 2000), the authors explain that the method has been tested on several images and that it is successful, some segmented images are presented in the papers in order to illustrate the performances.

In (Kuo, 2005), a more sophisticated subjective evaluation is used: a grading system is defined. The system grades the fitting into 5 different grades: "perfect", "good", "fair", "poor" and "wrong", depending on the general appearance of the estimated contour and on the fitting of 4 benchmark points (left, right, top and bottom corners of lips). Figure 30 gives an illustration of some of the considered grades. If both the global estimated contour and the position of lips corners are accurate, the segmentation is labeled as "perfect". When the accuracy of the global contour or when the accuracy of the lip corner decreases, the segmentation is labeled with the other grades.

Of course, the major limitation of the subjective method for the evaluation of the segmentation accuracy is that it depends on the human expert and it is not obvious that the performances will be esti-

Figure 30. from left to right, "perfect", "good", "fair" and "poor" labeled segmentation (Kuo, 2005)

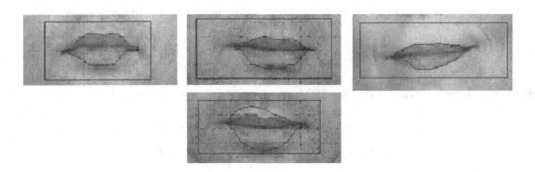

Figure 31. Performances evaluation based on the accuracy of the Qi keypoints

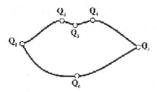

mated in the same way if the human expert changes. For example, in (Kuo, 2005), the authors do not say anything about the number of human experts who labeled the different lip segmentations.

Quantitative Evaluation

The quantitative evaluation may concern either the whole contour either only some specific points of the contour (generally the mouth corners positions).

In (Eveno, 2004), the mouth contour is associated to six key points Qi (Figure 31) and the performances of the proposed mouth contour extraction algorithm are evaluated by estimating the accuracy of these six estimated keypoints. More precisely, the key points of 300 images (extracted from 11 sequences) have been manually marked several times by different human operators. For each point, the ground-truth position is computed as the mean of all the hand checked positions. Then for each point the difference between the ground truth position and the estimated position is computed. Table 3 reports the quantitative performances.

The same six key points are considered in (Yokogawa, 2007) where the relative error is computed as the sum of the distances between the manually extracted points and the estimated points normalized by the distance between both mouth corners. As outlined by the authors themselves, one limitation of the method is that errors can occur when the expert establishes the ground truth by manually clicking the key points on an important series of images.

When the quantitative evaluation is focused on the whole contour, a reference global contour or a ground truth global contour is needed. The reference contour can be either manually extracted or automatically extracted with another segmentation method. Whatever the method for the reference contour, a perfect contour is not always guaranteed since errors can occur in the building of the ground truth. This limitation is brought out by all the authors proceeding to such a quantitative evaluation.

Table 3. Key points accuracy in (Eveno, 2004)

	Q_1	Q_2	Q_3	Q_4	Q_5	Q_6
Error (%)	4	2.4	1.8	1.9	3.3	3.6

In (Wu, 2002), the lip contours are hand-labeled and compared to the estimated results by computing an error ratio. If a pixel does not belong to both the hand-labeled mouth area and the mouth area estimated by the algorithm, the pixel is evaluated as an error pixel. The error ratio is computed by the ratio between the number of error pixels (NEP) and the total number of pixels of the hand-labeled mouth area. In (Wu, 2002), this method has been used in order to evaluate the lip contour extraction on a sequence of 126 frames. The same method has been used in (Stillittano, 2008) on a set of 507 images coming from the AR face database corresponding to two particular mouth shapes ("scream" and "smile") and on a set of 94 images coming from a database acquired by the authors with a head mounted camera pointing the mouth area (see Figure 32) for image examples and extracted contours with the method proposed in (Stillittano, 2008)).

The limitation of this quantitative method based on the whole lip contour is that the ratio criterion is related to the number of pixels inside the hand-labeled mouth area so that for a same number of error pixels, the ratio is lower for "scream" images (high number of pixels inside the mouth area) than for "smile" images (low number of pixels inside the mouth area).

Similar approach is proposed in (Liew, 2003). To have a ground truth, the authors manually fit a parametric lip model on 70 images randomly extracted from their database. For the performances evaluation, two measures are computed: the percentage of overlap between the segmented and the ground truth lip areas and a segmentation error measure which is the ratio between the miss-classified pixels and the number of lips pixels in ground truth.

In (Wakasugi, 2004), the segmentation accuracy is evaluated by computing the factor $F_c = S_{diff}/L_c^2$ where S_{diff} is the area between the real outer lip contour (hand-labeled ground truth) and the extracted contour and L_c is the length of the real contour. Both contours are supposed to be similar if Fc is below a threshold fixed to 0.04 which means that an admissible difference between both contours is about 4 pixels if L_c is 100 pixels.

In (Gacon, 2005) and (Bouvier, 2007) the objective evaluation is done by computing the distances between the contour points given by the ground truth and the corresponding points given by the author's algorithm. The distances are normalized by the width of the mouth.

Performances Evaluation with Respect to the Considered Application

When the lip segmentation algorithm has been developed for a specific application (lip reading or facial animation for example), the performances of the lip segmentation algorithm are evaluated in regards to the performances of the considered application. In such a case, the segmentation will be considered as

Figure 32. On the left, "smile" and "scream" examples from the AR database and on the right, author's database examples

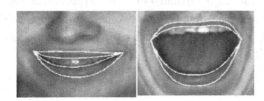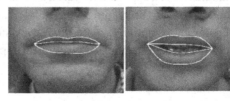

good if the corresponding application works well. This does not necessarily mean that the accuracy of the lip segmentation is very good.

In (Brand, 2001), the goal is to study the biometric potential of the lips for speaker recognition and the evaluation is done by computing the speaker recognition rates.

In (Chan, 1998; Chan, 2001; Chiou, 1997; Nefian, 2002), the purpose is lip reading and speech recognition. As a consequence, the accuracy of lip segmentation is evaluated through the recognition rates of the considered sentences. In (Seguier, 2003), the temporal evolution of height and the width of a speaking mouth are studied since these parameters are of high importance for automatic lip reading.

In (Gacon, 2005), a subjective evaluation related to the application of lip reading is done by testing the intelligibility improvement by adding the synthetic visual information in case of a subject telling phone numbers with different level of noise. Using the original video of the speaker telling phone numbers, the proposed algorithm based on Active Appearance Model is used to construct a video of the synthetic mouth telling the phone numbers. Then the audio channel is superposed to study intelligibility improvement and compared with the intelligibility of the original video with the audio.

In (Hsu, 2002), the authors develop a face detection algorithm for color image using a skin-tone color model and facial features. The goal is to develop a system that extracts faces from images with multiple subjects and then to compute features (eyes, lips) for subject identification. To evaluate the algorithm the face detection rate is calculated. The face is considered as "well detected" when the face ellipse, the eye and the mouth bounding boxes are found correctly. Thus they evaluate the performances of their algorithm for mouth segmentation.

In (Yin, 2002; Wu, 2002), the performances of lip segmentation algorithm are evaluated in the case of face synthesis and facial animation. The aim of evaluation is to see if the synthesized mouth movements have a realistic behavior or not. A visual comparison between the synthesized video and the original one is done. In (Wu, 2004), the evaluation is even done more objectively by comparing the Facial Animation Parameters generated from a hand-labeled lip contours and from the lip contours automatically extracted.

In (Seyedarabi, 2006), the authors are interested in facial Action Units automatic classification. The extracted lip feature points are used to extract some geometric features to form a feature vector which is used to classify lip images into AUs, using Probabilistic Neural Networks. Experimental results display the robustness of the lip edge detection since a reasonable classification with an average AUs recognition rate of 85.98% in image sequences is achieved.

APPLICATIONS OF LIP SEGMENTATION

Lip segmentation is a low level processing that is generally integrated to a higher level interpretation application. Though perfect lip segmentation would be the best case, the required accuracy of segmented lips could be different from an application to another. For example, less accuracy is needed for only visual evaluation based applications (facial animation for example) than for numerical parameters based applications (automatic lip reading for example). Here we are focusing on two particular applications that involve lip segmentation as a pre-processing step: lip reading and facial animation or synthesis. In the last section, we will mention some atypical applications.

Lip Reading

Lip reading application is probably the first application in computer vision that has required lip segmentation. The problem of lip reading has been studied first of all in the context of audio-visual speech recognition. Indeed, human speech perception is bimodal: we combine audio and visual information. An automatic visual speech recognition system is a significant complement to an audio speech recognition system when the audio system is used in a noisy environment. The reader can refer to the reference (Potamianos, 2004) for a complete overview about audio-visual automatic speech recognition. Our purpose here is not to make a comparison between the performances of the different audio-visual speech recognition system that have been developed. We aim at explaining how the segmented lip contours are used in the context of lip reading application.

The link between lip and oral message is included in the shape and the motion of the lips. So it is necessary first to extract the contours of the lips and second to characterize the lip shape with an efficient set of parameters. The first step for an automatic lip reading system being lip segmentation, many lip segmentation algorithms have been developed for that purpose. Lip segmentation in the context of speech reading is a very difficult task because:

- High accuracy is mandatory. Indeed speech reading is based on the analysis of measures computed from the estimated lip contours so that any error on lip contour extraction will have an immediate repercussion on the global speech recognition rate.
- Lip deformations and motions are numerous during speech sequence.

In (Sugahara, 2000), a particular set of parameters coming from the outer lip contour and made of the distances from the centre of the contour to 12 points of the contour equally spaced out and the deviations of these distances computed on the previous frames. As a result, the speech recognition process is based on 24 measures coming from the lip contour. In (Shinchi, 1998), the same 12 points are considered but the recognition is based on the analysis of the surface of the triangular areas defined by the lines coming from the centre point of the lip contour to the 12 edges points.

Most of the time, the features that are extracted from lip contour in order to characterize lip shape in the context of lip reading are based on mouth dimensions. In (Chan, 1998), (Barnard, 2002), the length and the width of the outer lips only are computed from the segmented lip. In (Seguier, 2003), in addition to the height and the width (H, L) of the outer lip contour, their temporal derivatives (δH, δL) and the percentage of light %W and dark pixels %B in the mouth area are considered. A more complete set of geometric features taking information from outer and inner lip contours is proposed in (Zhang, 2002). Figure 33 describes the geometric features that are computed from the extracted lip contours. The speech recognition results show that the global set of geometric features outperforms the case when only outer lip features are taken into account.

But as explained in (Rosenblum, 1996; Summerfield, 1989; Summerfield, 1992), not only the mouth dimensions are necessary but also the presence of teeth or tongue during speech is a very important visual cue. The methods developed in (Chan, 2001; Gacon, 2005; Zhang, 2002) give such additional information. The six geometric parameters and the information about the presence of teeth/tongue have been used for lip reading in (Chang 2001; Zhang 2002) and it has been shown that the recognition

Figure 33. Definition of the geometric features for lip reading application

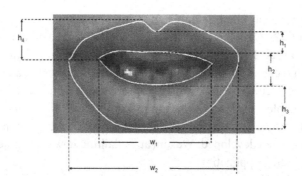

rates are higher than when only a partial set of this information is used. In (Aleksic, 2002), this idea of integrating lip deformations and information about teeth and tongue is also defended. The MPEG-4 Facial Action Parameters associated to the mouth, teeth and tongue are extracted from the lip contours and are used for the purpose of speech recognition.

As a conclusion, it is obvious that all the considered methods use numerical information about the lip shape and that the lip reading recognition rates are directly related to the accuracy of the lip segmentation. For the moment, the problem of lip reading for continuous speech with different speakers has not been solved partly due to the fact that an ideal lip contour is not yet achievable for any kind of speech sequences.

Virtual Face Animation

The second application which extensively uses lip segmentation is virtual face animation (Beaumesnil 2006; Kuo 2005; Yin 2002; Wu 2002)… The purpose is the building of a virtual face with realistic lip deformations and motion. We are not going to make an exhaustive comparison between the proposed methods for face animation but we prefer to focus on some examples in order to exhibit the way the different authors integrate lip segmentation results in their animation process.

In (Wu 2002; Wu 2004), the MPEG-4 Facial Action Parameters associated to the inner lip contour and to the outer lip contour are extracted from the segmented lip and are used in order to be the inputs of a facial animation MPEG-4 player. Figure 34 gives an example of generated virtual face.

In (Kuo, 2005), extracted lip contours are used to animate real faces. The animation in the mouth region consists in one Action Unit operation consisting in pulling the lip corner in order to generate smiling faces (see Figure 35 for an illustration).

In (Yin 2002), lip segmentation and tracking are presented for the purpose of realistic facial expression generation. Once the mouth contours have been extracted, the mouth feature vertices of a global 3D face model are fitted on some mouth point's contour.

Figure 34. Examples of MPEG-4 facial animation (Wu, 2004)

   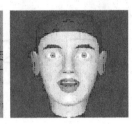

Figure 35. Example of animated face based on lip segmentation (Kuo, 2005)

Biometric Applications

In (Brand, 2001; Chibelushi, 1997; Hsu, 2002; Luettin, 1997; Wark, 1998; Wark, 1998b), lip segmentation is used for the purpose of speaker or subject identification. This tends to exploit the biometric potential of the lips and is based on geometrical and appearance based features computed on the segmented lips. In (Hammal, 2006; Hammal, 2007), five geometric distances are computed on a face skeleton including lip, eyes and brows contours (Figure 36). These five distances are then used in a facial expression classification process.

In the same way, geometric features are computed from the lip contours in (Seyedarabi, 2006) and are used to classify lip images into Action Units.

Figure 36. On the left, 5 geometric distances computed on the facial skeleton including the outer lip contour (mouth height and width); on the right, two examples of automatic facial expression recognition

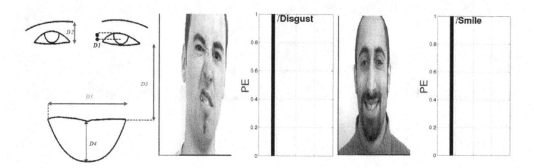

Finally, in (Yokogawa, 2007), the precise lip contour is used as a help for the treatment of cleft lip patients in order to plan the plastic surgery procedure. It is also used for dental treatments.

CONCLUSION

Lip modeling and lip segmentation have been extensively studied. Concerning the modeling of lip shape or lip pixels color distribution, different models have been proposed and none of them is really predominant in the literature. Concerning lip segmentation, region-based approaches and contour-based approaches have been proposed. Contour-based approaches lead to more accurate contours but suffer from difficulties for contour initialization. Region-based approaches do not depend on the initialization process but produce only rough accuracy around the contours. As a consequence, the current tendency is the combination of both approaches.

However that may be, the problem of lip segmentation is still open and will still be largely studied given the amount of industrial applications that would benefit from accurate lip contours.

REFERENCES

Aleksic, P. S., Williams, J. J., Wu, Z. & Katsaggelos, A. K. (2002). Audiovisual speech recognition using MPEG-4 compliant visual features. *EURASIP Journal on Applied Signal Processing, special Issue on Audio-Visual Speech Processing*, pp. 1213-1227, November.

ARbase The AR face database home page http://cobweb.ecn.purdue.edu/~aleix/aleix_face_DB.html

Ballerini, L. (1999). Genetic Snakes for Medical Images Segmentation. *Lecture Notes in Computer Science, 1596*, 59-73.

Barnard, M., Holden, E. J. & Owens, R. (2002). Lip Tracking using Pattern Matching Snakes. *The 5th Asian Conference on Computer Vision* (ACCV'2002), pp. 273-278, January.

Beaumesnil, B., Chaumont, M., & Luthon F. (2006). Liptracking and MPEG4 Animation with Feedback Control - *IEEE International Conference On Acoustics, Speech, and Signal Processing*, (ICASSP'2006), May.

Blake, A., Isard, M. A. & Reynard, D. (1995). Learning to track the visual motion of contours. *Artificial Intelligence*, 101-134.

Bouvier, C., Coulon, P. Y., & Maldague, X. (2007). Unsupervised Lips Segmentation Based on ROI Optimisation and Parametric Model. *International Conference on Image Processing*, ICIP2007.

Brand, J. (2001). Visual speech for speaker recognition and robust face detection. *PhD thesis*, University of Wales, United Kingdom.

Castañeda, B., & Cockburn, J. C. (2005). *Reduced support vector machine applied to real-time face tracking.* In *Proc. ICASSP, 2*, 673-676). Philadelphia, PA: IEEE.

Chan, M. T., Zhang, Y., & Huang, T. S. (1998). Real-time lip tracking and bimodal continuous speech recognition. In *Proc. IEEE Signal Processing Society Workshop on Multimedia Signal Processing*, pp. 65–70, Los Angeles, Calif, USA, December.

Chan, M. T. (2001). Hmm-based audio-visual speech recognition integrating geometric and appearance-based visual features. In *Workshop on Multimedia Signal Processing*.

Chen, S. C., Shao, C. L., Liang, C. K., Lin, S. W., Huang, T. H., Hsieh, M. C., Yang, C. H., Luo, C. H. & Wuo, C. M.. (2004). A Text Input System Developed by using Lips Image Recognition based LabVIEW for the seriously disabled. *International Conference of the IEEE Engineering in Medicine and Biology Society* (IEMBS'2004), *2*, 4940-4943.

Chen, Q. C., Deng, G. H., Wang, X. L., & Huang, H. J. (2006) An Inner Contour Based Lip Moving Feature Extraction Method for Chinese Speech. *International conference on Machine Learning and Cybernetics*, pp. 3859-3864.

Chibelushi, C. (1997). Automatic Audio-Visual Person Recognition. *PhD thesis*, University of Wales, Swansea.

Chiou, G., & Hwang, J. (1997). Lipreading from color video. In *Trans. on Image Processing, 6*(8),1192-1195, August.

Cohen, L. (1991). On Active Contour Models and Balloons - *CVGIP: Image Understanding, 53*(2), 211-218.

Coianiz, T., Torresani, L., & Caprile, B. (1996). 2D deformable models for visual speech analysis. In D. G. Stork & M. E. Hennecke (Eds.), *Speechreading by Humans and Machines: Models, Systems, and Applications* pp.391-398, New York: Springer-Verlag.

Cootes, T., Taylor, C., Cooper, D., & Graham, J. (1992). Training Models of Shape from Sets of Examples - *In D. Hogg and R. Boyle, editors, 3rd British Machine Vision Conference*, pp. 9–18. Springer-Verlag, September.

Cootes, T. F., Taylor, C. J., & Cooper, D. H. (1995). Active Shape Models - Their Training and Application. *Computer Vision and Image Understanding, 61*(1), 38-59.

Cootes, T. F., Edwards, G. J., & Taylor, C. J. (1998). *Active Appearance Model.* In Proc. *European Conference on Computer Vision, 2,* 484-498.

Cootes T. F., Walker K. N., & Taylor C. J. (2000). View-Based Active Appearance Models. In Proc. 4th International Conference on Automatic Face and Gesture Recognition, pp.227–232, Grenoble, France.

Cootes, T. F., & Taylor, C. J. (2001). Constrained Active Appearance Models. In Proc. *8th International Conference on Computer Vision, 1,* 748–754. Vancouver, Canada.

Cootes, T. (2004). Statistical Models of Appearance for Computer Vision - *Technical report,* free to download on http://www.isbe.man.ac.uk/bim/refs.html.

Cuavebase The CUAVE database homepage http://www.ece.clemson.edu/speech/cuave.htm

Daubias, P., & Deléglise, P. (2002). *Statistical* Lip-Appearance Models Trained Automatically Using Audio Information. *EURASIP Journal on Applied Signal Processing, 11,* 1202–1212.

Daubias, P., & Deleglise, P. (2003). The LIUM-AVS database: A Corpus to test Lip Segmentation and Speechreading systems in Natural Conditions. *Proc. 8th Eur. Conf. on Speech Communication and Technology,* Geneva, Switzerland, September, pp. 1569-1572.

Delmas, P., Coulon, P. Y., & Fristot, V. (1999). Automatic Snakes for Robust Lip Boundaries Extraction - *International Conference on Acoustics, Speech and Signal Processing, 6,* 3069-3072.

Delmas, P., Eveno, N., & Liévin, M. (2002). Towards Robust Lip Tracking. *International Conference on Pattern Recognition (*ICPR'02), *2,* 528-531.

Deng, G., & Cahill, L. W. (1993). *The Logarithmic Image Processing Model and Its Applications.* In Proc. Of The Twenty-Seventh Asilomar Conference, 2, 1047-1051.

Eveno, N., Caplier, A., & Coulon, P. Y. (2003). Jumping Snakes and Parametric Model for Lip Segmentation. *International Conference on Image Processing (ICIP'03),* Barcelona, Spain, September.

Eveno, N., Caplier, A., & Coulon, P. Y. (2004). Automatic and Accurate Lip Tracking *IEEE Transactions on Circuits and Systems for Video technology, 14*(5), May, 706-715.

Feretbase The Feret Database homepage http://www.itl.nist.gov/iad/humanid/feret/

Ford, A., & Roberts A. (1998). *Color Space Conversion* (Tech. Rep.). http://inforamep.net/poyton/PDFs/coloureq.pdf.

Gacon, P., Coulon, P. Y., & Bailly, G. (2005). Non-Linear Active Model for Mouth Inner and Outer Contours Detection. Proc. of *European Signal Processing Conference (EUSIPCO'05),* Antalya, Turkey.

Gong, Y., & Sakauchi, M. (1995). Detection of Regions Matching Specified Chromatic Features. *Computer Vision and Image Understanding, 61,* 263-269.

Gordan, M., Kotropoulos, C., & Pitas, I. (2001). Pseudo-automatic Lip Contour Detection Based on Edge Direction Patterns. *International Symposium on Image and Signal Processing and Analysis, (ISPA 2001)*, pp. 138-143, 2001.

Hammal, Z., Eveno, N., Caplier, A., & Coulon, P.Y. (2006). Parametric Model for Facial Features Segmentation. *Signal Processing, 86*, 399-413.

Hammal, Z., Couvreur, L., Caplier, A. & Rombaut, M. (2007). Facial Expression Classification: An Approach based on the Fusion of Facial Deformation unsing the Transferable Belief Model. *Int. Jour. of Approximate Reasonning*, doi: 10.1016/j.ijar.2007.02.003

Hennecke, M., Prasad, K., & Stork, D. (1994). Using deformable template to infer visual speech dynamics. *In Proc. 28ᵗʰ Annual Asilomar Conference on Signal, Systems and Computers*, pp.578-582.

Hsu, R. L., Abdel-Mottaleb, M., & Jain, A. K. (2002). Face Detection in Color Images. *IEEE Trans. Pattern Analysis and Machine Intelligence*, 24(5), 696-706.

Jang, K. S., Han, S., Lee, I., & Woo, Y. W. (2006). Lip Localization Based on Active Shape Model and Gaussian Mixture Model. In *Advances in Image and Video Technology, 4319*, 1049-1058. Springer Berlin / Heidelberg.

Kanade, T., Cohn, J. F., & Tian, Y. (2000). Comprehensive database for facial expression analysis. *Proceedings of the Fourth IEEE International Conference on Automatic Face and Gesture Recognition (FG'00)*, Grenoble, France, 46-53.

Kass, M., Witkin, A., & Terzopoulos D. (1987). Snakes: Active Contour Models. *International Journal of Computer Vision, 1*(4), 321-331.

Kaucic, R., & Blake, A. (1998). Accurate, Real-Time, Unadorned Lip Tracking. *International Conference on Computer Vision*, pp. 370-375.

Kuo, P., Hillman, P., & Hannah, J. M. (2005). Improved Lip Fitting and Tracking for Model-based Multimedia and Coding. *Visual Information Engineering*, pp. 251-258.

Leung, S.-H., Wang, S.-L., & Lau, W.-H. (2004). Lip Image Segmentation Using Fuzzy Clustering Incorporating an Elliptic Shape Function. *IEEE Transactions on Image Processing, 13*(1), 51-62.

Li, Z., & Ai, H. (2006). Texture-Constrained Shape Prediction for Mouth Contour Extraction and its State Estimation. In Proc. ICPR06 *II*, 88-91, Hong Kong.

Liévin, M., & Luthon, F. (2004). Nonlinear Color Space and Spatiotemporal MRF for Hierarchical Segmentation of Face Features in Video. *IEEE Transactions on Image Processing, 13*(1), 63-71.

Liew, A., Leung, S. H., & Lau, W. H. (2000). Lip Contour Extraction using a Deformable Model. *International Conference on Image Processing, 2*, 255-258.

Liew, A., Leung, S. H., & Lau, W. H. (2003). Segmentation of Color Lip Images by Spatial Fuzzy Clustering. *IEEE Transactions on Fuzzy Systems, 11*(1), 542-549.

Lucey, S., Sridharan, S., & Chandran, V. (2000). Initialised Eigenlip Estimator for Fast Lip Tracking Using Linear Regression. *International Conference on Pattern Recognition, 3*, 178-181.

Luettin, J. (1997). Visual speech and speaker recognition, *Ph.D. thesis*, University of Sheffield, Sheffield, UK.

M2VTSbase The M2VTS database homepage http://www.tele.ucl.ac.be/M2VTS/

Malciu, M., & Prêteux, F. (2000). Tracking Facial Features in Video Sequences Using a Deformable Model-based approach. *Proc. SPIE Mathematical Modeling, Estimation, and Imaging, 4121*, 51-62.

Martinez, A. M., & Benavente, R. (1998). *The AR Face Database - CVC Technical Report #24.*

Matthews, I., Cootes, T. F., Cox, S., Harvey, R., & Bangham, J. A. (1998). Lipreading using shape, shading and scale. In Proc. *Auditory-Visual Speech Processing (AVSP)*, pp. 73-78, Australia.

Matthews, I., & Baker, S. (2003). Active Appearance Models Revisited. *Technical Report CMU-RITR -03-02*, Carnegie Mellon University Robotics Institute, April 2003. http://citeseer.ist.psu.edu/matthews-04active.html

Messer, K., Matas, J., Kittler, J., & Jonsson, K. (1999). XM2VTSDB: The Extended M2VTS Database. *In Audio- and Video-based Biometric Person Authentication, AVBPA1999.*

Mirhosseini, A. R., Chen, C., Lam, K. M., & Yan, H. (1997). A Hierarchical and Adaptive Deformable Model for Mouth Boundary Detection. *International Conference on Image Processing, 2*, 756-759.

Nefian, A. V., Liang, L., Pi, X., Xiaoxiang, L., Mao, C., & Murphy, K. (2002). A Coupled HMM for Audio-Visual Speech Recognition. In Proc *2002 IEEE Int. Conf. on Acoustics, Speech and Signal Processing, 2*, 2013-2016.

Pantic, M., Tomc, M., & Rothkrantz, L. J. M. (2001). A hybrid Approach to Mouth Features Detection. *Proceedings of IEEE Int'l Conf. Systems, Man and Cybernetics (SMC'01)* - pp. 1188-1193, Tucson, USA, October.

Pardàs, M., & Sayrol, E. (2001). Motion Estimation Based Tracking of Active Contours. *Pattern Recognition Letters, 22*, 1447- 1456.

Patterson, E. K., Gurbuz, S., Tufekci, Z., & Gowdy, J. H. (2002). Moving-Talker, Speaker-Independent Feature Study and Baseline Results Using the CUAVE Multimodal Speech Corpus. *EURASIP Journal on Applied Signal Processing, Issue 11*, 1189-1201

Phillips, P .J., Moon, H., Rauss, P. J., & Rizvi, S. (2000). The FERET evaluation methodology for face recognition algorithms. *IEEE Transactions on Pattern Analysis and Machine Intelligence, 22*(10), October.

Pigeon, S., & Vandendorpe, L. (1997). The M2VTS multimodal face database. *In Lecture Notes in Computer Science: Audio- and Video- based Biometric PersonAuthentication* (J. Bigun, C. Chollet and G. Borgefors, Eds.), *1206*, 403-409.

Poggio, T., & Hulbert, A. (1998). Synthesizing a Color Algorithm from Examples. *Science, 239*, 482-485.

Potamianos, G., Neti, C., Luettin, J., & Matthews, I. (2004). Audio-Visual Automatic Speech Recognition : an Overview. *Issues in Visual and Audio-Visual Speech Processing*, G. Bailly, E. Vatikiotis-Bateson, and P. Perrier, MIT Press.

Radeva, P., & Marti, E. (1995). Facial Features Segmentation by Model-Based Snakes. *International Conference on Computer Vision.*

Rao, R., & Mersereau, R. (1995). On Merging Hidden Markov Models with Deformable Templates. *International Conference on Image Processing* (ICIP'1995), *3*, 556-559.

Rosenblum, D., & Saldana, M. (1996). An audiovisual test of kinematic primitives for visual speech perception. *Journal of Experimental Psychology: Human Perception and Performance, 22*(2), 318–331.

Sadeghi, M., Kittler, J., & Messer, K. (2002). Modelling and Segmentation of Lip Area in Face Images. *Vision, Image and Signal Processing, IEE Proceedings, 149*, 179-184.

Seguier, R., & Cladel, N. (2003). Genetic Snakes: Application on Lipreading. *International Conference on Artificial Neural Networks and Genetic Algorithms, (ICANNGA).*

Seo, K. H., & Lee, J. J. (2003). Object tracking using adaptive color snake model. *International Conference on Advanced Intelligent Mechatronics* (AIM'2003), *2*, 1406-1410.

Seyedarabi, H., Lee, W., & Aghagolzadeh, A. (2006). Automatic Lip Tracking and Action Units Classification using Two-step Active Contours and Probabilistic Neural Networks. *Canadian Conference on Electrical and Computer Engineering, (CCECE'2006)*, pp. 2021-2024.

Shinchi, T., Maeda, Y., Sugahara, K., & Konishi, R. (1998). Vowel recognition according to lip shapes by using neural network. In *The IEEE Int.l Joint Conf. on Neural Networks Proceedings and IEEE World Congress on Computational Intelligence, 3,*.1772-1777.

Stillittano, S., & Caplier, A. (2008). Inner Lip Contour Segmentation by Combining Active Contours and Parametric Models. *International Conference on Computer Vision Theory and Applications* (VISAPP 2008), Madeira, Spain, January.

Sugahara, K., Kishino, M., & Konishi, R. (2000). Personal computer based real time lip reading system. In *Signal Processing Proceedings, WCCC-ICSP2000, 2*, 1341-1346

Summerfield, A. Q., MacLeod, A., McGrath, M., & Brooke, M. (1989). Lips, teeth and the benefits of lipreading. In *Handbook of Research on Face Processing*, A. W. Young and H. D. Ellis, Eds., pp. 223–233, Elsevier Science Publishers, Amsterdam, North Holland.

Summerfield, A. Q. (1992). Lipreading and audio-visual speech perception. *Philosophical Transactions of the Royal Society of London, Series B, 335*(1273), 71–78.

Tian, Y., Kanade, T., & Cohn, J. (2000). Robust Lip Tracking by Combining Shape, Color and Motion. *4th Asian Conference on Computer Vision,* January.

Tomasi, C., & Kanade, T. (1991). Detection and Tracking of Point Features. *Technical Report* CMU-CS-91-132, Carnegie Mellon University.

Vogt, M. (1996). Fast Matching of a Dynamic Lip Model to Color Video Sequences Under Regular Illumination Conditions. *In D.G. Stork and M.E. Hennecke, editors, Speechreading by Humans and Machines, 150,* 399–407.

Wakasugi, T., Nishiura, M., & Fukui, K. (2004). Robust Lip Contour Extraction using Separability of Multi-Dimensional Distributions. *Proceedings of the Sixth IEEE International Conference on Automatic Face and Gesture Recognition* (FGR'2004), 415-420, May.

Wang, S. L., Lau, W. H., Liew, A. C., & Leung, S. H. (2007). Robust lip region segmentation for lip images with complex background - *PR(40)*, No. 12, December, 3481-3491.

Wark, T., Sridharan, S., & Chandran, V. (1998). An Approach to statistical lip modeling for speaker identification via chromatic feature extraction. In *Proc. 14th ICPR, I,* 123-125, Brisbane, Australia.

Werda, S., Mahdi, W., & Hamadou, A. B. (2007). Automatic Hybrid Approach for Lip POI Localization: Application for Lip-reading System. *ICTA'07*, April.

Wyszecki, G., & Stiles, W. S. (1982). *Color Science: Concepts and Methods, Quantitative Data and Formulae.* John Wiley & Sons, Inc., New York, New York, 2nd edition.

Wojdel, J. C., & Rothkrantz, L. J. M. (2001). Using aerial and geometric features in automatic lip-reading. In Proc. *7th Eurospeech, 4,* 2463-2466, Aalborg, Denmark.

Wu, Z., Petar, A. Z., & Katsaggelos, A. K. (2002). Lip Tracking for MPEG-4 Facial Animation. *Int. Conf. on Multimodal Interfaces (ICMI'02)*, Pittsburgh, PA, October.

Wu, Z., & Aleksic, P. S. (2004). Inner lip feature extraction for MPEG-4 facial animation. *International Conference on Acoustics, Speech and Signal Processing* (ICASSP'2004), *3,* 633-636.

XM2VTS base The XM2VTS face database homepage, http://www.ee.surrey.ac.uk/Research/VSSP/xm2vtsdb/

Xin, S., & Ai, H. (2005). Face Alignment under Various Poses and Expressions. *Affective computing and intelligent interaction, ACII 2005 First International conference, 3784,* 40-47. Beijing , China.

Xu, C., & Prince, J. L. (1998). Snakes, Shapes, and Gradient Vector Flow. *IEEE Transactions on Image Processing, 7,* 359-369.

Yang, J., & Waibel, A. (1996). A Real-Time Face Tracker. In *Proc. Of 3rd IEEE Workshop on Applications of Computer Vision*, pp.142–147, Sarasota, USA.

Yin, L., & Basu, A. (2002). Color-Based Mouth Shape Tracking for Synthesizing Realistic Facial Expressions. *International Conference on Image Processing* (ICIP'2002), pp. 161-164, September.

Yokogawa, Y., Funabiki, N., Higashino, T., Oda, M. & Mori, Y. (2007). A Proposal of Improved Lip Contour Extraction Method using Deformable Template Matching and its Application to Dental Treatment . *Systems and Computers in Japan –38,* 80-89, May.

Yuille, A., Hallinan, P., & Cohen, D. (1992). Features extraction from faces using deformable templates. *Int. Journal of Computer Vision, 8*(2), 99-111.

Zhang, L. (1997). Estimation of the Mouth Features using Deformable Template. *International Conference on Image Procesing* (ICIP'1997), *3*, 328-331, October.

Zhang, X., & Mersereau, R. M. (2000). *Lip Feature Extraction Towards an Automatic Speechreading System.* In Proc. *International Conference on Image Processing.* Vancouver, British Columbia, Canada: IEEE.

Zhang, X., Broun, C., Mersereau, R. & Clements, M. (2002). Automatic Speechreading with Applications to Human-Computer Interfaces. *Eurasip Journal on Applied Signal Processing, 11*, 1228-1247.

Zhang, B., Gao, W., Shan, S., & Wang, W. (2003). *Constraint Shape Model Using Edge Constraint and Gabor Wavelet Based Search.* Audio-and Video-Based Biometrie Person Authentication, 4th International Conference, (AVBPA 2003), Guildford, United Kingdom.

Zhiming, W., Lianhong, C., & Haizhou, A. (2002). A Dynamic Viseme Model for Personalizing a Talking Head. *International Conference on Signal Processing, 2*, 1015-1018.

Chapter IV
Visual Speech and Gesture Coding Using the MPEG–4 Face and Body Animation Standard

Eric Petajan
VectorMAX Corporation, USA

ABSTRACT

Automatic Speech Recognition (ASR) is the most natural input modality from humans to machines. When the hands are busy or a full keyboard is not available, speech input is especially in demand. Since the most compelling application scenarios for ASR include noisy environments (mobile phones, public kiosks, cars), visual speech processing must be incorporated to provide robust performance. This chapter motivates and describes the MPEG-4 Face and Body Animation (FBA) standard for representing visual speech data as part of a whole virtual human specification. The super low bit-rate FBA codec included with the standard enables thin clients to access processing and communication services over any network including enhanced visual communication, animated entertainment, man-machine dialog, and audio/visual speech recognition.

INTRODUCTION

In recent years the number of people accessing the internet or using digital devices has exploded. In parallel the mobile revolution is allowing consumers to access the internet on relatively powerful handheld devices. While the transmission and display of information is efficiently handled by maturing fixed and wireless data networks and terminal devices, the input of information from the user to the target system is often impeded by the lack of a keyboard, low typing skills, or busy hands and eyes. The last barrier to efficient man-machine communication is the lack of accurate speech recognition in real-world environments. Given the importance of mobile communication and computing, and the ubiquitous internetworking of all terminal devices, the optimal system architecture calls for compute-intensive processes to be performed across the network. Support for thin mobile clients with limited memory, clock speed, battery life, and connection speeds requires that visual speech and gesture information captured from the user be transformed into a representation that is both compact and computable on the terminal device.

The flow of audio/video data across a network is subject to a variety of bottlenecks that require lossy compression; introducing artifacts and distortion that degrade the accuracy of scene analysis. Video with sufficient quality for facial capture must be either stored locally or analyzed in real time. Real-time video processing should be implemented close to the camera to avoid transmission costs and delays, and to more easily protect the user's visual privacy. The recognition of the human face and body in a video stream results in a set of descriptors that ideally occur at the video frame rate. The human behavior descriptors should contain all information needed for the Human-Computer Interaction (HCI) system to understand the user's presence, pose, facial expression, gestures, and visual speech. This data is highly compressible and can be used in a communication system when standardized. The MPEG-4 Face and Body Animation (FBA) standard[1,2] provides a complete set of Face and Body Animation Parameters (FAPs and BAPs) and a codec for super low bit-rate communication. This chapter describes the key features of the MPEG-4 FBA specification, its application to visual speech and gesture recognition, and architectural implications.

The control of a computer by a human incorporating the visual mode is best implemented by the processing of video into features and descriptors that are accurate and compact. These descriptors should only be as abstract as required by network, storage capacity, and processing limitations. The MPEG-4 FBA standard provides a level of description of human facial movements and skeleton joint angles that is both highly detailed and compressible to 2 kilobits per second for the face and 5-10 kilobits per second for the body. The MPEG-4 FBA stream can be transmitted over any network and can be used for visual speech recognition, identity verification, emotion recognition, gesture recognition, and visual communication with the option of an alternate appearance. The conversion of video into an MPEG-4 FBA stream is a computationally intensive process which may require dedicated hardware and HD video to fully accomplish. The performance of recognition tasks on the FBA stream can be performed anywhere on the network without risking the violation of the users visual privacy when video is transmitted. When coupled with voice recognition, FBA recognition should provide the robustness needed for effective HCI. As shown in Figure 1, the very low bit-rate FBA stream enables the separation of the HCI from higher level recognition systems, applications and databases that tend to consume more processing and storage than is available in a personal device. This client-server architecture supports all application domains including human-human communication, human-machine interaction, and local HCI (non-networked). While the Humanoid Player Client exists today on mobile phones, a mobile Face and Gesture Capture Client is still a few years away.

MPEG-4 FBA streaming is commercially deployed today for delivery of animation to mobile phones in Europe within the AniTones™ application. Content is efficiently created using facial capture from ordinary video and combined with animated backgrounds and bodies. FAP and BAP data (including both body and background object animation) are compressed into one small package for delivery over any mobile IP network. The AniTones™ player maintains a frame-rate of fifteen frames per second with synchronized audio on a 109 MHz processor.

Figure 1. FBA enabled client-server architecture

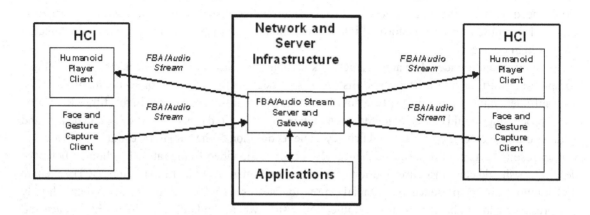

FACE ANIMATION

MPEG-4 contains a comprehensive set of tools for representing and compressing content objects and the animation of those objects. Virtual humans (faces and bodies) are treated as a special type of object in MPEG-4 with anatomically specific locations and associated animation parameters. While virtual humans can be treated as generic graphical objects, there are particular advantages to representing them with the Face and Body Animation (FBA) Coding specification.

As shown in Figure 2, Face Definition Parameter (FDP) feature points have been defined and located on the face. Some of these points only serve to help define the shape of the face. Those remaining are animated or displaced by FAPs, which are listed in Table 1. FAPs 1 and 2 are special sets of high level descriptors for visemes and expressions respectively, as described in Tables 2 and 3. Viseme and expression labels are a form of metadata that is subject to interpretation. The remaining FAPs (except for the rotation FAPs) are normalized in order to describe the motion of the face independently from the size, proportions, or geometry of a particular face. Normalization is achieved by measuring local facial dimensions on the source and destination faces and expressing FAPs in units that are relative to the local dimensions. Each FAP specifies either a normalized linear displacement in one axis aligned dimension (relative to the head) or one rotation. A given displacement FAP value is expressed as a fraction of the neutral face mouth width, mouth-nose distance, eye separation, iris diameter, or eye-nose distance. Another important feature of the FBA standard is the FAP interpolation policy that, for example, allows the transmission of FAPs for only one side of the face followed by copying to the other side before animation; reducing both data-rate and computation in the client.

Most FAPs are displacements of the feature points from their neutral face position. Neutral position is defined as mouth closed, eyelids tangent to the iris, gaze and head orientation straight ahead, teeth touching, and tongue touching the front teeth contact point. The head orientation FAPs are applied after all other FAPs have been applied within the face. In other words, all but the head orientation FAPs refer to the local face coordinate system. If the head is animated with a body, the head orientation FAPs express rotations relative to the top-most vertebrae (the connection point between the head and body is FDP 7.1 in Figure 2).

FAPs and BAPs are specified at a given frame rate that is typically equal to that of the captured facial video. FAPs that are not transmitted for a given frame may be interpolated by the decoder. For example, if the inner lip but not the outer lip FAPs are transmitted, the decoder is free to synthesize the motion of the outer lips. Since the outer lip motion closely follows the motion of the inner lips, a simple copying operation is sufficient for most applications. While the behavior of face models can vary in response to FAPs, lip and eyelid closure are guaranteed. Lip closure is mandated in the neutral face and is defined during animation when the corresponding upper and lower lip FAPs sum to zero. Eyelids are open and tangent to the iris in the neutral face. Since the eyelid FAPS are expressed in units of iris diameter, the eyelids will be closed during animation when the upper and lower eyelid FAPS sum to the iris diameter. Thus, lip and eyelid closure are known regardless of the vertical contact position.

FAPs are normalized to be proportional to one of the key facial dimensions listed in Table 4. The third column of Table 1 indicates the Facial Animation Parameter Units (FAPU) used for each FAP. The normalization of the FAPs gives the face model designer freedom to create characters with any facial proportions regardless of the source of the FAPs. The mouth and eyelids will close as expected, mouth opening will be proportional to the face, etc. FAP normalization also allows face models to be designed without the need to transmit the face model. MPEG-4 compliant face models can be embedded into decoders, stored on portable media (e.g. CDROM), downloaded as an executable from a website, or built into a web browser. From the user's perspective, MPEG-4 face models can be freely exchanged at any time, and FAP streams which are broadcast can be decoded as soon as the next I-frame is received within the compressed FBA stream. More advanced face models will allow the user to radically deform the model during the animation while maintaining proper facial movements. FAP normalization also enables visual speech recognition independent of the speaker and anywhere on the network.

BODY ANIMATION

The joints of the humanoid skeleton are named in the MPEG-4 FBA standard and these names are common with the H-Anim[4] standard. Body Animation Parameters (BAPs) are Euler angles for each joint. The first 10 BAPs out of 186 are shown in Table 5. The connection between the skull and the uppermost vertebrae is FDP 7.1; the center of rotation for the head rotation FAPS. Spinal BAPs are specified with a level of detail in order to support low power FBA players. BAPs can be captured with varying levels of accuracy and numbers of joints using body motion capture equipment, while purely passive or video-based body motion capture results are limited. BAPs can be synthesized or measured from any animated 3D character. Ultimately, virtual humans[5] will be fully synthesized and conversant with real humans with the help of this common language for representing human face and body behavior.

Figure 2. FDP Feature Points. Note that filled points are subject to displacement and/or rotation by FAPs

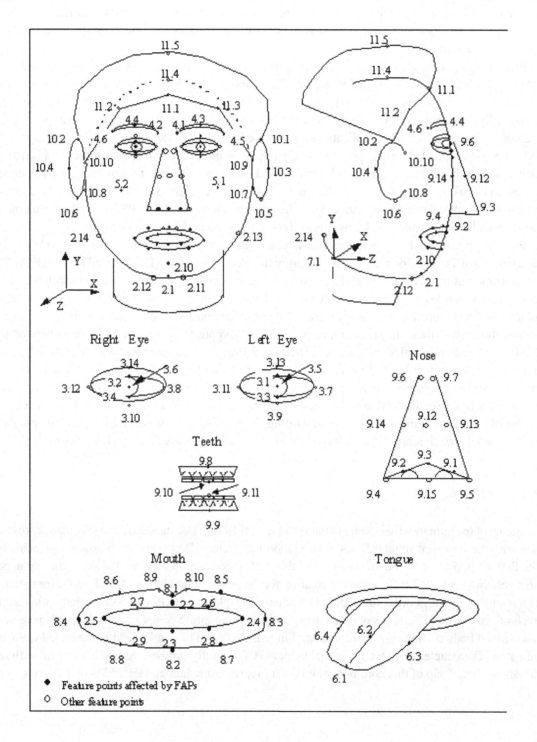

Table 1. Complete FAP list

#	FAP name	FAP description	units	Uni-orBidir	Positive motion	Group	F D P subgrp num
1	viseme	Set of values determining the mixture of two visemes for this frame (e.g. pbm, fv, th)	na	na	na	1	na
2	expression	A set of values determining the mixture of two facial expression	na	na	na	1	na
3	open_jaw	Vertical jaw displacement (does not affect mouth opening)	MNS	U	down	2	1
4	lower_t_midlip	Vertical top middle inner lip displacement	MNS	B	down	2	2
5	raise_b_midlip	Vertical bottom middle inner lip displacement	MNS	B	up	2	3
6	stretch_l_cornerlip	Horizontal displacement of left inner lip corner	MW	B	left	2	4
7	stretch_r_cornerlip	Horizontal displacement of right inner lip corner	MW	B	right	2	5
8	lower_t_lip_lm	Vertical displacement of midpoint between left corner and middle of top inner lip	MNS	B	down	2	6
9	lower_t_lip_rm	Vertical displacement of midpoint between right corner and middle of top inner lip	MNS	B	down	2	7
10	raise_b_lip_lm	Vertical displacement of midpoint between left corner and middle of bottom inner lip	MNS	B	up	2	8
11	raise_b_lip_rm	Vertical displacement of midpoint between right corner and middle of bottom inner lip	MNS	B	up	2	9
12	raise_l_cornerlip	Vertical displacement of left inner lip corner	MNS	B	up	2	4
13	raise_r_cornerlip	Vertical displacement of right inner lip corner	MNS	B	up	2	5
14	thrust_jaw	Depth displacement of jaw	MNS	U	forward	2	1
15	shift_jaw	Side to side displacement of jaw	MW	B	right	2	1
16	push_b_lip	Depth displacement of bottom middle lip	MNS	B	forward	2	3
17	push_t_lip	Depth displacement of top middle lip	MNS	B	forward	2	2
18	depress_chin	Upward and compressing movement of the chin (like in sadness)	MNS	B	up	2	10
19	close_t_l_eyelid	Vertical displacement of top left eyelid	IRISD	B	down	3	1
20	close_t_r_eyelid	Vertical displacement of top right eyelid	IRISD	B	down	3	2

Table 1. Complete FAP list (continued)

#	FAP name	FAP description	units	Uni- orBidir	Positive motion	Group	F D P s u b g r p num
21	close_b_l_eyelid	Vertical displacement of bottom left eyelid	IRISD	B	up	3	3
22	close_b_r_eyelid	Vertical displacement of bottom right eyelid	IRISD	B	up	3	4
23	yaw_l_eyeball	Horizontal orientation of left eyeball	AU	B	left	3	na
24	yaw_r_eyeball	Horizontal orientation of right eyeball	AU	B	left	3	na
25	pitch_l_eyeball	Vertical orientation of left eyeball	AU	B	down	3	na
26	pitch_r_eyeball	Vertical orientation of right eyeball	AU	B	down	3	na
27	thrust_l_eyeball	Depth displacement of left eyeball	ES	B	forward	3	na
28	thrust_r_eyeball	Depth displacement of right eyeball	ES	B	forward	3	na
29	dilate_l_pupil	Dilation of left pupil	IRISD	B	growing	3	5
30	dilate_r_pupil	Dilation of right pupil	IRISD	B	growing	3	6
31	raise_l_i_eyebrow	Vertical displacement of left inner eyebrow	ENS	B	up	4	1
32	raise_r_i_eyebrow	Vertical displacement of right inner eyebrow	ENS	B	up	4	2
33	raise_l_m_eyebrow	Vertical displacement of left middle eyebrow	ENS	B	up	4	3
34	raise_r_m_eyebrow	Vertical displacement of right middle eyebrow	ENS	B	up	4	4
35	raise_l_o_eyebrow	Vertical displacement of left outer eyebrow	ENS	B	up	4	5
36	raise_r_o_eyebrow	Vertical displacement of right outer eyebrow	ENS	B	up	4	6
37	squeeze_l_eyebrow	Horizontal displacement of left eyebrow	ES	B	right	4	1
38	squeeze_r_eyebrow	Horizontal displacement of right eyebrow	ES	B	left	4	2
39	puff_l_cheek	Horizontal displacement of left cheeck	ES	B	left	5	1
40	puff_r_cheek	Horizontal displacement of right cheeck	ES	B	right	5	2
41	lift_l_cheek	Vertical displacement of left cheek	ENS	U	up	5	3
42	lift_r_cheek	Vertical displacement of right cheek	ENS	U	up	5	4
43	shift_tongue_tip	Horizontal displacement of tongue tip	MW	B	right	6	1

Table 1. Complete FAP list (continued)

#	FAP name	FAP description	units	Uni- orBidir	Positive motion	Group	F D P s u b g r p num
44	raise_tongue_tip	Vertical displacement of tongue tip	MNS	B	up	6	1
45	thrust_tongue_tip	Depth displacement of tongue tip	MW	B	forward	6	1
46	raise_tongue	Vertical displacement of tongue	MNS	B	up	6	2
47	tongue_roll	Rolling of the tongue into U shape	AU	U	concave upward	6	3, 4
48	head_pitch	Head pitch angle from top of spine	AU	B	down	7	na
49	head_yaw	Head yaw angle from top of spine	AU	B	left	7	na
50	head_roll	Head roll angle from top of spine	AU	B	right	7	na
51	lower_t_midlip_o	Vertical top middle outer lip displacement	MNS	B	down	8	1
52	raise_b_midlip_o	Vertical bottom middle outer lip displacement	MNS	B	up	8	2
53	stretch_l_cornerlip_o	Horizontal displacement of left outer lip corner	MW	B	left	8	3
54	stretch_r_cornerlip_o	Horizontal displacement of right outer lip corner	MW	B	right	8	4
55	lower_t_lip_lm_o	Vertical displacement of midpoint between left corner and middle of top outer lip	MNS	B	down	8	5
56	lower_t_lip_rm_o	Vertical displacement of midpoint between right corner and middle of top outer lip	MNS	B	down	8	6
57	raise_b_lip_lm_o	Vertical displacement of midpoint between left corner and middle of bottom outer lip	MNS	B	up	8	7
58	raise_b_lip_rm_o	Vertical displacement of midpoint between right corner and middle of bottom outer lip	MNS	B	up	8	8
59	raise_l_cornerlip_o	Vertical displacement of left outer lip corner	MNS	B	up	8	3
60	raise_r_cornerlip_o	Vertical displacement of right outer lip corner	MNS	B	up	8	4
61	stretch_l_nose	Horizontal displacement of left side of nose	ENS	B	left	9	1
62	stretch_r_nose	Horizontal displacement of right side of nose	ENS	B	right	9	2
63	raise_nose	Vertical displacement of nose tip	ENS	B	up	9	3
64	bend_nose	Horizontal displacement of nose tip	ENS	B	right	9	3

Table 1. Complete FAP list (continued)

#	FAP name	FAP description	units	Uni-orBidir	Positive motion	Group	F D P subgrp num
65	raise_l_ear	Vertical displacement of left ear	ENS	B	up	10	1
66	raise_r_ear	Vertical displacement of right ear	ENS	B	up	10	2
67	pull_l_ear	Horizontal displacement of left ear	ENS	B	left	10	3
68	pull_r_ear	Horizontal displacement of right ear	ENS	B	right	10	4

Table 2. Values for viseme_select

visemeselect	phonemes	example
0	none	na
1	p, b, m	put, bed, mill
2	f, v	far, voice
3	T,D	think, that
4	t, d	tip, doll
5	k, g	call, gas
6	tS, dZ, S	chair, join, she
7	s, z	sir, zeal
8	n, l	lot, not
9	r	red
10	A:	car
11	e	bed
12	I	tip
13	Q	top
14	U	book

Table 3. Values for expression_select

expression_ select	expression name	textual description
0	na	na
1	joy	The eyebrows are relaxed. The mouth is open and the mouth corners pulled back toward the ears.
2	sadness	The inner eyebrows are bent upward. The eyes are slightly closed. The mouth is relaxed.
3	anger	The inner eyebrows are pulled downward and together. The eyes are wide open. The lips are pressed against each other or opened to expose the teeth.
4	fear	The eyebrows are raised and pulled together. The inner eyebrows are bent upward. The eyes are tense and alert.
5	disgust	The eyebrows and eyelids are relaxed. The upper lip is raised and curled, often asymmetrically.
6	surprise	The eyebrows are raised. The upper eyelids are wide open, the lower relaxed. The jaw is opened.

Table 4. Facial animation parameter units

IRISD0	Iris diameter (equal to the distance between upper ad lower eyelid)	IRISD = IRISD0 / 1024
ES0	Eye separation	ES = ES0 / 1024
ENS0	Eye - nose separation	ENS = ENS0 / 1024
MNS0	Mouth - nose separation	MNS = MNS0 / 1024
MW0	Mouth width	MW0 / 1024
AU	Angle Unit	10^{-5} rad

VISUAL SPEECH PROCESSING

FAPs were designed to satisfy a wide range of applications including visual speech processing for Automatic Speech Recognition (ASR)[5-17] and Text-To-Speech (TTS). The explicit timing information

Table 5. The first 10 (of 186) body animation parameters

BAP ID	BAP NAME	DESCRIPTION
1	sacroiliac_tilt	Forward-backward motion of the pelvis in the sagittal plane
2	sacroiliac_torsion	Rotation of the pelvis along the body vertical axis
3	sacroiliac_roll	Side to side swinging of the pelvis in the coronal plane
4	l_hip_flexion	Forward-backward rotation in the sagittal plane
5	r_hip_flexion	Forward-backward rotation in the sagittal plane
6	l_hip_abduct	Sideward opening in the coronal plane
7	r_hip_abduct	Sideward opening in the coronal plane
8	l_hip_twisting	Rotation along the thigh axis
9	r_hip_twisting	Rotation along the thigh axis
10	l_knee_flexion	Flexion-extension of the leg in the sagittal plane

provided with FAP data and the normalization of FAPs enables direct correlation of visual speech with voice features during audio/visual speech analysis and synthesis[18]. Figure 3 shows four frames from a video sequence that was processed using a commercial facial capture application called alterEGO. The inner lip contour, nostril centers, eyelid, pupil, and eyebrows are marked with a graphic overlay. Nostril and mouth tracking windows are also shown. Note that the inner lip contour is well estimated even when the mouth is nearly closed (second frame), and when teeth and tongue are visible (third and fourth frames). Complete mouth closure is properly identified in the first frame as indicated by the lack of bottom lip contour (green overlay). FAP data is output from this application after adaptive spatio-temporal filtering.

Figure 4 shows a screen shot from a commercial application for editing FAP data call FAPeditor. The upper left window is used to to select particular FAPs for editing, the lower left window shows a real-time preview of the FAP data on a particular face model while selected FAPS are shown as a function of frame number with a time aligned audio waveform. FAPs 4 and 5 (top and bottom midlip vertical displacement) are shown with the voice waveform for the utterance "Welcome my darling to your wireless daily horoscope. I am Madam Zora. Please tell me your astrological sign. I will wait. Ah, you are a Scorpio am I right?" Note that the framerate is 30 Hz and about 450 frames are shown. The bottom lip movement is positive in the up direction (shown in orange) and the top lip movement is positive in the down direction. Bilabial closure is occurring when FAPs 4 and 5 sum to zero as seen during the Ms and Ps in the utterance. Inspection of the timeline shows the closures centered at frames 48, 129, 158, 168, 211, 246, 412, and 421. Note that Ms and Ns are clearly distinguished from each other as are Ps and Ts. While lip closure is the most important visual speech feature, the remaining inner lip FAPs comprise a complete but compact set of visual speech features. If bilateral symmetry and a front view is assumed, only seven FAPs (3,4,5,6,8,10,12) need to be processed for visual speech analysis.

Figure 3. Facial capture results showing inner lip contour

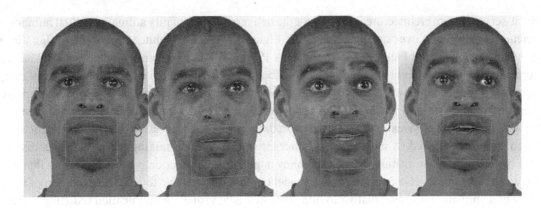

Figure 4. FAPs 4 and 5 with voice waveform

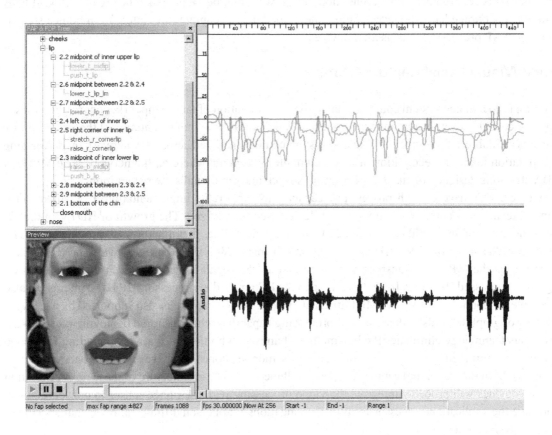

FBA CLIENT-SERVER ARCHITECTURE

A client-server system architecture is needed for the delivery of high quality animated virtual humans or characters to thin clients over any digital network. Figure 5 shows the architecture for the Audio/Visual Facial Capture Client and Figure 6 shows the FBA Player. While wired and wireless network speeds continue to rise, the availability of ubiquitous broadband internet connectivity is still many years away. Furthermore, the need for low latency communication for interactive applications (e.g. VoIP, multiplayer games, and dialog systems) places additional demands on networks that may be difficult or costly to achieve. The addition of visual communication to a dialog system places heavy demands on the network if video streaming is used. A more practical alternative is to present talking animated faces that are driven by low bit-rate animation streams. In many applications animation is more appealing than live video and acceptable levels of animated face model quality are available today. The evolution of facial capture and animation will eventually provide photo-realistic visual communication indistinguishable from natural video. The MPEG-4 FBA standard provides a comprehensive representation of human-oids and characters and very low bit-rate compression of Face and Body Animation Parameters. The MPEG-4 FBA standard also provides independence between a given face model and the source of the FAP data that drives it by normalizing the facial movements. This enables face models to be replaced by the user for entertainment purposes, or updated over the network during a session. Currently, 3D graphics APIs are provided with acceleration in a growing number of phones. The use of MPEG-4 FBA will also encourage hardware acceleration and embedding of computation intensive modules such as video-to-FAP processing in consumer devices.

Audio/Visual Facial Capture Client

User input to a dialog system could ultimately be a combination of tactile input (keyboard and mouse), voice, face and body gestures, and visual speech. When a real-time implementation of the facial capture client is available, a full duplex A/V dialog system could be realized across any network by performing computation intensive recognition tasks on compute servers anywhere on the network. The MPEG-4 FBA stream is designed to enable direct visual speech and emotional state recognition.

Current PCs have enough processing capacity to support its implementation. Consumer video camera technology continues to improve while being commoditized. The growth of HDTV in the US and other parts of the world has encouraged consumer electronics manufacturers to provide cheap HD video cameras using the 720P HD video scanning format (1280Hx720V progressive). The HDV video format uses the MPEG-2 Transport Stream format at 25 Megabits/second over Firewire to transmit lightly compressed HD video from the camera to the PC for further processing. IP HD cameras are also available for connection over 100 Mbit Ethernet or Wifi. Video capture is also supported by a growing number of graphics cards with associated processing capability while the rapid deployment of PCI-Express bus technology eliminates the bus-memory bandwidth bottleneck that was impeding HD video capture on commodity PC hardware. In a few years, mobile phones will have enough processing power to handle both the player and capture clients simultaneously. The architecture of these next-generation mobile devices will probably integrate the video processing with the image sensor to conserve power and save the application processor for utility applications like Personal Information Managers (PIM), Web browsing, and games.

A variety of Video-to-FAP systems have been developed during the last decade[19-21] but video cameras and PC processing power have only recently become economical enough to support full facial capture in real time. The FBA encoder does not require significant processor resources while voice encoding and processing is lightweight and accelerated on a typical PC sound card. The FBA stream contains timing information which supports synchronization with any voice bitstream. RTP can be easily be adapted to carry FBA streams with associated voice or audio streams over IP networks.

FBA Player Client

The FBA player is designed to be extremely light weight and to use as many standard/embedded APIs as possible. When implemented on a mobile phone, these include OpenGL-ES, JSR-184 and JSR-135 for mobile 3D and audio/video decoding. The talking animated character or virtual human can be composited onto a 2D scene or positioned in a 3D scene with other animated graphics, textual information or other animated characters. The low complexity of the FBA player makes it ideal for multiplayer networked games and 3D social environments. Current PCs are capable of supporting several concurrent FBA players driving a characters in a shared scene. A variety of MPEG-4 FBA compliant face models have been developed ranging from the simple 300 triangle mesh shown in Figure 4 to bones rigged mesh models with thousands of triangles[22-25].

Figure 5. Audio/visual facial capture client

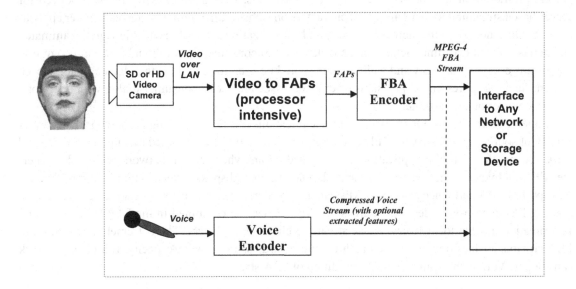

Figure 6. Simple FBA player client

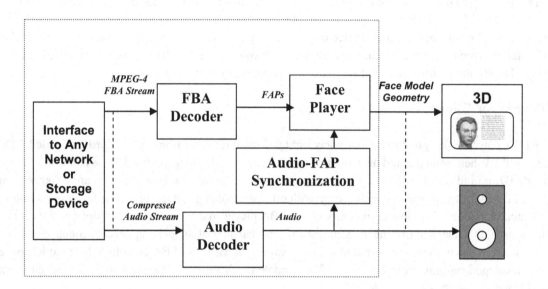

APPLICATION TO VISUAL SPEECH AND GESTURES PROCESSING

The compressed FBA stream driving a face typically occupies less than 2kilobits/sec of bitrate and can therefore be transmitted over any network that can support coded natural voice. As MPEG-4 FBA players proliferate in web browsers and wireless terminals, FBA streams will first be produced for server-based streaming to drive animated characters on websites. E-commerce and call center applications should benefit from the increased novelty and humanization associated with high quality animated characters. When real-time facial capture is deployed to consumers, speech and gesture recognition algorithms operating on FBA and audio streams could be used to search content databases for speech content, facial gestures and expressions of emotion associated with consumer dialog with operators, IVR systems or other consumers.

A reference architecture for network-based applications of FBA streaming is shown in Figure 7. A variety of sources and receivers of FBA streams are shown in this distributed architecture. Voice and FBA streams flow through application servers residing anywhere on the network while TTS generates FBA and voice from text and A/V speech recognition and speaker verification[26,27] are performed on captured FBA and voice streams. FAPs can also be derived from voice[28] to supplement or replace missing FAP data from video. All sources of FAP data can be combined in the FAP Unification and Interpolation module for delivery as one stream to client FBA players. The extremely low bit-rate of FBA streams enables this distributed architecture regardless of network capacity. If a given network can support VoIP then it can support the addition of FBA streams.

Figure 7. FBA networked application architecture

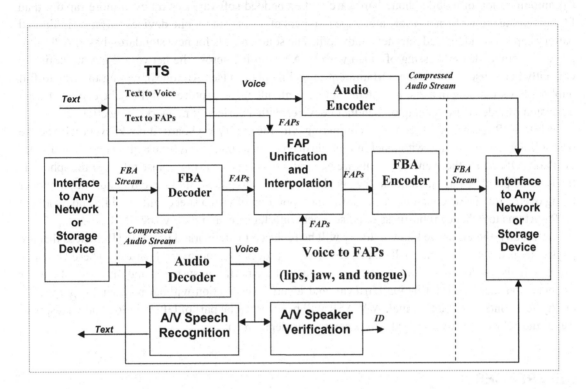

The perception of human speech incorporates both acoustic and visual communication modalities. Automatic speech recognition (ASR) systems have traditionally processed only the acoustic signal. While video cameras and video acquisition systems have become economical, the use of automatic lipreading to enhance speech recognition performance is an ongoing and fruitful research topic. During the last 20 years a variety of research systems have been developed which demonstrate that visual speech information enhances overall recognition accuracy, especially in the presence of acoustic noise. The client-server architecture proposed above should enable earlier deployment of audio-visual speech recognition on mobile devices by performing the recognition processing on the FBA stream on the server side of the network.

CONCLUSIONS

The greatest barrier to deployment of A/V speech recognition is the cost of high quality video cameras and processing power. Fortunately, the increasing commoditization of consumer HD video equipment is driving down camera costs and providing cost effective format and interconnect standards to PCs. Commoditization of mobile phone hardware and embedded software occurs even more rapidly than PCs given the higher turnover rate and huge numbers of users. But mobile devices suffer from limited battery capacity and limited internet bandwidth. The solution calls for new standards-based APIs supported by embedded processing of video with FBA streaming across the network. FBA streaming is currently being used to deliver entertainment to mobile phones (see Anitones); paving the way to full duplex FBA streaming in a dialog system[29]. Finally, mobile facial capture will likely be deployed as an extension of video conferencing on handheld devices with a variety of network connections.

While ASR has had a difficult time competing with the querty keyboard, it could eventually be the best solution for interacting with machines while driving, walking, or anytime a querty keyboard is not available. Of course, these environments are generally noisy and wearing a close talking microphone is likely to be problematic. In addition, the speaker may need to talk softly to avoid disturbing others or being overheard. These conditions call for the incorporation of visual speech into mobile and handheld ASR systems to enhance robustness to noise, vocal interference, and poor voice SNR.

Eventually, the PC as we know it today will be replaced by networked portable UI devices that are physically just displays with small embedded sensors, processors, radios, and battery. These UI appliances will also be found at retail businesses, in public transportation systems, and office buildings for financial transactions, information retrieval, and identity verification without requiring typing skills or physical contact with a terminal. A/V ASR will be an essential part of UI evolution and widespread use of the MPEG-4 FBA standard will accelerate its deployment.

REFERENCES

Adjoudani, A., & Benoit, C. (1995, September). Audio-visual speech recognition compared across two architectures. In *Proceedings of the Fourth European Conference on Speech Communication and Technology (Eurospeech '95) Madrid, Spain, September 18-21*. Bonn, Germany: Institute of Communication Sciences, University of Bonn.

Aleksic, P. S., & Katsaggelos, A. K. (2004). Speech-to-video synthesis using MPEG-4 compliant visual features. *IEEE Transactions on Circuits and Systems for Video Technology, Special Issue on Audio and Video Analysis for Multimedia Interactive Services*, 14(5), 682-692.

Aleksic, P. S., & Katsaggelos, A. K. (2006). *Audio-visual biometrics using FAPs as visual features*. In preparation for submission to EURASIP Journal on Applied Signal Processing, Special Issue on Robust Speech Recognition.

Aleksic, P. S., & Katsaggelos, A. K. (2006, March). Automatic facial expression recognition using facial animation parameters and multi-stream HMMs. *IEEE Transactions on Information Forensics and Security 1*(1), 3-11.

Aleksic, P. S., & Katsaggelos, A. K. (2006, November). Audio-visual biometrics. In *Proceedings of IEEE, Special Issue on Biometrics 94*(11), 2025-2044.

Aleksic, P. S., Williams, J. J., Wu, Z., & Katsaggelos, A. K. (2002, November). Audio-visual speech recognition using MPEG-4 compliant visual features. *EURASIP Journal on Applied Signal Processing: Special Issue on Audio-Visual Speech Processing, 2002*(11), 1213-1227.

Baldwin, J. F., Martin, T. P., & Saeed, M. (1999). Automatic Computer Lip-reading using Fuzzy Set Theory. In D. W. Massaro (Ed.) *Proceedings of AVSP'99 – International Conference on Auditory-Visual Speech Processing: University of California, Santa Cruz, California, August 7-10, 1999* (pp. 86-91). Santa Cruz, CA: Perceptual Science Laboratory, University of California.

Bregler, C., Omohundro, S., & Konig, Y. (1994). A hybrid approach to bimodal speech recognition. In Avtar Singh (Ed.) *Conference Record of the Twenty-eighth Asilomar Conference on Signals, Systems, & Computers: October 31-November 2, 1994, Pacific Grove, California* (pp. 556-560). New York, NY: IEEE Computer Society Press.

Capin, T. K., Petajan, E., & Ostermann, J. (2001). Efficient Modeling of Virtual Humans in MPEG-4. In *Proceedings of ICME 2000 – IEEE International Conference on Multimedia and Expo: Vol. 2* (pp. 1103-1106). New York, NY: IEEE Press.

Escher, M., Goto, T., Kshirsagar, S., Zanardi, C., & Magnenat Thalmann, N. (1999). User Interactive MPEG-4 Compatible Facial Animation System. In *Proceedings of International Workshop on Synthetic-Natural Hybrid coding and Three Dimensional Imaging (IWSNHC3DI'99)* (pp. 29-32). Santorini, Greece: IWSNHC3DI

Fries, G., Paradiso, A., Nack, F., & Shuhmacher, K. (1999). A Tool for Designing MPEG-4 Compliant Expressions and Animations on VRML Cartoon Faces. In D. W. Massaro (Ed.) *Proceedings of AVSP'99 – International Conference on Auditory-Visual Speech Processing: University of California, Santa Cruz, California, August 7-10, 1999* (pp. 145-150). Santa Cruz, CA: Perceptual Science Laboratory, University of California.

Goldschen, A., Garcia, O. & Petajan, E. (1994). Continuous optical automatic speech recognition. In Avtar Singh (Ed.) *Conference Record of the Twenty-eighth Asilomar Conference on Signals, Systems, & Computers: October 31-November 2, 1994, Pacific Grove, California* (pp. 572-577). New York, NY: IEEE Computer Society Press.

Grammalidis, N., Sarris, N., Deligianni, F., & Strintzis, M. G. (2002, October). Three-Dimensional Facial Adaptation for MPEG-4 Talking Heads. *EURASIP Journal on Applied Signal Processing: Special Issue on Audio-Visual Speech Processing, 2002*(10), 1005-1020.

Hovden, G. & Ling, N. (2003, November). Optimizing Facial Animation Parameters for MPEG-4. *IEEE Transactions on Consumer Electronics, 49*(4), 1354-1359.

Humanoid Animation Working Group: http://www.h-anim.org/

International Organization for Standardization ISO/IEC 14496-1:2004 (MPEG-4). *Information Technology – Coding of audio-visual objects, Part 1: Systems.* (2004). http://www.smalllinks.com/54F

International Organization for Standardization ISO/IEC 14496-2:2004 (MPEG-4). *Information Technology – Coding of audio-visual objects, Part 2: Visual.* (2004). http://www.smalllinks.com/54E

Luettin, J., Thacker, J. A., & Beet, S. W. (1995). Active shape models for visual speech feature extraction. In David G. Stork & Marcus E. Hennecke (Eds.) *Speechreading by Humans and Machines: Models, Systems, and Applications: Proceedings of the NATO Advanced Study Institute on Speechreading by*

Man and Machine, held in Castéra-Verzudan, France, Aug. 28-Sept. 8, 1995 (pp 383-390). New York, NY: Springer Publishing Company.

Movellan, J. R., & Mineiro, P. (1999). A Diffusion Network Approach to Visual Speech Recognition. In D. W. Massaro (Ed.) *Proceedings of AVSP'99 – International Conference on Auditory-Visual Speech Processing: University of California, Santa Cruz, California, August 7-10, 1999* (pp. 92-96). Santa Cruz, CA: Perceptual Science Laboratory, University of California.

Niyogi, P., Petajan, E., & Zhong, J. (1999). Feature based representation for audio-visual Speech Recognition. In D. W. Massaro (Ed.) *Proceedings of AVSP'99 – International Conference on Auditory-Visual Speech Processing: University of California, Santa Cruz, California, August 7-10, 1999* (pp. 97-102). Santa Cruz, CA: Perceptual Science Laboratory, University of California.

Petajan, E. D. (1984). *Automatic lipreading to enhance speech recognition.* Unpublished doctoral dissertation, University of Illinois at Urbana-Champagne.

Petajan, E. D. (1984). Automatic lipreading to enhance speech recognition. In *Proceedings of Globecom'84 – Global Telecommunications Conference* (pp. 265-272). New York, NY: IEEE Press.

Petajan, E. D. (2000). Approaches to Visual Speech Processing based on the MPEG-4 Face Animation Standard. In *Proceedings of ICME 2000 – IEEE International Conference on Multimedia and Expo: Vol. 2* (pp. 575-587). New York, NY: IEEE Press.

Raouzaiou, A., Tsapatsoulis, N., Karpouzis, K., & Kollias, S. D. (2002, October). Parameterized Facial Expression Synthesis Based on MPEG-4. *EURASIP Journal on Applied Signal Processing: Special Issue on Audio-Visual Speech Processing, 2002*(10), 1021-1038.

Senior, A., Neti, C. V., & Maison, B. (1999). On the use of Visual Information for Improving Audio-based Speaker Recognition. In D. W. Massaro (Ed.) *Proceedings of AVSP'99 – International Conference on Auditory-Visual Speech Processing: University of California, Santa Cruz, California, August 7-10, 1999* (pp. 108-111). Santa Cruz, CA: Perceptual Science Laboratory, University of California.

Silsbee, P. L., & Bovik, A. C. (1995). Medium vocabulary audiovisual speech recognition. In Antonio J. Rubio Ayuso & Juan M. López Soler (Eds.) *New Advances and Trends in Speech Recognition and Coding: Proceedings of the NATO Advanced Study Institute on New Advances and Trends in Speech Recognition and Coding, held in Bubión, Granada, Spain, June 28-July 10, 1993* (pp. 13-16). New York, NY: Springer Publishing Company.

Talle, B., & Wichert, A. (1999). Audio-visual Sensorfusion with Neural Architectures. In D. W. Massaro (Ed.) *Proceedings of AVSP'99 – International Conference on Auditory-Visual Speech Processing: University of California, Santa Cruz, California, August 7-10, 1999* (pp. 103-107). Santa Cruz, CA: Perceptual Science Laboratory, University of California.

www.f2f-inc.com

www.vectormax.com

FURTHER READING

Seltzer, M. L. & Raj, B. (2003, March). Speech-recognizer-based filter optimization for microphone array processing. IEEE Signal Processing Letters, 10(3), 69 – 71.

Massaro, D. W. (2001). Auditory visual speech processing. In Proceedings of the 7th European Conference on Speech Communication and Technology (Eurospeech'01) (pp. 1153-1156). Aalborg, Denmark.

Massaro, D. W. (2002). Multimodal Speech Perception: A Paradigm for Speech Science. In B. Granstrom, B., House, D., & Karlsson, I. (Eds.), Multilmodality in language and speech systems, (pp. 45-71). Dordrecht, The Netherlands: Kluwer Academic Publishers.

Massaro, D. W. (2003). Model Selection in AVSP: Some Old and Not So Old News. In Schwartz, J. L., Berthommier, F., Cathiard, M. A., & Sodoyer, D. (Eds.), Proceedings of Auditory-Visual Speech Processing (AVSP'03), ISCA Tutorial and Research Workshop on Audio Visual Speech Processing (pp. 83-88; also CD-ROM). St Jorioz, France.

Campbell, C. S., Shafae, M. M., Lodha, S. K.,& Massaro, D. W. (2003). Discriminating Visible Speech Tokens Using Multi-Modality. In Brazil, E., & Shinn-Cunningham, B. (Eds.), Proceedings of the 9th International Conference on Auditory Display, (ICAD'03). Boston, MA: Boston University Publications.

Massaro, D.W. (2004). A Framework for Evaluating Multimodal integration by Humans and A Role for Embodied Conversational Agents. In Proceedings of the 6th International Conference on Multimodal Interfaces, (ICMI'04) (pp.24-31). State College, PA. New York: ACM Press.

Guiard-Marigny, T., Tsingos, N., Adjoudani, A., Benoît, C., Gascuel, M. (1996). 3D Models Of The Lips For Realistic Speech Animation. In IEEE Computer Animation, 80-89. CA

Walsh, A. E. & Bourges-Sevenier, M. (2001). MPEG-4 Jump-Start. Upper Saddle River, NJ: Pearson Education.

Zhong, J. (1998). Flexible face animation using MPEG-4/SNHC parameter streams.. In Proceedings of IEEE International Conference on Image Processing, 1998 (ICIP 98). (pp. 924 – 928). New York, NY: IEEE Press.

Kim, S. H., & Kim, H. G. (2000). 3D Facial Feature Extraction and Global Motion Recovery Using Multi-modal Information. In Biologically Motivated Computer Vision First IEEE International Workshop BMCV 2000 Seoul, Korea, May 15–17, 2000 Proceedings. (pp. 385-394). Heidelberg, Germany: Springer Berlin.

Christian Babski: http://ligwww.epfl.ch/~babski/vrml.html

Papadogiorgakil, M., Grammalidis, N., Sarris, N., & Strintzis, M. G. (2004). Synthesis of virtual reality animation from sign language notation using MPEG-4 body animation parameters. In Proceedings 5th International Conference on Disability, Virtual Reality and Associated Technology (pp. 259-266). http://www.icdvrat.reading.ac.uk/2004/papers/S08_N5_Papadogiorgaki_ICDVRAT2004.pdf

Yoon, S., Kim, S., & Ho, Y. (2003). BAP generation for head movement based on MPEG-4 SNHC. In Proceedings of the 2003 Joint Conference of the Fourth International Conference on Information,

Communications and Signal Processing, 2003 and the Fourth Pacific Rim Conference on Multimedia (pp. 36- 40). Heidelberg, Germany: Springer-Verlag.

Kim, J., Song, M. Kim, I., Kwon, Y., Kim, H., & Ahn, S. (2000). Automatic FDP/FAP generation from an image sequence. In IEEE International Symposium on Circuits and Systems, 2000. (pp. 40-43). New York, NY: Wiley-IEEE Press.

Fernando, C., Pereira, N., & Ebrahimi, T. (2002). The MPEG-4 Book. New York, NY: Prentice Hall PTR.

Magnenat-Thalmann, N., & Thalmann, D. (2004). Handbook of Virtual Humans. New York, NY: John Wiley and Sons.

Gratch, J., Rickel, J., Andre, E., Cassell, J., Petajan, E., & Badler, N. (2002, July/August). Creating Interactive Virtual Humans: Some Assembly Required. In IEEE Intelligent Systems. (pp. 54-63). New York, NY: IEEE Press.

Sim, T., Zhang, S., Janakiraman, R., & Kumar,S. (2007). Continuous Verification Using Multimodal Biometrics. In IEEE Transactions on Pattern Analysis and Machine Intelligence, 29(4), 687-700.

Cheung, M., Mak, M. & Kung, S. (2005). A two-level fusion approach to multimodal biometric verification. In Proceedings of IEEE National Conference on Accoustics, Speech and Signal Processing. (ICASSP '05) (pp. 485-488). New York, NY: IEEE Press.

Low cost 720P Camcorder: http://www.smalllinks.com/54B

720P Camcorder: http://www.smalllinks.com/54C

720P Camcorder: http://www.smalllinks.com/54D

Painkras, E.& Charoensak, C. (2005). A Framework for the Design and Implementation of a Dynamic Face Tracking System. In Proceedings of TENCON 2005 IEEE Region 10 Conference. (pp. 1-6). New York, NY: IEEE Press.

Gallardo-Antolin, A., Díaz-de-María, F., & Valverde-Albacete, F. (1999). Avoiding distortions due to speech coding and transmission errors in GSM ASR Tasks. In Proceedings of IEEE International Conference on Acoustics, Speech and Signal Processing (ICASSP '99) (pp. 277-280). New York, NY: IEEE Press.

NIST Mark-III Microphone Array: http://www.nist.gov/smartspace/cmaiii.html

Brandstein, M. & Ward, D. (2001). Signal Processing Techniques and Applications. Heidelberg, Germany: Springer-Verlag.

CAIP Microphone Array Research: http://www.caip.rutgers.edu/multimedia/marrays/

Seltzer, M. L., & Raj, B. (2003). Speech-recognizer-based filter optimization for microphone array processing. In IEEE Signal Processing Letters (pp. 69-71). New York, NY: IEEE Press.

Section II
Lip Modeling, Segmentation, and Feature Extraction

Chapter V
Lip Region Segmentation with Complex Background

Shilin Wang
Shanghai Jiaotong University, China

Alan Wee-Chung Liew
Griffith University, Australia

Wing Hong Lau
City University of Hong Kong, Hong Kong

Shu Hung Leung
City University of Hong Kong, Hong Kong

ABSTRACT

*As the first step of many **visual speech recognition** and **visual speaker authentication** systems, robust and accurate lip region segmentation is of vital importance for lip image analysis. However, most of the current techniques break down when dealing with lip images with complex and inhomogeneous background region such as mustaches and beards. In order to solve this problem, a Multi-class, Shape-guided FCM (MS-FCM) clustering algorithm is proposed in this chapter. In the proposed approach, one cluster is set for the lip region and a combination of multiple clusters for the background which generally includes the skin region, lip shadow or beards. With the spatial distribution of the lip cluster, a spatial penalty term considering the spatial location information is introduced and incorporated into the objective function such that pixels having similar color but located in different regions can be differentiated. Experimental results show that the proposed algorithm provides accurate lip-background partition even for the images with complex background features.*

INTRODUCTION

Visual speech recognition has aroused the interest of many researchers (Chan 2001, Kaynak et al. 2001, Zhang et al 2001). The visual information of lip movement can help enhancing the accuracy of automatic speech recognition systems especially in noisy environments (Petajan 1985, Bregler et al. 1993). Accurate and robust lip region segmentation, as the first step of most lip extraction systems, is of key importance for subsequent processing.

Lip region segmentation aims to classify all the pixels in an image into two categories: the lip pixels and the background (non-lip) ones, and various techniques have been proposed to address this problem. In recent years, segmentation of color lip images has gained more popularity than segmentation from gray-scale images due to the availability of low-cost hardware and increasing computing power. Color can provide additional information that is not available in gray-scale images and thus it enhances the robustness of the lip segmentation algorithm. In addition, it is also easier for detecting the teeth and tongue, which are important for extracting the lip region accurately.

Various lip image segmentation methods have been proposed in the literature. Color space analyses such as preset color filtering (Wark et al. 1998) and color transformation (Eveno et al. 2001) have been used to enlarge the color difference between the lip and skin. Nevertheless, this kind of methods will result in large segmentation error if the color distribution of lip region overlaps with that of background region. Edge detection algorithms (Hennecke et al 1994, Caplier 2001) can produce accurate result if prominent and consistent intensity changes around the boundary exist. However, this condition may not be easily satisfied for people with low color contrast between the lip and skin. Spatial continuity has also been exploited in Markov random field based techniques to improve the robustness of segmentation (Lieven and Luthon 1999, Zhang and Mersereau 2000). These algorithms can reduce the segmentation error caused by "pepper" noise. **Fuzzy c-means** (FCM) clustering is another kind of widely used image segmentation techniques (Bezdek 1981). In FCM-based methods, neither prior assumption about the underlying feature distribution nor training is needed.

The methods mentioned above all produce satisfactory results to a certain extent for lip image without mustache or beards. However, most of them fail to provide accurate lip segmentation for lip images with beards. We have previously proposed a fuzzy clustering based algorithm that takes into consideration the lip shape, i.e., fuzzy c-means with shape function (FCMS) (Leung et al 2004), to segment the lip region. The FCMS exploits both the shape information and the color information to provide accurate segmentation results even for lip images with low contrast. However, it still fails for image with a complex background due to the insufficient background modeling.

In this chapter, a new fuzzy clustering based algorithm is proposed to solve the problem. The three distinctive features of the proposed lip segmentation algorithms are: (i) prior information of lip shape is seamlessly incorporated in the object function which can effectively differentiate pixels of similar color but located in different regions; (ii) multiple spheroidal-shaped clusters are employed to model the inhomogeneous background region and the proper number of clusters is determined automatically; (iii) with the information of probable lip location, inner mouth features such as teeth and oral cavity can be detected more accurately and thus the robustness of the lip segmentation result is improved.

The chapter is organized as follows. An example of lip image with complex background is illustrated and the major difficulties of accurate lip region segmentation are examined. Then we describe in detail the state-of-the-art fuzzy clustering based algorithm: the Multi-class, Shape-guided FCM (MS-FCM) clustering method (Wang et al. 2007) and elaborate the underlying mechanism of why the proposed algorithm is effective dealing with the lip images with complex background region. From the experimental results, we show that our method is able to provide accurate and robust lip region segmentation result even when the background region is complex.

PROBLEMS ENCOUNTED IN LIP SEGMENTATION WITH COMPLEX BACKGROUND

Segmenting lip images with mustaches and beards surrounding the lip region remains an open question for most existing lip segmentation techniques (Lievin and Luthon 1999). Fig. 1 illustrates an example

Figure 1. (a) original lip image, (b) color distribution of (a) in CIELAB color space, (c)-(e) color distribution projection on the L-a, b-a, L-b plane, respectively, (f) the edge map of the hue image, (g) the edge map of the luminance image

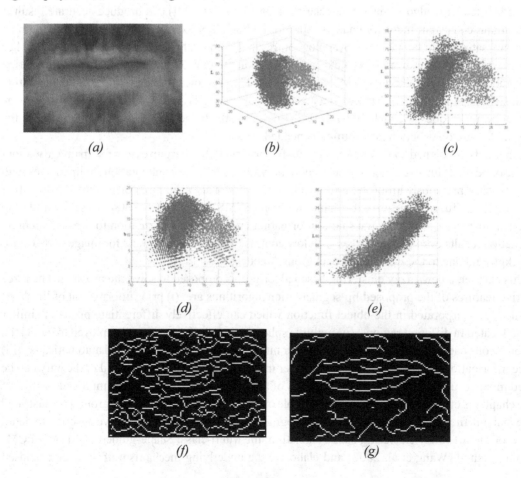

Table 1. Major difficulties for the traditional lip segmentation approaches

Lip segmentation approaches	Major difficulties
Color-based approaches (color filtering)	Similarity and overlap in the color space
Edge-detection approaches	Too many false-boundary edges
MRF-based approaches	Patches and holes can be usually found

of lip image and its corresponding color distribution of the lip and non-lip pixels in CIE-1976 CIELAB color space, where * and + represent the lip and background (or non-lip) pixels, respectively. The hue image, with the hue definition given in (Zhang and Mersereau 2000), and the edge map are also shown in Fig. 1.

Three major observations can be drawn from these figures. Firstly, the lip and background pixels overlap in the color space as shown from Fig. 1(b) to (e) and this will bring unsolvable troubles to those segmentation methods solely based on color information. Although MRF has been used to exploit the local spatial information to enhance the robustness, patches outside and holes inside the lip region are usually found if a large number of pixels of similar color are aggregated. Mislabeled pixels due to the color similarity will lead to undesirable disturbances to both membership map and color centroids for the conventional FCM algorithm. Secondly, the presence of beards causes many luminance and hue edges in the background region and the use of edge information to infer the lip boundary becomes unreliable. As a result, methods that solely or partially depend on the edge information will not deliver satisfactory performance. Finally, the traditional two-class partitioning methods are utterly not appropriate for lip images with beards since the background region is too complex and inhomogeneous. Due to these three major difficulties, most of the lip segmentation algorithms reported in the literatures cannot provide satisfactory segmentation results for lip images with beards. The difficulties in **lip segmentation** for the traditional methods can be briefly summarized in Table 1.

MULTI-CLASS, SHAPE-GUIDED FCM (MS-FCM) CLUSTERING METHOD

Objective and General Description

In order to overcome the difficulties mentioned above, a fuzzy-clustering based lip segmentation approach, the Multi-class Shape-guided FCM (MS-FCM) method is proposed.

Since it is an unsupervised learning method for which neither prior assumption about the underlying feature distribution nor training is required, fuzzy-clustering based algorithm is capable of handling lip and skin color variation caused by make-up. For feature selection in our algorithm, the color information of each pixel is adopted as the discriminative feature.

Since the lip and background pixels overlap in the color space, the color information alone cannot provide accurate segmentation results. As the lip pixels are usually aggregated to form a large patch, their physical distances towards the lip center provide supportive information for the lip-background differentiation. In MS-FCM, such **spatial information** is obtained from the prior lip shape and is seamlessly incorporated into the objective function to discriminate the non-lip pixels that have similar color but located at a distance away from the lip. As a result, the "Shape-guided" feature of our algorithm aims to exploit the prior lip shape information to better handle the color overlap problem between the lip and background.

In the fuzzy clustering, as Euclidean distance function is adopted to describe the difference between features, the clusters obtained are usually of spheroidal shapes. However, as observed from the Fig.1 (b)-(e), the color information of the background region has a multimodal distribution due to background inhomogeneity. Hence, one single cluster is not sufficient to model such complex background distribution and thus incur large segmentation error. In order to improve the modeling sufficiency, multiple clusters are employed to describe the complex background region as in Gaussian mixture modeling. The "Multi-class" feature of our algorithm helps to reduce the misclassification caused by inadequate background modeling.

The "Multi-class" and the "Shape-guided" features are the two key novelties of our algorithm and they work together to overcome the difficulties of segmenting lip images with complex background. Fig. 2 illustrates the typical segmentation results obtained from both the conventional **FCM** and the MS-FCM algorithm using different numbers of background clusters (where C is the total number of clusters). It is observed that the conventional FCM is unable to segment the lip region accurately for an image with multiple background features even with different setting of C; whereas MS-FCM is able to clearly segment the lip region for C larger than 2 since it requires at least 2 clusters to represent background region which contains two distinguishing parts, the beards and the skin. It is clear from the results that the use of prior shape information and multiple-background-cluster are both necessary. Without using multiple-background-cluster, large segmentation error occurs due to insufficient background model-

Figure 2. (a) Original lip image; lip-segmentation result obtained by the conventional FCM with (b) C=2, (c) C=3, (d) C=4; lip-segmentation result obtained by MS-FCM with (e) C=2, (f) C=3, (g) C=4

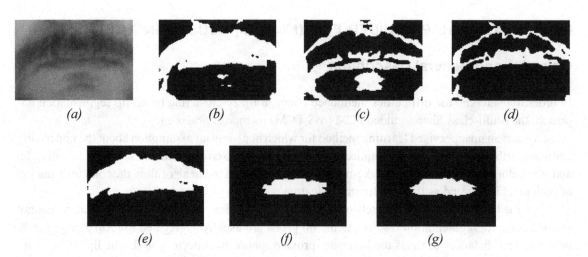

ing even if the shape information is considered (Fig. 2(f)). Without the prior shape information, poor segmentation result is obtained even if multiple background clusters are employed (Fig. 2(c)(d)(e)).

Details of the MS-FCM Algorithm

Objective *Function of MS-FCM*

Let's consider an image I of size N by M. $X = \{x_{1,1}, \ldots, x_{r,s}, \ldots, x_{N,M}\}$ denotes the set of feature vectors where $x_{r,s} \in R_q$ is a q-dimensional color vector for pixel located at (r,s). The Euclidean distance between the color feature vector $x_{r,s}$ and the color centroid vi of the ith cluster ($i = 0$ for the lip cluster and $i \neq 0$ for the background clusters) is represented by $d_{i,r,s}$. The **objective function** of MS-FCM is formulated as:

$$J = J_{CLR} + J_{SPA} = J_{CLR,OBJ} + J_{CLR,BKG} + J_{SPA,OBJ} + J_{SPA,BKG}$$

$$= \sum_{r=1}^{N}\sum_{s=1}^{M} u_{0,r,s}^m d_{0,r,s}^2 + \sum_{r=1}^{N}\sum_{s=1}^{M}\sum_{i=1}^{C-1} u_{i,r,s}^m d_{i,r,s}^2 + \sum_{r=1}^{N}\sum_{s=1}^{M} f(u_{0,r,s})g_{OBJ}(r,s) + \sum_{r=1}^{N}\sum_{s=1}^{M}\sum_{i=1}^{C-1} f(u_{i,r,s})g_{i,BKG}(r,s)$$

(1)

subject to

$$\sum_{i=0}^{C-1} u_{i,r,s} = 1, \quad \forall (r,s) \in I$$

(2)

where the N×M×C matrix $U \in M_{fc}$ is a fuzzy c-partition of X, $V = \{v_0, v_1, \ldots v_{C-1}\} \in R_{cq}$ with $v_i \in R_q$ is the set of fuzzy cluster centroids, $m \in (1, \infty)$ defines the fuzziness of the clustering, and $u_{i,r,s}$ is the membership value of the (r,s)-th pixel in cluster C_i.

The first and second terms in (1) are the **color penalty term**s for the lip ($i = 0$) and background classes ($i \neq 0$), respectively, which penalize the membership value of a certain cluster for a pixel whose color is dissimilar to the color centroid of the cluster. The **color penalty term**s result in a single spheroidal-shaped distribution for the lip region (only one cluster is assigned to the lip) and a mixture of spheroidal-shaped distributions for the background region which provides a better description of the background.

The third and fourth terms in (1) are the **spatial penalty terms** which help incorporate the prior lip shape information. The spatial penalty terms for the object (i.e. lip) cluster and the background clusters are the product of $f(u)$ and $g(r,s)$, where $f(u)$ is proportional to the membership u and $g(r,s)$ is only related to the spatial location (r,s) of the pixel. We note that any form of f and g is appropriate as long as the spatial penalty term satisfies: (i) For pixels inside the lip region, $J_{SPA,OBJ}$ is small while $J_{SPA,BKG}$ is large which penalizes the background membership in this region. Moreover, the closer to the lip center, the larger $J_{SPA,BKG}$ should be. (ii) For pixels near the lip boundary, both $J_{SPA,OBJ}$ and $J_{SPA,BKG}$ are small as pixels in this region have similar probability to be lip or background pixels. Spatial information in this region can hardly help differentiate between lip and background. (iii) For pixels faraway from the lip region, $J_{SPA,OBJ}$ is large while $J_{SPA,BKG}$ is small which penalizes the lip membership in this region. Moreover, the farther away from the lip center, the larger $J_{SPA,OBJ}$ should be. (iv) For different background cluster, the spatial penalty term $J_{i,SPA,BKG}$ should be the same since no prior spatial distribution of any background cluster is available.

Since the shape of the outer lip contour resembles an ellipse, the spatial location information is naturally defined as the elliptic distance of a pixel to the lip center. The elliptic distance can be described with the parameter set $p = \{x_c, y_c, w, h, \theta\}$ in which (x_c, y_c) is the center of the ellipse, w and h are respectively the semi-major axis and the semi-minor axis, and θ is the inclination angle about (x_c, y_c). For a pixel located at (r,s), the elliptic distance *dist* is formulated as

$$dist(r,s,\boldsymbol{p}) = \frac{((r-x_c)\cos\theta + (s-y_c)\sin\theta)^2}{w^2} + \frac{((s-y_c)\cos\theta - (r-x_c)\sin\theta)^2}{h^2}$$

and thus $g(r,s)$ can be directly expressed as $g(dist)$. In our algorithm, $f(u)$ is set to u^m for simplicity and g_{OBJ} and $g_{i,BKG}$ are in the sigmoidal form, i.e.,

$$g_{OBJ}(dist) = p_{OBJ}/(1+\exp(-(dist(r,s,\boldsymbol{p}) - m_{OBJ})/\sigma_{OBJ})) \tag{3}$$

$$g_{i,BKG}(dist) = g_{BKG}(dist) = p_{BKG}/(1+\exp((dist(r,s,\boldsymbol{p}) - m_{BKG})/\sigma_{BKG})) \tag{4}$$

where p_{OBJ} and p_{BKG} are the maximum penalty, m_{OBJ} and m_{BKG} are the mean values and σ_{OBJ} and σ_{BKG} control the steepness of the sigmoid curve.

The **objective function** J is now given by,

$$J(U,V,\boldsymbol{p}) = \sum_{r=1}^{N}\sum_{s=1}^{M}\sum_{i=0}^{C-1} u_{i,r,s}^m d_{i,r,s}^2 + \sum_{r=1}^{N}\sum_{s=1}^{M} u_{0,r,s}^m p_{OBJ}/(1+\exp(-(dist(r,s,\boldsymbol{p})-m_{OBJ})/\sigma_{OBJ}))$$
$$+ \sum_{r=1}^{N}\sum_{s=1}^{M}\sum_{i=1}^{C-1} u_{i,r,s}^m p_{BKG}/(1+\exp((dist(r,s,\boldsymbol{p})-m_{BKG})/\sigma_{BKG})) \tag{5}$$

Parameter Updating Formulae

Since the optimal solution for

$$\min_{M_{fc}\times R^{cq}\times R^5}\{J(U,V,\boldsymbol{p})\}$$

is the stationary point of the objective function, Picard iteration is used to solve for the optimum point (U^*, V^*, p^*). The derivation of the **parameter updating formulae** in each iteration is described in the following.

Let $\varphi: M_{fc} \to R$, $\varphi(U) = J(U,V,\boldsymbol{p})$ with $V \in R^{cq}$ and $p \in R^5$ remain unchanged. Taking the partial derivative of $\varphi(U)$ with respect to U subject to the constraint (2), the updated membership value $u_{i,r,s}^+$ can be obtained by setting the derivative to zero and it is given by:

$$u_{0,r,s}^+ = \left[1 + \sum_{j=1}^{C-1}\left(\frac{d_{0,r,s}^2 + g_{OBJ}(r,s)}{d_{j,r,s}^2 + g_{BKG}(r,s)}\right)^{1/(m-1)}\right]^{-1} \tag{6}$$

$$u_{i,r,s}^+ = \left[\left(\frac{d_{i,r,s}^2 + g_{BKG}(r,s)}{d_{0,r,s}^2 + g_{OBJ}(r,s)} \right)^{1/(m-1)} + \sum_{j=1}^{C-1} \left(\frac{d_{i,r,s}^2 + g_{BKG}(r,s)}{d_{j,r,s}^2 + g_{BKG}(r,s)} \right)^{1/(m-1)} \right]^{-1} \quad i \neq 0$$

(7)

Similarly, let $\psi : R^{cq} \to R$, $\psi(V) = J(U,V,p)$ with $U \in M_{fc}$ and $p \in R^5$ remain unchanged. The partial derivative of $\psi(V)$ with respect to V is given by:

$$\frac{d\psi}{dV} = \frac{\partial J}{\partial V} = \frac{\partial J_{CLR}}{\partial V} + \left(\frac{\partial J_{SPA,OBJ}}{\partial V} + \frac{\partial J_{SPA,BKG}}{\partial V} \right)$$

(8)

Since $J_{SPA,OBJ}$ and $J_{SPA,BKG}$ are constants when $U \in M_{fc}$ and $p \in R^5$ are fixed, the second term on the right hand side of (8) vanishes and the derivative

$$\frac{d\psi}{dV}$$

is identical to that of the FCM. Following the derivation in (Bezdek 1980), the updated centroid can be computed as follows:

$$\mathbf{v}_i^+ = \sum_{r=1}^{N} \sum_{s=1}^{M} u_{i,r,s}^m \mathbf{x}_{r,s} \bigg/ \sum_{r=1}^{N} \sum_{s=1}^{M} u_{i,r,s}^m$$

(9)

Finally, the partial derivative of $J(U, V, p)$ with respect to p is given by

$$\frac{\partial J(U,V,p)}{\partial p} = \frac{\partial J_{CLR}}{\partial p} + \left(\frac{\partial J_{SPA,OBJ}}{\partial p} + \frac{\partial J_{SPA,BKG}}{\partial p} \right)$$

(10)

The first term on the right hand side of (10) vanishes since J_{CLR} is a function of the color features and is independent of the spatial parameter set p. By setting the partial derivative in (10) to zero,

$$\sum_{r=1}^{N} \sum_{s=1}^{M} \left(\begin{array}{c} p_{OBJ} u_{0,r,s}^m \dfrac{\exp(-(dist(r,s,p) - m_{OBJ})/\sigma_{OBJ})}{(1 + \exp(-(dist(r,s,p) - m_{OBJ})/\sigma_{OBJ}))^2} \\[2mm] - \sum_{i=1}^{C-1} p_{BKG} u_{i,r,s}^m \dfrac{\exp((dist(r,s,p) - m_{BKG})/\sigma_{BKG})}{(1 + \exp((dist(r,s,p) - m_{BKG})/\sigma_{BKG}))^2} \end{array} \right) \frac{\partial dist(r,s)}{\partial p} = 0$$

(11)

Since direct solving p^+ with (11) is complex, the Conjugate Gradient (CG) method is adopted instead to solve p^+ numerically for its fast convergence.

Equations (6) and (9) together with p^+ obtained via CG form a Picard iteration to find the optimal solution (U^*, V^*, p^*). The iterative sequence converges to a local minimum since the objective function

J is a continuous function of (*U, V, p*), and *J* is positive and ever decreasing in each updating process of (*U, V, p*), and $x_{r,s}$ is bounded by R^q.

The computational cost for updating the spatial parameter vector *p* is quite expensive as it requires an iterative procedure. From the experimental results, it was observed that the optimized ellipse obtained by the CG method always lies close to the boundary of the lip cluster. Hence, the best-fit ellipse (Liew et al. 2002) for the lip cluster is a good approximation of p^+ which requires less computation to obtain. For a given *U*, the parameters of the best-fit ellipse are computed as follows:

$$\mu_{x,y} = \begin{cases} 1 & u_{0,x,y} \geq u_{i,x,y} \quad for\ any\ i \neq 0 \\ 0 & otherwise \end{cases} \tag{12}$$

$$x_c = \sum_{x=1}^{M}\sum_{y=1}^{N} x \cdot \mu_{x,y} \Big/ \sum_{x=1}^{M}\sum_{y=1}^{N} \mu_{x,y}, \quad y_c = \sum_{x=1}^{M}\sum_{y=1}^{N} y \cdot \mu_{x,y} \Big/ \sum_{x=1}^{M}\sum_{y=1}^{N} \mu_{x,y} \tag{13}$$

$$\theta = \frac{1}{2}\tan^{-1}\left\{\frac{2\eta_{11}}{\eta_{20}-\eta_{02}}\right\} \tag{14}$$

$$w = \left(\frac{4}{\pi}\right)^{1/4}\left[\frac{(I_y)^3}{I_x}\right]^{1/8}, \quad h = \left(\frac{4}{\pi}\right)^{1/4}\left[\frac{(I_x)^3}{I_y}\right]^{1/8} \tag{15}$$

where

$$\eta_{ij} = \sum_{x=1}^{M}\sum_{y=1}^{N}(x-x_c)^i(y-y_c)^j \mu_{x,y} \tag{16}$$

$$I_x = \sum_{x=1}^{M}\sum_{y=1}^{N}((y-y_c)\cos\theta - (x-x_c)\sin\theta)^2\mu_{x,y} \tag{17}$$

$$I_y = \sum_{x=1}^{M}\sum_{y=1}^{N}((x-x_c)\cos\theta + (y-y_c)\sin\theta)^2\mu_{x,y} \tag{18}$$

In order to reduce the effect of noise to the calculation of the best-fit ellipse, the membership map of each cluster is first smoothed by a 3 by 3 Gaussian low-pass filter.

By using p^+ obtained via the best-fit ellipse approach to perform the segmentation, it is observed that the convergence property of the Picard iteration has not been affected and the segmentation result is very close to that of using the p^+ obtained via the CG method.

Determining the Number of Background Clusters

Since the MS-FCM algorithm uses multiple clusters to represent the background region, the number of clusters used will affect both the processing time and segmentation quality. Setting an inadequate number of clusters may result in segmentation errors due to misclassifying some nearby background pixels as lip pixels since their color information is closer to that of the lip than other background features. Nevertheless, this kind of misclassifying error can be reduced by increasing the number of clusters at the expense of increasing processing time. To determine an adequate number of background clusters, the following method is used:

1. Set the initial number of clusters $C=2$.
2. Perform the MS-FCM segmentation algorithm with $C-1$ background cluster(s).
3. Calculate index-I of the fuzzy distribution.
4. Repeat step 2 with C increased by 1 if current index-I is greater than that of the previous iteration, otherwise stop.
5. The proper number of clusters is set to $C-1$.

In step 3, index-I is the cluster validity index to evaluate the partitioning by different number of clusters and is defined as follows (Maulik and Bandyopadhyay 2002):

$$I(C) = \left(\frac{1}{C} \times \frac{E_1}{E_C} \times D_C \right)^q \tag{19}$$

where C is the number of clusters and

$$E_C = \sum_{i=0}^{C-1} \sum_{r=1}^{N} \sum_{s=1}^{M} u_{i,r,s} d_{i,r,s}, \quad D_C = \max_{i,j=1}^{C} \left\| v_i - v_j \right\|, q=2.$$

Implementation Procedure

The lip images used in our experiments are in 24-bit RGB format. However, it is known that the RGB color space is not visually uniform (CIE 1986, Hunt 1991, Sharma 1998), it is preferred to transform the images to another color space such that the color distance between two pixels is proportional to their perceived color difference. The two approximately uniform color spaces, CIE-1976 CIELAB and CIELUV, are suitable color transformations for the purpose. With the reference white set equal to $\{R=G=B=255\}$, the color transformation procedure is described in (Hunt 1991) and the color vector $\{L^*, a^*, b^*, u^*, v^*\}$ is used to represent the color information of the pixels.

The presence of teeth pixels in the lip image is of concern for the proposed algorithm. Its presence will disturb the membership distribution by biasing the cluster centroids. According to (Liew et al. 2003), the teeth pixels are observed with low value of chromaticity information a^* and u^* compared to that of skin and lip pixels. However, due to the complex background with beards, robust estimation of the chromaticity information of the skin and lip pixels is not an easy task. Since the approximate boundary is estimated and described by p in each iteration, the teeth masking method in (Liew et al. 2003) can be modified as follows: (i) the mean and standard deviation of the chromaticity a^* and u^* of all the pixels inside the approximate boundary are calculated and denoted by μ_a, σ_a and μ_u, σ_u, respectively; (ii) the threshold of a^* and u^* are given by

$$t_a = \begin{cases} \mu_a - \sigma_a & \text{if } (\mu_a - \sigma_a) < 9 \\ 9 & \text{otherwise} \end{cases}$$

and

$$t_u = \begin{cases} \mu_u - \sigma_u & \text{if } (\mu_u - \sigma_u) < 29 \\ 29 & \text{otherwise} \end{cases};$$

(iii) possible teeth pixels, i.e., pixels inside the approximate boundary with $a^* \leq t_a$ or $u^* \leq t_u$, or with $L^* < 35\%$ of the reference white (which are possibly oral cavity pixels) are masked out from subsequent clustering process.

The procedures of the MS-FCM segmentation algorithm with C clusters are summarized as follows:

1. Initialize the values of the color centroids V.
2. Ignoring the spatial penalty term, compute the initial membership distribution U via (6) and (7).
3. Update V via (8) and compute the spatial parameter set p using the CG method or the approximate method.
4. With the approximate boundary described by p, detect and mask the teeth and oral cavity pixels by the method mentioned above.
5. Calculate the spatial penalty term and update U via (6) and (7).
6. Repeat steps 3 to 5 for k=1, 2, 3, ... until

$$\left\| U^{(k+1)} - U^k \right\|_\infty < \varepsilon_T \text{ or}$$

   $k \geq k_{\max}$, where ε_T is a small threshold and $k_{\max}$ is the maximum number of iterations.
7. Smooth the membership of each cluster using a 3x3 Gaussian low-pass filter and then apply a hard classification process by assigning each pixel to the cluster having the highest membership value.

To estimate the initial color centroids for step 1, the first frame of the lip sequence is analyzed by the conventional FCM. The color centroid of the cluster located at the center portion of the image is assigned as the lip cluster and the others as the background clusters. For subsequent frames, the centroids of the previous frame can be directly used as the initial centroids for the current frame.

Physical Interpretation of the Spatial Penalty Term

In order to elaborate the function of the spatial penalty term, we divide the entire lip image into five different regions as shown in Fig.3. The approximate lip-background boundary is denoted by a dashed-line ellipse shown in region III. And the spatial parameter set p is adopted to describe the boundary ellipse.

Figure 3. The five elliptic regions of a lip image

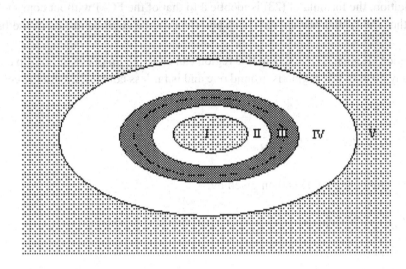

- Far inside the boundary (Region I): For pixels in this region, they are of high probability to be lip pixels. The spatial distance between any pixel in this region and the lip center is very small and thus g_{OBJ} is much smaller while g_{BKG} is much larger compared to the color distance $d_{i,r,s}^2$, i.e.:

$$g_{OBJ}(r,s) \ll d_{i,r,s}^2 \ll g_{BKG}(r,s) \tag{20}$$

According to (6) and (7), the updated membership values are given by

$$u_{0,r,s}^+ \approx 1, u_{i,r,s}^+ \approx 0 (i \neq 0) \tag{21}$$

From (21), it is observed that the spatial penalty term force the pixels in this region to be lip pixels.

- Far outside the lip region (Region V): Pixels in this region are not likely to be lip pixels since they are too far away from the lip region. The spatial distance between any pixel in this region and the lip center is very large and thus g_{BKG} is much smaller while g_{OBJ} is much larger compared to the color distance $d_{i,r,s}^2$, i.e.:

$$g_{BKG}(r,s) \ll d_{i,r,s}^2 \ll g_{OBJ}(r,s) \tag{22}$$

$$u_{0,r,s}^+ \approx 0, u_{i,r,s}^+ \approx \left[\sum_{j=1}^{C-1} \left(\frac{d_{i,r,s}}{d_{j,r,s}} \right)^{2/(m-1)} \right]^{-1} (i \neq 0) \tag{23}$$

From (23), it is observed that the spatial penalty term force the pixels in this region to be non-lip pixels. In addition, the formula of (23) is identical to that of the FCM without considering the lip cluster and thus the spatial penalty term has no effect on the color centroids of the background clusters.

- Boundary region (Region III): Pixels in this region can either be lip pixels or non-lip ones. Spatial distance of any pixel in this region is around one and is far less compared with the color dissimilarity, i.e.,

$$g_{OBJ}(r,s) << d_{i,r,s}^2, \ g_{BKG}(r,s) << d_{i,r,s}^2 \qquad (24)$$

The updated membership value is then given by:

$$u_{i,r,s}^+ \approx \left[\sum_{j=0}^{C-1} \left(\frac{d_{i,r,s}}{d_{j,r,s}} \right)^{2/(m-1)} \right]^{-1} \qquad (25)$$

From (25), it can be observed that in the boundary region, the spatial penalty term is disappeared and the membership value of a pixel in this region is solely based on its color information. Although the approximate boundary is described in an elliptic form, the proposed algorithm is suitable for various lip shapes segmentation since the elliptic function is a good approximation to most lip shapes.

- Inside the boundary (Region II): Pixels in this region are more likely to be lip pixels rather than non-lip ones. The spatial distance of any pixel is small in this region and thus g_{BKG} is comparable to the color distances $d_{i,r,s}^2$ and g_{OBJ} is negligible, i.e.:

$$g_{OBJ} << g_{BKG}, \ g_{OBJ} << d_{i,r,s}^2 \qquad (26)$$

The updated membership value is then given by:

$$\Rightarrow \frac{d_{0,r,s}^2 + g_{OBJ}(r,s)}{d_{i,r,s}^2 + g_{BKG}(r,s)} \approx \frac{d_{0,r,s}^2}{d_{i,r,s}^2 + g_{BKG}(r,s)} < \frac{d_{0,r,s}^2}{d_{i,r,s}^2} \quad for \ i \neq 0$$

$$\Rightarrow u_{0,r,s}^+ > \left[\sum_{j=0}^{C-1} \left(\frac{d_{0,r,s}}{d_{j,r,s}} \right)^{2/(m-1)} \right]^{-1} \qquad (27)$$

The spatial penalty term aims to increase the membership values inside Region II.

- Outside the boundary (Region IV): Pixels in this region are more likely to be background pixels rather than the lip ones. The spatial distance is large and thus g_{OBJ} is comparable to the color distances $d_{i,r,s}^2$ and g_{BKG} is negligible, i.e.:

$$g_{BKG} \ll g_{OBJ}, \; g_{BKG} \ll d_{i,r,s}^2 \tag{28}$$

The updated membership value is then given by:

$$\Rightarrow \frac{d_{0,r,s}^2 + g_{OBJ}(r,s)}{d_{i,r,s}^2 + g_{BKG}(r,s)} \approx \frac{d_{0,r,s}^2 + g_{OBJ}(r,s)}{d_{i,r,s}^2} > \frac{d_{0,r,s}^2}{d_{i,r,s}^2} \quad for \; i \neq 0$$

$$\Rightarrow u_{0,r,s}^+ < \left[\sum_{j=0}^{C-1} \left(\frac{d_{0,r,s}}{d_{j,r,s}} \right)^{2/(m-1)} \right]^{-1} \tag{29}$$

The spatial penalty term aims to decrease the membership values inside Region II.

Regions I to V will expand, shrink or even disappear with different parameter settings of the sigmoid function g_{OBJ} and g_{BKG}. It should be noted that g_{OBJ} and g_{BKG} in the spatial penalty term can be of other forms rather than the sigmoid function. Fig. 4 illustrates two different forms of spatial functions g_{OBJ} and g_{BKG}. For the first case, sigmoid functions with $p_{OBJ} = p_{BKG} = 200$, $m_{OBJ} = 1.5$, $m_{BKG} = 0.75$, $\sigma_{OBJ} = 1$ and $\sigma_{BKG} = 0.5$ are adopted. For the second case, polynomial functions are adopted:

$$g_{OBJ}(dist) = Coef \times dist^2 \text{ and } g_{BKG}(dist) = Coef \times dist^{-2} \tag{30}$$

where *Coef* is set to 40/3.

To avoid very large values of g_{BKG}, thresholding is performed on g_{BKG} with the threshold set to 10*Coef.

For the contour maps in Fig.4, the darker color represents smaller value of the spatial function and vice versa. From Fig.4, the following conclusions may be drawn: i) the two forms of spatial functions are both able to enhance the performance of clustering by introducing the spatial information. Both of them enhance the membership value of the lip cluster for pixels inside the lip boundary while reduce the membership values for pixels outside the boundary. ii) Compared with the polynomial function of g_{OBJ}, the sigmoid function has the following property: in the inner boundary region, the spatial function is always of a very small value while around the boundary region, the spatial function increases very fast and reaches a very large value (five times the average color distance) when the spatial distance exceed two times the boundary distance. From the experiments, the sigmoid function with the above parameter setting can provide more accurate segmentation results than the polynomial function and thus such setting is adopted in our experiments.

EXPERIMENTAL RESULTS

In order to test the performance of our MS-FCM algorithm, a database containing over 5000 lip images is built. Among them, 5000 lip images are collected from more than twenty individuals in our laboratory to test the proposed algorithm for images without beards. In addition, 500 lip images with beards also

Figure 4. Function of g_{OBJ} and g_{BKG} in the spatial penalty term compared with the average color distance for (a) sigmoid function, (b) polynomial function; the contour map of g_{OBJ} for (c) sigmoid function, (d) polynomial function; the contour map of g_{BKG} for (e) sigmoid function, (f) polynomial function

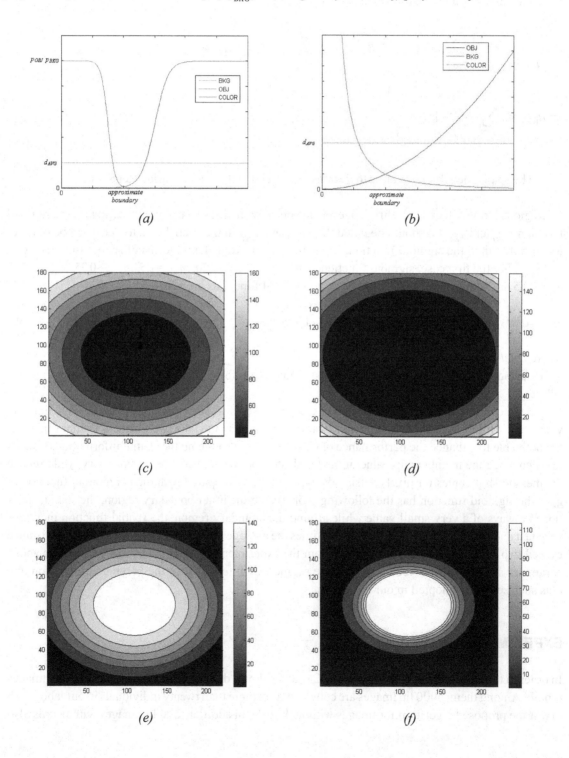

have been taken from the "AR Face Database" (Martinez and Benavente 1998) to test the performance of the proposed algorithm.

In Fig. 5, three lip images are used to compare the performance of the proposed algorithm with other methods including the conventional FCM, Lievin and Luthon's method (Lievin's for short) (Lievin and Luthon 1999), and Zhang and Mercereau's method (Zhang's for short) (Zhang and Mercereau 2000). The three original images are shown in Fig. 5(a1), 5(a2) and 5(a3). Fig. 5(b1), 5(b2) and 5(b3) are the corresponding segmentation results obtained via FCM. It can be seen that the conventional FCM can deliver acceptable results if the lip and the background are well differentiated (see Fig. 5(b1) with 3 clusters). However, when the lip color and part of the background color are close, the conventional FCM is unable to produce good segmentation even with more clusters (see Fig. 5(b3) with 5 clusters).

Fig. 5(c1)(c2)(c3) and 5(d1)(d2)(d3) show the segmentation results obtained from Lievin's and Zhang's methods, respectively. Lievin's and Zhang's methods basically use 2 clusters to segment the image from the hue information. When the hue for the lip region and the background are close, the two-class assumption becomes inappropriate. Zhang's method further makes use of the edge map information to aid the segmentation. It produces large segmentation errors since the edge map is quite noisy for lip image with beards.

Finally, Fig. 5(e1)(e2)(e3) show the segmentations obtained from the proposed algorithm with 3 clusters. It is seen that our algorithm outperforms the other 3 methods for lip images with mustaches and beards.

For quantitative comparison, the boundary of the lip region is manually drawn and compared with the segmented lip region. A quantitative index, Segmentation Error (*SE*) as defined in (Lee et al. 1990) and given in (23), is used to evaluate the performance of the proposed algorithm.

$$SE = P(O) \cdot P(B \mid O) + P(B) \cdot P(O \mid B) \tag{31}$$

where $P(B|O)$ is the probability of classifying background as object, $P(O|B)$ is the probability of classifying object as background. $P(O)$ and $P(B)$ are the a priori probabilities of the object and the background of an image, respectively. The segmentation error as well as the two misclassifying probability of the four algorithms are tabulated in Table 2.

Table 2. The P{B|O}, P{O|B} and SE of the conventional FCM, Lievin's, Zhang's and MS-FCM for the three lip images shown in Figure 5

	Fig. 5(a1)			Fig. 5(a2)			Fig. 5(a3)		
	$P(B|O)$	$P(O|B)$	SE(%)	$P(B|O)$	$P(O|B)$	SE(%)	$P(B|O)$	$P(O|B)$	SE(%)
FCM	0.125	0.033	5.40	1.683	0.080	26.77	2.214	0.032	19.15
Lievin's	0.847	0.046	23.10	1.400	0.013	17.53	1.601	0.005	12.18
Zhang's	0.538	0	12.51	3.119	0	36.56	7.026	0	51.40
MS-FCM	0.162	0.015	**4.87**	0.014	0.03	**2.81**	0.031	0.008	**0.95**

Figure 5. (a1),(a2),(a3) Original lip images. Segmentation results obtained from: (b1),(b2),(b3) conventional FCM, (c1),(c2),(c3) Lievin's method, (d1),(d2),(d3) Zhang's method, and (e1),(e2),(e3) MS-FCM

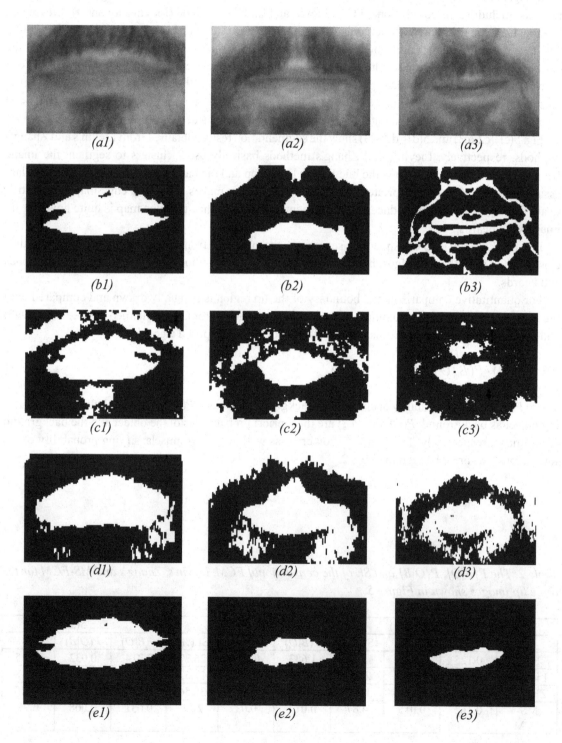

From Table 2, it is observed that the segmentation error of MS-FCM is much smaller than that of the other algorithms. More segmentation results for images with or without beards produced by MS-FCM are given in Fig. 6. The average segmentation error for the 500 lip images selected from the "AR Face Database" is around 3%. These results demonstrate that the segmented lip region obtained by our algorithm fits well to the lip.

Figure 6. More segmentation results obtained by MS-FCM with the segmented lip region shown in white

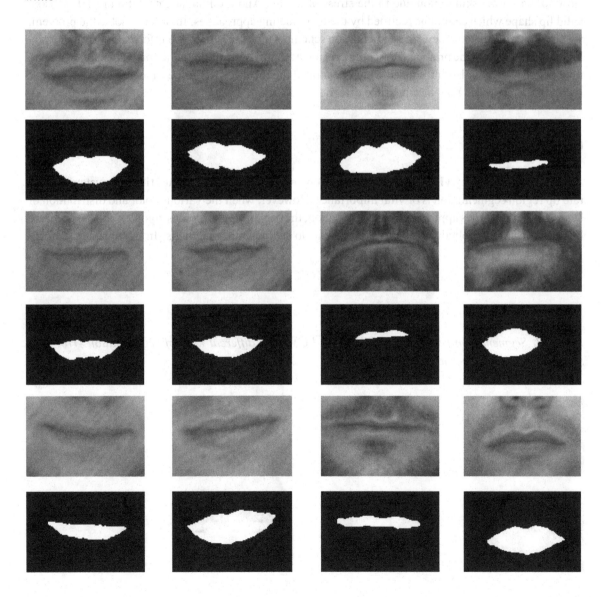

FUTURE WORKS

From the experimental results shown in the previous section, the proposed MS-FCM algorithm can achieve the lip region accurately. However, for some special cases (less than 5% of all the lip images we tested), the MS-FCM algorithm still cannot provide accurate segmentation results. Fig.7 demonstrates some of such lip images and it can be observed that the lip corners are classified as non-lip pixels because these pixels are of dark color which is similar to that of beard-pixels. Moreover, their location is close to the approximate boundary so that the prior lip shape cannot provide useful assistance. Such drawback in segmenting dark lip corners can be overcome by some lip modeling approaches with lip shape validation since the major part of lip region is correctly identified.

For the last figure in Fig.7, the lower part of the lip region is segmented as non-lip since its color is close to that of the skin region due to the stress of the lip. And the final segmentation result is also a valid lip shape which cannot be rectified by the lip modeling approaches. In order to solve the problem, we are now working on a new lip segmentation scheme which takes both the information from current lip image and it from the previous lip sequences into account. In addition to the spatial penalty term, the time penalty term is also introduced which penalized the incoherence in the time domain. We believe such kind of approach may be a possible direction to follow.

CONCLUSIONS

As the first step of many **visual speech recognition** and **visual speaker authentication** systems, accurate lip region segmentation is of vital importance. However, when the various color and distribution of beards and moustaches appear around the lip region, the background becomes complex and the accurate lip region cannot be obtained by most of current lip segmentation methods. In this chapter, a fuzzy

Figure 7. Segmentation results obtained by MS-FCM with different kind of segmentation error (the segmented lip region is shown in white)

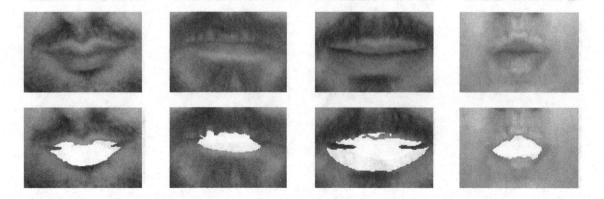

clustering based lip segmentation method, the Multi-class, Shape-guided FCM (MS-FCM) clustering algorithm, is proposed to solve this problem. A spatial penalty term based on the lip shape information is introduced in the dissimilarity measure which encourages the lip cluster membership value for pixels inside the lip region while penalizes them for those outside the lip region. With the spatial penalty term, pixels with similar color while located in different regions can be differentiated. From the experimental results, it is observed that our approach consistently produce superior results compared with some existing techniques. In our future work, a general scheme considering all the color, spatial and time consistence information will be our research focus.

REFERENCES

Bezdek, J. C. (1980). A convergence theorem for the fuzzy ISODATA clustering algorithms. *IEEE Transactions on Pattern Analysis and Machine Intelligence, 2*, 1-8.

Bezdek, J. C. (1981). *Pattern recognition with fuzzy objective function algorithms*. Plenum Press, New York, 1981.

Bregler, C., Hild, H., Manke, S., Waibel, A. (1993). Improving connected letter recognition by lipreading. *Proc. of IEEE International Conference on Acoustics, Speech, Signal Processing*, pp. 557-560.

Caplier, A. (2001). *Lip Detection and Tracking, Proc. of 11th International Conference on Image Analysis and Processing*. Palermo, Italy, pp. 8-13.

Chan, M. T. (2001). HMM-based audio-visual speech recognition integrating geometric and appearance-based visual features. *IEEE Fourth Workshop on Multimedia Signal Processing*, Cannes, France, pp. 9-14.

CIE (1986). *Colorimetry*, CIE Pub. No. 15.2, Bureau Central de la CIE, Vienna, Austria.

Eveno, N., Caplier, A., Coulon, P. Y. (2001). New color transformation for lips segmentation. *Proc. of IEEE Fourth Workshop on Multimedia Signal Processing*, Cannes, France, pp.3-8.

Hennecke, M. E., Prasad, K. V., & Stork, D. G. (1994). Using deformable templates to infer visual speech dynamics. *1994 Conference Record of the Twenty-Eighth Asilomar Conference on Signals, Systems and Computers, 1*, 578-582. Pacific Grove, CA, USA.

Hunt, R. W. G. (1991). *Measuring Color*, 2nd Ed., Ellis Horwood Series in Applied Science and Industrial Technology, Ellis Horwood Ltd.

Kaynak, M. N., Zhi, Qi, Cheok, A. D., Sengupta, K., Chi Chung, Ko (2001). Audio-visual modeling for bimodal speech recognition. *Proc. of IEEE International Conference on Systems, Man, and Cybernetics*, Tucson, AZ, USA, vol.1, pp. 181-186.

Lee, S. U., Chung, S. Y., Park, R. H. (1990). A comparative performance study of several global thresholding techniques for segmentation. *Computer Vision, Graphics and Image Processing, 52*, 171-190.

Leung, S. H., Wang, S. L., & Lau, W. H. (2004). Lip image segmentation using fuzzy clustering incorporating an elliptic shape function. *IEEE Transactions on Image Processing, 13*(1), 51-62.

Lievin, M., & Luthon, F. (1999). Lip features automatic extraction. *Proc. of IEEE International Conference on Image Processing*, Chicago, IL, USA, 3, 168-172.

Liew, A. W. C., Leung, S. H., & Lau, W. H. (2003). Segmentation of color lip images by spatial fuzzy clustering. *IEEE Transactions on Fuzzy Systems, 11*(4), 542-549.

Liew, A. W. C., Leung, S. H., Lau, W. H. (2002). Lip contour extraction from color images using a deformable model. *Pattern Recognition, 35,* 2949-2962.

Martinez, A. M., Benavente, R. (1998). The AR face database, [Online] CVC Technical Report #24.

Maulik, U., & Bandyopadhyay, S. (2002). Performance Evaluation of Some Clustering Algorithms and Validity Indices. *IEEE Transactions on Pattern Analysis and Machine Learning, 24*(12), 1650-1654.

Petajan, E. D. (1985). Automatic lipreading to enhance speech recognition. *Proc. of IEEE Conference on Computer Vision and Pattern Recognition*, 40-47.

Sharma, G., Vrhel, M. J., Trussell, H. J. (1998). Color imaging for multimedia. *Proceedings of the IEEE, 86,* 1088 –1108.

Shi-Lin Wang, Wing-Hong Lau, Alan Wee-Chung Liew and Shu-Hung Leung (2007). Robust Lip Region Segmentation for Lip Images with Complex Background, Pattern Recognition, vol. 40, issue 12, pp. 3481-3491.

Wark, T., S. Sridharan, V. Chandran (1998). An approach to statistical lip modelling for speaker identification via chromatic feature extraction. *Proc. of Fourteenth International Conference on Pattern Recognition, Brisbane, Australia, 1,* 123-125.

Zhang, X., & Mersereau, R. M. (2000). Lip feature extraction towards an automatic speechreading system. *Proc. of IEEE ICIP'2000, 3,* 226-229, Vancouver, Canada.

Zhang, X., & Mersereau, R. M. (2000). Lip feature extraction towards an automatic speechreading system. *Proc. of IEEE International Conference on Image Processing, 3,* 226-229. Vancouver, BC, Canada.

Zhang, Y., Levinson, S., & Huang, T. (2000). Speaker independent audio-visual speech recognition, *Proc. of IEEE International Conference on Multimedia and Expo, 2,* 1073-1076. New York, USA.

ADDITIONAL READING

T. Coianiz, L. Torresani, B. Caprile (1995). 2D deformable models for visual speech analysis, NATO Advanced Study Institute: Speech reading by Man and Machine, pp. 391-398.

T. F. Cootes, A. Hill, C. J. Taylor, J. Graham (1994). Use of active shape models for locating structures in medical images, Image and Vision Computing, vol.12, pp.355-365.

T. F. Cootes, G. J. Edwards, C. J. Taylor (2001). Active appearance models, IEEE Transactions on Pattern Analysis and Machine Intelligence, vol.23, issue 6, pp.681-685.

N. Eveno, A. Caplier, P. Coulon (2003). Jumping snakes and parametric model for lip segmentation, Proc. of 2003 International Conference on Image Processing, vol.2, pp.867-870.

M. Gordan, C. Kotropoulos, I. Pitas (2001). Pseudoautomatic lip contour detection based on edge direction patterns, Proc. of the 2nd International Symposium on Image and Signal Processing and Analysis (ISPA 2001). Pula, Croatia, pp.138-143.

M. Lievin, P. Delmas, P. Y. Coulon, F. Luthon and V. Fristot (1999). Automatic lip tracking: Bayesian segmentation and active contours in a cooperative scheme, Proc. of IEEE International Conference on Multimedia Computing and Systems, Florence, Italy, vol.1, pp. 691-696.

J. Luettin, N. A. Thacker, S. W. Beet (1996). "Visual speech recognition using active shape models and hidden Markov models," Proc. of IEEE International Conference on Acoustics, Speech and Signal Processing, vol.2, pp. 817-820, Atlanta, USA.

J. Luettin (1997). Visual speech and speaker recognition, PhD thesis, University of Sheffield.

I. Matthews, T.F Cootes, J.A Bangham, S. Cox, R. Harvey (2002). Extraction of visual features for lipreading, IEEE Transactions on Pattern Analysis and Machine Intelligence, vol.24, issue 2, pp.198-213.

G. Rabi, S. W. Lu (1997). Energy minimization for extracting mouth curves in a facial image, Proc. of IEEE International Conference on Intelligent Information Systems, IIS'97, pp.381-385.

P. Scanlon and R. Reilly (2001). Feature analysis for automatic speechreading, Proc. 2001 IEEE Fourth Workshop on Multimedia Signal Processing, Cannes, France, pp.625-630.

K. L. Sum, W.H. Lau, S.H. Leung, A.W.C Liew, K.W. Tse (2001). A new optimization procedure for extracting the point-based lip contour using active shape model, Proc. of IEEE International Conference on Acoustics, Speech and Signal Processing, Salt Lake City, USA, Vol. 3, pp. 1485-1488.

Alan L. Yuille, David S. Cohen, and Peter W. Hallinan (1989). Feature extraction from faces using deformable templates, Proc. of Computer Vision and Pattern Recognition '89, pp.104-109.

X. Zhang, R.M. Mersereau, M. Clements and C.C. Broun (2002). Visual speech feature extraction for improved speech recognition, Proc. of IEEE International Conference on Acoustics, Speech, and Signal Processing, Orlando, Florida, USA, vol.2, pp.1993-1996.

Chapter VI
Lip Contour Extraction from Video Sequences under Natural Lighting Conditions

Marc Lievin
Avid Technology Inc., Canada

Patrice Delmas
The University of Auckland, New Zealand

Jason James
The University of Auckland, New Zealand

Georgy Gimel'farb
The University of Auckland, New Zealand

ABSTRACT

An algorithm for lip contour extraction is presented in this chapter. A colour video sequence of a speaker's face is acquired under natural lighting conditions without any particular set-up, make-up, or markers. The first step is to perform a logarithmic colour transform from RGB to HI colour space. Next, a segmentation algorithm extracts the lip area by combining motion with red hue information into a spatio-temporal neighbourhood. The lip's region of interest, semantic information, and relevant boundaries points are then automatically extracted. A good estimate of mouth corners sets active contour initialisation close to the boundaries to extract. Finally, a set of adapted active contours use an open form with curvature discontinuities along the mouth corners for the outer lip contours, a line-type open active contour when the mouth is closed, and closed active contours with lip shape constrained pressure balloon forces when the mouth is open. They are initialised with the results of the pre-processing stage. An accurate lip shape with inner and outer borders is then obtained with reliable quality results for various speakers under different acquisition conditions.

INTRODUCTION

In this chapter we present an algorithm for lip contour tracking under natural lighting conditions. Our algorithm accurately extracts the inner and outer lip borders from a colour video sequence of a subject's face. No predefined set-up, make-up, or markers are necessary. The only requirement is that the whole mouth region remains in the field of view at all times. The output is a set of adapted active contours that model the lip boundaries.

An image or sequences of images is captured using a digital still or video camera. These images are then processed in three steps. In step one the mouth area is segmented using colour and movement information from the face skin. The second step detects the mouth corners that will be used to initialise the active contours. The third step extracts lip contours using adapted active contours.

Our algorithm offers a very low bit-rate coding of lip contour dynamics and could be readily implemented in applications such as automatic speech recognition, videoconferencing, and face synthesis under natural lighting conditions with few assumptions.

BACKGROUND

The mouth is a highly changeable (in morphology, topology, colour and texture) 3D object. It is composed of more than two hundred distinct muscles displaying different behaviour patterns depending on the language spoken. Fast and accurate tracking of lip movements has been a goal of the computer vision community for at least 30 years. Initially, most research focussed on multimodal speech analysis, where visual and audio information are processed together to improve speech and/or speaker recognition. More recently, there has been rapid growth in the number and diversity of multimedia applications requiring accurate lip movement parameters for modelling and animation.

One of the first lip-tracking systems was developed by Petajan in the mid 1980s. A camera fixed with respect to the head looks upward facilitating, via a binary thresholding of the image, the detection of nostrils (as the darkest blobs on the face). Anthropometric heuristics (regarding distances between eyes, nose, mouth and eyes) then help delineate the mouth area. Another thresholding process segments the aperture between the lips (as the darkest blob in the vicinity of the mouth region) and associated parameters (lip aperture, protrusion, stretching and jaw aperture) correlated to speech generation. Opening parameters of the mouth (surface, perimeter, height and aperture area) were combined with the output of a speech recognition module to recognise isolated letters (Petajan, 1985). A modified version saw the binary masks used to build a mouth shape database for viseme recognition (Petajan, Bischoff, Bodoff, & Brooke, 1988).

The first attempts to integrate video into speech analysis systems were made to resolve cases of greatly degraded speech, such as situations where "cocktail party" effects dominate or the signal to noise ratio is too low. Often the goal was to help increase the recognition rate of speech processing systems by detecting the utterance of separated letters (using closure of mouth detection) such as the so-called VCV (vowel-consonant-vowel) sequences.

The 1990s saw the advent of face tracking and recognition techniques based on colour, contour points, geometrical models (Yuille, Hallinan, & Cohen, 1992), and classification techniques. For most of these applications, the mouth region was the prime area of study as it carries most of the information conveyed by a talking face. Amongst others, algorithms can be classified as ``template matching'' by temporal warping (Pentland & Mase, 1989), neural networks (Bregler & Konig, 1994), or Hidden Markov Models (Goldschen, Garcia & Petajan, 1994; Silsbee,1994; Guiard-Marigny, Tsingos, Adjoudani, Benoît, & Gascuel, 1996). Systems then evolved towards a more global approach of the face, integrating colours (Petajan & Graf, 1996; Vogt in Stork & M. Hennecke, 1996), and more specifically hue for face and lip detection and tracking (Hennecke, Prasad, & Stork, 1996; Lievin & Luthon, 1998; Coianiz in Stork & Hennecke, 1996).

Another application saw warping techniques used to normalise speech processing sequences processed via template matching algorithms (Petajan & Graf, 1996). Using the same visual analysis principles Goldstein, Garcia, & Petajan (1996) and Stork & Hennecke (1996) demonstrated that integrating variations of labial parameters (through the lip opening (co-articulation) parameters and their derivatives) improved the recognition scores of purely audio systems. Subsequently most recognition systems refined these fundamental principles to improve their recognition scores or to derive new applications.

The mouth area was sometimes tracked using markers (Basu, Oliver, & Pentland, 1998) or make-up (Abry & Lallouache, 1991). While such artefacts are not suitable outside research lab facilities, they allowed reliable real-time acquisition of the mouth area parameters. Higher level information was progressively introduced to track/detect lip contours, integrating techniques such as Deformable Templates (Yuille, Hallinan, & Cohen, 1992), Active Contours (Leroy, Herlin, & Cohen, 1996), Active Shape Models (Luettin, Thacker, & Beet, 1996), and Active Appearance Models (Stegmann, 2000).

While primarily designed to support speech recognition tasks, visual parameter tracking systems have progressively been oriented towards applications including, but not limited to, the synthesis of human face, creation of 3D avatars (Akimoto, Suenaga, & Wallace, 1993; Azarbayejani, Starner, Horowitz, & Pentland, 1993; Eisert & Girod, 1998), enhanced visiophony (Zhang, 1997; Bailly, Reveret, Borel, & Badin, 2000), teleconferencing, (Valente & Dugelay, 2000) and more generally, navigation and interactivity in virtual reality (Gratch, Wang, Okhmatovskaia, Lamothe, Morales, Van der Werf, & Morency, 2007). Integration of a predefined set of talking face 3D points in the MPEG4 coding standard recognised the importance of visual cues for multi-media applications and allowed straightforward positioning of communicant avatars in virtual environments.

LIP CONTOUR EXTRACTION ALGORITHM

We consider a RGB video sequence that contains as a minimum the region of the face spanning from chin to nostrils, but may include the whole face.

The processing is conducted in three steps:

- *Step One*: Lip Segmentation.
    - o   Logarithmic colour-space transform: *RGB* to *HI*.
    - o   Segmentation of the mouth area.
- *Step Two*: Determine Mouth Characteristics.
    - o   Mouth corner detection.
- *Step Three:* Evaluate Lip Contours.
    - o   Snake initialisation from mouth corners.
    - o   Convergence of automatic snake (outer) and balloon snake (inner).
    - o   Convergence validation, reinitialisation, and final convergence.

Step One: Lip Segmentation

Detection of face features is often luminance dependent. Because of unreliable viewing conditions and the wide variety of application environments, several approaches have been proposed in the literature. The first category uses only the luminance of the image (e.g. Luettin in Stork & Hennecke, 1996). In this case, applications are sensitive to lighting conditions and analysis of the mouth must be restricted to a small area. The second category computes the hue for a suitable colour space. These approaches attempt to gain independence from viewing conditions (e.g. Coianiz in Stork & Hennecke, 1996). It appears that colour processing is efficient enough to provide robust information for further processing such as dynamic contours (e.g. Dalton in Stork & Hennecke, 1996). The latest research has been focussing on providing skin segmentation under adverse conditions, e.g. facial hair (Wang, Lau, Liew, & Leung, 2007). The complexity of real world examples often requires the inclusion of a training stage (Petajan, Bischoff, Bodoff, & Brooke, 1998). Our approach is intended to be robust to real-world viewing conditions.

Logarithmic Colour Transform

To gain independence from lighting conditions, we compute a logarithmic colour transform. Angular transforms are known to give poor results in noisy environments, e.g. indoor or cloudy conditions. Therefore, a logarithmic hue transform is defined using the G and B channels from RGB colour space.

We compute the hue in a mathematical framework based on a logarithmic image processing model (Leroy, Herlin, & Cohen, 1996). The intensity I of an image is represented by its associated grey tone function $i = M(1 - \frac{I}{I_0})$.

This model satisfies the saturation characteristics of the human visual system and should not be confused with the normalised colour space, rgb. The difference between the logarithmic tone of the channels G and R corresponds to the logarithmic hue tone h. With few assumptions (I_0 close to the maximum value of white M), the logarithmic difference becomes a ratio between the G and R components. This ratio is simple enough to enable real-time implementation on portable systems and reliable enough to provide very good discrepancy in face and lip hue. Finally, from the RGB colour space, a HI logarithmic colour space is defined (Equation 1) and displayed in Figure 1.

$$H = 256 \times \frac{G}{R} \text{ and } I = \frac{R + G + B}{3}$$

$$(1)$$

Hue and Motion Observations

As the red hue can saturate and lose its discrepancy, motion is used to bring additional and complementary information. The first step combines motion with hue information. From the HI colour space, two observations o are derived (Equation 2). The hue observation $h(s)$ consists of filtering the hue value $H(s)$ at pixel s with a parabola centred on the mean value of lip hue H_{lip} with a standard deviation of the hue value Δ_H. Avoiding the standard Gaussian definition allows the segmentation process to converge in a

Figure 1. HI Colour transforms. Top: *typical colour images for the lower face;* Bottom: *the corresponding hue images*

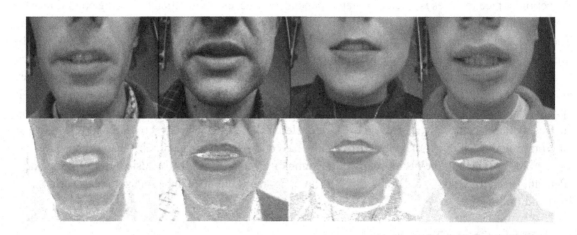

few iterations. The motion observation *fd(s)* is defined as the unsigned difference between the luminance of two consecutive images. *I(s)* represents the intensity (or luminance) at pixel *s*.

$$h(s) = \left[256 - \left(\frac{H(s) - H_{lip}}{\Delta_H} \right)^2 \right] \times 1_{\frac{|H(s) - H_{lip}| \leq 16}{\Delta_H}}$$

$$fd(s) = |I_t(s) - I_{t-1}(s)|$$

(2)

The notation $1_{condition}$ denotes a binary function that takes the value 1 if the condition is true or 0 otherwise.

Parameter Estimation

The hue observation needs three parameters to be estimated: H_{lip}, Δ_H, θ_h. For this purpose, the hue histogram is a useful representation of the hue distribution over the image. Two main hue modes can be detected; the first for the lip and face skin, the second for the background. In natural conditions, the lip mode and the skin mode overlap (Figure 2).

In order to estimate H_{lip} accurately we use the following steps:

- Estimate the main mode that corresponds to the hue skin H_{skin} from the global hue distribution computed over the whole image (*Left* of Figure 2).
- Cluster all pixels respecting the condition given in Equation 2 with H_{skin} instead of H_{lip} (*Middle* of Figure 2).
- Evaluate H_{lip} from the hue distribution after discarding all pixels belonging to skin mode. Only the lip (*black* in Figure 2) and background modes remain.

The threshold hue field is then defined by $h > \theta_h$.

The algorithm requires an appropriate threshold θ_{fd} to suppress the camera noise without causing significant temporal changes. We compute the entropy $E_{fd}(S)$ over an image. The threshold motion field is then defined by $fd > \theta_{fd}$ with $\theta_{fd}(S) = 2^{E_{fd}(S)}$.

The fields after thresholding appear non-homogeneous and noisy. We need an additional relaxation process to segment the lips more accurately.

The Segmentation Algorithm

Observations and Labels are in a Markov Random Field (MRF) Framework. From the motion and hue observations four initial labels (a_0, a_1, b_0, b_1), are introduced to code four distinct pixel classes. Pixels with ($_1$) or without ($_0$) motion, belonging (*a*) or not belonging (*b*) to red hue areas. The label field follows the main MRF () property related to a *spatiotemporal neighbourhood structure* (Figure 3), *i.e.* the label l_s of the current pixel s depends only on the labels of its spatiotemporal neighbours n.

Maximizing the A-Posteriori probability (MAP criterion) of the label field is equivalent to minimizing a global energy function (Geman, & Geman, 1984):

Figure 3. Left: Spatiotemporal neighbourhood structure η with binary cliques c = (s, n). s is the current pixel (in black), n is any spatiotemporal neighbour of s (in grey); Right: corresponding elementary cube C_{xyt}

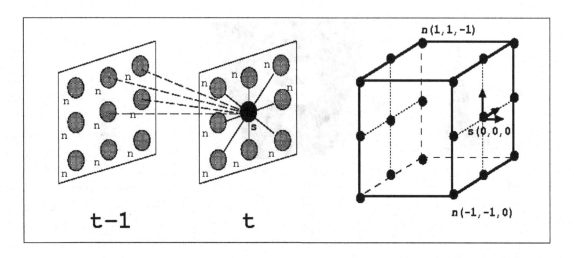

$$W(S) = \sum_{o \in \{fd,h\}} U_o(S) + \alpha.U_m(S)$$

(3)

where U_o and U_m respectively represent the *attachment energies* (expressing the link between labels and observations, (Equation 4) and the *model energy* (corresponding to spatial and temporal a priori constraints) (Equation 5) over the image S, with α a weighting coefficient between the two energies. U_o is given as:

$$U_o(S) = \sum_{s \in S} \left[\frac{[o_s - \psi_o(l_s)]^2}{2\sigma_o^2} \right]$$

(4)

where ψ_o is an attachment function, defined as the mean value of the observation o over S, and σ_o^2 is the corresponding variance. Both are estimated on a local neighbourhood, typically a 9 by 9 pixel window. The *a priori model energy* is defined as the sum of interaction potential functions over the neighbourhood:

$$U_m(S) = \sum_{s \in S} \left[\sum_{n \in \eta(s)} V_{st}(l_n, l_s) \right]$$

(5)

The spatiotemporal potential function V_{st} is defined as the inverse of the Euclidian distance between two neighbours. The distance integrates two elementary potentials β_s and β_t as scale factors:

$$V_{st}(l_n, l_s) = \frac{\beta_s(l_n, l_s)\beta_t(l_n, l_s)}{\sqrt{\beta_t(l_n, l_s)^2 \left(\delta_x^2 + 4\delta_y^2\right) + \beta_s(l_n, l_s)^2 \delta_t^2}}$$

(6)

where

$$\overrightarrow{(s, n)} = (\delta_x, \delta_y, \delta_t) \text{ and } \delta \in \{-1; 0; 1\}.$$

The elementary potentials β_s and β_t are defined within the range $\{-1, +1\}$ to constrain the model respective to spatial homogeneity of labels and temporal homogeneity of hue when no motion is detected.

An iterative deterministic algorithm (Iterated Conditional Modes) is implemented to compute the minimum energy at each site, starting from the initial label configuration L_t^0. At each pixel site, all values corresponding to all possible combinations of labels are evaluated. The configuration that minimizes the local energy is taken. After a few iterations (typically around 10) on the label field, a local minimum is reached. Homogeneous red hue and motion lip fields are obtained.

Red Hue Labels and Region of Interest

From the final label fields red hue relevant labels are extracted (a_0 and a_1, middle-bottom images of Figure 4). Those results are shown with a Region of Interest (ROI). The computation of the ROI follows a very simple rule: a cost function representing the ratio between the number of lip labels and the ROI area is maximized.

Typical sequences have been tested, some with a soft natural red make-up, others with very poor lighting conditions without any make-up. The results demonstrate the robustness of the algorithm to the variability of the lighting conditions.

Summary of the Lip Segmentation Step of the Lip Contour Extraction Algorithm

At the pre-processing stage, the lip segmentation results remain robust across a range of lighting conditions and provide:

- ROI Automatic mouth location (e.g. see Figure 5).
- Unsupervised segmentation of the mouth shape.
- Semantic information: open/close detection.

Results are accurate and reliable but the mouth borders sometimes appear irregular when tongue or gum areas are segmented with the lips (e.g. see Figure 5 bottom row, second image). The segmentation is also imprecise when close to the mouth corners (e.g. see Figure5 top row); the inner contour is not segmented when the mouth is not clearly open (e.g. see Figure 5). To improve these results we need a higher level lip contour extraction algorithm such as adapted active contours.

Figure 4. Lip mask extraction. From top to bottom: sequence of luminance images; initial labels; label fields after relaxation: the 4 labels are shown in grey levels (from white to black: b_1, a_1, b_0, a_0); sequence of hue relevant label images (a_0 and a_1), final masks

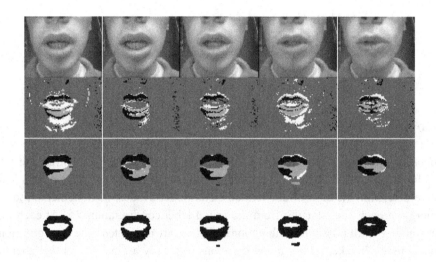

Figure 5. Two sequences of final lip hue fields with ROI superposed on the corresponding luminance

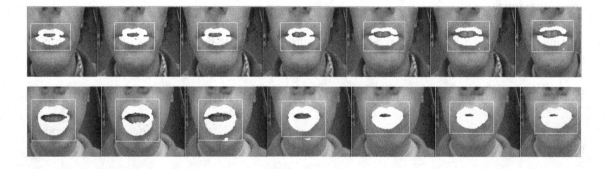

Step Two: Mouth Corner Detection

Location of characteristic points (commissures and vertical extrema of the mouth) is a mandatory step in accurate contour extraction methods (Fua, & Brechbühler, 1996). Characteristic points of the face are the primary way to anchor face analysis on the right area of the image. An absence of pre-determined anchor points for lip models has often been the reason for failure (including but not limited to Deformable Templates (Yuille et al., 1992), Active Shape Models (Luettin et al., 1996), and Active Contours (Leroy et al., 1996)) to properly extract lip contours. Characteristic points of the face have traditionally been located by segmenting the darkest blobs of the image (Petajan, 1985), the darkest line for the lips separation when mouth is closed, or the extremas of the image rows respective to column projection (Radeva, Serrat, & Marti, 1995; Delmas, Coulon, & Fristot, 1999) of the lips vertical extremas (Figure 6 left and middle). There has been a revival of such techniques (Xie, Cai, & Zhao, 2004), associated with very straightforward differential or morphological operators, to determine face feature locations, but these attempts often fail when there is no prior knowledge/segmentation of the face features and their locations. The vertical extrema of the inner and outer lip contours are readily available with the masks computed during our lip segmentation step, but the mouth corners must be obtained separately by combining several approaches integrating different image information and heuristics.

Irrespective of natural or artificial illumination, areas of darkness usually occur at the inner border of lips on horizontal mouth transitions (i.e.: upper lips and teeth, teeth and mouth interior, teeth and lower lips) when the mouth is closed. Once the image area investigated is limited to the close vicinity of the mouth, the study of vertical minima of the image can help locate mouth corners.

The mouth corners are estimated with the following steps:

- The location of the grey level minima over image columns are found;
- Their vertical distribution is computed using a centred weighted distribution:

$$\zeta_j = e^{-4(1-2\frac{j}{N_{col}})^2}$$

(7)

where N_{col} is the number of columns of the image, j is the current column. The weighting coefficient ζ_j varies from **0** to **1**, from the border to the centre of the image taking into account the position and orientation of the mouth as obtained from the lip masks. As a heuristic it uses the largest width whether it be the width of the image or twice the width of the lip mask bounding box.

An accumulation vector V_{ROI}, is the sum of the weighted projection of the minima previously extracted. Let's suppose, for a given column j, that the luminance minima lie on the ith row. Then, the ith component of vector V_{ROI} is incremented by ζ_j which correspond to the weighted score for column j. V_{ROI} extrema usually gives the position of the mouth's horizontal symmetry axis.

- Lip corners are extracted by following the line of minima, from the centre of the image to the left and right.
- Finally, a good estimate of the width of the mouth can be found.

When the mouth is open and under bright illumination conditions (or when reflection of the light on the teeth generates bright or saturated regions) this scheme may fail. This usually results in the mouth corners being wrongly detected inside the mouth region. This is usually due to the line of minima being broken before reaching the actual position of the mouth corner. In such cases, a multi-scale curvature-based (e.g. looking for curvature extremas) corner detector (Moktharian, 1998) processes the pixels in the vicinity of the bounding box obtained from step one (see Figure 5). Only corners in the regions delineated by the central horizontal tier and outer vertical tiers of the bounding box are considered. Using the symmetry of the mouth and proximity to the line of minimas, a pair of corners is selected (Figure 7). Once detected in a given frame the mouth corners can be tracked on consecutive frames using a modified Kanade-Lucas feature tracking algorithm (Delmas, Eveno, & Lievin (2002)).

Step Three: Evaluate Lip Contours

The final step in the algorithm is to produce a set of adapted active contours that accurately represent the inner and outer boundaries of the lips.

In this section we will define the mathematical concepts behind the active contours formalism. We

Figure 6. Mouth corner detection. From left to right: vertical minima (minima in grey, extrema in white) on a grey level image; the corresponding counting per row; mouth corner position for an open mouth

Figure 7. Mouth corner detection for various speaker and illumination conditions

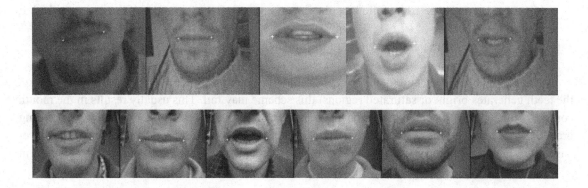

will then provide a non-exhaustive list of energy functionals introduced in the literature that will support lip contour extraction under varying initial conditions. The active contours numerical derivation from a continuous formal problem to its matricial form will be given. The equation for the snake rigidity matrix will be developed for constant active contours' internal energy parameters. Appendix A will for the first time further derive the unique literal inversion of the snake rigidity matrix.

Background

Active contours or snakes appeared in the mid 1980s following joint work by Kass, Witkin, and Terzopoulos (1987) on physically-constrained models as solutions to variational problems in Image Processing and Computer Vision. Snakes rapidly met success thanks to their ability to integrate both edge detection and contour point chaining into a single process. Their adaptable framework made them suitable for a wide range of applications from Medical Imaging (McInerney & Terzopoulos, 1997) to object tracking (Sundaramoorthi, Yezzi, Mennucci, & Sapiro, 2007). They were the first global contour extraction technique, soon followed by the likes of Deformable Templates (Yuille, Hallinan, & Cohen, 1992), Hybrid Active Shape Models (Luettin et al., 1996), Active Appearance Models (Stegmann, 2000) and derived variations.

Active contours search for chained curves, under an energy-based minimisation paradigm. They evolve from a pre-defined initial shape towards the desired features of an image, following steepest gradient descent formalism under internal constraints. Active contours' energy minimisation lets them evolve under constrained geometry (as allowed by their internal energy) towards image features specified by their external energy. Their external energy is defined by a combination of terms each taking its minimal values at the desired points of interest.

Active Contours Theoretical Derivation

Active contours are deformable curves which evolve to minimize their associated energy $\phi(v)$. They deform to minimize their attached energy from their initial position towards a final position which depends on the respective influence of the considered energy terms. The snake total energy is grouped in two separate categories, conventionally named internal and external energy. Internal energy comprises the regularisation terms as well as any additional shape constraint terms. The external energy term comprises "adequation to data" terms and any other terms (e.g. balloon forces (Cohen, 1992)) which may drive the active contours towards desired features using image information.

Active Contour Energies

Let C be a deformable curve over time t and space s. The overall length of the curve is usually normalized to 1 when s represents the curvilinear abscissa. Let $v(s, t)$ be the position of a curve point, x and y its associated Cartesian coordinates. By definition:

$$v(s,t) = (x(s,t), y(s,t)), \ \forall (s,t) \ \varepsilon \ [0,1] \times [0,\infty[\tag{8}$$

The snake functional energy is given by:

$$\phi(v) : v(s,t) \quad \rightarrow \quad E_{int}(v(s,t)) + E_{ext}(v(s,t))$$

(9)

The internal energy takes into account tension and curvature deformation via coefficients α and β.

$$E_{int}(s) \quad = \quad \int_0^1 \left(\alpha(s) |v'(s)|^2 + \beta(s) |v''(s)|^2 \right) ds$$

(10)

where v' and v'' are the first and second derivatives of v with respect to s. Energy derived in Equation 10 corresponds to Tikhonov stabilisers up to order **2** (Tikhonov, 1974). The snake energy model was also introduced (Kass et al., 1987) as a thin plate-membrane model.

External energy takes into account information related to the image and can be of explicit or implicit nature. The explicit form must approach the known features targeted for extraction while respecting smoothing constraints. This is often performed with least square operator type (e.g. $\int_\Omega (f(x) - x)^2 dx$, $f(x)$ regularised form of data x) functions. However Active contours use an implicit form for the external energy functional. They will converge towards the minimum of this function; minima which are not known a-priori. Most introduced functions usually drive active contours towards regions of high gradients, high luminosity contrast, or connected patches (often through colour distribution statistics). The external energy can be defined as:

$$E_{ext} \quad = \quad \int_{v \, \varepsilon \, C(s,t)} P(v(s,t)) dv$$

(11)

where P, external potential, refers to its physics equivalent which has extrema in the regions of interest e.g. convergence. The associated derived force is given by:

$$F_{ext}(v) \quad = \quad -\nabla(P(v))$$

(12)

where ∇ is the gradient operator:

$$\nabla . = \begin{pmatrix} \partial / \partial x \\ \partial / \partial y \end{pmatrix}$$

Active contours converge towards the minima of the external energy functional under regularising constraints as defined in the internal energy functional. Introducing new energy functionals allows us to modify the behaviour (both internally and externally) of active contours. Constraints on active contour deformation, introduction of new physical properties, or modifications of the image features used to extract lip contours are further described below.

Internal Energy

Difficulty in determining the optimal snake energy functional (for the extraction of specific features) led some authors to remove one of the internal energy terms. This simplified addressing the respective influence of the remaining internal term and the external energy term (Bossart, David, Dinten, & Chassery, 1997; Fua & Leclerc, 1990). However this also leads to the degradation of the active contour's shape evolution and convergence appearance. Forcing α to 0 suppresses tension constraints which ensure the even distribution of points during evolution. It also generates accumulation points close to high gradient values area. Forcing β to 0 suppresses shape contour curvature smoothing and allows irregular shapes (Fu, Erdem, & Tekalp, 1998; , Fua & Brechbhler, 1996; Ip & Yu, 1996).

Forces and External Energy Potential

External energy terms drive the snake towards the desired features. Their choices strongly influence the snake convergence behaviour.

Gradient

Widely used to directly relate snake convergence and contour detection, the image gradient functional is given by:

$$E_{edge} = -\int_C |\nabla I(x,y)|^2 \, dC$$

Fua and Leclerc (1990) established that, on the condition of weak curve curvature, the minimisation of the above functional was driving the curve C points towards contours. To reduce gradient inherent noise and discretisation effects, a low-pass filtering of the original image is often performed first. The derived potential and associated force are written as:

$$F_{edge}(x,y) = \nabla(|\nabla I_{g_\sigma}(x,y)|^2)$$
$$E_{edge}(x,y) = -\int_C |\nabla I_{g_\sigma}(x,y)|^2 \, dC \tag{13}$$

where I_{g_σ} is the Gaussian (with standard deviation σ) filtered version of the original image.

Line

This potential allows active contour convergence towards darker or lighter areas of the image:

$$F_{ligne}(x,y) = \mp \nabla I(x,y)$$
$$E_{ligne}(x,y) = \pm I(x,y) \tag{14}$$

A good example of a potential application is shown in (Kass, Witkin, & Terzopoulos, 1987) where it is used to extract growth rings in sliced trunk images. This force is particularly useful when the expected final features lie along a unique line (e.g. closed lips separation line).

Balloon Force

To counter active contour's tendency to evolve slowly (literally snake their way through the image) in regions where the external potential have weak values, several solutions were tried. One of the first attempts was to derive a pressure force pushing the snake towards regions of interest (Cohen, 1992; Cohen & Cohen, 1993). This force is applied perpendicularly to the snake points:

$$F_{ballon}(s) = k_2 \overrightarrow{n(s)}$$

(15)

where $\vec{n}(s)$ is the unit vector normal to the curve at point v(s) of curvilinear abscissa s. The associated potential can be seen as the minimisation/maximisation of the surface A contained within the active contour's curve:

$$E_{ballon} = -k_2 \int_0^d dA$$

(16)

where k_2 is a signed constant. A combination of k_2, positive, respectively negative, and an increase of the surface A generates a force normal to the contour (Cohen, 1990). To further stabilize the snake evolution process, Cohen normalised the external forces:

$$F_{norm}(v(s)) = k_2 \vec{n}(s) - k_1 \frac{\nabla P_{ext}}{\left\| \nabla P_{ext} \right\|} (v(s))$$

(17)

This works only when the gradient vector field does not have "hot" points within the regions of interest or presents gradients of roughly equal strength.

Close to equilibrium, the balloon force ought to balance the remaining external forces related to the features to extract. To achieve this, the value of k_2 is chosen close to, but smaller than k_1 to make sure a contour point is locally able to stop the active contour's evolution. When k_2 is of opposite sign (contraction), the balloon force contracts, thus accelerating the active contour's natural tendency to shrink. This helps avoid being trapped around spurious/isolated edges. Further, the normalisation of the external forces vector field implies that the only gradient influence is angular. Therefore, the above balloon force only works when the features of interest are roughly located along circular patterns. We will introduce later on, a modified balloon force suited to inner lip contour detection.

We have described a few examples of the active contour's great adaptability to problems through the diversity of internal and external energy driving their evolution dynamics and final state. However, the introduced external energy functionals are often non convex. It follows that active contours will often converge towards a local minimum of their energy functional depending on the active contours initial conditions (Cohen & Gorre, 1995).

Euler-Lagrange: From Functional System to Differential Equations

An active contour can be seen as a physical object with elastic hybrid properties (thin layer, membrane), v (Terzopoulos, Witkin, & Kass, 1988), of given mass density μ, evolving in a viscous medium (with given viscosity coefficient γ) and deforming itself through time (at a rate controlled by parameter v) under the influence of forces $f(v)$ which are related to the evolving medium model (in our case the image and its derivatives). The energy functionals $E(v)$ describing this model are Spline functions with controlled continuity (Terzopoulos, 1986). The Lagrangian equations governing the physical object evolution are:

$$\partial / \partial t (\mu \partial v / \partial t) + \gamma \partial v / \partial t + \partial E(v) / \partial v = f(v) \tag{18}$$

The right most term of the left side of Equation 18 is the variational derivative of the elastic deformation model, usually known as internal energy. Using the deformation energy previously introduced in Equation 10, one can rewrite Equation18 as:

$$\partial / \partial t (\mu \partial v / \partial t) + \gamma \partial v / \partial t - (\alpha(s) v_s) + (\beta(s) v_{ss}) = F_{ext} + F_{gravitation} \tag{19}$$

where v_s and v_{ss} are the first and second derivatives of vector v with respect to s.

We derive the evolving scheme of active contours, from the differential scheme to the matricial scheme as first briefly introduced by the active contours creators (Kass, Witkin, & Terzopoulos, 1988). Equation 19 can be obtained through the Euler-Lagrange theorem by minimisation. Let ϕ be the function defined as:

$$\phi(s, v, v_s, v_{s^n}) = \int_0^l f(s, v, v_s, \ldots, v_{s^n}) ds \tag{20}$$

For v to minimise Equation 21, f must verify the following Euler equation:

$$\sum_{i=1}^{n-1} (-1)^i \partial^i / \partial s^i (\partial f / \partial v_{s^i}) = 0 \tag{21}$$

where v_{s^i} represents the ith derivative of v with respect to s ($v_{s^i} = \partial^i v / \partial s^i$). The active contour's energy functional integrates derivatives of v up to order 2:

$$-\partial / \partial s (\alpha (\partial v'^2 / \partial v')) + \partial^2 / \partial s^2 (\beta (\partial v''^2 / \partial v'') + \partial E_{ext} / \partial v = 0 \tag{22}$$

The Euler-Lagrange variational formulation only provides the solution to the static problem. We will first derive the static problem. The above equation transforms into:

$$-(\alpha(s) v_s(s)) + (\beta(s) v_{ss}(s)) = F_{ext}(v(s)) \tag{23}$$

The active contour's internal parameters $\alpha(s)$ and $\beta(s)$, are supposed to be able to vary along the curvilinear abscissa s and through time. From now on, $\alpha(s)$ and $\beta(s)$ will refer to varying coefficients while α and β will refer to constant parameters. Equation 23 transforms into:

$$-\alpha(s) v^{(2)}(s) - \alpha'(s) v'(s) + \beta(s) v^{(4)}(s) + \beta^{(2)}(s) v^{(2)}(s) + 2\beta'(s) v^{(3)}(s) = F_{ext}(v(s)) \tag{24}$$

For parameters α and β constant, equation 24 transforms into the classic elliptical differential equation (Kass, Witkin, & Terzopoulos, 1988) characterising the active contour's behaviour:

$$-\alpha v''(s) + \beta v^{(4)}(s) \quad = \quad F_{ext}(v(s))$$

(25)

Note that when there is no influence from external forces the differential equation can be directly solved (Cohen, 1992). If $\beta = 0$, $v(s) = as + b$, which is the equation of a line. If $\alpha = 0$, $v(s) = ae^{-\delta s} + be^{\delta s}$ which is the parametric equation of a spline. When there is no external force applied, it can be seen experimentally that active contours slowly shrink to a unique point as expected by considering their associated energy minimisation principles (Chassery & Elomary, 1993).

Numerical Implementation

The above differential equations are directly resolved only when there are no external forces to account for. A discretisation scheme is necessary to transform the elliptic differential equations system into a linear matricial system.

Finite Difference Discretisation Scheme

Considering a constant sampling step h between consecutive points along a given curve, the curve derivatives can be written as:

$$v'(ih) = \frac{v(ih) - v((i-1)h)}{h}$$
$$v''(ih) = \frac{v((i+1)h) - 2v(ih) + v((i-1)h)}{h^2}$$
$$\tilde{\beta}_i = \beta(ih)$$

(26)

$$\tilde{\alpha}_i = \alpha(ih)$$

Assuming that the following simplifications apply for all i:
$$v_i^{(n)} = v^{(n)}(ih) = \frac{\partial v^n}{\partial s^n}(ih)$$

(27)

Considering first the variable structural functions $\alpha(s)$ and $\beta(s)$:

$$\frac{\partial \beta}{\partial s}(i) \quad = \quad (\tilde{\beta}_i - \tilde{\beta}_{i-1})/h$$

$$\frac{\partial^2 \beta}{\partial s^2}(i) \quad = \quad (\tilde{\beta}_{i+1} - 2\tilde{\beta}_i + \tilde{\beta}_{i-1})/h^2$$

(28)

Using equation 23 and applying a finite difference discretisation scheme, one obtains:

$$(\widetilde{\beta}_{i-1} / h^4)v_{i-2}$$
$$+(-\widetilde{\alpha}_i / h^2 - 2\widetilde{\beta}_{i-1} / h^4 - 2\widetilde{\beta}_i / h^4)v_{i-1}$$
$$+(\widetilde{\alpha}_i / h^2 + \widetilde{\alpha}_{i+1} / h^2 + \widetilde{\beta}_{i-1} / h^4 + 4\widetilde{\beta}_i / h^4 + \widetilde{\beta}_{i+1} / h^4)v_i$$
$$+(-\widetilde{\alpha}_{i+1} / h^2 - 2\widetilde{\beta}_i / h^4 - 2\widetilde{\beta}_{i+1} / h^4)v_{i+1}$$
$$+(\widetilde{\beta}_{i+1} / h^4)v_{i+2}$$
$$= F_{ext}(v_i) \tag{29}$$

Introducing $\alpha_i = \widetilde{\alpha}_i / h^2$ and $\beta_i = \widetilde{\beta}_i / h^4$

$$\beta_{i-1}v_{i-2}$$
$$-(\alpha_i + 2\beta_{i-1} + 2\beta_i)v_{i-1}$$
$$+(\alpha_i + \alpha_{i+1} + \beta_{i-1} + 4\beta_i + \beta_{i+1})v_i$$
$$-(\alpha_{i+1} + 2\beta_i + 2\beta_{i+1})v_{i+1} + \beta_{i+1}v_{i+2}$$
$$= F_{ext}(v_i) \tag{30}$$

Constant Coefficients

While there are equations (Cohen L.D., 1992) allowing variable constraint coefficients $\alpha(s)$ and $\beta(s)$ for each control point of the snake, it has not been shown yet how they may improve convergence. In most published work, active contours' conformal parameters α and β are spatially constant. Equations 23 and 30 demonstrate that rigidity and curvature terms (e.g. involving α and β) can be regrouped in a unique matrix. Using Equation 30 for constant coefficients and with i varying from 0 to $N-1$, the static active contour linear equations are given by:

$$\beta v_{i-2} - (\alpha + 4\beta)v_{i-1} + (2\alpha + 6\beta)v_i \ (\alpha + 4\beta)v_{i+1} + \beta)v_{i+2} = F_{ext}(v_i) \tag{31}$$

which can be written in matricial form as:

$$AV = F_{ext} \tag{32}$$

A, is known as the rigidity matrix of the active contours, referring to their elastic properties. V is the snake control points (or snaxels) vector and F_{ext} represents the external forces vector:

$$V = \begin{pmatrix} v_0 \\ v_1 \\ \vdots \\ v_i \\ \vdots \\ v_{N-1} \end{pmatrix}, \boldsymbol{F}_{ext} \begin{pmatrix} f_{ext}(v_0) \\ f_{ext}(v_1) \\ \vdots \\ f_{ext}(v_i) \\ \vdots \\ f_{ext}(v_{N-1}) \end{pmatrix} \tag{33}$$

Closed Snake

In the case of a closed form, $v(N) = v(0)$ up to $v^i(N) = v^i(0)$, for all i integer up to N. A takes the form of a symmetric Toeplitz matrix of band width 5 (or quasi-pentadiagonal):

$$A = \begin{pmatrix}
2\alpha+6\beta & -\alpha-4\beta & \beta & 0 & \cdots & 0 & \beta & -\alpha-4\beta \\
-\alpha-4\beta & 2\alpha+6\beta & -\alpha-4\beta & \beta & 0 & \cdots & 0 & \beta \\
\beta & -\alpha-4\beta & 2\alpha+6\beta & -\alpha-4\beta & \beta & 0 & \cdots & 0 \\
0 & \ddots & \ddots & \ddots & \ddots & \ddots & \ddots & \vdots \\
\vdots & \ddots & \ddots & \ddots & \ddots & \ddots & \ddots & 0 \\
0 & \cdots & 0 & \beta & -\alpha-4\beta & 2\alpha+6\beta & -\alpha-4\beta & \beta \\
\beta & 0 & \cdots & 0 & \beta & -\alpha-4\beta & 2\alpha+6\beta & -\alpha-4\beta \\
-\alpha-4\beta & \beta & 0 & \cdots & 0 & \beta & -\alpha-4\beta & 2\alpha+6\beta
\end{pmatrix}$$

Open Snakes with Fixed Extremities

Here extremity points V(0) and V(N-1) are fixed (e.g. both spatially and through time). Matrix A is now of dimension $(N-2)$. Starting again from Equation (30) one can define (Berger, 1991) the curve derivatives in v(1) and v(N-1). The active contours are now described through the matricial system $AV = F + V_{fix}$ with:

$$A = \begin{pmatrix}
2\alpha+5\beta & -\alpha-4\beta & \beta & 0 & \cdots & \cdots & \cdots & 0 \\
-\alpha-4\beta & 2\alpha+6\beta & -\alpha-4\beta & \beta & 0 & \cdots & \cdots & \vdots \\
\beta & -\alpha-4\beta & 2\alpha+6\beta & -\alpha-4\beta & \beta & 0 & \cdots & \vdots \\
0 & \ddots & \ddots & \ddots & \ddots & \ddots & \ddots & \vdots \\
\vdots & \ddots & \ddots & \ddots & \ddots & \ddots & \ddots & 0 \\
\vdots & \cdots & 0 & \beta & -\alpha-4\beta & 2\alpha+6\beta & -\alpha-4\beta & \beta \\
\vdots & \cdots & \cdots & 0 & \beta & -\alpha-4\beta & 2\alpha+6\beta & -\alpha-4\beta \\
0 & \cdots & \cdots & \cdots & 0 & \beta & -\alpha-4\beta & 2\alpha+5\beta
\end{pmatrix}$$

The vector V_{fix} integrates the relations between the fixed points ($v(0)$ and $v(N-1)$), and their two closed neighbours ($v(1)$ and $v(N-2)$) in the computation of first and second order derivatives:

$$V_{fix} = \begin{bmatrix} (\alpha + 2\beta)v(0) \\ -\beta v(0) \\ 0 \\ \vdots \\ \vdots \\ 0 \\ -\beta v(N-1) \\ (\alpha + 2\beta)v(N-1) \end{bmatrix}$$

(34)

Comparing open and closed snake rigidity matrices, one sees that a discontinuity in curvature or tension on a single point leads to the modification of six or nine matrix coefficients respectively, irrespective of its size.

Dynamic Scheme

For closed snakes, the rigidity matrix is ill-conditioned (Berger, 1991) and cannot be inverted. A minimization process of the gradient descent type is introduced via a first order temporal term and associated parameter. The latter controls the temporal evolution step of the active contours. While a constant is often chosen it may be set variable; larger in areas with no gradient information, smaller when reaching regions with contours points (Fua & Lecler, 1990).

Recalling Equation 18, the differential equation presented in Equation 19 can be transformed into the following dynamic matricial scheme:

$$\mu \frac{d^2 V}{dt^2} + \gamma \frac{dV}{dt} + AV(t) = F(V(t-1))$$

(35)

where τ is the snake evolution temporal step ($\gamma = 1/\tau$). μ is the system mass previously introduced. For both coefficient constant using backward temporal discrete schemes, the above equation transforms into:

$$\mu(V(t) - 2V(t-1) + V(t-2)) + V(t) - V(t-1)\tau + AV(t) = F(V(t-1))$$

(36)

and:

$$V(t) = (A + (\gamma + \mu)I)^{-1}\big((\gamma + 2\mu)V(t-1) - \mu V(t-2) + F(V(t-1))\big) \tag{37}$$

The classic snake evolution formula is obtained for a zero mass system:

$$V(t) \;=\; (A + \gamma I)^{-1}(\gamma V(t-1) + F(V(t-1))) \tag{38}$$

An explicit formulation of the above equation is sometimes applied to avoid inverting the dynamic rigidity matrix $((A + \gamma I))$:

$$V(t) \;=\; (A - \gamma I)(\gamma V(t-1) + F(V(t-1))) \tag{39}$$

However this scheme has been shown to be unstable (Leymarie & Levine, 1993). A new direct inversion of the dynamic rigidity matrix is fully derived in Appendix A.

Snake Performance

The active contour's behaviour is strongly dependent on the parameters α, β and γ. Information about these coefficients' behaviour is often overlooked in the available bibliography. Understanding this behaviour is useful in properly calibrating the active contour's evolution process. Through these coefficients, the matricial system behaviour depends on its conditioning and eigenvalues.

Eigenvalues

All eigenvalues must be positive to avoid large oscillations during convergence as demonstrated by (Berger, 1991). Eigenvalues for A are given as:

$$\lambda_k \;=\; \frac{4}{h^4}\sin^2\frac{k\pi}{N}\left(4\beta \sin^2\frac{k\pi}{N} + h^2\alpha\right) \tag{40}$$

For all k between 0 and N-1, It can be seen that one eigenvalue is equal to zero while the others have values between 0 and $4(4\beta + h^2\alpha)$. This demonstrates that A is ill-conditioned, i.e. the static problem is unstable and requires the introduction of a dynamic scheme with associated parameter γ. Eigenvalues for $M = (I + A\gamma)^{-1}$ are:

$$\mu_k \;=\; \frac{1}{1 + \dfrac{\lambda_k}{\gamma}} \tag{41}$$

γ and λ_k set the dynamic rigidity matrix eigenvalues. They will directly influence the conditioning of the matricial system (Berger, 1991) as well as the dynamic behaviour of the active contours.

Setting γ

$1/\gamma$ controls the gradient descent process. It can vary during the active contours' temporal evolution to accelerate or slow down their final convergence. Fua & Leclerc (1990) linked γ to the variation of the gradient information in the vicinity of the active contour's control points. In practise, after every few iterations (approximately 10), γ is updated through:

$$\gamma = \frac{\sqrt{2N}}{\Delta} \left| \frac{\partial E}{\partial v} \right|$$

(42)

where Δ is the initial spatial step value and E the snake total energy. An increase in the snake total energy over the course of p iterations translates in an increase of γ, hence a decrease of τ, snake temporal evolution. The snake evolution is slowed on the presence of high gradient values (e.g. likely contour points). If the active contours progress through an image area with weak gradients, using Equation 42 γ decreases over time thus increasing the snake's evolution time step.

While this method offers a better control of the snake evolution, it is not able to assess its "satisfactory" convergence as it generates snakes oscillations when close to convergence. A specific convergence indicator, further detailed below, is usually required.

Active Contours Experimental Implementation

Three major problems are classically encountered when using snakes. They are: initialization, parameter estimation, and convergence. The initialization is often performed manually using close approximations to the desired features to provide fast convergence.

The snake evolution depends on its parameter values, which are usually evaluated heuristically. The lip segmentation step and mouth corner detection step provide case-specific (e.g. mouth closed or open) active contour initialisation points close to the desired lip contours. Irrespective of semantic information, both inner and outer active contours have fixed control points at the mouth corners. The outer active contour is always a closed form

When the mouth is closed, the inner active contour is initialised as a single line open snake. When the mouth is open the inner active contour is initialised as a closed form.

Hue Based Statistics for Inner and Outer Snake Convergence

The major problems encountered when extracting lip contours centre around detection of the outer-lower lip and inner lip contours. The outer-upper lip contour is always well detected thanks to a clear edge and texture transition between the skin and the upper-lip. Usually, outside the lip corner area (where shadows complicate the image), the hue, derived from the HS space, is a good estimator of the lip region. A lip colour statistic can be derived from the study of the pixels situated:

- on a few lines under the upper-outer lip contour (as the upper lip is thin).
- on 2/3 of the columns under the lip boundary (to avoid the colourless corners area).

The mean (m_{lip}) and variance (σ_{lip}) of the hue over the previously defined area is computed. Assuming the distribution of hue values over the lip area follows a Gaussian law, the probability of a pixel $p(x, y)$ belonging to the lip area is given by $P_{m\sigma}(p(x, y)) \geq \eta$ with:

$$P_{m,\sigma}(p(x,y)) = \frac{1}{\sqrt{2}\sigma}\exp\left(\frac{-\left(p(x,y) - m_{lip}\right)^2}{2\sigma^2}\right) \tag{43}$$

Equilibrium is reached when a criterion, based either on quadratic distance of consecutive re-sampled snake curves or on gradient values inside a narrow band along the active contour, is satisfied. This can be combined with the re-initialisation criterion developed in Equation 43 to ensure that the active contours converge towards the desired features. Figure 8 shows a case-study where the active contours were intentionally initialised inside the lips. Upon convergence, the above criterion (Equation 43) separates lip and non-lip pixels (Figure 8 middle). A good convergence will be achieved when the contours lie in or near transitions between lip and non-lip labelled pixels. A simple majority count of the central snake points is performed. If convergence is not ensured, the inner active contour points are re-initialised on the first pixels marked as "not belonging to the lip region", encountered inwards from the outer active contours. The process is repeated until convergence is reached.

RESULTS

Our algorithm was tested on a database designed to cover a wide range of mouth shapes and deformations including verbal and non-verbal lip movements. Speakers were asked to utter sentences including French VCVCV stimuli ("c'est pas VCVCV") where $V \in \{a, i, y\}$ and $C \in \{b, v, r, l, z\}$) under varying illumination conditions. The data was gathered from several fixed or head-mounted video acquisition systems. The database contains approximately 1200 colour (*RGB*, 8 bits/pixel/colour) images (stills or short videos) of 17 different subjects (15 males and 2 females). Video-sequences (up to 150 frames or 6 seconds) were gathered from two different generations of head-mounted cameras with attached LED lighting (Bailly et al., 2000). Sequences were acquired in QCIF and CIF format video. An additional set of short sequences (typically 50 consecutive frames at 25fps) and still-frames displaying full face regions with mouths and lips in various states of extreme mouth movement and sidewise motion of the jaw were acquired with a fixed Pan-tilt-zoom Sony EVi-D70 video camera (resolution 768 by 494 pixels). The head-mounted video sequences feature a 200 by 100 pixel close-up view of the mouth region. They are mostly used to demonstrate the validity of our accurate lip contour extraction. The shorter video-sequences and stills display full faces and demonstrate the validity of our face to mouth region extraction framework. An additional set of sequences, referred to as the ATR recording set (Reveret, 1999), were acquired for benchmarking. A specific setup (NTSC-RGB input from a Tri CCD camera and two 100W light sources) was used to acquire the same VCVCV stimuli sequences from one subject. For bench-marking, a speech processing expert manually delineated the inner and outer lip contours of the images corresponding to the VCVCV stimuli. Video-sequences of the database can be obtained

Figure 8. Outer snake re-initialisation. From left to right: snake initialisation, unsatisfactory convergence, lips/non-lips labelling; re-initialisation, final convergence

freely by emailing the second author of this chapter.

The results presented here, include various speakers with different lip shapes and pilosity (Figure 9) showing a closed or open mouth. Some of the images have been acquired via a camera-mounted with respect to the head (Figure 10, Figure 11, Figure 12), others have been obtained with the widely used Sony EVI-D100 camera or unspecified web-cameras.

Figure 9 demonstrates the robustness of our hierarchical scheme. Such images do not respect any of the heuristics (whether it be minimal or maximal values, etc...) usually associated with face feature extraction methods (Radeva et al., 1995; Brunelli & Poggio, 1995; Goecke et al., 2007). Our lip segmentation step localises the mouth region. From there the search for mouth corners and the initial points for active contours is greatly simplified.

Figure 10 shows the ability of our method to extract asymmetric contours. Note that the asymmetric opening of the mouth is a typical feature encountered with most speakers. The lower-outer lip contours for the second image is definitely out of position. This is due to very fast jaw opening. The interlaced frames (odd-even lines) display a different position resulting in two edge lines for the lower lip contour. A frame rate above 60fps would be necessary to catch such fast lip opening movements.

Figure 9. Lip contours extracted from a user with beard displaying horizontal sidewise jaw movements

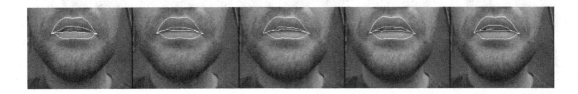

Figure 11 shows a complete video sequence of lips opening and closing. The lips' contours are well tracked in all images. Note that in the last inner lip contours detected, the open snake had some difficulties converging and does not show a perfectly correct mouth line. Increasing both α and β for inner active contours when the mouth is closed would probably solve this problem by further binding the points and restricting changes in curvature.

Figure 12 shows some of the problems that may be encountered when mouth corners are erroneously detected away from their actual positions. The binding forces pull the active contours in such a way that weak edges (often describing the lip-skin boundaries close to the commissures) are not able to retain active contours points. This can be solved by allowing the active contours to move from the mouth corners. The closed form outer active contours with fixed $V(0)$ and $V(N/2)$ are not attached directly to the mouth corners but to springs anchored to the mouth corners.

Figure 13 shows extracted lip contours on two of the APR benchmark images acquired under asymmetric lighting conditions. The contours have been delineated by a speech processing expert for the sake of comparison. Although the maximum vertical distance between both (manually delineated and obtained with our algorithm) contours never exceed five pixels, it was found inadequate for speech-from-image applications by speech processing experts. Close scrutiny of the lip contours manually extracted by the speech processing expert reveals that the extracted inner contours rely more on inside knowledge of the spoken sequence than image processing information such as edges, clustered areas, and region consistency. It does not however invalidate the potential of lip contours extraction for all other multi-media applications.

A subset of 300 images containing meaningful lip movements were selected for performance testing. The subset included sequences with poorly illuminated lip regions to test the algorithm in adverse conditions. Step one was able to locate the mouth area in 85% of the images. The algorithm failed when the scene was very poorly illuminated. Step two extracted the mouth corners in 97% of the images successfully segmented in step one. Corners were missed in images with very poor illumination. Step three extracted satisfactory outer active contours in most cases (see Table 1, 2nd colum, third row). In-

Figure 10. Lip contours extraction from seven consecutive frames. Top: outer lip contour initialisation points; Middle: inner lip contour initialisation points; Bottom: final lip contours

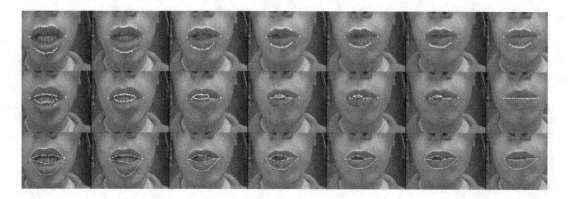

Figure 11. Final lip contours on consecutives images extracted from a video sequence

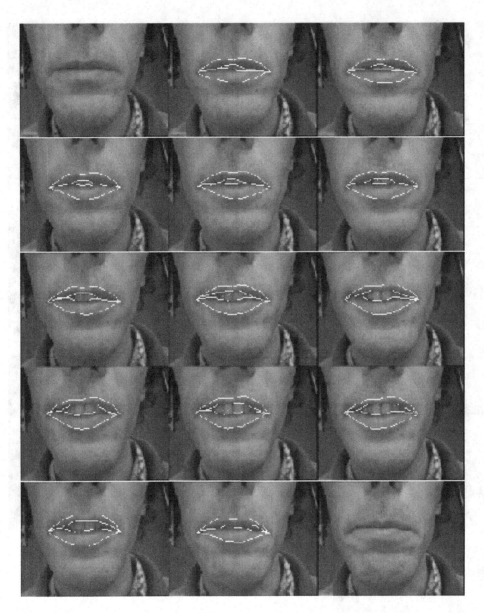

ner contours were always detected when the mouth was closed. The detection of inner lip contours was complicated where tongue and gum tissue appeared in the image, and under very poor illumination. Overall, the framework performance over a range of subjects is satisfactory.

Figure 12. Head mounted consecutive frames and extracted lip contours

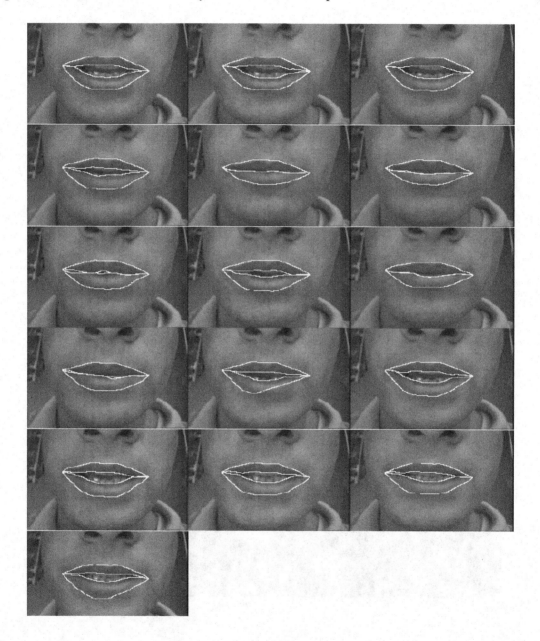

An accuracy test was performed on a subset of the manually benchmarked APR video sequences. The average contour point location error (between extracted and benchmarked lip contours) was 0.53 pixels with a standard deviation of 0.08 for outer lip contours. Average error was computed at 0.88 pixels

Figure 13. Lip contours extracted by our algorithm and manually delineated by a speech processing expert (Reveret, 1999). From left to right: Mouth area under asymmetric illumination; lip contours delineated by the expert; lip contours extracted by our algorithm; ground truth and extracted contours superimposed

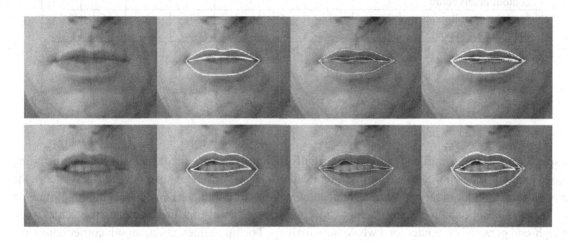

(stddev at 0.11) for inner lip contours. No error of more than seven pixels was recorded with more than 85% of the extracted lip contours located less than 2 pixels away from the benchmark pixels.

CONCLUSIONS

In this chapter, the theory behind the logarithmic hue-like colour space has been briefly developed. A hierarchical spatiotemporal colour segmentation algorithm integrating hue and motion information has been successfully applied to several video sequences with no specific model of the speaker and variable illumination conditions. Mouth commissures of the lips are detected by combining corner detectors and between-lips lines of minima. Some improvements of active contours theory, applied to lip contour extraction, have enhanced the robustness of the results. Comparison between the results expected by

Table 1. Closed/Open lips convergence performance

	Outer contour	Inner contour	
Lip status	Open/Closed	Closed	Open
Successful convergence	93%	100%	68%

Table 2. Distance errors between final active contours and contours delineated by the expert

Error in pixels	0	1	2	3	4	5	6	>6
% of the overall outer contour pixels count	80.0	10.4	1.6	1.3	1.2	1.1	4.2	0
% of the overall inner contour pixels count	72	7	6	3	3	2	6	0

a speech processing expert and our results partially demonstrated the inadequacy of image processing based methods for audio-visual recognition applications. However, it does not reduce the relevance of the proposed method for other applications in need of lip contour parameters such as 3D mouth animation for face synthesis and low-bit rate coding videoconferencing. Real-time processing can be achieved on a high-end personal computer for a whole face analysis. The lip segmentation, mouth corner detection, and active contour evolution steps are processed at 15 frames per second. We still have difficulty accurately detecting inner lip contours when gum and tongue appear, as these two features have the same hue, motion, and texture information as the lips. This is probably due to the fact that inner lip contours have no physical existence but are determined by the appearance of the lips when speaking. The application developed in this book's chapter (Gastelum et al., 2008) is an attempt at accurately animating lips without a need for inner lip contours detection.

FUTURE DIRECTIONS

The current algorithm has excellent potential for 3D lip tracking which is of increasing importance in a wide range of multi-media applications. Reducing the search region to the near vicinity of the lips makes stereo matching a potential solution for 3D lip contours extraction. This is even true for real time applications with passive illumination, as the matching algorithm performs well for face features (Leclercq, Liu, Woodward, & Delmas, 2004). After extensive studies of webcam based stereovision systems we concluded that satisfactory rectification could not be achieved because of the poor/inconsistent quality of the equipment. We are currently looking at higher quality firewire cameras and external triggering for synchronisation of the video streams. Custom made stereo systems are available on the market but they are both too expensive for widespread applications and currently provide inadequate resolution for accurate results on the important parts of the face. While still in development, preliminary results on direct extraction of lip contours from textured 3D face surfaces using a new technique inspired by Geodesic Active Contours for surfaces algorithm (Krueger, Delmas, & Gimel'farb, 2007) show promising results. We believe the future of visual lip tracking lies with high resolution 3D data.

REFERENCES

Akimoto, T., Suenaga, Y., & Wallace, R. (1993). Automatic creation of 3D facial models. *Computer Graphics and Applications, 13*(5), 16-22.

Abry, C., & Lallouache, T. (1991). Audibility and Stability of Articulatory Movements: Deciphering two experiments on anticipatory rounding in French. *Proceedings of the 12th International Congress of Phonetic Sciences, 1,* 220-225. Aix-en-Provence, France.

Azarbayejani, A., Starner, T., Horowitz, B., & Pentland, A. (1993). Visually controlled graphics. *IEEE Transactions on Pattern Analysis and Machine Intelligence, 15*(6), 602-605.

Bailly, G., Reveret, L., Borel, P., Badin, P. (2000, Sept.). *Hearing by eyes thanks to the ``labiophone'': exchanging speech movements.* Presented at the COST254 workshop: Friendly Exchanging through the Net, Bordeaux, France.

Basu, S., Oliver, N., & Pentland, A. (1998). 3D modeling of human lip motions. *Proceedings of the International Conference on Computer Vision,* (pp. 337-343). Bombay, India: Narosa Publishing House.

Berger, M. O. (1991). *Active contours: modelisation, behaviour, convergence* (in French). Unpublished Doctoral dissertation, National Polytechnic Institute of Lorraine.

Bossart, P. L., David, D., Dinten, J. M., & Chassery, J. M. (1997). Détection de contours réguliers dans des images bruitées et texturées (in french). *Traitement du Signal, 14*(2), 209-225.

Bregler, C., & Konig, Y. (1994). Eigenlips for robust speech recognition. *Proceedings of the International Conference on Acoustics, Speech and Signal Processing,* (pp. 669-672). Adelaide, Australia: IEEE Press.

Chassery, J-M., & Elomary, Y. (1993). Cooperation between active contours and multi-resolution for edge-based segmentation. *Proceedings of the IMDSP Conference,* (pp. 206-207). Cannes, France: IEEE Press.

Chen, T., & Rao, R. R. (1998). Audio-visual integration in multimodal communication. *Special Issue on Multimedia Signal Processing. IEEE Proceedings, 86*(5), 837-852.

Cohen, I. (1992). *Modèles déformables 2-D et 3-D: Application à la segmentation d'images médicales (in french).* Unpublished doctoral dissertation, University Paris IX-Dauphine.

Cohen, L. D. (1990). *Etude des modèles de contours actifs et d'autres techniques de traitement d'images.* Unpublished doctoral disseertation, University of Paris-sud-Orsay.

Cohen, L. D., & Cohen, I. (1993). Finite element methods for active contour models and balloons for 2-D and 3-D images. *IEEE Transactions on Pattern Analysis and Machine Intelligence, 15*(11), 1131-1147.

Cohen, L. D., & Gorre, A. (1995, September). *On the convexity of the active contour energy.* Presented at the GRETSI symposium on Signal and Image Processing, Juan-les-Pins, France.

Delmas, P., Coulon, P. Y., Fristot, V. (1999). Automatic snakes for robust lip boundaries extraction. *Proceedings of the international conference on acoustics, speech, and signal processing, 6,* 3069-3072. Phoenix, Az., USA: IEEE Press.

Delmas, P., Eveno, N., & Lievin, M. (2002). Towards Robust Lip Tracking. *Proceedings of the International Conference in Pattern Recognition, 2*, 528-531. Quebec-city, Canada: IEEE Press.

Eisert, P., & Girod, B. (1998). Analyzing facial expressions for virtual conferencing. *Animating Virtual Humans, 18*(5), 70-78.

Fu, Y., Erdem, A. T., & Tekalp, A. M. (1998). Occlusion adaptive motion snake. *Proceedings of the International Conference on Image Processing, 3*, 633-637. Chicago, Ill., USA: IEEE Press.

Fua, P., & Brechbühler, C. (1996). Imposing hard constraints on soft snakes. *Proceedings of the European Conference on Computer Vision*, (LNCS 1064, pp. 495-506). Cambridge, UK: Springer.

Fua, P., & Leclerc, Y. G. (1990). Model driven edge detection. *Machine Vision and Applications, 3*, 1-11.

Geman, S., & Geman, D. (1984). Stochastic relaxation, Gibbs distributions and the Bayesian restoration of images. *IEEE Transactions on Pattern Analysis Machine Intelligence, 6*(6), 721-741.

Goldschen, A. J., Garcia, O. N., & Petajan, E. (1994). Continuous optical automatic speech recognition by lipreading. *Proceedings of the 28th Annual Asilomar Conference on Signals Systems and Computers, 1*, 572-577. Pacific Grove, Cal., USA: IEEE Press.

Gratch, J., Wang, N., Okhmatovskaia, A., Lamothe, F., Morales, M., Van der Werf, R. J., & Morency, L. P. (2007). Can Virtual Humans Be More Engaging Than Real Ones?. *Proceedings of the Human-Computer Interaction Conference*, (LNCS 4552, pp. 286-297). Beijing, China: Springer.

Guiard-Marigny, T., Tsingos, N., Adjoudani, A., Benoît, C., & Gascuel, M.P. (1996) 3D Models of the Lips For Realistic Speech Animation. In J.A. Jacko (Ed.), *Proceedings of Computer Animation*, (pp. 80-89). Geneva, Switzerland: IEEE Press.

Hadamard, J. (1902): Sur les problèmes aux dérivées partielles et leur signification physique (in french). *Princeton University Bulletin*, 49-52.

Hennecke, M., Prasad, K., & Stork, D. (1996). Automatic speech recognition system using acoustic and visual signals. *Proceedings of ASILOMAR-29*, (pp. 1214-1218). Pacific Grove, Cal., USA: IEEE Press.

Ip, H. H. S., & Yu, R.P.K. (1996). Recursive splitting of active contours in multiple clump segmentation. *Electronics Letters, 32*(17), 1564-1566.

Krueger, M., Delmas, P., & Gimel'farb, G. (2007). Towards Feature Extraction on Implicit Surfaces using Geodesic Active Contours. *In M. Cree (Ed.), Proceedings of the Image and Vision Computing New Zealand Conference*, (pp. 294-299). Hamilton, New Zealand: Waikato University Press.

Leclercq, P., Liu, J., Woodward, A., & Delmas, P. (2004). Which Stereo Matching Algorithm for Accurate 3D Face Creation?. In R. Klette & J. Zunic (Eds), *Proceedings of the International Workshop in Combinatorial Image Analysis*, (LNCS 3322, pp. 690-704). Auckland, New Zealand: Springer.

Li, S. Z. (1995). On discontinuity-adaptive smoothness priors in computer vision. *IEEE Transactions on Pattern Analysis and Machine Intelligence, 17*(6), 576-586.

Lievin, M. & Luthon, F. (1998) Lip features automatic extraction. *Proceedings of the International Conference on Image Processing*, (pp. 168-172). Chicago, Ill., USA: IEEE Press.

Leroy B., Herlin I. L., & Cohen L. D. (1996). Face identification by deformation measure. *Proceedings of the International Conference on Pattern Recognition*, *3*, 633-637. Vienna, Austria: IEEE Press.

Luettin, J., Thacker, N. A., & Beet, S. W. (1996). Visual speech recognition using Active Shape Models and hidden Markov models. *Proceedings of the International Conference on Acoustics Speech and Signal Processing*, (pp. 817-820). Atlanta, Ga., USA: IEEE Press.

Pentland, A., & Mase, K. (1989). *Lip reading: Automatic visual recognition of spoken words* (Tech. Rep. 117). Cambridge, Mass., USA: MIT, Media Lab.

Petajan, E.D. (1985). An architecture for automatic lipreading to enhance speech recognition. *Proceedings of the International Conference on Computer Vision and Pattern Recognition*, (pp 40-47). San Francisco, Cal., USA: IEEE Press.

Petajan, E. D., Bischoff, B., Bodoff, D., & Brooke, N. M. (1988). An improved automatic lipreading system to enhance speech recognition. *Proceedings of the Computer/Human Interaction Conference*, (pp 19-25). Washington DC, USA: ACM Press.

Petajan, E. D., & Graf, H. P. (1996). Robust face feature analysis for automatic speachreading and character animation. *Proceedings of the International Conference on Automatic Face and Gesture Recognition*, (pp 357-362). Killington, Ve., USA: IEEE Press.

Radeva, P., Serrat, J., & Marti, J. (1995). A snake for model-based segmentation. *Proceedings of the Fifth International Conference on Computer Vision*, (pp 816-821). Cambridge, Mass., USA: IEEE Press.

Reveret, L. (1999). *Design and evaluation of a video tracking system of lip motion in speech production* (in french). Unpublished doctoral dissertation, National Polytechnic Institute of Grenoble, France.

Sundaramoorthi, G., Yezzi, A., Mennucci, A. (2007). Sobolev Active Contours. *International Journal of Computer Vision*, *73*(3), 345-366.

Silsbee, S. L. (1994). Sensory integration in audiovisual automatic speech recognition. *Proceedings of the 28th Annual Asilomar Conference on Signals Systems and Computers*, *1*, 561-565. Pacific Grove, Cal., USA: IEEE Press.

Stegmann, M. B. (2000). *Active Appearance Models: Theory, Extensions and Cases* (Tech. Rep.). Informatics and Mathematical Modelling, Technical University of Denmark.

Stork, D., & Hennecke, M. (1996). Speechreading by Humans and Machines, *NATO ASI Series F: Computer and System Sciences*, *150*. Springer-Verlag, Berlin.

Terzopoulos, D. (1986) Image analysis using multi-grid relaxation methods. *IEEE Transactions on Pattern Analysis and Machine Intelligence*, *8*(2), 129-139.

Terzopoulos, D., Witkin, A., & Kass, M. (1988). Constraints on deformable models: Recovering 3D shape and non-rigid motion. *Artificial Intelligence*, *36*, 91-123.

Tikhonov, A., & Arsenine, V. (1974). *Méthodes de résolution de problèmes mal poses (in french)*. MIR Eds.

Valente, S., & Dugelay, J. L. (2000). Face tracking and realistic animations for telecommunicant clones. *IEEE Multimedia Magazine, 7*(1), 34-43.

Wang, S.-L., Lau, W.-H., Liew, A.W.-C., Leung, S.-H. (2007). Robust lip region segmentation for lip images with complex background. *Pattern Recognition, 40*, 3481-3491.

Xie, L., Cai, X-L., & Zhao, R-C. (2004). A robust hierarchical lip tracking approach for lipreading and audio visual speech recognition. *Proceedings of the International Conference on Machine Learning and Cybernetics, 6*, 3620-3624. Shanghai, China: IEEE Press.

Yuille, A.L., Hallinan, P.W., & Cohen, D.S. (1992). Feature extraction from faces using deformable templates. *International Journal of Computer Vision, 8*(2), 99-111.

Zhang, L. (1997). Tracking a face for knowledge-based coding of videophone sequences. *Signal Processing: Image Communication, 10*, 93-114.

ADDITIONAL READING

Benson, A., & D.J. Evans, D.J. (1977). A normalized algorithm for the solution of positive definite symmetric quindiagonal systems of linear equations. *ACM Transations on Mathematical Software, 3*(1), 96-103.

Berger, M.O., & Mohr, R. (1990). Towards autonomy in active contours models. *Proceedings of the International Conference on Pattern Recognition,* (pp. 847-851). Atlantic City, NJ, USA: IEEE Press.

Berger, M.O., Mozelle, G., & Laprie, Y. (1995). Cooperation of active contours and optical flow for tongue tracking in X-ray motion pictures. In G. Borgefors (Eds.), *Proceedings of the Scandinavian Conference on Image Analysis,* (pp. 913-920). Uppsala, Sweden: SCAIA Press.

Black, M.J., Sapiro, G., Marimont, D.H. & Heeger, D. (1998). Robust anisotropic diffusion. *IEEE Transactions on Image Processing, 7*(3), 421-432.

Bradski, G.R. (1998). Computer vision face tracking for use in a perceptual user interface. *Intel Technology Journal Q2*, 1-15, 1998.

Bregler, C., & Omohundro, S. (1995). Nonlinear manifold learning for visual speech recognition. *Proceedings of the International Conference on Computer Vision,* (pp. 494-499). Cambridge, Mass., USA: MIT Press.

Brunelli, R., & Poggio, T. (1995). Face recognition: Features versus Templates. *IEEE Transactions on Pattern Analysis and Machine Intelligence, 15*(10), 1042-1052.

Caselles, V., Catte, F., Coll, T., & Dibos, F. (1993). A geometric model for active contours in image processing. *Numerische Mathematik, 66*, 1-31.

Caselles, V., Kimmel, R., & Sapiro, G. (1997). Geodesic active contours. *International Journal of Computer Vision*, 22(1), 61-79.

Cetintemel, G.D., & Burlina, P. (1998). On-the-fly snake construction from video. *Proceedings of the International Conference on Image Processing*, (vol.3, pp. 638-642). Chicago, Ill., USA: IEEE Press.

Chan, M., Chen, C.F., Barton, G., Delmas, P., Gimel'farb, G., Leclercq, P., & Fisher, T. (2003). A strategy for 3D face Analysis and Synthesis. In D. Bailey (Ed.), *Proceedings of the Image Vision Computing New Zealand*, (pp. 384-389), Palmerston North, New Zealand: Massey University Press.

Chan, T., & Vese, L. (2001). Active Contours without Edges. *IEEE Transactions on image processing*, 10(2), 233-277.

Cootes, T.F. Taylor, T.J., Cooper, D.H., & Graham, J. (1995). Active shape models: Their training and application. *Computer Vision and Image Understanding*, 61(1), 38-59.

Delmas, P., Woodward, A., & Leclercq, P. (2004). Can Stereo-matching algorithms accurately render face features?. In P. Bones (Ed.), *Proceedings of the Image and Vision Computing New Zealand Conference*, (pp. 29-34). Akaroa, New Zealand: Landcare Research Ltd. Press.

Deriche, R., & Giraudon, G. (1991). *Accurate corner detection: an analytical study*, (INRIA Research Report 1420). Institut National de Recherche en Informatique et Automatique, France.

Essa, I.A., & Pentland, A.P. (1995). Facial expression recognition using a dynamic model and motion energy. *Proceedings of the International Conference on Computer Vision*, (pp. 360-367). Cambridge, Mass., USA: MIT Press.

Goecke, R., Tran, Q.N., Millar, J.B., Zelinsky, A., & Robert-Ribes, J. (2000). Validation of an Automatic Lip-Tracking Algorithm and Design of a Database for Audio-Video Speech Processing. *Proceedings of the 8th Australian International Conference on Speech Science and Technology*, (pp. 92-97). Canberra, Australia: ASSTA Press.

Gunn, S.R., & Nixon, M.S. (1997). A robust snake implementation: A dual active contour. *IEEE Transactions on Pattern Analysis and Machine Intelligence,* 19(1), 63-67.

Hill, A., & Taylor, C.J. (1992). Model-based image interpretation using genetic algorithms. *Image and Vision Computing*, 10, 295-300.

Horbelt, S., & Dugelay, J.L. (1995). Active contours for lipreading - combining snakes with templates. *Proceedings of the GRETSI symposium on Signal and Image Processing*, (pp. 717-720). Juan Les Pins, France: GRETSI Press.

Horbelt, S. (1995). *Automatic lipreading on the basis of image sequences to support speech recognition*. Unpublished Diploma disertation, University Erlangen-Nuremberg.

Jourlin, M., & Pinoli, J-C. (1995). Image dynamic range enhancement and stabilization in the context of the logarithmic image processing model. *Signal Processing*, 41(2), 225-237.

Kass, M., Witkin, A., & Terzopoulos, D. (1988). Snakes: Active contours models. *International Journal of Computer Vision*, 321-331.

Kervrann, C., & Heitz, F. (1994). Robust tracking of stochastic deformable models in long image sequences. *Proceedings of the International Conference on Image Processing,* (pp. 88-92). Austin, TX, USA: IEEE Press.

Kervrann, C., & Heitz, F. (1999). Statistical deformable model-based segmentation of image motion. *IEEE Transactions on Pattern Analysis and Machine Intelligence,* 8(4), 583-588.

Kutulakos, K.N., & Seitz, S.M. (2000). A theory of shape by space carving. *International Journal of Computer Vision,* 38(3), 199-218.

Lanitis, A., Taylor, T.J., & Cootes, T.F. (1997). Automatic interpretation and coding of face images using flexible models. *IEEE Transactions on Pattern Analysis and Machine Intelligence,* 19(7), 743-755.

Larsen, O.V., Mikaelsen, F., & Gronkjaer, L.G. (1995). Tracking and segmenting dividing objects using multiple and dividing snakes. In G. Borgefors (Ed.), *Proceedings of the Scandinavian Conference on Image Analysis,* (pp. 921-929). Uppsala, Sweden: SCAIA Press.

Lee, W.S., Escher, M., Sannier, G., & Thalmann, N. (1999). Mpeg-4 compatible faces from orthogonal photos. *Proceedings of the International Conference on Computer Animation,* (pp.186-194). Geneva, Switzerland: IEEE Press.

Leymarie, F., & M.D. Levine, M.D. (1992). Simulating the grass-fire transform using an active contour model. *IEEE Transactions on Pattern Analysis and Machine Intelligence,* 14(1), 56-75.

Li, N., Dettmer, S., & Shah, M. (1995). *Lipreading Using Spatiotemporal Eigen Decomposition* (Tech. Rep. 95-13). Orlando, Florida: University of Central Florida, Computer Vision Lab.

Lievin, M., & Luthon, F. (2000). A hierarchical segmentation algorithm for face analysis. *Proceedings of the International Conference on Multimedia and Expo,* (vol. 2, pp. 1080-1088). New-York, NY, USA: IEEE Press.

Malladi, R., Sethian, J.A., & Vemuri, B.C. (1995). Shape modeling with front propagation: A level set approach. *IEEE Transactions on Pattern Analysis and Machine Intelligence,* 17(2), 158-175.

McInerney, T., & Terzopoulos, D. (1997). Medical image segmentation using topologically adaptable surfaces. *Proceedings of the CVRMed'97 Conference,* (LNCS 1205, pp. 1-10). Grenoble, France: Springer.

Mokhtarian, F., & Suomela, R. (1998). Robust image corner detection through curvature scale space. *IEEE Transactions on Pattern Analysis and Machine Intelligence,* 20(12), 1376-1381.

Noble, J.A. (1988). Finding corners. *Image and Vision Computing,* 6, 121-128.

Neuenschwander, W., Fua, P., Iverson, L., Szekely, G., & Kubler, O. (1997). Ziplock snakes. *International Journal of Computer Vision,* 25(3), 191-201.

Osher, S., & Sethian, J.A. (1988). Fronts propagating with curvature dependent speed: Algorithms based on Hamilton-Jacobi formulations. *Journal of Computational Physics,* 79, 12-49.

Parke, F.I., & Waters, K. (1996). *Computer Facial Animation,* A.K. Peters Press.

Petajan, E.D., & Graf, H. P. (1996). Robust face feature analysis for automatic speech-reading and character animation. *Proceedings of the International Conference on Automatic Face and Gesture Recognition,* (pp 357-362). Killington, VT, USA: IEEE Press.

Poon, C.S., & Braun, M. (1997). Image segmentation by a deformable contour model incorporating region analysis. *Physics in Medicine and Biology,* 42, 1833-1841.

Ranganath, S. (1995). Contour extraction from cardiac MRI studies using snakes. *IEEE Transactions on Medical Imaging,* 14(2), 328-338.

Ronfard, R. (1994). Region-based strategies for active contour models. *International Journal of Computer Vision,* 13(2), 229-251.

Sapiro, G. (1996). Vector (self) snakes: A geometric framework for colour, texture and multiscale image segmentation. *Proceedings of the International Conference on Image Processing,* (pp. 817-820). Lausanne, Switzerland: IEEE Press.

Sapiro, G. (1997). Color snakes. *Computer Vision and Image Understanding,* 68(2), 247-253.

Salkauskas, K. (1974). C1 splines for interpolation of rapidly varying data. *Rocky Moutain Journal of Mathematics,* 14(1), 239-250.

Scharcanski, J., & Venetsannopoulos, A.N. (1995). Colour image edge detection using directional operators. *Proceeding of the 1995 Workshop on Nonlinear Signal and Image Processing,* (pp. 511-514). Halkidiki, Greece: IEEE Press.

Smith, G.D., (1974). *Numerical Solution of Partial Differential Equations: Finite Difference Methods.* Oxford: Clarendon Press.

Staib, L.H., & Duncan, J.S. (1992). Boundary finding with parametrically deformable models. *IEEE Transactions on Pattern Analysis and Machine Intelligence,* 14(11), 1061-1075.

Tsang, P.W. & W.H. Tsang, W.H. (1996). Edge detection on object color. *Proceedings of the International Conference on Image Processing,* (pp. 1049-1052). Lausanne, Switzerland: IEEE Press.

Vogt, M. (1997). Interpreted multi-state lip models for audio-video speech recognition. *Proceedings of the Audio-Visual Speech Processing, Cognitive and Computational Approaches Workshop,* (pp. 125-128). Rhodes (Greece): ESCA Press.

Wolff, G.J., Prasad, K.V., Stork, D.G. & Hennecke, M. (1993). Lip-reading by neural networks: Visual pre-processing, learning and sensory integration. *Proceedings of the Neural Information Processing Systems Conference NIPS-6,* (pp. 1027-1034). Denver, CO, USA: Morgan Kaufmann Press.

Xiao, J., Baker, S., Matthews, I., & Kanade, T. (2004). Real-time Combined 2D+3D Active Appearance Models. *Proceedings of the IEEE International Conference on Computer Vision and Pattern Recognition,* (Vol. 2, pp. 535-542). Washington, DC, USA: IEEE Press.

Xu, C., & Prince, J.L. (1998). Snakes, shapes and gradient vector flow. *IEEE Transactions on Image Processing,* 7(3), 359-369.

APPENDIX A

Active Contours Stiffness Matrix Inverse Computation

An internal energy of Tikhonov stabilizer of order up to N can be written as:

$$E_{int}(v) = \sum_{r=1}^{N} \int_0^1 a_r v^{(r)}(s) ds$$

(44)

Minimizing the snake functional leads to:

$$\sum_1^N \int_0^1 (-1)^{(r)} (a_r v^{(r)}(s))^{(r)} ds + \nabla E_{ext} = 0$$

(45)

and for a_r constant:

$$\sum_1^N \int_0^1 (-1)^r a_r v^{(2r)}(s) ds + \nabla E_{ext} = 0$$

(46)

Using a backward finite difference scheme when the number of discrete points is larger than the order of the Tikhonov stabilizer gives:

$$\sum_{r=1}^{N} (-1)^r a_r \sum_{j=0}^{2r} (-1)^j v(s-r+j) + \nabla E_{ext} = 0$$

$$\sum_{r=1}^{N} \sum_{j=0}^{2r} (-1)^{r+j} a_r v(s-r+j) + \nabla E_{ext} = 0$$

(47)

We show that the snake stiffness inverse matrix is a symmetrical Toeplitz matrix having, dimension parity depending on,

$$\frac{N+1}{2} \text{ (odd case) or } \frac{N}{2}+1 \text{ (even case)}$$

distinct values. The computation of the inverse matrix used M crossing matrices P and its diagonal matrix Δ_M. The matrix $M = I + A\gamma$ can be written (Berger, 1991) as the following sum $cI + bJ + aJ^2 + aJ^{n-2} + bJ^{n-1}$ where J, unitary matrix is defined as:

$$J = \begin{pmatrix} 0 & 1 & 0 & \cdots & \cdots & \cdots & 0 \\ 0 & 0 & 1 & 0 & \cdots & \cdots & 0 \\ 0 & \cdots & 0 & 1 & 0 & \cdots & 0 \\ 0 & \cdots & \cdots & \ddots & \ddots & \ddots & \vdots \\ \vdots & \cdots & \cdots & \cdots & 0 & 1 & 0 \\ 0 & \cdots & \cdots & \cdots & \cdots & 0 & 1 \\ 1 & 0 & \cdots & \cdots & \cdots & \cdots & 0 \end{pmatrix}$$

with :

$$
\begin{aligned}
a &= \beta \\
b &= -h^2 \alpha - 4\beta \\
c &= -2a - 2b + \gamma
\end{aligned}
\qquad (48)
$$

Let's define P, the crossing matrix of J, hence of M, and Δ_J its diagonal matrix in the eigenvector reference frame. This leads to:

$$
\begin{aligned}
M &= I + A\gamma \\
&= cI + bJ + aJ^2 + aJ^{N-2} + bJ^{N-1} \\
&= cPIP^{-1} + bP\Delta_J P^{-1} + aP\Delta_J^2 P^{-1} + aP\Delta_J^{N-2} P^{-1} + bP\Delta_J^{N-1} P^{-1} \\
&= P(cI + b\Delta_J + a\Delta_J^2 + a\Delta_J^{N-2} + b\Delta_J^{N-1})P^{-1} \\
&= P\Delta_M P^{-1}
\end{aligned}
\qquad (49)
$$

It can easily be demonstrated that, J has its eigenvalues equal to w^k, k varying from 0 to $N-1$ and w equal to

$$e^{2\frac{j\pi}{N}}.$$

Straightforwardly, the eigenvector associated with the eigenvalue w^i, is equal to $(1, w^i, w^{2i}, ..., w^{i(N-2)}, w^{i(N-1)})^T$.

Eigenvalues

Noticing that M and J have the same eigenvectors we can compute the eigenvalues μ_k of M as:

$$
\begin{aligned}
\mu_k &= c + bw_k + aw_k^2 + aw_k^{N-2} + bw_k^{N-1} \\
&= c + b\left(w_k + 1w_k\right) + a\left(w_k^2 + 1w_k^2\right) \\
&= \gamma + 2a - 2b + b\left(e^{-2j\frac{k}{N}} + e^{2j\frac{k}{N}}\right) + a\left(e^{-4j\frac{k}{N}} + e^{4j\frac{k}{N}}\right) \\
&= \gamma + 2a - 2b + 2b\cos\left(2\pi\,\frac{k}{N}\right) + 4a\cos\left(4\pi\,\frac{k}{N}\right) \\
&= \gamma + 2a - 2b + 2b\left(1 - 2\sin^2\left(\frac{\pi k}{N}\right)\right) + 4a\left(2\left(1 - 2\sin^2\left(\frac{\pi k}{N}\right)\right)^2 - 1\right) \\
&= \gamma + 4\sin^2\left(\frac{\pi k}{N}\right)\left(4a\sin^2\left(\frac{\pi k}{N}\right) - b - 4a\right) \\
&= \gamma + 4\sin^2\left(\frac{\pi k}{N}\right)\left(4\beta\,\sin^2\left(\frac{\pi k}{N}\right) + k\alpha^2\right)
\end{aligned}
\tag{50}
$$

Therefore, P is a Vandermonde matrix of rank N with a general element ω, N^{th} root of the unit. It is defined as:

$$
P = \frac{1}{\sqrt{N}}
\begin{pmatrix}
1 & 1 & \cdots & \cdots & \cdots & 1 \\
\vdots & \omega & \omega^2 & \cdots & \cdots & \omega^{N-1} \\
\vdots & \omega^2 & \omega^4 & \cdots & \cdots & \omega^{2(N-1)} \\
\vdots & \omega^3 & \omega^6 & \cdots & \cdots & \omega^{3(N-1)} \\
\vdots & \vdots & \cdots & \cdots & \cdots & \vdots \\
1 & \omega^{N-1} & \omega^{2(N-1)} & \cdots & \cdots & \omega^{(N-1)^2}
\end{pmatrix}
$$

P^{-1} is given as:

$$
P^{-1} = \frac{1}{\sqrt{N}}
\begin{pmatrix}
1 & 1 & \cdots & \cdots & \cdots & 1 \\
\vdots & \overline{\omega} & \overline{\omega}^{-2} & \cdots & \cdots & \overline{\omega}^{-N-1} \\
\vdots & \overline{\omega}^{-2} & \overline{\omega}^{-4} & \cdots & \cdots & \overline{\omega}^{-2(N-1)} \\
\vdots & \overline{\omega}^{-3} & \overline{\omega}^{-6} & \cdots & \cdots & \overline{\omega}^{-3(N-1)} \\
\vdots & \vdots & \cdots & \cdots & \cdots & \vdots \\
1 & \overline{\omega}^{-N-1} & \overline{\omega}^{-2(N-1)} & \cdots & \cdots & \overline{\omega}^{-(N-1)^2}
\end{pmatrix}
$$

where $^-$ denotes the complex conjugate.
and the inverse of M as:

$$
M^{-1} = P\Delta_M^{-1}P^{-1}
\tag{51}
$$

where Δ is the diagonal matrix of the eigenvalues μ_k of the matrix M. Defining $(m'_{ij})_{(i,j)\varepsilon[1,N]^2}$ as the general element of M^{-1}, one reads:

$$
\begin{aligned}
m'_{ij} &= \sum_{k=1}^{N} p_{ik} \frac{1}{\mu_k} \overline{p_{kj}} \\
&= \frac{1}{N}\sum_{k=1}^{N} \omega^{(i-1)(k-1)} \frac{1}{\mu_k} \overline{\omega}^{-(k-1)(j-1)} \\
&= \frac{1}{N}\sum_{k=1}^{N} \frac{1}{\mu_k} \omega^{(i-j)(k-1)}
\end{aligned}
\tag{52}
$$

The inverse (if it exists) of a symmetric matrix is symmetric which leads to m'_{ij} real:

$$
\begin{aligned}
m'_{ij} &= \frac{1}{N}\sum_{k=1}^{N} \frac{1}{\mu_k} \Re(\omega^{(i-j)(k-1)}) \\
&= \frac{1}{N}\sum_{k=1}^{N} \frac{1}{\mu_k} \cos\left(\frac{2(i-j)(k-1)\pi}{N}\right) \\
&= \frac{1}{N}\sum_{k=1}^{N} \frac{\cos\left(\dfrac{2(i-j)(k-1)\pi}{N}\right)}{1+\dfrac{\dfrac{4}{h^4}\sin^2\dfrac{k\pi}{N}(4\beta\sin^2\dfrac{k\pi}{N}+h^2\alpha)}{\gamma}}
\end{aligned}
\tag{53}
$$

Looking at eq. (52) one sees that same diagonal elements are equal. It is then straightforward to demonstrate that the matrix M^{-1} bears

$$E(\frac{N}{2}+1)$$

distinct elements. For N even: let's define

$$j_s = i + \frac{N}{2} - 1.$$

The associated matrix element is given by:

$$
\begin{aligned}
m'_{ij_s} &= \frac{1}{N}\sum_{k=1}^{N} \frac{1}{\mu_k} \omega^{(1-N2)(k-1)} \\
&= \frac{1}{N}\sum_{k=1}^{N} \frac{1}{\mu_k} \omega^{(1-N+N2)(k-1)} \\
&= \frac{1}{N}\sum_{k=1}^{N} \frac{1}{\mu_k} \omega^{(1+N2)(k-1)} \text{ as } \omega^N \quad 1
\end{aligned}
\tag{54}
$$

and since (52):

$$m'_{ij_s} = m'_{i_d j} \quad \text{with } \bar{i}_d \quad i + \frac{N}{2} + 1$$
$$= m'_{ij_s} + 2 \tag{55}$$

A symmetric leads to:

$$m'_{ii + \frac{N}{2} - k} = m'_{ii + \frac{N}{2} + k}$$

In the even case, $(I + A\gamma)^{-1}$ is given by:

$$
\begin{pmatrix}
m'_1 & m'_2 & \ddots & m'_{N/2} & m'_{N/2+1} & m'_{N/2} & \ddots & m'_2 \\
m'_2 & m'_1 & \ddots & \ddots & \ddots & \ddots & \ddots & \ddots \\
\ddots & \ddots & \ddots & \ddots & \ddots & \ddots & \ddots & m'_{N/2} \\
m'_{N/2} & \ddots & \ddots & \ddots & \ddots & \ddots & \ddots & m'_{N/2+1} \\
m'_{N/2+1} & \ddots & \ddots & \ddots & \ddots & \ddots & \ddots & m'_{N/2} \\
m'_{N/2} & \ddots & \ddots & \ddots & \ddots & \ddots & \ddots & \ddots \\
\ddots & \ddots & \ddots & \ddots & \ddots & \ddots & m'_1 & m'_2 \\
m'_2 & \ddots & m'_{N/2} & m'_{N/2+1} & m'_{N/2} & \ddots & m'_2 & m'_1
\end{pmatrix}
\tag{56}
$$

It can be easily demonstrated that in the odd case it is equal to:

$$
\begin{pmatrix}
m'_1 & m'_2 & \ddots & m'_{N+1/2} & m'_{N+1/2} & \ddots & m'_3 & m'_2 \\
m'_2 & m'_1 & \ddots & \ddots & \ddots & \ddots & \ddots & m'_3 \\
\ddots & \ddots & \ddots & \ddots & \ddots & \ddots & \ddots & \ddots \\
m'_{N+1/2} & \ddots & \ddots & \ddots & \ddots & \ddots & \ddots & m'_{N+1/2} \\
m'_{N+1/2} & \ddots & \ddots & \ddots & \ddots & \ddots & \ddots & m'_{N+1/2} \\
\ddots & \ddots & \ddots & \ddots & \ddots & \ddots & \ddots & \ddots \\
m'_3 & \ddots & \ddots & \ddots & \ddots & \ddots & m'_1 & m'_2 \\
m'_2 & m'_3 & \ddots & m'_{N+1/2} & m'_{N+1/2} & \ddots & m'_2 & m'_1
\end{pmatrix}
\tag{57}
$$

with m_l element of the diagonal l, $l \geq 1$, given as:

$$
m_l = \frac{1}{N} \sum_{k=1}^{N} \frac{\cos\left(\dfrac{2(l-1)(k-1)\pi}{N}\right)}{1 + \dfrac{\dfrac{4}{h^4}\sin^2\dfrac{k\pi}{N}\left(4\beta\sin^2\dfrac{k\pi}{N} + h^2\alpha\right)}{\gamma}}
\tag{58}
$$

212

Chapter VII
3D Lip Shape SPH Based Evolution Using Prior 2D Dynamic Lip Features Extraction and Static 3D Lip Measurements

Alfonso Gastelum
The University of Auckland, New Zealand, & Image Analysis Visualization Laboratory,
CCADET-UNAM, Mexico

Patrice Delmas
The University of Auckland, New Zealand

Jorge Marquez
Image Analysis Visualization Laboratory, CCADET-UNAM, Mexico

Alexander Woodward
The University of Auckland, New Zealand

Jason James
The University of Auckland, New Zealand

Marc Lievin
Avid Technology Inc., Canada

Georgy Gimel'farb
The University of Auckland, New Zealand

ABSTRACT

This chapter describes a new user-specific 2D to 3D lip animation technique. 2D lip contour position and corresponding motion information are provided from a 2D lip contour extraction algorithm. Static face measurements are obtained from 3D scanners or stereovision systems. The data is combined to generate an initial subject-dependent 3D lip surface. The 3D lips are then modelled as a set of particles whose dynamic behaviour is governed by Smooth Particles Hydrodynamics. A set of forces derived from ellipsoid muscle encircling the lips simulates the muscles controlling the lips motion. The 3D lip model is comprised of more than 300 surface voxels and more than 1300 internal particles. The advantage of the particle system is the possibility of creating a more complex system than previously introduced surface models.

INTRODUCTION

It has been shown that the lip area carries more than half of the speaking face's visual information in both the English (McGrath, 1985; Summerfield et al., 1989) and French (Benoit, Lallouache, Mohamadi & Abry, 1992) languages. There is strong evidence (Benoit et al., 1992) that 3-Dimensional (3D) face representation carries more information than its 2-Dimensional (2D) equivalent in the understanding of speech. Experiments (Benoit, 1996) have shown that speech intelligibility (under audio-visual stimuli) steadily increases when presenting a listener with audio stimuli, visual displays of 3D synthetic lips alone and a 3D synthetic representation of the face area (Guiard-Marigny, Tsingos, Adjoudani, Benoît & Gascuel, 1995). There is a growing need for interactive communication devices that facilitate communication between both humans (using realistic 3D face models), and computers (using avatars). Generating a fast and realistically animated 3D talking face that accurately conveys visual lip information is an important research area.

BACKGROUND

There has been a wealth of research and publications dealing with static and dynamic 2D lip-region study, extraction and analysis over the last three decades, but there are only a limited set of publications dealing with direct (without any a-priori assumptions about the expected surfaces) 3D lip information extraction. Research is concentrated on dynamic 2D lip parameter extraction for model-based 3D animation or static 3D lip-information extraction.

Recently, the movie industry has developed cumbersome dynamic systems to, partially or fully, recover fine (both in resolution and accuracy) 3D information from the face. These systems are essentially marker based and use pattern projection, infra-red sensitive dyes, or a combination of both. Data acquisition is via massively parallel multiple cameras. The data is extensively processed for Computer Graphics reconstruction. This requires specialist hardware and has no practical applications outside character generation and animation for motion pictures.

Ahlberg (2001) used the front and side images of a face, and a generic 3D face mesh model (based on the original Candide face model) assuming cylindrical geometry. After a planar projection, a subset of 3D model meshes and corresponding image face features were manually mapped, allowing a complete registration of the 2D face texture onto the 3D face model. Specifically designed models for 3D lips were derived by Basu, S., Oliver, N., & Pentland, A. (1998). First a limited set of 3D lip surface points (painted on the mouth as black dots) were manually extracted from video-sequences. Next, the 3D lips surface deformation manifold was restricted to statistically learned shapes via Principal Component Analysis

(PCA). Reveret, Borel, & Badin (2000) used 3D lip surfaces interpolated from manually delineated 2D lip contours projected on a 3D torus. The allowed motion was restricted to deformations statistically learned (again using PCA) from a group of 23 French visemes.

Zhang, Liu, Adler, Cohen, Hanson, & Shan (2004) used a calibrated web-camera and structure from motion principles to semi-automatically (the user must manually select a small set of face feature points in two consecutive frames) create a low resolution textured 3D model of the human subject detected in the scene. Readers seriously interested in 3D face modelling analysis and synthesis should read Wen and Huang's book (2004).

A large number of 3D face animation techniques have been developed; many have been focused on the mouth region. The use of computer technology to produce 3D static and animated human faces began in the early 1970s. Parke (1972) created the first animation of a 3D face by hand digitizing expressions and facial geometry and then defining key positions. Animation of the face resulted from interpolation between the key frames. To overcome the model complexity he later developed a parametric facial model based on empirical and traditional hand-drawn animation methods (Parke, 1974). The parameters define a linear interpolation between two extremes and are divided into conformation parameters and expression parameters. The conformation parameters define the shape of the face and the expression parameters are used to create the animation. It uses the previous work of Ekman (1972), which describes facial expressions as the result of activities of specific facial muscles. Montgomery (1980) augmented earlier work with the addition of nonlinear interpolation between frames, as well as forward and backward co-articulation approximation, thus integrating lip-reading ability. Terzopoulos (1990) developed a physics-based 3D face model taking into account the anatomy of the face with the representation of several layers (bones, muscles and skin). Essa (1994) "solved" the associated inverse problem: given a sequence of images describing a facial expression, find which group of muscles caused the motion and then deduce the expression using previous knowledge about facial expressions and the corresponding pattern motion using optical flows. An excellent example of the realistic animation potential of physics driven facial muscle models can be found in Sifakis, Selle, Robinson-Mosher, and Fedkiw (2006). It requires 8 high-speed synchronised cameras, 250 markers on the subjects face to acquire data and 7 minutes (on a high-end 3.4 GhZ PC) to generate an accurate representation of a single motion-capture frame. While the hardware requirements make it unrealistic at the time of writing it probably represents the future of visually and phonetically correct 3D face and lips animation.

Despite a large amount of work in the field, there is still no passive system using off-the-shelf cameras and PC hardware able to perform full 3D face analysis at a processing speed close to real-time, and then reproduce a dynamic facsimile (3D clone) of the subject's face or lips at a remote location.

There are a variety of different techniques that can be used for facial animation. These range from simple methods suitable for real-time applications to complex ones that produce a high level of physical accuracy. There are also different methods for representing the data comprising a face (e.g. geometrically defined meshes or volumetric objects). The most appropriate reference for an overview of such techniques is (Neumann & Noh, 1998).

With the advent of higher-performance hardware, a renaissance in advanced and physically accurate techniques for facial animation is taking place. Realistic 3D human faces have found application in many situations. The easily recognisable human face provides an emotive bridge that personalises many human-computer interactions in today's society. Face models based on real people are widely sought after. Facial animation is used in a wide range of applications. These include the gaming and cinema industries where there is convergence between expected 3D realism and customer experience (via lifelike and believable characters which greatly enhance the immersion and emotional content), medicine (e.g. realistic surgery training, simulation of facial tissue for skin incisions and wound closure, and aesthetical impact of planned orthodontic surgery), social agents and avatars (used in places such as kiosks; their main purpose is to humanise and communicate information), and teleconferencing methods to reduce communication overheads (e.g. using computer vision to extract facial properties and transmit only the parameters to control a 3D face model over the network).

As readily available dynamic 3D face information is not available at the current stage of research, we introduce a 2D to 3D lip animation scheme. User-dependent information on the lips is obtained from:

- Dynamic 2D lip contours
- Static 3D lip surfaces

2D lip contours are obtained using an algorithm that combines mouth region segmentation with hue and motion observations, followed by a set of lip shape adapted active contours. 3D lip surfaces are manually delineated and extracted from face surfaces.

We present a 2D to 3D lip rendering algorithm. Firstly, a user-specific animated 3D lip model (integrating Smooth Particle Hydrodynamics (SPH) theory and a virtual muscular system) is generated using 3D data obtained from a 3D scanner or very precise stereovision system. Secondly, 2D lip contours are obtained from live or offline video sequences using a hierarchical approach combining Hidden Markov Model segmentation and active contours. The extracted 2D outer lip contour points are then mapped to an animated 3D lip model. This produces a realistic 3D lip animation using only 2D lip motion and 3D static data. The main contribution of this chapter is the design and animation of the SPH-based 3D lip model. For more details on 3D face acquisition the reader should refer to Woodward et al. (2006) and Chan, Delmas, Gimel'farb & Leclercq (2005). For more details on 2D lip tracking, the reader should refer to this book's chapter (Lievin and Delmas, 2008).

DATA ACQUISITION

3D Static Data Acquisition

Facial data is represented as a set of points in 3D space. This data can be derived from real world models or humans (i.e. as a computer vision and image processing task), or from a modelling package (an artistic approach). There are several techniques for creating 3D facial models using 2D images. Leclerc & Fua (1996) use a rectified stereo pair of images to find pixel correspondence and generate a disparity map. A depth map can then be constructed. Another approach is to calibrate a pair of cameras and obtain the 3D world coordinates of each pair of pixels in the images by using triangulation. Finding correspondence between the stereo pairs can be performed via automatic pattern localisation or by manually finding similarities. A third approach, using only one camera, is orthogonal views (Yin & Ip, 1996). Two images are taken; one from the front and the other from the side. The front-view image provides the X- and Y-coordinates, while the side-view provides the Z-coordinate of the pixel corresponding to the same feature in both images. (Arai & Kurihara, 1991) detect facial features from colour images and apply the orthogonal views technique to obtain their 3D positional values. Photometric stereo (Woodham, 1980) is based on the way images of 3D objects are formed. Objects can be seen because they reflect light. The surface normal and other characteristics of the surface (e.g. depth) can be obtained using prior knowledge of the scene illumination geometry and the nature of surface reflection. Stereo-vision matching and registration of 3D information using structured lighting are by far the most active research avenues and common commercial solutions for the retrieval of 3D face data.

In our experiments the volume representing the lips is constructed using 3D face data retrieved on location at our photogrammetry laboratory. We used a Solutionix Rexcan 400 3D scanner (with sub-mm accuracy in all directions) or a rectified stereovision system comprised of Canon EOS 30D cameras coupled with active illumination (in our case, Gray code stripe patterns). The Rexcan system provides high density data (300,000 points) in a short time (0.7 sec) and scans the important regions of the face with minimal movements from the subjects. The scanner uses structured light technology associated with a 640 by 480 pixel camera. The halogen light source projects multiple striped patterns to recover the object's shape. We used the scanner at a standoff scan distance to the target of approximately 600 to 700 mm, and with a field of view of 400 by 300 mm. The resolution is 0.625mm both horizontally and vertically and the depth accuracy is 0.5 mm. Advantages over classic laser scanners are safety and fast acquisition with 24 bit colour texture. A cheaper alternative to the 3D scanner is to use an active or passive acquisition system with one or more coupled cameras. Using a framework and test bench for passive and active 3D acquisition systems using three different approaches (binocular stereo, photometric stereo and structured lighting) and twelve algorithms we proved that an active acquisition system consisting of high resolution stereo cameras in epipolar position coupled with a Gray code pattern was able to produce the same accuracy as obtained by the Rexcan scanner (Woodward et al. 2006). This offers a higher resolution (both for texture and depth) of about 4 Mpixels for the face and a cheaper alternative.

2D Lip Contour Extraction

We obtain the 2D lip contour information using an algorithm described by Delmas and Lievin (2008). The algorithm accurately extracts the inner and outer lip borders from an image of a subject's face. No predefined set-up, make-up, or markers are necessary and normal illumination (natural or from ceiling lights) is expected. The only requirement is that the whole mouth region remains in the field of view at all times. The output is a set of adapted active contours that model the lip boundaries. The algorithm comprises three distinct steps:

Step One: Lip Segmentation:

- Logarithmic colour-space transform: *RGB* to *HI* (Figure 1. left; first and second rows).
  We work with a nonlinear colour space based on a logarithmic transform robust to lighting conditions. It is a logarithmic image processing model inspired by biological considerations that yields good contrast enhancement (Lievin & Luthon, 2004).
- Segmentation of the mouth area:
  A coarse-to-fine approach for face feature identification is defined. A hierarchical iterated algorithm for segmenting N face features is used. To detect face regions, motion information is combined with red hue information in a statistical Markov Random Field framework (Figure 1 right). Lip contour extraction is achieved by applying the algorithm with 2-pass segmentation, the first pass corresponds to the face tracking implementation, and the second pass segments the lips.

Step Two: Determine Mouth Characteristics:

- Mouth corner detection:
  Mouth corners (anchor points for the active contour extremities) are detected by combining heuristics, initial curve fitting using the mask obtained in step one, and several classic corner detectors.

Step Three: Evaluate Lip Contours:

- Snake initialisation from mouth corners:
  Mask boundaries extracted from step one are discretised and combined with mouth corner points obtained in step two to provide a snake initialisation close to the desired solution (as seen in Figure 2 first two rows).

Figure 1. Step 1 algorithm description. The mouth area is extracted using the steps described (right) and the corresponding results from a sequence of mouth region images are given (left)

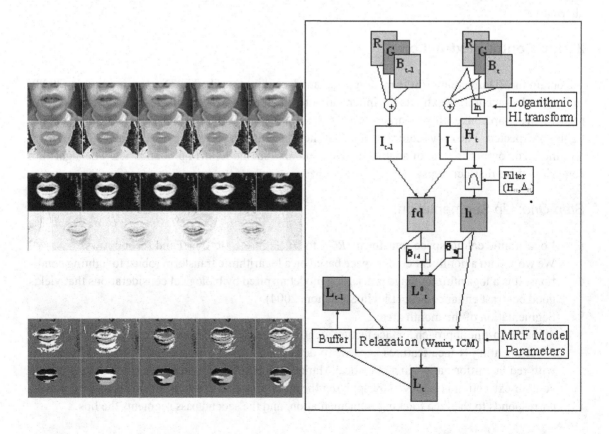

Figure 2. Step 2 and 3 algorithm results on a video sequence of lips. From top to bottom: outer (top) and inner (middle) lip contour (including mouth corners) initialisation for active contours; final active contours (bottom)

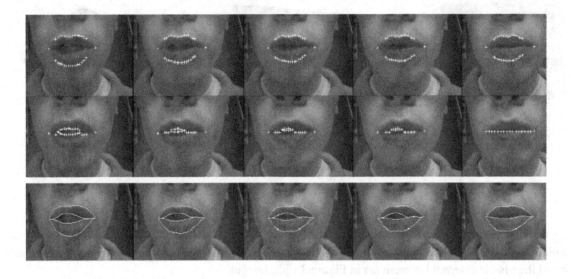

- Convergence of automatic snake (outer) and balloon snake (inner):
  The pace of outer active contours evolution is controlled with a varying energy-based time step coefficient. Inner snakes' convergence is helped by a specifically designed balloon force which takes into account the expected shape of the lips.
- Convergence validation, reinitialisation, and final convergence:
  Convergence is attained when the overall active contours' energy over several iterations does not vary above a given threshold. Good convergence is tested using statistical analysis of the internal area adjacent to the contour boundary. Final convergence is attained when both the above criterion are satisfied.

3D Lip Model Construction

Our dynamic 3D system needs a closed 3D surface of the mouth region as an input. These models can be created using CAD modelling programs or acquired directly from live subjects using 3D acquisition systems.

There are various approaches to representing face data and building surfaces that are topologically equivalent to a human face. Our model is based on a face surface obtained from our 3D acquisition system (as described in the data acquisition section). The initial cloud of 3D data points (representing the face surface) is tessellated to form a mesh of polygons. We then delineate surface of the lips. Using

Figure 3. 3D lip surface acquisition. Left: 3D face surface; middle: corresponding triangle representation of the mouth region surface; right: close-up of the simplified lip mesh

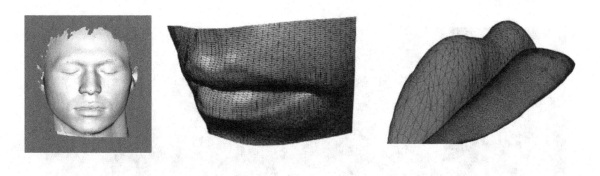

correspondences between the face surface and texture obtained with our 3D acquisition system, we find pixels on the lip boundaries and their corresponding nearest face surface mesh triangles. We then build the visible external lip mesh (as in Figure 3 right image).

Next we apply the Ray-Triangle Intersection algorithm to build the volumetric set of points which will describe the 3D lips. The Ray-Triangle Intersection algorithm requires a closed surface as input. As the input surface obtained from the Rexcan scanner is not closed, we implemented a surface closing

Figure 4. Surface closing procedure: a) Schematic procedure showing the Boolean intersection operation between two surfaces. b) Resulting closed surface lip after application of the Boolean operation

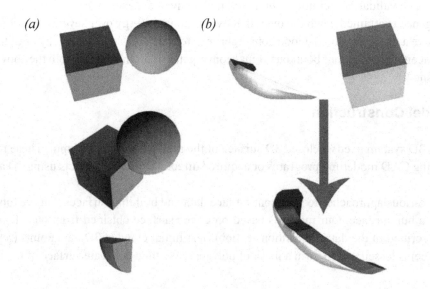

procedure using simple Boolean intersection operations between the upper and lower lips and a 3D box (as shown in Figure 4). We use this final surface as the initial input to our SPH particle model.

Our mechanical model is based on a particle system. Our first step is to obtain the position of the initial particles that conform to the 3D lip model. The Ray-Triangle Intersection algorithm tests whether a point is located inside or outside the closed surface of the 3D lips. The set of points tested are distributed isotropically within a discrete cubic field. All points inside the boundaries of the tested surfaces will be included in the lips' particle system (as shown in Figure 5).

Figure 5 shows the process applied to obtain the set of internal particles necessary for the definition of the SPH model. As SPH depends on the object discretisation, the interior particles must accurately describe the object's mechanical properties.

At the end of this step we have two representations of the lips: the triangle mesh surface and the volume of particles. The mesh is only used for visualisation purpose while the particles model the mechanical behaviour of the lips (as in Figure 6)

The lip comprises the skin on the outside and the oral mucosa supported by skeletal muscle on the inside (Figure 7). The vermilion border (Figure 7a) forms the transition between the external epidermis and the oral mucosa on the inside. Each layer exhibits specific mechanical properties which reinforce the concept of a multilayer model with properties depending on density and elastic constraints.

Figure 5. a) Schematic view in 2D of the test to verify if a particle is inside a surface. b) Schematic view in 3D showing the classification of a discrete field of points, gray outside the surface and black inside. c) Algorithm results from different particles resolutions

(a)   *(b)*   *(c)*

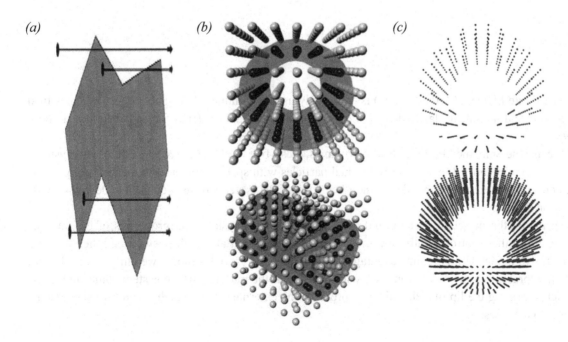

Figure 6. 3D lip model composed of a surface triangle mesh and a volumetric particle system. Dots represent the surface mesh nodes and the internal particle points.

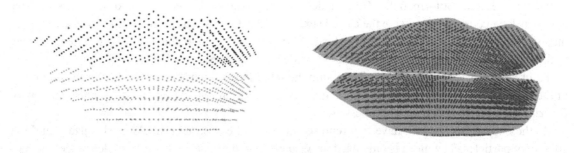

Figure 7. Lip tissue section; a) Vermillion border. b) Skin. c) Mucosa. d) Gland

The Finite Element Method (FEM) is commonly used to simulate deformable object (such as lips) behaviour and nonlinear elastic deformation, due to external and internal forces (Cheung & Leung, 1991).

We use the Smoothed Particles Hydrodynamics, mesh-free method (Liu & Liu, 2003). SPH systems employ a model formed by a set of individual particles with specific material properties and governing conservation equations that define their behaviour. SPH systems have been used to describe solids (Jansson & Vergeest, 2002).

To model the muscular system, and the anatomical and physiological properties of the muscles (Gray, 2000) that control mouth movements, we obtain the spatial mouth position and then define a constitutive model. Utilising the advantages of the smoothed particles model we build a particle field system representing the mouth muscles, with one side of the muscle particle system connected to the particles forming the lip model. This field provides the external forces which control the movements of the lip particles.

Description of the Smooth Particle System

The particle system constructed in the previous section follows the governing laws of Continuum Mechanics and the equations are solved using SPH. SPH follow a Lagrangian approach and has been used to solve problems in fluid mechanics and astronomy. SPH has also recently been extended to model the deformation of solid objects (Jansson & Vergeest, 2002).

In our model the solid is defined by a set of n particles. We use the letter i to define the particle of interest and $V(i)$ to define the set of particles within the vicinity of i. Each particle has an associated mass m_j and density ρ_j with j defining a particle element in $V(i)$. The continuous integral representation of the equation to solve the continuum volume of the solid is replaced by a discrete summation over all the neighbouring particles j of the discrete volume defined around i.

$$A_i = \sum_j m_j \frac{A_j}{\rho_j} W(r_i - r_j, h)$$

(1)

where A_i is the function value in the r_i position and $W(r_i - r_j, h)$ is a smoothing kernel. h is the support radius and is referred to as the smoothing length. $r_i - r_j$ is the distance between the particle i and a neighbourhood particle j. The value of A at the location r_j is denoted by A_j (Monaghan, 2005). The support radius is the maximum distances between interacting particles. The smoothing kernel establishes how the distance between particles affects their interaction. We use the smoothing kernel specifically defined for elastic materials (Solenthaler, 2007):

$$W(r,h) = \begin{cases} c\frac{2h}{\pi}\cos\left(\frac{(r+h)\pi}{2h}\right) + c\frac{2h}{\pi} & 0 \le r \le h \\ 0 \end{cases}$$

(2)

where c is a normalization factor equal to:

$$c = \frac{\pi}{8h^4\left(\frac{\pi}{3} - \frac{8}{\pi} + \frac{16}{\pi^2}\right)}$$

The gradient of the function ∇A_i of the function A_i of the particle i is defined as:

$$\nabla A_i = \frac{1}{\rho_i}\sum_j m_j (A_j - A_i)\nabla W(r_i - r_j, h)$$

(3)

In their initial state, all particles are considered to be in a resting (zero stress) state. The initial mass properties for each particle is set using an appropriate density value for lip tissues, $\rho = 1000.0$ kg/m^3, defined by Duck (1990).

The density variations over time depend on the particle configuration, where density is defined as:

Figure 8. a) Smoothing kernel values for smoothing length h=1. b) Gradient of the smoothing kernel

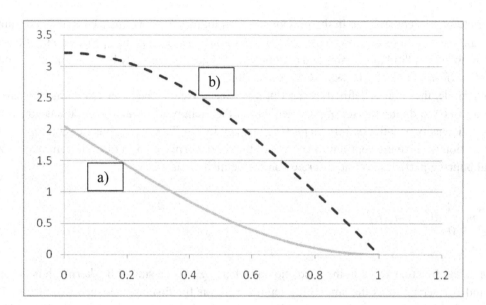

$$\rho_i = \sum_j m_j W(r_i - r_j, h)$$

(4)

The continuity of the system and the accuracy of the solution are ensured by constructing a neighbourhood with an adequate number of particles for each particle i. The number of particles that are neighbours of i is determined using the smoothing length where two particles are neighbours if:

$$D_{ij} < scale * h_{ij}$$

(5)

D_{ij} is the distances between particles and h_{ij} is given by:

$$h_{ij} = \frac{h_i + h_j}{2}$$

(6)

where h_i, h_j are the smoothing length of particles i and j. The scale factor adjusts the number of neighbouring particles. In our case the minimum number of particles in each neighbourhood was set at 20. The neighbourhood search is made using an octree algorithm. The same octree algorithm will be used later in the collision calculations.

In order to obtain a fast computational solution we implemented a modified octree-space search algorithm (described in Figure 9) We used the initial space neighbours to classify groups of particles, then built a branch of the tree containing the particles that are neighbours in space (this vicinity is different from the one used for SPH). This helps organise the neighbour data and accelerates the SPH computation process.

Each branch of the octree contains the particles situated in a specific volume region (in our case a cube). The number of particles and the total volume depends on the scale-level of the branch, each branch is a new discrete volume representation (considered as a particle at the current scale), with an associated mass equal to the sum of all the particles' mass contained in the branch. The object's volume is represented here as a discrete approximation (as in Figure 9); the higher the scale-level the less accurate the approximation. The associated discrete volume has a new smooth kernel and vicinity which is computed using only branches at the same scale-level.

Figure 9 describes how the object volume is divided using the octree algorithm. The first image (from left to right) shows the first space, encompassing the object's volume in continuous representation, divided into 8 cubes. The second image is the result of zooming into one of the first image's cubes and the subsequent division of this cube into 8 smaller cubes. Again, the next image shows a view of the approximation of one of the previous image's cubes. Upon reaching particle resolution, the diagram

Figure 9. Octree sub-division. From left to right: multi-scale representation of a multi-particle object. The right image shows the last stage of the octree division where cubes contain either a unique particle or none

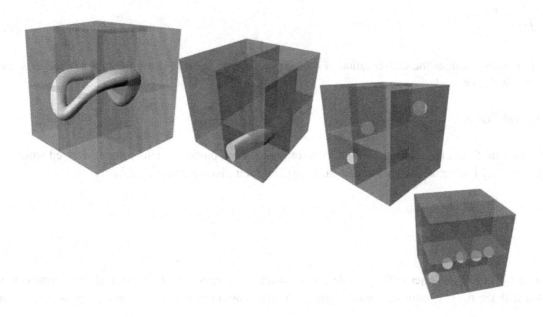

Figure 10. Multi-resolution voxel-particles representation. Left: surface model; middle left: Each voxel is represented by a particle, this is the lowest resolution of the octree search; middle right: Each particle is now grouping a set of voxels; right: Highest level of the octree; the voxels forming the particle is increased.

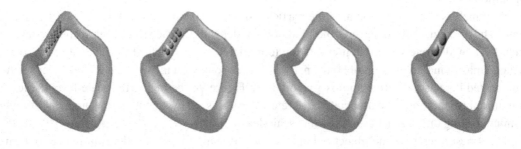

shows the discrete approximation instead of the continuous surface representation. At the last octree stage, each cube contains only one particle or is empty.

Model Behaviour

Following the rules of Continuum Mechanics, particle acceleration is described by:

$$\rho \frac{Dv_i}{Dt} = Fi_i + Fe_i$$

(7)

Equation 7 defines the conservation of momentum where Fi_i and Fe_i are the internal and external forces for each particle.

Internal Forces

The internal forces reduce to the elastic constraints between particles. This force is derived from the strain energy (potential energy store in each particle) for a given particle as:

$$U_i = \frac{1}{2}V_i(\varepsilon_i \bullet \sigma_i)$$

(8)

where U_i is the strain energy for particle i, ε_i its strain, σ_i its stress and V_i its equivalent volume calculated with the density value defined in equation 6. The relation between strain and stress for an elastic material is given by Hooke's law:

$$\sigma = C\varepsilon \tag{9}$$

The relation between stress and strain is modified to take into account the behaviour of soft tissues. Equation 9 is rewritten as:

$$\sigma = 2\mu(\varepsilon + T_r\dot{\varepsilon}) + \delta_{ij}\lambda(\varepsilon + T_r\dot{\varepsilon}) \tag{10}$$

where μ and λ are the Lame constants and T_y the relaxation time of the material.

Using the Green Saint Venant strain tensor (Müller 2004), the strain is given as:

$$\varepsilon = \nabla u + \nabla u^T + \nabla u \nabla u^T \tag{11}$$

where ∇u is the gradient of the vector displacement with respect to the original position of the particle in the reference shape (original shape in equilibrium).

The force exerted over the particle j by i is defined as:

$$F_{ji} = -\nabla u_j U_i = -V_i\sigma_i\nabla u_j\varepsilon_i$$

$$F_{ji} = -2V_i(I + \nabla u_i^T)\sigma_i\frac{\partial \nabla u_i}{\partial u_j} \tag{12}$$

We can express this equation using SPH laws (Equations 1 and 3):

$$\nabla u_i = \frac{1}{\rho_i}\sum_j m_j(u_j - u_i)\nabla W(r_i - r_j, h) \tag{13}$$

and

$$\frac{\partial \nabla u_i}{\partial u_j} = V_j\nabla W(r_i - r_j, h) \tag{14}$$

External Forces

Equation 7 requires the definition of the external forces acting on the particle system in order to fully describe the system. Two types of external force act on the 3D lip model. The first force takes into account the collisions between particles. The second force is generated by the muscles governing the lips' movements.

The first external force considered is the interaction between particles Fe^c. Collision only relates to particles which belong to different neighbourhoods. The collisions occur between two particles at a time and the final velocity is a sum over all the pairs for each particle.

$$v_i = \sum_j \left(\frac{1}{m_i + m_j} \right) \left[(m_i - m_j) \frac{\upsilon_i}{N_i} + 2m_j \frac{\upsilon_j}{N_j} \right]$$

$$v_j = \sum_i \left(\frac{1}{m_i + m_j} \right) \left[2m_i \frac{\upsilon_i}{N_i} + (m_j - m_i) \frac{\upsilon_j}{N_j} \right] \tag{15}$$

where v_i and v_j is the final velocity after the collision and υ_i y υ_j the velocity before, N_i contains the number of individual collisions for the particle i and N_j contains the number of collisions for j. The instant force after a collision is:

$$Fe^c_i = m_i \left(\frac{v_i - \upsilon_i}{dt} \right) \tag{16}$$

Another type of interaction occurs when the smoothing kernels of two particles are interacting in a resting contact. A new acceleration that opposes the one being produced in the particles is introduced to avoid penetration.

$$Fe^c_i = -m_i a_i \tag{17}$$

where a_i is the acceleration of the particle i.

The acceleration caused by the muscles can be expressed such that for a particle i, the force due to a muscle is simply the sum of all the forces generated by all the muscles in contact with that particle:

$$Fe^{m_r}_i = \sum_k Fe^m_k \tag{18}$$

Each muscle is connected to the lips' particle system at one end and is fixed at the other. Each muscle is considered to be an independent object, but where two or more muscles, or the muscle and the lips, intersect, we consider those particles to belong to all the objects in the intersection, and to be affected by the internal forces of all objects.

The acceleration of the muscle and how it affects the lips is solved in the SPH implementation. We introduce a new external force $Fe^{m'}$ for each muscle. This force acts in the particles of the muscle that belong to the insertion area. The force is computed together with the internal force of the muscle particle system $Fi^{m'}$ so we obtain the total Fe^m acting on the particles of the lips:

Figure 11. Top: arrangement of fibres for the Orbicularis Oris muscles (Yamashita & Kubota, 2001); bottom: force field representation of the muscles driving the particle system model (in grey)

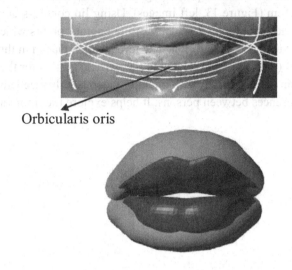

Orbicularis oris

Figure 12. Schematic representation of the connection between the muscle (dark particles) and the tissue (white particles), the grey particles show the connection between both systems

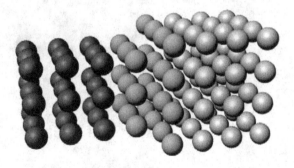

$$Fe^m = Fi^{m'} + Fe^{m'} \tag{19}$$

As the particles of the muscles and lips interconnect in the area of insertion, the final acceleration of the muscle is also affected by the resistance from the lips and other muscles.

RESULTS

The correspondence between the initial lip tracking and the final model is given by the points obtained from the lip tracking system (Figure 13, left images). Using lip contours extracted from consecutive images, we compute the acceleration and velocity of the contour points which we directly relate to a resulting force value for each 3D contour point. The force is then placed in the corresponding position in the particle field model (total sum) and related to the particle system for the respective contour.

The muscle description obtained from a lip tracking video is only a general measurement for modelling lip movement differences between persons. It helps explore the limit values using the following evolution law formulas:

$$F = ma$$
$$a = \frac{\partial v}{\partial t}$$

(20)

Figure 13. 2D lip contours and associated 3D lips surfaces. Left: Delineation of 2D lip boundaries (contours and active contours initialisation points); right: 3D lip model evolution (front and side)

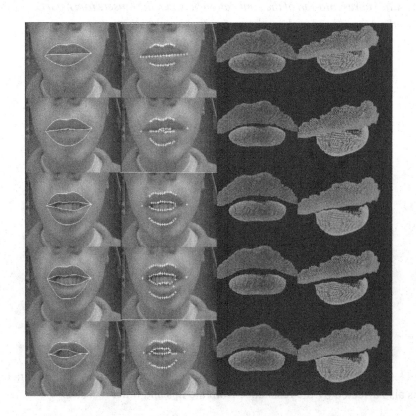

Figure 14. Representation of a dynamic collision between two horizontal objects moving towards each other. Top: initial stage, two objects (black and white particles); middle: The objects are colliding; bottom: Last stage of the initial collision

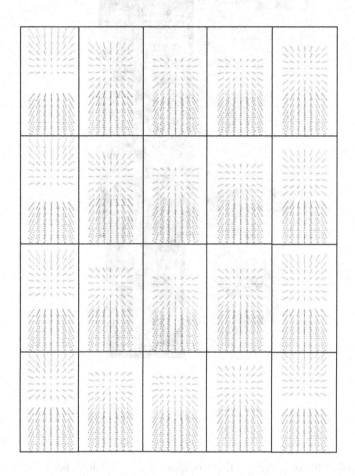

The mass is again related to the particle property. We can therefore relate the range of lip movement to the particle system properties. Extreme lip movements can be used as calibration points (see Figure 15).

Figure 14 shows a particular representation of the collision between two planar surfaces. The collision is calculated using the octree algorithm. As the collision is calculated using particles, we use the conservation of momentum law after a collision. The resulting force and momentum start the internal deformation in both surfaces. Overlapping surfaces increase internal particle deformation.

The use of an octree improves the computational time, and allows the possibility of running the model at different resolutions (in particle components) so it can be adapted to a range of conditions. The

Figure 15. Different 2D lip level of opening and corresponding 3D particle model

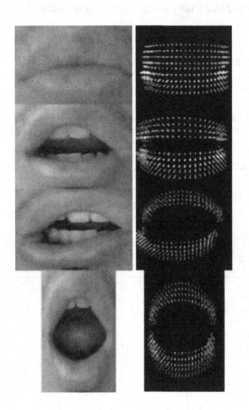

system anticipates collisions of particles, first computing the collisions between branches (containing a set of particles and a defined volume). If there is a collision, the algorithm further searches down the affected branches to see if there is a collision between the component particles. This eliminates the need for particle-by-particle computations.

Collision detection needs some further improvement as we obtained some particle penetration after a collision (See Figure 14). This needs to be avoided as it produces an incorrect graphical representation with some mesh triangles overlapping.

CONCLUSIONS

3D facial data, acquired by 3D acquisition systems, and 2D lip contours extracted from video-sequences of the same subject are processed to build a 3D lip model comprised of more than 300 surface voxels and more than 1300 internal particles. The model dynamics are governed by Smooth Particles Hydro-dynamics. The lip muscles behaviour is similarly modelled.

The motion and acceleration data obtained from the lip tracking algorithm are used as calibration input to describe the group of forces necessary to produce a gesture. The set of forces is arranged to resemble the anatomical position of the muscles in the face. The particles model maintains the lips' anatomical properties while allowing complex collision scenarios.

The advantage of the particle system is the possibility of creating a more complex system than previously introduced surface models. Instead of the current three layer model, we could define additional layers and assign different particles density according to the tissue properties.

An interesting challenge would be to compare the results obtained from the particles model with the ones obtained from a multi-layer mass-spring face model controlled by physics-based muscles.

Some lip deformations may require a more complex muscular structure, but the advantage of using fields representing vector forces is clear: we can add more fields and sum the resulting force over a set of particles. The SPH model and the constitutive modelling technique will readily determine the resulting internal response to the force and the changes in the triangular mesh shape associated with the particle system.

FUTURE DIRECTIONS

One of our future research directions is to extend the amount of muscular system integrated into our model. An increased set of muscles will improve the reality of the computed motion while allowing more complex results. There is however an obvious computational time/complexity trade-off which needs to be taken into account.

Currently we use a particles system that uses a unique constant density value for all particles. We are working on a more complex system allowing the particles' density to vary depending on the tissue modelled (e.g. surface or depth specific). This will benefit from new data we will gather in late 2008 using Magnetic Resonance Elastography. This will allow us, to map a different density value for each voxel of the volume acquired. The obvious advantage of this new system is to obtain a better description of the tissue and a more realistic solution of the constitutive model.

We are currently investigating several ways to improve both the quality of data gathered and the model properties and behaviour. Preliminary results on the extraction of 3D contours from implicit surfaces (Krueger, Delmas, & Gimel'farb, 2007) show that extracting the 3D lip surfaces may be done automatically. Using synchronised video cameras, placed along converging axis, for lip tracking, may help obtain more accurate peripheral lip contours (i.e. closer to the lip corners) that would improve the particles system's force computation. Long term we hope to model the particles system with data gathered through dynamic 3D lip contour tracking using synchronised video camera systems (Woodward, Delmas, & Gimel'farb, 2007), accurate 3D face surface generation (Gimel'farb, Delmas, Morris, & Shorin, 2007) and 3D contour extraction (Krueger et al. 2007).

REFERENCES

Ahlberg, J. (2001). *CANDIDE-3 - an updated parametrized face* (Tech. Rep. LiTH-ISY-R-2326), Linkoping University, Sweden, Department of Electrical Engineering.

Arai, K., & Kurihara, T. (1991). A transformation method for modeling and animation of the human face from photographs. *Proceedings of Computer Animation*, (pp. 45-58). Tokyo: Japan: Springer.

Basu, S., Oliver, N., & Pentland, A. (1998). 3D modeling of human lip motions. *Proceedings of the International Conference on Computer Vision*, (pp. 337-343). Bombay, India: IEEE Press.

Benoit, C., Lallouache, M. T., Mohamadi, T. M., & Abry, C. (1992). A set of French visemes for visual speech synthesis. In G. Bailly & C. Benoit (Eds), *Talking Machines: Theories, Models, and Designs* (pp. 485-503). Amsterdam, Holland: Elsevier Science Publishers.

Benoit, C. (1996). Synthesis and automatic recognition of audio-visual speech. *Proceedings of the Colloquium Integrated Audio-Visual Processing for Recognition, Synthesis and Communication,* (Digest No: 1996/213, pp.1/1-1/6). London, UK: IEEE Press.

Chan, M., Delmas, P., Gimel'farb, G., & Leclercq, P. (2005). Comparative study of 3D face acquisition techniques. In A. Gagalowicz & W. Philips, eds., *Proceedings of the International Conference on Computer Analysis of Images and Patterns,* (LNCS 3691, pp. 740-747). Versailles, France: Springer.

Cheung, Y. K., & Leung, A. Y. T. (Eds). (1991). *Finite Element Methods in Dynamics*, New York: Science Press.

Duck, F. A. (Ed.). (1990). *Physical Properties of Tissue*, London: Academic Press.

Ekman, P. (1972). Universals and cultural differences in facial expressions of emotion. In J. Cole (Ed.), *Proceedings of the Nebraska symposium on motivation*, (pp. 207-282). Lincoln: University of Nebraska Press.

Essa I. (1994). *Analysis, Interpretation, and Synthesis of Facial Expressions.* Unpublished doctoral dissertation, Cambridge, Mass., USA: MIT, Department of Media Arts and Sciences.

Gimel'farb, G., Delmas, P. J., Morris, J., & Shorin, A. S. (2007). Robust face matching under large occlusions. In R. Cucchiara (Ed.), *Proceedings of the 14th International Conference on Image Analysis and Processing*, (pp.448-453). Modena, Italy: IEEE Press.

Goecke, R., Millar, J. B., Zelinsky, A., & Robert-Ribes, J. (2001). *Stereo-vision lip-tracking for audio-video speech processing.* Paper presented at the IEEE International Conference on Acoustics, Speech, and Signal Processing. Salt Lake City, USA.

Gray, H. (2000). Anatomy of the Human Body. *Bartleby's online edition.* Retrieved October 10, 2007, from http://www.bartleby.com/107/

Guiard-Marigny, T., Tsingos, N., Adjoudani, A., Benoît, C., & Gascuel, M. P. (1996). 3D Models of the Lips for Realistic Speech Animation. In J.A. Jacko (Ed.), *Proceedings of Computer Animation*, (pp. 80-89). Geneva, Switzerland: IEEE Press.

Hieber, S. E., Walther, J. H., & Koumoutsakos, P. (2004). Remeshed smoothed particle hydrodynamics simulation of the mechanical behavior of human organs. *Care, 12*(4), 305-314.

Hoover, Wm. G. (Eds). (2006). *Particle Applied Mechanics: The State of the Art.* Hackensack, NJ: World Scientific Publishing.

Jansson, J., & Vergeest, J. S. M. (2002). A discrete mechanics model for deformable bodies. *Computer-Aided Design, 34*, 913-928.

Krueger, M., Delmas, P. J., & Gimel'farb, G. (2007). Towards feature extraction on implicit surfaces using geodesic active contours. In *Proceedings of Image and Vision Computing New Zealand 2007 Conference*, 5-7 December 2007, (pp. 294-299). Hamilton, New Zealand: Waikato University Press.

Leclerc Y. G., & Fua, P. (1996). Taking advantage of image based and geometry-based constraints to recover 3-D surfaces. *Computer Vision Image Understanding, 64*(1), 111-127.

Lievin, M., & Luthon, F. (2004). Nonlinear color space and spatiotemporal MRF for hierarchical segmentation of face features in video. *IEEE Transactions on Image Processing, 13*(1), 63-71.

Liu, G. R., & Liu, M. B. (Eds). (2003). *Smoothed particle hydrodynamics: a mesh-free particle method.* Hackensack, NJ: World Scientific Publishing.

McGrath, M. (1985). *An examination of cues for visual and audio-visual speech perception using natural and computer-generated faces.* Unpublished doctoral dissertation, University of Nottingham, UK.

Monaghan, J. J. (1992). Smoothed particle hydrodynamics. *Annual Review of Astronomy and Astrophysics, 30*, 543-574.

Monaghan, J. (2005). Smoothed particle hydrodynamics. *Reports on Progress in Physics, 68*, 1703-1759.

Montgomery, A. A. (1980). Development of a model for generating synthetic animated lip shapes. *Journal of the Acoustical Society of America, 68*, S58 (abstract).

Müller, M., Schirm, S., Teschner, M., Heidelberger, B., & Gross, M. (2004). Interaction of fluids with deformable solids. *Journal of Computer Animation and Virtual Worlds, 15*(3-4), 159-171.

Neumann, U., & Noh, J. (1998). *A survey of facial modeling and animation techniques* (Tech. Rep. 99-705). Los Angeles, Cal.: University of Southern California, Department of Computer Science.

Parke, F. I. (1972). Computer Generated Animation of Faces. *Proceedings of the ACM Annual Conference, 1*, 451-457. Boston, Mass, USA: ACM Press.

Parke, F. I. (1974). *A parametric model for human faces* (Tech. Rep. 75-047). Salt Lake City, Utah: University of Utah, Department of Computer Science.

Sifakis, E., Selle, A., Robinson-Mosher, A., & Fedkiw, R. (2006). Simulating Speech with a Physics-Based Facial Muscle Model. In M.-P. Cani & J. O'Brien (Eds), *Proceedings of the Eurographics/SIGGRAPH Symposium on Computer Animation*, (pp. 261-270). Boston, Mass., USA: ACM Press.

Solenthaler, B., Schläfli, J., & Pajarola, R. (2007). A Unified Particle Model for Fluid-Solid Interactions. *Computer Animation and Virtual Worlds, 18*(1), 69-82.

Summerfield, Q. (1992). Lipreading and Audio-Visual Speech Perception. *Philosophical Transactions: Biological Sciences, 335*(1273), 71-78.

Terzopoulos, D., & Waters, K. (1990). Physically-Based Facial Modeling, Analysis, and Animation. *Journal of Visualization and Computer Animation, 1*(2), 73-80.

Wen, Z., & Huang, T. S (Eds). (2004). *3D Face Processing: Modeling, Analysis and Synthesis.* Kluwer Academic Publication Press.

Woodham R. J. (1980). Photometic method for determining surface orientation from multiple images. *Optimal Engineering, 19,* 139-144.

Woodward, A., An, D., Lin, Y., Delmas, P. Gimel'farb, G., & Morris, J. (2006). An evaluation of three popular computer vision approaches for 3-D face synthesis. *Proceedings of the Joint International Workshops on Statistical, Structural, and Syntactic Pattern Recognition,* (LNCS 4109, pp. 270-278). Hong Kong, China: Springer.

Woodward, A. M., Delmas, P. J., & Gimel'farb, G. (2007). Low cost virtual face performance capture using stereo Web cameras. In D. Merry & L. Rueda (Eds), *Pacific-Rim Symposium on Image and Video Technology,* (LNCS 4872, pp. 763-776). Santiago, Chile: Springer.

Yamashita, Y., & Kubota, M. (2001). Imaging of elastic modulus of incompressible biological soft tissue from a knowledge of displacement measurements. *Proceedings of the International Conference on Image Processing,* (vol. 1, pp. 321-324). Thessalonica, Greece: IEEE Press.

Zhang, Z., Liu, Z., Adler, D., Cohen, M. F., Hanson, E., & Shan, Y. (2004). Robust and Rapid Generation of Animated Faces from Video Images: A Model-Based Modeling Approach. *International Journal of Computer Vision, 58*(2), 93-119.

ADDITIONAL READING

Basu, S., Oliver, N., & Pentland, A. (1998). 3D Modeling and Tracking of Human Lip Motions. *Proceedings of the Sixth International Conference on Computer Vision,* (pp. 337-343). Bombay, India: IEEE Press.

Bell, N., Yu, Y., & Mucha, P. (2005). Particle-based simulation of granular materials. *Proceedings of the SIGGRAPH/Eurographics Symposium on Computer Animation,* (pp. 77-86). Los Angeles, Cal., USA: ACM Press.

Cameron, J. (1991). Physical Properties of Tissue. A Comprehensive Reference Book, edited by Francis A. Duck. *Medical Physics, 18*(4), 834-834.

Capell, S., Green, S., Curless, B., Duchamp, T., & Popovi, Z. (2002). A multiresolution framework for dynamic deformations. *Proceedings of the SIGGRAPH/Eurographics symposium on Computer animation,* (pp. 41-47). San Antonio, NM, USA: ACM Press.

Chabanas, M., Luboz, V., & Payan, Y. (2003). Patient specific finite element model of the face soft tissues for computer-assisted maxillofacial surgery. *Medical Image Analysis, 7,* 131-151.

Choe, B., Lee, H., & Ko, H. S. (2001). Performance-driven muscle-based facial animation. *The Journal of Visualization and Computer Animation, 12,* 67-79.

Deng, Z., & Noh, J. (2007). Computer Facial Animation: A Survey. In Z. Deng & U. Neumann (Eds), *Data-Driven 3D Facial Animation* (pp. 1-28). London, UK: Springer.

Ishikawa, T., Sera, H., Morishima, S., & Terzopoulos, D. (1997). 3D estimation of facial muscle parameter from the 2D marker movement using neural network. In R. T. Chin & T.-C. Pong *Proceedings of the Asian Conference on Computer Vision* (LNCS 1352, pp. 671-678). Honk-Kong: Springer.

Kawashima, Y., & Sakai, Y. (2007). Large Deformation Analysis of Hyperelastic Materials Using SPH Method. *e-Journal of Soft Materials, 3*, 21-28.

Kensler, A., & Shirley, P. (2006). Optimizing Ray-Triangle Intersection via Automated Search. *Proceedings of the Symposium on Interactive Ray Tracing*, (pp. 33-38). Salt lake City, USA: IEEE Press.

Kwon, O.-H. (1999). Automatic estimation of 2D facial muscle parameter using neural network. *Proceedings of the Fifth Asia-Pacific Conference on Optoelectronics and Communications Conference,* (vol. 2, pp. 994-997). Yokohama, Japan: IEEE Press.

Liu, G. R., Liu, M. B., & Li, S. (2004). Smoothed particle hydrodynamics a meshfree method. *Computational Mechanics, 33*, 491-491.

Garcia, C., Mendoza, C., Pastor, Rodriguez, L. (2006). Optimized linear FEM for modeling deformable objects. *Computer Animation and Virtual Worlds,* 17(3-4), 393-402.

Monaghan, J. J. (2005). Smoothed particle hydrodynamics. *Reports on Progress in Physics, 68*(8), 1703-1759.

Morishima, S., Ishikawa, T., & Terzopoulos, D. (1998). Facial muscle parameter decision from 2D frontal image. Proceedings of the *Fourteenth International Conference on Pattern Recognition*, (vol. 1, 160-162). Brisbane, Australia: IEEE Press.

Mueller, M., Charypar, D., & Gross, M. (2003). Particle-based fluid simulation for interactive applications. *Proceedings of the SIGGRAPH/Eurographics symposium on Computer animation*, (pp. 154-159). San Diego, Cal., USA: ACM Press.

Mueller, M., Keiser, R., Nealen, A., Pauly, M., Gross, M., & Alexa, M. (2004). Point based animation of elastic, plastic and melting objects. *Proceedings of the SIGGRAPH/Eurographics Symposium on Computer Animation*, (pp. 141-151). Los Angeles, Cal., USA: ACM Press.

Mueller, M., Solenthaler, B., Keiser, R., & Gross, M. (2005). Particle-based fluid-fluid interaction. *Proceedings of the SIGGRAPH/Eurographics Symposium on Computer Animation*, (pp. 237-244). Los Angeles, Cal., USA: ACM Press.

Picinbono, G., Delingette, H., & Ayache, N. (2003). Non-linear anisotropic elasticity for real-time surgery simulation. *Graphical Models, 65*(5), 305-321.

Solenthaler B., Schläfli J., Pajarola R. (2007). A unified particle model for fluid-solid interactions. *Computer Animation and Virtual Worlds, 18*, 69-82.

Sera, H., Morishima, S., & Terzopoulos, D. (1996). Physics-based muscle model for mouth shape control. *Proceedings of the 5th International Workshop on Robot and Human Communication*, (pp. 207-212). Tsukuba, Japan: IEEE Press.

Silver, F. H., Freeman, J. W., & DeVore, D. (2001). Viscoelastic properties of human skin and processed dermis. *Skin Research and Technology, 7*, 18-23.

Simon, C., Philippe, B., & Pierre, P. (2005). Particle-based viscoelastic fluid simulation. *Proceedings of the SIGGRAPH/Eurographics Symposium on Computer Animation*, (pp. 219-228). Los Angeles, Cal., USA: IEEE Press.

Hieber, S.E., Walther, J.H., Koumoutsakos, P. (2004). Remeshed smoothed particle hydro-dynamics simulation of the mechanical behavior of human organs. *Technology and Health Care, 12*(4), 305-314.

Steinhauser, M. O., Grass, K., Thoma, K., & Blumen, A. (2006). Impact dynamics and failure of brittle solid states by means of non-equilibrium molecular dynamics simulations. *EPL (Europhysics Letters), 73*(1), 62-68.

Tang, S.-S., Yan, H., & Liew, A. W.-C. (2003). A NURBS-based vector muscle model for generating human facial expressions. *Proceedings of the Joint Conference of the Fourth International Conference on Information, Communications and Signal Processing and Pacific Rim Conference on Multimedia*, (vol. 2, pp. 758-762). Hong-Kong, China: IEEE Press.

Yamashita, Y., & Kubota, M. (2001). Imaging of elastic modulus of incompressible biological soft tissue from a knowledge of displacement measurements. *Proceedings of the International Conference on Image Processing,* (vol. 1, pp. 321-324). Thessalonica, Greece: IEEE Press.

Zhang, Y., Prakash, E. C., & Sung, E. (2001). A physically-based model for real-time facial expression animation. *Proceedings of the Third International Conference on 3-D Digital Imaging and Modeling,* (pp. 399-406). Quebec-city, Canada: IEEE Press.

Zhang, Y., Prakash, E. C., & Sung, E. (2001). A physically-based model with adaptive refinement for facial animation. *Proceedings of the Fourteenth Conference on Computer Animation,* (pp. 28-252). Seoul, Korea: IEEE Press.

Zhang, Y., Prakash, E. C., & Sung, E. (2001). Real-time physically-based facial expression animation using mass-spring system. *Proceedings of the Computer Graphics International Conference*, (pp. 347-350). Hong-Kong, China: IEEE Press.

Zhang, Y., Prakash, E. C., & Sung, E. (2002). Synthesis of facial expressions using a 3D anatomical model. *Proceedings of the 7th International Conference on Control, Automation, Robotics and Vision*, (vol. 2, pp. 704-709). Singapore: Cedar Press.

Zhang, Y., Prakash, E. C., & Sung, E. (2004). A new physical model with multilayer architecture for facial expression animation using dynamic adaptive mesh. *IEEE Transactions on Visualization and Computer Graphics, 10*(3), 339-352.

Chapter VIII
How to Use Manual Labelers in the Evaluation of Lip Analysis Systems?

Shafiq ur Réhman
Umeå University, Sweden

Li Liu
Umeå University, Sweden

Haibo Li
Umeå University, Sweden

ABSTRACT

*The purpose of this chapter is not to describe any lip analysis algorithms but rather to discuss some of the issues involved in evaluating and calibrating labeled lip features from human operators. In the chapter we question the common practice in the field: using manual lip labels directly as the **ground truth** for the evaluation of lip analysis algorithms. Our empirical results using an Expectation-Maximization procedure show that subjective noise in manual labelers can be quite significant in terms of quantifying both human and algorithm extraction performance. To train and evaluate a lip analysis system one can measure the performance of human operators and infer the "ground truth" from the manual labelers, simultaneously.*

INTRODUCTION

Lip image analysis (lip detection, localization and segmentation) plays an important role in many real world tasks, particularly in visual speech analysis/synthesis applications (e.g. application area mentioned by Mathew et al., 2002; Daubias et al., 2002; Potamianos et al., 2004; Cetingul et al., 2005; Wark et al., 1998; Chan et al., 1999; Chetty et al., 2004; Wang et al., 2004; Tian et al., 2000; Luthon et al., 2006, Réhman et al., 2007). Although impressive achievement has been made in the field (Wang et al., 2007; Caplier et al., 2008) (e.g. it is reported that the maximum mean lip tracking error has been reached to 4% of the mouth width (Eveno et al., 2004)); from an engineering viewpoint, automatic lip analysis today still presents a significant challenge to current capabilities in computer vision and pattern recognition. An important research problem is *how to boost the technology development of lip analysis to achieve an order-of-magnitude improvement*? An order-of-magnitude improvement in the performance of lip analysis will reach usual mean human performance: lip tracking with an accuracy of one-pixel for CIF lip images (position error around 0.5% of the mouth width).

Researchers from lip image analysis (especially lip-tracking and localization) should consider lessons from the work of face recognition vendor test (FRVT) (Phillips et al., 2000), which is a series of U.S. Government sponsored face recognition technology evaluations. Under its impressive effort in thirteen years, face recognition performance has improved by two orders of magnitude. To expect a similar order-of-magnitude improvement with lip analysis technologies, an urgent issue is *to establish performance benchmarks for lip analysis, assess the advancement in the state-of-the-art in the technology,* and *identify the most promising approaches for further development.*

Currently positive activities in the establishment of common test databases are in progress. Examples of publicly available databases include e.g. TULIPS 1.0 (Movellan, 1995), BioID (Jesorsky et al., 2001), (X) M2VTS (Messer et al., 1999), BANCA (Bailly-Bailliere et al., 2003), and JAFFE (Lyons et al., 1999). However, the evaluation criteria are not agreed on common ground yet. Lack of well accepted evaluation protocols makes it impossible even for experts in the field to have a clear picture of the state of the art lip analysis technology.

A common practice in the (*quantitative*) evaluation of a lip analysis technology is to collect *reference* examples with manual labeling by having the human operators examine a lip image on the computer screen and then use a mouse to indicate where they think the lips or the key points are. These manual labeling-marks of the lip area are used as the "ground truth" for the training and evaluation of lip analysis systems.

A critical question is: ***Can the manual labelers be served as the ground truth?***

We suggest that one should *not directly* use the manual labelers for evaluation because:

- There can be considerable ambiguity in lip labeling: for the same lip image, individual operators can produce different labels, and even the same person can produce different labels over time.
- Ignoring subjective uncertainty in human lip labeling can lead to significant overconfidence in terms of performance estimation for both humans and computers.
- Most lip analysis algorithms are learning based and heavily relied on the training data (reference). Inherent ambiguity in lip labelers will significantly lower the performance of the trained algorithms.

We further question a common implication in the evaluation that *human will perform (much) better than the algorithms.* In fact, it has been shown in the FRVT 2006 (Phillips et al., 2006) that it is not always human outperforms better than image analysis algorithms, and it was the first time that measuring human face recognition capability was integrated into evaluation. From experiments, it has found that algorithms are capable of human performance levels, and that at false accept rates in the range of 0.05, the algorithms even can out-perform humans (Phillips et al., 2006). Similar claims can be found in lip analysis literatures that some algorithms are comparable to human performance (Eveno et al., 2004) or even better than human in the detection of certain feature points (Goecke et al., 2000).

In this chapter we introduce a new way of using manual labeling to evaluate lip analysis systems. The key points are

- Measure the quality of human operators as well as manual labels;
- Infer the "ground truth" from the manual labels weighted by the quality;
- Replace manual labels with the inferred ground truth for the training and evaluation of lip analysis algorithms.

In present work BioID database (Jesorsky et al., 2001) is used as a show case of our new evaluation paradigm. We demonstrate how to generate a consensus ground truth for assessment of how well human operators are performing based on the fact that they cannot label the lip features with 100% correction. Our empirical results by an Expectation-Maximization procedure show that subjective noise from manual labelers can be quite significant in terms of quantifying both human and algorithm lip detection performance. Measuring the quality of human operators and manual labeling is a key step to achieve an unbiased evaluation.

MANUAL LIP LABELLING

Typically, manual lip labeling, used in the evaluation of lip analysis algorithms is performed by asking human operators (more often, students or researchers) to mark some semantic feature points around the mouth, e.g., left and right corners of the mouth, middle points of upper and lower lips. The spatial positions of the marked feature points are used directly as the "ground truth" for the evaluation of algorithms. One can see some problems here, *first* the definition of the feature points itself may be fuzzy and quite often no distinct positions exist in images. Depending on the quality of lip images, performance of the operators will be varying (this is called *intra-person variation*); *second* the labeling is person dependent, which will generate so-called *inter-person variation*. Therefore, it is necessary to handle both intra- and inter-person variations. To do so, we have to measure the performance (quality) of individual operators.

To measure the performance of each operator, we have to know the ground truth of the feature points. Although physical or digital phantoms of the lips can provide a level of known "ground truth", as noted in Warfield et al. (2004); they have so far been unable to reproduce the full range of imaging characteristics. One alternative is to infer the "ground truth" from manual labelers. In the medical image segmentation area Warfield et al. developed a technique to simultaneously estimate both ground true of image segmentation and operator quality based on an EM algorithm (Warfield et al., 2004). Here we reformulate the lip localization problem into a segmentation problem so that the algorithm proposed by Warfield et al. can be applied. More specifically, when feature points are marked, a closed contour is formed from the feature points. The contours from feature points labeled by 4 operators around the mouth of a sample lip image are shown in Fig.1

One can see that the four human labelers performed differently. The mouth area can be segmented by taking interior of the closed lip contour. Here we assume that the quality of segmentation of the mouth

Figure 1. Sample example of human labeling given on the BioID face database. One can see that lips drawn from manual labeling from 4 human operators vary. ©2008 Shafiq ur Réhman. Used with permission.

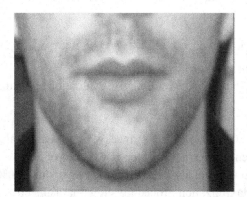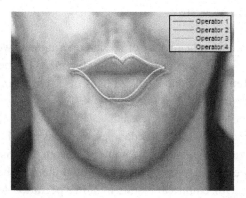

is a measure of the quality of the feature points. If the ground truth of the mouth region is known, the performance of individual operators can be assessed by measuring the quality of their segmentation.

Following (Warfield et al., 2004), the performance of operators is specified by two terms: *sensitivity* and *specificity*. The *sensitivity* is defined as how well the operator marked the true area under consideration, and *specificity* is how well the operator differentiated the rest of the image area from the true mouth area. The performance parameter p represents the "true negative fraction" or specificity, and q represents the "true positive fraction" or sensitivity. This is summarized in table I

These two parameters are the classification probabilities $\{p, q\}$ and are assumed to be person specific. For any segmentation **D** and the ground true **T**, $\{p, q\}$ can be calculated as (see Fig. 2)

$$p = \frac{\overline{D} - \overline{D} \cap T}{\overline{T}}$$

$$q = \frac{T \cap D}{T}$$

Table 1

D/T	0 (non-mouth)	1 (mouth)
0 (non-mouth)	p	$1-q$
1 (mouth)	$1-p$	q
Marginal Total	1	1

Figure 2. Segmentation D and ground truth T

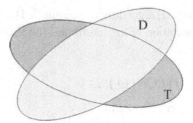

The key is how to get the ground truth **T** and further assess performance of individual operator given the segmentation **D**.

INFERRING GROUND TRUTH FROM HUMAN DATA

Since the "ground truth" of segmentation is not known (or missing) we have to figure out how to estimate the "ground truth" from the segmentation made by the operators. One solution is to use the Expectation-Maximization (EM) technique to infer the ground truth (Dempster et al., 1977). For our purpose, we extend the algorithm STAPLE developed by Warfield et. al. (2004) so that it could handle annotated images from a database.

Formally, let **D** be the $N \times M \times J$ matrix representing the binary decisions of J operators on M mouth areas. The number of pixels in a lip image is N. **T** be the $N \times M$ matrix representing M binary "truth" mouth regions in which *1*'s are for mouth-pixels and *0*'s for non-mouth pixels. Let (**D**; **T**) be the complete data and the probability mass function of the complete data is given as $f(D, T/\Theta)$ where the performance parameters are $\theta_j = (p_j, q_j), j = J$. The log likelihood function of the complete data is expressed as

$$\ln L_{complete} \Theta = \ln f(D, T/\Theta)$$

In theory the operator parameters $\Theta = \{\theta_1, \theta_2...\}^T$ could be estimated by maximizing the log likelihood function of the complete data; i.e.

$$\widehat{\Theta} = \arg\max_{\Theta} \ln f(D, T / \Theta)$$

Unfortunately it doesn't work here simply because the "ground truth" of the mouth region is unknown. One strategy to overcome the difficulty is to compute the conditional expectation of the complete-data log-likelihood function instead,

$$\Theta = \arg\max_{\Theta} E_T\{\ln f(D,T \mid \Theta) \mid D\}$$

The Expectation-Maximization (EM) algorithm can be applied to estimate the operator performance parameters Θ. The conditional expectation of log likelihood function can be further written as

$$\begin{aligned}
\Theta &= \arg\max_{\Theta} E_T\{\ln f(D,T \mid \Theta) \mid D\} \\
&= \arg\max_{\Theta} E_T\left[\ln \frac{f(D,T,\Theta)}{f(\Theta)} \mid D\right] \\
&= \arg\max_{\Theta} E_T\left[\ln \frac{f(D,T,\Theta)f(T,\Theta)}{f(\Theta)} \mid D\right]
\end{aligned}$$

Since the ground true **T** is independent of the performance parameters

$$f(T,\Theta) = f(T)f(\Theta)$$

Hence we have

$$\Theta = \arg\max_{\Theta} E_T\left[\ln f(D \mid T,\Theta)f(T) \mid D\right] \tag{1}$$

Omitting **T**, we have

$$\Theta = \arg\max_{\Theta} E_T\left[\ln f(D \mid T,\Theta) \mid D\right] \tag{2}$$

Let Θ° be initial value for parameter Θ and assuming the operator decisions are conditionally independent given operator performance parameters and the ground truth. The **E-Step** calculates

$$\begin{aligned}
Q(\Theta \mid \Theta^\circ) &\equiv E_T\{\ln f(D \mid T,\Theta) \mid D,\Theta^\circ\} \\
&= \sum_T f(T \mid D,\Theta^\circ)\ln f(D \mid T,\Theta)
\end{aligned}$$

and **M**-step requires the maximization of $Q(\Theta \mid \Theta^\circ)$ over the parameter space of Θ; i.e. choosing Θ^1 such that $Q(\Theta^1 \mid \Theta^\circ) \geq Q(\Theta \mid \Theta^\circ)$. For each iteration k, the current estimate of Θ^k and segmentation decision **D** are used to calculate the conditional expectation of the complete-data log-likelihood function and then the estimate of Θ^{k+1}, which is found by the maximization of $Q(\Theta \mid \Theta^k)$.

The **E**- and **M**- steps are iterated until convergence. Local convergence is guaranteed when likelihood has an upper bound.

The ground truth and performance parameters can be estimated iteratively:

Estimation of the Ground Truth given Operator Performance Parameters

The ground truth can be estimated by

$$f\left(T \mid D, \Theta^k\right) = \frac{f\left(D, T \mid \Theta^k\right)}{f\left(D \mid \Theta^k\right)}$$

$$= \frac{f\left(D \mid T, \Theta^k\right) f(T)}{\sum_T f\left(D \mid T, \Theta^k\right) f(T)}$$

where $f(T)$ is the priori probability of the ground true **T**.

Estimation of the Performance Parameters of the Operators

Given D^r_{ij} decision of the ***jth***-operator for ***rth***-image and ground truth T^r_i, the operator performance parameters $\{p_j, q_j\}$ sensitivity and specificity are

$$p_j = \sum_{ir} \Psi(D^r_{ij} = 1 \mid T^r_i = 1), \quad q_j = \sum_{ir} \Psi(D^r_{ij} = 0 \mid T^r_i = 0);$$

Where Ψ is the conditional probability of the segmentation when the ground truth is known.

It is assumed that segmentation decisions are all conditionally independent given the "ground truth" (i.e. T^r_j) and the performance parameter $p_j, q_j \in [0,1]$, i.e.

$$(D^r_j \mid T^r, \Theta_j) \perp (D^r_{\hat{j}} \mid T^r, \Theta_{\hat{j}}); \quad \forall \, j \neq \hat{j}$$

If p^{k-1}_j and q^{k-1}_j are the previous estimate of the operator performance parameters, according to equation 2 then we have

$$(p^k_j, q^k_j) = \underset{p,q}{\arg\max} \, E_T\left[\ln f(D/T, p, q).f(T)\} \mid D, p^{k-i}_j, q^{k-1}_j\right]$$

$$= \underset{p,q}{\arg\max} \sum_r \sum_i E_T\left[\ln f(D^r_{ij}/T^r_i, p_j, q_j) \mid D^r_{ij}, p^{k-i}_j, q^{k-1}_j\right] \tag{3}$$

AN EXPERIMENT ON COMPARING HUMAN AND ALGORITHM PERFORMANCE

To demonstrate the concept proposed in this chapter we select the database BioID (Jesorsky et al., 2001) as a case study. The BioID Face Database is used within the FGnet project of the European Working Group on face and gesture recognition (FGnet-IST-2000). The BioID Face Database has been recorded and was published to give all researchers working in the area of face detection the possibility to compare the quality of their face detection algorithms with others. During the recording special emphasis has been laid on "real world" conditions. Therefore, the test set features a large variety of illumination, background and face size. The dataset consists of 1521 gray level images with a resolution of 384 x 286 pixels. Each one shows the frontal view of a face of one out of 23 different test persons. For comparison purposes the set contains manually set facial features points. Two PhD students from the department of Imaging Science and Biomedical Engineering at the University of Manchester marked up the images from the BioID Face Database. They selected important feature points (as shown in Fig. 3-a), which are very useful for facial analysis and gesture recognition. Four points around the mouth are marked:

Figure 3. a) Example of human labeling points given on the BioID database. b) Four feature p around the mouth. ©2008 Shafiq ur Réhman. Used with permission.

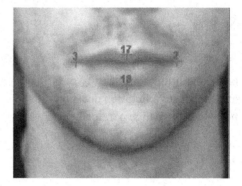

Figure 4. A lip spline, mouth image and segmented mouth area after the EM algorithm based on performance parameters. ©2008 Shafiq ur Réhman. Used with permission.

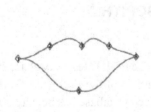
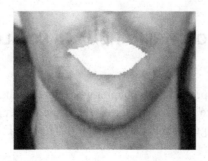

- No. 2 = right mouth corner
- No. 3 = left mouth corner
- No. 17 = center point on outer edge of upper lip
- No. 18 = center point on outer edge of lower lip

To compare the quality of different face detection algorithms on the test set, the following distance based quality measure is suggested: Estimate the facial feature (eye or lip) positions with the test algorithm and calculate the absolute pixel distance from the manually set positions so that two distance values will be received. The distances will be used to measure the performance of the algorithm.

The current results challenge the way of directly using the manual annotation as the "ground truth" for evaluation of algorithms. We do by estimating of the quality of the annotation. We invited three students from our university to mark the four points around the mouth for all face images (as shown in Fig. 3-b). To form a nice mouth region, two additional points are interpolated from the corner and center

Figure 5. Sample lip area marked by operator 1,2,3,4 respectively. ©2008 Shafiq ur Réhman. Used with permission.

Figure 6. a) Sensitivity of human operators after iterations. b) Specificity of human operator after complete convergence

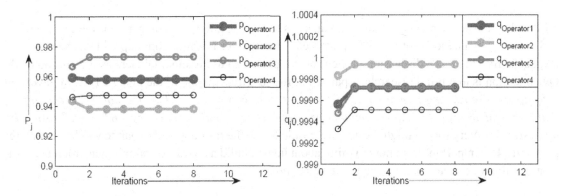

Table 2. The computed sensitivity and specificity of four operators

OPERATOR	P	Q
1	0.9583509	0.9778526
2	0.939260	0.9910173
3	0.9740195	0.9775210
4	0.9463833	0.9545102

points for all lips. In this way we have total six points and a closed lip contour can be formed by spline curves. We overlay lip contours over face images as shown in Fig. 4). One can see that the decision on mouth regions varies from person to person (Fig. 5).

To quantitatively assess the performance of individual operators we calculate the performance parameters. The interior of the lip contour is segmented and used for estimation of ground truth. The initial values of performance parameters were set to 0.9 and initialization probabilities of being mouth pixel and non-mouth pixel were 0.5; $p_j = q_j = 0.9$ and $P_r(T_i = 1) = P_r(T_i = 0) = 0.5$. The algorithm converges quite fast as shown in Fig. 6. The converged result is listed in table II. It can be seen from table II that the performance parameters, *sensitivity* and *specificity* differ from person to person. It is very interesting to notice that the annotation provided with the BioID face database don't do the top job. They are just ranked No. 3. It is questionable to use a bad annotation which has been known *a prior* to judge the performance of computer algorithms. One can see also that there is a space to improve the quality of manual annotation for evaluation. It is worth mentioning that in our formulae we show how to estimate the ground true for mouth segmentation but not how to estimate the ground true of the feature points

CONCLUDING REMARKS

To speed up the development of human lip analysis technology, it is extremely important to have a fair and objective evaluation protocol. The purpose of this chapter is not to come up with such evaluation protocols. Instead, it is a discussion of the problem of how to use manual labelers as the ground truth. Our intention is to remind researchers particular the researchers new in the field of 1) *being aware of subjective noise existing in manual labelers and there are ways to reduce the noise*; 2) *recognizing that technical progress has made computer programs close to and even better than human for some lip analysis tasks*. Very soon it might be no longer valid to use the results from human to validate computer programs. It is important from now to think about how to build a common and fair evaluation platform where both program and human can be treated *equally*.

FURTHER READINGS

We highly recommend the work done in the following research areas to the readers who want to learn more about the topic

1. **Face Recognition Vendor Test (FRVT)** (Phillips et al., 2000, 2000b, 2005, 2006; O'Toole et al., 2007), which is a series of U.S. Government sponsored face recognition technology evaluations. One can see how "standardization" or evaluation process to boost significantly technical progress.

2. **Automatic Eye Detection and Validation** (Jesorsky et al., 2001; Wang et al., 2005; Asteriadis et al., 2006; Cristinacce et al., 2004). Technically this is quite similar to the problem of automatic lip localization. Noticeably, kind of standard databases, XM2VTS (Messer et al. 1999) and BioID (Jesorsky et al., 2001) have been widely used in the area and the ROC curve over the databases is commonly adopted; which greatly facilities the comparison between different techniques. However, as in the lip analysis area, manual labelers are used as the ground true. The problem of subjective noise in manual labelers has not been addressed.

3. **Evaluation in Medical Image Analysis** (Warfield et al., 2002, 2004, and 2008): The work of Warfield et al. on evaluation in the medical image segmentation area is very inspired. One can see how manual labelers given by medical experts are treated and evaluated.

ACKNOWLEDGMENT

This work was supported by the Tactile Video Project and by Swedish Research Council (i.e., Vetenskapsrådet www.vr.se).

REFERENCES

Asteriadis, S., Nikolaidis, N., Hajdu, A., & Pitas, I. (2006). A novel eye-detection algorithm utilizing edge-related geometrical information. *In 14th European Signal Processing Conference (EUSIPCO06).*

Bailly-Bailliere, E., Bengio, S., Bimbot, F., Hamouz, M., Kittler, J., Mariethoz, J., Matas, J., Messer, K., Popoviciand, V., Poree, F., Ruiz, B., & Thiran, J. P. (2003). The BANCA Database and Evaluation Protocol. In Lecture Notes in Computer Science. *4th International Conference on Audio- and Video-Based Biometric Person Authentication*, 2688, 625–638.

Caplier, A., Stillittano, S., Bouvier, C., & Coulon, P. (2008). *Lip Modelling and Segmentation. Visual Speech Recognition: Lip Segmentation and Mapping* (To appear).

Cetingul, H. E., Yemez, Y., Erzin, E., & Tekalp, A. M. (2005). Robust Lip-motion Features for Speaker Identification. *In Proceeding of the IEEE International Conference on Acoustics, Speech and Signal Processing*, 509 – 512.

Chan, S., Ngo, C., W., & Lai, K. (1999). Motion tracking of human mouth by generalized deformable models. *Pattern Recognition Letters, 20*(9), 879-887.

Chetty G., & Wagner, M. (2004). Liveness verification in audio-video speaker authentication. In *Proceedings of 10th Australian Conference on Speech Science and Technology*, 358-363.

Cristinacce, D., Cootes, T., & Scott, I. (2004). A multi-stage approach to facial feature detection. *In 15th British Machine Vision Conference*, London, England, 277–286.

Daubias, P., & Deleglise, P. (2002). Statistical Lip-Appearance Models Trained Automatically using Audio Information. *Journal on Applied Signal Processing, 2002*(11), 1202–1212.

Dempster, A. P., Laird, N. M., & Rubin, D. B. (1997). Maximum Likelihood from Incomplete Data via the EM Algorithm. *Journal of the Royal Statistical Society: Series B, 39*(1).

Eveno, N., Caplier, A., & Coulon, P. (2004). Automatic and Accurate Lip Tracking. *IEEE Transactions on Circuits and Systems for Video technology, 14(5)*, 706–715.

FGnet-IST-2000-26434. *Face and Gesture Recognition Working Group*. http://www-prima.inrialpes.fr/FGnet/html/home.html.

Goecke, R., Tran, Q., Millar, J., Zelinsky, A., & Robert-Ribes, J. (2000). Validation of an Automatic Lip-Tracking Algorithm and Design of a Database for Audio-Video Speech Processing. *In Proceedings of the 8th Australian International Conference on Speech Science and Technology*, 92–97.

Jesorsky, O., Kirchberg, K., & Frischholz, R. (2001). Robust Face Detection Using the Hausdorff Distance. *In Proceeding of 3rd Int. Conf. on Audio- and Video-based Biometric Person Authentication*, 90–95.

Luthon, F., & Beaumesnil, B. (2006). Real Time lip Tracking for Synthetic face animation with feedback loop. *In Proceedings of international Conference on Computer Vision Theory and Applications, 2*, 402-407.

Lyons, M., Budynek, J., & Akamatsu, S. (1992). Automatic Classification of Single Facial Images. *IEEE Transactions on Pattern Analysis and Machine Intelligence, 21*(12), 1357–1362.

Matthews, I., Cootes, T., Bangham, J., Cox, S., & Harvey, R. (2002). Extraction of Visual Features for Lipreading. *IEEE Transactions on Pattern Analysis and Machine Intelligence, 24*(2), 198 – 213.

Messer, K., Matas, J., Kittler, J., Luettin, J., & Maitre, G. (1999): XM2VTSDB: The Extended M2VTS Database. *In Proceeding of 2nd International Conference on Audio- and video-based person authentication*, 72 – 77.

Movellan, J.R. (1995). Visual Speech Recognition with Stochastic Networks. In G. Tesauro, D. Toruetzky, T. Leen (Eds.), *Advances in Neural Information Processing Systems,* MIT Pess, Cambridge, 7.

O'Toole, A. J., Phillips, P. J., Jiang, F., Ayyad, J., Penard, N., & Abdi, H. (2007). Face recognition algorithms surpass humans matching faces over changes in illumination. *IEEE Transactions on Pattern Analysis and Machine Intelligence, 29*(9), 1642–1646.

Phillips, P. J., Martin, A., Wilson, C., & Przybocki, M. (2000). An Introduction to Evaluating Biometric Systems. *Computer, 33*(2), 56–63.

Phillips, P. J., Moon, H., Rizvi, S. A., & Rauss, P. J. (2000b). The FERET Evaluation Methodology for Face-recognition Algorithms. *IEEE Transactions on Pattern Analysis and Machine Intelligence, 22*(10), 1090–1104.

Phillips, P. J., Flynn, P., Scruggs, T., Bowyer, K., Chang, J., k. Hoffman, Marques, J., Jaesik, M., & Worek, W. (2005). Overview of the Face Recognition Grand Challenge. *IEEE Computer Society Conference on Computer Vision and Pattern Recognition, 1*(20–25), 947–954.

Phillips, P. J., Scruggs, W. T., OToole, A. J., Flynn, P. J., Bowyer, K. W., Schott, C. L., & Sharpe, M. (2006). *FRVT 2006 and ICE 2006 Large-Scale Results*. Evaluation Report: NISTIR 7408.

Potamianos, G., Neti, C., Luettin, J., & Matthews, I. (2004). Audio-Visual Automatic Speech Recognition: An Overview. In G. Bailly, E. Vatikiotis-Bateson, and P. Perrier (Ed.), MIT Press.

Réhman, S. U., Liu, L., & Li H. (2007). Lipless Tracking and Emotion Estimation. *In Proceeding of 3rd International Conference on Signal-Image Technology & Internet- based Systems*, Shanghai, China

Tian, Y. L., Kanade, T., & Cohn, J. (2000). Robust lip tracking by combining Shape, Color and Motion. *In Proceedings of the 4th Asian Conference on Computer Vision*, 1040-1045.

Warfield, S. K., Zou, K. H., & Wells-III, W. M. (2002). Validation of image segmentation and expert quality with an expectation maximization algorithm. *In Fifth International Conference on Medical Image Computing and Computer Assisted Intervention*, 298–306.

Warfield, S. K., Zou, K. H., Wells, W. M. (2008). Validation of image segmentation by estimating rater bias and variance. *Philos. Transact. A. Math. Phys. Eng. Sci., 366*, 2361–2375.

Warfield, S. K., Zou, K. H., & Wells, W. M. (2004). Simultaneous Truth and Performance Level Estimation (STAPLE): An Algorithm for the Validation of Image Segmentation. *IEEE Transactions on Medical Imaging, 23*(7), 903–921.

Wark, T., Dridharan, S., & Chandran, V. (1998). An approach to statistical lip modeling for speaker identification via chromatic feature extraction. *In Proceedings of the 14th IEEE International Conference on Pattern Recognition, 1*, 123-125.

Wnag, Y., Ai, H., Wu, B., & Huang C. (2004). Real time facial expression recognition with ada boost. *In Proceedings of IEEE 7th International Conference on Pattern Recognition*, 926 - 929.

Wang, S. L., Lau, W. H., Liew, A. W. C., & Leung, S. H. (2007). Robust Lip region Segmentation for lip images with Complex Background. *Pattern Recognition, 40*(12), 3481–3491.

Wang, P., Green, M. B., Ji, Q., & Wayman, J. (2005). Automatic eye detection and its validation. In: *Proceedings of the 2005 IEEE Computer Society Conference on Computer Vision and Pattern Recognition – Workshops, 164*.

ADDITIONAL READINGS

Asteriadis, S., Nikolaidis, N., Hajdu, A., & Pitas, I. (2006). A Novel eye-detection algorithm utilizing edge-related geometrical information. *In 14th European Signal Processing Conference (EUSIPCO06).*

Barnard, M., Holden, E.J., & Owens, R. (2002). Lip tracking using pattern matching snakes. *In Proceedings of the 5th Asian Conference on Computer Vision.*

Basu, S., Oliver, N., & Pentland, A. (1998). 3D lip shapes from video: A combined physical-statistical model. *Speech Communication, 26*(12), 131–148.

Bailly-Bailliere, E., Bengio, S., Bimbot, F., Hamouz, M., Kittler, J., Mariethoz, J., Matas, J., Messer, K., Popoviciand, V., Poree, F., Ruiz, B., & Thiran, J. P. (2003). The BANCA Database and Evaluation Protocol. In Lecture Notes in Computer Science. *4th International Conference on Audio- and Video-Based Biometric Person Authentication, 2688,* 625–638.

Black, M. J., Fleet, D. J., & Yacoob, Y. (1998). A framework for modeling appearance change in image sequences. *In Proceedings of 6th IEEE International Conference on Computer Vision,* 660–667.

Caplier, A., Stillittano, S., Bouvier, C., & Coulon, P. (2008). *Lip Modelling and Segmentation. Visual Speech Recognition: Lip Segmentation and Mapping (To appear).*

Cetingul, H. E., Yemez, Y., Erzin, E., & Tekalp, A. M. (2005). Robust Lip-motion Features for Speaker Identification. *In Proceeding of the IEEE International Conference on Acoustics, Speech and Signal Processing,* 509 – 512.

Chan, S., Ngo, C. W., & Lai, K. (1999). Motion tracking of human mouth by generalized deformable models. *Pattern Recognition Letters, 20*(9), 879-887.

Chetty G., & Wagner, M. (2004). Liveness verification in audio-video speaker authentication. *In Proceedings of 10th Australian Conference on Speech Science and Technology,* 358-363.

Cootes, T. F., Cooper, D. H., Taylor, C. J., & Graham, J. (1992). Trainable method of parametric shape description. *Image and Vision Computing, 10*(5), 289–294.

Cootes, T. F., Taylor, C., Cooper, D., & Graham, J. (1995) Active shape models -their training and applications. *Computer Vision and Image Understanding, 61*(1), 38–59.

Cristinacce, D., Cootes, T., & Scott, I. (2004) A multi-stage approach to facial feature detection. *In 15ᵗʰ British Machine Vision Conference,* London, England, 277–286.

Daubias, P., & Deleglise, P. (2002). Statistical Lip-Appearance Models Trained Automatically using Audio Information. *Journal on Applied Signal Processing, 2002*(11), 1202–1212.

Dempster, A. P., Laird, N. M., & Rubin, D. B. (1997). Maximum Likelihood from Incomplete Data via the EM Algorithm. *Journal of the Royal Statistical Society: Series B, 39*(1).

Eveno, N., Caplier, A., & Coulon, P. (2004). Automatic and Accurate Lip Tracking. *IEEE Transactions on Circuits and Systems for Video technology, 14*(5), 706–715.

FGnet-IST-2000-26434. *Face and Gesture Recognition Working Group.* http://www-prima.inrialpes. fr/FGnet/html/home.html.

Guizatdinova, I., & Surakka, V. (2005). Detection of facial landmarks from neutral, happy, and disgust facial images. In *Proceedings of the 13th International Conference in Central Europe on Computer Graphics, Visualization and Computer Vision*, 55-62.

Goecke, R., Tran, Q., Millar, J., Zelinsky, A., & Robert-Ribes, J. (2000). Validation of an Automatic Lip-Tracking Algorithm and Design of a Database for Audio-Video Speech Processing. In *Proceedings of the 8th Australian International Conference on Speech Science and Technology*, 92–97.

Graf, H. P., Cosatto, E., Gibbon, D., Kocheisen, M., & Petajan, E. (1996). Multi-modal system for locating heads and faces. In *Proceedings of the 2nd International Conference on Automatic Face and Gesture Recognition*, 88–93.

Hjelmas, E., & Low, B. K. (2001). Face detection: A survey. *Computer Vision and Image Understanding, 83*, 236–274.

Iyengar, G., & Neti, C. (2001). Detection of faces under shadows and lighting variations. In *Proceedings of the 4th IEEE Workshop on Multimedia Signal Processing*, 15–20.

Jesorsky, O., Kirchberg, K., & Frischholz, R. (2001). Robust Face Detection Using the Hausdorff Distance. In *Proceeding of 3rd Int. Conf. on Audio- and Video-based Biometric Person Authentication*, 90–95.

Kass, M., Witkin, M. A., & Terzopoulos, D. (1988). Snakes: Active contour models. *International Journal on Computer Vision, 1*(4), 321–331.

Kaucic, R., Dalton, B., & Blake, A., (1996). Real-time lip tracking for audio-visual speech recognition applications. In Proceeding of European Conference of Computer vision , 376–387.

Kaucic. R., & Blake, A. (1998).Accurate, real-time, unadorned lip tracking. In *Proceedings of the 6th International Conference on Computer Vision*, 370–375.

Kelly, P. H., Hunter, E. A., Kreutz-Delgado, K., & Jain, R.(1998). *Lip posture estimation using kinematically constrained mixture models.* British Machine Vision Association.

Kumar, V. P., & Poggio, T. (2000). Learning-based approach to real time tracking and analysis of faces. In *Proceedings of the 4th IEEE International Conference on Automatic Face and Gesture Recognition*, 96-101.

Leung, S. H., Wang, S. L., & Lau, W. H. (2004). Lip image segmentation using fuzzy clustering incorporating an elliptic shape function. *IEEE Transactions on Image Processing, 13*(1), 51–62.

Lievin, M., Delmas, P., Coulo, P., Luthon, F. & Fristot, V. (1999). Automatic lip tracking: Bayesian segmentation and active contours in a cooperative scheme. In *Proceedings of IEEE International Conference on Multimedia Computing and Systems*, 1, 691–696.

Liew, A. W. C., Leung, S. H., & Lau, W. H. (2002). Lip contour extraction from color images using a deformable model. *Pattern Recognition, 35*, 2942–2962.

Lucey, S., Sridharan, S., & Chandran, V. (2002). Adaptive mouth segmentation using chromatic features. *Pattern Recognition Letters, 23*, 1293–1302.

Lucey S., Matthews, I., Ambadar, Z., Hu, C., Frade, F., & Cohn, J. (2006). AAM derived face representations for robust facial action recognition. In *Proceedings of the 7th IEEE International Conference on Automatic Face and Gesture Recognition,* 155 – 160.

Luettin, J., Thacker, N. A., & Beet, S. W. (1996). Active shape models for visual speech feature extraction. *Speechreading by Humans and Machines, 150*, 383–390.

Luettin J., & Thacker, N. A. (1997). Speech reading using Probabilistic Models. *Computer Vision and Image Understanding, 65*(2), 163–178.

Luthon, F., & Beaumesnil B. (2006). Real-time Lip Tracking for Synthetic Face Animation with Feedback Loop. In *Proceedings of the International Conference on Computer Vision Theory and Applications, 2*, 402–407.

Lyons, M., Budynek, J., & Akamatsu, S. (1992). Automatic Classification of Single Facial Images. *IEEE Transactions on Pattern Analysis and Machine Intelligence, 21*(12), 1357–1362.

MacKenzie I. S., & Ware, C. (1993). Lag as a determinant of human performance in interactive systems. In *Proceedings of the SIGCHI Conference on Human Factors in Computing Systems*, 488–493.

Matthews, I., Cootes, T. F., Cox, S., Harvey, R., & Bangham, J. (1998). Lipreading using shape, shading and scale. In Proceedings *of the International Conference on Auditory-Visual Speech Processing*, 73–78.

Mase, K., & Pentland, A., (1991). Automatic lipreading by optical-flow analysis. *Systems and Computer, 22*(6), 67–76.

Marcel, S. (2002). Gestures for multi-modal interfaces: A review. IDIAP Technical Report IDIAP-RR 02-34.

Meier, U., Huerst, W., & Duchnowski, P., (1996). Adaptive bimodal sensor fusion for automatic speechreading. In *Proceedings of the IEEE International Conference on Acoustics, Speech and Signal Processing*, 833–836.

Meier, U., Stiefelhagen, R., Yang, J., & Waibel, A. (2000) . Towards unrestricted lip reading. *International Journal of Pattern Recognition and Artificial Intelligence, 14*(5), 571–586.

Messer, K., Matas, J., Kittler, J., Luettin, J., & Maitre, G. (1999): XM2VTSDB: The Extended M2VTS Database. In *Proceeding of 2nd International Conference on Audio- and video-based person authentication, 72 – 77.*

Movellan, J. R. (1995). Visual Speech Recognition with Stochastic Networks. In G. Tesauro, D. Toruetzky, T. Leen (Eds.), *Advances in Neural Information Processing Systems*, MIT Pess, Cambridge, vol 7.

Nordstrand, M., Granstrom, B., Svanfeldt, G., & House, D. (2003) Measurements of articulatory variation and communicative signals in expressive speech. In *Proceedings of the ISCA Tutorial and Research Workshop on Auditory-Visual Speech Processing*, 233–237.

Nefian, A., Liang, L., Pi, X., Xiaoxiang, L., Murphy K., & Mao C. (2002). A coupled HMM for audio-visual speech recognition. In *Proceedings of the IEEE International Conference on Acoustics, Speech and Signal Processing, 2*, 2013–2016.

Otsuka, T., & Ohya, J. (1998). Extracting facial motion parameters by tracking feature points. In *Proceedings o f the 1st International Conference on Advanced Multimedia Content Processing*, 442–453.

O'Toole, A. J., Phillips, P. J., Jiang, F., Ayyad, J., Penard, N., & Abdi, H. (2007). Face recognition algorithms surpass humans matching faces over changes in illumination. *IEEE Transactions on Pattern Analysis and Machine Intelligence, 29*(9), 1642–1646.

Petajan, E. D., & Graf, H. P. (1996). Robust face feature analysis for automatic speachreading and character animation. *Speech reading by Humans and Machines, 150*, 425–436.

Phillips, P. J., Martin, A., l. Wilson, C., & Przybocki, M. (2000). An Introduction to Evaluating Biometric Systems. *Computer, 33*(2), 56–63.

Phillips, P. J., Moon, H., Rizvi, S. A., & Rauss, P. J. (2000b). The FERET Evaluation Methodology for Face-recognition Algorithms. *IEEE Transactions on Pattern Analysis and Machine Intelligence, 22*(10), 1090–1104.

Phillips, P. J., Flynn, P., Scruggs, T., Bowyer, K., Chang, J., k. Hoffman, Marques, J., Jaesik, M., & Worek, W. (2005). Overview of the Face Recognition Grand Challenge. *IEEE Computer Society Conference on Computer Vision and Pattern Recognition, 1*(20–25), 947–954.

Phillips, P. J., Scruggs, W. T., OToole, A. J., Flynn, P. J., Bowyer, K. W., Schott, C. L., & Sharpe, M. (2006). *FRVT 2006 and ICE 2006 Large-Scale Results*. Evaluation Report: NISTIR 7408.

Potamianos, G., Cosatto, E., Graf, H., & Roe, D. (1997). Speaker independent audio-visual database for bimodal ASR. In *Proceedings of ESCA Workshop on Audio-Visual Speech Processing*, 65-68.

Potamianos, G., Verma, A., Neti, C., Iyengar, G., & Basu, S. (2000). A cascade image transform for speaker independent automatic speechreading. In *Proceedings of the IEEE International Conference on Multimedia and Expo, 2*, 1097–1100.

Potamianos, G., Neti, C., Luettin, J., & Matthews. I. (2004). Audio-Visual Automatic Speech Recognition: An Overview, In G. Bailly, E. Vatikiotis-Bateson, and P. Perrier (Ed.), *Issues in Visual and Audio-Visual Speech Processing*, MIT Press (In Press).

Réhman, S. U., Liu L., & Li, H. (2006). *Lip Segmentation: Performance Evaluation Criteria*, DML Technical Report: DML-TR-2006:02, ISSN Number: 1652-8441, 2006.

Reveret L., & Benoyt, C. (1998). A new 3D Lip model for analysis and synthesis of lip motion. In *Proceedings of the International Conference on Auditory-Visual Speech Processing*, 207–212.

Scanlon P., & Reilly, R. (2001). Feature Analysis for automatic Speech Reading. In *Proceedings of the 4th IEEE Workshop on Multimedia Signal Processing*, 625–630.

Senior A. W. (1999). Face and Feature finding for a Face Recognition System. In *Proceedings of the 2nd International Conference on Audio and Video-based Biometric Person Authentication*, pp. 154–159.

Stiefelhagen, R., Meier, U., & Yang, J. (1997). *Real-time lip-tracking for lipreading. In Proceeding of Eurospeech*, 2007–2010.

Turk, M. A., & Pentland, A. (1991). Eigenfaces for Recognition. *Journal of Cognitive Neroscience, 3*(1), 71–86.

Tian, Y. L., Kanade, T., & Cohn, J. (2000). Robust lip tracking by combining Shape, Color and Motion. In *Proceedings of the 4th Asian Conference on Computer Vision*, 1040-1045.

Warfield, S. K., Zou, K. H., & Wells-III, W. M. (2002). Validation of image segmentation and expert quality with an expectation maximization algorithm. In *Fifth International Conference on Medical Image Computing and Computer Assisted Intervention*, 298–306.

Warfield, S. K., Zou, K. H., Wells, W. M. (2008). Validation of image segmentation by estimating rater bias and variance. *Philos. Transact. A. Math. Phys. Eng. Sci., 366*, 2361–2375.

Warfield, S. K., Zou, K. H., & Wells, W. M. (2004). Simultaneous Truth and Performance Level Estimation (STAPLE): An Algorithm for the Validation of Image Segmentation. *IEEE Transactions on Medical Imaging, 23*(7), 903–921.

Wark, T., Dridharan, S., & Chandran, V. (1998). An approach to statistical lip modeling for speaker identification via chromatic feature extraction. In *Proceedings of the 14th IEEE International Conference on Pattern Recognition, 1*, 123-125.

Wnag, Y., Ai, H., Wu, B., & Huang C. (2004). Real time facial expression recognition with ada boost. In *Proceedings of IEEE 7th International Conference on Pattern Recognition*, 926 - 929.

Wang, S. L., Lau, W. H., Liew, A. W. C., & Leung, S. H. (2007). Robust Lip region Segmentation for lip images with Complex Background. *Pattern Recogn., 40*(12), 3481–3491.

Wang, P., Green, M. B., Ji, Q., & Wayman, J. (2005). Automatic eye detection and its validation. In: *Proceedings of the 2005 IEEE Computer Society Conference on Computer Vision and Pattern Recognition – Workshops*, 164.

Wakasugi, T., Nishiura, M., & Fukui, K. (2004). Robust lip contour extraction using separability of multidimensional distributions. In *Proceedings of the 6th International Conference on Automatic Face and Gesture Recognition*, 415–420.

Yang, J., Stiefelhagen, R., Meier, U., & Waibel, A. (1998). Real-time face and facial feature tracking and applications. In *Proceedings of the International Conference on Auditory-Visual Speech Processing*, 79–84.

Zhang, X., Broun, C., Mersereau, R. M., & Clements, M. A. (2002) Automatic speechreading with applications to human-computer interfaces. *Journal on Applied Signal Processing, 2002*(11), 1228–1247.

APPENDIX I

Here we extended the **STAPLE** algorithm (Warfield et al., 2002) to estimate both human performance parameters and ground true from a marked face database.

E-Step: Estimation of Ground Truth

The E-step drives the estimation for unobserved true segmentation based of following steps:

1) Compute the conditional probability density function of the true segmentation for each pixel based on observed segmentation (i.e. expert decisions) and previous estimate of the expert performance parameters.
2) Then label each pixel respectively.

If $f(T)$ is the priori probability of 'T', then true segmentation is estimated

$$f(T^r \mid D^r, \Theta^k) = \frac{f(D/T, \Theta^{k-1})f(T)}{\sum_{T'} f(D/T, \Theta^{k-1})f(T)}$$

$$= \frac{\prod_i \left[\prod_j f(D_{ij}^r / T_i^r, \Theta_j^{k-1}) \right] f(T_i^r)}{\sum_{T_1^{'r}}^{T_N^{'r}} \prod_i \left[\prod_j f(D_{ij}^r / T_i^{'r}, \Theta_j^{k-1}) \right] f(T_i^r)}$$

$$= \frac{\prod_i \left[\prod_j f(D_{ij}^r / T_i^r, p_j^{k-1}, q_j^{k-1}) \right] f(T_i^r)}{\prod_i \left[\sum_{T_i^r} \prod_j f(D_{ij}^r \mid T_i^r, p_j^{k-1}, q_j^{k-1}) \right] f(T_i^r)}$$

Now for each pixel 'i' per image 'r', we have

$$f(T_i^r \mid D_i^r, p^{k-1}, q^{k-1}) = \frac{\prod_j f(D_{ij}^r \mid T_i^r, p^{k-1}, q^{k-1}) f(T_i^r)}{\sum_{T_i} \prod_j f(D_{ij}^r \mid T_i^r, p^{k-1}, q^{k-1}) f(T_i^r)}$$

(4)

Considering the true segmentation as the binary random variable, if the estimate of probability of the true segmentation at each pixel 'i' in image 'r' $T_i^r = 1$; then probability that $T_i^r = 0$ is $1 - f(T_i^r = 1 \mid D_i^r, \Theta^{k-1})$. As p_j is the sensitivity i.e. "true positive fraction" and q_j is specificity i.e. "true negative fraction" of j-th expert, then from equation (4)

$$\alpha^k \equiv f(T_i^r = 1) \prod_j f(D_{ij}^r \mid T_i^r = 1, p_j^k, q_j^k)$$

$$\equiv f(T_i^r = 1) \prod_{j:D_{ij}^r=1} p_j^k \prod_{j:D_{ij}^r=0} (1 - p_j^k) \tag{5}$$

Similarly,

$$\beta^k \equiv f(T_i^r = 0) \prod_j f(D_{ij}^r \mid T_i^r = 0, p_j^k, q_j^k)$$

$$\equiv f(T_i^r = 0) \prod_{j:D_{ij}^r=0} q_j^k \prod_{j:D_{ij}^r=1} (1 - q_j^k) \tag{6}$$

Where $j:D_{ij} = 1$ represents the set of indices for which expert 'j' marked pixel 'i' as 1; where $j:D_{ij} = 0$ represents the set of indices for which expert 'j' valued pixel 'i' as 0. After estimation of the prior-probability labeling of the probability map of all the pixels for the r-th image is done using the W_i^r;

$$\left[W_i^r\right]^{k-1} \equiv f(T = 1 \mid D_i^r, p^{k-1}, q^{k-1})$$

$$\equiv \frac{\alpha_i^{k-1}}{\alpha_i^{k-1} + \beta_i^{k-1}} \tag{7}$$

Equation 7 represents the normalized prior probability of $Ti = 1$, and $\left[W_i^r\right]^{k-1}$ is the probability of the true segmentation for rth-image at pixel 'i' being equal to one; for complete E-step. The expression for the conditional expectation of the complete-data log-likelihood function mentioned in equation 1 is needed. The complete-data log-likelihood function is derived in M-Step.

M-Step: Estimation of Performance Parameters

Considering the conditional probability of the true segmentation for each ***rth***-image calculated from equation 7, p^k, q^k are derived which maximize the conditional expectation of complete-data log-likelihood function. Considering the equation 3, for each expert *'j'*:

$$(p_j^k, q_j^k) = \underset{p_j, q_j}{\arg\max} \sum_{r,i} E\left[\ln f(D_{ij}^r \mid T_i^r, p_j, q_j) \mid D, p^{k-1}, q^{k-1}\right]$$

$$= \underset{p_j, q_j}{\arg\max} \sum_{r,i} \left(\begin{array}{l} \left[W_i^r\right]^{k-1} \ln f\left(D_{ij}^r \mid T_i^r = 1, p_j, q_j\right) + \\ \left(1 - \left[W_i^r\right]^{k-1}\right) \ln f\left(D_{ij}^r \mid T_i^r = 0, p_j, q_j\right) \end{array} \right)$$

$$= \underset{p_j, q_j}{\arg\max} \sum_r \left(\begin{array}{l} \sum_{i:D_{ij}=1} \left[W_i^r\right]^{k-1} \ln p_j + \\ \sum_{i:D_{ij}=1} \left[1 - W_i^r\right]^{k-1} \ln(1 - q_j) + \\ \sum_{i:D_{ij}=0} \left[W_i^r\right]^{k-1} \ln(1 - p_j) + \\ \sum_{i:D_{ij}=0} \left[1 - W_i^r\right]^{k-1} \ln q_j \end{array} \right)$$

Here at maximum the first derivative with respect to p_j of the above expression will become zero. Similarly, differentiating $Q(\Theta/\Theta_k)$ w. r. t. p_j and setting it zero yields the values of the expert parameters that maximizes the expectation of the log likelihood function as

$$
\begin{aligned}
p^k_j &\equiv \sum_r \left(\frac{\sum_{i:D^r_{ij}=1}\left[W^r_{ij}\right]^{k-1}}{\sum_{i:D^r_{ij}=1}\left[W^r_i\right]^{k-1} + \sum_{i:D^r_{ij}=0}\left[W^r_i\right]^{k-1}} \right) \\
&\equiv \sum_r \left(\frac{\sum_{i:D^r_{ij}=1}\left[W^r_{ij}\right]^{k-1}}{\sum_i W^r_i} \right)
\end{aligned}
\tag{8}
$$

Similarly

$$
\begin{aligned}
q^k_j &\equiv \sum_r \left(\frac{\sum_{i:D^r_{ij}=0}\left[W^r_{ij}\right]^{k-1}}{\sum_{i:D^r_{ij}=1}\left[1-W^r_i\right]^{k-1} + \sum_{i:D^r_{ij}=0}\left[1-W^r_i\right]^{k-1}} \right) \\
&\equiv \sum_r \left(\frac{\sum_{i:D^r_{ij}=0}\left[W^r_{ij}\right]^{k-1}}{\sum_i (1-W^r_i)} \right)
\end{aligned}
\tag{9}
$$

where 'r' is total no of image in the data-set. Each iteration provides the belief in estimated true segmentation. The STAPLE algorithm estimates true best segmentation which is based on the expert performance parameters iteratively. In first step the true best segmentation is estimated from equation 7 and the expert quality parameters from equation 8+9. The true best segmentation is achieved when the algorithm is converged. The algorithm convergences, when $p_j^k = p_j^{k-1}$; for **jth**-expert.

Section III
Visual Speech Recognition

Chapter IX
Visual Speech Processing and Recognition

Constantine Kotropoulos
Aristotle University of Thessaloniki, Greece

Ioannis Pitas
Aristotle University of Thessaloniki, Greece

ABSTRACT

This chapter addresses both low- and high-level problems in visual speech processing and recognition In particular, mouth region segmentation and lip contour extraction are addressed first. Next, visual speech recognition with parallel support vector machines and temporal Viterbi lattices is demonstrated on a small vocabulary task.

INTRODUCTION

Audio-visual speech recognition is an emerging research field, where multi-modal signal processing is required. The motivation for using the visual information in performing speech recognition lays on the fact that the human speech production is bimodal by its nature (Campbell, 1998; Massaro, 1987; Reisberg, 1987; Sumby, 1954; Summerfield, 1987). Although human speech is produced by the vibration of the vocal cords, it depends also on articulators that are partly visible, such as the tongue, the teeth, and the lips. Furthermore, the muscles that generate the facial expressions are also employed in speech production. Consequently, speech can be partially recognized from the information of the visible articulators involved in its production and in particular the image region comprising the mouth (Benoît, 1992; Chen, 1998; Chen, 2001).

Undoubtedly, the acoustic signal carries the most useful information for speech recognition. However, when speech is degraded by noise, integrating the visual information with the acoustic one reduces significantly the word error rate (Lombard, 1911; McGurk, 1976). Indeed, under noisy conditions, it has been proved that the use of both modalities in speech recognition offers an equivalent gain of 12 dB to the signal-to-noise ratio of the acoustic signal (Chen, 2001). For large vocabulary speech recognition tasks, the visual signal can yield a performance gain, when it is integrated with the acoustic signal, even for clean acoustic speech (Neti, 2001). It is worth noting that lipreading cannot replace the normal auditory function, because its largest weakness is the difficulty of interpreting voicing, prosody, and the manner of production of consonants (Ebrahimi, 1991).

Despite the variety of existing methods in visual speech processing and recognition (Stork, 1996; Neti 2002; Potamianos, 2003; Aleksic, 2006) there is still ongoing research attempting to: 1) find the most suitable features and classification techniques to discriminate effectively between the different mouth shapes, while preserving the mouth shapes produced by different individuals that correspond to one phone in the same class; 2) require minimal processing of the mouth image, to allow for a real time implementation of mouth detection, lip contour extraction, and mouth shape classifier; and 3) facilitate the easy integration of audio and video speech recognition modules. This chapter addresses both low and high level problems in visual speech processing and recognition summarizing and extending past results (Gordan 2001; Gordan 2002a; Gordan 2002b) and contributing to just-mentioned points 1) and 2). Mouth region segmentation is described first. Next, lip contour extraction is discussed. Finally, an SVM-based approach to visual speech recognition with a dynamic network is studied.

BACKGROUND

Fuzzy C-means algorithm is one of the most successful algorithms for segmenting an image into homogeneous regions. It has been successfully applied to medical image analysis, soil structure analysis, satellite imagery, and color lip image segmentation (Crane, 1999; Palm, 1999; Thitimajshima, 2000; Liew, 2003). Whenever only the gray level uniformity is examined, the standard fuzzy C-means yields spatially discontinuous regions. Although variants of fuzzy C-means exist, which incorporate geometric constraints, such as the geometric properties of the pixels in 3×3 neighborhoods, in order to update the fuzzy partition, still the results are not satisfactory, because the variants resort to the gray levels (or color component intensities) of the pixels only (Nordam, 2000; Pham, 2001; Tolias, 1998). The just described observations motivated us to modify the fuzzy C-means algorithm in order to ensure spatially continuous regions. The approach discussed in this chapter includes explicitly the information about the spatial position of the pixels in addition to their gray level values. For the time being, we use the easiest way to include the spatial information. That is, each pixel is represented by its luminance, its x and y coordinates. For small-size images, this approach allows us to obtain very good segmentation results, superior to those obtained by the standard fuzzy C-means and the spatially constrained fuzzy C-means (Pham, 2001; Tolias, 1998) without requiring any manually marked contour points.

A relatively large class of lipreading algorithms resort to lip contour extraction in the first frame of an audio-visual image sequence and lip contour tracking in the subsequent frames (Kaucic, 1996; Luettin, 1996; Matthews, 1998). While well-performing automatic lip contour tracking algorithms exist whenever a good initial estimate of the mouth contour is provided, such an estimate is not always available due to the lack of a-priori information for the position, size, and approximate shape of the mouth. Several approaches were proposed in order to extract a good lip contour initially. For example, region-based image segmentation and edge detection were found to work quite well in profile images as well as frontal images, whenever speakers' lips were marked by either lipstick or reflective markers. The above-mentioned approaches unfortunately fail without lip marking. Lip contour extraction becomes even harder in the gray-level images, where the chromatic information differentiating between the lips and the skin cannot be exploited. Gray-level images of the mouth region usually exhibit a low contrast, so region-based segmentation and edge detection algorithms fail (Kaucic, 1996; Luettin, 1996). In such cases, several points are manually marked on the lip contour and the lip contour can be found by either interpolation assuming a particular geometric model or manually drawing it. Typical lip contour tracking algorithms (Luettin, 1996; Sanchez, 1997) resort to a large number of points (approximately 50-100) marked on the lip contour. Such markers can be used without any further preprocessing to represent the lip contour in lipreading based on *active shape models* (Luettin, 1997) and *active appearance models* (Matthews, 1998). Alternatively, an interpolation (e.g. B-splines) can be applied in order to obtain the entire lip contour (Sanchez, 1997). When a small number of points (e.g. 6 points) are marked on the lip contour, these markers are used to derive the parameters of lip contour models, such as the widely used ellipsoidal model (Hennecke, 1994) or the parabolic one (Tian, 2000). In the latter case, the accuracy of lip contour extraction is limited by the fitness of the model to the real lip contour. For example, in the case of an asymmetric mouth image (say due to a displacement of the video camera), the derived model-based lip contour representation might be different than the real lip contour. Such an example from the Tulips1 database (Movellan, 1995) is depicted in Figure 1.

In this chapter, we present an approach for lip contour extraction in gray level images, which is based on edge detection using gradient masks and edge following. The motivation for the solution being proposed is the following: Since we know that mouth images have, typically, a low contrast in the lip-to-skin area, and accordingly false edges can appear in this area, we do not resort to edge magnitude in lip contour detection, but we exploit the edge direction in contour following. Indeed, it is well known that the edge direction on the lip contours is approximately piecewise constant and follows a given pattern in all mouth images, while the "false edges" inside the lip and skin areas are random and omni-directional. Taking this observation into account, we develop a piecewise edge following algorithm that builds on the constancy of the edge direction as the following criterion. The experimental results have demonstrated the successful performance of the proposed algorithm. However, the manual demarca-

Figure 1. Example of an asymmetric mouth from Tulips 1 database

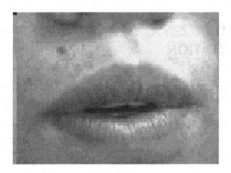

tion of the start and end point of the lip contour in each mouth region of interest is still required by the algorithm developed. Best results are obtained when the points are marked directly on a color map used for representing the edge directions. Although not completely automatic, the proposed algorithm has the advantage of providing a reliable lip contour without any geometric model assumption, while requiring a small number of points (6 to 12) to be manually demarcated.

Visual speech recognition refers to the recognition of spoken words based only on the visual examination of speaker's face. Visual speech recognition is also known as *lipreading*, since the most important visible part of the face examined for information extraction during speech is the mouth area. Different shapes of the mouth (i.e., different mouth openings, different position of the teeth and tongue) realized during speech cause the production of different sounds. One can establish a correspondence between the mouth shape and the phone produced, even if this correspondence is not one-to-one, but one-to-many, due to invisible articulators are involved in speech production as well. For small vocabulary word recognition tasks, we can perform good quality speech recognition using the visual information conveyed by the mouth shape only. Several methods have been proposed for visual speech recognition. They vary widely with respect to: 1) the feature types, 2) the classifier used, and 3) the class definition. For example, Bregler and Omohundro used time delayed neural networks (TDNN) for classification and the outer lip contour coordinates as features (Bregler, 1995). Luettin and Thacker used active shape models to represent the different mouth shapes and gray level distribution profiles (GLDPs) around the outer and/or inner lip contours as feature vectors, and finally built whole-word Hidden Markov Model (HMM) classifiers for visual speech recognition (Luettin, 1997). Movellan employed also HMMs to build the visual word models, but he used directly the gray levels of the mouth images as features after simple preprocessing to exploit the vertical symmetry of the mouth (Movellan, 1995). Very good results were reported, when partially observable stochastic differential equations (SDE) were integrated in a network instead of HMMs (Movellan, 2001). A comparative study for a series of different features based on Principal Component Analysis (PCA) and Independent Component Analysis (ICA) in an HMM-based visual speech recognizer was presented (Gray, 2001). The suitability of support vector machines (SVMs) for visual speech recognition is studied. SVMs have been proved powerful classifiers in various pattern recognition applications, such as face detection (Buciu, 2001; Fazekas, 2001; Kotropoulos, 2001), face verification/recognition, (Li, 2000; Terrillon, 2000; Tefas, 2001), etc. Very good results in audio speech recognition using SVMs were reported as well (Ganapathiraju, 2000). SVMs are not popular in automatic speech recognition partially due to the fact that SVMs are static classifiers, while speech is a dynamic process, where the temporal information is essential for recognition. This drawback can be alleviated by a combination of HMMs with SVMs (Ganapathiraju, 2000). We shall use Viterbi lattices to create dynamically visual word models.

SPATIALLY CONSTRAINED FUZZY C-MEANS ALGORITHM APPLIED TO MOUTH REGION SEGMENTATION

Figure 2 (b) demonstrates the segmentation obtained when the standard fuzzy *C*-means algorithm is applied to mouth regions of interest from four typical grayscale images, namely, "Girl", "Lena", "Lisa", and "Anthony" from Tulips1 (Movellan, 1995). The latter is split into four sub-regions shown in the rightmost image of Figure 2 (a). Clearly, the standard fuzzy *C*-means algorithm does not yield compact regions, meaning that the separation of lip and skin regions is not accurate. That is, the information of pixel gray levels is not enough to differentiate between the lips and the skin due to the low contrast of the images. As a consequence, many outliers are present in both regions, which can not be filtered out. Since both lip and skin areas are spatially continuous regions, a plausible solution to circumvent this deficiency is to keep in the same region neighboring pixels having similar gray levels by taking into account both the spatial distance as well as the gray level distance between the resulting regions. The most straightforward approach is to consider that each pixel is represented by its spatial coordinates x and y as well as its gray level ℓ. Let W, H, and L_{max} denote the image width, height, and maximum gray level (e.g. 256), respectively. The ith pixel of the mouth image, $i = 1, 2, ..., WH$, is represented by an integer-valued three-dimensional (3-D) feature vector $\mathbf{q}_i$ in a 3-D space:

$$\mathbf{q}_i = \begin{pmatrix} x_i & y_i & \ell_i \end{pmatrix}^T \tag{1}$$

where $x_i \in [1, 2, ..., W]$, $y_i \in [1, 2, ..., H]$, and $\ell_i \in [0, 1, ..., L_{max} - 1]$. All the three components of the feature vector admit integer values. Although, mouth image segmentation should result into two classes, namely the skin and the lips, sometimes it is more advantageous to partition the skin into two convex regions, which leads to $C = 3$ classes instead of 2. Let $\mathbf{U} = [u_{ij}]$ be the $C \times WH$ partition matrix, which contains the membership degrees to the C classes, and $\mathbf{v}_j = (v_{xj}, v_{yj}, v_{\ell j})^T, j = 1, 2, ..., C$ be the class centers derived by the fuzzy C-means algorithm. The partition matrix should satisfy the same constraints as in the standard fuzzy C-means. If we assume a Euclidean distance between $\mathbf{q}_i$ and $\mathbf{v}_j$, the cost function to be minimized becomes:

$$J_m(\mathbf{U}, \mathbf{V}) = \sum_{i=1}^{WH} \sum_{j=1}^{C} u_{ij}^m (\mathbf{q}_i - \mathbf{v}_j)^T (\mathbf{q}_i - \mathbf{v}_j) \quad \mathbf{V} = \{\mathbf{v}_1, \mathbf{v}_2, ..., \mathbf{v}_C\} \tag{2}$$

The steps of the spatially constrained fuzzy C-means algorithm are the following:

Step 1. Set $C = 2$ or 3 and e=0.001%.
Step 2. Reset the iteration index, $k = 0$. Initialize randomly the partition matrix $\mathbf{U} = \mathbf{U}^0$.
Step 3. If

$$\max_{\substack{j=1,2,...,C \\ i=1,2,...,WH}} \left(u_{ij}^k - u_{ij}^{k-1} \right) > \varepsilon$$

go to Step 4; Otherwise, go to Step 5.
Step 4. (a) Increase the iteration index $k = k + 1$; (b) Compute the class centers:

$$\mathbf{v}_j^k = \frac{\sum_{i=1}^{WH} \left(u_{ij}^{k-1} \right)^2 \cdot \mathbf{q}_i}{\sum_{i=1}^{WH} \left(u_{ij}^{k-1} \right)^2}, \quad j = 1, 2, ..., C; \tag{3}$$

(c) Update the fuzzy partition:

$$u_{ij}^k = \left(\sum_{c=1}^{C} \left(\frac{\left(\mathbf{q}_i - \mathbf{v}_j^k\right)^T \left(\mathbf{q}_i - \mathbf{v}_j^k\right)}{\left(\mathbf{q}_i - \mathbf{v}_c^k\right)^T \left(\mathbf{q}_i - \mathbf{v}_c^k\right)} \right)^2 \right)^{-1}, \quad i=1,2,\dots,WH \text{ and } j=1,2,\dots,C;$$

(4)

(d) Go to Step 3.

Step 5. Set the final partition matrix as $\mathbf{U} = \mathbf{U}^k$ and the final class centers as $\mathbf{V} = \mathbf{V}^k$. Upon convergence, the ith pixel is assigned to class j, if

$$j = \arg\max_c \; u_{ic}.$$

(5)

The final step of the proposed segmentation approach eliminates the outliers inside each region. A pixel in the segmented image is treated as outlier, if the majority of pixels within a 3 × 3 neighborhood centered on it have been assigned to a different class than that of it. In this case, the pixel is marked as an outlier and will be moved toward the class to which most of its neighbors belong to. By doing so, smooth compact image regions result.

The spatially constrained fuzzy C-means algorithm was tested for mouth image segmentation on the objective to improve lip contour extraction afterwards. Having segmented a mouth image, lip contour extraction can be easily conducted using edge detection between image regions. When $C = 3$, an extra-boundary between the 2 skin regions or inside the lip region emerges, that does not represent a lip boundary. The false boundaries can be easily identified with respect to their shape, the area they enclose, or the fact that they do not form a closed contour, as lip contour must be.

As has already been stated, the critical factor is the low contrast of gray-level mouth images. In the following, we differentiate between two mouth image categories, where two different approaches are described. In the case of medium or low contrast gray level mouth images with slightly variable illumination, the entire mouth image can be processed at once, but due to the variation of illumination within the mouth image and the non-convexity of the skin region, segmentation to $C = 3$ classes is recommended. The first class represents then the lips and the remaining other two classes represent the skin areas. In the case of very-low contrast gray level mouth images with variable illumination, the variant of fuzzy C-means algorithm described fails when it is applied to the entire mouth image. A remedy is to divide the mouth image into four sub-images, namely the upper-left, the upper-right, the lower-left and the lower-right ones. After having segmented each sub-image and extracting the lip contour in each segmented sub-image, a piecewise approximation of the full lip contour is obtained and the lip contour segments can be finally joined with interpolation. It is worth noticing that mouth sub-images can easily be segmented into $C = 2$ classes, because the skin region is convex. An example of such mouth image splitting into 4 sub-images is given in Figure 2 (a).

Let us confine our discussion to lip contour extraction in images depicting a closed mouth. For open-mouth images, the number of classes will increase in order to create separate regions for the teeth, the tongue, etc. The assessment of the results has been done by visual examination of the segmentation and the extracted lip contour overlaid on the original mouth image for a set of different gray level mouth images. Two sets of mouth images have been considered: (i) manually defined rectangular regions of

Figure 2. From left to right: mouth images from "Girl", "Lena", "Lisa" and the subject "Anthony" in Tulips1. (a) Original mouth images; (b) Segmentations obtained by the standard fuzzy C-means algorithm; (c) Segmentations obtained by the described fuzzy C-means algorithm; (d) Segmentations obtained by the RB-NE fuzzy C-means algorithm

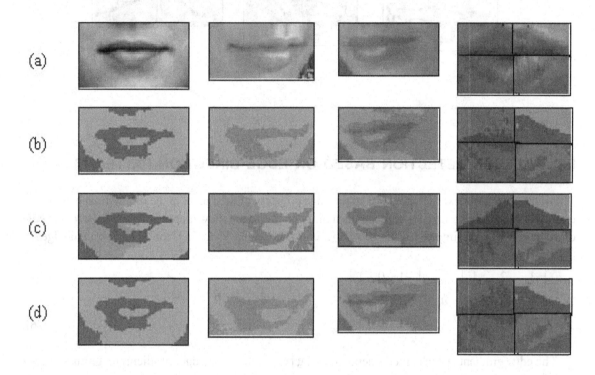

interest with medium or low contrast from gray level images "Lena", "Lisa" and "Girl" depicted in the first three images in Figure 2 (a); (ii) rectangular regions of interest with very low contrast from the audio-visual database Tulips1 (Movellan, 1995), such as closed-mouth images of the subjects Anthony, Ben, Candace, and George. The latter images were split into four sub-images prior to segmentation as shown for the region of interest defined on the mouth image of subject Anthony (last image in Figure 2 (a)). The segmentation obtained by the developed segmentation algorithm (Figure 2 (c)) is compared to that obtained by the standard fuzzy C-means algorithm (Figure 2 (b)), and the one derived by the rule-based neighborhood enhancement (RB-NE) fuzzy C-means (Tolias, 1998) (Figure 2 (d)). The visual inspection of Figure 2 verifies that the developed algorithm performs better than the standard fuzzy C-means algorithm and the RB-NE fuzzy C-means in all the cases but one. Indeed the described algorithm fails in the lower half of the mouth image from Tulips 1 database like the other algorithms.

The lip boundaries extracted after having segmented several mouth images into regions by the described algorithm are shown overlaid on the original mouth image/sub-images in Figure 3.

Figure 3. Examples of lip region boundaries extracted after having applied the described fuzzy C-means algorithm variant. From left to right: mouth images of "Lena", "Lisa", and "Anthony" (Tulips1)

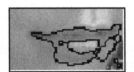 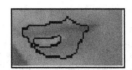 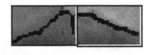

LIP CONTOUR DETECTION BASED ON EDGE DIRECTION PATTERNS

The outer lip contour extraction resorts to the edge property of each pixel in the mouth image. Since the quality of the extracted lip contour depends mainly on the edge follower applied in a later step, the edge detector can be very simple, e.g. the two Sobel convolution masks for horizontal and vertical edges:

$$h_x = \begin{bmatrix} 1 & 2 & 1 \\ 0 & 0 & 0 \\ -1 & -2 & -1 \end{bmatrix} \quad h_y = \begin{bmatrix} -1 & 0 & 1 \\ -2 & 0 & 2 \\ -1 & 0 & 1 \end{bmatrix}$$

(6)

The edge gradient at each pixel is denoted by $|\mathbf{g}| e^{i\alpha_g}$, where the edge (gradient) magnitude $|g|$, and the edge (gradient) direction α_g are given by

$$|\mathbf{g}| = \sqrt{g_x^2 + g_y^2}$$

(7)

$$\alpha_g = \arctan(\frac{g_y}{g_x}), \quad -\pi \leq \alpha_g < \pi$$

(8)

with g_x obtained at each pixel by convolving the mouth image with the horizontal Sobel mask h_x and g_y obtained at each pixel by convolving the mouth image with the vertical Sobel mask h_y. When the edges are being represented by their magnitude, as is usually done in image processing, a gray level image is sufficient to visualize the edges. However, if one wants to represent visually the edge direction, one additional image component besides the luminance is needed. The most straightforward solution is to map the edge property of every pixel to a 3-component color. Accordingly, the edge image is visualized as a color image. Since the edge direction is an angular measure, for a good edge magnitude-direction mapping in the color domain, we choose the Hue Luminance Saturation (HLS) color space, where the hue H is angle and the luminance L is equal to the edge magnitude. The third component, the saturation, S, is set a-priori to its maximum permissible value, i.e., pure and saturated colors are considered. The edge measures to color mapping is explicitly given by

$$L = \frac{255 - |\mathbf{g}|}{255}, \quad L \in [0,1]$$

$$H = 180 + \frac{\alpha_g}{\pi} 180, \quad 0 \le H < 180$$

$$S = \begin{cases} 0 & \text{if } L = 1 \\ 1 & \text{if } L \ne 1 \end{cases}.$$

(9)

To improve the color representation of edge images, an enhancement of the edge magnitude is needed as a preprocessing step. The block diagram of the edge detection and color mapping process is shown in Figure 4. The original mouth image X, its edge magnitude image, and the resulting color map E of the edge magnitude and edge direction for one frame from Tulips1 database are shown in Figure 5.

Examining Figure 5, it is rather easy to verify that although the edge magnitude image is too poor to allow the detection of the lip contour, the color map of the edge magnitude and edge direction facilitates the extraction of 6 outer lip contour segments that are differentiable by their hue. One may also notice that the manual demarcation of the start and end point of each lip contour segment is easily done based on the color attribute. Figure 5 (d) shows an example of such a manual demarcation.

In the following, the outer lip contour extraction algorithm is detailed. The extraction of the inner lip contour can be performed similarly by checking edge direction patterns in the inner mouth area. To extract a good outer lip contour, the algorithm starts with the computation of the edge magnitude and edge direction. After the manual demarcation of 6 point pairs, representing the start and end points of 6 mouth segments, the lip contour extraction is performed within each mouth region yielding a piecewise lip contour approximation and finally a linear contour interpolation is performed in order to close the lip contour. Although the proposed algorithm still needs user intervention, the latter is kept to a minimum and is facilitated a lot since the end points are easily located on the artificially created color map that visualizes the edge information. The edge following algorithm is based on the heuristic search technique described in (Pitas, 2000). In particular, the edge direction information is exploited

Figure 4. Block diagram of the visual representation of edge magnitude and edge direction by a color map

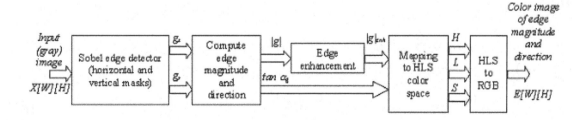

Figure 5. (a) Original mouth image; (b) Edge magnitude image; (c) Color map for edge magnitude and edge direction; (d) Manually marked points are shown overlaid, which define 6 non-overlapping lip contour segments

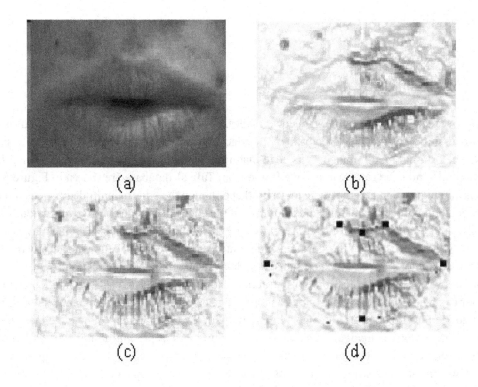

in the cost function of the heuristic edge following algorithm. That is, the cost function of the heuristic edge following algorithm for a path connecting the start point $\mathbf{q}_1$ to the end point $\mathbf{q}_N$ is a weighted sum of the individual costs of all the pixels in the path given by:

$$C(\mathbf{q}_1, \mathbf{q}_2, ..., \mathbf{q}_N) = \sum_{k=1}^{N} |\alpha_{gmed}(\mathbf{q}_k) - \alpha_g(\mathbf{q}_k)|$$

(10)

where

$$\alpha_{gmed}(\mathbf{q}_k) = \begin{cases} \dfrac{\alpha_g(\mathbf{q}_1) + \sum_{i=2}^{k-1} 2^{i-2} \cdot \alpha_g(\mathbf{q}_i)}{2^{k-2}} & k \geq 3 \\ \alpha_g(\mathbf{q}_k) & k = 1, 2 \end{cases} .$$

(11)

In (10), the absolute difference between the mean direction of all the pixels found so far in the path and the direction of the next candidate pixel is used. Accordingly, the probability that the following algorithm takes a (spurious) wrong direction is reduced. Furthermore, instead of using a 3 × 3 search neighborhood centered on each pixel within the 6 mouth image sub-regions, a priori knowledge regarding the allowable lip-contour directions is exploited. Accordingly, only the 2 × 2 search neighborhoods for each lip contour segment, shown in Figure 6, are considered. The overall algorithm for lip contour extraction based on the edge following can be described algorithmically by the following steps:

For each region/segment $r = 1, 2,..., 6$ do:

Step 1. Read the starting point $\mathbf{q}_{r_1} = (x_{r_1}, y_{r_1})$ and the end point $\mathbf{q}_{r_N} = (x_{r_N}, y_{r_N})$.

Step 2. Select the 2 × 2 search neighborhood, denoted by M_r, to be used in the edge following algorithm.

Step 3. Apply the heuristic edge following:

$$\mathbf{q}_{r_k} = \arg\min_{j \in M_r(\mathbf{q}_{r_{k-1}})} C\left(\mathbf{q}_{r_1}, \mathbf{q}_{r_2}, ..., \mathbf{q}_{r_{k-1}}, \mathbf{q}_{r_j}\right) \ k = 2, 3, ..., N$$

Figure 6. The six 2×2 search neighborhoods. From left to right: NE neighborhood; SE neighborhood; NE neighborhood; SE neighborhood; SW neighborhood; NW neighborhood

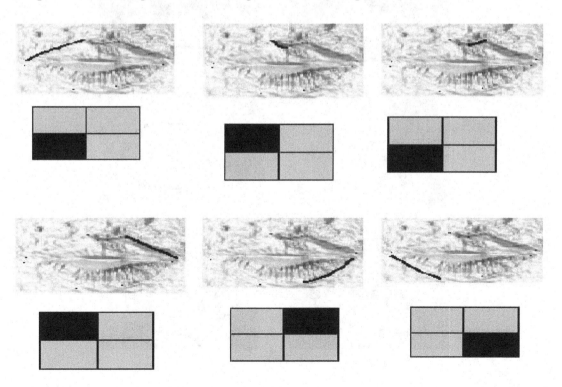

Obtain the closed lip contour by linear interpolation between either $\mathbf{q}_{r_N} = (x_{r_N}, y_{r_N})$ and $\mathbf{q}_{(r+1)_1} = (x_{(r+1)_1}, y_{(r+1)_1})$, for $r = 1, 2, ..5$ or (x_{6_N}, y_{6_N}) and (x_1, y_1).

To test the performance of the proposed lip contour extraction algorithm, mouth images from two databases frequently employed in speechreading experiments were used, namely the Tulips1 database (Movellan, 1995) and the M2VTS database (Pigeon, 1997). The quality of the results is assessed visually.

In the case of mouth images from the Tulips1 database, three different mouth images (frames) were used for the subject Anthony, while only one mouth image per subject was used for subjects Ben, Can-

Figure 7. Three outer lip contour extraction examples for 3 subjects from the Tulips1 database. (a) Subject Anthony. (b) Subject Candace. (c) Subject Cynthia. From left to right: Original mouth image and extracted outer lip contour shown overlaid on the mouth image. (a) Subject Anthony. (b) Subject Candace. (c) Subject Cynthia

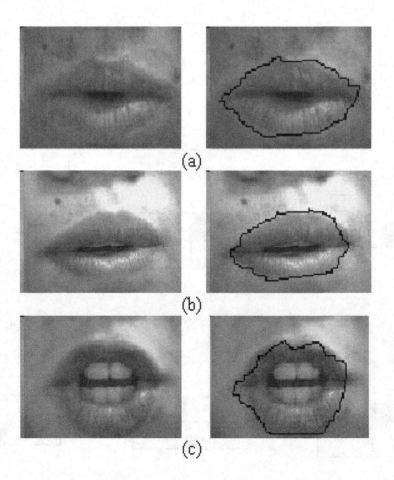

(a)

(b)

(c)

Figure 8. Outer lip contour extraction for subject sv from M2VTS database. From left to right: the original mouth image; the extracted outer lip contour by the described algorithm; the outer lip contour tracked with B-splines

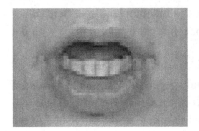  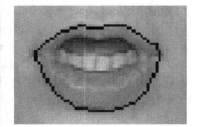

dace, Cynthea, Regina, George, and Oliver. The latter image was chosen to exhibit the largest variation with respect to the degree of mouth opening, the asymmetry of mouth image, the mouth shape, and the lip-to-skin contrast. In all cases, the lip contour extracted was qualified to be good and sometimes very good. Some results for the Tulips 1 database are depicted in Figure 7. In mouth images from the Tulips1 database, the contrast between lips and skin regions is lower than that in mouth images from the M2VTS database. Accordingly, the correct extraction of the lip contour in images from the Tulips1 database is more difficult than in images from the M2VTS database.

In the case of images from M2VTS database, a rectangular region of interest containing the mouth was selected manually first. Then, the lip contour extraction algorithm was applied to the selected region of interest. The results were compared to the similar ones reported in (Ramos, 2000). Results from M2VTS database are demonstrated in Figure 8. Although there are some differences in the shape obtained, the extracted lip contour by the described algorithm can be qualified to be good.

VISUAL SPEECH RECOGNITION WITH A SUPPORT VECTOR MACHINE-BASED DYNAMIC NETWORK

Two classes of approaches to build word models can be found, namely those, where whole word models are developed (Movellan, 1995; Luettin, 1997; Ganapathiraju, 2000) and others, where viseme-oriented word models are derived (Goldschen, 1993; Goldschen, 1996; Rogozan, 1999). In this section, we adopt the latter approach, because it is more suitable for an SVM implementation. Furthermore, it maintains the dictionary of basic visual models, needed for word modeling, into a reasonable limit, and generalizes easily to large vocabulary word recognition tasks without a significant increase in storage requirements.

The word recognition rate (WRR) obtained is at the level of the best previously reported rates, although the state transition probabilities are not learned. When very simple features (i.e., pixels) are used, the achieved word recognition rate is higher than the ones reported in the literature. Accordingly

SVMs offer a promising alternative to visual speech recognition. It is well known that the Morton-Massaro law (MML) holds when humans integrate audio and visual speech (Movellan, 2001). Experiments have demonstrated that MML holds also for audio-visual speech recognition systems. That is, the audio and visual speech signals may be treated as if they were conditionally independent without significant information loss about speech categories. This observation supports the independent treatment of audio and visual speech and yields an easy integration of the visual speech recognition module with the acoustic speech recognition module.

The section is organized as follows. SVM classifiers are briefly reviewed. The concepts of visemes and phonemes are described next. The SVM-based approach to visual speech recognition is discussed then. Experimental results for a small vocabulary visual speech recognition task (i.e., the visual recognition of the first four digits in English) are reported and compared to other results published in the literature.

Support Vector Machines Overview

SVMs constitute a principled technique to train classifiers that stems from statistical learning theory (Vapnik, 1998; Cristianini; 2000). Their root is the optimal hyperplane algorithm. They minimize a bound on the empirical error and the complexity of the classifier at the same time. Accordingly, they are capable of learning in sparse high-dimensional spaces with relatively few training examples. Let $\{\mathbf{q}_i, l_i\}$, $i = 1, 2,..., N$, denote N training examples where $\mathbf{q}_i$ comprises an M-dimensional pattern and l_i be its class label. Without any loss of generality we shall confine ourselves to the two-class pattern recognition problem. That is, $l_i \in \{-1, 1\}$. We agree that $l_i = 1$ is assigned to positive examples, whereas $l_i = -1$ is assigned to counterexamples.

The data to be classified by the SVM might be linearly separable in their original domain or not. If they are separable, then a simple linear SVM can be used for their classification. However, the power of SVMs is demonstrated better in the nonseparable case, when the data cannot be separated by a hyperplane in their original domain. In the latter case, we can project the data into a higher dimensional Hilbert space and attempt to linearly separate them in the higher dimensional space using kernel functions. Let Φ denote a nonlinear map $\Phi: \mathbb{R}^M \to H$, where H is a higher-dimensional Hilbert space. SVMs construct the optimal separating hyperplane in H. Therefore, their decision boundary is of the form:

$$f(\mathbf{q}) = \text{sign}\left(\sum_{i=1}^{N} \alpha_i \, l_i \, K(\mathbf{q}, \mathbf{q}_i) + \beta \right)$$

(12)

where $K(\mathbf{q}_1, \mathbf{q}_2)$ is a kernel function that defines the dot product between $\Phi(\mathbf{q}_1)$ and $\Phi(\mathbf{q}_2)$ in H, and α_i are the nonnegative Lagrange multipliers associated with the quadratic optimization problem that aims to maximize the distance between the two classes measured in H subject to the constraints

$$\mathbf{w}^T \Phi(\mathbf{q}_i) + \beta \geq 1 \quad \text{for } l_i = +1$$
$$\mathbf{w}^T \Phi(\mathbf{q}_i) + \beta \leq 1 \quad \text{for } l_i = -1$$

(13)

where $\mathbf{w}$ and β are the parameters of the optimal separating hyperplane in H. That is, $\mathbf{w}$ is the normal vector to the hyperplane,

$$|\beta| \Big/ \|\mathbf{w}\|$$

is the perpendicular distance from the hyperplane to the origin, and $\|\mathbf{w}\|$ denotes the Euclidean norm of vector $\mathbf{w}$.

The use of kernel functions eliminates the need for an explicit definition of the nonlinear mapping Φ, because the data appear only as dot products of their mappings in the training algorithm of SVM. Frequently used kernel functions are the polynomial kernel, $K(\mathbf{q}_i, \mathbf{q}_j) = m\mathbf{q}_i^T\mathbf{q}_j + n)^k$ and the Radial Basis Function (RBF) kernel, $K(\mathbf{q}_i, \mathbf{q}_j) = \exp\{-g|\mathbf{q}_i - \mathbf{q}_j|^2\}$. In the following, we will omit the sign function from the decision boundary (12) that simply makes the optimal separating hyperplane an indicator function.

To enable the use of SVM classifiers in visual speech recognition when we model the speech as a temporal sequence of symbols corresponding to the different phones, we shall employ the SVMs as nodes in a Viterbi lattice. But the nodes of such a Viterbi lattice should generate the posterior probabilities for the corresponding symbols to be emitted (Young, 1999), and the standard SVMs do not provide such probabilities as output. Several solutions are proposed in the literature to map the SVM output to probabilities: the cosine decomposition proposed in (Vapnik, 1998), the probabilistic approximation by applying the evidence framework to SVMs (Kwok, 1999), and the sigmoidal approximation (Platt, 1999). In this chapter, the sigmoidal approximation is adopted, since it is a simple solution, which was already used in a similar application of SVMs to audio speech recognition (Ganapathiraju, 2000).

The solution proposed by Platt shows that having a trained SVM, we can convert its output to probability by training the parameters a_1 and a_2 of a sigmoidal mapping function so that it produces a good mapping from SVM margins to probability. In general, the class-conditional densities on either side of the SVM hyperplane are exponential. Accordingly, the Bayes' rule (Hastie, 1998) applied to 2 exponentials suggests the use of the following parametric form of a sigmoidal function

$$P(l = +1 \mid f(\mathbf{q})) = \frac{1}{1 + \exp(a_1 f(\mathbf{q}) + a_2)}$$

(14)

where l is the label of $\mathbf{q}$, given by the sign of $f(\mathbf{q})$, that is $l = +1$, $iff f(\mathbf{q}) > 0$; $f(\mathbf{q})$ is the output of an SVM classifier at the feature vector $\mathbf{q}$ to be classified; a_1 and a_2 are the sigmoidal mapping parameters to be derived for the currently trained SVM with $a_1 < 0$. $P(l = -1 \mid f(\mathbf{q}))$ can be defined similarly. However, since each SVM represents only one data category (i.e., the positive examples), we are interested only in the probability given by (14). Equation (14) gives directly the posterior probability to be used in a Viterbi lattice. The parameters a_1 and a_2 are derived from a training set $(\mathbf{q}_i, l_i)$, $i = 1, 2,...,N$ by creating the new set $(f(\mathbf{q}_i), t_i)$, $i = 1, 2,...,N$, where t_i are the target probabilities defined as follows. When a positive example (i.e., $l_i = 1$) is observed at a value $f(\mathbf{q}_i)$, we assume that this example is probably in the class represented by the SVM, but there is still a small finite probability ϵ_+ for getting the opposite label at the same $f(\mathbf{q}_i)$ for some out-of-sample data. Thus, $t_i = t_+ = 1 - \epsilon_+$. When a negative example (i.e., $l_i = -1$) is observed at a value $f(\mathbf{q}_i)$, we assume that this example is not probably in the class represented by the SVM, but there is still a small finite probability $\in_-$ for getting the opposite label at the same $f(\mathbf{q}_i)$ for some out-of-sample data. Thus, $t_i = t_- = \in_-$. Let us denote by N_+ and N_- the number of positive and negative examples in the training set, respectively. We set

$$t_+ = \frac{N_+ + 1}{N_+ + 2}$$

and

$$t_- = \frac{1}{N_- + 2}.$$

The parameters a_1 and a_2 are found by minimizing the negative log likelihood of the training data, which is a cross-entropy error function given by

$$\mathcal{E}(a_1, a_2) = -\sum_{i=1}^{N} [t_i \log(p_i) + (1 - t_i) \log(1 - p_i)]$$

(15)

where

$$t_i = \begin{cases} t_+, & \text{for } l_i = +1 \\ t_-, & \text{for } l_i = -1 \end{cases}$$

(16)

and

$$p_i = \frac{1}{1 + \exp(a_1 f(\mathbf{q}_i) + a_2)}.$$

(17)

In Eqs. (15) and (17), p_i, $i = 1, 2, ..., N$, is the value of the sigmoidal mapping for the training example $\mathbf{q}_i$ and $f(\mathbf{q}_i)$ is the real valued output of the SVM at this training example. Due to the negative sign of a_1, p_i tends to 1 if $f(\mathbf{q}_i) > 0$ and to 0 otherwise.

Visemes and Phonemes

The basic units of the acoustic speech are the phones. Roughly speaking, a phone is an acoustic realization of a phoneme, a theoretical unit for describing how speech conveys linguistic meaning. The acoustic realization of a phoneme depends on the speaker's characteristics, the word context, etc. The variations in the pronunciation of the same phoneme are called allophones. In the technical literature, a clear distinction between phones and phonemes is seldom made.

In this section, we are dealing with speech recognition in English, so we shall focus on this particular case. The number of phones in the English language varies in the literature (Deller, 1993; Rabiner, 1993). Usually there are about 10-15 vowels or vowel-like phones and 20-25 consonants. The most commonly used computer-based phonetic alphabet in American English is ARPABET, which consists of 48 phones (Chen, 1998). To convert the orthographic transcription of a word in English to its phonetic transcription, one can use the publicly available CMU pronunciation dictionary (CMUdict). The CMU pronunciation dictionary uses a subset of the ARPABET consisting of 39 phones. For example, the CMU phonetic transcription of the word "one" is "W-AH-N".

Similarly to the acoustic domain, we can define the basic unit of speech in the visual domain, the viseme. In general, in the visual domain, we observe the image region of the speaker's face that contains the mouth. Therefore, the concept of viseme is usually defined related to the mouth shape and the mouth movements. An example where the concept of viseme is related to the mouth dynamics is the viseme OW, which represents the movement of the mouth from a position close to O to a position close to W (Chen, 1998). In such a case, to represent a viseme, we would need to use a video sequence, a fact that would complicate the processing of the visual speech to some extent. However, fortunately, most of the visemes can be approximately represented by stationary mouth images. Two examples of visemes defined in relationship to the mouth shape during the production of the corresponding phones are given in Figure 9.

To be able to perform visual speech recognition, ideally we would like to define for each phoneme its corresponding viseme. In this way, each word could be unambiguously described according to its pronunciation in the visual domain. Unfortunately, invisible articulatory organs are also involved in speech production. Accordingly, the mapping of phonemes to visemes is many-to-one. Thus, there are phonemes that cannot be distinguished in the visual domain. For example, the phonemes /P/, /B/, and /M/ are all produced with a closed mouth and are visually indistinguishable, so they will be represented by the same viseme. We also have to consider the dual aspect corresponding to the concept of allophones in the acoustic domain. The same viseme can have different realizations represented by different mouth shapes due to the speaker variability and the context.

Unlike the phonemes, in the case of visemes there are no commonly accepted viseme tables by all researchers (Chen, 2001), although several attempts toward this direction have been undertaken. For

Figure 9. From left to right: mouth shape during the realization of phone /O/ and phone /F/ by subject Anthony in the Tulips1 database (Movellan, 1995)

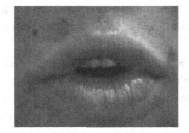 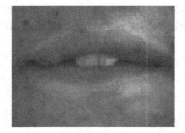

Table 1. The most used viseme groupings for the English consonants (Chen, 2001)

Viseme group index	Corresponding consonants
1	/F/; /V/
2	/TH/; /DH/
3	/S/; /Z/
4	/SH/; /ZH/
5	/P/; /B/; /M/
6	/W/
7	/R/
8	/G/; /K/; /N/; /T/; /D/; /Y/
9	/L/

example, it is commonly agreed that the visemes of the English consonants can be grouped into 9 distinct groups, as in Table 1 (Chen, 2001). To obtain the viseme groupings the confusions in stimulus-response matrices measured on an experimental basis are analyzed. In such experiments, subjects are asked to visually identify syllables in a given context, such as vowel-consonant-vowel (V-C-V) words. Then the stimulus-response matrices are tabulated and the visemes are identified as those clusters of phonemes in which at least 75 % of all responses are correct. This strategy will lead to a systematic, application-independent, mapping of phonemes to visemes. Average linkage hierarchical clustering (Goldschen, 1993) and self-organizing maps (Rogozan, 1999) were employed to group visually similar phonemes based on geometric features. Similar techniques could be applied for raw images from mouth regions as well.

However, in this chapter we do not resort to such strategies, because the main goal is to evaluate the proposed visual speech recognition method. Thus, only the visemes, that are strictly needed to represent the visual realization of the small vocabulary used in the application, are defined and the training images are manually classified to a number of predefined visemes.

The Proposed Approach to Visual Speech Recognition

Each visual word model can be represented afterwards as a temporal sequence of visemes. Thus, the structure of the visual word modeling and recognition system can be regarded as a two-level structure:

1. At the first level, viseme classes are built so that one class of mouth images is defined for each viseme. Accordingly, mouth shape recognition problem is treated as a pattern recognition problem. In particular, the classification of mouth shapes to viseme classes is formulated as a two-class (binary) pattern recognition problem, where there is one SVM dedicated for each viseme class.

2.   At the second level, the abstract visual word models are built, that are described as temporal sequences of visemes. The visual word models are implemented by means of the Viterbi lattices, where each node generates the emission probability of a certain viseme at one particular time instant.

One may notice that the aforementioned two-level approach is very similar to some techniques employed for acoustic speech recognition (Ganapathiraju, 2000), justifying thus our expectation that the proposed method will ensure an easy integration of the visual speech recognition subsystem with a similar acoustic speech recognition subsystem.

In this section, we will focus on the first level of the proposed algorithm for visual speech modeling and recognition. The second level involves the development of the visual symbolic sequential word models using the Viterbi lattices. The latter level is discussed only in principle.

Let us first treat the discrimination between different mouth shapes during speech production as a pattern recognition problem. The set of patterns comprises the feature vectors $\{\mathbf{q}_i\}$, $i = 1, 2,...,P$, where each of them represents a mouth image. For example, a feature vector could be the collection of the gray levels from a rectangular image region containing the mouth, some parameters quantifying mouth geometry (i.e., mouth width, height, perimeter, etc.) or the coefficients of a linear transformation of the mouth image. Let us assume that all feature vectors $\mathbf{q}_i \in \mathbb{R}^M$. Let us denote the pattern classes by C_j, $j = 1, 2,...,Q$, where Q is the total number of classes. Each class C_j is a group of patterns that represent mouth shapes corresponding to one viseme.

A network of Q parallel SVMs is designed where each SVM is trained to classify test patterns in class C_j or its complement C_j^C. We will slightly deviate from the notation introduced in Section 2.2, because a test pattern $\mathbf{q}_k$ could be assigned to more than one classes. It is convenient to represent the class label of a test pattern $\mathbf{q}_k$ by a $(Q \times 1)$ vector $\mathbf{l}_k$ whose jth element l_{kj} admits the value 1 if $\mathbf{q}_k \in C_j$ and -1 otherwise. More than one elements of $\mathbf{l}_k$ may have the value 1 if $f_j(\mathbf{q}_k) > 0$, where $f_j(\mathbf{q}_k)$ is the decision function of the jth SVM. To derive an unambiguous classification, we will use SVMs with probabilistic outputs. That is, the output of the jth SVM classifier will be the posterior probability for the test pattern $\mathbf{q}_k$ to belong to the class C_j, $P(l_j = 1 \mid f_j(\mathbf{q}_k))$, given by (14). This pattern recognition problem can be applied to visual speech recognition in the following way: Each unknown pattern represents the image of the speaker's face at a certain time instant; Each class label represents one viseme. Accordingly, we shall identify what is the probability of a viseme to be produced at any time instant in the spoken sequence. This gives the solution required at the first level of the proposed visual speech recognition system, to be passed to the second level. The network of Q parallel SVMs is shown in Figure 10.

The phonetic transcription represents each word by a left-to-right sequence of phonemes. Moreover, the visemic model corresponding to the phonetic model of a word can be easily derived using a phoneme-to-viseme mapping. However, the aforementioned representation shows only which visemes are present in the pronunciation of the word, not the duration of each viseme. Let T_i, $i = 1, 2,...,S$ denote the duration of the ith viseme in a word model of S visemes. Let T be the duration of the video sequence that results from the pronunciation of this word. In order to align the video sequence of duration T with the symbolic visemic model of S visemes, we can create a temporal Viterbi lattice containing as many states as the frames in the video sequence. Such a Viterbi lattice that corresponds to the pronunciation of the word "one" is depicted in Figure 11. In this example, the visemes present in the word pronunciation have been denoted with the same symbols as the underlying phones.

Figure 10. Illustration of the parallel network of binary classifiers for viseme recognition

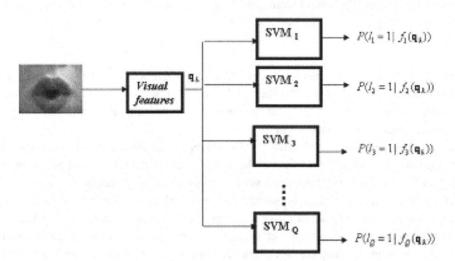

Figure 11. A temporal Viterbi lattice for the pronunciation of the word "one" in a video sequence of 5 frames

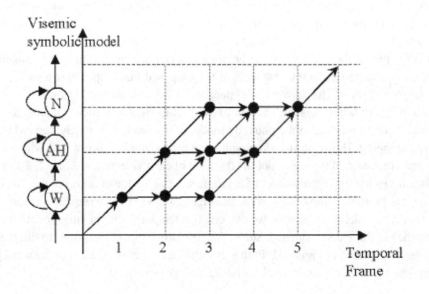

Let D be the total number of visemic models defined for the words in the vocabulary. Each visemic model, w_d, $d = 1, 2,...,D$ has its own Viterbi lattice. For example, in the lattice of Figure 11, each node is responsible for the generation of one observation that belongs to a certain class at each time instant. Let $l_k = 1, 2,...,Q$ be the class label where the observation o_k generated at time instant k belongs to. Let us denote the emission probability of that observation by $b_{l_k}(o_k)$. Each solid line between any two nodes in the lattice represents a transition probability between two states. Let us denote by $a_{l_k, l_{k+1}}$ the transition probability from the node corresponding to the class l_k at time instant k to the node corresponding to the class l_{k+1} at time instant $k + 1$. The class labels l_k and l_{k+1} may be different or not.

Having a video sequence of T frames for a word and a Viterbi lattice for each visemic word model, w_d, $d = 1, 2,...,D$ we can compute the probability that the visemic word model w_d is realized following a path $\wp$ in the Viterbi lattice as

$$p_{d,\wp} = \prod_{k=1}^{T} b_{l_k}(o_k) \cdot \prod_{k=1}^{T-1} a_{l_k, l_{k+1}}.$$

(18)

The probability that the visemic word model w_d is realized can be computed by

$$p_d = \max_{\wp}^{\mathcal{P}} p_{\wp}$$

(19)

where $\mathcal{P}$ is the number of all possible paths in the lattice. Among the words that can be realized following any possible path in any of the D Viterbi lattices, the word described by the model whose probability p_d, $d = 1, 2,...,D$, is maximum. That is, the most probable word is finally recognized.

In the visual speech recognition approach discussed, the emission probability $b_{l_k}(o_k)$ is given by the corresponding SVM, SVM_{l_k}. To a first approximation, we assume equal transition probabilities $a_{l_k, l_{k+1}}$ between any two states. Accordingly, it is sufficient to take into account only the $b_{l_k}(o_k)$, $k = 1, 2,...,T$, in the computation of the path probabilities $p_{d,\wp}$ which yields the simplified equation

$$p_{d,\wp} = \prod_{k=1}^{T} b_{l_k}(o_k).$$

(20)

Of course, learning the probabilities $a_{l_k, l_{k+1}}$ from word models would yield a more refined modeling. This could be a topic of future work.

Experimental Results

To evaluate the recognition performance of the proposed SVM-based visual speech recognizer, we choose to deal with the recognition of the first four digits in English. Towards this end we used the small audiovisual database Tulips1 (Movellan, 1995), frequently used in similar visual speech recognition experiments. While the number of the words is small, this database is challenging due to the differences in illumination conditions, ethnicity and gender of the subjects. Also we must mention that, despite the small number of words pronounced in the Tulips1 database compared to vocabularies for real-world applications, the portion of phonemes in English covered by these four words is large enough: 10 out of 48 appearing in the ARPABET table, i.e., approximately 20%. Since we use viseme-oriented models, and the visemes are actually just representations of phonemes in the visual domain, we can consider the results described in this section as significant.

Solving the proposed task requires first the design of a particular visual speech recognizer. The design involves the following steps: (1) to define the phoneme to viseme mapping; (2) to build the

Table 2. Viseme classes defined for the four words of the Tulips1 database (Movellan, 1995)

Viseme group index	Symbolic notation	Viseme description
1	(W)	small rounded open mouth state
2	(AO)	larger rounded open mouth state
3	(WAO)	medium rounded open mouth state
4	(AH)	medium ellipsoidal mouth state
5	(N)	medium open, not rounded, mouth state; teeth visible
6	(T)	medium open, not rounded, mouth state; teeth and tongue visible
7	(TH)	medium open, not rounded
8	(IY)	longitudinal open mouth state
9	(F)	almost closed mouth position; upper teeth visible; lower lip moved inside

Table 3. Phoneme-to-viseme mapping in the experiments conducted on the Tulips1 database (Movellan, 1995)

Viseme group index	Corresponding phonemes
1, 2, or 3 (depending on speaker's pronunciation)	/W/, /UW/, /AO/
1 or 3 (depending on speaker's pronunciation)	/R/
4	/AH/
5	/N/
6	/T/
7	/TH/
4 or 8 (depending on speaker's pronunciation)	/IY/
9	/F/

SVM network; (3) to train the SVMs for viseme classification; (4) to generate and implement the word models as Viterbi lattices. The trained visual speech recognizer is used then to assess its recognition performance in test video sequences.

Let us start with the definition of the viseme classes for the first four digits in English. First, the phonetic transcriptions of the first four digits in English are obtained using the CMU pronunciation dictionary (CMU): "one"→"W-AH-N"; "two"→"T-UW"; "three"→"TH-R-IY"; "four"→"F-AO-R".

Next, the viseme classes are defined so that each viseme class includes as few phonemes as possible and as few different visual realizations of the same viseme as possible. The definition of viseme classes was done based on the visual examination of the video part from the Tulips1 database. The clustering of the different mouth images into viseme classes was done manually based on the visual similarity of these images. By this procedure we obtained the viseme classes described in Table 2 and the phoneme-to-viseme mapping given in Table 3.

One SVM has to be defined and trained for each viseme. To employ SVMs, one should define the features to be used to represent each mouth image and select the kernel function to be used. Since the recognition and generalization performance of each SVM is strongly influenced by the selection of the kernel function and the kernel parameters, we devoted much attention to these issues. We trained each SVM using as kernel function the linear, the polynomial, and the RBF one. In the case of the polynomial kernel, the degree of the polynomial k was varied between 2 and 6. For each trained SVM, we compared the predicted error, precision, and recall on the training set, as computed by SVMLight (Joachims, 1999), for the different kernels and kernel parameters, and finally the simplest kernel is selected that yields the best values for these estimates. That kernel was the polynomial kernel of degree $k = 3$. The RBF kernel gave the same performance estimates with the polynomial kernel of degree $k = 3$ on the training set, but at the cost of a larger number of support vectors. A simple choice of a feature vector such as the collection of the gray levels from a rectangular region of fixed size containing the mouth, scanned row by row, is proved suitable whenever SVMs have been used for visual classification tasks (Buciu, 2001).

More specifically, we used two types of features to conduct the visual speech recognition experiments: (i) The first type comprised the gray levels of a rectangular region of interest around the mouth, down-sampled to the size 16×16. Each mouth image is represented by a feature vector of length 256. (ii) The second type represented each mouth image frame at the time T_f by a vector of double size (i.e., 512) that comprised the gray levels of the rectangular region of interest around the mouth down-sampled to the size 16×16, as previously, and the temporal derivatives of the gray levels normalized to the range $[0, L_{max} - 1]$, where L_{max} is the maximum gray level value in mouth image. The temporal derivatives are simply the pixel by pixel gray level differences between the frames T_f and T_{f-1}. These differences are the so-called delta features.

Some preprocessing of the mouth images was needed before training and testing the visual speech recognition system. It concerns the normalization of the mouth in scale, rotation, and position inside the image. Such a preprocessing is needed due to the fact that the mouth has different scale, position in the image, and orientation toward the horizontal axis from utterance to utterance, depending on the subject and on its position in front of the camera. To compensate for these variations we applied the normalization procedure of mouth images with respect to scale, translation and rotation (Luettin, 1997).

The visual speech recognizer was tested for speaker-independent recognition using the leave-one-out testing strategy for the 12 subjects in the Tulips1 database. This implies training the visual speech recognizer 12 times, each time using 11 subjects for training and leaving the 12th out for testing. In each case, we trained first the SVMs, and then the sigmoidal mappings for converting the SVMs output to probabilities. The training set for each SVM is selected manually. Only the video sequences of the so-called Set 1 in the Tulips1 database were used for training. The labeling of all the frames from Set 1 (a total of 48 video sequences) was done manually by visual examination of each frame. We examined the video only in order to label all the frames according to Table 3. Finally, we compared the similarity of the frames corresponding to the same viseme and different subjects, and decided if the classes could be merged. The disadvantage of this approach is the large time needed for labeling, which would not be needed if HMMs were used for segmentation. A compromise solution for labeling could be the use of an automatic solution for phoneme-level segmentation of the audio sequence and the use of this segmentation on the aligned video sequence also.

Once the labeling was completed, only the unambiguous positive viseme examples and the unambiguous negative viseme examples were included in the training sets. The feature vectors used in the training sets of all SVMs were the same. Only their labeling as positive or negative examples differs from one SVM to another. This leads to an unbalanced training set in the sense that the negative examples are frequently more than the positive ones.

The configuration of the Viterbi lattice depends on the length of the test sequence through the number of frames T_{tst} of the sequence (as illustrated in Fig. 11), and it was generated automatically at runtime for each test sequence. The number of Viterbi lattices can be determined in advance, because it is equal to the total number of visemic word models. Thus, taking into account the phonetic descriptions for the four words of the vocabulary and the phoneme-to-viseme mappings in Table 3, we have 3 visemic word models for the word "one", 3 models for "two", 4 models for "three", and 6 models for "four". The multiple visemic models per word are due to the variability in speakers' pronunciation.

In each of the 12 leave-one-out tests, we have as test sequences the video sequences corresponding to the pronunciation of the four words and there are two pronunciations available for each word and speaker. This leads to a sub-total of 8 test sequences per system configuration, and a total of $12 \times 8 = 96$ test sequences for the visual speech recognizer.

Two visual speech recognizers were implemented, trained, and tested. They differ in the type of features used. The first system (without delta features) did not include temporal derivatives in the feature vector, while the second (with delta features) included also temporal derivatives between two frames in the feature vector.

Next, experimental results are presented that were obtained by the proposed system with and without delta features.. Moreover, we compare these results to others reported in the literature for the same experiment on the Tulips1 database. The WRRs have been averaged over the 96 tests obtained by applying the leave-one-out principle. Five objective measures are employed: (1) The WRR per subject obtained by the proposed method when delta features are used is shown in Table 4 and compared to that in (Luettin, 1997); (2) The overall WRR for all subjects and pronunciations with and without delta features is reported in Table 5 and compared to that obtained in (Luettin, 1997; Movellan, 1995; Gray, 2001; Movellan, 2001); (3) The 95% confidence intervals (CI) for the WRRs of the several systems included in the comparisons, which provide an estimate of the performance of the systems for a much larger number of subjects. (4) The confusion matrix between the words actually presented to the classifier and the words recognized is shown in Table 6 and compared to the average human confusion matrix (Table 7) in percentage, that is cited in (Movellan, 1995) ; (4) The accuracy of the viseme segmentations resulting from the Viterbi lattices.

Table 4. WRR for each subject in Tulips1, using (a) SVM dynamic network with delta features; (b) AAM for inner and outer lip contours and HMM with delta features (Luettin, 1997)

Subject	1	2	3	4	5	6	7	8	9	10	11	12
Accuracy [%] (SVM-based dynamic network)	100	75	**100**	**100**	87.5	100	**87.5**	100	100	62.5	87.5	87.5
Accuracy [%] (AAM & HMM)	100	87.5	87.5	75	100	100	75	100	100	75	100	87.5

We would like to note that normal hearing subjects untrained in lipreading achieved under similar experimental conditions a WRR of 89.93% whereas the hearing impaired had an average performance of 95.49% (Movellan, 1995). From the examination of Table 5, it can be seen that the reported WRR is

Table 5. The overall WRR and its 95% confidence interval of the SVM dynamic network compared to those of other techniques

Method	SVM-based dynamic network without delta features	SVM-based dynamic network with delta features	AAM and HMM shape + intensity inner + outer lip contour without delta features (Luettin, 1997)	AAM and HMM shape + intensity inner + outer lip contour with delta features (Luettin, 1997)	HMMs without delta features (Movellan, 1995)	HMMs with delta features (Movellan, 1995)
WRR [%]	76	90.6	87.5	90.6	60	89.93
CI [%]	[66.6, 83.5]	[83.1, 94.7]	[79.4, 92.7]	[83.1, 94.7]	[49.9, 69.2]	[82.3, 94.5]
Method	Global PCA and HMMs (Gray, 2001)	Global ICA and HMMs (Gray, 2001)	Blocked filter bank PCA/ local ICA (Gray, 2001)	Unblocked filter bank PCA/local ICA (Gray, 2001)	Diffusion network shape + intensity (Movellan, 2001)	
WRR [%]	79.2	74	85.4	91.7	91.7	
CI [%]	[70.0, 86.1]	[64.4, 81.7]	[76.9, 91.1]	[84.4, 95.7]	[84.4, 95.7]	

equal to the best one in (Luettin, 1997) and just 1.1% below the reported rates in (Gray, 2001; Movellan, 2001). However the features used in the proposed method are simpler than those used with HMMs to obtain the same or higher WRRs. For the shape + intensity models (Luettin, 1997) the gray levels should be sampled in the exact subregion of the mouth image containing the lips, around the inner and outer lip contours, and should exclude the skin areas. Accordingly, the method in (Luettin, 1997) requires the tracking of the lip contour in each frame, which increases the processing time of visual speech recognition. For the method in (Gray, 2001), a large amount of local processing is needed, by the use of a bank of linear shift invariant filters with unblocked selection whose response filters are ICA or PCA kernels of very small size (12 × 12 pixels). The obtained WRR is higher than those reported in (Movellan, 1995), where similar features are used, namely the gray levels of the region of interest comprising the mouth, after some simple preprocessing steps. The preprocessing in (Movellan, 1995) was vertical symmetry enforcement of the mouth image by averaging, followed by low pass filtering, sub-sampling, and thresholding.

To assess the statistical significance of the rates observed, we model the ensemble {test patterns, recognition algorithm} as a source of binary events, 1 for correct recognition and 0 for an error, with probability p of drawing a 1 and $(1-p)$ of drawing a 0. These events can be described by Bernoulli trials. Let us denote by $\hat{p}$ the estimate of p. The exact ϵ confidence interval of p is the segment between the two roots of the quadratic equation (Papoulis, 1991):

$$(p - \hat{p})^2 = \frac{z^2_{(1+\epsilon)/2}}{K} \, p \, (1-p)$$

(21)

where z_u is the u-percentile of the standard Gaussian distribution having zero mean and unit variance, and $K = 96$ is the total number of tests conducted. We computed the 95% confidence intervals ($\epsilon = 0.95$) for the WRR of the proposed approach and the WRRs reported in (Luettin, 1997; Movellan, 1995; Gray, 2001; Movellan, 2001), as summarized in Table 5.

Another measure of the performance assessment is given by comparing the confusion matrix of the proposed system (Table 6) with the average human confusion matrix (Table 7) provided in (Movellan, 1995). The accuracy of the viseme segmentation that results from the best Viterbi lattices was computed

Table 6. Confusion matrix for visual word recognition by the dynamic network of SVMs with delta features

		Digit recognized			
		one	two	Three	four
Digit presented	One	95.83%	0%	0%	4.17%
	Two	0%	95.83%	4.17%	0%
	Three	16.66%	12.5%	70.83%	0%
	Four	0%	0%	0%	100%

Table 7. Average human confusion matrix (Movellan, 1995)

		Digit recognized			
		one	Two	three	four
Digit presented	one	89.36%	0.46%	8.33%	1.85%
	two	1.39%	98.61%	0%	0%
	three	9.25%	3.24%	85.64%	1.87%
	four	4.17%	0.46%	1.85%	93.52%

using as reference the manually performed segmentation of frames into the viseme classes (Table 3) as a percentage of the correctly classified frames. We obtained an accuracy of 89.33%, which is just 1.27% lower than the WRR.

The results obtained demonstrate that the SVM-based dynamic network is a very promising alternative to the existing methods for visual speech recognition. An improvement of the WRR is expected when training of the transition probabilities is implemented and the trained transition probabilities are incorporated in the Viterbi decoding lattices.

The complexity of the SVM structure can be estimated by the number of SVMs needed for the classification of each word, as a function of the number of frames T in the current word pronunciation. For the experiments reported here, if we take into account the total number of symbolic word models, that is 16, and the number of possible states as a function of the frame index, we get: 6 SVMs for the classification of the first frame, 7 for the second frame, 8 for the before-last frame, 6 for the last frame, and 9 SVMs for all remaining frames. This yields a total of $9 \times T - 9$ SVMs. As it can be seen, the number of SVM outputs to be estimated at each time instant is not large. Therefore the recognition could be done in real-time, since the number of frames per word is small (on the order of 10) in general. Of course, when scaling the system to an LVCSR application, a significantly larger number of context dependent viseme SVMs will be required, thus affecting both training and recognition complexity.

CONCLUSIONS

In this chapter, starting from the well known fuzzy C-means algorithm, a modification has been introduced that includes pixel spatial coordinates in the feature vectors. This algorithm enables fully automated mouth region segmentation.

Next, a solution to the problem of lip contour extraction in gray-level images based on image gradient information was proposed. Compared to other similar algorithms, this solution has the advantage of providing a reliable lip contour without any geometric model assumption, while requiring a small number of points (6 to 12) to be manually demarcated.

Third, a method for visual speech recognition that employs SVMs has been described. The SVM classifiers have been integrated into a Viterbi decoding lattice. Each SVM output was converted to a posterior probability, and then the SVMs with probabilistic outputs were integrated into Viterbi lattices as nodes. We have tested the method on a small visual speech recognition task, namely the recognition of the first four digits in English. The used features were the simplest possible, that is, the raw gray level values of the mouth image and their temporal derivatives. Under these circumstances, we obtained a word recognition rate that competes with that of the state-of-the-art methods. Accordingly, SVMs are found to be promising classifiers for visual speech recognition tasks. The existing relationship between the phonetic and visemic models can also lead to an easy integration of the visual speech recognizer with its audio counterpart.

FUTURE RESEARCH DIRECTIONS

The fuzzy C-means algorithm can be further enhanced by examining the inclusion of texture features in the feature vector as well as the use of more elaborated distance measures from Riemannian geometry (Jost, 1995) than the Euclidean distance. Moreover, the algorithm can be tested on color images and its performance can be assessed against the methods in (Oliver, 1997; Sadeghi, 2001), because the color information can significantly improve the efficiency and robustness of lip feature extraction (Zhang, 2000).

As a feature work, the edge following algorithm can be made completely automatic by learning the directional patterns from a set of training mouth images and using the learned patterns to initialize the cost function.

The performance of visual speech recognizer can be improved by training the state transition probabilities of the Viterbi decoding lattice. Another topic of interest would be the integration of this type of visual recognizer with an SVM-based audio recognizer, to perform audio-visual speech recognition. Another line of research could be the use of one-class SVMs instead of two-class SVMs within the dynamic network and the assessment of their performance compared to that of two-class SVMs. One-class SVMs (Manevitz, 2001) have been less-studied than two-class SVMs, but have recently attracted the interest of the research community. The treatment of large vocabulary visual speech recognition problems using databases such as CUAVE (Patterson, 2002), and the Bernstein Lipreading Corpus (Bernstein, 1991) is another topic of future research.

Viseme clustering is frequently employed in visual speech synthesis and computer graphics animation (Bregler, 1997; Ezzat, 1998; Jones, 1997). Several past works (Lavagetto, 1995; Williams, 1998) are devoted to the systematic derivation of viseme clusters, a topic that deserves a systematic treatment. Viseme clusterings can be further validated by employing visuphones. A visuphone is the extension of the notion of viseme (Vignoli, 2000). It encompasses a set of speech, video, and 3-D articulatory gesture measurements related to the trajectory and the dynamics of visible articulators during the production of the corresponding phone.

REFERENCES

Benoît, C., Lallouache, T., Mohamadi, T., & Abry, C. (1992). A set of French visemes for visual speech synthesis. In G. Bailly and C. Benoît (Eds.), *Talking Machines: Theories, Models, and Designs* (pp. 485-504). Amsterdam, The Netherlands: North Holland Elsevier.

Bregler, C., & Omohundro, S. (1995). Nonlinear manifold learning for visual speech recognition. In *Proc. IEEE Int. Conf. Computer Vision* (pp. 494-499).

Buciu, I., Kotropoulos, C., & Pitas, I. (2001). Combining support vector machines for accurate face detection. In Proc. *2001 IEEE Int. Conf. Image Processing, 1,* 1054-1057.

Burges, C. J. C. (1998). A tutorial on support vector machines for pattern recognition. *Data Mining and Knowledge Discovery, 2*(2), 121-167.

Cawley, G. (1996). *The Application of Neural Networks to Phonetic Modelling.* Ph. D. Thesis, University of Essex, England.

CMUdict. The Carnegie Mellon University Pronouncing Dictionary. www.speech.cs.cmu.edu/ cgi-bin/cmudict

Chen, T. (1998). Audio-visual integration in multimodal communication. *Proceedings of the IEEE, 86*(5), 837-852.

Chen, T. (2001). Audiovisual speech processing. *IEEE Signal Processing Magazine, 18*(1), 9-21.

Crane, S. E., & Hall, L. O. (1999). Learning to identify fuzzy regions in magnetic resonance images. In *Proc. 18th Int. Conf. NAFIPS* (pp. 352 -356).

Cristianini, N., & Shawe-Taylor, J. (2000). *An Introduction to Support Vector Machines.* Cambridge, U.K.: Cambridge University Press.

Deller, J. R., Proakis, J. G., & Hansen, J. H. L. (2000). *Discrete-Time Processing of Speech Signals.* N.Y.: Wiley-Interscience, IEEE Press.

Dupont, S., & Luettin, J. (2000). Audio-visual speech modeling for continuous speech recognition. *IEEE Trans. Multimedia, 2*(3), 141-151.

Fazekas, A., Kotropoulos, C., Buciu, I., & Pitas, I. (2001). Support vector machines on the space of Walsh functions and their properties. In *Proc. 2nd Int. Symp. Image and Signal Processing and Applications* (pp. 43-48).

Fletcher, R. (1987). *Practical Methods of Optimization,* 2/e. N. Y.: J. Wiley & Sons.

Ganapathiraju, A., Hamaker, J., & Picone, J. (2000). Hybrid SVM/HMM architectures for speech recognition. In Proc. *Speech Transcription Workshop.*

Goldschen, A. J. (1993). *Continuous Automatic Speech Recognition by Lipreading.* Ph. D. Thesis,

George Washington University, Washington, DC.

Goldschen, A. J., Garcia, O. N., & Petajan, E. D. (1996). Rationale for phoneme-viseme mapping and feature selection in visual speech recognition. In D. G. Stork and M. E. Hennecke (Eds.), *Speechreading by Humans and Machines* (pp. 505-515), Berlin,Germany: Springer.

Gordan, M., Kotropoulos, C., & Pitas, I. (2001). Pseudoautomatic lip contour detection based on edge direction patterns. In *Proc. 2nd Int. Symp. Image and Signal Processing and Applications* (pp. 138-143).

Gordan, M., Kotropoulos, C., & Pitas, I. (2002a). A support vector machine based-dynamic network for visual speech recognition applications. *Journal Applied Signal Processing, 2002* (11), 1248-1259.

Gordan, M., Kotropoulos, C., Georgakis, A., & Pitas, I. (2002b). A new fuzzy C-means segmentation strategy. In *Proc. A&QT-R 2002 (THETA-13) 2002 IEEE TTTC Int. Conf. Automation, Quality, and Testing, Robotics.*

Gray, M. S., Sejnowski, T. J., & Movellan, R. J. (2001), A comparison of image processing techniques for visual speech recognition applications. In T. Leen, G. Dietterich, and V. Tresp (Eds.), *Advances in Neural Information Processing Systems, 13,* 939-945. Cambridge, MA: MIT Press.

Hastie, T., & Tibshirani, R. (1998). Classification by pairwise coupling. *The Annals of Statistics, 26*(1), 451-471.

Hennecke, M. E., Prasad, K. V., & Stork, D. G. (1994). Using deformable templates to infer visual speech dynamics. In Proc. 28th Asilomar Conf. Signals, Systems, and Computers (pp. 578-582). Pacific Grove, CA.

Joachims, T. (1999). Making large-scale SVM learning practical. In B. Scoelkopf, C. Burges, and A. Smola, (Eds.), *Advances in Kernel Methods - Support Vector Learning*: (pp. 169-184). Cambridge, MA: The MIT Press.

Kaucic, R., Dalton, B., & Blake, A. (1996). Real-time lip tracking for audio-visual speech recognition applications. In *Proc. European Conf. Computer Vision* (pp. 376-387).

Kotropoulos, C., Bassiou, N., Kosmidis, T., & Pitas, I. (2001). Frontal face detection using support vector machines and back-propagation neural networks. In Proc. *2001 Scandinavian Conf. Image Analysis* (pp. 199-206).

Kwok, J. T. –Y. (1999). Moderating the outputs of support vector machine classifiers. *IEEE Trans. Neural Networks, 10*(5), 1018-1031.

Li, Y., Gong, S., & Liddell, H. (2000). Support vector regression and classification based multi-view face detection and recognition. In Proc. *Fourth IEEE Int. Conf. Automatic Face and Gesture Recognition* (pp. 300-305).

Liew, A. W. – C., Leung, S. H., & Lau W. H. (2003). Segmentation of color lip images by spatial fuzzy clustering. *IEEE Trans.Fuzzy Systems, 11*(4), 542-549.

Luettin, J., Thacker, N. A., & Beet, S. W. (1996). Active shape models for visual speech feature extraction. In *Speechreading by Humans and Machine, NATO ASI Series, Series F: Computer and Systems Sciences, 150,* 383-390. Berlin: Springer Verlag.

Luettin, J., & Thacker, N. A. (1997). Speechreading using probabilistic models. *Computer Vision and Image Understanding, 65*(2), 163-178.

Matthews, I., Cootes, T., Cox, S., Harvey, R., & Bangham, J. A. (1998). Lipreading using shape, shading, and scale. In *Proc. Auditory-Visual Speech Processing* (pp. 73-78). Sydney, Australia.

Movellan, J. R. (1995). Visual speech recognition with stochastic networks, In G. Tesauro, D. Toruetzky, and T. Leen, (Eds.), *Advances in Neural Information Processing Systems*, 7, 851-858. Cambridge, MA: The MIT Press.

Movellan, J. R., & McClelland, J. L. (2001). The Morton-Massaro law of information integration: Implications for models of perception, *Psychological Review*, 108(1), 113-148.

Movellan, J. R., Mineiro, P., & Williams, R. J. (2001), Partially observable SDE models for image sequence recognition tasks. In T. Leen, G. Dietterich, and V. Tresp (Eds.), *Advances in Neural Information Processing Systems*, 13, 880-886. Cambridge, MA: The MIT Press.

Neti, G., Potamianos, G., Luettin, J., Matthews, I., Glotin, H., & Vergyri, D. (2001). Large-vocabulary audio-visual speech recognition: A summary of the Johns Hopkins summer 2000 workshop. In Proc. *IEEE Workshop Multimedia Signal Processing* (pp. 619-624).

Noordam, J. C., & van den Broek, W. H. A. M. (2000). Geometrically guided fuzzy c-means clustering for multivariate image segmentation. In *Proc. Int. Conf. Pattern Recognition* (pp. 462-465).

Pahm, D. L., & Prince, J. L. (1999). Adaptive fuzzy segmentation of magnetic resonance images. *IEEE Transactions on Medical Imaging*, 18(9), 737-752.

Pham, T. D. (2001). Image segmentation using probabilistic fuzzy c-means clustering. In *Proc. 2001 IEEE Int. Conf. Image Processing*, 1, 722-725.

Papoulis, A. (1991). *Probability, Random Variables, and Stochastic Processes*, 3/e. N.Y.: McGraw-Hill.

Platt, J. (2000). Probabilistic outputs for support vector machines and comparisons to regularized likelihood methods. In A. Smola, P. Bartlett, B. Scholkopf, and D. Schuurmans (Eds.), *Advances in Large Margin Classifiers*: (pp. 61-74). Cambridge, MA: MIT Press.

Pigeon, S., & Vandendorpe, L. (1997). The M2VTS multimodal face database. In J. Bigun, C. Chollet, and G.. Borgefors (Eds.), *Lecture Notes in Computer Science: Audio- and Video-based Biometric Person Authentication*, 1206, 403-409.

Pitas, I. (2000). *Digital Image Processing: Algorithms and Applications*. London, UK: John Wiley & Sons, Inc.

Rabiner, L., & Juang, B.-H. (1993). *Fundamentals of Speech Recognition*. Englewood Clffs, N. J.: Prentice Hall PTR.

Ramos, M. U., Matas, J., & Kittler, J. (1997). Statistical chromaticity models for lip tracking with B-splines. In In J. Bigun, C. Chollet, and G.. Borgefors (Eds.), *Lecture Notes in Computer Science: Audio- and Video-based Biometric Person Authentication*, 1206, 69-76.

Ramos, M. U., Li, Y., Matas, J., & Kittler, J. (2000). Lip tracking on the XM2VTS database. http://www.ee.surrey.ac.uk/CVSSP/xm2vtsdb/results/lips

Rogozan, A. (1999). Discriminative learning of visual data for audiovisual speech recognition. *Int. Journal Artificial Intelligence Tools*, 8(1), 43-52.

Tefas, A., Kotropoulos, C., & Pitas, I. (2001). Using support vector machines to enhance the performance of elastic graph matching for frontal face authentication. *IEEE Trans. Pattern Analysis and Machine Intelligence, 23*(7), 735-746.

Terrillon, T. J., Shirazi, M. N., Sadek, M., Fukamachi, H., & Akamatsu, S. (2000). Invariant face detection with support vector machines. In Proc. *15th Int. Conf. Pattern Recognition, 4,* 210-217.

Thitimajshima, P. (2000). A new modified fuzzy c-means algorithm for multispectral satellite images segmentation. In *Proc. Geoscience and Remote Sensing Symposium, 4,* 1684 -1686.

Tian, Y., Kanade, T., & Cohn, J. F. (2000). Robust lip tracking by combining shape, color, and motion. In *Proc. ACCV* (pp. 1040-1045).

Tolias, Y. A., & Panas, S. M. (1998). On applying spatial constraints in fuzzy image clustering using a fuzzy rule-based system. *IEEE Signal Processing Letters, 5*(10), 245-247.

Vapnik, V. N. (1998). *Statistical Learning Theory.* N.Y.: J. Wiley.

Young, S., Kershaw, D., Odell, J., Ollason, D., Valtchev, V., & Woodland, P. (1999). *The HTK Book.* Cambridge, U.K.: Entropic Ltd., HTK version 2.2.

ADDITIONAL READING

Aleksic, P. S., & Katsaggelos, A. K. (2006). Audio-visual biometrics. *Proceedings of the IEEE, 94*(11), 2025-2044.

Bernstein, L., & Eberhardt, S. (1991). *Johns Hopkins lipreading corpus V & VI.* (Tech. Rep.). Baltimore, MD: Johns Hopkins University.

Bregler, C., Covell, M., & Slaney, M. (1997). Video rewrite: Driving visual speech with audio. In Proc. *ACM SIGGRAPH,* (pp. 353-360).

Campbell, R., Dodd, B., & Burnham, D. (Eds.). (1998). *Hearing by Eye II.* Hove: Psychology Press.

Desorby, F., Davy, M., & Doncarli, C. (2005). An online kernel change detection algorithm. *IEEE Trans. Signal Processing, 53*(8) Part B, 2961-2974.

Ebrahimi, D., & Kunov, H. (1991). Peripheral vision lipreading aid. *IEEE Trans. Biomedical Engineering, 38*(10), 944-952.

Ezzat, T., & Poggio, T. (1998). MikeTalk: A talking facial display based on morphing visemes. In Proc. *Computer Animation Conf.,* (pp. 96-102).

Jones, C. M., & Dlay, S. S. (1997). Automated lip synchronization for human-computer interaction and special effect animation. *In Proc. IEEE Int. Conf. Multimedia Computing Systems,* (pp. 589-596).

Jost, J. (1995*). Riemannian geometry and geometric analysis.* Berlin: Springer.

Lavagetto, F. (1995). Converting speech into lip movements: A multimedia telephone for hard of hearing people. *IEEE Trans.Rehabilitation Engineering, 3*(1), 90-102.

Lombard, E. (1911). Le Signe de l' elevation de la voix. *Ann. Maladies Oreille, Larynx, Nez, Pharynx, 37*.

Massaro, D. W. (1987). Speech perception by ear and eye. In B. Dodd, and R. Campbell (Eds.*), Hearing by eye: The psychology of lip-reading* (pp. 53-83). London: Lawrence Erlbaum.

Mavenitz, L., & Yousef, M. (2001). One-class SVMs for document classification. *Journal of Machine Learning Research, 2*, 139-154.

McGurk, H., & MacDonald, J. (1976). Hearing lips and seeing voices. *Nature, 264*, 746-748.

Neti, C., Potamianos, G., Luettin, J., & Vatikiotis-Bateson, E. (Eds.). (2002). Special issue on joint audio-visual speech processing. *EURASIP Journal on Applied Signal Processing*, 2002 (11).

Oliver, N., Pentland, A. P., & Berard, F. (1997). LAFTER: Lips and face real time tracker. In Proc. *IEEE Computer Vision and Pattern Recognition*, (pp. 123-129).

Patterson, E. K., Gurbuz, S., Tufecki, Z., & Gowdy, J. N. (2002). CUAVE: A new audi-visual database for multimodal human-computer interface research. In Proc. *IEEE Int. Conf. Acoustics, Speech, and Signal Processing, II*, 2017-2020.

Potamianos, G., Neti, C., Gravier, G., Garg, A., & Senior, A. W. (2003). Recent advances in automatic recognition of audiovisual speech. *Proceedings of the IEEE, 91*(9), 1306-1326.

Reisberg, D. (1987). Easy to hear but hard to understand: A lip-reading advantage with intact auditory stimuli. In B. Dodd, and R. Campbell (Eds.*), Hearing by eye: The psychology of lip-reading* (pp. 97-113). London: Lawrence Erlbaum.

Sadeghi, M., Kittler, J., & Messer, K. (2001). Segmentation of lip pixels for lip-tracker initialization. In *Proc. IEEE Int. Conf. Image Processing, 1*, 50-53.

Stork, D. G., & Hennecke, M. E. (1996). Speechreading: An overview of image processing, feature extraction, sensory integration, and pattern recognition techniques. Recent advances in automatic recognition of audiovisual speech. *In Proc. Face and Gesture Recognition* (pp. xvi-xxvi).

Sumby, W. H., & Pollock, I. (1954). Visual contribution to speech intelligibility in noise. *Journal Acoustical Society of America, 26*, 212-215.

Summerfield, Q. (1987). Some preliminaries to a comprehensive account of audio-visual speech perception. In B. Dodd, and R. Campbell (Eds.*), Hearing by eye: The psychology of lip-reading* (pp. 3-51). London: Lawrence Erlbaum.

Vignoli, F. (2000). From speech to talking faces: Lip movements estimation based on linear approximators. In *Proc. IEEE Int. Conf. Acoustics, Speech, and Signal Processing, 4*, 2381-2384).

Williams, J. J., Rutledge, J. C., & Katsaggelos, A. K. (1998). Frame rate and viseme analysis for multimedia applications to assist speechreading. *Journal of VLSI Signal Processing, 20*, 7-23.

Zhang, X., & Mersereau, R. M. (2000). Lip feature extraction towards an automatic speechreading system. In *Proc. IEEE Int. Conf. Image Processing, 3*, 226-229.

Chapter X
Visual Speech Recognition Across Multiple Views

Patrick Lucey
Queensland University of Technology, Australia

Gerasimos Potamianos
IBM T. J. Watson Research Center, USA

Sridha Sridharan
Queensland University of Technology, Australia

ABSTRACT

It is well known that visual speech information extracted from video of the speaker's mouth region can improve performance of automatic speech recognizers, especially their robustness to acoustic degradation. However, the vast majority of research in this area has focused on the use of frontal videos of the speaker's face, a clearly restrictive assumption that limits the applicability of audio-visual automatic speech recognition (AVASR) technology in realistic human-computer interaction. In this chapter, the authors advance beyond the single-camera, frontal-view AVASR paradigm, investigating various important aspects of the visual speech recognition problem across multiple camera views of the speaker, expanding on their recent work. The authors base their study on an audio-visual database that contains synchronous frontal and profile views of multiple speakers, uttering connected digit strings. They first develop an appearance-based visual front-end that extracts features for frontal and profile videos in a similar fashion. Subsequently, the authors focus on three key areas concerning speech recognition based on the extracted features: (a) Comparing frontal and profile visual speech recognition performance to quantify any degradation across views; (b) Fusing the available synchronous camera views for improved recognition in scenarios where multiple views can be used; and (c) Recognizing visual speech using a single pose-invariant statistical model, regardless of camera view. In particular, for the latter, a feature normalization approach between poses is investigated. Experiments on the available database are reported in all above areas. This chapter constitutes the first comprehensive study on the subject of visual speech recognition across multiple views.

INTRODUCTION

Recent algorithmic advances in the field of automatic speech recognition (ASR) together with progress in technologies such as speech synthesis, natural language understanding, and dialog modeling have allowed deployment of many automatic systems for human-computer interaction. Of course, these systems require highly accurate ASR to achieve successful task completion and user satisfaction. Although this in general is attainable in relatively quiet environments and for low- to medium-complexity recognition tasks, ASR performance degrades significantly in noisy acoustic environments, especially under conditions mismatched to training data (Junqua, 2000).

One possible avenue proposed for improving ASR robustness to noise is to incorporate visual speech information extracted from a speaker's face into the speech recognition process – thus giving rise to audio-visual ASR (AVASR) systems. Indeed, over the past two decades, significant progress has been achieved in this field, and many researchers have been able to demonstrate dramatic gains in bimodal ASR accuracy, in line with expectations from human speech perception studies (Sumby and Pollack, 1954). Overviews of such efforts can be found in Chibelushi et al. (2002) and Potamianos et al. (2003), among others. In spite however of this progress, practical deployments of AVASR systems have yet to emerge. This we believe is mainly due to the fact that most research in this field has neglected addressing robustness of the AVASR visual front-end component to realistic video data. One of the most critical overseen issues is speaker head pose variation, or in other words the camera view-point of the speaker's face.

Indeed, with a few exceptions reviewed in the Background section, nearly all work in the literature has concentrated on the case where the speaker's face is captured in a fully frontal pose – a rather restrictive human-computer interaction scenario, a fact also made clear in Figure 1. For example, one potential AVASR application is speech recognition using mobile devices such as cell phones. Device placement with respect to the head does not allow frontal AVASR in this case. Another interesting scenario is that of in-vehicle AVASR. Due to frequent driver head movement, a frontal pose cannot be guaranteed, regardless of camera placement – for example at the rear-view mirror, the cabin driver-side column, or the instrument console. Other possibilities include the design of an audio-visual headset, where a miniature camera is placed next to the microphone in the wearable boom. Requiring frontal views of the speaker mouth means that the device may be designed to protrude unnecessarily in front of the mouth, creating headset instability and usability issues (Gagne et al., 2001; Huang et al., 2004). In contrast, placing the camera to the side of the face would allow a significantly shorter boom, hence resulting in a lighter and easier to use headset. Finally, an interesting scenario is this of AVASR during meetings and lectures inside smart rooms. There, pan-tilt-zoom (PTZ) cameras can track the meeting speaker(s) providing high resolution views. However, due to the camera fixed placements in space, frontal speaker views cannot be guaranteed. This latter scenario motivates our work. It is discussed in more detail later on in this book chapter, together with the audio-visual database collected in this domain to drive our research.

Motivated by the above, in this chapter, we advance beyond the single-camera, frontal-view AVASR paradigm that has hindered progress in the field. Since the subject of non-frontal AVASR is still at its infancy, we focus on a simplified version of the problem, by considering two fixed views: the traditional *frontal* view and an extreme case, namely that of *profile* views. To allow a comprehensive study of the relevant issues, we consider the case where data are available synchronously from both views via a multi-camera setting (see also Figure 2). In addition, in this study we bypass the problem of head-pose

Figure 1. Examples of practical scenarios where frontal AVASR is inadequate: (a) Driver data inside an automobile; (b) Mouth region data from a specially designed audio-visual headset; (c) Data from a lecturer captured by a pan-tilt-zoom camera inside a smart-room.

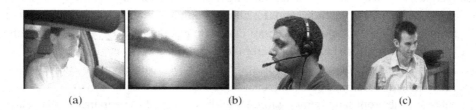

(a)   (b)   (c)

estimation, assuming that in the resulting data the view-point (frontal or profile) is a-priori known. Furthermore, we concentrate entirely on the problem of visual speech recognition (also known as automatic speechreading or lipreading). Such focus prevents our comparative results from being skewed by the audio modality and the audio-visual fusion component used. Finally, to allow meaningful speechreading results (in terms of recognition accuracies achieved and their "spread") and to keep data collection size requirements manageable, we focus our study on a small-vocabulary recognition task, namely that of connected-digit strings.

We first develop an appearance-based visual front-end that extracts features for frontal and profile videos in a similar fashion. The adopted algorithmic approach shares common components across views, without favoring one over the other, and allows easy generalization to additional views in the future. In more detail, it is based on AdaBoost statistical classifiers of faces and facial features (Viola and Jones, 2001) that are used to track rectangular region-of-interests containing the mouth with the same resolution across views. Visual features are then extracted using the identical procedure for both views. It should be noted that the problem is significantly more challenging in the profile case, due to the more limited area where the facial features are contained and the fact that some are occluded, hence removing redundancy and symmetries present in the frontal case – see also Figure 2. Nevertheless, our proposed approach results in satisfactory tracking performance.

Following visual feature extraction, the remainder of the chapter focuses on three key issues with respect to automatic speechreading across the two views of interest:

a. Comparing frontal and profile visual speech recognition to quantify the performance degradation;
b. Fusing the available synchronous camera views for improved recognition in scenarios where both views are available for use; and
c. Recognizing visual speech using a single pose-invariant statistical model, regardless of which of the two camera views the test data belongs to.

Figure 2. Synchronous (a) frontal and (b) profile views of a subject recorded in the IBM smart-room. In the latter case, visible facial features are "compacted" within approximately half the area compared to the frontal face case, thus increasing tracking difficulty.

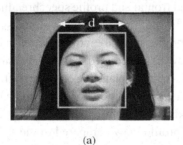 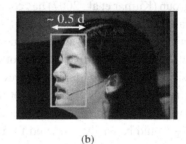

(a)   (b)

Specifically, for the latter, a feature normalization approach between poses is investigated. This approach, based on a linear regression technique, is analyzed in more detail later on. Following this analysis, a description of the basic visual speech recognition system employed in this work, including a brief description of the fusion of the two camera views is given. The latter part of this book chapter describes our experiments and provides results concerning system performance investigating points (a)–(c) above. We then conclude the chapter with a brief summary and hypothesize possible avenues for future work, respectively.

BACKGROUND

Although nearly all audio-visual speech research focuses on frontal data of the speaker's face or mouth region, there exists some work that discusses non-frontal views. Following on from the early work of Sumby and Pollack (1954), Neely (1956) conducted some human perception studies that found the when the angle from the frontal view was increased, there was a decrease in speech intelligibility. Similarly, Jordan & Thomas (2001) found that human identification of visual speech becomes more difficult as the angle (from frontal to profile view) increases – a rather intuitive finding. Profile views have also been used in visual speech synthesis, often in conjunction with frontal views, or as part of a 3D head model (Morishima et al., 1989; Lavagetto, 1995; Hovden & Ling, 2003). Finally, with respect to automatic speechreading and AVASR, only three research groups – to our knowledge – have focused on the use of non-frontal data. A brief overview of their work follows.

The first group has considered profile-only AVASR, in work reported by Yoshinaga et al. (2003, 2004) and Iwano et al. (2007). In these papers, the authors extract up to four-dimensional visual speech features from profile videos of the mouth region of Japanese speakers uttering connected digit strings, and then fuse them with the audio channel, resulting in improved ASR performance. The visual features are geometric-based (profile lip angle and its first derivative) and/or appearance-based (optical flow).

They conducted these experiments on a database which consisted of 38 male speakers who uttered 50 sequences of 4 connected Japanese digits. No visual-only recognition results are reported, and no comparison with frontal AVASR is made. Thus, none of the three focal issues (a)–(c) of our study are addressed.

The second group (Kumar et al., 2007) has conducted frontal and profile speechreading and AVASR comparisons on a speaker-dependent isolated word set. The authors employ low-dimensional geometric visual features in these comparisons and conclude that profile speechreading is better than frontal. This finding seems rather counter-intuitive as the profile view has a reduced amount of visible articulators available as noted previously (see Figure 2). However, this result is plausible considering the database (10 speakers, each uttering 150 words 10 times, captured in easy conditions with a chroma keyed uniform background), as well as the simple geometric feature extraction technique used. This is because the lip edges and corners would be easily extracted from the profile view compared to the frontal view, due to their contrast to the background. It would be expected however, that if state-of-the-art appearance-based features were used, this would no longer be the case, due to their ability to capture more than just corner and edge information. In summary, the study does examines (a) and (b), albeit in a primitive way. It does not however discuss issue (c).

An additional effort is reported by Kumatani & Stiefelhagen (2007). There, the authors consider AVASR on a large-vocabulary continuous speech database with three available synchronized camera views of the speaker (frontal, profile, and at 45 degrees), using appearance-based visual features. Their database consists of 39 male and 5 female speakers, uttering sentences from the TIMIT database. In the paper, the authors compare AVASR performance between the frontal and 45-degree views, an investigation similar to issue (a) of this chapter, but they do not discuss the other two topics of interest in our study.

Other than these three bodies of work, no other attempt has been made to address the problem of non-frontal AVASR. Clearly therefore, this chapter advances the state-of-the-art in the field by comprehensively discussing all three issues, (a)–(c), within the same experimental framework. It also constitutes a natural continuation of our earlier research reported in Lucey & Potamianos (2006) and Lucey et al. (2007) that separately treated issues (a, b) and (c), respectively. In particular, this chapter for the first time introduces a visual front-end that extracts features for frontal and profile videos in a similar fashion, without favoring one over the other, thus providing truly unbiased results in our study. Furthermore, the feature normalization approach across poses, first introduced in Lucey et al. (2007), is discussed in great detail, accompanied by a large number of experiments later on in this book chapter to quantify its effectiveness with respect to feature vector size, test data distribution across views, and the introduction of a third view.

THE IBM SMART-ROOM DATABASE

As discussed in the Introduction, the scenario of interest that has been the driving force of our work is that of meetings or lectures inside smart rooms (Pentland, 1998; Gatica-Perez et al., 2005; CHIL). These rooms are equipped with a number of audio-visual sensors, including microphone arrays, fixed and pan-tilt-zoom (PTZ) cameras. This scenario has been of central interest in the recently concluded "Computers in the Human Interaction Loop" (CHIL) integrated project, funded by the European Union.

A schematic diagram of one of the smart rooms developed for this project, in particular the one located at IBM Research, is depicted in Figure 3(a).

Clearly, audio-visual speech technologies, such as speech activity detection, source separation, and speech recognition, are of prime interest in this scenario, due to overlapping and noisy speech, typical in multi-person interaction, captured by far-field microphones. Data from the smart room fixed cameras are of insufficient quality to be used for this purpose, as they typically capture the participants' faces in low resolution – see also Figure 3(b). On the other hand, video captured by the PTZ cameras can provide high resolution data, assuming that successful active camera control is employed, based on tracking the person(s) of interest (Zhang et al., 2007). Nevertheless, since the PTZ cameras are fixed in space, they cannot necessarily obtain frontal views of the speaker. It is therefore apparent that speechreading from non-frontal views is required in this scenario, as well as fusion of multiple camera views, if available. This scenario is the prime focus in the book chapter.

Figure 3. (a) A schematic diagram of the IBM smart-room developed for the purpose of the CHIL project. Notice the fixed and PTZ cameras, as well as the far-field table-top and array microphones. (b) Examples of image views captured by the IBM smart-room cameras. In contrast to the four cameras (two upper rows), the two PTZ cameras (lower row) provide closer views of the lecturer, albeit not necessarily frontal.

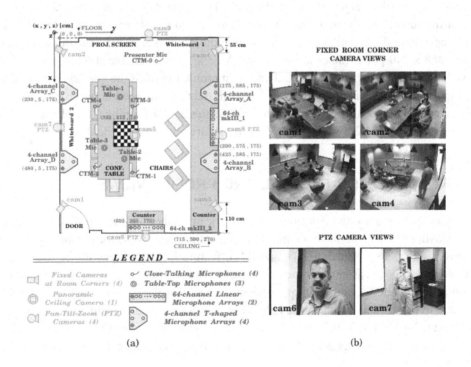

(a)   (b)

Figure 4. Examples of synchronous frontal and profile video frames of four subjects from the audio-visual database used in this chapter.

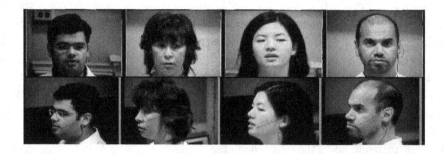

To facilitate our investigation into automatic speechreading across multiple views, we have collected an audio-visual database in this smart room under the constrained conditions described in the Introduction. We refer to the resulting corpus as the *IBM smart-room database* (which due to proprietary constraints is currently not publicly available). In particular, a total of 38 subjects uttering connected-digit strings have been recorded, using two microphones and three PTZ cameras. Of the two microphones, one is head-mounted (close-talking channel – see also Figure 4), and the other is omni-directional, located on a wall close to the recorded subject (far-field channel). The three PTZ cameras record frontal and two side views of the subject, and feed a single video channel into a laptop via a quad-splitter and an S-video-to-DV converter. As a result, two synchronous audio streams at 22 kHz and three visual streams at 30 Hz and 368 x 240-pixel frames are available. Among these available streams, two video views are employed in this work, namely the frontal and right profile (which is the one "closest" to the profile pose – see Figure 4). A total of 1661 utterances from this database are used in the chapter experiments, partitioned using a multi-speaker paradigm into 1198 sequences for training (1 hr 51 min in duration), 242 for testing (23 min), and 221 sequences (15 min) that are allocated to a held-out set.

VISUAL FRONT-END FOR FRONTAL AND PROFILE VIEWS

For this book chapter, we use the AdaBoost framework of Viola & Jones (2001), later extended by Leinhart & Maydt (2002), to perform the mouth region-of-interest (ROI) localization and extraction. This framework allows us to generate face and facial feature localizers specific for each view-point, but nevertheless using a consistent approach across both views. These classifiers are trained using the OpenCV libraries (OpenCV), and their application requires that the speaker pose is first determined (an issue that is overlooked in this chapter). Following this step, ROIs are obtained for each view at the same resolution (32 x 32 pixels), and visual feature vectors extracted using the same approach for both views. The following subsections detail the specific tracking process for each view-point, followed by the visual feature extraction stage.

Frontal ROI Localization and Tracking

The positive examples used for training the AdaBoost classifiers were obtained from a set of 847 training frontal images, chosen at random from the training set sequences of the database discussed in the previous section, and each manually annotated with 17 facial points. Among these points, it was deemed that nine were sufficient to assist in extracting the frontal mouth ROI. These points were the left and right eyes, nose, the left and right mouth corners, top and bottom of the mouth, the mouth center and chin – see also Figure 5.

The resulting 847 positive examples for the face were further augmented by including rotations in the image plane by ±5 and ± 10 degrees, as well as mirroring the images, providing a total of 5082 positive examples. All were normalized to 16 x 16 pixels, based on an inter-eye distance of 6 pixels. The negative face examples consisted of a random collection of approximately 5000 images that did not contain any faces. Some of them were of the frame background, as well as random objects.

In contrast to the face examples, since a number of facial features were located so close to each other (a matter of pixels in some cases), it was decided not to include rotations to the set of 847 positive examples of each of the nine facial features. In terms of template size, the eye classifiers were trained using image templates of size 20 x 20, the nose and chin employed a template size of 15 x 15, and the right, top, left and bottom mouth templates were chosen to be 10 x 10. Finally, the mouth center templates were of size 24 x 24.

In particular, the latter classifier was used to find a coarse ROI, so that further refinement could take place, hence the larger template size. Notice that all these templates were obtained from normalized face images of size 64 x 64, based on an inter-eye distance of 32 pixels. As the face localization step limits the facial feature search space, the negative examples for the various facial features only consisted of

Figure 5. Nine points used for facial feature localization on frontal faces: (a) right eye, (b) left eye, (c) nose, (d) right mouth corner, (e) top mouth, (f) left mouth corner, (g) bottom mouth, (h) mouth center, and (i) chin

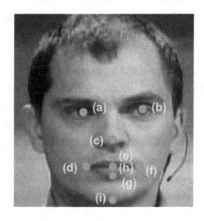

Table 1. Facial feature detection for frontal head pose. The four features considered for ROI normalization are depicted in bold.

Facial Feature	Localization Accuracy (%)
Right Eye	91.08
Left Eye	89.47
Nose	89.47
Right Mouth	91.08
Top Mouth	81.08
Left Mouth	89.47
Bottom Mouth	83.78
Center Mouth	89.47
Chin	67.57

images of other facial features. This was done to alleviate confusions that might have occurred due to various facial features looking alike, for example an open mouth could appear like an eye under certain illumination conditions.

To validate the approach and determine which features could be reliably employed for ROI localization, all classifiers were tested on a small set of 37 frontal images. The detection accuracy results of the nine facial feature classifiers are depicted in Table 1. There, a feature is considered accurately detected when the distance between its estimated position and annotated location is less than 10% of the inter-eye distance in the frame – similarly to the work of Jesorsky et al. (2001). As it can be seen from Table 1, most of the facial features were located at a pretty high rate, except the chin and top and bottom mouth. Since the final extracted mouth ROI needed to be normalized for scale and rotation to enforce alignment across all ROI images, two geometrically aligned points had to be found for this to happen. In the literature, normally eye locations are used for such an alignment. However, it was found heuristically that this metric was not ideal for scaling the mouth, as there is a great deal of variability in mouth shape and size, which is not highly correlated to the inter-eye distance. As such, it was determined that the left and right mouth corners be used instead, since these gave much better reference points for scale and rotation normalization.

The frontal mouth localizer and tracker used to extract the mouth ROI for the frontal pose was as follows. Given the video of a spoken utterance, face localization was first applied to estimate the position of the speaker's face. Once the face was located, the eyes were searched for over specific face regions (based on training data statistics). Once the eyes were localized, a general mouth search region was specified. The mouth center classifier was then used to refine this search region. The resulting mouth region was subsequently used as the search region to locate the right and left mouth corners. Once these two points were found, the extracted mouth ROI was rotated so that these two points were aligned horizontally and scaled to be 20 pixels apart to yield a final 32 x 32 pixel ROI. Notice that the ROI was

Figure 6. Mouth ROI extraction examples. The upper rows show examples of the localized face, eyes, mouth region, and mouth corners. The lower row shows the corresponding normalized mouth ROIs (32 x 32 pixels).

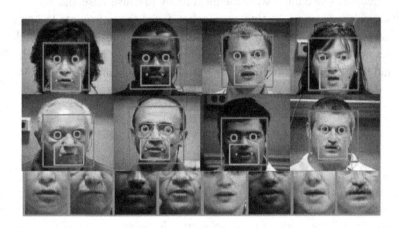

downsampled from much higher resolution (approximately 80 x 80 pixels on average). Such downsampling keeps dimensionality low without adversely affecting lipreading performance, as reported in the work of Jordan & Sergeant (1998). Notice also that the final ROI contained most of the lower part of the face, which is known to benefit lipreading by both machines (Potamianos & Neti, 2001) and humans (Summerfield, 1989).

Following ROI localization, the ROI is tracked over consecutive frames. If the detected ROI is too far away compared to a previous frame, then this is regarded as a detection failure, and the previous ROI location is used. A mean filter is then employed to smooth tracking. Due to the speed of the Viola-Jones algorithm, this process is performed at every frame. Prior to the start of the full process, an initialization phase is executed to obtain a first "lock" on the location of the various facial features. Figure 6 depicts face and facial feature localization examples from the visual front-end and the final extracted mouth ROIs.

Profile ROI Localization and Tracking

The ROI localization and tracking for the profile view was developed in a similar manner to its frontal counterpart. Due to the compactness of the facial features in the profile view, only seven of the 17 manually annotated facial features were used. These were the left eye, nose, the top, center, and bottom of the mouth, the left mouth corner, and the chin, as depicted in Figure 7. Similarly to the frontal data, a set of 847 images were available for training and 37 images for validation purposes. This provided 847 positive examples for each of the seven facial feature classifiers. The resulting face training set also included rotations in the image plane by ±5 and ±10 degrees, providing 4235 positive examples. A similar amount of negative examples of the background were also employed in training. Approximately 5000 negative examples were used for each facial feature, consisting of images of the other facial features that surrounded its location, since these were the most likely to cause false alarms.

One difficulty experienced was selecting appropriate facial feature points to use for the training image normalization (scaling and rotation). In the frontal face scenario, eyes are predominately used for this purpose, but in the profile-view case a pair of geometrically aligned features does not exist. Instead, the nose and the chin were chosen, with a normalized constant distance of 64 pixels between

Figure 7. Points used for facial feature localization on the profile pose: (a) left eye, (b) nose, (c) top mouth, (d) mouth center, (e) bottom mouth, (f) left mouth corner, and (g) chin. The center of the depicted bounding box around the left eye defines the actual feature location.

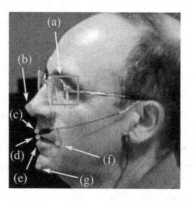

Table 2. Facial feature detection for profile head pose. The two features considered for ROI normalization are depicted in bold.

Facial Feature	Localization Accuracy (%)
Left Eye	86.49
Nose	81.08
Top Mouth	78.37
Center Mouth	81.08
Bottom Mouth	72.97
Left Mouth Corner	86.49
Chin	62.16

them. This choice was dictated by the head pose variation within the dataset that had less of an effect on the chosen metric, compared to other possibilities (such as eye-to-nose distance, etc.). Based on the resulting normalized training faces, the left mouth corner and the top, center, and bottom mouth classifiers were trained on templates of size 10 x 10 pixels. Both nose and chin classifiers were trained on templates of size 15 x 15 pixels, whereas the eye template was slightly larger, at 20 x 20 pixels.

The localization results of the various facial features from this validation set provided an indication of what particular features would give the best chance of reliably tracking the ROI. These results are shown in Table 2, where a feature is considered incorrectly localized if the location error is larger than 10% of the annotated nose-to-chin distance. From these localization results, it can be seen that along with the left eye, the left mouth corner yielded the best performance. This shows the usefulness of employing a corner for facial feature localization, as it provides a unique shape within the face which is hard to get confused with other objects. As the left eye and left mouth corner yielded the best results, it was decided to use these two points for scale normalization. The only difference between using the left eye and left mouth corner, compared to the nose and chin was changing the scaling factor from 64 to 45 pixels.

The whole procedure of ROI localization and tracking was similar to that for the frontal pose. Given the video of a spoken utterance, face localization was first applied to estimate the location of the speaker's face. Once the face was located, the left eye and nose were searched over specific regions of the face (based on training data statistics). From these locations, a generalized mouth region was estimated, and

Figure 8. Examples of accurate (a-d) and inaccurate (e,f) results of the localization and tracking system. In (f), it can be seen that the subject exhibits a somewhat more frontal pose compared to the profile view of the other subjects.

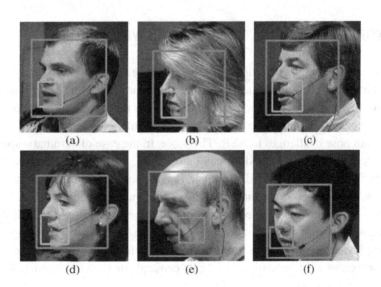

from this the left mouth corner was located. The next step was to define a scaling metric, so that all ROI images would be normalized to the same size. As mentioned previously, the ratio of the vertical distance between the left eye and left mouth corner over the normalization constant of 45 pixels was used to achieve this. A 48 x 48 normalized ROI based on the left mouth corner was then extracted. The ROI was subsequently downsampled to 32 x 32 pixels, for use in the lipreading system. Following ROI localization, the ROI was tracked like in the frontal scenario. Overall, the accuracy of the profile visual front-end was very good. Examples of the extracted profile ROIs are shown in Figure 8. A major factor affecting performance was random head movement and some head pose variability, where subjects exhibit a somewhat more frontal pose than the majority – see also Figure 8(f).

Visual Feature Extraction

For both frontal and profile view-points, the same visual feature extraction process was applied. Following ROI extraction, the mean ROI over the utterance was removed. This approach is very similar to cepstral mean subtraction (CMS) in the audio domain and is known as feature mean normalization (FMN). Our implementation is similar to that of Potamianos et al. (2003), however in our approach we performed normalization in the image domain instead of the feature domain. A two-dimensional, separable, discrete cosine transform (DCT) was then applied on the resulting mean-removed ROI, with the $M = 100$ top DCT coefficients retained, according to a zig-zag pattern. An intra-frame linear discriminate analysis (LDA) step was then used to project the features down to $N = 30$ dimensions, resulting in a "static" visual feature vector.

Subsequently, in order to incorporate dynamic speech information, five of these neighboring static feature vectors over $\pm J$ adjacent frames were concatenated, and were projected via an inter-frame LDA step to yield a "dynamic" visual feature vector, extracted at the video frame rate of 30 Hz. For the experiments in the next section, dynamic features of dimensionality P ranging from 10 to 70 will be analyzed, in order to examine the effect on the transformation approach introduced in the next section. The classes used for LDA matrix calculation were the hidden Markov model (HMM) states, based on forced alignment employing an audio-only HMM on the far-field audio channel of the database.

VISUAL FEATURE NORMALIZATION ACROSS VIEWS

Visual features extracted using the techniques discussed above contain important speech information. This can be exploited, when the features are fed into an automatic speechreading system, as discussed in the next section. However, although their extraction follows the same approach for both frontal and profile views, one expects the feature spaces to "differ" significantly across the two views. Feature mismatch is known to pose challenges to ASR. Therefore, in the case of automatic speechreading, the use of view-dependent visual speech models may be required, an approach that does not scale well if a continuum of possible views is expected. However, if some sort of feature-space invariance could be determined, then the use of a view-independent visual speech model becomes viable. This latter method has the advantage that it removes the need of training and keeping multiple models active, when the camera-speaker view-point may vary.

Seeking feature invariance to reduce train/test mismatch for improved classification is an active research topic. For example, in acoustic-only ASR, cepstral mean subtraction (CMS) and RASTA processing (Mammone et al., 1996; Hermansky & Morgan, 1994) are known approaches, aiming to reduce mismatch caused by channel conditions and noise. In the visual domain, techniques such as linear regression have been used in face recognition, as a means to project undesired non-frontal face images into frontal ones. Blanz et al. (2005) cite that the advantage of doing so is due to the fact that most state-of-the-art face recognition systems are optimized for frontal faces, with their performance degrading significantly when presented with non-frontal faces. Interestingly, linear regression has also been investigated in the audio-visual speech literature for speech enhancement, namely as a means to estimate clean audio features from a noisy audio-visual feature vector (Girin et al., 2001; Goecke et al., 2002).

Motivated by these works, this section introduces a linear regression based approach that normalizes visual speech features into the feature space of a desired view-point, allowing speech modeling by a single statistical model. The approach is summarized in the following two subsections, further delving into implementation details.

Linear Regression for View-Invariance

Blanz et al. (2005) cite two possible ways of performing view-invariant face recognition, either via a view-point transform or a coefficient-based approach. The view-point transform approach acts in a pre-processing manner to transform/warp a face representation (i.e. image or feature vector) of an undesired view into the desired one – a one-to-one mapping. Coefficient-based recognition on the other hand attempts to estimate the face representation under all views given a single one (i.e., given just one view of the face, all other potential views are estimated such as right profile, 45° right, frontal, 45° left, left profile etc.), otherwise called the lightfield of the face (Gross et al., 2004) – a one-to-many mapping process. Although it is not clear which approach is superior, the view-point transform approach is employed in this chapter as only one view is required. The reason behind this choice is the fact that almost all automatic speechreading systems to date have been optimized for frontal views and using the view with the most visible articulators present seems like a viable approach. This is similar to the motivation cited by Blanz et al. (2005) for their face recognition system.

The most common way to perform this approach is to estimate a linear regression (transformation) matrix $\mathbf{W}$ between a training set consisting of N examples of the undesirable viewpoint $\mathbf{X}$, and their synchronized target examples in the preferred viewpoint $\mathbf{T}$ (Bishop, 2006). Matrix $\mathbf{W}$ is then computed by minimizing

$$tr[(\mathbf{WT} - \mathbf{X})^T (\mathbf{WT} - \mathbf{X})] + \lambda \cdot tr[\mathbf{W}^T \mathbf{W}],$$ (1)

where $\mathbf{X} = \{\mathbf{x}_1, ..., \mathbf{x}_N\}$, $\mathbf{T} = \{[\mathbf{t}_1, 1]^T, ..., [\mathbf{t}_{N,1}]^T\}$ and $\mathbf{x}_n$ and $\mathbf{t}_n$ are synchronous data vectors. A unit bias has been added to $\mathbf{T}$ to allow for any fixed offset in the data. In addition, regularization term λ has been introduced into (1) as a means to avoid over-fitting, a common issue in linear regression that is further discussed in the next subsection. Based on (1), the solution for $\mathbf{W}$ becomes (Bishop, 2006)

$$\mathbf{W} = \mathbf{TX}^T (\mathbf{XX}^T + \lambda \mathbf{I})^{-1}.$$ (2)

Figure 9. Schematic of visual feature normalization for view-invariance: Features x_n extracted from an undesired view (e.g. profile) are transformed into features t_n in the target view space (e.g. frontal) via a linear regression matrix W. The matrix is calculated offline based on synchronized visual features T and X from the two views.

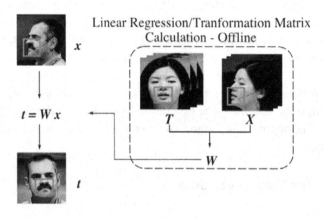

Figure 10. Quality of profile ROI projection into the desirable frontal view, based on the regression training set size and the value of the regularization parameter.

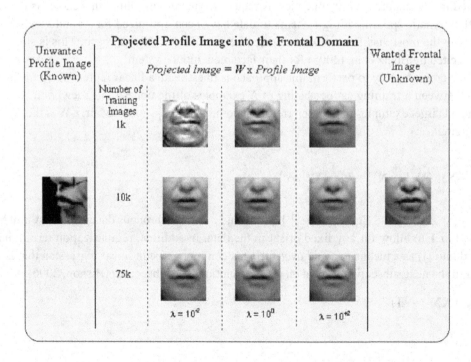

In our AVASR experiments described at the end of the chapter, transformation matrix **W** was estimated using the input visual speech features of a particular viewpoint, **X**, obtained in parallel with synchronized features extracted from the desirable viewpoint, **T**. This was deemed preferable to transforming the entire raw image patch of mouth data (ROI), as it reduced vector dimensionality (*P* varies from 10 to 70, compared to the mouth ROI vector that has a dimensionality of 32 x 32 = 1024). Matrix **W**, therefore, was used to project visual speech features ($\mathbf{x}_n$) of an unwanted viewpoint into estimates of desirable viewpoint features ($\hat{\mathbf{t}}_n$). This process is depicted in Figure 9.

Importance of the Regularization Term (λ)

The regularization term, λ, was introduced in the previous subsection to control the problem of overfitting. Overfitting refers to the situation where a model has too many parameters compared to the amount of available training data, as a result perfectly fitting to that data, but unsuitable to model unseen events. In the context of the linear regression in (1), λ allows a complex model to be produced, by weighting values not supported by the training data towards zero. In the practical application of (1), the following issues are of interest:

- *What value of λ should be used?*
- *What impact does the amount of training data have on the value of λ?*

To help address these issues, we proceed to a demonstration of the effectiveness of linear regression over various values of λ and across a different number of training images. In this experiment, matrix **W** was trained from whole frontal and profile grayscale ROI images (32 x 32 pixels), instead of their corresponding visual features. Different **W**s were calculated for $\lambda = \{10^{-2}, 10^0, 10^2\}$ and for three sizes of the training image set, namely 1k, 10k, and 75k. These training images were randomly selected from the entire training set (~ 200k images). The resulting regression matrices were then used to project a previously unseen undesirable profile ROI image into the desired frontal view. The process is depicted in Figure 10.

As can be seen from Figure 10, the resemblance of the actual frontal ROI image and the projected profile ROI varies according to the number of training images used and the value of λ. For example, when only 1k training images were used and $\lambda = 10^{-2}$, the projected profile ROI looks like a noisy ghost-like ROI, a far-cry from the original frontal one, due to overfitting. In comparison, when the value of λ was increased to 10^0 and 10^2 using 1k training images, the respective projected profile ROIs looked a lot more like the original. Once however the number of training images used is increased (10k and 75k), the value of λ has little to no observable difference on the projected profile ROI quality.

This experiment highlights the importance of the regularization term λ as it alleviates the problem of overfitting, when the number of training examples is limited. However, when there is an abundance of training examples, the value of the regularization term is insignificant, as the large amount of training data ensures that a model which generalizes well across the data can be obtained. As such, for the experiments conducted at the end of the Chapter, the value of λ was set to 10^0, even though it was not important as the number of training frames was close to 200k.

VISUAL SPEECH RECOGNITION AND STREAM INTEGRATION

In the previous two sections we discussed how to extract visual speech features for the frontal and profile views and how to transform them across views. As already mentioned, such features can be fed into an automatic speechreading system to yield an estimate of the spoken word sequence. In this work, we employ a hidden Markov model (HMM) based ASR system for this purpose. In particular, for the connected-digit recognition task considered here, eleven nine-state, left-to-right, whole-word models are used, one for each digit (both "oh" and "zero" are included), with seven Gaussian mixtures per state. A silence and short-pause model are also employed. All models are bootstrapped from a segmentation of the audio channel of the database, obtained by an audio-only HMM with identical topology, and trained

Figure 11. The various automatic speechreading modeling scenarios considered in this chapter: (a) Single-view modeling for dedicated frontal or profile camera views. (b) Fused multi-view system using two synchronous cameras capturing both frontal and profile views. (c) Single-camera, view-independent system, possibly using view-normalized visual features.

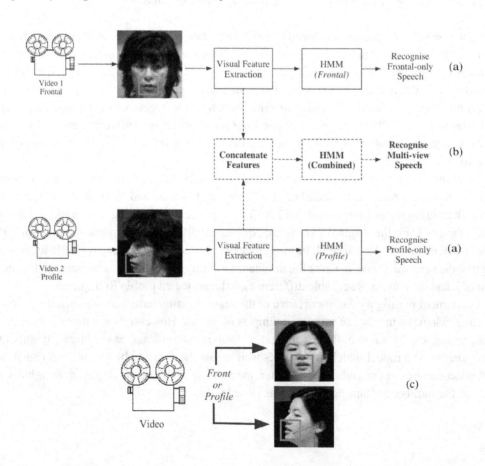

by the expectation-maximization algorithm. For testing, Viterbi decoding is used with no grammar or language model present (i.e., no constraints are imposed on the digit string length). The HTK toolkit is utilized for both system training and testing (Young et al., 2002).

As discussed in our Introduction, we are interested in three particular aspects of the problem of visual speech recognition concerning the two available views, also depicted in Figure 11. The first (see Figure 11(a)) concerns the automatic speechreading of videos at a consistent view (frontal or profile), using a dedicated HMM for the particular view in question. These HMMs are of course trained on visual speech features of the corresponding view. Experiments concerning this approach are reported in the first part of the next section and are of interest in addressing the question of how profile speechreading compares to the traditional frontal one.

The second scenario of interest is the "multi-view" one, where the speaker's head is captured by multiple synchronized cameras, each viewing the face at a fixed view. In the simplified investigation of this chapter, the scenario translates into combining (fusing) the frontal and profile view feature streams, aiming at improved recognition compared to either single-view system alone (Figure 11(b)). Such combination can be achieved using the feature or decision fusion strategies (Potamianos et al., 2003). In the former, visual features extracted from the two streams are concatenated, and the resulting features projected by LDA to a lower-dimensional space (for example, equaling that of the initial streams), in order to avoid the curse of dimensionality. Due to the fact that LDA is also used in the single-stream visual feature extraction, this process is referred to by Potamianos et al. (2003) as hierarchical LDA (HiLDA).

In contrast, in decision based fusion, the concatenated features are considered generated by a multi-stream HMM (MSHMM) – in our case, a two-stream one. This HMM arises by combining two single-stream HMMs of identical topology (states and transitions), one modeling the frontal- and one the profile-view visual features. The state-conditional observation log-likelihood of the resulting HMM is a linear combination of the ones of its two single-stream HMM components. In the multi-view experiments reported in the next section, the multi-view MSHMM parameters are obtained using the expectation-maximization algorithm (Young et al., 2002). The weights used in the linear combination of the two log-likelihoods are estimated at the end of the training procedure, by minimizing the word error rate on the held-out data set (see database and multi-view experiment descriptions).

The third scenario of interest is the one that a single camera captures a subject in a view that may vary within a set of pre-defined views. In our simplified study, this set contains two "extreme" views (frontal and profile), with each utterance being available at the frontal or profile view, known a-priori, with no significant view variation over its duration (see also Figure 11(c)). For automatic speechreading in this scenario, one can consider a system that has both frontal and profile HMMs available, using the appropriate view-dependent model. This approach however requires training and storing both HMMs – a situation that does not scale well as the number of possible views increases. A much more desirable alternative is to use a single HMM that can generalize well over both views. This can be achieved based on the feature normalization technique discussed in the previous section. Use of such features, for example, allows a single-stream frontal HMM to be applied to profile views. Of course, this requires training and storing feature regression matrices, but both requirements are significantly less than those for training and storing HMMs. The technique is investigated in the view-invariant speechreading experiments, and it is compared against the alternative modeling approach of using a single-stream HMM trained on all available data (i.e., on both frontal and profile views).

EXPERIMENTS

We now proceed to our experiments, with the first three experiments investigating issues (a), (b), and (c), as stated in the Introduction and depicted in Figure 11. Particular emphasis is placed on (c), namely single-camera, view-independent speechreading, with two additional sessions devoted to it. One analyzes performance with respect to test data distribution across views (for both frontal and right profile data), and another discusses the scenario where a third view is introduced (frontal, right profile and left profile data).

Frontal vs. Profile Speechreading

Visual-only ASR performance for both frontal and profile views is depicted in Figure 12. There, various values of J (one-side temporal window) and P (final visual feature dimensionality – see also the Visual Feature Extraction section) are considered. As it can be observed in Figure 12(a), performance of frontal features improves when the temporal window J is increased from 1 to 2, which highlights the importance of incorporating temporal information into the feature set. When however J increases past 2, performance levels off with no real improvement gained. It must also be noted that there is no real difference between $P = 30$ to 60 features for $J \geq 2$. In summary, the lowest word error rate (WER)

Figure 12. Comparison of the automatic speechreading performance in word error rate (WER), %, between: (a) frontal and (b) profile views, using dedicated HMMs trained on the particular view. Performance is depicted as a function of feature dimensionality, P, and of one-side length of temporal window, J, used to incorporate dynamic speech information.

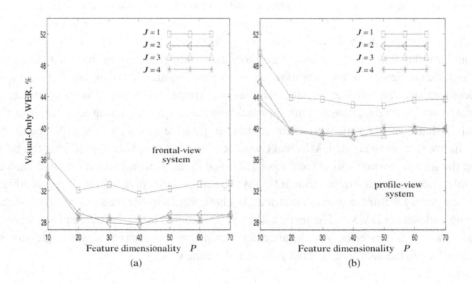

attained is 27.66%, achieved for $J = 2$ and $P = 40$. For the profile features (see Figure 12(b)), a similar trend to the frontal view can be observed. The best performance is obtained for $P = 40$ features and $J = 2$, resulting in a WER of 38.88%. This corresponds to an absolute degradation of 11.22% in WER, or a 40% relative WER increase, compared to the frontal-view system.

The degradation from frontal to profile speechreading can be attributed to the visible articulators that the system has available in the respective views. For example, in the frontal scenario, the teeth, lips, tongue, and jaw may be visible. In the profile view however, only the lips and jaw are available. An additional difficulty with the profile view lies in the background. In the frontal scenario, a small localization/tracking error may cause slight only appearance changes, due to the somewhat uniform background around the lips (i.e., speaker skin). In contrast, poor localization/tracking in the profile view may capture an excessive amount of non-facial background, causing significant ROI appearance changes. To counteract this, a face contour algorithm could be applied. However, this can introduce errors into the system due to poor detection, while also being computationally expensive (see Potamianos et al. (2003) for details).

Considering the difficulties in extracting visual speech from the profile view, the 38.88% WER achieved is still extremely useful, and much better than pure chance. This becomes apparent when the profile visual stream is fused with the audio channel. Although the combined audio-visual scenario is outside the scope of this book chapter, it is worth mentioning that Lucey et al. (2006) report substantial ASR gains over audio-only results.

Multi-View Speechreading

Although profile automatic speechreading is significantly inferior to using frontal data, there may still exist useful information in profile data not captured in the frontal view. Under this hypothesis, fusing visual speech representations from both views may be advantageous, assuming that synchronous data streams are available from both. Following the presentation in the Visual Speech Recognition and Stream Integration section, we employ both feature fusion (HiLDA) and decision-based integration (using MSHMMs) for combining frontal and profile visual features. Based on the results of the previous subsection, 40-dimensional features are extracted from each view and concatenated. Under HiLDA fusion, the resulting 80-dimensional vectors are projected to 40 dimensions by means of LDA. In the MSHMM implementation, two systems are considered: One that employs all 40 dimensions from each of the two streams, and a second one that uses the top 20 only features from each view (thus resulting to a 40-dimensional concatenated vector). In both cases, MSHMM integration weights are estimated to 0.8 and 0.2 for the frontal and profile streams, based on minimizing the WER on the held-out set.

The results of the above experiments are depicted in Table 3. There, it can be observed that combining the two views is beneficial, reducing WER in all cases, compared to single-view speechreading. The best performance is achieved by the MSHMM that uses 20 features per stream. The resulting 25.36% WER represents a 2.3% absolute WER reduction (8% relative) over the frontal view. This demonstrates that there indeed exists speech information in the profile view, not captured in frontal data. This is possibly due to lip protrusion visibility in profile views. In terms of the fusion approach employed, Table 3 suggests that MSHMM-based decision fusion is superior to plain feature combination. This may be due to the explicit modeling of the reliability / information content of the two feature streams, possible in the MSHMM formulation via the use of combination weights. This fact becomes even more important, when there exists inter- or even intra-utterance variation in the quality of the two feature streams

Table 3. Multi-view automatic speechreading performance in WER, %, using both feature fusion (HiLDA) and decision fusion (MSHMM) based systems. Frontal- and profile-view system performance is also shown.

View	Features	WER, %
Frontal	40	27.66
Profile	40	38.88
Multi-view	HiLDA – 40	27.50
Multi-view	MSHMM (20 + 20)	25.36
Multi-view	MSHMM (40 + 40)	26.19

– due to poor tracking, or other sources of visual degradation, for example. Such variation cannot be explicitly modeled in the feature fusion framework (Potamianos et al., 2003).

View-Invariant Speechreading

We now proceed to the third aspect of our investigation, namely that of employing a single statistical model to recognize visual features from multiple views. To simplify our discussion, we denote by F a set containing frontal data only, by R a set containing profile data (recall from the database description that we used the *right*-profile view of our data), and by (F_a, R_b) a set containing $a\%$ of frontal and $b\%$ of right profile data, where of course $a + b = 100$. In addition, we denote projected data (in the visual feature space) using the linear regression approach by $\bullet'$; for example F' denotes frontal features projected onto the profile feature space, and R' stands for profile ones projected to the frontal-view feature space. In general, we are interested in the performance of single-view HMMs (trained on either F or R data), as well as of HMMs trained on multi-view data (i.e., combination of F and R data – similarly to "multi-style" training in the ASR literature), when presented with various test sets containing F and/or R data. This means that the feature normalization approach introduced will only be considered at testing, but not during training.

In particular, in this section we consider three systems, developed on training set data:

- F, i.e., all 1198 frontal videos;
- R, namely, their synchronous 1198 profile videos; and
- (F_{50}, R_{50}), i.e., trained on 599 frontal and 599 profile videos, chosen by a random split of the 1198 training set videos among the two available views.

The systems are evaluated on sets F, R, and (F_{50}, R_{50}) of the database *test* set. Similarly to the training set split, the latter is made up by 121 frontal and 121 profile test video sequences, obtained by a random selection of the 242 test videos among the two views. In addition to the above, test sets F' (projected frontal features into profile), R' (profile into frontal), (F'_{50}, R_{50}) and (F_{50}, R'_{50}) are also considered.

An additional goal of these experiments is to investigate the effect of the feature dimensionality on the effectiveness of the regression approach. For this purpose, all systems are trained and tested using features of dimensions ranging from $P = 10$ to 60. It is also worth mentioning that all transformation matrices are calculated offline by means of (2). For example, transformation matrix $\mathbf{W}_R$, which projects profile features into the frontal view, is calculated employing the full set of training frontal features (F) as the target variable $\mathbf{T}$, and the full set of training profile features (R) as the input variable $\mathbf{X}$. Similarly, transformation matrix $\mathbf{W}_F$, which projects the frontal features into the profile view, is estimated using the opposite configuration.

A first set of experiments is summarized in Figure 13. There, the three trained systems (i), (ii), and (iii), shown left-to-right, are evaluated on test sets F, R, F', and R'. The first observation to make is that the best performance achieved on sets F and R is under matched training and testing conditions, namely by the frontal-view system tested on F and by the profile-view system tested on R. The best such numbers have already been reported in the frontal vs profile speechreading experiments (see also Figure 12 and Table 2), as 27.66% and 38.88% WERs respectively, both for $P = 40$.

As expected, when each system is tested on features of the other view, the features are essentially recognized as noise, due to the extreme train/test mismatch. In both cases (frontal-view system tested on R, or profile-view one tested on F), the WER reaches approximately 87%. Such mismatch can be effectively reduced by the projection approach: For example, the frontal-view system (i) exhibits dra-

Figure 13. Visual-only WER, %, of three automatic speechreading systems: (i) trained on frontal data; (ii) trained on profile views; and (iii) multi-style trained, 50% on frontal and 50% on profile views. All systems are tested on frontal and profile views. In addition, systems (i) and (ii) are tested on view-normalized features to reduce training/test mismatch, when presented with the opposite view. Results are depicted as a function of visual feature dimensionality, P, ranging from 10 to 60.

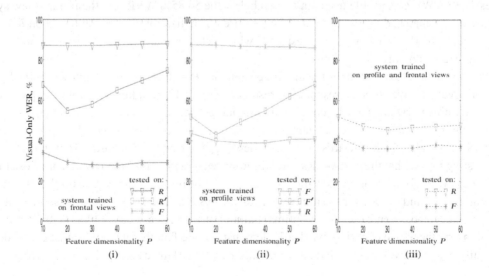

Table 4. Visual-only WER, %, of three trained systems considered, evaluated on a variety of test sets, all reported for feature dimensionality P = 20.

system trained on	system tested on						
	F	R	R′	F′	(F_{50}, R_{50})	(F_{50}, R'_{50})	(F'_{50}, R_{50})
(i): F	29.18	87.07	54.85	-	58.03	42.02	-
(ii): R	87.45	39.88	-	42.97	63.93	-	42.24
(iii): (F_{50}, R_{50})	36.41	47.39	-	-	41.73	-	-

matic WER improvement from 87.07% (when tested on R) to 54.85% (on $R′$). Similarly, the WER of profile-view system (ii) on frontal data gets reduced from 87.45% (when tested on F) to 42.97% (on $F′$). These results are reported for feature dimensionality $P = 20$ that yields the highest improvements. When the number of features however is increased, the projection approach gradually looses its effectiveness, with WER increasing from 54.85% (when $P = 20$) to 74.78% (for $P = 60$) for the frontal system tested on $R′$ data, and from 42.97% (when $P = 20$) to 67.97% (for $P = 60$) for the profile system tested on $F′$. In a sense, the effective number of model parameters in (1) are adapted automatically to the training set data size (Bishop, 2006).

Another interesting observation concerns the performance of system (iii), trained on multi-view data (F_{50}, R_{50}), compared to the two single-view systems. As already mentioned, the single-view models are superior when tested on matched data. However, even after feature normalization, they lag behind the multi-view system (iii), when tested on mismatched views. More precisely, multi-view system (iii) achieves 47.39% WER on profile test data R, well below the 54.85% WER that the frontal-view system (i) reaches on mismatched profile test data after feature normalization (i.e., when tested on $R′$). Similarly, it achieves 36.41% WER on frontal test set F, which is better than the 42.97% that the profile-view system (ii) reaches on normalized data $F′$.

The above results are reported for feature dimensionality $P = 20$, and are summarized at the left side of Table 4, together with other corresponding results of Figure 13. In addition, Table 4 depicts results of the three trained systems (i)–(iii) on three additional test sets that contain 50% frontal-view video sequences and 50% profile-view ones. The first of these test sets is unnormalized, (F_{50}, R_{50}), whereas the other two are normalized, one towards the frontal view (F_{50}, R'_{50}), and one towards the profile, (F'_{50}, R_{50}). It is interesting to note that the best WERs of all three systems in this combined test set are close to each other: 42.02% WER for the frontal-view models, 42.24% for the profile-view system (both following test set normalization), and 41.73% for the multi-view trained system. The latter exhibits a somewhat lower WER, which becomes even better if the optimal number of features are used (40.83% for $P = 30$).

In summary, the above experiments clearly demonstrate the fact that a single statistical model can successfully recognize visual speech data from multiple views. This can be achieved by using models trained on either of the two available views, but in conjunction with appropriate feature normalization of test views mismatched to the training view, or by employing a model trained on data from both views. The experiments in this section show that the second approach is preferable, when data from both views are equally likely. In the next section, we investigate what happens when the latter assumption is violated.

View-Invariant Speechreading Biased Towards Frontal View

In a practical speechreading application it may occur that one view is more frequent than another. We are then interested to investigate how the single-model systems of the previous section compare to each other. We therefore consider a hypothetical test case, where the frontal view is dominant, at let's say 80% of the time, with the profile view occurring at 20%. Three automatic speechreading systems are then investigated: System (i) used in the previous subsection, trained on 100% frontal-view videos, system (iii) used in previous subsection, built on training set (F_{50}, R_{50}), and a new one, system (iv), estimated on training set (F_{80}, R_{20}), consisting of 80% of the frontal data (958 utterances) and 20% of the profile data (240 sequences), i.e., matching the composition of the testing scenario. Note that the profile-view system is not tested, since these experiments are now biased towards the frontal view.

All three systems are evaluated on a set consisting of 80% of the frontal-view sequences of the test set (194 sequences) and 20% of profile-view ones (48 videos). In addition to the resulting (F_{80}, R_{20}) test set composition, the feature-normalized version (F_{80}, R'_{20}) is also considered. Results are depicted in Table 5, reported for feature dimensionality $P = 20$. It is clear that the best performance is achieved by system (i), trained on frontal-view data, reaching a WER of 33.90%. This result is of course reported on set (F_{80}, R'_{20}), i.e., after regression-based feature normalization of the profile data; without it, WER degrades to 40.09% on (F_{80}, R_{20}). It is interesting to note that this result is significantly better to both multi-view trained systems (iii) and (iv), even for the system trained on the same $80\% - 20\%$ data ratio among the two views as the test set.

These results demonstrate the merit of the feature normalization approach introduced. Evidently, when the models are biased towards one particular view, such as the frontal one here, it is advantageous

Table 5. Visual-only WER, %, in a scenario where the frontal view dominates the test set. The best performance is achieved by system (i), trained on frontal-view data, of course after the necessary regression-based normalization of the test set profile views. All results are reported for feature dimensionality $P = 20$.

training-set composition	test-set composition	WER (%)
(i): F	(F_{80}, R'_{20})	33.90
(iii): (F_{50}, R_{50})	(F_{80}, R_{20})	39.61
(iv): (F_{80}, R_{20})	(F_{80}, R_{20})	37.33

Figure 14. The automatic speechreading systems considered now recognizes visual speech from frontal, right- and left-profile view videos using a single model.

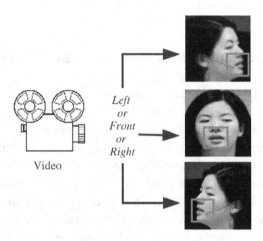

Video

Left
or
Front
or
Right

to normalize all views into the better trained one, when testing. It would also be expected that when the number of non-dominant views increases, the result will be even more dramatic, as these non-dominant views increase data variation. This scenario is the focus of the experiments reported next.

View-Invariant Speechreading Including an Additional Pose

In the previous section, it is hypothesized that if the number of views increased, the benefit of feature normalization across views would become even more pronounced. To investigate this, a left profile view is introduced. Therefore, the speechreading paradigm shifts from the one depicted in Figure 11(c) to that of Figure 14. In addition to systems (i) and (iv) discussed earlier, a new speechreading system – denoted by (v) – is introduced to accommodate the additional view. This is trained on data dominated by the frontal view. For this purpose, a (F_{80}, R_{10}, L_{10}) training set data composition is employed, where L denotes the left profile view. In particular, among the 1198 sequences of the training set, 958 frontal-view videos, 120 right-profile, and 120 left-profile ones are picked at random.

The systems are evaluated on test sets consisting of frontal-view data (F), right-profile data (R), compositions (F_{80}, R_{20}), (F_{80}, R_{10}, L_{10}), and appropriately normalized versions of most above sets towards the frontal-view feature space. Notice that test set (F_{80}, R_{10}, L_{10}) consists of 194 frontal sequences and 24 for each of the two profile views. For these experiments, the left profile data set is constructed by horizontally mirroring the right profile ROI images. Once these ROIs are obtained, the visual feature extraction step is performed as described previously. Since the left profile ROIs are just the mirrored

Table 6. Automatic speechreading results in WER, %, showing the effect that an additional pose has on performance for P = 20.

system trained on	system tested on						
	F	R	R′	(F_{80}, R_{20})	(F_{80}, R'_{20})	(F_{80}, R_{10}, L_{10})	$(F_{80}, R'_{10}, L'_{10})$
(i): F	29.18	87.07	54.85	40.09	33.90	40.07	33.81
(iii): (F_{80}, R_{20})	32.46	62.55	57.98	37.33	36.61	41.23	40.76
(v): (F_{80}, R_{10}, L_{10})	32.51	69.74	58.02	38.19	37.31	39.96	36.82

right profile images, this means that the features are effectively the same due to the DCT step in the visual feature extraction process. As the DCT is a laterally symmetrical function (Potamianos and Scanlon, 2005), the only difference between left and right profile features is that the odd frequency components have opposite polarity, which in turn results in essentially the same visual feature vectors being obtained for both the profile poses (after the LDA step). As such, visual-only recognition results using each of these views are identical. Table 6 shows the results of the experiments for visual feature dimensionality $P = 20$. From these, it can be seen that when data of another view is added, the benefit from view normalization, used in conjunction with the frontal-view trained system, is more substantial, compared to training multi-view systems. Indeed, when only two views are used, system (iv) performance on the (F_{80}, R_{20}) set reaches 37.33% WER, compared to 33.90% of system (i) on set (F_{80}, R'_{20}). However, when all three views are present, i.e. for test set (F_{80}, R_{10}, L_{10}), system (v) obtains a worse WER of 39.96%, which is a degradation of around 2.6%, while system (i) performance remains approximately steady at 33.81%.

Similarly to the previous experiments, this can be attributed to the lack of classification power the system possesses to accurately model features across the different views. In comparison, projecting the features into a uniform view does not alter speechreading performance. It is expected that further degradation would occur to the combined systems when more views are included into the system (i.e., ±30°, ±45°, ±60°, etc.). However, by utilizing the view-normalizing step, degradation to the overall speechreading performance can be minimized.

CONCLUSIONS

Over the past twenty years, literally hundreds of articles have been dedicated to illustrating the benefit of using the visual speech information from a speaker's mouth in addition to the audio signal for the task of speech recognition. Even though all these works have shown that including the visual channel to the speech recognition system greatly improves the recognition performance in the presence of acoustic noise, no deployed AVASR systems exist to date. A major reason for this is that nearly all research in the field has failed to focus on undesirable visual data variability, such as head pose. In an attempt to remedy this situation, the work in this book chapter has concentrated on researching and developing methods to recognize visual speech across multiple views.

Within this broad problem, the following three objectives set out in the Introduction were achieved:

- The automatic speechreading performance of the profile view was compared to its synchronous counterpart in the frontal view. Reasonable speechreading performance was obtained from the profile view, albeit, degraded when compared to the frontal view (38.88% vs. 27.66% WER).
- A novel system which fuses both frontal and profile synchronous features was described, referred to as a multi-view visual speech recognition system. It was shown that there does exist complimentary information in the profile view, which in turn improved the overall speechreading performance (multi-view WER was 25.36%, compared to the frontal WER of 27.66%).
- A unified approach to automatic speechreading was presented, by normalizing all views to a single uniform view. Given only one camera, this view-invariant visual speech recognition system used a transformation matrix based on linear regression to project the features of the undesired view (profile) into a preferable view (frontal). These experiments were performed for the stationary scenario, where the speaker was fixed in one view (i.e. frontal or profile) for the entire utterance, known a-priori. This view-normalization step was shown to lessen the train/test mismatch between the two views and was shown to be of particular benefit when the speaker was in one view more than the other (i.e. frontal over profile). When more non-dominant views were included (such as the other profile view), the normalizing step also proved to be of benefit.

FUTURE RESEARCH DIRECTIONS

In this book chapter, the first steps towards finding solutions for the problem of visual speech recognition from multiple views were investigated, with results from a multitude of experiments involving non-frontal views presented for the small-vocabulary task of connected-digit recognition. Experiments in this book chapter have focused on the situation where the speaker's head is constant in one pose throughout the entire utterance, which is a slightly unrealistic scenario.

To make this more realistic, there are a couple of scenarios which should be looked at. The first one would be to conduct automatic speechreading experiments on the situation where the speaker head moves during the utterance. A further progression on this would be to look at instances where the speaker is out of view for a particular camera for a portion of the time, or one particular view may be partially or fully occluded by some object such as a speaker's hand. This particular problem highlights the benefit of the multi-view approach as there would be more of a chance that the speaker's mouth would be in at least one of the camera views. Future work in terms of the multi-view visual speech recognition system would need to be conducted on dynamically adapting the weights for the various visual streams and audio streams. Similar work can be done for single camera systems as well.

In addition to these scenarios, visual variability such as illumination, appearance, speaking style, image alignment (registration) and speaker emotion and expression need to be investigated as well. A much more robust AVASR system could be obtained if research into speechreading across these variables were investigated. But it must be noted that speaker movement and varying visual environments are the most pressing issues facing visual speech recognition and AVASR in general, as very accurate face localization and tracking is required, which is an extremely difficult endeavor. However, success in this area is imperative if this technology is going to be viable for commercial use in the near future.

Future research on robustness to visual channel variabilities also needs to be conducted on large-vocabulary data. To facilitate these types of research endeavors, databases which contain such data need to become available which can be problematic due to the cost involved in collecting such data as well as proprietary issues.

ACKNOWLEDGMENT

The QUT portion of this work was supported by the Australian Research Council Grant No: LP0562101

REFERENCES

Bishop, C. (2006). Pattern Recognition and Machine Learning. Springer.

Blanz, V., Grother, P., Phillips, P., & Vetter, T. (2005). Face recognition based on frontal views generated from non-frontal images. In *Proceedings of the International Conference on Computer Vision and Pattern Recognition – CVPR* (vol. 2, pp. 454-461). San Diego, CA, USA.

Chibelushi, C. C., Deravi, F., & Mason, J. S. D. (2002). A review of speech-based bimodal recognition. *IEEE Transactions on Multimedia, 4,* 23-37.

CHIL project: Computers in the Human Interaction Loop. [online] http://chil.server.de

Gagné, J.-P., Laplante-Lévesque, A., Labelle, M., & Doucet, K. (2001). Evaluation of an Audiovisual-FM System (AudiSee): The Effects of Visual Distractions on Speechreading Performance (Technical Report). École d'orthophonie et d'audiologie, Faculté de medicine, Université de Montreal: Montreal, Canada.

Gatica-Perez, D., Lathoud, G., Odobez, J.-M., & McCowan, I. (2005). Multimodal multispeaker probabilistic tracking in meetings. In *Proceedings of the International Conference on Multimodal Interfaces – ICMI.* Trento, Italy.

Girin, L., Schwartz, J. -L., & Feng, G. (2001). Audio-visual enhancement of speech in noise. *Journal of the Acoustical Society of America, 109,* 3007-3020.

Goecke, R., Potamianos, G., & Neti, C. (2002). Noisy audio feature enhancement using audio-visual speech data. In *Proceedings of the International Conference on Acoustics, Speech and Signal Processing – ICASSP* (pp. 2025-2028). Orlando, FL, USA.

Gross, R., Matthews, I., & Baker, S. (2004). Appearance-based face recognition and light-fields. *IEEE Transactions on Pattern Analysis and Machine Intelligence 26*(4), 449-465.

Hermansky, H., & Morgan, N. (1994). RASTA processing of speech. *IEEE Transactions on Speech and Audio Processing 2*(4), 578-589.

Hovden, G., & Ling, N. (2003). Optimizing facial animation parameters for MPEG-4. *IEEE Transactions on Consumer Electronics, 49*(4), 1354-1359.

Huang, J., Potamianos, G., Connell, J., & Neti, C. (2004). Audio-visual speech recognition using an infrared headset. *Speech Communication, 44*(4), 83-96.

Iwano, K., Yoshinaga, T., Tamura, S., & Furui, S. (2007). Audio-visual speech recognition using lip information extracted from side-face images. *EURASIP Journal on Audio, Speech, and Music Processing, 2007*, 1.

Jesorsky, O., Kirchberg, K., & Frischholz, R. (2001). Robust face detection using the Hausdorff distance. In *Proceedings of the International Conference on Audio and Video Biometric Person Authentication – AVBPA* (pp. 90-95). Halmstad, Sweden.

Jordan, T., & Sergeant, P. (1998). Effects of facial image size on visual and audio-visual speech. R. Campbell, B. Dodd, & D. Burnham (Eds.), *Hearing by Eye II* (pp. 155-176). Hove, United Kingdom: Psychology Press Ltd. Publishers.

Jordan, T., & Thomas, S. (2001). Effects of horizontal viewing angle on visual and audiovisual speech recognition. *Journal of Experimental Psychology: Human Perception and Performance, 27*, 1386-1403.

Junqua, J. –C. (2000). Robust Speech Recognition in Embedded Systems and PC Applications. Springer.

Kumar, K., Chen, T., & Stern, R. M. (2007). Profile view lip reading. In *Proceedings of the International Conference on Acoustics, Speech and Signal Processing – ICASSP* (vol. 4, pp. 429-432). Honolulu, HI, USA.

Kumatani, K., & Stiefelhagen, R. (2007). State synchronous modeling on phone boundary for audio visual speech recognition and application to multi-view face images. In *Proceedings of the International Conference on Acoustics, Speech and Signal Processing – ICASSP* (vol. 4, pp. 417-420). Honolulu, HI, USA.

Lavagetto, F. (1995). Converting speech into lip movements: A multimedia telephone for hard of hearing people. *IEEE Transactions on Rehabilitation Engineering*, 3(1), 90-102.

Leinhart, R., & Maydt, J. 2002. An extended set of Haar-like features. *In Proceedings of the International Conference on Image - ICIP* (pp. 900-903). Rochester, NY, USA.

Lucey, P., & Potamianos, G. 2006. Lipreading using profile versus frontal views. In *Proceedings of the IEEE International Workshop on Multimedia Signal Processing – MMSP* (pp. 24-28).

Lucey, P., Potamianos, G., & Sridharan, S. (2007). A unified approach to multi-pose audio-visual ASR. In *Proceedings of the Conference of the International Speech Communication Association – Interspeech* (pp. 650-653). Antwerp, Belgium.

Mammone, R. J., Zhang, X., & Ramachandran, R. P. (1996). Robust speaker recognition: A feature based approach. *IEEE Signal Processing Magazine, 13*, 58-70.

Morishima, S., Aizawa, K., & Harashima, H. (1989). An intelligent facial image coding driven by speech and phoneme. In *Proceedings of the International Conference on Acoustics, Speech and Signal Processing – ICASSP* (pp. 1795-1798). Glasgow, United Kingdom.

Neely, K. (1956). Effect of visual factors on the intelligibility of speech. *Journal of the Acoustic Society of America, 28*, 1275-1277.

OpenCV: Open Source Computer Vision Library. [online] http://sourceforge.net/projects/opencvlibrary

Pentland, A. (1998). Smart rooms, smart clothes. In *Proceedings of the International Conference on Pattern Recognition – ICPR* (vol. 2, pp. 949-953). Brisbane, Australia.

Potamianos, G., & Neti, C. (2001). Improved ROI and within frame discriminant features for lipreading. In *Proceedings of International Conference on Image Processing – ICIP* (vol. 3, pp. 250-253). Thessaloniki, Greece.

Potamianos, G., Neti, C., Gravier, G., Garg, A., & Senior, A. W. (2003). Recent advances in the automatic recognition of audio-visual speech. *Proceedings of the IEEE, 91*(9), 1306-1326.

Potamianos, G., Neti, C., Iyengar, G., Senior, A. W., & Verma, A. (2001). A cascade visual front end for speaker independent automatic speechreading. *International Journal of Speech Technology, 4*(3-4), 193-208.

Potamianos, G., & Scanlon, P. (2005). Exploiting lower face symmetry in appearance-based automatic speechreading. In *Proceedings of the Auditory-Visual Speech Processing International Conference – AVSP* (pp. 79-84). British Columbia, Canada.

Sumby, W., & Pollack, I. (1954). Visual contribution to speech intelligibility. *Journal of the Acoustical Society of America, 26*(2), 212-215.

Summerfield, A., MacLeod, A., McGrath, M., & Brooke, M. (1989). Lips, teeth, and the benefits of lipreading. In A. Young & H. Ellis (Eds.), *Handbook of Research on Face Processing* (pp. 223-233). Amsterdam, The Netherlands: Elsevier Science Publishers.

Viola, P., & Jones, M. (2001). Rapid object detection using a boosted cascade of simple features. In *Proceedings of the International Conference on Computer Vision and Pattern Recognition – CVPR* (vol. 1, pp. 511-518).Kauai, HI, USA.

Yoshinaga, T., Tamura, S., Iwano, K., & Furui, S. (2003). Audio-visual speech recognition using lip movement extracted from side-face images. In *Proceedings of the Workshop on Auditory Visual Speech Processing – AVSP* (pp. 117-120). St. Jorioz, France.

Yoshinaga, T., Tamura, S., Iwano, K., & Furui, S. (2004). Audio-visual speech recognition using new lip features extracted from side-face images. In *Proceedings of the Workshop on Robustness Issues in Conversational Interaction – ROBUST.* Norwich, England.

Young, S., Everman, G., Hain, T., Kershaw, D. Moore, G., Odell, J., et al. (2002). *The HTK Book (for HTK Version 3.2.1)*. Entropic Ltd.

Zhang, Z., Potamianos, G., Senior, A. W., & Huang, T. S. (2007). Joint face and head tracking inside multi-camera smart rooms. *Signal, Image and Video Processing, 1*, 163-178.

ADDITIONAL READINGS

Adjoudani, A., & Benoit, C. (1996). On the integration of auditory and visual parameters in an HMM-based ASR. In Stork D. G., & Hennecke, M. E. (Eds.), *Speechreading by Humans and Machines* (pp. 461-471). Berlin, Germany: Springer.

Aleksic, P. S., Williams, J. J., Wu, Z., & Katsaggelos, A. K. (2002). Audio-visual speech recognition using MPEG-4 compliant visual features. *EURASIP Journal on Advances in Signal Processing, 2002*(11), 1213-1227.

Bregler, C., & Konig, Y. (1994). 'Eigenlips' for robust speech recognition. In *Proceedings of the International Conference on Acoustics, Speech and Signal Processing – ICASSP* (pp. 669-672). Adelaide, Australia.

Cox, S., Matthews, I., & Bangham, A. (1997). Combining noise compensation with visual information in speech recognition. In *Proceedings of the European Tutorial and Workshop on Audio-Visual Speech Processing – AVSP* (pp. 53-56). Rhodes, Greece.

Duchnowski, P., Meier, U., & Waibel, A. (1994). See me, hear me: Integrating automatic speech recognition and lip-reading. In *Proceedings of the International Conference on Spoken Language Processing – ICSLP* (pp. 547-550).Yokohama, Japan.

Dupont, S., & Luettin, J. (2000). Audio-visual speech modeling for continuous speech recognition. *IEEE Transactions on Multimedia, 2*, 141-151.

Gordan, M., Kotropoulos, C., & Pitas, I. (2002). A support vector machine-based dynamic network for visual speech recognition applications. *EURASIP Journal on Advances in Signal Processing, 2002*(11), 1248-1259.

Heckmann, M., Berthommier, F., & Kroschel, K. (2002). Noise adaptive stream weighting in audio-visual speech recognition. *EURASIP Journal on Advances in Signal Processing, 2002*(11), 1260-1273.

Hennecke, M. E., Stork, D. G., & Prasad, K. V. (1996). Visionary speech: Looking ahead to practical speechreading systems. In Stork D. G., & Hennecke, M. E. (Eds.), *Speechreading by Humans and Machines* (pp. 331-349). Berlin, Germany: Springer.

Jiang, J., Alwan, A., Keating, P. A.,Chaney, B., Auer, Jr., E. T., & Bernstein, L. E. (2002). On the relationship between face movements, tongue movements, and speech acoustics. *EURASIP Journal on Advances in Signal Processing, 2002*(11), 1174-1188.

Kittler, J., Hatef, M., Duin, R. P. W., & Matas, J. (1998). On combining classifiers. *IEEE Transactions on Pattern Analysis and Machine Intelligence, 20*, 226-239.

Lippmann, R. P. (1997). Speech recognition by machines and humans. *Speech Communication, 22,* 1-15.

Massaro, D. W., & Stork, D. G. (1998). Speech recognition and sensory integration. *American Scientist, 86,* 236-244.

McGurk, H., & MacDonald, J. (1976). Hearing lips and seeing voices. *Nature, 264,* 746–748.

Nakamura, S. (2001). Fusion of audio-visual information for integrated speech processing. In Bigun, J., & Smeraldi, F. (Eds.) *Audio-and Video-Based Biometric Person Authentication* (pp. 127-143). Berlin, Germany: Springer-Verlag.

Nefian, A. V., Liang, L., Pi, X., Liu, X., & Murphy, K. (2002). Dynamic Bayesian networks for audio-visual speech recognition. *EURASIP Journal on Advances in Signal Processing, 2002*(11), 1274-1288.

Neti, C., Potamianos, G., Luettin, J., Matthews, I.,Glotin, H., Vergyri, D., Sison, J., Mashari, A., & Zhou, J. (2000). Audio-*Visual Speech Recognition (Final Workshop 2000 Report).* Center for Language and Speech Processing, The Johns Hopkins University: Baltimore, MD, USA.

Patterson, E. K., Gurbuz, S., Tufekci, Z., & Gowdy, J. N. (2002). Moving talker, speaker-independent feature study, and baseline results using the CUAVE multimodal speech corpus. *EURASIP Journal on Advances in Signal Processing, 2002*(11), 1189-1201.

Petajan, E. D. (1984). Automatic lipreading to enhance speech recognition. In *Proceedings of the Global Telecommunications Conference – Globecom* (pp. 265-272). Atlanta, GA, USA.

Potamianos, G., & Graf, H. P. (1998). Discriminative training of HMM stream exponents for audio-visual speech recognition. In *Proceedings of the International Conference on Acoustics, Speech and Signal Processing – ICASSP* (pp. 3733-3736). Seattle, WA, USA.

Rabiner, L., & Juang, B.-H. (1993*). Fundamentals of Speech Recognition.* Englewood Cliffs, NJ, USA: Prentice Hall.

Rogozan, A. (1999). Discriminative learning of visual data for audiovisual speech recognition. *International Journal on Artificial Intelligence Tools, 8,* 43-52.

Silsbee, P. L., & Bovik, A. C. (1996). Computer lipreading for improved accuracy in automatic speech recognition. *IEEE Transactions on Speech and Audio Processing, 4,* 337-351.

Sodoyer, D., Schwartz, J.-L., Girin, L., Klinkisch, J., & Jutten, C. (2002). Separation of audio-visual speech sources: A new approach exploiting the audiovisual coherence of speech stimuli. *EURASIP Journal on Advances in Signal Processing, 2002*(11), 1165-1173.

Teissier, P., Robert-Ribes, J., & Schwartz, J.-L. (1999). Comparing models for audiovisual fusion in a noisy-vowel recognition task. *IEEE Transactions on Speech and Audio Processing, 7,* 629-642.

Yehia, H., Rubin, P., & Vatikiotis-Bateson, E. (1998). Quantitative association of vocal-tract and facial behavior. *Speech Communication, 26,* 23-43.

Zhang, X., Broun, C. C., Mersereau, R. M., & Clements, M. (2002). Automatic speechreading with applications to human-computer interfaces. *EURASIP Journal on Advances in Signal Processing, 2002*(11), 1228-1247.

Chapter XI
Hidden Markov Model Based Visemes Recognition, Part I:
AdaBoost Approach

Say Wei Foo
Nanyang Technological University, Singapore

Liang Dong[a]
National University of Singapore, Singapore

ABSTRACT

Visual speech recognition is able to supplement the information of speech sound to improve the accuracy of speech recognition. A viseme, which describes the facial and oral movements that occur alongside the voicing of a particular phoneme, is a supposed basic unit of speech in the visual domain. As in phonemes, there are variations for the same viseme expressed by different persons or even by the same person. A classifier must be robust to this kind of variation. In this chapter, the author's describe the Adaptively Boosted (AdaBoost) Hidden Markov Model (HMM) technique (Foo, 2004; Foo, 2003; Dong, 2002). By applying the AdaBoost technique to HMM modeling, a multi-HMM classifier that improves the robustness of HMM is obtained. The method is applied to identify context-independent and context-dependent visual speech units. Experimental results indicate that higher recognition accuracy can be attained using the AdaBoost HMM than that using conventional HMM.

INTRODUCTION

Brief Review of Research in Lip-Reading

The technique of retrieving speech content from visual clues such as the movement of the lips, tongue and teeth is commonly known as automatic lip-reading.

It has long been observed that the presence of visual cues such as the movement of lips, facial muscles, teeth and tongue may enhance human speech perception (Sumby, 1954). It has also been shown (Petajan, 1984; Morishima, 2002; Adjoudani, 1996; Silsbee, 1996; Tomlinson, 1996; Chen, 1998; Finn, 1988) that the performance of a purely acoustic based speech recognition system will improve with additional input from the visual speech elements, especially when the speech sound is swarmed by environmental noise. Visual speech processing can also be applied to areas such as speaker verification, multimedia telephony for the hearing impaired, cartoon animation and video games.

In 1984, Petajan developed probably the first visual speech processor. In this system, the distance of geometric measures among different mouth shapes was computed for identifying the visual representations of word productions. In 1993, Goldschen extended Petajan's design by using Hidden Markov Model as the visual classifier. Subsequent researches on implementing visual speech processing/visual-audio integration include Neural Network (Yuhas, 1989), time-delayed Neural Network (TDNN) (Stork, 1992; Bregler, 1995), fuzzy logics (Silsbee, 1996) and Boltzmann zippers (Stork, 1996).

Among the various techniques for visual speech processing studied so far, Hidden Markov Model (HMM) holds the greatest promise due to its capabilities in modeling and analyzing temporal processes. In Goldschen's system, HMM classifiers were explored for recognizing a closed set of TIMIT sentences based on speech sounds (Goldschen, 1994). In 1990, Welch *et al* explored audio-to-visual mapping using HMM for building speech-driven models. Silsbee and Bovik (1993) applied HMM to identify isolated words based on sounds alone. Tomlinson *et al* (1996) suggested a cross-product HMM topology, which allows asynchronous processing of visual signals and acoustic signals. Luettin *et al* (1996) used HMMs with an early integration strategy for both isolated digit recognition and connected digit recognition. In recent years, coupled HMM, product HMM and factorial HMM are explored for audio-visual integration (Zhang, 2002; Gravier, 2002; Nefian, 2002; Dupont, 2000).

Other studies relating to lip-reading include: the psychology of lip-reading (Dodd and Campbell, 1987); lip tracking by Yuille *et al* (1992), Coianiz *et al* (1996), Hennecke *et al* (1994), Eveno *et al* (2004), speaker identification by Cetingul *et al* (2006) and visual contribution to the perception of consonants by Binnie *et al* (1974).

Visemes and Viseme Classifiers

The most conspicuous element in visual speech perception is the oral movement. The sequence of movement of the lips for a phonetic sound is regarded as the most representative feature of a viseme (Owens, 1985). It indicates a short period of lip movement repeatable for the same sound. Like phonemes, which are the basic building blocks of sound of a language, visemes are the basic constituents for the visual representations of spoken words. A visual speech recognition system may be designed to recognize words by recognizing the visemes that constitute the words. For notational convenience, we shall identify the visemes by the names of the phonemes they represent. As our focus is on oral movement, we shall refer to the movement of mouth when voicing a particular phoneme as a viseme.

However, the relationship between phonemes and visemes is not a one-to-one but a many-to-one mapping. For example, although phonemes /b/, /m/, /p/ are acoustically distinguishable sounds, they are grouped into one viseme category as they are visually confusable. An early viseme grouping was suggested by Binnied *et al* (1974) and was applied to some identification experiments (Greenwood, 1997). Viseme groupings suggested by Owens *et al* (1985) are obtained by analyzing the stimulus-response matrices of the perceived visual signals. The MPEG-4 multimedia standard adopted the same viseme

Table 1. Viseme table adopted in MPEG-4

Viseme Number	Corresponding phonemes	Examples
0	none	(silence and relax)
1	p, b, m	push, bike, milk
2	f, v	find, voice
3	T, D	think, that
4	t, d	teach, dog
5	k, g	call, guess
6	tS, dZ, S	check, join, shrine
7	s, z	set, zeal
8	n, l	note, lose
9	r	read
10	A:	jar
11	e	bed
12	I	tip
13	Q	shock
14	U	good

grouping strategy for face animation, in which fourteen viseme groups are included (Tekalp, 2000). This grouping is shown in Table 1. However, different groupings are adopted by different research groups to fulfill specific requirements (Morishima, 2002).

For each viseme category in Table 1, there are only subtle differences in change of lips between different phoneme productions, e.g. /tS/, /dZ/ and /S/. A classifier with good discriminative power is thus required to distinguish the productions within a viseme category.

A viseme may be represented by a time sequence of lip shapes. Selected frames of the sequence of images of the mouth uttering the word 'hot' are given in Fig.1. However, when extracted from spoken sentences, the same phonetic sound may have slightly different sets of lip shapes as they are affected by the adjoining sounds/visemes. For example, the visual representations of the vowel /ai/ are very different when extracted from the words *hide* and *right*. Thus visemes demonstrate polymorphism under various contexts. For some visemes, there is a wide spread of features for the same viseme. This calls for a classifier that is also robust to the variation.

A classifier that is both discriminative and robust is thus required to distinguish the subtle difference between certain groups of visemes while at the same time able to cope with the variation of visemes of the same group. The traditional single-HMM classifier (Rabiner, 1993), e.g. the Maximum Likelihood (ML) model trained with the Baum-Welch method, is most of the time not able to provide these discriminative power and robustness required for viseme recognition. In this chapter, we describe the

Figure 1. Selected frames of the sequence of images in the pronunciation of the word 'hot' and the corresponding speech signal

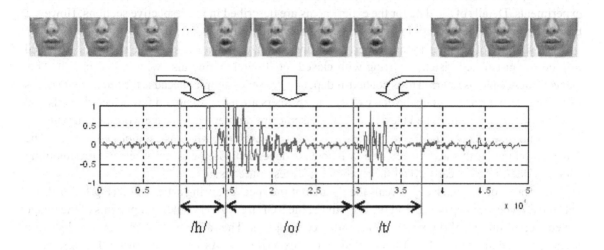

AdaBoost HMM classifier that is capable of improving robustness. Two discriminative approaches are presented in the next chapter.

Most of the HMM-based visual-only systems reported in literature take an individual word as the basic recognition unit and an HMM is trained to model it. Such an approach works well with limited vocabulary such as digit set (Luettin, 1996; Chen, 2001) or a small number of *AVletters* (Matthews, 2002), isolated words or nonsense words, but it is difficult to extend such methods to cover a large vocabulary because a great number of samples have to be collected to train all the possible word models that may appear in the speech.

A text-independent speech recognition system, on the other hand, not only is able to identify words within its vocabulary, but is also able to recognize new words. To make a visual speech recognition system text-independent, one approach is to use basic visual speech units such as visemes. By modeling and recognizing visemes, the system may be further trained to recognize words by breaking them into a sequence of visemes. Words and connected-visemes may then be identified by constructing HMM chains using exhaustive means such as level building (Rabiner, 1993).

Databases of Visemes

In the acoustic speech processing domain, a number of speech databases, e.g. TIMIT, DARPA, YOHO, etc. have been developed. These databases are widely used in speech recognition and become the benchmark for measuring the performance of a certain speech recognizer. In visual speech processing, although some audio-visual speech databases (Chibelushi, 1996; Potamianos, 1997) have been proposed in recent years, they are not widely accepted by multimedia community. The data used in most visual speech experiments are independently recorded.

For experiments conducted for the methods proposed, different sets of visemes are used for different experiments. Details of the data for the experiments are described in the respective sections. However, the treatment of the recordings to extract the lip shape and position is the same.

The samples of visemes for our experiments are obtained in two ways. 1) The speakers are asked to produce an isolated viseme, starting with closed mouth and ending also with closed mouth. This category of samples is referred to as context-independent viseme samples because the temporal features of a viseme are not affected by the context. 2) The speakers are asked to utter a few selected words that contain the target viseme. The video clips of the viseme are segmented from the word productions using the image sequences and the corresponding acoustic waveform, which is exemplified in Fig.1. The samples obtained in this way are referred to as context-dependent viseme samples because the adjoining sounds/visemes may greatly affect the temporal features of the viseme.

Each frame of the video clip reveals the lip area of the speaker during articulation (Fig.1). To eliminate the effect caused by changes in the brightness, the RGB (red, green, blue) components of the image are converted into HSV (hue, saturation, value) components. The RGB to HSV conversion algorithm proposed in (Potamianos, 1997) is adopted in our experiments. As illustrated in the histograms of distribution of hue component shown in Fig.2, the hue factors of the lip region and the remaining lip-excluded image occupy different regions of the histogram. A threshold may be manually selected to segment the lip region from the entire image as shown in Fig. 2a. This threshold usually corresponds

Figure 2. Isolation of the lip region from the entire image using hue distribution. (a) Histogram of the hue component for the entire image. (b) Histogram of the hue component for the actual lip region. (c) Histogram of the hue component for the actual lip-excluded image.

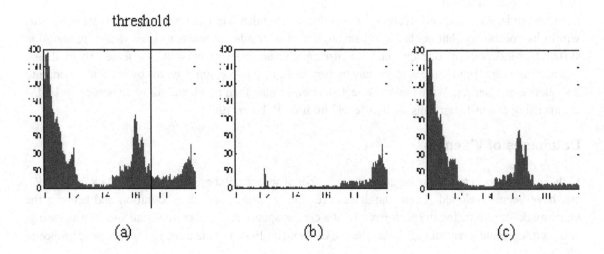

to a local minimum point (valley) in the histogram. Note that for different speakers and lighting conditions, the threshold may be different.

The boundaries of the lips are tracked using a geometric template with dynamic contours to fit an elastic object (Bregler, 1995; Adjoudani, 1996). As the contours of the lips are simple, the requirement on the selection of the dynamic contours that build the template is thus not stringent. Results of lip tracking experiments show that Bezier curves can well fit the shape of the lip (Stork, 1996). To extract the feature of the lips and mouth, we make use of a template consisting of ten Bezier curves as shown in Fig.3d. Eight of which characterize the lip contours and two curves describe the tongue when it is visible. The template is controlled by points marked as small circles in Fig.3d. Lip tracking is carried out by fitting the template to minimize certain energy function. The energy function comprises the following four terms:

$$E_{lip} = -\frac{1}{R_1} \int_R H(x)dx \tag{1a}$$

$$E_{edge} = -\frac{1}{C_1 + C_2} \int_{C_1 + C_2} |H^+(x) - H(x)| + |H^-(x) - H(x)| \, dx \tag{1b}$$

$$E_{hole} = -\frac{1}{R_2 - R_3} \int_{R_2 - R_3} H(x)dx \tag{1c}$$

$$E_{inertia} = \| \Gamma_{t+1} - \Gamma_t \| \tag{1d}$$

where R_1, R_2, R_3, C_1 and C_2 are areas and contours as illustrated in Fig. 3d. $H(x)$ is a function of the hue of a given pixel; $H^+(x)$ is the hue function of the closest right-hand side pixel and $H^-(x)$ is that of the closest left-hand side pixel. Γ_{t+1} and Γ_t are the matched templates at time $t+1$ and t. $\|\Gamma_{t+1}-\Gamma_t\|$ indicates the Euclidean distance between the two templates (further details may be found in (Adjoudani, 1996)). The overall energy of the template E is the linear combination of the components as given by

$$E = c_1 E_{lip} + c_2 E_{edge} + c_3 E_{hole} + c_4 E_{inertia} \tag{2}$$

While tracking the boundaries of the lips from the image sequence, the parameters of the template are updated to minimize E in a number of epochs. A detailed discussion is given in (Bregler, 1995; Silsbee, 1996; Adjoudani, 1996). The matched template and the actual lip boundary are pictured in Fig.3d and Fig.3e, respectively. It can be seen that the matched template is symmetric and smooth, and is therefore easy to process.

Ten geometric parameters as shown in Fig.3f are then extracted to form a feature vector from the matched template. These features indicate the thickness of various parts of the lips, the positions of some key points and the curvatures of the lips. They are chosen as they uniquely determine the shape of the lips and they best characterize the movement of the lips.

For each viseme listed in Table 1, 70 context-independent samples and 100 context-dependent samples from each of one male English speaker (Speaker M) and one female English speaker (Speaker F) are recorded. Thus 140 context-independent samples and 200 context-dependent samples are collected for training and testing the viseme classifiers. The features of these visemes are extracted and Principal Components Analysis (PCA) is carried out to reduce the dimension of the feature vectors from ten to seven. The resulting feature vectors are clustered into groups using *K-means* algorithm. In the experiments conducted, 128 clusters are created for the vector database. The means of the 128 clusters form the symbol set $O^{128}=(O_1,O_2, ..., O_{128})$ of the HMM. This set of data is used in training and testing the conventional HMM system mentioned in Section 2 and the AdaBoost HMM in Section 4.

Organization of the Chapter

The organization of the chapter is as follows. Following this introductory section is a brief review of the HMM principles and the performance of conventional HMM in lip-reading. A review of adaptive boosting is presented in Section 3. Detailed description of the AdaBoost HMM is given in Section 4. In Section 5, the application of the AdaBoost HMM classifier to viseme recognition and its performance

Figure 3.(a) original image, (b) lip localization, (c) segmented lip area, (d) parameterized lip template, (e) actual lip shape, (f) geometric measures extracted from matched lip shape: 1:thickness of the upper bow, 2:thickness of the lower bow, 3:thickness of the lip corner, 4:position of the lip corner, 5:position of the upper lip, 6:position of the lower bow, 7:curvature of the upper-exterior boundary, 8:curvature of the lower-exterior boundary, 9:curvature of the upper-interior boundary, and 10:curvature of the lower-interior boundary.

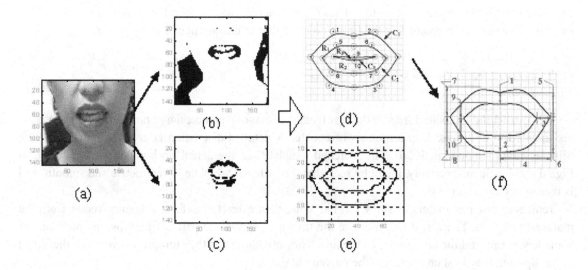

are discussed. The issue on computational load of AdaBoost HMM is addressed in Section 6 followed by the concluding remark in Section 7.

CONVENTIONAL HMM

Review of Hidden Markov Models (HMMs)

The block diagram of a conventional HMM classifier is shown in Fig.4. In a system of identifying K visemes, K classifiers are included. The input to the system is the T-length vector sequence of an unknown viseme production, denoted by x^T. In the traditional approach, each sub-classifier is a single HMM that is trained with the samples of a specific viseme. Each HMM determines the probability of occurrence of the unknown viseme. By comparing the probabilities $P_1, P_2, \ldots P_K$, a decision is made about the identity of the unknown viseme. Traditional approaches for optimizing the viseme classifier focuses mainly on improving the performance of the individual HMM, e.g. setting proper HMM parameters, maximizing the probabilities of the given samples, minimizing the cross-entropy and so on.

Hidden Markov Model (HMM) is essentially a division of a process into a number of discrete states. While using an HMM to analyze a stochastic process, the observation sequence, say $o^T=(o_1,o_2,\ldots,o_t,\ldots,o_T)$ where o_t is the t-th symbol appeared in the sequence, is assumed to be emitted from a sequence of hidden states $s^T=(s_1,s_2,\ldots,s_T)$, where $s_i \in S^N$ and $S^N =(S_1,S_2,\ldots,S_N)$ is the set of states of the HMM. Each state maintains a probability function or probability density function to indicate the likelihood of emitting certain symbols. The states are interconnected with each other through state transition probability, which indicate the likelihood of a state repeating itself or transiting to another state.

Figure 4. Block diagram of the conventional HMM recognition system

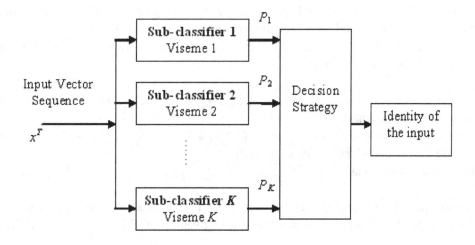

Figure 5. The relation between the observation sequence and the state sequence of an HMM with N states

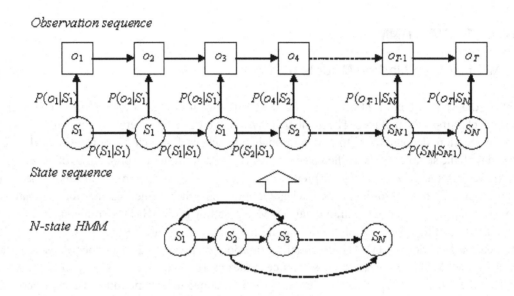

The relationship between the explicit process (observations), the hidden process (states) and the HMM is depicted in Fig.5, where $P(S_j|S_i)$ (i,j = 1,2,...N) is the likelihood of transition from S_i to S_j and $P(o_t|S_i)$ (t=1,2,...T) is the likelihood of emitting o_t in state S_i. If the output of an HMM takes discrete and finite values, e.g. from a finite symbol set $O^M = (O_1, O_2, ..., O_M)$, the HMM is called discrete; if the output takes infinite continuous values, the HMM is called continuous. For ease of subsequent discussion on other HMM based systems, the mathematical model of discrete HMMs is summarized in the following paragraphs.

The beauty of HMM is that it is able to reveal the underlying process of signal generation even though the properties of the signal source remain unknown. Assume that $O^M = (O_1, O_2, ..., O_M)$ is the set of discrete symbol alphabet and $S^N = (S_1, S_2, ..., S_N)$ is the set of states. An N-state-M-symbol HMM $\theta(\pi, A, B)$ is determined with the following three components:

1. The probabilities of the initial states $\pi = [\pi_i]_{1 \times N} = [P(s_1 = S_i)]_{1 \times N}$ $(1 \leq i \leq N)$, where s_1 is the first state in the state chain.
2. The state transition matrix $A = [a_{ij}]_{N \times N} = [P(s_{t+1} = S_j | s_t = S_i)]_{N \times N}$ $(1 \leq i, j \leq N)$, where s_{t+1} and s_t are the t+1-th and the t-th states respectively.
3. The symbol emission matrix $B = [b_{ij}]_{N \times M} = [P(O_j | S_i)]_{N \times M}$ $(1 \leq i \leq N, 1 \leq j \leq M)$.

In a K-class identification problem, assume that $x^T = (x_1, x_2, ..., x_T)$ is a sample of a particular class, say Class d_i. The probability of occurrence of the sample x^T given the HMM $\theta(\pi, A, B)$, denoted by $P(x^T|\theta)$, is computed using either the forward or backward process. The optimal hidden state chain is revealed using Viterbi matching (Rabiner, 1993). Training of the HMM is the process of determining the parameters set $\theta(\pi, A, B)$ to fulfill certain criterion function such as $P(x^T|\theta)$ or the mutual information (Bahl, 1986). For training of the HMM, the Baum-Welch training algorithm is popularly adopted, which leads to Maximum Likelihood (ML) estimation θ_{ML} that maximizes the probability $P(x^T|\theta)$. Mathematically,

$$\theta_{ML} = \arg\max_{\theta}[P(x^T|\theta)]$$

(3)

The Baum-Welch training can be realized at relatively high speed as the Expectation-Maximization (EM) estimation is adopted in the training process. However, the parameters of the HMM are solely determined by the correct samples while the relationship between the correct samples and incorrect ones is not taken into consideration. The method, in its original form, is thus not developed for fine recognition. If another sample y^T of Class d_j ($j \neq i$) is similar to x^T, the scored probability $P(y^T|\theta)$ may be close to $P(x^T|\theta)$, and θ_{ML} may not be able to distinguish x^T and y^T. One solution to this problem is to adopt a training strategy that maximizes the mutual information $I_M(\theta, x^T)$ defined as

$$I_M(\theta, x^T) = \log P(x^T|\theta) - \log \sum_{all\, \theta' \neq \theta} P(x^T|\theta')P(\theta')$$

(4)

This method is referred to as maximum mutual information (MMI) estimation (Bahl, 1986). It increases the *a posteriori* probability of the model corresponding to the training data, and thus the overall discriminative power of the HMM obtained is guaranteed. However, analytical solutions to Eqn.(4) are difficult to realize and implementation of MMI estimation is tedious. Computationally less intensive metric and approach are desirable.

Configuration of the Hidden Markov Model for Viseme

The movement of the lips can be partitioned into three phases during the production of a text-independent viseme. The initial phase begins with a closed mouth and ends with the start of sound production. The intermediate phase is the articulation phase, which is the period when sound is produced. The third phase is the end phase when the mouth restores to the relaxed state. Fig.6 illustrates the change of the lips in the three phases and the corresponding acoustic waveform when the phoneme /u/ is uttered.

To associate the HMM with the physical process of viseme production, three-state left-right HMM structure as shown in Fig.7 is adopted.

Using this structure, the state transition matrix A has the form

$$A = \begin{bmatrix} a_{1,1} & a_{1,2} & 0 & 0 \\ 0 & a_{2,2} & a_{2,3} & 0 \\ 0 & 0 & a_{3,3} & a_{3,4} \\ 0 & 0 & 0 & 1 \end{bmatrix},$$

Figure 6. The three phases of viseme production. (a) Initial phase, (b) Articulation phase and (c) End phase

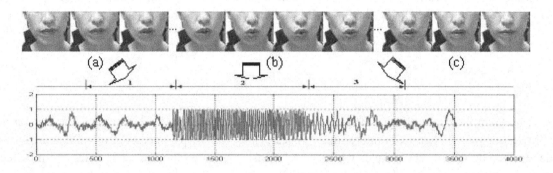

Figure 7. Three-state left-right viseme model

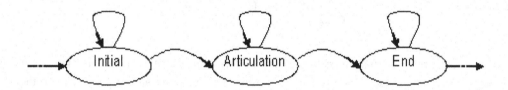

where the 4th state is a null state that indicates the end of viseme production. The initial values of the coefficients in Matrices A and B are set according to the statistics of the three phases. Given a viseme sample, the approximate initial phase, articulation phase and end phase are manually segmented from the image sequence and the acoustic signal, and the duration of each phase is counted. The coefficients $a_{i,i}$ and $a_{i,i+1}$ are initialized with these durations. For example, if the duration of State S_i is T_i, the initial value of $a_{i,i}$ is set to be

$$\frac{T_i}{T_i + 1}$$

and the initial value of $a_{i,i+1}$ is set to be

$$\frac{1}{T_i + 1}$$

as they maximize $a_{ij}^T a_{ij+1}$. Matrix B is initialized in a similar manner. If symbol O_j appears $T(O_j)$ times in State S_i, the initial value of b_{ij} is set to be

$$\frac{T(O_j)}{T_i} \,.$$

For such arrangement, the states of the HMM are aligned with the three phases of viseme production.

Performance of Conventional HMM in Viseme Recognition

For the purpose of comparison, the performance of the conventional HMM method is evaluated. For the experiments, the visemes from the database mentioned in Section 1.3 are used. For each viseme, its samples are divided into two groups: 40 context independent samples and 100 context-dependent samples are training samples, respectively, and the remaining 100 context independent samples and 100 context-dependent samples are testing samples, respectively.

For each viseme, single-HMM classifier is configured as in Section 2.2 and trained using the Baum-Welch algorithm and training samples. For the context-independent samples, the average classification accuracy is above 80%, especially for the vowels, where the accuracy is more than 90%.

In the second experiment, context-dependent samples are used for training and validation. The recognition rates of the HMMs are also given in Table 2. It is observed that the recognition rates of

Table 2. Recognition rates of viseme samples using conventional HMM

Viseme Number		context-independent		context-dependent	
		Speaker 1	Speaker 2	Speaker 1	Speaker 2
1	p, b, m	87%	63%	80%	29%
2	f, v	96%	72%	73%	32%
3	T, D	89%	81%	66%	35%
4	t, d	85%	66%	50%	10%
5	k, g	85%	60%	83%	10%
6	tS, dZ, S	90%	75%	79%	25%
7	s, z	96%	81%	55%	51%
8	n, l	81%	46%	21%	32%
9	r	82%	36%	44%	14%
10	A:	99%	78%	78%	70%
11	e	92%	70%	66%	48%
12	I	99%	90%	90%	66%
13	Q	93%	89%	65%	62%
14	U	93%	93%	91%	69%

identifying context-dependent samples are much lower than those of the context-independent samples. For the vowels, the average accuracy is in the region of 60%. For the consonants, the accuracy is much lower.

REVIEW OF ADAPTIVE BOOSTING

The procedures of Adaptive Boosting are presented as a flow chart in Fig. 8. Assume that in the two-class identification problem (*Class* 1 vs. *Class* 2), the training set is comprised of R samples $\{y_1,d_1\}$, $\{y_2,d_2\},\ldots, \{y_R,d_R\}$. y_i is the observed data and $d_i=\{-1,+1\}$ is the label identifier where $d_i=-1$ denotes *Class* 1 and $d_i=+1$ denotes *Class* 2. The process of Adaptive Boosting involves of a series of rounds $(t=1,2,\ldots,T)$ of weight-adjusting and classifier-training (Schapire, 1999). Let $D_t(i)$ stand for the weight that is assigned to the i-th training sample in the t-th Boosting round and D_t denote the set of the weights $\{D_t(1),D_t(2),\ldots D_t(R)\}$. The steps of Adaptive Boosting are presented below:

1. Initially, assign the weight $D_t(i)=1/R$ $(i=1,2,\ldots R)$ to the R training samples $\{y_1,d_1\}$, $\{y_2,d_2\},\ldots, \{y_R,d_R\}$. Note that $D_1(i)=1/R$ $(i=1,2,\ldots R)$ follows a uniform distribution.
2. Train the t-th classifier θ_t in the t-th Boosting round using the distribution D_t, starting with $t=1$.
3. Formulate the hypothesis, $h_t(y_i)\rightarrow\{-1,+1\}$ $(i=1,2,\ldots R)$ and calculate the error $\varepsilon_t = P(h_t(y_i) \neq d_i)$ for θ_t.
4. Calculate

$$w_t = \frac{1}{2}\ln(\frac{1-\varepsilon_t}{\varepsilon_t}),$$

    which weights the importance of the classifier θ_t.
5. Update the distribution using the following expression.

$$D_{t+1}(i) = \frac{D_t(i)}{Z_t} \times \begin{cases} e^{-w} & if\ h_t(y_i) = d_i \\ e^{w} & if\ h_t(y_i) \neq d_i \end{cases}$$

(5)

where Z_t is a normalization factor to make D_{t+1} a distribution.

Step 2 to Step 5 are repeated until the error rate of the classifier exceeds 0.5 or after a given number of training epochs. A series of classifiers $\theta_1,\theta_2,\ldots\theta_T$ and weights $w_1,w_2,\ldots w_T$ are obtained at the end of the above procedures. In this chapter, the T sub-classifiers, together with the weights assigned to them, are looked as an integral entity and are referred to as an AdaBoost-classifier. For an unknown input y, the sub-decisions made by the T composite classifiers are synthesized using

$$H(y) = sign(\sum_{t=1}^{T} w_t h_t(y))$$

Figure 8. *Steps of Adaptive Boosting algorithm*

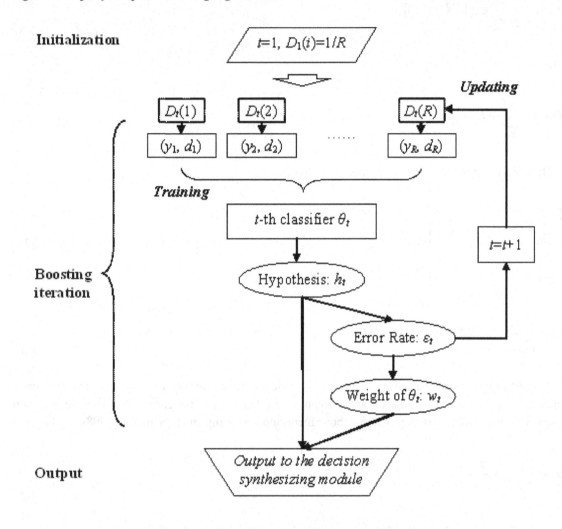

If $H(y) < 0$, $y \in Class\ 1$, otherwise $y \in Class\ 2$.

The objective of boosting is to minimize the training error

$$\varepsilon(H) = \frac{1}{R} \sum_{i=1}^{R} [i : H(y_i) \neq d_i]$$

of the final hypothesis. Schapire and Singer (1998) proved that $\varepsilon(H)$ is bounded as follows.

$$\varepsilon(H) \le \frac{1}{R} \sum_{i=1}^{R} \exp[-d_i f(y_i)]$$

(6)

where

$$f(y_i) = \sum_{t=1}^{T} w_t h_t(y_i)$$

.

By unraveling the recursive definition of D_t, we have

$$\frac{1}{R} \sum_{i=1}^{R} \exp[-d_i f(y_i)] = \prod_{t=1}^{T} Z_t$$

(7)

where

$$Z_t = \sum_{i=1}^{R} D_t(y_i) \exp[-w_t d_i h_t(y_i)]$$

(8)

Eqn.(6) suggests that the training error can be reduced most rapidly by choosing w_t and h_t at each round to minimize Z_t. In the case of binary hypotheses, this leads to the choice of w_t in the expression below, which is adopted in Step 4 of the above mentioned boosting steps (Schapire, 1998).

$$w_t = \frac{1}{2} \ln(\frac{1 - \varepsilon_t}{\varepsilon_t})$$

(9)

If the training error of θ_t (the classifier obtained at the t-th Boosting round) is less than 0.5, say

$$\varepsilon_t = \frac{1}{2} - \gamma_t \ (\gamma_t > 0)$$

,

it is also proved in (Freund, 1997) that the training error is bounded as in the inequality below.

$$\varepsilon(H) \le 2^T \prod_{t=1}^{T} \sqrt{\varepsilon_t(1 - \varepsilon_t)} = \prod_{t=1}^{T} \sqrt{1 - 4\gamma_t^2} \le \exp(-2\sum_{t=1}^{T} \gamma_t^2)$$

(10)

The above inequality shows that if only the individual classifier has a classification error less than 0.5 (or equivalently a classification rate greater than 0.5), the overall error rate should decrease exponentially. The boosted classifier may generate a hypothesis with an arbitrary low rate of error as boosting continues.

ADABOOST HMM CLASSIFIER

Base Training Algorithm

For a K-class identification problem, there are K sub-classifiers. The block diagram of the structure of a typical sub-classifier of the AdaBoost HMM is shown in Fig. 9. It is expected that by synthesizing the decisions made by the multiple HMMs, a more complex decision boundary can be obtained to cover the relevant clusters of data.

Boosting is carried out during the training phase of the composite HMMs. For the K class identification problem, the purpose of HMM AdaBoosting is to train a set of HMMs that represent or span the distribution of the training samples. In the application of AdaBoosting strategy to the construction of a multi-HMM classifier, the following two important issues arise: 1) The choice of base training algorithm and 2) the measurement of classification error. 1) is discussed in this section and 2) in the following section.

It is known that the Baum-Welch estimation can be implemented efficiently by repeating the Expectation-Maximization (EM) iterations. The resulting HMM is a good model to the target process but is not good at differentiating similar samples. The Maximum Mutual Information (MMI) estimation,

Figure 9. Block diagram of adaptively boosted HMM classifier as a sub-classifier

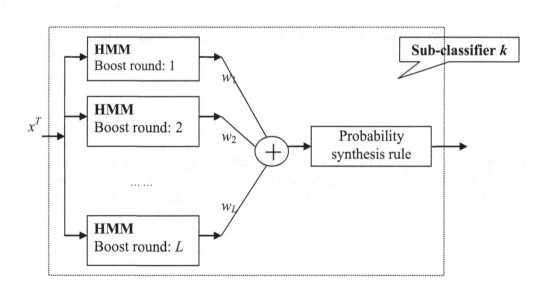

on the other hand, may ensure good discrimination power but its implementation is complicated and time-consuming.

Adaptive Boosting has loose requirements on the selection of base classifiers. As long as the training error of the individual classifier is less than 0.5, the training error of the AdaBoost-classifier will drop. The same requirements apply to HMMs. If the training error of the composite HMMs is forced to be less than 0.5, the error rate of the AdaBoost-HMM classifier will also decrease as boosting continues. Besides this, since each of the multiple HMMs has to be individually trained, reduction of the computational load per HMM is also an important consideration. Considering these two factors, the Baum-Welch algorithm, which is less computationally intensive, is adopted.

Assume that $X_k = \{x_1^k, x_2^k, \cdots x_R^k : d_k\}$ are R_k training samples (sequences) of Class d_k, where $x_i^k = (o_1^{k,l}, o_2^{k,l}, \cdots, o_T^{k,l})(l=1,2,\ldots R_k)$ is a T_l-length observation sequence and $o_i^{k,l}$ $(i=1,2,\ldots T_l)$ is the i-th symbol appeared in the sequence. For the N-state-M-symbol HMM $\theta(\pi,A,B)$, we define the forward variables $\alpha_t^{k,l}(i) = P(o_1^{k,l}, o_2^{k,l}, \cdots o_t^{k,l}, s_t = S_i | \theta)$ and backward variables $\beta_t^{k,l}(i) = P(o_{t+1}^{k,l}, o_{t+2}^{k,l}, \cdots o_T^{k,l} | s_t = S_i, \theta)$ for x_i^k, the parameters of the HMM are then estimated through the following Expectation-Maximization (EM) recursion.

$$\bar{a}_{ij} = \frac{\sum_{l=1}^{R} \frac{1}{P_l} \sum_{t=1}^{T-1} \alpha_t^{k,l}(i) a_{ij} b_j(o_{t+1}^{k,l}) \beta_{t+1}^{k,l}(j)}{\sum_{l=1}^{R} \frac{1}{P_l} \sum_{t=1}^{T-1} \alpha_t^{k,l}(i) \beta_{t+1}^{k,l}(j)}$$

(11a)

$$\bar{b}_j(O_m) = \frac{\sum_{l=1}^{R} \frac{1}{P_l} \sum_{\substack{t=1 \\ s.t. o_t^{k,l}=O_m}}^{T-1} \alpha_t^{k,l}(j) \beta_t^{k,l}(j)}{\sum_{l=1}^{R} \frac{1}{P_l} \sum_{t=1}^{T-1} \alpha_t^{k,l}(j) \beta_t^{k,l}(j)}$$

(11b)

where O_m is the m-th symbol in the symbol set and $P_l = P(x_l^k | \theta)$. In Eqn.(11.b),

$$\sum_{\substack{t=1 \\ s.t. o_t^{k,l}=O_m}}^{T_l-1} \alpha_t^{k,l}(j) \beta_t^{k,l}(j)$$

is the sum of the products of the forward and backward variables when the t-th observed symbol $o_t^{k,l} = O_m$ i.e. $\alpha_t^{k,l}(i) = P(o_1^{k,l}, o_2^{k,l}, \cdots o_t^{k,l} = O_m, s_t = S_i | \theta)$. In the above mentioned strategy, all the samples are treated equally. If weight D_l is assigned to the l-th sample x_l^k, then Eqn.(11) becomes,

$$\overline{a}_{ij} = \frac{\sum_{l=1}^{R} \frac{D_l}{P_l} \sum_{t=1}^{T-1} \alpha_t^{k,l}(i) a_{ij} b_j(o_{t+1}^{k,l}) \beta_{t+1}^{k,l}(j)}{\sum_{l=1}^{R} \frac{D_l}{P_l} \sum_{t=1}^{T-1} \alpha_t^{k,l}(i) \beta_{t+1}^{k,l}(j)}$$

(12a)

$$\overline{b}_j(O_m) = \frac{\sum_{l=1}^{R} \frac{D_l}{P_l} \sum_{\substack{t=1 \\ s.t.\ o_t^l = O_m}}^{T-1} \alpha_t^{k,l}(j) \beta_t^{k,l}(j)}{\sum_{l=1}^{R} \frac{D_l}{P_l} \sum_{t=1}^{T-1} \alpha_t^{k,l}(j) \beta_t^{k,l}(j)}$$

(12b)

For the above equations, Arslan and Hansen (1999) proved that weighting of the training samples does not violate the convergence property of the maximum likelihood training. A local maximum point of $P(X_k|\theta)$ will be attained after a sufficient number of training epochs. Since different samples are treated differently in estimating the parameters, Eqn.(12) have the potential to be applied to HMM AdaBoosting. In this chapter, the above mentioned training strategy shall be referred to as the biased Baum-Welch estimation.

Cross-Validation for Error Estimation

Unlike Neural Network or other classifiers, HMM gives a probabilistic measure rather than a definite Boolean result. The decision about the identity of the input is usually obtained by comparing the probabilities measured of all HMMs.

Assume that at a certain Boosting round, Class d_l ($l=1,2,...K$) has L_l sub-classifiers (HMMs) – $\Theta_l = \{\theta_1^l, \theta_2^l, \cdots, \theta_L^l\}$. For a given training sample $x_i^k \in X_k$, the probabilities of x_i^k, given all the HMMs, are computed and compared with one another. The HMM that gives the maximum likelihood is chosen as the identity of x_i^k.

$$\theta^* = \underset{\theta}{\arg\max}\, P(x_i^k | \theta_j^l) \quad \forall l = 1,2,\cdots K, j = 1,2,\cdots L_l$$

(13)

The decision made in this way is a *one vs. the rest* classification. If the correct model scores greater likelihood than the others, the result is correct; otherwise, an error occurs. As a result, the following hypothesis is made upon an HMM classifier in d_k, e.g. θ_p^k ($1 \leq p \leq L_k$):

$$h_p^k(x_i^k) = \begin{cases} 1 & if\ P(x_i^k | \theta_p^k) > P(x_i^k | \theta_q^j) \quad \forall j = 1,2,\cdots K,\ j \neq k,\ q = 1,2,\cdots L_j \\ -1 & otherwise \end{cases}$$

(14)

The training error of θ_p^k is estimated by summarizing the weighted hypotheses over all the training samples in X_k.

$$\varepsilon_p^k = \frac{D(x_i^k)E(h_p^k(x_i^k)=-1)}{R_k} = \sum_{\substack{i=1 \\ s.t.h_p^k(x_i^k)=-1}}^{R} \frac{D(x_i^k)}{R_k}$$

(15)

From Eqns.(14) and (15), it can be seen that the error rate not only depends on the classifier itself but also relates to the other classifiers. The HMM obtained at Boosting round t, e.g. θ_t^k, will therefore influence the error rate of all the HMMs trained at the previous Boosting rounds, e.g. θ_τ^k ($j=1,2,\dots K$, $\tau < t$). AdaBoosting requires that the composite classifiers have an error rate less than 0.5. As a result, not only the recently boosted HMM but also all the existing HMMs have to be validated. Clearly the computations involved in calculating and comparing the probabilities are intensive. In our system, the following measures are taken to facilitate the processing.

As illustrated in Fig. 10, each class, say d_k, maintains a maximum probability array. The elements in the array are the R_k greatest probabilities of the training samples $X_k = \{x_1^k, x_2^k, \cdots x_{R_k}^k\}$ that are scored by the HMMs of Class d_j ($\forall j \neq k$). These maximum probabilities are denoted as $P_{\max}(x_1^k|\bar{\theta})$, $P_{\max}(x_2^k|\bar{\theta})$,... $P_{\max}(x_{R_k}^k|\bar{\theta})$ in the figure, where $\bar{\theta}$ denotes any HMM of the class other than d_k.

At Boosting round L_k+1, after a new HMM of Class d_k is trained, say $\theta_{L_k+1}^k$, the probabilities of all the training samples of Classes d_1, d_2, ... d_K, given $\theta_{L_k+1}^k$ are computed. For Class d_l as an example, if $P(x_i^l|\theta_{L_l+1}^k) > P_{\max}(x_i^l|\bar{\theta})$ ($i=1,2,\dots R_l$), $P_{\max}(x_i^l|\bar{\theta})$ is replaced with $P(x_i^l|\theta_{L_l+1}^k)$. The following hypothesis, which is concluded from (10), is made for a training sample of Class d_k, say x_i^k.

$$h_{L_k+1}^k(x_i^k) = \begin{cases} 1 & if \ P(x_i^k|\theta_{L_k+1}^k) > P_{\max}(x_i^k|\bar{\theta}) \quad i=1,2,\cdots R_k \\ -1 & otherwise \end{cases}$$

(16)

Figure 10. Data structure for implementing error estimation

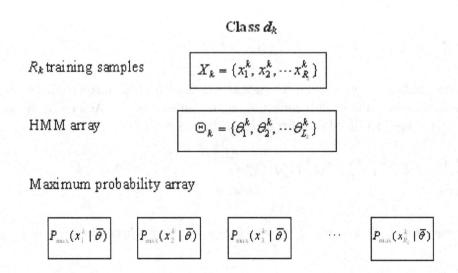

The training error of $\theta^k_{L_k+1}$ is then computed using Eqn.(15). In this way, the training error of any composite HMM, say θ^l_t ($t=1,2,...L_l$), can be easily obtained by comparing $P(x^l_i|\theta^l_t)$ ($i=1,2,...R_l$) with the corresponding value in its maximum likelihood array – $P_{\max}(x^l_i|\bar{\theta})$.

If the error rates of $\theta^k_{L_k+1}$ and the existing HMMs are all less than 0.5, $\theta^k_{L_k+1}$ is retained as a qualified boosted classifier; otherwise, $\theta^k_{L_k+1}$ is discarded. The above mentioned strategy provides an easily programmable approach for evaluating and computing the training error of the AdaBoost-HMM classifiers. Because the error rates are computed by comparing the probabilities scored by the individual HMMs, the above mentioned procedure shall be referred to as cross-validation.

Step-by-Step Procedures

The step-by-step procedures of HMM AdaBoosting for a *K*-class problem are given below.

Step 1. For training set of Class d_k with R_K samples $X_k = \{x^k_1, x^k_2, \cdots x^k_{R_k}\}$, initially, assign a uniform distribution $D_1(x^k_j) = 1/R_k$, ($\forall k=1,2,...,K; j=1,2,...,R_k$) to $x^k_1, x^k_2, \cdots x^k_{R_k}$. The boosting token k is initialized to be equal to 1.

Step 2. Train a new HMM for the k-th class θ^k_t using the biased Baum-Welch algorithm with the distribution $D_t(x^k_j)$.

Step 3. Formulate the binary hypothesis $h^k_t(x^k_j) \rightarrow \{-1,+1\}$ for θ^k_t according to the following equation.

$$h^k_t(x^k_j) = \begin{cases} 1, & if\ P(x^k_i|\theta^k_p) > (x^k_i|\theta^k_q),\ \forall j \neq k, q=1,2,...L_j \\ -1, & otherwise \end{cases} \tag{17}$$

The error rate of θ^k_t, ε^k_t, and the error rates of all the existing HMMs of other classes θ^j_l, ($j=1,2,\cdots K, j \neq k, l=1,2\cdots R_j$) are estimated and verified using the cross-validation and the following equation.

$$\varepsilon^k_p = D(x^k_i)E(h^k_p(x^k_i) = -1) = \sum_{i=1,s.t.h^k_p(x^k_i)=-1}^{R_k} D(x^k_i) \tag{18}$$

If the new model is valid, go on to Step 4; otherwise, the boosting token is passed to the next class

$$k = \begin{cases} k+1 & if\ k < K \\ 1 & if\ k = K \end{cases}$$

and then Step 2 is repeated.

Step 4. Calculate

$$w^k_t = \frac{1}{2}\ln(\frac{1-\varepsilon^k_t}{\varepsilon^k_t})$$

for θ_t^k, where ε_t^k is the error rate. If the error rate of some existing HMM, say θ_l^j, changes, the corresponding

$$w_l^j = \frac{1}{2}\ln(\frac{1-\varepsilon_l^j}{\varepsilon_l^j})$$

is also recomputed.

Step 5. Update the distribution:

$$D_{t+1}(x_j^k) = \frac{D_t(x_j^k)}{Z_t} e^{w_t^k h_t^k (x_j^k)}$$

($h_t^k(x_j^k) = 1$ or -1), where Z_t is the normalization factor.

The procedure terminates when boosting for all the classes are completed. Assume that Θ_k is the AdaBoost-HMM classifier for Class d_k (k=1,2,...K) that has been "boosted" for L_k rounds. Then Θ_k consists of L_k HMMs - $\theta_1^k, \theta_2^k, \cdots \theta_{L_k}^k$ and L_k weights - $w_1^k, w_2^k, \cdots w_{L_k}^k$. The normalized log likelihood of an observed sequence x^T given Θ_k is defined below.

$$\overline{P}(x^T \mid \Theta_k) = \frac{1}{L_k} \sum_{t=1}^{L_k} \log[w_t^k P(x^T \mid \theta_t^k)] \tag{19}$$

The final decision is made by comparing the $\overline{P}(x^T \mid \Theta_k)$ for all the classes (k=1,2,...K). The one that gives the maximum probability is chosen as the identity of x^T.

$$ID(x^T) = \arg\max_k \overline{P}(x^T \mid \Theta_k) \quad (1 \le k \le K) \tag{20}$$

Conceptual Interpretation of HMM AdaBoosting

The improvement of the performance of the AdaBoost-HMM classifiers can be interpreted conceptually as follows. Given enough training samples (the number of samples does not have to be very large but they should cover the entire sample space), the boosted HMMs can be trained to cover the widely spread samples. Assume that $X_k = \{x_1^k, x_2^k, \cdots x_{R_k}^k\}$ are training samples of Class d_k. In the first round of boosting, the samples are treated equally ($D_1(x_j^k) = 1/R_k \ \forall k = 1,2\cdots K, j = 1,2\cdots R_k$) and the HMM obtained θ_1^k is a normal ML model. Most of the samples, say $X_{k,ideal} = \{x_1^{k,ideal}, x_2^{k,ideal}, \cdots x_{R_{k,ideal}}^{k,ideal}\}$, where $X_{k,ideal} \subset X_k$ and $R_{k,ideal}$ is the number of the samples in $X_{k,ideal}$, have greater likelihood values such that $P(x_i^{k,ideal} \mid \theta_1^k) > P(x_i^{k,ideal} \mid \theta_1^j)$ ($\forall j = 1,2,\cdots K, j \ne k, i = 1,2,\cdots R_{k,ideal}$). These samples are referred to as the ideal samples because the normal ML model is able to identify them correctly. However, the likelihood values of some other samples $X_{k,hard} = \{x_1^{k,hard}, x_2^{k,hard}, \cdots x_{R_{k,hard}}^{k,hard}\}$, where $X_{k,hard} \subset X_k$ and $R_{k,hard}$ is the number of the samples in $X_{k,hard}$, determined by $\theta_1^k - P(x_i^{k,hard} \mid \theta_1^k)$ (i=1,2,...$R_{k,hard}$) may be smaller than that determined by incorrect HMMs. These samples are called hard samples because the ML model is not able to identify them correctly.

As boosting continues, new HMMs $\theta_2^k, \theta_3^k, \cdots \theta_{L_k}^k$ tend to bias towards these hard samples. For example, if θ_t^k is obtained at Round t, the scored likelihood of a certain group of hard samples $P(x_i^{k,hard} | \theta_t^k)$ increases as t increases. The cost is that the likelihood of some ideal samples will normally decrease. By synthesizing the likelihood according to Eqn.(19), the decision boundaries formed will properly cover both the ideal samples and hard samples. Fig. 11 gives conceptual illustrations of the difference between a single HMM classifier and an AdaBoost-HMM classifier. A single HMM may identify the ideal samples with good accuracy but may be unable to take into consideration the hard or outlier samples as well. After boosting, a more complex decision boundary is formed. The hard samples can then be classified with good credibility.

For different classes, the number of rounds the boosted HMM can pass cross-validation are different and hence different classes may have different number of HMMs. However, the unequal number of HMMs for different classes does not affect the final decision because $\bar{P}(x^T | \Theta_k)$ in Eqn.(19) is normalized with the number of HMMs in a class.

Another aspect of the proposed strategy that should be stressed is that the error rate computed by Eqn.(15) only accounts for part of the classification error. It indicates the samples in X_k being misclassified into some wrong category d_j ($j \neq k$). This kind of error is normally referred to as False Rejection Rate (FRR) or Type II error. Another source of the error indicates the samples of other classes X_j ($j \neq k$) are erroneously accepted by Θ_k. This portion of error is referred to as False Acceptance Rate (FAR) or Type I error. However, FAR is not considered in the proposed HMM AdaBoosting algorithm because it cannot work with the biased Baum-Welch estimation. As illustrated in Eqn.(12), the biased Baum-Welch algorithm only uses the correct training samples for parameter estimation. An erroneously accepted sample cannot be applied to train the parameters of the HMMs. FRR can weight the correct training

Figure 11. A conceptual illustration: the decision boundaries formed by a single HMM (left) and an AdaBoost-HMM (right)

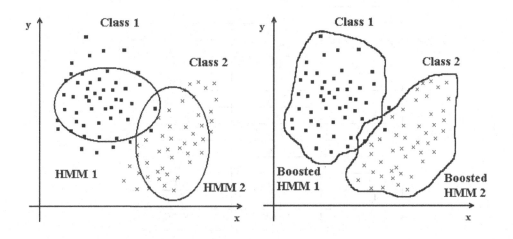

samples in Eqn.(12) as it is an indicator of the goodness-of-fit of the correct samples, while FAR, which is a statistical measure for the incorrect samples (irrelevant to the correct samples), cannot be applied for the proposed method. This is why FAR is not computed in the boosting steps given in Section 4.3.

APPLICATION OF THE ADABOOST-HMM CLASSIFIER TO VISEME RECOGNITION

Experiments are carried out to assess the performance of the AdaBoost-HMM in recognition of visemes. Comparison is also made with the performance of the single HMM classifiers.

The same set of data for assessing the conventional HMM mentioned in Section 2 are used. The 140 vector sequences for context-independent visemes are divided into two groups: 40 of them are used as the training samples and the other 100 are used as the testing samples. For each isolated viseme, an AdaBoost-HMM classifier that consists of 15 to 20 HMMs is trained with the proposed strategy given in Section 4.3.

According to Eqn.(20), for a testing sample x^T of Class d_k, a correct classification is made if $ID(x^T)=d_k$. The classification error (FRR) of the AdaBoost-HMM classifier Θ_k is then computed using the expression below.

Table 3. Classification errors in recognition of context-independent visemes

Viseme Categories	Classification Error (FRR)	
	Single-HMM Classifier	AdaBoost-HMM Classifier
1 p, b, m	13%	8%
2 f, v	4%	5%
3 T, D	11%	4%
4 t, d	35%	17%
5 k, g	24%	9%
6 tS, dZ, S	10%	10%
7 s, z	4%	4%
8 n, l	19%	20%
9 r	18%	7%
10 A:	1%	4%
11 e	8%	11%
12 I	1%	4%
13 Q	7%	10%
14 U	7%	9%
Average	11.6%	8.7%

$$FRR(\Theta_k) = 1 - \frac{number\ of\ correctly\ classified\ samples\ of\ d_k}{number\ of\ all\ the\ testing\ samples\ of\ d_k}$$

(21)

The classification errors of the AdaBoost viseme classifiers are listed in Table 3. A single-HMM classifier is also trained for each isolated viseme using the same 40 training samples. The single-HMM classifier is an ML HMM as mentioned in Section 2. The classification errors of the single-HMM classifiers are computed using Eqn.(21) and are also listed in Table 3 for comparison.

From Table 3, it can be seen that both the single-HMM classifiers and AdaBoost-HMM classifiers can identify the context-independent visemes with reasonable accuracy. An average classification error below 20% is obtained with either approach. The classification error is lower for the vowels as the movement

Figure 12. Rate of training error vs. boosting round – Viseme classifiers of (a) /e/, (b) /s, z/, (c) /T, D/, and (d) /t, d/

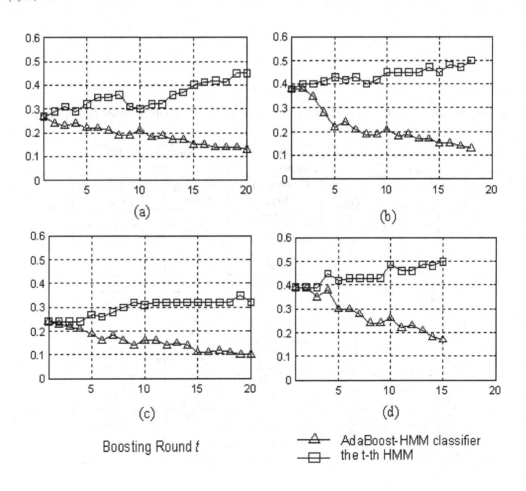

349

of the lips is more. The performance of the AdaBoost-HMM classifiers and that of the single-HMM classifiers are not significantly different. The samples obtained for the context-independent visemes demonstrate good homogeneity as they are independently produced.

In the second experiment, the 200 samples of context-dependent visemes are used. 100 samples are used for training and the other 100 for testing. The corresponding vector sequences are then determined from the images and a series of boosted HMMs is trained for each viseme with the proposed strategy.

As mentioned in Section 4.3, the training error of an AdaBoost-HMM classifier shows tendency of decreasing as boosting continues. To illustrate such change, the training errors of four AdaBoost-HMM classifiers and the t-th HMM (the HMM trained in the t-th Boosting round) of the classifiers are presented in Fig.12. Take Fig.12a as an example, the training error of the AdaBoost-HMM classifier decreases from 0.27 to 0.13 for the 20 rounds while the training error of the t-th HMM increases from 0.27 to 0.45. This is so as the composite HMM biases more and more to the outlier samples as boosting continues.

For the experiments carried out, the boosted sub-classifier for each viseme consists of 12 to 20 HMMs. The training errors and classification errors (FRR) of the testing samples are listed in Table 4 together with the corresponding errors using the single-HMM classifiers. It is observed that the accuracy of recognition is significantly improved (smaller error rate) using AdaBoost-HMM classifier.

Compared with the classification errors listed in Table 3, the classification accuracy of the single-HMM classifiers decreases dramatically in identifying context-dependent visemes. The classification

Table 4. Training and classification errors (FRR) in recognition of context-dependent visemes

Viseme Categories	Single-HMM Classifier		AdaBoost-HMM Classifier	
	Training Error	Classification Error	Training Error	Classification Error
1 p, b, m	14%	20%	6%	15%
2 f, v	15%	27%	11%	25%
3 T, D	24%	34%	10%	18%
4 t, d	39%	50%	17%	19%
5 k, g	17%	17%	16%	16%
6 tS, dZ, S	17%	21%	5%	9%
7 s, z	39%	45%	13%	17%
8 n, l	40%	79%	22%	33%
9 r	21%	54%	22%	37%
10 A:	14%	18%	5%	5%
11 e	27%	33%	13%	7%
12 I	9%	10%	0%	2%
13 Q	10%	35%	4%	11%
14 U	4%	9%	1%	7%
Average	21%	32%	10%	16%

rates of some consonants are even less than 50%. The reason underlying the high identification error is the distribution of the samples. As the samples of a context-dependent viseme are extracted from various words (contexts), the "shapes" of the samples of even the same viseme are different. In statistics jargon, the samples of a context-dependent viseme demonstrate a spread-out distribution. The single-HMM classifiers cannot cover such a distribution well. However, the classification accuracy can be greatly improved with the application of AdaBoost-HMM classifiers. As illustrated in Table 4, although the classification errors are larger compared with those listed in Table 3, an average recognition accuracy of 70%~80% is still attainable, which is about 16% better than the single-HMM classifiers. The improvement can be attributed to the fact that a more complex decision boundary is formulated using the AdaBoost-HMM classifier than using the single-HMM classifier. Therefore, the AdaBoost-HMM classifiers can better cover the spread-out distribution for both the testing samples and the training samples. This is validated by the experimental results. If the context-dependent visemes are looked as isolated visemes distorted by adjoining visemes, it is concluded that the AdaBoost-HMM classifiers provide better robustness on identifying visemes than single-HMM classifiers.

COMPUTATIONAL LOAD OF ADABOOST HMM

The computations involved in HMM AdaBoosting are estimated as follows. For the 3-state-128-symbol discrete HMM applied in the experiments, with 100 training samples ranging from 15~50 frames for each viseme, about 10^6 computations (computations include multiply and division) are required to train an HMM with the biased Baum-Welch estimation. Most of the computations are for calculating the forward variables and backward variables. For example, if the length of a training sample is 30 frames (average length), about 1200 multiplies are required to build a probability trellis to compute the forward variables and backward variables (Rabiner, 1993). Assume that all the 100 training samples have the same length of 30 frames, about 1.2×10^5 computations are required to compute these variables. The forward variables and backward variables have to be computed more than once because expectation-maximization (EM) iterations are taken in the Baum-Welch estimation. If ten iterations are used (in our experiments, the probability scored for the training samples becomes stable after about 10 iterations), 1.2×10^6 computations are required. The number of computations involved in estimating the state transition coefficients and symbol emission probabilities is small compared with this quantity. As a result, it is reasonable to conclude that computations of the order of 10^6 are required to train a single-HMM classifier.

For AdaBoost-HMM classifier comprising 20 HMMs, approximately 2×10^7 computations are required for training the classifier. The additional number of computations including error estimation using cross-validation and calculation of weights is small compared with the number of computations required for the Baum-Welch estimation. The total number of computations is thus approximately 2×10^7 This is a modest amount of computations for the modern computers or signal processor chips.

The computational load in the recognition phase is far less than that in the training phase. For the single-HMM classifiers, the likelihood of an input sequence is computed using the forward process. If the input sequence is 30-frame in length, about 1200 multiplies are performed. As the identity of the input sequence is determined out of fourteen viseme categories, the total number of computations will be approximately 1.7×10^4. For AdaBoost-HMM classifiers, the input sequence is evaluated by a total of 280 (20×14) HMMs, where about 3.4×10^5 multiplies are carried out. The number of computations involved in probability synthesis is small compared with this quantity. Thus about 3.4×10^5 computations are required for recognition by AdaBoost-HMM classifiers.

CONCLUSION

The basic units of visual speech are the visemes, the most conspicuous component of the visual speech is the oral movement. However, many basic sounds have the same sequence of movement of the lips. The mapping between phonemes and visemes is not one-to-one but many-to-one. Also, the visemes for the same phoneme appearing in different words (contexts) may be different.

A classifier of visemes must be discriminative to distinguish the subtle difference between certain groups of visemes. It must also be robust to cope with the variation of visemes of the same group.

To improve the robustness of the HMM to cope with context-dependent visemes which have a spread-out distribution, Adaptively Boosted HMM is proposed. Results show that significant improvement over the conventional HMM can be achieved at the cost of additional computational load.

REFERENCES

Adjoudani, A., & Benoit, C. (1996). On the Integration of Auditory and Visual Parameters in an HMM-based ASR. *Speechreading by Humans and Machines,* Edited by D. G. Stork and M. E. Hennecke,NATO ASI Series, 461-472.

Bahl, L. R., Brown, P. F., De Souza,P. V., & Mercer, R. L. (1986). Maximum mutual information estimation of hidden Markov model parameters for speech recognition. *IEEE Int. Conf. on Acoustics, Speech, and Signal Processing, 1,* 49-52.

Binnie, C., Montgomery, A., & Jackson, P. (1974). Auditory and visual contributions to the perception of consonants. *Journal of Speech Hearing and Research, 17,* 619-630.

Bregler, C., & Omohundro, S. (1995). Nonlinear manifold learning for visual speech recognition. *IEEE Int. Conf. on Computer Vision,* 494-499.

Chen, T. (2001). Audiovisual Speech Processing. *IEEE Signal Processing Magazine.*

Chen, T., & Rao, R. R. (1998). Audio-Visual Integration in Multimodal Communication. *IEEE Proc, 86(5),* 837-852.

Chibelushi, C. C., Gandon, S., Mason, J. S. D., Deravi, F., & Johnston, R. D. (1996). Design issues for a digital audio-visual integrated database. *IEE Colloquium on Integrated Audio-Visual Processing, No. 1996/213,* 7/1-7/7.

Cetingul, H. E., Yemez, Y., Erzin, E., & Tekalp, A.M. (2006). Discriminative Analysis of Lip Motion Features for Speaker Identification and Speech-Reading. *IEEE Trans. on Image Processing, 15*(10), 2879-2891.

Coianiz, T., Torresani, L., & Caprile, B. (1996). 2D Deformable Models for Visual Speech Analysis. *Speech Reading by Humans and Machines*, Edited by D. G. Stork and M. E. Hennecke, NATO ASI Series, 391-398.

Dodd, B., & Campbell, R. (1987). *Hearing by Eye: The psychology of lip-reading.* Lawrence Erlbaum Associates,London.

Dong, L., & Foo, S. W. (2002). Boosting of Hidden Markov Models and the application to visual speech analysis. *Recent Trends in Multimedia Information Processing. The 9th Int. Workshop on Systems, Signals and Image Processing,* 358-364.

Dupont, S., &. Luettin, J. (2000). Audio-visual speech modeling for continuous speech recognition. *IEEE Trans. Multimedia, 2(3),* 141-151.

Eveno, N., Caplier, A., & Coulon, P.Y. (2004). Accurate and Quasi-Automatic Lip Tracking, *IEEE Trans. on Circuits & Systems for Video Technology, 14*(5), 706-715.

Finn, K. E., & Montgomery, A. A. (1988). Automatic optically-based recognition of speech," *Pattern Recognition Letters, 8(3),* 159-164.

Foo, S. W., & Dong, L. (2003). A boosted multi-HMM classifier for recognition of visual speech elements. *IEEE Int. Conf. on Acoustics, Speech, and Signal Processing,(ICASSP '03). 2003, 2,* 285 -288.

Foo, S. W., Lian, Y., & Dong, L. (2004). Recognition of Visual Speech Elements Using Adaptively Boosted Hidden Markov Models. *IEEE Trans. on Circuits and Systems for Video Technology, 14(5),* 693-705.

Goldschen, A. J. (1993). *Continuous automatic speech recognition by lipreading,* Ph.D thesis, George Washington University, Washington.

Goldschen, A. J., Garcia, O. N., & Petajan, E. (1994). Continuous optical automatic speech recognition by lipreading. *The 28th Asilomar Conf. on Signals, Systems, and Computers, 1,* 572-577.

Gravier, G., Potamianos, G., & Neti, C. (2002). Asynchrony modeling for audio-visual speech recognition. *Int. Conf. of Human Language Technology,* available on proceeding CD, USA.

Greenwood, G. W. (1997). Training partially recurrent neural networks using evolutionary strategies. *IEEE Trans. Speech and Audio Processing, 5(2),* 192-194.

Hennecke, M. E., Prasad, K. V., & Stork, D. G. (1994). Using Deformable Templates to Infer Visual Speech Dynamics. *The 28ᵗʰ Asilomar Conf. on Signals,Systems and Computers, 1,* 578-582.

Luettin, J., Thacker, N. A., & Beet, S. W. (1996). Speechreading using shape and intensity information. *Int. Conf. on Spoken Language Processing,* 58-61.

Matthews, I., Cootes, T. F., Bangham, J. A., Cox, S., & Harvey, R. (2002). Extraction of visual features for lipreading. *IEEE Trans. on Pattern Analysis and Machine Intelligence, 24(2),* 198 -213.

Morishima, S., Ogata, S., Murai, K., & Nakamura, S. (2002). Audio-visual speech translation with automatic lip synchronization and face tracking based on 3-D head model. *IEEE Int. Conf. on Acoustics, Speech, and Signal Processing, 2,* 2117-2120.

Nefian, A. V., Liang, L., Pi, X., Liu, X., & Murphy, K. (2002). Dynamic Bayesian networks for audio-visual speech recognition," *EURASIP Journal of Applied Signal Processing, 2002(11)*, 1274-1288.

Owens, E., &. Blazek, B. (1985). Visemes Observed by Hearing Impaired and Normal Hearing Adult Viewers. *Journal of Speech Hearing and Research, 28*, 381-393.

Petajan, E. D. (1984). *Automatic lipreading to enhance speech recognition*, Ph.D thesis, University of Illinois at Urbana-Champaign.

Potamianos, G., Cosatto, F., Graf, H. P., & Roe, D. B. (1997). Speaker independent audio-visual database for bimodal ASR. *ESCA Workshop Audio-Visual Speech Processing*, 65-68.

Rabiner, L. R., & Juang, B. H. (1993). *Fundamentals of speech recognition*, Prentice Hall International Inc. Signal Processing Series.

Silsbee, P., & Bovik, A. (1996). Computer Lipreading for Improved Accuracy in Automatic Speech Recognition. *IEEE Trans. Speech and Audio Processing, 4(5)*, 337-351.

Silsbee, P. L., & Bovic, A. C. (1993). Medium vocabulary audiovisual speech recognition. *NATO ASI New Advances and Trends in Speech Recognition and Coding*, 13-16.

Silsbee, P. L., & Bovic, A. C. (1993). Visual lipreading by computer to improve automatic speech recognition accuracy. *Technical Report TR-93-02-90*, University of Texas Computer and Vision Research Center, Austin, TX, USA.

Stork, D. G., & Lu, H. L. (1996). Speechreading by Boltzmann zippers. *Machines that learn*, Snowbird, UT.

Stork, D. G., Wolff, G., & Levine, E. (1992). Neural network lipreading system for improved speech recognition. *Int. Joint Conf. on Neural Network*, 285-295.

Sumby, W. H., & Pollack, I. (1954). Visual contributions to speech intelligibility in noise. *Journal of the Acoustical Society of America, 26*, 212-215.

Tekalp, A. M., & Ostermann, J. (2000). Face and 2-D mesh animation in MPEG-4. *Signal Processing: Image Communication, Special Issue on MPEG-4, 15, 387-421.*

Tomlinson, M., Russell, M., & Brooke, N. (1996). Integrating audio and visual information to provide highly robust speech recognition. *IEEE Int. Conf. on Acoustics, Speech, and Signal Processing,2,821-824.*

Yuhas, B. P., Goldstein, M. H., & Sejnowski, T. J. (1989). Integration of acoustic and visual speech signals using neural networks. *IEEE Communication Magazine*, 65-71.

Yuille, A., & Hallinan, P. (1992). Deformable Templates. *Active Vision,* Edited by Andrew Blake and Alan Yuille. *The MIT Press,* 21-38.

Zhang, X. Z., Mersereau, R. M., & Clements, M. A. (2002). Audio-visual speech recognition by speechreading. *The 14th Int. Conf. on Digital Signal Processing, 2*, 1069 -1072.

ENDNOTE

[a]   Liang Dong was with the University when the research was carried out and is currently with the Healthcare Department, Philips Research Asia – Shanghai, China

Chapter XII
Hidden Markov Model Based Visemes Recognition, Part II:
Discriminative Approaches

Say Wei Foo
Nanyang Technological University, Singapore

Liang Dong[a]
Nanyang Technological University, Singapore

ABSTRACT

The basic building blocks of visual speech are the visemes. Unlike phonemes, the visemes are, however, confusable and easily distorted by the contexts in which they appear. Classifiers capable of distinguishing the minute difference among the different categories are desirable. In this chapter, we describe two Hidden Markov Model based techniques using the discriminative approach to increase the accuracy of visual speech recognition. The approaches investigated include Maximum Separable Distance (MSD) training strategy (Dong, 2005) and Two-channel training approach (Dong, 2005; Foo, 2003; Foo, 2002) The MSD training strategy and the Two-channel training approach adopt a proposed criterion function called separable distance to improve the discriminative power of an HMM. The methods are applied to identify confusable visemes. Experimental results indicate that higher recognition accuracy can be attained using these approaches than that using conventional HMM.

INTRODUCTION

Viseme Classifiers for Fine Discrimination

In the previous chapter, we have described an AdaBoost-HMM classifier to deal with the variations of a particular viseme appearing in different contexts. However, the method does not specifically deal with the fine discrimination of different phonemes which may be confusable.

Table 1. Viseme table adopted in MPEG-4

Viseme Number	Corresponding phonemes	Examples
0	none	(silence and relax)
1	p, b, m	push, bike, milk
2	f, v	find, voice
3	T, D	think, that
4	t, d	teach, dog
5	k, g	call, guess
6	tS, dZ, S	check, join, shrine
7	s, z	set, zeal
8	n, l	note, lose
9	r	read
10	A:	jar
11	e	bed
12	I	tip
13	Q	shock
14	U	good

In MPEG-4 multimedia standard the relationship between phonemes and visemes is a many-to-one mapping (Tekalp, 2000). For example, there are only subtle differences in change of mouth shape between phoneme productions of /f/ and /v/, and thus they are clustered into one viseme category. If there is a classifier that is able to distinguish the small difference between them, the accuracy of visual speech recognition will be greatly improved.

For training of the single-HMM classifier, the Baum-Welch training algorithm making use of Maximum Likelihood (ML) model (Rabiner, 1993) is popularly adopted. However, the parameters of the HMM are solely determined by the correct samples while the relationship between the correct samples and incorrect ones is not taken into consideration. The method, in its original form, is thus not developed for fine recognition. One solution to this problem is to adopt a training strategy that maximizes the mutual information. The method is referred to as Maximum Mutual Information (MMI) estimation (Bahl, 1986). It increases the *a posteriori* probability of the model corresponding to the training data, and thus the overall discriminative power of the HMM obtained is guaranteed. However, it is difficult to realize such a strategy and implementation of MMI estimation is tedious. A computationally less intensive metric and approach are desirable.

In this chapter, we describe two Hidden Markov Model based techniques to increase the discriminative power of visual speech recognition. We name the two techniques as the Maximum Separable Distance (MSD) training strategy (Dong, 2005), and the Two-channel training approach (Dong, 2005; Foo, 2003; Foo, 2002).

Organization of the Chapter

The organization of the chapter is as follows. The proposed new metric Maximum Separable Distance (MSD) is described in Section 2. The MSD HMM and the Two-channel HMM are presented in Sections 3 and 4 respectively. The concluding remark is given in Section 5. Some suggestions for future work are outlined in Section 6.

SEPARABLE DISTANCE FUNCTION

Definition and Estimation of Parameters

In this section, a new metric to measure the difference between two observation sequences is described. We shall name the metric '*separable distance*'.

Let an HMM be represented by $\theta(\pi, A, B)$, where π denotes the probabilities of the initial states, A denotes the state transition matrix and B denotes the symbol emission matrix. In addition, let $O^M = (O_1, O_2, \ldots, O_M)$ be the set of discrete symbol alphabet and $S^N = (S_1, S_2, \ldots, S_N)$ be the set of states.

Assume that in a two-class identification problem, $\{x^T : d_1\}$ and $\{y^T : d_1\}$ are a pair of training samples, where x^T and y^T are observation sequences of length T and d_1 and d_2 are the class labels. Assume that $x^T = (x_1^T, x_2^T, \cdots, x_T^T)$ is a true sample while $y^T = (y_1^T, y_2^T, \cdots, y_T^T)$ is a false sample. The observed symbols in x^T and y^T are from the symbol set O^M. $P(x^T|\theta)$ and $P(y^T|\theta)$ are the scored probabilities for x^T and y^T given HMM θ, respectively. The pair of training samples x^T and y^T must be of the same length so that their probabilities $P(x^T|\theta)$ and $P(y^T|\theta)$ can be suitably compared. Such comparison is meaningless if the samples are of different lengths; the shorter sequence may give larger probability than the longer one even if it is not the true sample of θ.

Define a new function $I(x^T, y^T, \theta)$, called the separable-distance function, as follows.

$$I(x^T, y^T, \theta) = \log P(x^T|\theta) - \log P(y^T|\theta) \tag{1}$$

A large value of $I(x^T, y^T, \theta)$ would mean that x^T and y^T are more distinct and separable. The strategy then is to determine the HMM θ_{MSD} (MSD for maximum separable-distance) that maximizes $I(x^T, y^T, \theta)$. Mathematically,

$$\theta_{MSD} = \arg\max_{\theta} [I(x^T, y^T, \theta)] \tag{2}$$

As the first step towards the maximization of the separable-distance function $I(x^T, y^T, \theta)$, a Lagrangian $F(x^T, y^T, \theta, \lambda)$ involving $I(x^T, y^T, \theta)$ and the parameters of B is defined as below,

$$F(x^T, y^T, \theta, \lambda) = I(x^T, y^T, \theta) + \sum_{i=1}^{N} \lambda_i \left(1 - \sum_{j=1}^{M} b_{ij}\right) \tag{3}$$

where λ_i is the Lagrange multiplier for the i-th state and

$$\sum_{j=1}^{M} b_{ij} = 1$$

($i = 1, 2, \ldots N$). By maximizing $F(x^T, y^T, \theta, \lambda)$, $I(x^T, y^T, \theta)$ is also maximized. Differentiating $F(x^T, y^T, \theta, \lambda)$ with respect to b_{ij} and setting the result to 0, we have,

$$\frac{\partial \log P(x^T \mid \theta)}{\partial b_{ij}} - \frac{\partial \log P(y^T \mid \theta)}{\partial b_{ij}} = \lambda_i$$

(4)

Since λ_i is positive, the optimum value obtained for $I(x^T, y^T, \theta)$ is the maximum as solutions for b_{ij} must be positive. In Eqn.(2), $\log P(x^T|\theta)$ and $\log P(y^T|\theta)$ may be computed by summing up all the probabilities over time T.

$$\log P(x^T \mid \theta) = \sum_{\tau=1}^{T} \log \sum_{i=1}^{N} P(s_\tau^T = S_i) b_i(x_\tau^T)$$

(5)

Note that the state transition coefficients a_{ij} do not appear explicitly in Eqn.(5), they are included in the term $P(s_\tau^T = S_i)$.

The two partial derivatives in Eqn.(4) may be evaluated separately as follows,

$$\frac{\partial \log P(x^T \mid \theta)}{\partial b_{ij}} = \sum_{\substack{\tau=1 \\ s.t. x_\tau^T = O_j}}^{T} P(s_\tau^T = S_i \mid \theta, x^T) = b_{ij}^{-1} \sum_{\tau=1}^{T} P(s_\tau^T = S_i, x_\tau^T = O_j \mid \theta, x^T)$$

(6a)

$$\frac{\partial \log P(y^T \mid \theta)}{\partial b_{ij}} = \sum_{\substack{\tau=1 \\ s.t. y_\tau^T = O_j}}^{T} P(s_\tau^T = S_i \mid \theta, y^T) = b_{ij}^{-1} \sum_{\tau=1}^{T} P(s_\tau^T = S_i, y_\tau^T = O_j \mid \theta, y^T)$$

(6b)

By defining

$$E(S_i, O_j \mid \theta, x^T) = \sum_{\tau=1}^{T} P(s_\tau^T = S_i, x_\tau^T = O_j \mid \theta, x^T)$$

(7)

$$E(S_i, O_j \mid \theta, y^T) = \sum_{\tau=1}^{T} P(s_\tau^T = S_i, y_\tau^T = O_j \mid \theta, y^T)$$

(8)

$$D_{ij}(x^T, y^T, \theta) = E(S_i, O_j \mid \theta, x^T) - E(S_i, O_j \mid \theta, y^T)$$

(9)

Eqn.(4) can be written as,

$$\frac{E(S_i, O_j \mid \theta, x^T) - E(S_i, O_j \mid \theta, y^T)}{b_{ij}} = \frac{D_{ij}(x^T, y^T, \theta)}{b_{ij}} = \lambda_i \quad 1 \le j \le M \tag{10}$$

By making use of the fact that

$$\sum_{j=1}^{M} b_{ij} = 1,$$

it can be shown that

$$b_{ij} = \frac{D_{ij}(x^T, y^T, \theta)}{\sum_{j=1}^{M} D_{ij}(x^T, y^T, \theta)} \quad i = 1, 2, \cdots, N, \; j = 1, 2, \cdots M \tag{11}$$

The set $\{b_{ij}\}$ ($i = 1, 2, \dots N$, $j = 1, 2, \dots M$) so obtained gives the maximum value of $I(x^T, y^T, \theta)$. However, b_{ij} may not be estimated by applying Eqn.(11) alone, other considerations shall be taken into account such as when $D_{ij}(x^T, y^T, \theta)$ is less than or equal to 0. Further discussion on the determination of values of b_{ij} is given in Section 2.2.

Convergence of the MSD Estimation

Eqn.(11) suggests an iterative approach to maximize $I(x^T, y^T, \theta)$. The convergence of the method is proved by using the standard Expectation-Maximization (EM) optimization techniques (McLanchlan, 1997). By considering x^T and y^T as the observed data and the state sequence $s^T = (s_1^T, s_2^T, \cdots, s_T^T)$ as the hidden or unobserved data, the estimation of $E_\theta(I) = E[I(x^T, y^T, s^T \mid \tilde{\theta}) \mid x^T, y^T, \theta]$ from incomplete data x^T and y^T is then given by

$$E_\theta(I) = \sum_{s^T \in S} I(x^T, y^T, s^T \mid \tilde{\theta}) P(x^T, y^T, s^T \mid \theta)$$

$$= \sum_{s^T \in S} [\log P(x^T, s^T \mid \tilde{\theta}) - \log P(y^T, s^T \mid \tilde{\theta})] P(x^T, y^T, s^T \mid \theta) \tag{12}$$

where θ and $\tilde{\theta}$ are the HMM before training and the HMM after training respectively, and S denotes all the state combinations with length T. The estimation converges if only the updated values of b_{ij} increase $E_\theta(I)$ (McLanchlan, 1997; Tanner, 1996). This can be proven by applying the Baum's auxiliary function (Q function) (Baum, 1967). Using the auxiliary function $Q_x(\tilde{\theta}, \theta)$ given by

$$Q_x(\tilde{\theta}, \theta) = \sum_{s^T \in S} \log P(x^T, s^T \mid \tilde{\theta}) P(x^T, s^T \mid \theta) \tag{13}$$

Eqn.(12) can then be written as

$$E_\theta(I) = Q_x(\widetilde{\theta},\theta)P(y^T \mid s^T,\theta) - Q_y(\widetilde{\theta},\theta)P(x^T \mid s^T,\theta) \tag{14}$$

$Q_x(\widetilde{\theta},\theta)$ and $Q_y(\widetilde{\theta},\theta)$ may be further analyzed by breaking up the probability $P(x^T,s^T \mid \widetilde{\theta})$ as in Eqn.(15) below,

$$P(x^T,s^T \mid \widetilde{\theta}) = \widetilde{\pi}(s_0)\prod_{\tau=1}^{T} \widetilde{a}_{s_{\tau-1},s_\tau} \widetilde{b}_{s_\tau}(x_\tau) \tag{15}$$

where $\widetilde{\pi}$, $\widetilde{a}$ and $\widetilde{b}$ are the parameters of $\widetilde{\theta}$. Here, we assume that the initial distribution starts at $\tau=0$ instead of $\tau=1$ for notational convenience. The Q function then becomes,

$$Q_x(\widetilde{\theta},\theta) = \sum_{s^T \in S} \log \widetilde{\pi}(s_0)P(x^T,s^T \mid \theta) + \sum_{s^T \in S}(\sum_{\tau=1}^{T} \log \widetilde{a}_{\tau-1,\tau})P(x^T,s^T \mid \theta)$$
$$+ \sum_{s^T \in S}(\sum_{\tau=1}^{T} \log \widetilde{b}_\tau(x_\tau))P(x^T,s^T \mid \theta) \tag{16}$$

$Q_y(\widetilde{\theta},\theta)$ is decomposed in a similar manner. The parameters to be optimized are now separated into three independent terms.

From Eqns.(14) and (16), $E_\theta(I)$ can also be divided into the following three terms,

$$E_\theta(I) = E_\theta(\widetilde{\pi},I) + E_\theta(\widetilde{a},I) + E_\theta(\widetilde{b},I) \tag{17}$$

where

$$E_\theta(\widetilde{\pi},I) = \sum_{s^T \in S} \log \widetilde{\pi}(s_0)[P(x^T,y^T,s^T \mid \theta) - P(x^T,y^T,s^T \mid \theta)] = 0 \tag{18a}$$

$$E_\theta(\widetilde{a},I) = \sum_{s^T \in S}\sum_{\tau=1}^{T} \log \widetilde{a}_{\tau-1,\tau}[P(x^T,y^T,s^T \mid \theta) - P(x^T,y^T,s^T \mid \theta)] = 0 \tag{18b}$$

$$E_\theta(\widetilde{b},I) = \sum_{s^T \in S}[\sum_{\tau=1}^{T} \log \widetilde{b}_\tau(x_\tau) - \sum_{\tau=1}^{T} \log \widetilde{b}_\tau(y_\tau)]P(x^T,y^T,s^T \mid \theta) \tag{18c}$$

$E_\theta(\widetilde{\pi},I)$ and $E_\theta(\widetilde{a},I)$ are associated with the hidden state sequence s^T. It is assumed that x^T and y^T are drawn independently and emitted from the same state sequence s^T, hence both $E_\theta(\widetilde{\pi},I)$ and $E_\theta(\widetilde{a},I)$ become 0. $E_\theta(\widetilde{b},I)$, on the other hand, is associated with the symbols in x^T and y^T. It is not equal to 0 if x^T and y^T are different. By enumerating all the state combinations, we have,

$$E_\theta(\widetilde{b}, I) = \sum_{i=1}^{N} \sum_{\tau=1}^{T} [\log \widetilde{b}_i(x_\tau^T) - \log \widetilde{b}_i(y_\tau^T)] P(x^T, y^T, s_\tau^T = S_i \mid \theta) \qquad (19)$$

If

$$\sum_{\tau=1}^{T} [\log \widetilde{b}_i(x_\tau^T) - \log \widetilde{b}_i(y_\tau^T)]$$

is arranged according to the order of appearance of the symbols (O_j) within x^T and y^T, we have,

$$E_\theta(\widetilde{b}, I) = \sum_{i=1}^{N} \sum_{j=1}^{M} \log \widetilde{b}_{ij} \sum_{\tau=1, s.t. x_\tau^T = y_\tau^T = O_j}^{T} [P(x_\tau^T = O_j, s_\tau^T = S_i \mid \theta, x^T)$$

$$- P(y_\tau^T = O_j, s_\tau^T = S_i \mid \theta, y^T)] P(x^T, y^T \mid \theta) \qquad (20)$$

Let

$$E(S_i, O_j \mid \theta, x^T) = \sum_{\tau=1, s.t. x_\tau^T = y_\tau^T = O_j}^{T} P(x_\tau^T = O_j, s_\tau^T = S_i \mid \theta, x^T) \qquad ,$$

Eqn.(20) can be written as

$$E_\theta(\widetilde{b}, I) = \sum_{i=1}^{N} \sum_{j=1}^{M} \log \widetilde{b}_{ij} [E(S_i, O_j \mid \theta, x^T) - E(S_i, O_j \mid \theta, y^T)] P(x^T, y^T \mid \theta) \qquad (21)$$

In the M-step of the EM estimation, $\widetilde{b}_{ij}$ is adjusted to maximize $E_\theta(\widetilde{b}, I)$ or $E_\theta(I)$. Since

$$\sum_{j=1}^{M} \widetilde{b}_{ij} = 1$$

and Eqn.(21) has the form
$$K \sum_{j=1}^{M} w_j \log v_j \qquad ,$$

which attains a global maximum at the point

$$v_j = \frac{w_j}{\sum\limits_{j=1}^{M} w_j}$$

($j = 1, 2, \ldots M$), the re-estimated value of $\widetilde{b}_{ij}$ of $\widetilde{\theta}$ that lead to the maximum $E_\theta(I)$ is given by

$$\widetilde{b}_{ij} = \frac{E(S_i, O_j \mid \theta, x^T) - E(S_i, O_j \mid \theta, y^T)}{\sum\limits_{j=1}^{M} [E(S_i, O_j \mid \theta, x^T) - E(S_i, O_j \mid \theta, y^T)]} = \frac{D_{ij}(x^T, y^T, \theta)}{\sum\limits_{j=1}^{M} D_{ij}(x^T, y^T, \theta)} \tag{22}$$

The same conclusion is reached as in Eqn.(11). The above derivations strictly observe the standard optimization strategy (McLanchlan, 1997), where the expectation of the value of the separable-distance function, $E_\theta(I)$, is computed in the E-step and the coefficients b_{ij} are adjusted to maximize $E_\theta(I)$ in the M-step. The convergence of the method is therefore guaranteed.

It is also clear from Eqns.(18.a) and (18.b) that modification to π_i and a_{ij} will not increase the value of $E_\theta(I)$ explicitly. As a result, although changes to π_i and a_{ij} may lead to different values of $I(x^T, y^T, s^T \mid \widetilde{\theta})$, they cannot be adjusted toward a larger value of $I(x^T, y^T, s^T \mid \widetilde{\theta})$ using the EM estimation. This is the reason why only b_{ij} is adjusted in the MSD estimation.

MSD HMM CLASSIFIER

The MSD Training Strategy

The MSD training strategy is the process of increasing the separable-distance between two confusable classes. For the true sample $\{x^T: d_1\}$ and false sample $\{y^T: d_2\}$ mentioned in Section 2.1, the separable-distance measure between x^T and y^T is given below by using the definition given in Eqn.(1),

$$I(x^T, y^T, \theta) = \log P(x^T \mid \theta) - \log P(y^T \mid \theta) \tag{23}$$

where θ is the HMM for discriminating Class d_1 and d_2, x^T is the true sample and y^T is the false sample of θ. $I(x^T, y^T, \theta)$ can be maximized by changing the elements of Matrix B of the HMM as given in Eqn.(22).

Although Eqn.(22) indicates that b_{ij} can be estimated by computing the expectations $E(S_i, O_j \mid \theta, x^T)$ and $E(S_i, O_j \mid \theta, y^T)$, it cannot be applied to parameter training directly because $D_{ij}(x^T, y^T, \theta)$ may be less than 0 while b_{ij} cannot be negative values. As a result, some additional processing has to be carried out in the training strategy. These considerations are taken into account in the following steps of MSD estimation.

Step 1: Parameter Initialization

For the discrete HMM discussed in this chapter, the selection of the initial values is relatively easy. Parameters in Matrix A can take arbitrary or uniform values provided that the probability constraints

$$\sum_{n=1}^{N} a_{mn} = 1$$

and $a_{mn} \geq 0$ ($m,n = 1,2,\ldots N$) are met. The initial values of the elements in Matrix B can also take arbitrary or uniform values. In specific identification task, however, the parameters of an HMM should be set according to the statistical/temporal features of the training samples.

Step 2: Compute the Expectations

The expectations $E(S_i,O_j|\theta,x^T)$ and $E(S_i,O_j|\theta,y^T)$ are computed in this step. For x^T, the forward variable $\alpha_t^x(i)$ and backward variable $\beta_t^x(i)$ at time t ($1 \leq t < 1$), given θ, are defined as $\alpha_t^x(i) = P(o_1^1, o_2^1, \cdots o_t^1, s_t^1 = S_i \mid \theta)$, $\beta_t^x(i) = P(o_{t+1}^1, o_{t+2}^1, \cdots o_T^1 \mid s_t^1 = S_i, \theta)$ and are computed by building a probability trellis with $N \times T$ nodes (Rabiner, 1993). Using $\alpha_t^x(i)$ and $\beta_t^x(i)$, the following probability is computed.

$$\gamma_t^x(i) = P(s_t^x = S_i \mid x^T, \theta) = \sum_{j=1}^{N} \frac{\alpha_t^x(i) a_{ij} b_j(x_{t+1}^T) \beta_{t+1}^x(j)}{\sum_{i=1}^{N} \sum_{k=1}^{N} \alpha_t^x(i) a_{ij} b_k(x_{t+1}^T) \beta_{t+1}^x(k)}$$

(24)

Let $\gamma_t^x(i,O_j)$ denote $\gamma_t^x(i)$ with the t-th observed symbol $o_t^x = O_j$. By counting the number of $\gamma_t^x(i,O_j)$ over time T, we have,

$$E(S_i,O_j \mid \theta, x^T) = \sum_{t=1}^{T} \gamma_t^1(i,O_j)$$

(25)

For y^T, $\gamma_t^y(i)$ and $E(S_i,O_j|\theta,y^T)$ are computed in the same manner and $D_{ij}(x^T,y^T,\theta)$ is then computed.

Step 3: Parameter Modification

It is seen from Eqn.(22) that to maximize $I(x^T,y^T,\theta)$, b_{ij} should be set proportional to $D_{ij}(x^T,y^T,\theta)$. However, for certain symbol, e.g. O_p, the expectation $D_{ip}(x^T,y^T,\theta)$ may be less than 0. In this case, a small value ε, e.g. $\varepsilon = 10^{-3}$, is assigned to the corresponding $b_i(O_p)$. As a result, if there are L occurrences of $D_{ip}(x^T,y^T,\theta) \leq 0$, i.e.

$$L = number\ of\ D_{ip}(x^T, y^T, \theta) \leq 0 \qquad p = 1,2,\cdots M$$

(26)

$\tilde{b}_{ij}$ is estimated according to the following expression

$$\tilde{b}_{ij} = \begin{cases} \Sigma_D^{-1} D_{ij}(x^T, y^T, \theta)(1 - L\varepsilon) & if \quad D_{ij}(x^T, y^T, \theta) > 0 \\ \varepsilon & otherwise \end{cases}$$

(27)

where Σ_D is the sum of $D_{ij}(x^T,y^T,\theta)$ provided that $D_{ij}(x^T,y^T,\theta) > 0$.

$$\Sigma_D = \sum_{j=1}^{M} D_{ij}(x^T, y^T, \theta) \qquad\qquad if \quad D_{ij}(x^T, y^T, \theta) > 0 \qquad\qquad (28)$$

Step 4: State Duration Validation

The proposed MSD estimation requires that the values of the training pair x^T and y^T are fairly similar such that their state durations are comparable. If the durations of State S_i, say $E(S_i|\theta,x^T)$ and $E(S_i|\theta,y^T)$, differ too much, $D_{ij}(x^T,y^T,\theta)$ becomes meaningless. For example, if $E(S_i|\theta,x^T) \ll E(S_i|\theta,y^T)$, even the symbol O_j takes much greater portion in $E(S_i|\theta,x^T)$ than in $E(S_i|\theta,y^T)$, the computed $D_{ij}(x^T,y^T,\theta)$ may also be less than 0. The consequence is that $b_i(O_j)$ is always set to be equal to ε rather than adjusted to increase $I(x^T,y^T,\theta)$. As a result, the state durations of x^T and y^T should be validated after each training cycle. Using the forward and backward variables, the state duration of $\hat{x}_1$ is computed as follows.

$$E(S_i|\theta,x^T) = \sum_{t=1}^{T} \frac{\alpha_t^x(i)\beta_t^x(i)}{\sum_{i=1}^{N}\alpha_t^x(i)\beta_t^x(i)} \qquad i = 1,2,\cdots,N \qquad\qquad (29)$$

$E(S_i|\theta,y^T)$ is computed in the same manner. Training continues if $E(S_i|\theta,x^T) \approx E(S_i|\theta,y^T)$ (not necessary to be the same), e.g.

$$1.2 > E(S_i|\theta,x^T)/E(S_i|\theta,y^T) > 0.8 \quad i = 1,2,\cdots,N \qquad\qquad (30)$$

otherwise training stops even $I(x^T,y^T,\theta)$ shows trend of increasing.

Step 5: Termination

Step 2 and Step 3 are repeated in each training cycle. After each cycle, Step 4 is implemented to verify the state durations. The procedures are repeated until either premature termination occurs, i.e. $E(S_i|\theta,x^T)$ and $E(S_i|\theta,y^T)$ differ too much, or the difference of $I(x^T,y^T,\theta)$ between consecutive training cycles is smaller than a predefined threshold, or the specified number of training cycles is met.

Extensions to the MSD Estimation

In Eqn.(22), both training samples x^T and y^T have the same length T. This condition is necessary in order to compare on the same basis the probabilities scored for two sequences. Otherwise, the shorter sequence tends to score greater likelihood even it is not the true sample. However, the MSD estimation can be extended to training samples of different lengths in the following manner. Assume that the length of the training pair $x^{T_1} = (x_1^{T_1}, x_2^{T_1}, \cdots x_{T_1}^{T_1})$ and $y^{T_2} = (y_1^{T_2}, y_2^{T_2}, \cdots y_{T_2}^{T_2})$ are T_1 and T_2, respectively. By carrying out linear adjustment, it is easy to prove that $\tilde{b}_j$ can be estimated via the following equation.

$$\widetilde{b}_{ij} = \frac{T_2 E(S_i, O_j \mid \theta, x^{T_1}) - T_1 E(S_i, O_j \mid \theta, y^{T_2})}{\sum_{j=1}^{M} [T_2 E(S_i, O_j \mid \theta, x^{T_1}) - T_1 E(S_i, O_j \mid \theta, y^{T_2})]}$$

(31)

In Step 4 of the MSD training strategy, the duration of state S_i for x^{T_1}, $E(S_i \mid \theta, x^{T_1})$, is then compared with $T_1 E(S_i \mid \theta, y^{T_2})/T_2$.

The MSD estimation can also be extended to the case of multiple training samples. Assume that the training pair are two labeled sample sets: $X = \{x^{(1)}, x^{(2)}, \cdots x^{(R_1)} : d_1\}$ denote the true samples and $Y = \{y^{(1)}, y^{(2)}, \cdots y^{(R_2)} : d_2\}$ denote the false samples, where $x^{(i)}$ and $y^{(i)}$ indicate the i-th training samples of Class d_1 and Class d_2, respectively, and R_1 is the number of samples of Class d_1, R_2 is the number of samples of Class d_2. The separable distance is computed using the expression below.

$$I(X, Y, \theta) = R_1^{-1} \sum_{i=1}^{R_1} \log P(x^{(i)} \mid \theta) - R_2^{-1} \sum_{i=1}^{R_2} \log P(y^{(i)} \mid \theta)$$

(32)

If all the training samples in X and Y have the same length, it is concluded that $\widetilde{b}_j$ should be estimated as follows.

$$\widetilde{b}_{ij} = \frac{R_1^{-1} \sum_{m=1}^{R_1} E(S_i, O_j \mid \theta, x^{(m)}) - R_2^{-1} \sum_{n=1}^{R_2} E(S_i, O_j \mid \theta, y^{(n)})}{\sum_{j=1}^{M} [R_1^{-1} \sum_{m=1}^{R_1} E(S_i, O_j \mid \theta, x^{(m)}) - R_2^{-1} \sum_{n=1}^{R_2} E(S_i, O_j \mid \theta, y^{(n)})]}$$

(33)

While validating the state durations, the term

$$R_1^{-1} \sum_{m=1}^{R_1} E(S_i \mid \theta, x^{(m)})$$

is computed and compared with

$$R_2^{-1} \sum_{n=1}^{R_2} E(S_i \mid \theta, y^{(n)})$$.

If

$$R_1^{-1} \sum_{m=1}^{R_1} E(S_i \mid \theta, x^{(m)}) \approx R_2^{-1} \sum_{n=1}^{R_2} E(S_i \mid \theta, y^{(n)})$$,

the training cycle is repeated; otherwise, the training terminates. In a more complex situation where the training samples in X and Y have different lengths, they can be linearly scaled first as in Eqn.(31), and then clustered as in Eqn.(33).

Decision Strategy

In the two-class problem, with Class d_1 vs. Class d_2, let $\theta_{i,j}$ ($i, j = 1, 2$) be the MSD estimation of the HMM (abbreviated as MSD HMM) with the samples of Class d_i being the true training samples and the samples of Class d_j being the false training samples. The identity of an unknown input z^T can be determined using the following equation.

$$ID(z^T) = \begin{cases} d_1 & \text{if } P(z^T|\theta_{1,2}) > P(z^T|\theta_{2,1}) \\ d_2 & \text{otherwise} \end{cases}$$

(34)

In multi-class cases, say with Classes $d_1, d_2, ..., d_K$, (K-1) number of MSD HMMs are trained for each class to separate its true samples out of those of a specific class. For Class d_i as an example, K-1 HMMs– $\theta_{i,1,}$ $\theta_{i,2}$, ... $\theta_{i,j}$, ... $\theta_{i,K}$ ($i,j = 1,2,...$ K, $i \neq j$) are trained using the MSD estimation, where $\theta_{i,j}$ denotes the MSD HMM with the samples of Class d_i being the true training samples and the samples of Class d_j being the false training samples. For the K classes, there are totally $K(K$-1) MSD HMMs involved. For an unknown observation sequence z^T that belongs to one of the K classes, the identity of z^T is determined in the following steps.

1. $2K$ MSD HMMs $\theta_{1,2}$, $\theta_{2,1}$, $\theta_{2,3}$, $\theta_{3,2}$, $\theta_{3,4}$, $\theta_{4,3}$, ... $\theta_{K,1}$, $\theta_{1,K}$ are put into K groups with each of them consisting of two HMMs. The probabilities $P(z^T|\theta_{i,j})$ and $P(z^T|\theta_{j,i})$ are computed (denoted as $P_{i,j}$ in Fig. 1) .

Figure 1. The process for determining the identity of the input sample in multi-class identification

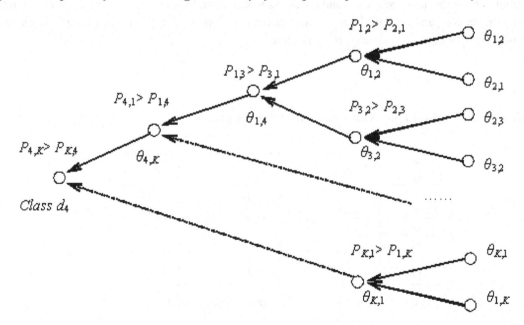

2.   If $P(z^T|\theta_{i,j}) > P(z^T|\theta_{j,i})$, Class d_i is more likely to be the identity of z^T than Class d_j and Class d_i is selected as the winning class in this group. The MSD HMMs of the winning classes are regrouped.

The decision strategy mentioned above employs elimination series to determine the identity of z^T. The number of winning classes halves after each decision round as depicted in Fig. 1. Steps 1 and 2 are repeated until only one winning class remains. Using this approach, it is usually unnecessary to compute all the probabilities that are scored by the $K(K-1)$ MSD HMMs.

Application of MSD HMM to the Recognition of Confusable Visemes

Data Selection and Model Training

The proposed MSD HMM is applied to recognize and distinguish confusable context-independent visemes. Its performance is compared with that of the ML estimation of HMM (abbreviated as ML HMM) trained using the Baum-Welch method. To highlight the discriminative power of the MSD HMM, 18 phonemes listed in Table 2 are chosen as some of them bear close similarity to another. According to the phoneme-viseme mapping given in Table 1, these phonemes are clustered into 6 viseme categories as shown in Table 2. Here, for notational convenience, we still use the term "viseme" to indicate the visual representation of each selected phoneme.

A professional English speaker is asked to produce each viseme 100 times. The video clips of these visemes are manually truncated/stretched such that all the visemes have uniform duration of 1 second, or equivalently 25 frames. Among these 100 samples (video clips), 50 are applied for training while the remaining 50 are for testing.

To associate the HMM with the physical process of viseme production, three-state left-right structure consisting of initial state, articulation state and end state, is used (see Section 2.2, Chapter XI). Given a viseme sample, the approximate initial phase, articulation phase and end phase are manually segmented from the image sequence and the acoustic signal, and the duration of each phase is counted. The coefficients $a_{i,i}$ and $a_{i,i+1}$ of Matrix A are initialized with these durations. For example, if the duration of State S_i is T_i, the initial value of $a_{i,i}$ is set to be

Table 2. Visemes selected for the MSD and ML HMM classifiers

Viseme Category*	Viseme 1	Viseme 2	Viseme 3	Viseme 4
1	/p/	/m/	/b/	
6	/th/	/sh/	/tZ/	/dZ/
10	/a:/	/ai/	/æ/	
12	/ei/	/i/	/j/	/ie/
13	/o/	/oi/		
14	/eu/	/au/		

(The viseme categories are numbered according to MPEG-4)*

$$\frac{T_i}{T_i + 1}$$

and the initial value of $a_{i,i+1}$ is set to be

$$\frac{1}{T_i + 1}$$

as they maximize $a_{i,i}^{T_i} a_{i,i+1}$. For Matrix B, uniform values are assigned to b_{ij}. The HMM initialized in this way is put through the Baum-Welch estimation to obtain ML HMM, and MSD estimation to obtain MSD HMMs, respectively.

For each viseme category, a number of MSD HMMs are trained to differentiate the confusable visemes in the category. In Category 1, for example, there are 6 MSD HMMs named $\theta_{1,2}$, $\theta_{1,3}$, $\theta_{2,1}$, $\theta_{2,3}$, $\theta_{3,1}$, and $\theta_{3,2}$, where $\theta_{1,2}$ is the MSD HMM with the training samples of /p/ being the true samples and the training samples of /m/ being the false samples.

Experimental Results

The average separable distance, which is computed using Eqn.(32), changes during the MSD estimation. In most cases, the separable distance increases rapidly at first and then slowly with increasing training cycles. Early termination may happen when the state duration condition mentioned in Step 4 (Section 3.1) is violated. These phenomena will be discussed later in Section 4.4.2.

The separable distances measured for the testing samples of Category 1 by the ML HMMs and the corresponding MSD HMMs are depicted in Table 3. Note that "/p/ vs /m/" indicates that the ML HMM is trained using the samples of /p/, and the MSD HMM is trained using both the samples of /p/ (as true samples) and those of /m/ (as false samples). It is seen that the separable distances obtained by the MSD HMMs are much larger than those scored by the ML HMMs. Thus the MSD HMMs is better able to tell apart the true viseme out of the confusable false visemes than the ML HMMs.

For each viseme category, the MSD HMMs are paired as in Fig. 1 and the decision strategy described in Section 3.3 is adopted. The labeled testing samples of each viseme are identified by ML HMMs and MSD HMMs, respectively. As an example, 50×3=150 testing samples in Category 1 are recognized within a closed set of 3 visemes. For the ML HMMs, a correct classification is made for a labeled sample if its corresponding HMM scores higher probability than other HMMs; and for the MSD HMMs, a correct classification is made if the final winning class matches the label of the sample. The classification rates computed in this way are illustrated in Table 4.

It can be observed from Table 4 that the MSD HMMs can better classify the selected visemes than the ML HMMs. The average improvement on classification rate is approximately 20%. Based on this significant difference in classification rate, it may be concluded that the MSD estimation is able to improve the discriminative ability of HMM in identifying confusable visemes.

Table 3. The separable distances between viseme samples of viseme category 1

	Separable distance (*true samples* vs *false samples*)					
	/p/ vs /m/	/p/ vs /b /	/m/ vs /p/	/m/ vs /b/	/b/ vs /p/	/b/ vs /m/
ML HMM	2.55	2.10	0.89	1.06	1.32	2.44
MSD HMM	7.12	4.47	2.11	3. 07	4.01	4.32

Table 4. Classification rates of the viseme samples of the 6 categories

	Category 1	Category 6	Category 10	Category 12	Category 13	Category 14
ML HMMs	41%	34%	49%	54%	78%	75%
MSD HMMs	62%	63%	68%	80%	88%	85%

TWO-CHANNEL HMM CLASSIFIER

Structure

The MSD training method mentioned in Section 3 may guarantee a good separable distance between true samples and false samples. However, the scored probability for a true sample, say $P(x^T|\theta)$, may be small. This is due to the fact that maximization of $P(x^T|\theta)$ is not considered in the training process given in Section 3.1. To apply the separable distance criterion function to ensure good discriminative power and at the same time, to guarantee a high probability of the true sample given the target HMM, a Two-channel HMM structure and training method are proposed in this section.

The block diagram of the Two-channel HMM is given in Fig. 2. It consists of a static-channel HMM and a dynamic-channel HMM. For the static-channel, a parameter-smoothed ML HMM is used and kept unchanged during the training process. For the dynamic-channel HMM, to maintain synchronization of the duration and transition of states, the same set of values for π and A as derived for the static-channel HMM is used, only the parameters of Matrix B of this channel are adjusted to maximize the separable distance as according to Eqn.(22).

The elements (b_{ij}) of Matrix B of the Two-channel HMM are decomposed into two parts as

$$b_{ij} = b_{ij}^{s} + b_{ij}^{d} \qquad \forall i = 1,2,\cdots,N,\ j = 1,2,\cdots,M \tag{35}$$

b_j^s for the static-channel and b_j^d for the dynamic-channel. The dynamic-channel coefficients b_j^d are the key source of the discriminative power. b_j^s s are computed using parameter-smoothed ML HMM and weighted. As long as b_{ij} computed from Eqn.(22) to maximize separable distance is greater than b_j^s, b_j^d is determined as the difference between b_{ij} and b_j^s according to Eqn.(35), otherwise b_j^d is set to be 0.

To avoid the occurrence of zero or negative probability, b_j^s ($\forall i = 1, 2, \cdots, N, \forall j = 1, 2, \cdots, M$) should be kept greater than 0 in the training procedure and at the same time, the dynamic-channel coef-

Figure 2. Block diagram of a Two-channel HMM

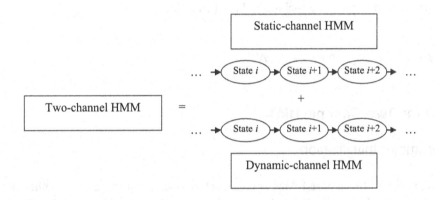

Figure 3. The two-channel structure of the i-th state of a left-right HMM

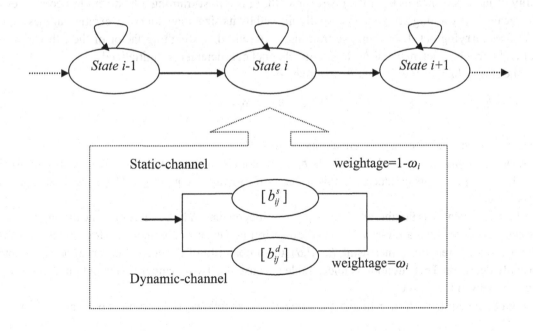

ficient b_{ij}^d ($\forall i = 1,2,\cdots,N, \forall j = 1,2,\cdots,M$) should be non-negative. Thus the probability constraint $b_{ij} = b_j^s + b_j^d \geq b_j^s > 0$ is met.

In addition, the relative weightage of the static-channel and the dynamic-channel may be controlled by the credibility weighing factor ω_i ($i=1,2,\ldots N$) (different states may have different values). If the weightage of the dynamic-channel is set to be ω_i by scaling of the coefficients,

$$\sum_{j=1}^{N} b_{ij}^d = \omega_i \quad 0 \leq \omega_i < 1 \quad \forall i = 1,2,\cdots,N$$

(36)

then the weightage of the static-channel has to be set as follows.

$$\sum_{j=1}^{N} b_{ij}^s = 1 - \omega_i \quad 0 \leq \omega_i < 1 \quad \forall i = 1,2,\cdots,N$$

(37)

Training of the Two-Channel HMM

Step 1: Parameter Initialization

For the Two-channel HMM, a base HMM is constructed using the parameter-smoothed ML HMM of x^T, $\tilde{\theta}_{ML}^x$, which is trained using the Baum-Welch estimation. The static-channel HMM is derived from the base HMM after applying the scaling factor. Parameter smoothing is carried out for $\tilde{\theta}_{ML}^x$ to prevent the occurrence of zero probability. Parameter smoothing is the simple management that b_{ij} is set to some minimum value, e.g. $\varepsilon=10^{-3}$, if the estimated conditional probability $\tilde{b}_{ij} = 0$ (Rabiner, 1989, Rabiner, 1993). As a result, even though symbol O_j never appears in the training set, there is still a non-zero probability of its occurrence in $\tilde{\theta}_{ML}^x$. Parameter smoothing is a post-training adjustment to decrease error rate because the training set, which is usually limited by its size, may not cover erratic samples.

Before carrying out discriminative training, ω_i (credibility weighing factor of the i-th state), b_j^s (static-channel coefficients) and b_j^d (dynamic-channel coefficients) are initialized.

The static-channel coefficients b_j^s are given by

$$\{b_{i1}^s \ b_{i2}^s \cdots b_{iM}^s\} = (1-\omega_i)\{\tilde{b}_{i1} \ \tilde{b}_{i2} \cdots \tilde{b}_{iM}\} \quad 1 \leq i \leq N, 0 \leq \omega_i < 1$$

(38)

where $\tilde{b}_{ij}$ is the symbol emission probability of $\tilde{\theta}_{ML}^x$.

As for the dynamic-channel coefficients b_j^d, a random or uniform initial distribution usually works well. In the experiments conducted in this paper, uniform values equal to ω_i/M are assigned to b_j^ds as initial values.

The selection of ω_i is flexible and largely problem-dependent. A large value of ω_i means large weightage is assigned to the dynamic-channel and the discriminative power is enhanced. However, as we adjust b_j^d toward the direction of increasing $I(x^T,y^T,\theta)$, the probability of the correct observation $P(x^T|\theta)$ will normally decrease. This situation is undesirable because the Two-channel HMM obtained is unlikely to generate even the correct samples.

A guideline for the determination of the value of ω_i is as follows. If the training pairs are very similar to each other such that $P(x^T | \widetilde{\theta}_{ML}^x) \approx P(y^T | \widetilde{\theta}_{ML}^x)$, ω_i should be set to a large value to guarantee good discrimination; on the other hand, if $P(x^T | \widetilde{\theta}_{ML}^x) >> P(y^T | \widetilde{\theta}_{ML}^x)$, ω_i should be set to a small value to make $P(x^T|\theta)$ reasonably large. In addition, different values shall be used for different states because they contribute differently to the scored probabilities. However, the values of ω_i for the different states should not differ greatly.

Based on the above considerations, the following procedures are taken to determine ω_i. Given the base HMM $\widetilde{\theta}_{ML}^x$ and the training pair x^T and y^T, the optimal state chains are searched using the Viterbi algorithm. Let $P(x^T, s^T | \widetilde{\theta}_{ML}^x)$ denote the probability of generating the optimal state chain s^T and the training sample x^T. If $\widetilde{\theta}_{ML}^x$ is a left-right model and the expected (optimal) duration of the i-th state ($i=1,2,\ldots,N$) of x^T is from t_i to $t_i+\tau_i$, $P(x^T, s^T | \widetilde{\theta}_{ML}^x)$ can then be written as the product of the segments of the state chain as follows.

$$P(x^T, s^T | \widetilde{\theta}_{ML}^x) = P(x_{t_1}^T, \cdots, x_{t_1+\tau_1}^T, S_1 | \widetilde{\theta}_{ML}^x) P(x_{t_2}^T, \cdots, x_{t_2+\tau_2}^T, S_2 | \widetilde{\theta}_{ML}^x) \cdots P(x_{t_N}^T, \cdots, x_{t_N+\tau_N}^T, S_N | \widetilde{\theta}_{ML}^x) \quad (39)$$

$P(y^T, s^T | \widetilde{\theta}_{ML}^x)$ is decomposed in the same way.

Let $P_{dur}(x^T, S_i | \widetilde{\theta}_{ML}^x) = P(x_{t_i}^T, \cdots, x_{t_i+\tau_i}^T, S_i | \widetilde{\theta}_{ML}^x)$, which indicates the probability of generating a segment of observation symbols within the duration $[t_i, t_i+\tau_i]$ and the state being S_i. This probability may be computed as follows.

$$P_{dur}(x^T, S_i | \widetilde{\theta}_{ML}^x) = \prod_{t=t_i}^{t_i+\tau_i} [P(s_t^T = S_j) b_j(x_t^T)]$$

$$(40)$$

$P_{dur}(x^T, S_i | \widetilde{\theta}_{ML}^x)$ may also be computed using the forward variables

$$\alpha_t^x(i) = P(x_{t_i+1}^T, \cdots, x_{t_i+t}^T, s_{t_i+t}^T = S_i | \widetilde{\theta}_{ML}^x)$$

or/and the backward variables

$$\beta_t^x(i) = P(x_{t_i+t+1}^T, \cdots, x_{t_i+\tau_i+1}^T | s_{t_i+t}^T = S_i, \widetilde{\theta}_{ML}^x).$$

However, if $\widetilde{\theta}_{ML}^x$ is not a left-right model but an ergodic model, the expected duration of a state will consist of a number of separated time slices, for example, k slices such as t_{i1} to $t_{i1}+\tau_{i1}$, t_{i2} to $t_{i1}+\tau_{i2}$ and t_{ik} to $t_{ik}+\tau_{ik}$. $P_{dur}(x^T, S_i | \widetilde{\theta}_{ML}^x)$ is then computed by multiplying them together as shown in the equation below.

$$P_{dur}(x^T, S_i | \widetilde{\theta}_{ML}^x) = P(x_{t_{i1}}^T, \cdots, x_{t_{i1}+\tau_{i1}}^T, S_i | \widetilde{\theta}_{ML}^x) P(x_{t_{i2}}^T, \cdots, x_{t_{i2}+\tau_{i2}}^T, S_i | \widetilde{\theta}_{ML}^x)$$

$$\cdots P(x_{t_{ik}}^T, \cdots, x_{t_{ik}+\tau_{ik}}^T, S_i | \widetilde{\theta}_{ML}^x) \quad (41)$$

The value of ω_i is derived by comparing the corresponding $P_{dur}(x^T, S_i | \widetilde{\theta}_{ML}^x)$ and $P_{dur}(y^T, S_i | \widetilde{\theta}_{ML}^x)$. If $P_{dur}(x^T, S_i | \widetilde{\theta}_{ML}^x) >> P_{dur}(y^T, S_i | \widetilde{\theta}_{ML}^x)$, this indicates that the coefficients of the i-th state of the base model are good enough for discrimination, ω_i should be set to a small value to preserve the original ML configurations. If $P_{dur}(x^T, S_i | \widetilde{\theta}_{ML}^x) < P_{dur}(y^T, S_i | \widetilde{\theta}_{ML}^x)$ or $P_{dur}(x^T, S_i | \widetilde{\theta}_{ML}^x) \approx P_{dur}(y^T, S_i | \widetilde{\theta}_{ML}^x)$, this indicates that State S_i is not able to distinguish between x^T and y^T, ω_i must be set to a value large enough to ensure $P_{dur}(x^T, S_i | \widetilde{\theta}) > P_{dur}(y^T, S_i | \widetilde{\theta})$, where $\widetilde{\theta}$ is the two channel HMM. In practice, ω_i can be manually selected according to the conditions mentioned above, or they can be computed using the following expression.

$$\omega_i = \frac{1}{1 + Cv^D} \tag{42}$$

where

$$v = \frac{P_{dur}(x^T, S_i | \widetilde{\theta}_{ML}^x)}{P_{dur}(y^T, S_i | \widetilde{\theta}_{ML}^x)}.$$

C ($C > 0$) and D are constants that jointly control the smoothness of ω_i with respect to v. Since $C > 0$ and $v > 0$, $\omega_i < 1$, by using suitable values of C and D, a set of credibility factors ω_i are computed for the states of the target HMM. For example, if the range of v is $10^{-3} \sim 10^5$, a typical setting is $C = 1.0$ and $D = 0.1$.

Once the values of ω_i ($i = 1, 2, ..., N$) are determined, they shall not be changed in the training process.

Step 2: Partition of the Observation Symbol Set

Let θ denote the HMM with the above initial configurations, the coefficients of the dynamic-channel are adjusted according to the following procedures. First, $E(S_i, O_j | \theta, x^T)$ and $E(S_i, O_j | \theta, y^T)$ are computed through the counting process as described in Section 3.1, Step 2.

It is shown in Eqn.(22) that to maximize $I(x^T, y^T, \theta)$, b_{ij} should be set proportional to $D_{ij}(x^T, y^T, \theta)$. However, for certain symbols, e.g. O_p, the expectation $D_{ip}(x^T, y^T, \theta)$ may be less than 0. Since the symbol emission coefficients cannot take negative values, these symbols have to be specially treated. For this reason, the symbol set $O^M = \{O_1, O_2, ..., O_M\}$ is partitioned into the subset $V = \{V_1, V_2, ..., V_K\}$ and its complement set $U = \{U_1, U_2, ..., U_{M-K}\}$ ($O^M = U \cup V$) according to the following criterion.

$$\{V_1, V_2, \cdots, V_K\} = \arg_{O_j}[\frac{E(S_i, O_j | \theta, x^T)}{E(S_i, O_j | \theta, y^T)} > \eta] \qquad (\eta \geq 1) \tag{43}$$

where η is the threshold with a typical value of 1. η shall be set to a larger value if it is required that the set V shall contain fewer dominant symbols. With $\eta \geq 1$, $E(S_i, V_j | \theta, x^T) - E(S_i, V_j | \theta, y^T) > 0$. As an illustration, the distributions of the values of $E(S_i, V_j | \theta, x^T)$ and $E(S_i, V_j | \theta, y^T)$ for different symbol labels are shown in Fig. 4a. The filtered symbols in set V when η is set 1 are shown in Fig. 4b.

Figure 4. (a) Distributions of $E(S_i, V_j | \theta, x^T)$ and $E(S_i, V_j | \theta, y^T)$ for all symbols. (b) Distribution of $E(S_i, V_j | \theta, x^T)$ for the symbols in V

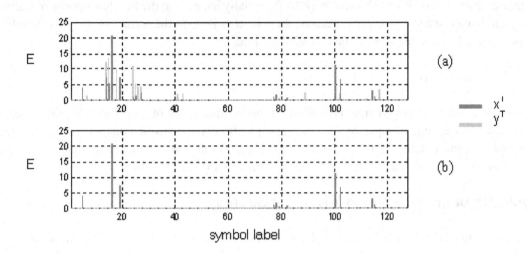

Step 3: Modification to the Dynamic-Channel

For each state, the symbol set is partitioned according to the procedures described in the previous section. As an example, consider the i-th state, for symbols in the set U, the symbol emission coefficient $b_i(U_j)$ ($U_j \in U$) should be set as small as possible. Let $b_i^d(U_j) = 0$, and so $b_i(U_j) = b_i^s(U_j)$. For symbols in the set V, the corresponding dynamic-channel coefficient $b_i^d(V_k)$ is computed according to the following expression, which is derived from Eqn.(22).

$$b_i^d(V_k) = P_D(S_i, V_k, x^T, y^T)(\omega_i + \sum_{j=1}^{K} b_i^s(V_j)) - b_i^s(V_k) \qquad k = 1, 2, \cdots, K$$

(44)

where

$$P_D(S_i, V_k, x^T, y^T) = \frac{E(S_i, V_k | \theta, x^T) - E(S_i, V_k | \theta, y^T)}{\sum_{j=1}^{K} [E(S_i, V_j | \theta, x^T) - E(S_i, V_j | \theta, y^T)]}$$

However, some coefficients obtained may still be negative, e.g. $b_i^d(V_l) < 0$ because of large value of $b_i^s(V_l)$. In which case, it indicates that $b_i^s(V_l)$ alone is large enough for separation. To prevent negative values appearing in the dynamic-channel, the symbol V_l is transferred from V to U and $b_i^d(V_l)$ is set to 0. The coefficients of the remaining symbols in V are re-estimated using Eqn.(44) until all $b_i^d(V_k)$s are greater than 0. This situation (some $b_i^d(V_l)<0$) usually happens at the first few epochs of training and it is not conducive to convergence because there is steep jump in the surface of $I(x^T,y^T,\theta)$. To relieve this problem, a larger value of η in Eqn.(43) shall be used.

Step 4: Termination

Optimization is done through iteratively calling of the training epoch of Step 2 and Step 3 mentioned above. After each epoch, the separable-distance $I(x^T,y^T,\tilde\theta)$ of the HMM $\tilde\theta$ obtained, is calculated and compared with that obtained in the last epoch. If $I(x^T,y^T,\tilde\theta)$ does not change more than a predefined value, training is terminated and the target Two-channel HMM is established.

Properties of the Two-Channel Training Strategy

The Two-channel HMM is a bit more complicated than the MSD HMM in terms of the model structure and training implementations, and in turn brings additional computations. However, the Two-channel method has some advantages over the MSD method. First, it enables weighing of static channel, dynamic channel, and even the individual states, which allows much flexibility of tuning between discriminative power and modeling accuracy of an HMM. Second, the adjustment of symbol output coefficients can be confined to a few dominant distinguishable features or be extended to a wider range of non-dominant distinguishable features (see Step 2 in Section 4.2). Such management may balance the computation load and the goodness of the modeling of the distinguishable features.

State Alignment

Similar to MSD training as mentioned in Section 3.1 (Step 4), the Two-channel training strategy also requires the state durations of the training pair, say x^T and y^T, are comparable. For this purpose, the state durations, $E(S_i|\theta,x^T)$ and $E(S_i|\theta,y^T)$ are first computed as in Eqn.(29). Based on which, the training process has to terminate prematurely if the condition given in Eqn.(30) is not met. In this case, If $I(x^T,y^T,\tilde\theta)$ of the final HMM $\tilde\theta$ does not meet certain discriminative requirement, e.g. $I(x^T,y^T,\tilde\theta)$ is less than a desired value, a new base HMM or smaller ω_i should be used instead.

Speed of Convergence

As discussed in the Section 2.2, the convergence of the parameter-estimation strategy proposed in Eqn.(22) is guaranteed according to the EM optimization principles. In the implementation of discriminative training, only some of the symbol emission coefficients in the dynamic-channel are modified according to Eqn.(22) while the others remain unchanged. However, the convergence is still assured because firstly the surface of $I(x^T,y^T,\theta)$ with respect to b_{ij} is continuous, and also adjusting the dynamic-channel elements according to the Two-channel training strategy leads to increased $E_\theta(I)$. A conceptual illustration is given in Fig.5 on how b_{ij} is modified when the symbol set is divided into subsets V and U. For ease of explanation, we assume that the symbol set contains only three symbols O_1, O_2 and O_3

with $O_1, O_2 \in V$ and $O_3 \in U$ for State S_i. Let θ_t denote the HMM trained at the t-th round and θ_{t+1} denote the HMM obtained at the $t+1$-th round. The surface of the separable-distance (I surface) is denoted as $I'=I(x^T, y^T, \theta_{t+1})$ for θ_{t+1} and $I=I(x^T, y^T, \theta_t)$ for θ_t. Clearly $I' > I$. The I surface is mapped to b_{i1}-b_{i2} plane (Fig.5a) and b_{i1}-b_{i3} plane (Fig.5b). In the training phase, b_{i1} and b_{i2} are modified along the line $b_{i1}^d + b_{i2}^d = \omega_i$ to reach a better estimation θ_{t+1}, which is shown in Fig.5a. In the b_{i1}-b_{i3} plane, b_{i3} is set to the constant b_{i3}^s while b_{i1} is modified along the line $b_{i3} = b_{i3}^s$ with the direction $\vec{d}$ as shown in Fig.5b. The direction of parameter adjustment given by Eqn.(22) is denoted by $\vec{d}'$. In the Two-channel approach, since only b_{i1} and b_{i2} are modified according to Eqn.(22) while b_{i3} remains unchanged, $\vec{d}$ may lead to lower speed of convergence than $\vec{d}'$ does.

Measure of Improvement of the Discriminative Power

The improvement to the discriminative power may be estimated as follows. Assume that $\tilde{\theta}$ is the Two-channel HMM obtained. The lower bound of the probability $P(y^T \mid \tilde{\theta})$ is given by

$$P(y^T \mid \tilde{\theta}) \geq (1 - \omega_{max})^T P(y^T \mid \tilde{\theta}_{ML}^x) \qquad (45)$$

where $\omega_{max} = \max(\omega_1, \omega_2, \ldots \omega_N)$.

Because the base HMM is the parameter-smoothed ML HMM of x^T, it is reasonable to assume that $P(x^T \mid \tilde{\theta}_{ML}^x) \geq P(x^T \mid \tilde{\theta})$. The upper bound of the separable-distance is given by the following expression

Figure 5. The surface of I and the direction of parameter adjustment

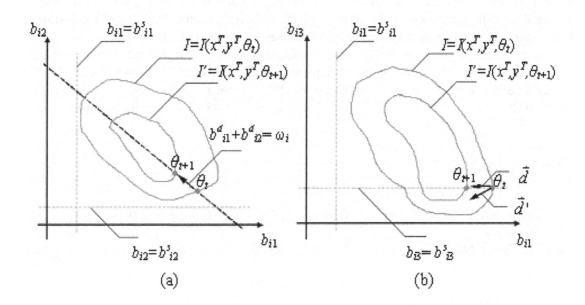

(a)   (b)

$$I(x^T, y^T, \tilde{\theta}) \le \log \frac{P(x^T | \tilde{\theta}_{ML}^x)}{(1 - \omega_{max})^T P(y^T | \tilde{\theta}_{ML}^x)} = -T \log(1 - \omega_{max}) + I(x^T, y^T, \tilde{\theta}_{ML}^x)$$

(46)

In practice, the gain of $I(x^T, y^T, \tilde{\theta})$ is much smaller than the theoretical upper bound. It depends on the resemblance between x^T and y^T, and the setting of ω_i.

Extensions of the Two-Channel Training Algorithm

The Two-channel training strategy is ready to be extended to the cases where the training samples are of different lengths. Similar to the MSD training extensions mentioned in Section 3.2, linear adjustment as given in Eqn.(31) can be carried out. For multiple training samples, the clustered separable distance may be computed via Eqn.(32) and the probability coefficients are estimated using Eqn.(33).

Application of Two-Channel HMM to Viseme Recognition

The 18 visemes described in Section3.4.1 are used to validate the performance of the Two-channel HMMs. As stated earlier, some visemes are so similar with each other that they are clustered into one viseme category in MPEG-4. Therefore, they are good for verifying the discriminative power of the viseme classifiers. Besides, the visemes of different viseme categories are different and can be identified by traditional means, say ML HMMs. This well fits the structure of the viseme classifier and decision strategy that to be discussed in the following section.

Viseme Classifier

The block diagram of a hierarchical viseme classifier is given in Fig.6. In Layer 1, ML HMMs are used for coarse classification and Two-channel HMMs are employed in Layer 2 for fine classification, two visemes at a time. For visemes that are too similar to be separated by the normal ML HMMs, they are clustered into one macro class. In the figure, θ_{Mac1}, θ_{Mac2}, ..., θ_{MacR} are the R number of ML HMMs for the R macro classes. The similarity between the visemes is measured as follows.

Assume that $X_i = \{x_1^i, x_2^i, \cdots, x_{l_i}^i : d_i\}$ is the training samples of viseme d_i (i=1,2,..., N, as N visemes are involved), where x_j^i is the j-th training sample and l_i is the number of the samples. An ML HMM is trained for each of the N visemes using the Baum-Welch estimation. Let $\theta_1, \theta_2, ..., \theta_N$ denote the N number of ML HMMs. For $\{x_1^i, x_2^i, \cdots, x_{l_i}^i : d_i\}$, the joint probability scored by θ_j is computed as follows.

$$P(X_i | \theta_j) = \prod_{n=1}^{l_i} P(x_n^i | \theta_j)$$

(47)

A viseme model θ_i is able to separate visemes d_i and d_j if the following condition applies,

$$\log P(X_i | \theta_i) - \log P(X_i | \theta_j) \ge \rho \qquad \forall j = 1, 2, \cdots, N, j \ne i$$

(48)

where ρ is a positive constant that is set according to the length of the training samples. For long training samples, large value of ρ is desired. For the 25-length samples adopted in our experiments, ρ is set to be equal to 2. If the condition stated in Eqn.(48) is not met, visemes d_i and d_j are categorized into the same macro class. The training samples of d_i and d_j are jointly used to train the ML HMM of the macro class. θ_{Mac1}, θ_{Mac2}, ..., θ_{MacR} are obtained in this way.

For an input viseme z^T to be identified, the probabilities $P(z^T|\theta_{Mac1})$, $P(z^T|\theta_{Mac2})$,..., $P(z^T|\theta_{MacR})$ are computed and compared with one another. The macro identity of z^T is determined by the HMM that gives the largest probability.

A macro class may consist of several similar visemes. Fine recognition within a macro class is carried out at the second layer using Two-channel HMMs. Assume that Macro Class i comprises L visemes: V_1, V_2,..., V_L. $L(L-1)$ number of Two-channel HMMs are trained to separate each pair of the visemes. We shall denote these Two-channel HMMs by $\theta_{j,k}$ ($j,k=1,2,...,L, j\neq k$) as shown in Fig.6. Take $\theta_{1,2}$ as an example, the parameter-smoothed ML HMM of V_1 is adopted as the base HMM for $\theta_{1,2}$; the samples of V_1 being the true class and the samples of V_2 being the false class.

Figure 6. Flow chart of the hierarchical viseme classifier

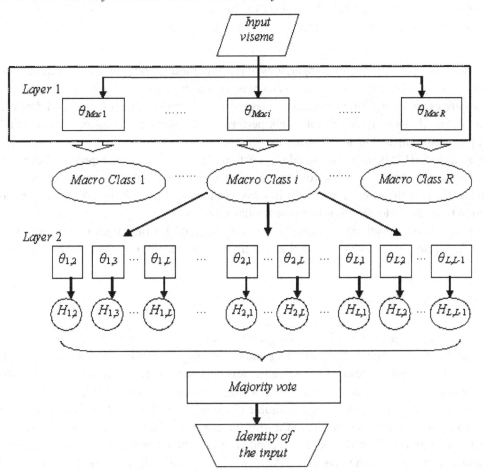

For an input viseme z^T to be identified, the following hypothesis is made,

$$H_{i,j} = \begin{cases} i & \text{if} \quad \log P(z^T|\theta_{i,j}) - \log P(z^T|\theta_{j,i}) > \rho \\ 0 & \text{otherwise} \end{cases} \quad (49)$$

Where ρ is the positive constant as defined in Eqn.(48) and $\rho=2$ here. $H_{i,j}=i$ indicates a vote for V_i. The decision about the identity of z^T is made by majority vote of all the Two-channel HMMs. The viseme class that has the maximum number of votes is chosen as the identity of z^T, denoted by $ID(z^T)$. Mathematically,

$$ID(z^T) = \max_i [\text{Number of } H_{i,j} = i] \qquad \forall i, j = 1,2,\cdots L, i \neq j \quad (50)$$

If two viseme classes, say V_i and V_j, receive the same number of votes, the decision about the identity of z^T is made by comparing $P(z^T|\theta_{i,j})$ and $P(z^T|\theta_{j,i})$. Mathematically,

$$ID(z^T) = \begin{cases} i & \text{if} \quad \log P(z^T|\theta_{i,j}) > \log P(z^T|\theta_{j,i}) \\ j & \text{otherwise} \end{cases} \quad (51)$$

The decision is based on pairwise comparisons of the hypotheses. The proposed hierarchical structure greatly reduces the computational load and increases the accuracy of recognition because pairwise comparisons are carried out within each macro class, which comprises much fewer candidate classes than the entire set. If coarse identification is not performed, the number of classes increases and the number of pairwise comparisons goes up rapidly.

The Two-channel HMMs act as the boundary functions for the viseme they represent. Each of them serves to separate the correct samples from the samples of another viseme. A conceptual illustration is given in Fig. 7 where the macro class comprises five visemes V_1, V_2, ..., V_5. $\theta_{1,2}$, $\theta_{1,3}$, ..., $\theta_{1,5}$ build the decision boundaries for V_1 to delimit it from the similar visemes.

The proposed Two-channel HMM model is specially tailored for the target viseme and its "surroundings". As a result, it is more accurate than the traditional modeling method that uses single ML HMM.

Performance of the System

As for experiments described in Section 3.4.1, of the 100 samples of a viseme, 50 are used for training and the remaining 50 for testing. By computing and comparing the probabilities scored by different viseme models using Eqns.(47) and (48), the visemes are clustered into 6 macro classes as presented in Table 8. Note that the clustering is the same as the MPEG-4 categorization in Table 2.

The results of fine recognition of some confusable visemes are listed in Table 6. Each row in Table 6 shows the two similar visemes that belong to the same macro class. The first viseme label (in boldface) is the target viseme and is denoted by x. The second viseme is the incorrect viseme and is denoted by y. $\tilde{\theta}_{ML}^x$ denotes the parameter-smoothed ML HMMs that are trained with the samples of x. With $\tilde{\theta}_{ML}^x$

Figure 7. Viseme boundaries formed by the Two-channel HMMs

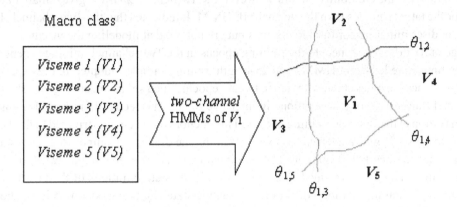

being the base HMM, two Two-channel HMMs: θ_1 and θ_2 are trained with the samples of x being the target training samples and the samples of y being the incorrect training samples. Different sets of the credibility factors (ω_1, ω_2, ω_3 for the three states) are used for θ_1 and θ_2. $\overline{P}$ is the average log probability scored for the testing samples and is computed as in Eqn.(52) below.

$$\overline{P} = \frac{1}{l}\sum_{i=1}^{l} \log P(x_i \mid \theta)$$

(52)

where x_i is the i-th testing sample of viseme x and l is the number of the testing samples. The average separable-distance is defined as follows.

$$\overline{I} = \frac{1}{l^2}\sum_{i=1}^{l}\sum_{j=1}^{l} I(x_i, y_j, \theta)$$

(53)

The value of $\overline{I}$ gives an indication of the discriminative power, the larger the value of $\overline{I}$, the higher the discriminative power.

For all settings of (ω_1, ω_2, ω_3), the Two-channel HMMs give a much larger separable-distance than the ML HMMs. It shows that better discrimination capabilities are attained using the Two-channel

Table 5. The macro classes for coarse identification

Macro class	Visemes	Macro class	Visemes
1	/a:/, /ai/, /æ/	4	/o/, /oi/
2	/ei/, /i/, /j/, /ie/	5	/th/, /sh/, /tZ/, /dZ/
3	/eu/, /au/	6	/p/, /m/, /b/

viseme classifiers than using the ML HMM classifiers. In addition, different levels of capabilities can be attained by adjusting the credibility factors. However, the Two-channel HMM gives smaller average probability for the target samples than the normal ML HMM. It indicates that the Two-channel HMMs perform well at discriminating confusable visemes but are not good at modeling the visemes.

The change of $I(x,y,\theta)$ with respect to the training epochs in the Two-channel training is depicted in Fig.8. For the three-state left-right HMMs and 25-length training samples adopted in the experiment, the separable-distance becomes stable after ten to twenty epochs. Such speed of convergence shows that the Two-channel training is not computationally intensive for viseme recognition. It is also observed that $I(x,y,\theta)$ may drop at the first few training epochs. This phenomenon can be attributed to the fact that some symbols in subset V are transferred to U while training the dynamic-channel coefficients. Fig.8d illustrates the situation of early termination. The training process stops even though $I(x,y,\theta)$ still shows the tendency of increasing. As explained in Section 4.3.1, if the state durations of the target training samples and incorrect training samples differ greatly, i.e. the state alignment condition is violated, the Two-channel training should terminate immediately. As for the MSD HMM mentioned in Section 3.4.2, the separable distance shows the same trend of increasing and early termination as shown in Fig.8.

The performance of the proposed hierarchical system is compared with that of the conventional recognition system where ML HMMs (parameter-smoothed) are used as the viseme classifiers. The False Rejection Error rates (FRR) or Type II error of the two types of viseme classifiers are computed for the 50 testing samples of each of the 18 visemes. It is found that 6 of the 18 visemes can be accurately identified by both the ML HMMs with FRRs less than 10%. The improvement resulting from the Two-channel training approach is not prominent for these visemes. As a result, only the FRRs of the remaining 12 confusable visemes are listed in Table 7.

Table 6. The average values of probability P and separable-distance I

Viseme pair		ML HMM $\widetilde{\theta}_{ML}^x$		Two-channel HMM θ_1		Two-channel HMM θ_2				
x	y	$\overline{P}$	$\overline{I}$	$\overline{P}$	$\overline{I}$	$\overline{P}$	$\overline{I}$	ω_1	ω_2	ω_3
/a:/	/ai/	-14.1	1.196	-17.1	5.571	-18.3	6.589	0.5	0.5	0.5
/ei/	/i/	-14.7	2.162	-19.3	5.977	-20.9	7.008	0.6	0.8	0.6
/au/	/eu/	-15.6	2.990	-18.1	5.872	-18.5	6.555	0.6	0.5	0.6
/o/	/oi/	-13.9	0.830	-17.5	2.508	-18.7	3.296	0.5	0.5	0.5
/th/	/sh/	-15.7	0.602	-19.0	2.809	-18.5	2.732	0.4	0.4	0.4
/p/	/m/	-16.3	1.144	-19.0	3.102	-17.1	2.233	0.4	0.5	0.4

(For θ_1, ω_1, ω_2 and ω_3 are set according to Eqn.(42), with C =1.0 and D =0.1. For θ_2, ω_1, ω_2 and ω_3 are manually selected.)

Compared with the conventional ML HMM classifier, the classification error of the proposed hierarchical viseme classifier is reduced by about 20%. Thus the Two-channel training algorithm is able to increase the discriminative ability of HMM significantly for identifying confusing visemes.

CONCLUSION

In this chapter, two HMM based methods are presented. The MSD estimation and Two-channel training strategy proposed are both discriminative training methods of HMM as they amplify the minor

Table 7. Classification errors ε_1 of the ML HMM and ε_2 of the Two-channel HMM

Viseme	ε_1	ε_2	Viseme	ε_1	ε_2
/a:/	64%	12%	/o/	46%	28%
/ai/	60%	40%	/oi/	36%	8%
/ei/	46%	22%	/th/	18%	16%
/i/	52%	32%	/sh/	20%	12%
/au/	30%	18%	/p/	36%	12%
/eu/	26%	16%	/m/	32%	32%

Figure 8. Change of I(x, y, θ) during the training process

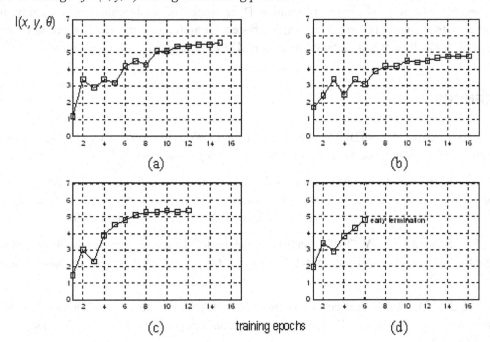

difference between a pair of confusable training samples. Experimental results indicate that by using these methods, the classification accuracy of confusable visemes is improved by about 20% over the traditional method.

For the implementation of the two training strategies, the Two-channel HMM employs a ML HMM as its static channel to guarantee a high probability of the true samples, and updates its dynamic channel for higher separable distance for better discrimination. The MSD HMM, on the other hand, can be more easily implemented as the requirement on the base model is not stringent, and the parameter estimation is based on some simple manipulations to the criterion function.

The MSD HMM and Two-channel HMM are specially designed for discerning minor difference between two classes. As a result, they are not good at dealing with variations of a class. That is why they are not fit for identifying context-dependent visemes. In applications, both classifiers should be used within a closed set of a few confusable classes, or in conjunction with other classifiers for fine recognition after coarse recognition is done. To cope with the variations of the classes, and especially the context-dependent samples of the same visemes, another training method such as AdaBoost HMM described in the previous chapter may be adopted.

FUTURE RESEARCH DIRECTION

Ventriloquists can speak with the mouth virtually closed. Some speakers do not have conspicuous mouth movement, especially for the consonant sounds. So it is a challenge to have a speaker dependent lip-reading system.

The speech information conveyed by the movement of the lips is far less than that of the acoustic signals. As a result, it is not feasible to develop a reliable speech recognition system based solely on this visual aspect of speech. Incorporation of audio recognition engine to the visual speech processing system is necessary for accurate speech recognition. Development of good techniques to integrate audio and visual aspects of speech in speech recognition systems is an important research direction. The application of phonetic, lexical and semantic rules to HMM modeling may also be explored.

REFERENCES

Baum, L. E., & Eagon, J. A. (1967). An inequality with applications to statistical estimation for probabilistic functions of Markov processes and to a model for ecology. *Bull. Amer. Math. Soc., 73*, 360-363.

Dong, L., Foo, S. W., & Lian, Y. (2005). A Two-channel training algorithm for Hidden Markov Model and its application to lip-reading. *EURASIP Journal on Applied Signal Processing, Special issue on Anthropomorphic Processing of Audio and Speech, 2005, No. 9*, 1382-1399,June,2005

Dong, L., Foo, S. W., & Lian, Y. (2005). Maximum Separable Distance estimation for Hidden Markov Model and the Application to Visual Speech Processing. *GESTS International Trans. Speech Science and Engineering, 2(1)*.

Foo, S. W., & Dong, L. (2002). A supervised Two-channel learning method for Hidden Markov Model and application to lip-reading. *IEEE Int. Conf. on Advanced Learning Technologies*, 334-338.

Foo, S. W., Lian, Y., & Dong, L. (2003). A Two-channel training algorithm for hidden Markov model to identify visual speech elements. *Int. Symposium on Circuits and Systems (ISCAS '03), 2,* 572-575.

McLanchlan, G. J., & Krishnan, T.(1997). *The EM Algorithm and Extensions.* Wiley Series in Probability and Statistics, John Wiley and Sons.

Rabiner, L. R., & Juang, B. H. (1993). *Fundamentals of speech recognition.* Prentice Hall International Inc. Signal Processing Series.

Tanner, M. A. (1996).*Tools for statistical inference: methods for the exploration of posterior distributions and likelihood functions.* Springer series in statistics,New York.

Tekalp, A. M., & Ostermann, J. (2000). Face and 2-D mesh animation in MPEG-4. *Signal Processing: Image Communication,Special Issue on MPEG-4, 15,387-421.*

ADDITIONAL READINGS

Baker, J. K. (1975). The Dragon System – An Overview. *IEEE Trans. on Acoustics,speech and Signal Processing, 23,* 24-29.

Baum, L. E. (1972). An inequality and associated maximization technique in statistical estimation for probabilistic functions of Markov processes. *Inequalities, 3,* 1-8.

Baum, L. E., & Petrie, T. (1966). Statistical inference for probabilistic functions of finite state Markov chains. *Ann. Math. Statist. 73,* 1554-1563.

Baum, L. E., & Sell, G. R. (1968). Growth functions for transformations on manifolds. *Pacific Journal of Mathematics,* 27(2),211-227.

Campbell, R. (1996). Seeing brains reading speech: A review and speculations. *Speech Reading by Humans and Machines,* edited by D. G. Stork and M. E. Hennecke,NATO ASI Series, 115-133.

Campbell, R., &. Dodd, B. (1980). Hearing by eye. *Quarterly Journal of Experimental Psychology, 32,* 85-99.

Dong, L., Foo, S. W., & Lian, Y. (2003). Cross-Speaker Viseme Mapping Using Hidden Markov Models. *4th Int. Conf. Information,Communications & Signal Processing,4th IEEE Pacific-Rim Conf. on Multimedia (ICICS-PCM 2003), 3,* 1384-1388.

Dong, L.,Foo, S. W., & Lian, Y. (2004). Level-Building on AdaBoost HMM Classifiers and the Application to Visual Speech Processing. *IEICE Trans. on Information and Systems, E87-D,No. 11,* 2460-2472.

Ephraim,Y., Dembo, A., & Rabiner, L. R. (1987). A minimum discrimination information approach for hidden Markov modeling. *IEEE Int. Conf. Acoustics,Speech,and Signal Processing,* 49-52.

Foo, S. W., & Dong, L. (2002). Recognition of Visual Speech Elements Using Hidden Markov Models. *Advances in Multimedia Information Processing. The 3rd IEEE Pacific Rim Conf. on Multimedia,* 607-614.

Foo, S. W., & Lim, E. G. (2003). Speaker Recognition using Adaptively Boosted Classifiers. *IEICE Trans. on Information and Systems, Special Issue on Speech Information Processing, E86-D, 3,* 474-482.

Foo, S. W., Lian, Y., & Dong, L. (2003). A Simplified Viterbi Matching Algorithm for Word Partition in Visual Speech Processing. *4th European Workshop on Image Analysis for Multimedia Interactive Services (WIAMIS 2003),* Session 5.

Foo, S. W., Lian, Y., & Dong, L. (2003). Using 3D Deformable Template Trellis to Describe the Movement of the Lip. *4th European Workshop on Image Analysis for Multimedia Interactive Services (WIAMIS 2003),* Session 5.

Goldschen, A. J., Garcia, O. N., & Petajan, E. D. (1997). Continuous Automatic Speech Recognition by Lipreading. *Computational Imaging and Vision, 14,* 321-343.

Jelinek, F. (1976). Continuous speech recognition by statistical methods. *Proc. IEEE, 64,* 532-556.

Lewis, T. W., & Powers, D. M. W. (2000). Lip feature extraction using red exclusion. *Selected papers from the Pan-Sydney Workshop on Visualization, 2,* 61 – 67.

Massaro, D. W. (1987). *Speech perception by ear and eye: A paradigm for psychological inquiry.* Lawrence Erlbaum Associates, Hillsdale, HJ.

M2VTS Multimodal Face Database Release 1.00. Available online, URL: http://www.tele.ucl.ac.be/PROJECTS/M2VTS/m2fdb.html

McGurk, H., & MacDonald, J. (1976). Hearing lips and seeing voices. *Nature, 264,* 746-748.

McLanchlan, G. J., & Krishnan, T.(1997). *The EM Algorithm and Extensions.* Wiley Series in Probability and Statistics,John Wiley and Sons.

Neely, K. K. (1956). Effect of visual factors on the intelligibility of speech. *Journal of the Acoustical Society of America, 28(6),* 1275-1277.

Petrie, T. (1969). Probabilistic functions of finite state Markov chains. *Ann. Math. Statist. 40(1),* 97-115.

Rabiner, L. R. (1989). A tutorial on Hidden Markov Models and selected applications in speech recognition. *Proc. IEEE, 77(2),* 257-286.

Reisberg, D., McLean, J., & Goldfield, A. (1987). Easy to hear,but hard to understand: A lip-reading advantage with intact auditory stimuli. *Hearing by Eye,* edited by B. Dodd and R. Campbell,Lawrence Erlbaum Associates, 97-113.

Schalkoff, R. J. (1992). *Pattern Recognition: Statistical,Structural and Neural Approaches.* John Wiley and Sons.

Silsbee, P. L., & Bovic, A. C. (1993). Visual lipreading by computer to improve automatic speech recognition accuracy. *Technical Report TR-93-02-90,* University of Texas Computer and Vision Research Center, Austin, TX, USA.

Stork, D. G., & Hennecke, M. E. (1996). Speechreading: An overview of image processing, feature extraction, sensory integration and pattern recognition techniques. *The Second Int. Conf. on Automatic Face Gesture Recognition*, xvi-xxvi.

Welsh, W. J., Simon, A. D., Hutchinson, R. A., & Searby, S. (1990). A speech-driven 'talking-head' in real time. *Proceedings of Picture Coding Symposium*, 7.6-1 - 7.6-2.

Williams, J. J., & Katsaggelos, A. K. (2002). An HMM-based speech-to-video synthesizer. *IEEE Trans. Neural Networks, 13*(4), 900-915.

Zhang, X. Z., Broun, C., Mersereau, R. M., & Clements, M. A. (2002). Automatic speechreading with applications to human-computer interfaces. *EURASIP Journal on Applied Signal Processing, Special Issue on Joint Audio-Visual Speech Processing*, 1228-1247.

ENDNOTE

[a] Liang Dong was with the University when the research was carried out and is currently with the Healthcare Department, Philips Research Asia – Shanghai, China

Chapter XIII
Motion Features for Visual Speech Recognition

Wai Chee Yau
RMIT University, Australia

Dinesh Kant Kumar
RMIT University, Australia

Hans Weghorn
BA University of Cooperative Education Stuttgart, Germany

ABSTRACT

The performance of a visual speech recognition technique is greatly influenced by the choice of visual speech features. Speech information in the visual domain can be generally categorized into static (mouth appearance) and motion (mouth movement) features. This chapter reviews a number of computer-based lip-reading approaches using motion features. The motion-based visual speech recognition techniques can be broadly categorized into two types of algorithms: optical-flow and image subtraction. Image subtraction techniques have been demonstrated to outperform optical-flow based methods in lip-reading. The problem with image subtraction-based method using difference of frames (DOF) is that these features capture the changes in the images over time, but do not indicate the direction of the mouth movement. New motion features to overcome the limitation of the conventional image subtraction-based techniques in visual speech recognition are presented in this chapter. The proposed approach extracts features by applying motion segmentation on image sequences. Video data are represented in a 2-D space using grayscale images named as motion history images (MHI). MHIs are spatio-temporal templates that implicitly encode the temporal component of mouth movement. Zernike moments are computed from MHIs as image descriptors and classified using support vector machines (SVMs). Experimental results demonstrate that the proposed technique yield a high accuracy in a phoneme classification task. The results suggest that dynamic information is important for visual speech recognition.

INTRODUCTION

Speech recognition technologies provide the flexibility for users to control computer through speech. The difficulty of speech recognition systems based on acoustic signals is the sensitivity of such systems to variations in acoustic conditions. The performance of audio speech recognizers degrades drastically when the acoustic signal strength is low, or in situations with high ambient noise levels. To overcome this limitation, there is an increasing trend in applying non-acoustic modalities in speech recognition. A number of alternatives have been proposed, such as visual (Petajan, 1984), recording of vocal cords movements through electroglottograph (EGG) (Dikshit, 1995) and recording of facial muscle activity (Arjunan, 2007). Vision-based techniques are non intrusive and do not require the placement of sensors on a speaker's face and hence are the more desirable options.

The use of visual signals in computer speech recognition is consistent with the way human perceive speech. Human speech perception consists of audio and visual modalities which are demonstrated by McGurk effect. McGurk effect occurs in situations when normal hearing adults are presented with conflicting visual and audio speech signals, the perception of sound is changed (McGurk & MacDonald, 1976). An example is when a listener hears a sound of /ba/ and sees a lip movement of /ga/, the sound /da/ is perceived. This indicates that substantial amount of speech information is encoded in visual signals. Visual speech information has been demonstrated to improve robustness of audio-only speech recognition systems (Stork & Hennecke 1996; Potamianos, Neti, Gravier, Garg, & Senior, 2004; Aleksic & Katsaggelos, 2005).

The visual cues contain far less classification power for speech as compared to audio data and hence it is to be expected that the visual-only speech recognition would support only a small vocabulary. High accuracies are achievable for small vocabulary, speaker-dependent visual-only speech recognition problems as reported in (Nefian, Liang, Pi, Liu & Murphy, 2002; Zhang, Mersereau, Clements & Broun, 2002; Foo & Dong, 2002). An increase in the number of speakers and size of the vocabulary would result in degradation of the accuracy of visual speech recognition. This is demonstrated by the high error rates reported by Potamianos et al. (2003) and Hazen (2006) in large vocabulary visual-only speech recognition task, with errors of the order of 90%. Further, these errors are also attributed to the large inter-subject variations caused by the differences in lip movements for the same utterance spoken by different speakers. The use of visual speech information for speaker recognition (Luettin, Thacker & Beet, 1996; Faraj & Bigun 2007) indicates the large variations that exit between the speaking styles of different people. This difference is even greater if we transgress across the geographic and cultural boundaries.

A typical visual speech recognition technique consists of three phases, (i) recording and preprocessing of video data, (ii) extraction of visual speech features and (iii) classification. One of the main challenges in visual speech recognition is the selection of features to represent lip dynamics. Visual speech features contain information on the visible movement of speech articulators such as lips, teeth and jaw. Various visual speech features have been proposed in the literature. These features can be broadly categorized into shape-based (model-based), appearance-based and motion features. Shape-based features rely on the geometric shape of lips.

Visual speech recognition was first proposed by Petajan (1984) using shape-based features such as height and width of the mouth. Researchers have reported the use of artificial markers on user's mouth to extract lip contours (Kaynak, Qi, Cheok, Sengupta, & Chung, 2001). The use of artificial markers is not natural and hence not suitable for practical speech-controlled applications. Stork & Hennecke (1996) have investigated the use of deformable templates to extract lip contours for lip-reading applications. Wang, Lau, Liew & Leung (2006) proposed a lip segmentation method that utilises colour and spatial information obtained from colour images. Active shape models (ASM) have been applied in visual speech recognition to extract model-based features (Perez, Frangi, Solano &. Lukas, 2005). ASM obtains the lip shape information by fitting a statistical shape model of the lip to the video frames. An extension to the ASM technique is active appearance model (AAM) that combines a shape model with a statistical model of the grey levels in the mouth region. The performance of AAM is demonstrated to outperform ASM in lip tracking (Matthews, Cootes, Cox, Harvey, Bangham, 1998). While such top-down approaches are less sensitive to image noise and illumination variations, these techniques use lip contours information only and omit information of other speech articulators movement.

Appearance-based features assume that the pixel values within the region of interest (ROI) contain important speech information (Potamianos et al., 2003). Such features are extracted directly from the pixel values of the mouth image. The raw image intensity values in the ROI result in high dimension data. To reduce the size of the feature vector, feature extraction and transform techniques such as Principal Component Analysis (PCA), Linear Discriminant Analysis (LDA) and Discrete Cosine Transform (DCT) have been proposed (Potamianos et al., 2004; Hazen, 2006; Liang, Liu, Zhao, Pi, & Nefian, 2002). Appearance-based features can represent visual information of the lips, within the mouth cavity and surrounding face region (Potamianos et al, 2003). As opposed to shape-based approach, these techniques do not explicitly extract lip feature points. One of the disadvantages of appearance-based features is the sensitivity of such features to varying imaging conditions such as illumination and view angle of the camera.

In both, shape-based and appearance-based techniques, features are extracted from the static frames and these can be considered as static features. To implicitly include the dynamic information to capture visual speech dynamics, one technique proposed by Potamianos et al is to augment these DCT coefficients by the first and second-order derivatives computed over multiple frames (Potamianos et al., 2004).

One advantage of using motion features is that these are independent of the static image and background and directly represent mouth movement. Few researchers have focused on applying motion features for visual speech recognition. Important information in lip-reading lies in the temporal change of lip positions and not solely on the absolute lip shape (Bregler & Konig, 1991). This chapter reviews number of different visual speech recognition techniques using motion features.

Motion history image (MHI) is a spatio-temporal template created by temporal integration of the video data and assigning greater weights to more recent movement (Bobick & Davis, 2001). The resultant MHI is a 2-D grayscale image that is suitable for representing short duration actions such as facial movement. This chapter presents a study of different features of MHI of the mouth movement during utterance of the phones. This chapter is organised as follows: the second section outlines the background on the importance of motion information for visual speech perception by human. The third section presents the state of the art lipreading techniques using motion features by computers and the available visual speech databases for evaluation. The fourth section presents the MHI based technique developed by the authors. The fifth section describes experiments conducted to evaluate this approach and the results. The last section concludes the chapter and future recommendations related to possible improvements and possible applications of visual speech recognition systems are given.

BACKGROUND

Visual speech information can be described in terms of the static and dynamic components (Rosenblum & Saldaa, 1998). Features extracted from static mouth images are static (pictorial) features. These features characterise the appearance or shape of the mouth in these frames. Motion features directly represent mouth movement without regards to the underlying static mouth appearance and shape.

Significance of Motion Information for Visual Speech Perception

A number of studies has demonstrated the significance of time-varying information for visual speech perception. While static features describe the underlying static poses of the mouth such as the lip shape and visibility of teeth and tongue, time-varying features represent the dynamics of articulation that correspond to facial movements.

An investigation using computer-generated faces demonstrated that subjects were able to distinguish vowels based on time-varying features extracted from the lips and jaw movements (Brooke & Summerfield, 1983). Experiments using point-light displays by Rosenblum & Saldaa (1998) obtained similar results that validated the significance of time-varying information in visual speech perception. The point-light display method is a method to measure time-varying information and this is achieved by applying small lights to different key facial feature points of a darkened speaker's face. Three different configurations for the point light displays were studied by Rosenblum and Saldaa (1998). It was observed that the point-light display configuration with lights attached to the lips, tongue and teeth provides the highest classification rate. The lowest accuracy was produced using the configuration with the most number of point light displays attached to the face (points on the mouth, cheeks and chin).

These experiments demonstrate that dynamic features characterizing the speech articulators' movements are salient features for speechreading. Humans' cognitive abilities in speech perception encompass multiple modalities with different temporal, spatial and sensing characteristics. The insights gained from studies of human visual speech perception provide clues that suggest which visual aspects of speech events are important for computer lip-reading. Results from human perceptual experiments demonstrate that the dynamic features extracted from facial movements contain significant cues useful for recognition of visual speech. Movements in the lower face region of the speaker which encloses the mouth, lips, teeth, tongue and jaw are found to be most informative for identifying utterances by humans. The region of interest for lip-reading systems should contain the lower face region for efficient decoding of visual speech.

STATE OF THE ART MACHINE-BASED LIPREADING TECHNIQUES USING MOTION FEATURES

The high sensitivity of human vision to motion tracking and dynamic information of visual speech suggest that motion features are useful for visual speech recognition. The motivation for using motion features is because significant visual speech information is reflected by the temporal change of lip positions and not solely on the absolute lip shape (Bregler & Konig, 1994). Another reason in favour of using temporal image data is the psychophysical evidence suggesting that biological visual systems are well adapted to process temporal information. The results from human perceptual studies by Rosenblum & Saldaa (1998) have validated that time-varying information is important for visual speech perception.

Research on machine lip-reading conducted by Goldschen et al. (1994) demonstrated that motion features are more discriminative as compared to static features. In their experiments, seven static features from the oral cavity such as the perimeter along the edge of the oral cavity, width and height of the oral cavity are used. They had extracted motion features as a combination of the first and second derivative of the static features and analysed the motion and static features using PCA. The results of their analysis indicate that most of the motion features are more informative than the static features. Despite the significance of speech dynamics in utterance recognition, few studies have focused on applying motion features for computer lip-reading as compared to static features.

The significance of lip motion in visual speech recognition is investigated by Cetingül et. al. (2006) for speaker and speech recognition. Their work compared different feature sets that consist of the lip motion, lip texture and audio information. The audio information is represented using the Mel-frequency cepstral coefficients (MFCC) and the first and second derivatives of MFCC. Lip texture is represented using the 2D-DCT coefficients of the luminance component within a bounding box around the region of interest (ROI) whereas the lip motion is extracted through discriminative analysis of the dense motion vectors within the ROI. Their results indicate that by including the lip motion features, the performance of the speech recognition system is improves as compared to fusion of audio and lip texture alone.

The techniques used to extract motion features reported in literature can be broadly classified into two: optical-flow and image subtraction. This chapter discusses these two techniques and looks at the different dynamic features associated with each of these. The chapter also discusses methods used to classify these motion features to identify speech from visual data.

Optical Flow-Based Motion Features

Optical-flow is a motion estimation technique for visual data. Optical-flow can be defined as the distribution of apparent velocities associated with the changes in spatial location of brightness patterns in an image. Different optical flow estimation techniques have been proposed in the literature and two of the widely used algorithms are reported by Horn & Schunck (1981) and Lucas & Kanade (1981).

In the Horn-Schunck technique, the image brightness at any coordinate (x, y) at time t is denoted by E(x, y, t). Assuming that brightness of each point is constant during a movement for a very short period, the following equation is obtained:

$$\frac{dE}{dt} = \frac{\partial E}{\partial x}\frac{dx}{dt} + \frac{\partial E}{\partial y}\frac{dy}{dt} + \frac{\partial E}{\partial t} = 0 \tag{1}$$

Let the vectors u denote the apparent horizontal velocity and v denote the apparent vertical velocity of brightness constrained by this equation.

$$u = \frac{dx}{dt}; v = \frac{dy}{dt} \tag{2}$$

A single linear equation defined as

$$E_x \cdot u + E_y \cdot v + E_t = 0 \tag{3}$$

The optical flow velocity (u, v) cannot be determined only by using Eq. (3). Hence, an additional constraint, named as the smoothness constraint is used. This constraint minimizes the square magnitude of the gradient of the optical-flow velocity and is given by:

$$\left(\frac{\partial u}{\partial x}\right)^2 + \left(\frac{\partial u}{\partial y}\right)^2, \left(\frac{\partial v}{\partial x}\right)^2 + \left(\frac{\partial v}{\partial y}\right)^2 \tag{4}$$

Solving Eq. (3) and (4), an optical flow pattern can be obtained, provided that the apparent velocity of the brightness pattern changes smoothly in the image. The flow velocity of each point is iteratively computed using the average of flow velocities estimated from neighbouring pixels in the image.

Based on the Horn & Schunck (1981) algorithm, an optical-flow based visual speech recognition technique was proposed by Mase & Pentland (1991) to estimate the velocity of lip motions measured from optical-flow data as motion features. These features were extracted from optical-flow of four windows around the edges of the mouth (each window represents one of four designated facial muscles is activated during speech). The performance of their system is comparable to the speech perception ability of human in an English digit recognition task.

A different optical flow estimation technique using 3-D structure method that applies eigenvalue analysis of multidimensional structure tensor is reported in (Bigun, Granlund, & Wiklund, 1991). The 3-D tensor structure method was applied in 2-D subspaces of the 3-D spatiotemporal space to estimate the lip contour motion for digit and speaker recognition applications in (Faraj & Bigun 2007).

Carboneras et. al. (2007) have compared the performance of low-dimensional motion features (extracted using optical flow algorithm) with the commonly used appearance-based, static features, 2D-DCT coefficients, in a digit recognition task. The motion feature vectors consisted of only three values, i.e., the vertical and horizontal relative movement, and the average luminance of the center of the mouth. These motion features are from the differences between the optical flow vectors computed on different regions of the speaker's mouth. The low-dimensional motion features are demonstrated to outperform the DCT-based features when tested using hidden Markov models (HMM) trained with both feature fusion and with decision fusion. The use of low-dimensional features requires only a small training data set and increases the training and testing speed of the system.

Iwano et. al. (2007) have investigated the performance of static and motion features for audio-visual speech recognition using side-face images. They have examined the lip-contour geometric (static) features and lip-motion features extracted using optical flow algorithm. The motion features are found to be useful for onset prediction and the static features are demonstrated to be effective for increasing the phoneme discrimination capacity. Combining the static and motion features can increase the noise robustness of the proposed visual speech recognition technique. The experimental results also show that for small vocabulary speech recognition, the noise robustness of the proposed method is increased by combining this visual information with audio information.

Image Subtraction-Based Motion Features

Image subtraction is a commonly used in motion detection and recognition. Image subtraction process involves the computation of the difference between adjacent frames and produces a delta image, also known as Difference of Frames (DOF). DOF is produced by subtracting the intensity values between successive frames of the image sequence. The intensity values of the DOF at pixel location with coordinates (x, y) of the tth frame is defined as

$$DOF_t(x, y) = \mid I_t(x, y) - I_{t-1}(x, y) \mid$$

(5)

It (x, y) represents the intensity values of the tth frame. One of the key advantages of the image subtraction method is the computational simplicity of the algorithm. Figure 1 shows two consecutive mouth images and the corresponding DOF.

Image subtraction was applied to extract motion features for visual speech recognition by Scanlon, Reilly & De Chazal (2003). They have suggested that the temporal difference between two adjacent frames is relatively small and does not provide significant temporal information. Hence, they have proposed the use of DOF between current frame and a frame much further back in the image sequence (multiple-frame DOF) as motion features. Multiple-frame DOFs are computed for cth and (c-k)th frame by

$$DOF_t(x, y) = \mid I_t(x, y) - I_{t-k}(x, y) \mid$$

(6)

For k=1, N/3, N/2, N*2/3, N*5/6 and N-1 with N being the total number of frames. They compared the motion features with static features computed using discrete cosine, Haar and Hadamard transform and demonstrated that motion features yield three times higher accuracies than static features. Image subtraction method for visual speech recognition has also been reported by Le et al (Lee, Lee & Lee, 2005). Lee et al coupled it with principal component analysis (PCA) and independent component analysis (ICA). They tested motion features obtained from both- single-frame and multiple-frame DOFs.

A comparison between image subtraction and optical-flow based motion features are reported in (Gray, Movella & Sejnowski, 1996). Motion features extracted from DOFs were demonstrated to outperform features extracted from optical-flow techniques. Gray et. al. (2006) have evaluated five type of motion features using: (i) pixel values of low pass filtered gray scale image (named as form) and DOF, (ii) form and PCA of DOFs, (iii) optical flow fields, (iv) optical flow information and acceleration (the difference between subsequent optical flow fields) (v) form and optical-flow. The accuracies of technique (i) using low pass filtered image and DOFs features produced the highest accuracies among the various dynamic techniques tested. The technique that combines DOF and grayscale image pixels yield 15% higher recognition rate as compared to the approach using optical flow fields and image pixels.

One of the possible reasons for the poorer performance of the optical-flow algorithm is due to the presence of noise in the resultant optical flow field. Another possible reason argued by Gray et. al (1996) is that the optical flow algorithm evaluated assumes rigidity of the objects (lips) and small pixel movement of features between frames. These assumptions do not hold for mouth images since the lips are non rigid and large pixel movement may occur for utterance spoken in high velocity. Moreover, the optical flow approaches become unstable if there are less than two directions (texture) in the local patch due to the aperture problem. When applying the optical-flow techniques to the lip images, the aperture-problem is a significant source of noise that affects the performance of optical flow for visual speech recognition. (Faraj & Bigun 2007).

Nevertheless, Scanlon et al. (2003) have pointed out that one of the drawbacks using image subtraction method based on single-frame DOF in visual speech recognition is the limited dynamic information between two adjacent frames. If multiple-frame DOFs are used as motion features, part of the movement information between the current frame, c and (c-k)th frames may have been lost. The selection of a suitable k value is not straight forward and may vary depending on the speed of utterance. Another issue related to the use of DOF is that these images capture information about the changes in the mouth image over time but do not indicate the direction of the mouth movement.

To overcome these limitations, this chapter investigates the use of a different segmentation algorithm to capture lip dynamics through temporal integration of image sequence into a 2-D spatio-temporal template named motion history image (MHI) technique (Bobick & Davis, 2001). MHI contain information on the spatial location and temporal information (history) of mouth movement.

MOTION HISTORY IMAGES FOR MOUTH MOVEMENT SEGMENTATION

MHI technique is a motion segmentation approach proposed by (Bobick & Davis, 2001). This technique can be viewed as an extension of the image subtraction method. This chapter presents a novel visual speech recognition method using motion features extracted from motion history images (MHI).

MHI is a grayscale image computed by applying accumulative image differencing on the video data. MHI is a spatial-temporal template that shows where and when the movements of speech articulators (lips, teeth, jaw, facial muscles and tongue) occur in an image sequence (Yau, Kumar & Weghorn, 2007). The pixel intensity of a MHI corresponds to a function of the temporal history of motion at that pixel location. The gray levels of a MHI are the temporal descriptors of the motion.

The pixels in the region of movement have higher intensity compared with the pixels where there is no movement. Thus motion segmentation is performed based on identifying regions that have intensity greater than a threshold. Thresholding is performed on the DOFs to produce binary images, Bt(x, y). The threshold value may be dynamically selected based on the statistical properties of the DOF or selected empirically. This chapter reports a fixed threshold value, a selected empirically. Bt (x, y) is defined as

$$B_t(x, y) = \begin{cases} 1 & if \;\; DOF_t(x, y) \geq a \\ 0 & otherwise \end{cases}$$

(7)

At any instant of time t, the intensity value of the MHI at pixel location (x, y) of the tth frame is given by

$$MHI_t(x, y) = \max \bigcup_{t=2}^{N} B_t(x, y).t$$

(8)

Figure 1. Example of DOFs and MHI computed from an image sequence with twelve frames (from left to right showing frame 1 to frame 12)

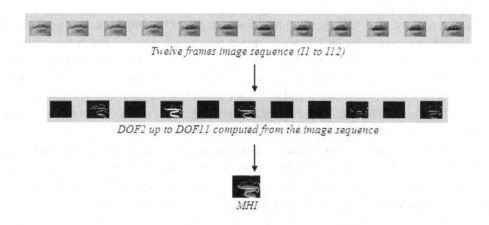

N is the total number of frames used to capture the facial movements. The delimiters for the start and stop of the motion are manually inserted into the image sequence of every utterance.

In Eq. (8), the binary images have been multiplied with a linear ramp function of time to implicitly encode the temporal information of the facial movements into the MHI. The maximum value obtained from the union of the multiplication of $Bt(x, y)$ and t is the pixel value of the $MHIt(x, y)$. By computing the MHI values for all pixels values of the image sequence using Eq. (8) produces a grayscale image (MHI) where the brightness of the pixels indicates the recency of motion in the image sequence. MHI contains pixels corresponding to spatial location of more recent facial movements brighter with larger intensity values. Figure 1 shows the three steps process (based on Eq 5-8) in calculating MHI from video data.

The motivation of using MHI in visual speech recognition is the static elements of the images are not present in the MHI and only the short duration (facial) movements are preserved. MHI is invariant within limits to the skin colour of the speakers due to the image subtraction process involved in the generation of MHI . Another advantage of using MHI is the low computational complexity of this motion segmentation approach.

The speed of phonation of the speaker might vary for each pronunciation of a phone and might be different for each recording. The variations in the speed of utterance result in the variations of the overall duration and there maybe variations in the micro phases of the utterances. The details of such variations are difficult to model due to the large inter-subject and inter-experiment variations. Our proposed approach approximates the variations in speed of speech by normalizing the overall duration of utterance. This is achieved by normalizing the intensity values of MHI to [0...1] to minimize the differences in MHIs of a same utterance pronounced with different velocity. MHI is a view-sensitive, motion representation technique. MHI generated from the sequence of images is dependent on factors such as position, orientation and distance of the speaker's face from the camera. Another factor that can affect the motion representation of MHI is the illumination variations.

Intensity values of MHIs in the spatial domain are not suitable to be used as features to represent the mouth movement due to the large dimension of image data. Further, the pixel values are dependent upon the local variation of the image intensity. The pixel values of MHIs vary with changes such as the tilt of speaker's mouth, or when there is a relative shift of the camera and mouth. To represent MHI with a smaller set of descriptors, suitable features need to be extracted.

FEATURE DESCRIPTORS

The gray level of each pixel in a MHI indicates the temporal characteristics of facial movement at that particular location. The pixel values of MHI contain spatial and temporal information of movement. For such images, global region-based feature descriptors are useful in characterizing the intensity distribution of MHIs as opposed to boundary-based features. Image descriptors evaluated in this chapter are Zernike moments and discrete cosine transform (DCT) coefficients.

Zernike Moment

Zernike moments (ZM) are a type of orthogonal image moments (Teague, 1980). One of the motivations for using ZM is due to the simple rotational properties of ZM. ZM has been adopted in MPEG-7 standard as a region-based shape descriptor (Zhang & Lu, 2004; Jeannin, 2000). ZM are demonstrated to outperform other image moments such as geometric moments, Legendre moments and complex moments in terms of sensitivity to image noise, information redundancy and image representation capability (The & Chin, 1988).

ZM is computed by projecting image function f(x, y) onto the orthogonal Zernike polynomial, Vnl. ZM is defined within a unit circle (i.e.: x2 + y2 ≤1). Zernike moments Znl of order n and repetition l is given by

$$Z_{nl} = \left[\frac{n+1}{\pi} \right] \int_0^{2\pi} \int_0^\infty V_{nl}(\rho,\theta) \, d\rho \, d\theta$$

(9)

$|l| \leq n$ and $(n - |l|)$ is even. $f(\rho, \theta)$ is the intensity distribution of MHI mapped to a unit circle of radius ρ and angle θ where $x = \rho\cos\theta$ and ρ. Zernike polynomial, Vnl is defined as

$$V_{nl}(\rho,\theta) = R_{nl}(\rho)e^{-\hat{j}l\theta} \qquad \hat{j} = \sqrt{-1}$$

(10)

where Rnl is the real-valued radial polynomial defined as

$$R_{nl}(\rho) = \sum_{k=0}^{\frac{n-|l|}{2}} -1^k \frac{(n-k)!}{k!(\frac{n+|l|}{2}-k)!(\frac{n-|l|}{2}-k)!} r^{n-2k}$$

(11)

ZM are independent features due to the orthogonality of the Zernike polynomial Vnl (Teague, 1980).

For ZM to be orthogonal, MHIs have to be scaled and bounded to be within a unit circle centered at the origin before computing ZM from MHIs. MHIs are bounded by the unit circle. The center of the image is taken as the origin and the pixel coordinates are mapped to the range of the unit circle i.e.: x2 + y2 ≤ 1. Figure 2 illustrates the square-to-circular transformation that maps the square image function (f(x, y)) to a circular image function (f(ρ, θ))in terms of i-j axes. The entire MHI is enclosed within the circular i-j coordinates to ensure that no information is lost in the square-to-circular transformation.

To illustrate the rotational characteristics of Zernike moments, consider β as the angle of rotation of the image. The resulting rotated Zernike moment is

$$Z'_{nl} = Z_{nl}e^{-jl\beta}$$

(12)

Znl is the Zernike moment of the original image. Equation (12) demonstrates that rotation of an image results in a phase shift on the Zernike moments (Khontazad & Hon, 1990). The absolute value of

Figure 2. Square-to-circular transformation of the image functions for computation of Zernike moments

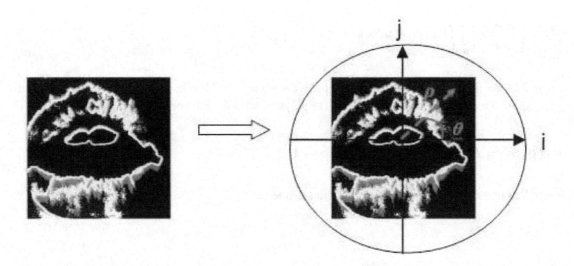

Table 1. List of the 64 Zernike Moments from 0th to 12th Order

Order	Moments
0	Z00
1	Z11
2	Z20Z22
3	Z31Z33
4	Z40Z42Z44
5	Z51Z53Z55
6	Z60Z62Z64Z66
7	Z71Z73Z75Z77
8	Z80Z82Z84Z86Z88
8	Z91Z93Z95Z97Z99
9	Z91Z93Z95Z97Z99
10	Z10,0Z10,2Z10,4Z10,6Z10,8Z10,10
11	Z11,1Z11,3Z11,5Z11,7Z11,9Z1,11
12	Z12,0Z12,2Z12,4Z12,6Z12,8Z12,10Z12,12
13	Z13,1Z13,3Z13,5Z13,7Z13,9Z13,11Z13,13
14	Z14,0Z14,2Z14,4Z14,6Z14,8Z14,10 Z14,12Z14,14

Zernike moments are rotation invariant. Zernike moments are not scale and translation invariant. To ensure scale and translation invariance, the image is first subjected to a normalization process using its regular moments before computing the Zernike moments from the normalized image.

This chapter adopts the absolute value of the Zernike moments, |Znl| as motion features to represent MHI. By including higher order moments, more image information is represented but this will increase the feature size and results in the features being more prone to noise. An optimum number of Zernike moments should be selected to ensure a balance trade-off between the feature dimensionality and the image information represented. The number of moments required is determined empirically by additive method. 64 ZM that comprise of 0th order up to 14th order moments have been used as features to represent each MHI of size 72x72 (a total of 5184 pixels). Table 1 lists the 64 Zernike moments used in our proposed approach.

Discrete Cosine Transform

2-D discrete cosine transform (DCT) is a linear transform technique widely used in image compression. DCT produces a compact energy representation of an image. DCT combines related frequencies into a value and focuses energy into top left corner of the resultant image. DCT is closely related to discrete Fourier transform. The 2-D DCT resultant image, Dpq where $0 \leq p \leq M-1$ and $0 \leq q \leq N-1$ of an input image, B with M rows and N columns are be defined as

$$D_{pq} = \alpha_p \alpha_q \sum_{m=0}^{M-1} \sum_{n=0}^{N-1} B_{mn} \cos \frac{\pi(2m+1)p}{2M} \cos \frac{\pi(2n+1)q}{2N}$$

(13)

$$\alpha_p = \begin{cases} \dfrac{1}{\sqrt{M}} & p = 0 \\ \sqrt{\dfrac{2}{M}} & 1 \le p \le M-1 \end{cases}$$

(14)

$$\alpha_p = \begin{cases} \dfrac{1}{\sqrt{N}} & q = 0 \\ \sqrt{\dfrac{2}{N}} & 1 \le q \le N-1 \end{cases}$$

(15)

2-D separable DCT coefficients have been as feature descriptors in visual speech recognition by a number of researchers (Potamianos et al., 2004; Heckmann, Kroschel, Savariaux, & Berthommier, 2002; Hong, Yao, Wan & Chen, 2006). DCT features can be extracted from images by applying (i) DCT on the entire image or (ii) applying DCT on small blocks (e.g. 8 x 8 blocks) of an image. Hong et al. (2006) has demonstrated that DCT features extracted using method (i) and method (ii) produced similar results for visual speech recognition (VSR). Potamianos, Verma, Neti, Iyengar & Basu (2000) have demonstrated that DCT features that are selected based on maximum energy criteria outperforms discrete wavelet transform (DWT) and principal component analysis (PCA) in VSR applications.

The experiments described in this chapter evaluate DCT features obtained by applying 2-D DCT on MHI. For the purpose of comparison of DCT and ZM features, the number of DCT coefficients extracted from each image has been kept the same as ZM, i.e., 64 values. DCT coefficients on the top left corner of the resultant image after applying 2-D DCT are used as features. Triangles with side lengths of 8 are taken from the top left of DCT images and 'flattened' into features vectors with length of 64 values.

PERFORMANCE EVALUATION

Experiments were conducted to evaluate the performance of the proposed visual speech recognition approach. The experiments were approved by the Human Experiments Ethics Committee of RMIT University.

The experiments were tested on a vocabulary consisting of fourteen English visemes. Visemes are the smallest visually distinguishable facial movements when articulating a phoneme. The motivation of using viseme as the recognition unit is because visemes can be concatenated to form words and sentences, thus providing the flexibility to extend the vocabulary.

The total number of visemes is much less than phonemes because speech is only partially visible (Hazen, 2006). While the video of the speaker's face shows the movement of the lips and jaw, the movements of other articulators such as tongue and vocal cords are often not visible. Hence, each viseme can correspond to more than one phoneme, resulting in a many-to-one mapping of phonemes-to-visemes.

There is no definite consensus about how the sets of visemes in English are constituted (Hazen, 2006). The number of visemes for English varies depending on factors such as the geographical loca-

Table 2. Fourteen visemes defined in MPEG-4

Viseme number	Corresponding phonemes	Vowel/ consonant
1	/p/, /b/ , /m/	consonant
2	/f/,/v/	consonant
3	/th/, /dh/	consonant
4	/t/, /d/	consonant
5	/k/, /g/	consonant
6	/ch/,/sh/,/jh/	consonant
7	/s/, /z/	consonant
8	/n/,/l/	consonant
9	/r/	consonant
10	A	vowel
11	E	vowel
12	I	vowel
13	O	vowel
14	U	vowel

Table 3. Audio visual speech databases

Database	Number of speakers	Recording conditions
CUAVE	36	Subjects moving
AVOZES	20	Studio
IBM AV	290	Studio
XM2VTS	295	Studio
M2VTS	37	Studio
VidTIMIT	43	Noisy office

tion, culture, education background and age of the speaker. The geographic differences in English are most obvious where the sets of phonemes and visemes changes for different countries and even for areas within the same country. It is difficult to determine an optimal and universal viseme set that is suitable for all speakers.

These experiments used visemes defined in the Facial Animation Parameters (FAP) of MPEG-4 standard. MPEG-4 defines a face model using Facial Animation Parameters (FAP) and Facial Definition Parameters (FDP). Visemes are one of the high level parameter of FAP (Kshirsagar, Escher, Sannier & Magnenat-Thalmann, 1999). Table 2 shows the fourteen visemes defined in MPEG-4 standard (The visemes chosen for experiments for highlighted in bold fonts).

Visual Speech Databases

The number of publicly available audio visual speech databases is less than audio speech databases. A number of the visual speech databases are recorded in ideal studio environments with controlled lighting. Table 3 lists some of the available visual speech databases and the different characteristics of these databases.

To evaluate the performance of the approach in a real world environment, video data was recorded using an inexpensive web camera in a typical office environment. This was done towards having a practical voiceless communication system using low resolution video recordings. The camera focused on the mouth region of the speaker and was kept stationary throughout the experiment. The following factors were kept the same during the recording of videos: window size and view angle of the camera, background and illumination. 2800 utterances (20 repetitions of each viseme) were recorded from ten subjects (5 males and 5 females) and stored as AVI files. Due to the large inter-speaker variations, the experiments were conducted for a speaker dependent task. Histogram equalization was applied on the images before computing the MHI to minimize the effects of uniform illumination variations.

One MHI of size 240 x 240 was generated for each phoneme and down sampled to 72 x 72. Fourteen visemes (highlighted in bold fonts in Table 2) were evaluated in the experiments. MHIs for 14 visemes of Subject 1 and Subject 2 are shown in Figure 3 and Figure 4. MHIs of the two subjects are different which is expected due to the large inter-subject variations.

Two types of image descriptors evaluated in the experiments were Zernike moments (ZM) and discrete cosine transform (DCT) coefficients. The optimum number of ZM features required for classification of the fourteen visemes was determined empirically. The number of features for DCT coefficients was kept the same as ZM to compare the image representation ability of these two image descriptors.

Classification

Zernike moments and discrete cosine transform (DCT) features were fed into support vector machines (SVMs) classifier as input vectors. SVMs are discriminative classifiers that are trained based on statistical learning theory. SVMs can be designed to classify linearly and non-linearly separable data. One of the strength of SVM is the good generalization achieved by regulating the trade-off between structural complexity of the classifier and empirical error. SVM is capable of finding the optimal separating hyperplane between classes in sparse high-dimensional spaces with relatively few training data. SVMs were selected due to the ability of SVMs to find a globally optimum decision function to separate the different classes of data. Unlike HMM, training of SVM is not susceptible to local maximas. SVM is

Fig 3. MHI of fourteen visemes of Subject 1

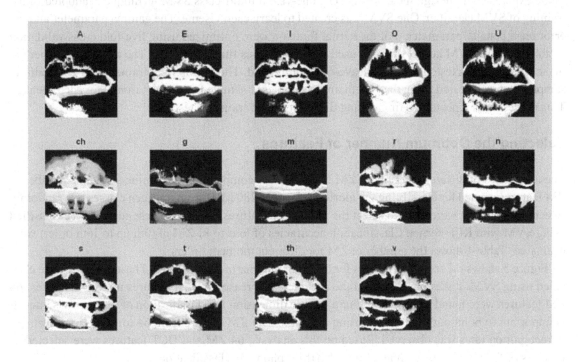

Fig 4. MHI of fourteen visemes of Subject 2

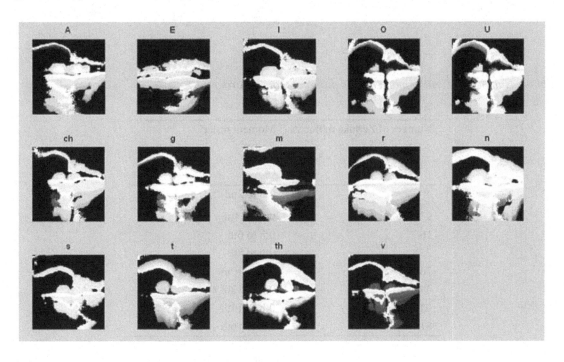

demonstrated to be a stable classifier by (Buciu, 2006). LIBSVM toolbox (Chang & Lin, 2001) was used in the experiment to design the c-SVMs. The one-vs.-all multi-class SVM technique is adopted in the training of SVM classifier. One SVM was created to learn each viseme. The gamma parameter and the error term penalty parameter, c of the kernel function were optimized using five-fold cross validation on the data. The SVM kernel function used was radial basis function (RBF). The classification performance of SVM was tested using the leave-one-out method. The SVMs were trained with 266 training samples and were tested using the 14 remaining samples (1 sample from each viseme) for each speaker. This process was repeated 20 times using different sets of train and test data.

Selecting the Optimum Number of Features

The accuracies of different number of ZM features were compared to determine a suitable number of ZM features needed for classifying the fourteen visemes. 280 MHI from fourteen classes of a randomly selected participant were used to select the number of features required. These features are classified using SVM with RBF kernel. Classification accuracies of four to 81 ZM of (0th up to 16th order) were evaluated. Table 4 shows the number of ZM for different moment orders.

Figure 5 shows the recognition rates for different number of ZM features. These features were classified using SVM. It was observed that the accuracies increased from 4 features up to 64 features. 64 ZM features were found to be the optimum feature dimension for classification of fourteen visemes. It is important to point out that by increasing the number of ZM feature from 64 to 81, no improvement in recognition rates was observed. Based on this analysis, 64 ZM and DCT features were selected as two sets of feature vectors computed from MHI for phoneme classification.

Table 4. Number of Zernike moments for different moment order

Number of Zernike moments	Moment order
4	0th to 2nd
9	0th to 4th
16	0th to 6th
25	0th to 8th
36	0th to 10th
49	0th to 12th
64	0th to 14th
81	0th to 16th

Figure 5. Recognition rates for different number of Zernike moments

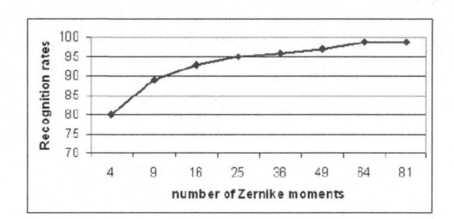

Statistical Analysis of Features

Multivariate analysis of variance (MANOVA) was applied on the Zernike moments (ZM) and discrete cosine transform (DCT) features in the experiments to analyse the data. MANOVA is an extension of One-Way Analysis of Variance (ANOVA) that can be applied to analyse multiple variable. MANOVA analyses the means of variables and determine whether the mean of these variables differ significantly between groups. In multivariate analysis of variance, canonical analysis was performed to find the linear combination of the original variables that has the largest separation between groups. Canonical variables are linear combinations of the mean-centred original variables. A grouped scatter plot of the first two canonical variables showed more separation between groups then a grouped scatter plot of any pair of original variables of ZM and DCT. Figure 6 and 7 shows the grouped scatter plot of ZM and DCT for Subject 1.

From Figure 6 and 7 we can clearly observe that there is overlapping between classes of ZM and DCT features, as indicated by the regions enclosed in dashed lines. The results of MANOVA analysis applied ZM and DCT features indicate that the fourteen classes may not be linearly separable. This reconfirms the choice of using non-linear support vector machines (SVM) to classify the features.

Rotational Sensitivity Analysis

The second part of the experiments was to test the sensitivity of DCT and ZM features to changes of mouth orientation in the images. Mouth orientation of a user may not always be the same with respect to the camera axis. Variations in mouth orientation will results in rotational changes of mouth in images. To investigate the rotational sensitivity of DCT and ZM features, 280 MHIs (from Subject 3) generated

Figure 6. Grouped scatter plot of first two canonical variables computed from fourteen visemes ZM features for Subject 1

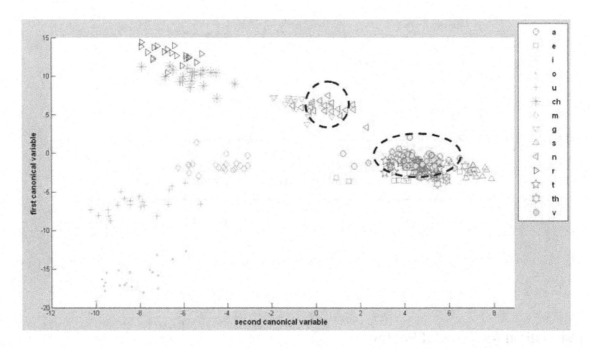

Figure 7. Grouped scatter plot of first two canonical variables computed from fourteen visemes of DCT features for Subject 1

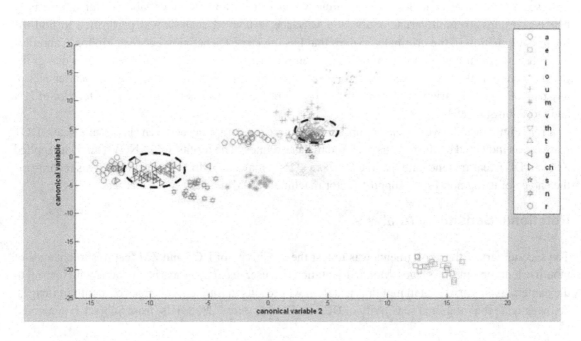

Figure 8. (left to right) MHI of vowel /A/ and MHI of /A/ rotated anticlockwise with an angle of 20 degrees

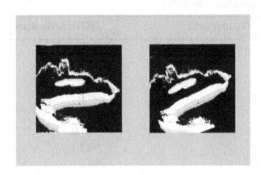

in the previous steps were rotated 20 degrees anticlockwise. Figure 8 shows an example of the rotated MHI of vowel /A/. 64 Zernike moments (ZM) and 64 DCT coefficients were computed from MHIs. The rotation factor was selected based on the maximum expected during experiments. The performance of the image descriptors in representing rotated mouth images was compared.

Support vector machines (SVMs) were trained using ZM and DCT features extracted from 280 MHIs before rotation. 280 rotated MHIs were used as testing samples. ZM and DCT features computed from rotated MHIs were presented to the trained SVMs to evaluate the sensitivity of the features to rotational changes.

RESULTS AND DISCUSSION

The first part of the experiments investigates the performance of Zernike moments (ZM) and discrete cosine transform (DCT) features in classifying MHIs of 14 phonemes. The mean SVM classification rates of ZM and DCT features are comparable, i.e., 97.4%and 99% respectively. The accuracies of each viseme are shown in Table 5 below.

It is observed that the error rates for all visemes are less than 5% using DCT and ZM features. The results indicate a high level of accuracy for the proposed technique in identifying phonemes from video data when there is no relative shift between the camera and the mouth.

One of the factors for misclassifications is the occlusion of articulators' movement. The investigated approach using MHI is a movement-based technique hence it is dependent on the distinctness of mouth movement patterns and is sensitive to motion occlusion. For example, motion occlusion occurs during the pronunciation of consonant /n/ which has the highest error rate based on Table 5. The movement of the tongue within the mouth cavity is not visible (occluded by the teeth) in the video data when pronouncing /n/. Therefore the tongue movement is not encoded in the resultant MHI. The movement of

Table 5. Mean SVM classification accuracies for Zernike moments and DCT features

Viseme	Recognition Rates (%)	
	Zernike moments	DCT coefficients
A	97.5	99.0
E	98.5	99.5
I	96.5	99.0
O	98.0	99.0
U	98.5	99.5
/m/	98.0	100.0
/v/	98.0	99.5
/th/	96.0	98.5
/t/	97.0	98.0
/g/	97.5	99.0
/ch/	96.0	99.0
/s/	98.5	98.5
/n/	96.8	98.5
/r/	98.0	99.5

the tongue tip touching the alveolar ridge (back of the front teeth) is not visible in the video of /n/. This reduces the amount of visual speech information represented in the MT of /n/.

The second part of the experiment evaluated the sensitivity of ZM and DCT features to rotational changes between camera and mouth. Table 6 shows the average classification rates using ZM and DCT features extracted from (i) original (non rotated) MHIs and (ii) rotated MHIs. ZM features demonstrated to have better tolerance to rotational changes of images as compared to DCT-based method.

The recognition rate of ZM features is approximately twice as good as the recognition rate of DCT feature in representing rotated images. DCT features are observed to be highly sensitive to rotational

Table 6. Average classification accuracies of Zernike moments DCT features

Features	Accuracies of original image	Accuracies of rotated image
Zernike moments	97.4%	84.6%
DCT coefficients	99.0%	36.8%

changes. The accuracies of ZM and DCT features were reduced to 84.6% and 36.8% when the mouth was rotated in the images. In the process of rotating the images, a small part of MHIs may have been cropped to ensure that the rotated images have the same size as original images (72 x 72). This may results in lost of information of MHIs and resulted in misclassifications of rotated MHIs using ZM and DCT features. The results suggest that DCT features require accurate normalization of mouth orientation. ZM is more resilient to rotational changes as compared to DCT features. Our results validate the good rotational property of ZM reported in the literature (Khontazad & Hon, 1990).

To compare the results of the proposed approach with other related work is inappropriate due to the different video corpus and recognition tasks used. Researchers who worked on a similar visual-only speech recognition task has reported approximately 10% higher error rate using shape-based features (geometric measures of the lip) extracted from static images (Foo & Dong, 2002). The encouraging results obtained in the experiments indicate that the proposed motion features is suitable for phoneme identification based on mouth movement, without regard to the static shape of mouth.

CONCLUSION

This chapter presents an overview of motion features for visual speech recognition. A brief comparison of different techniques has been provided and a technique based on motion history image (MHI) that overcomes some of the limitations is also presented. The study has made a comparison of the important global features, i.e., Zernike moments (ZM) and discrete cosine transform (DCT) coefficients used to represent and classify the MHI. The results indicate that the proposed technique can produce high success rates of 99% and 97% using DCT and ZM features when there is no relative shift between mouth and camera. ZM features were demonstrated to be more resilient to rotational changes as compared to DCT features. The results indicate that the reliability of such a system using ZM and DCT features drops by approximately 10% and 40% respectively when there is a relative rotation of the camera by 20 degrees. The results demonstrate that the proposed technique can reliably identify English phonemes.

FUTURE RESEARCH DIRECTIONS

Dynamic visual speech information is important for visual speech recognition. Human perceptual studies indicate that time-varying speech information is essential in speechreading (lip-reading). The number visual speech recognition techniques using motion features proposed in the literature is much less than appearance-based and model-based features extracted from static frames. These static visual speech features have been demonstrated to be useful for visual speech recognition. Nevertheless, the use of motion segmentation techniques to extract visual speech features provides a new paradigm to capture lip dynamics. Such approaches may provide valuable insights in machine recognition of visual speech.

Motion features extracted using techniques such as image subtraction, optical-flow and motion history image (MHI) in visual speech recognition can be seen as analogous to the delta features commonly used in audio speech recognizers. A few issues related to research on motion features for visual speech recognition that may be interesting and worthwhile to examine are: (i) Is complementary visual speech information exists in between motion features and static features? (ii) If time-varying and time-independent visual speech information is complementary, what would be the suitable framework for fusing the static and dynamic features? (iii) Is motion-based features important for speech activity detection and temporal segmentation of utterances?

REFERENCES

Arjunan, S. P., Weghorn, H., Kumar, D. K., & Yau, W. C. (2007). Silent bilingual vowel recognition - using fSEMG for HCI based speech commands. *Ninth International Conference on Enterprise Information Systems, 5*, 68-75.

Bigun, J., Granlund, G., & Wiklund, J. (1991). Multidimensional orientation estimation with applications to texture analysis of optical flow. *IEEE Trans. Pattern Analysis and Machine Intelligence, 13(* 8), 775-790.

Bobick, A. F., & Davis, J. W. (2001). The recognition of human movement using temporal Templates. *IEEE Transactions on Pattern Analysis and Machine Intelligence, 23*(3), 257-267.

Brooke, M., & Summerfield, Q. (1983) Analysis, synthesis and perception of visible articulatory movements. *Journal of Phonetics, 63–76.*

Buciu, Kotropoulos, I. C., Pitas., I. (2006). Demonstrating the stability of support vector machines for classification. *Signal processing, 86*, 2364-2380

Bregler, C., Omohundro, S. M., & Konig, Y. (1994). A hybrid approach to bimodal speech Recognition. *IEEE Proceedings of the 28th Asilomar Conference on Signals, Systems and Computers, 1*, 556–560.

Carboneras, A. V., Gurban, M., & Thiran, J. (2007) Low-dimensional motion features for audio-visual speech recognition. *15th European Signal Processing Conference (EUSIPCO), Poland*, pp. 297-301.

Chang, C. C., & Lin, C. J. (2001). LIBSVM: A library for support vector machines. *Software available at http://www.csie.ntu.edu.tw/ cjlin/libsvm.*

Cetingül, H. E., Erzin, E., Yemez, Y., & Tekalp (2006). Multimodal speaker/speech recognition using lip motion, lip texture and audio. *Signal Processing, 86*(12), 3549-3558.

Dikshit, P., & Schubert, R. W. (1995) Electroglottograph as an additional source of information in isolated word recognition. *14th Southern Biomedical Engineering Conference .*

Faraj, M., & Bigun, J. (2007). Synergy of lip-motion and acoustic features in biometric speech and speaker recognition. *IEEE Transactions on Computers, 5*(9), 169-1175.

Foo, S. W., & Dong, L. (2002). Recognition of visual speech elements using hidden Markov Models. *Lecture notes in computer science.* Springer-Verlag.

Goldschen, A. J., Garcia, O. N., & Petajan, E. D. (1994). Continuous optical automatic speech recognition by lipreading. *28th Annual Asilomar Conference on Signal Systems and Computer.*

Gordan, M., Kotropoulos, C., & Pitas, I. (2002) Application of support vector machines classifiers to visual speech recognition. *International Conference on Image Processing, 3.*

Gray, M. S., Movella, J. R., Sejnowski, T. J. (1996) Dynamic features for visual speechreading: A systematic comparison. *3rd joint symposium on neural computation, CA, 6*, 222-230.

Hazen, T. J. (2006). Visual model structures and synchrony constraints for audio-visual speech recognition. *IEEE Transactions on Speech and Audio Processing, 14*(3), 1082-1089.

Heckmann, M., Kroschel, K., Savariaux, C., & Berthommier, F. (2002). DCT-based video features for audio-visual speech recognition. *7th Int. Conf on Spoken LanguageProcessing.*

Hong, X., Yao, H., Wan, Y., & Chen, R. (2006). A PCA based visual DCT feature extraction method for lip-reading. *International Conference on Intelligent Information Hiding and Multimedia Signal Processing.*

Horn, B. K. P., & Schunck, B. G. (1981). Determining optical flow. *Artificial Intelligence, 17*,185-203.

Iwano, K., Yoshinaga, T., Tamura, S., & Furui, S. (2007). Audio-visual speech recognition using lip information extracted from side-face images. *EURASIP Journal on Audio, Speech and Music Processing.*

Jeannin, S. (2000) *MPEG-7 Visual part of experimentation model version 5.0*, ISO/IEC JTC1/SC29/WG11/N3321.

Kaynak, M. N., Qi, Z., Cheok, A. D., Sengupta, K., & Chung, K. C. (2001). Audio-visual modeling for bimodal speech recognition. *Proceedings of IEEE International Conference on Systems, Man and Cybernetics, 1*, 818-186.

Khontazad, A., & Hon, Y. H. (1990). Invariant image recognition by Zernike moments. *IEEE Transactions on Pattern Analysis and Machine Intelligence, 12*, 489.

Kshirsagar, S., Escher, M., Sannier, G., & M.-Thalmann, N. (1999). Multimodal animation system based on the MPEG-4 standard. *Proceedings of Multimedia Modeling*, (pp. 215-232).

Lee, S., & Yook, D. (2002) Viseme recognition experiment using context dependent hidden Markov models. *Intelligent Data Engineering and Automated Learning.*

Lee, K. D., Lee, M. J., & Lee, S. (2005) Extraction of frame-difference features based on PCA and ICA for lip-reading. *International Joint Conference on Neural Networks*, (pp 232-237).

Liang, L., Liu, X., Zhao, Y., Pi, X., & Nefian, A.V. (2002). Speaker independent audio-visual continuous speech recognition. *International Conference on Multimedia & Expo (ICME '02).*

Lucas, B. D., & Kanade, T. (1981). An iterative image registration technique with an application to stereo vision. *International Joint Conference Artificial Intelligence*, (pp. 674-679).

Luettin, J., Thacker, N. A., Beet, S. W. (1996). Speaker identification by lipreading. *Proc. of International Conference on Spoken Language Processing.*

Matthews, I., Cootes, T., Cox, S., Harvey, R. & Bangham, J. A. (1998), Lipreading using shape,shading and scale. *Proc. Auditory-Visual Speech Processing*, (pp. 73–78).

McGurk, H., & MacDonald, J. (1976). Hearing lips and seeing voices. *Nature, 264*, 746-748.

Nefian, A. V., Liang, L., Pi, X., Liu, X., & Murphy, K.(2002). Dynamic Bayesian Networks for Audio-Visual Speech Recognition. *EURASIP Journal on Applied Signal Processing, 11*, 1274-1288.

Perez, J. F. G., Frangi, A. F., Solano, E. L., & Lukas, K. (2005). Lip reading for robust speech recognition on embedded devices. *IEEE International Conference on Acoustics, Speech and Signal Processing, ICASSP '05.*

Petajan, E. D. (1984).Automatic lip-reading to enhance speech recognition. *IEEE Communication Society Global Telecommunications Conference.*

Potamianos, G., Verma, A., Neti , C., Iyengar, G., & Basu, S. (2000). A cascade image transform for speaker independent automatic speechreading. *IEEE International Conference on Multimedia and Expo.*

Potamianos, G., Neti, C., Gravier, G., Garg, A., & Senior, A. W. (2003). Recent advances in automatic recognition of audio-visual speech. *Proc of IEEE, 91.*

Potamianos, G., Neti, C., Gravier, G., Huang, J., Connell, J. H., Chu, S., Libal, V., Marcheret, E., Haas, N., & Jiang, J. (2004). Towards practical deployment of audio-visual speech recognition. *Proceedings of IEEE International Conference on Acoustics, Speech, and Signal Processing, 3,* 777-780.

Rosenblum, L. D., & Saldaa, H. M. (1998). Time-varying information for visual speech perception. *Hearing by Eye: Part 2, The Psychology of Speechreading and Audiovisual Speech, (Campbell, R.,Dodd, B. &Burnham, D. Ed).* Earlbaum: Hillsdale, NJ, 61–81

Scanlon, P., Reilly, R. B., & De Chazal, P. (2003) Visual feature analysis for automatic speechreading. *Audio Visual Speech Processing Conference, France.*

Stork, D.G., & Hennecke, M. E. (1996). Speechreading: an overview of image processing feature extraction, sensory integration and pattern recognition technique. *2nd International Conference on Automatic Face and Gesture Recognition (FG'96).*

Teague, M. R., (1980). Image analysis via the general theory of moments. *Journal of the Optical Society of America, 70,* 920-930.

Teh, C. H., & Chin, R. T. (1988). On image analysis by the methods of moments. *IEEE Transactions on Pattern Analysis and Machine Intelligence, 10*(4), 496-513.

Wang, S. L., Lau, W. H., Liew, A. W. C., & Leung, S. H.(2006). Fuzzy clustering-based approaches in automatic lip segmentation from color images. *Advances in Image and Video Segmentation, (Yu-Jin Zhang Ed.), Idea Group Inc.,14,* 292-317

Yau, W. C., Kumar, D. K., & Weghorn, H. (2007). Visual speech recognition using motion features and hidden Markov models. *12th International Conference. on Computer Analysis of Images and Patterns (CAIP 2007).*

Zhang, D., & Lu, G. (2004). Review of shape representation and description techniques. *Pattern Recognition Letters, 37,* 1-19.

Zhang, X., Mersereau, R. M., Clements, M., Broun, C. C. (2002). Visual speech feature extraction for improved speech recognition. *IEEE International Conference on Acoustics, Speech and Signal Processing (ICASSP '02), 2*, 1993-1996.

ADDITIONAL READING

Aleksic, P. S., Potamianos, G., & Katsaggelos, A. K. (2005). Exploiting Visual Information in Automatic Speech Processing. *Handbook of Image and Video Processing, Second Edition, Al. Bovic (Ed.), Ch. 10.8,* pp. 1264-1289, Elsevier Academic Press, MA.

Aleksic, P. S., Williams, J. J., Wu, Z., & Katsaggelos, A. K. (2002). Audio-visual speech recognition using MPEG-4 compliant visual features. *EURASIP Journal on Applied Signal Processing, Special Issue on Joint Audio-Visual Speech Processing,* 1213-1227.

Bobick, A., & Davis, A. (1997). Action recognition using temporal templates. *Motion-Based Recognition, M.Shah and R. Jain (eds),* pp. 125-146.

Burges, C. J. C. (1998). A tutorial on support vector machines for pattern recognition. *Data Mining and Knowledge Discovery, 2*(2), 955–974.

Campbell, R. (1998). Hearing by eye (II): the psychology of speechreading and auditory-visual speech. *Psychology Press Ltd.*

Campbell, R., Dodd, R., Burnham, D. (1998). Hearing by eye II: advances in the psychology of speechreading and auditory-visual speech : Pt. 2. *Psychology Press Ltd.*

Chen, T. (2001). Audiovisual speech processing. *IEEE Signal Processing Magazine, 18*, 9-21.

Chibelushi, C. C., Deravi, F., & Mason, J. S. D. (2002).A review of speech based bimodal recognition. *IEEE Trans. Multimedia, 4*, 23–37.

Daubias, P., & Deleglise, P., (2002) Automatically building and evaluating statistical models for lipreading. *EURASIP Journal of Appied. Signal Processing,* 2002, 1202–1212.

Duda, R.O., Hart, P.E., Stork, D.G. (2000). *Pattern classification.* Wiley-Interscience.

Dupont, S., & Luettin, J. (2000). Audio-visual speech modeling for continuous speech recognition. *IEEE Transactions on Multimedia, 2*, 141-151.

Furui, S. (2000). *Digital speech processing, synthesis and recognition,* CRC.

Goecke, R. (2005). Current trends in joint audio-video signal processing: a review. *IEEE International Symposium on Signal Processing and Its Applications ISSPA,* (pp. 70-73).

Goldschen, A. J., Garcia, O. N., & Petajan, E. D. (1996) Rationale for phoneme-viseme mapping and feature selection in visual speech recognition. *Speechreading by Humans and Machines, D. G. Stork and M. E. Hennecke,* Eds. Berlin, Germany: Springer.

Gonzalez, R. C., & Woods, R. E. (2002). *Digital image processing.* Prentice Hall.

Gordan, M., Kotropoulos, C., Pitas, I. (2002). A temporal network of support vector machine classifiers for the recognition of visual speech. *Lecture Notes in Computer Science. Methods and Applications of Artificial Intelligence: Second Hellenic Conference on AI, SETN,* 2308, 744-745.

Hu, M. K. (1962). Visual pattern recognition by moment invariants. *IEEE Transactions on Information Theory, 8,* 179-187.

Huang, J., Potamianos, G., Connell, J., & Neti, C. (2004). Audio-visual speech recognition using an infrared headset. *Speech Communication, 44,* 83-96.

Jiang, J., Alwan, A., Bernstein, L. E., Keating, P., & Auer, E. T. (2002). On the correlation between face movements, tongue movements and speech acoustics. *EURASIP Journal on Applied Signal Processing, 11,* 1174-1188.

Liew, A. W. C., Leung, S. H., & Lau, W. H. (2003). Segmentation of color lip images by spatial fuzzy clustering. *IEEE Transactions on Fuzzy Systems, 11*(4), 542-549.

Luettin, J., Thacker, N. A., & Beet, S. W. (1996). Active shape models for visual speech feature extraction. *Speechreading by Humans and Machines.*

Luettin, J., & Thacker, N. A. (1997). Speechreading using probabilistic models. *Computer Vision Image Understanding, 65,* 163–178.

Lippmann, R. P. (1997). Speech recognition by machines and humans. *Journal Speech Communication, 22,* 1-15.

Matthews, I., Cootes, T. F., Bangham, J. A., Cox, S., & Harvey, R. (2002). Extractin of visual features for lipreading. *IEEE Transactions on Pattern Analysis and Machine Intelligence, 24*(2), 198-213.

Mukundan, R., & Ramakrishnan, K. R. (1998). *Moment functions in image analysis – theory and applications.* World Scientific.

Neti, C., Potamianos, G., Luettin, J., Matthews, I., Glotin, H., Vergyri, D., Sison, J., Mashari, A., & Zhou, J. (2000). Audio-visual speech recognition. *Final Workshop 2000 Report .Center for Language and Speech Processing,* The Johns Hopkins University, Baltimore, MD.

O'Shaughnessy, D. (1999). *Speech communications: human and machine,* Wiley-IEEE Press.

Rabiner, L., & Juang, B. (1993) *Fundamentals of speech recognition.* US: Prentice Hall.

Saenko, K., Livescu, K., Glass, J., & Darrell, T. (2005). Production domain modeling of pronunciation for visual speech recognition, *IEEE International Conference on Acoustics, Speech and Signal Processing (ICASSP).*

Stork, D. G., & Hennecke, M. E. (1996). *Speechreading by humans and machines: models, systems and applications.* New York: Springer-Verlag.

Sumby, W. H., &. Pollack, I. (1952). Visual contribution to speech intelligibility in noise. *J. Acoustical Society America, 26,* 212–215.

Vapnik, V. (1998). *Statistical learning theory*: Wiley.

Vatikiotis-Bateson, E., Bailly, G., & Perrier, P. (Eds.) *Audio-visual speech processing.* MIT Press.

Zhang, X, Broun, C. C., Mersereau, R. M., & Clements, M. (2002). Automatic speechreading with applications to human-computer interfaces. *EURASIP Journal Applied Signal Processing, 2002*, 1228–1247.

Chapter XIV
Recognizing Prosody from the Lips:
Is It Possible to Extract Prosodic Focus from Lip Features?

Marion Dohen
GIPSA-lab, France

Hélène Lœvenbruck
GIPSA-lab, France

Harold Hill
ATR Cognitive Information Science Labs, Japan
University of Wollongong, Australia

ABSTRACT

The aim of this chapter is to examine the possibility of extracting prosodic information from lip features. The authors used two lip feature measurement techniques in order to evaluate the "lip pattern" of prosodic focus in French. Two corpora with Subject-Verb-Object (SVO) sentences were designed. Four focus conditions (S, V, O or neutral) were elicited in a natural dialogue situation. In the first set of experiments, they recorded two speakers of French with front and profile video cameras. The speakers wore blue lipstick and facial markers. In the second set, the authors recorded five speakers with a 3D optical tracker. An analysis of the lip features showed that visible articulatory lip correlates of focus exist for all speakers. Two types of patterns were observed: absolute and differential. A potential outcome of this study is to provide criteria for automatic visual detection of prosodic focus from lip data.

INTRODUCTION

For a spoken message to be understood (be it by machine or human being), the segmental information (phones, phonemes, syllables, words) needs to be extracted. Supra-segmental information, however, is also crucial. For instance, two utterances with exactly the same segmental content can have very different meanings if the supra-segmental information (conveyed by prosody) differs, as Lynne Truss (2003) nicely demonstrates:

> *A woman, without her man, is nothing.*
> *A woman: without her, man is nothing.*

Prosodic information has indeed been shown to play a critical role in spoken communication. Prosodic cues are crucial in identifying speech acts and turn-taking, in segmenting the speech flow into structured units, in detecting "important" words and phrases, in spotting and processing disfluencies, in identifying speakers and languages, or for detecting speaker emotions and attitudes. The fact that listeners use prosodic cues in the processing of speech has led some researchers to try to draw information from prosodic features to enhance automatic speech recognition (see *e.g.* Pagel, 1999; Waibel, 1988; Yousfi & Meziane, 2006).

Prosodic information involves acoustic parameters, such as intensity, fundamental frequency (F0) and duration. But prosodic information is not just acoustic, it is also articulatory, and in particular it involves visible lip movements. Although prosodic focus typically involves acoustic parameters, several studies have suggested that articulatory modifications—and more specifically visible lip and jaw motion—are also involved (*e.g.*, Cho, 2005; Dohen *et al.*, 2004, 2006; Erickson, 2002; Erickson *et al.*, 2000; Harrington *et al.*, 1995; Vatikiotis-Bateson & Kelso, 1993; Kelso *et al.*, 1985; Lœvenbruck, 1999, 2000; Summers, 1987; De Jong, 1995). More specifically, correlates of prosodic focus have been reported on the lips, as will be outlined below. If visual cues are associated with prosodic focus, then one can expect that prosodic focus should be detectable visually.

Despite these facts, the addition of dynamic lip information to improve automatic speech recognition robustness has been limited to the segmental aspects of speech: lip information is generally used to help phoneme (or word) categorization. Yet visual information about the lips does not only carry segmental information but also prosodic information. The question addressed in this chapter is whether there are potentially extractable visual lip cues to prosodic information. If a visual speech recognition system is able to detect prosodic focus, it will better identify the information put forward by the speaker, a function which can be crucial in a number of applications.

BACKGROUND

A review of speech perception studies suggests that the extraction of prosodic information from visual lip features may be possible. These studies have mostly examined the perception of "prosodic focus", or "emphasis", the aim of which is to highlight a constituent in an utterance, without change to its segmental content. It consists for the speaker in putting forward the part of the utterance he/she wants to communicate as being the most informative (see *e.g.*, Birch & Clifton, 1995; Gussenhoven, 1983; Halliday, 1967; Ladd, 1996; Nølke, 1994; Selkirk, 1984). Focus attracts the listener's attention to one particular constituent of the utterance and is very often used in speech communication. Among the different types of focus, contrastive focus is particularly interesting because it has clear acoustic consequences (for discussions on the distinction between different focus types, see *e.g.*, Bartels & Kingston, 1994; Di Cristo, 2000; Pierrehumbert & Hirshberg, 1990; Touati, 1987). Contrastive focus consists in selecting a constituent in the paradigmatic dimension. It is used to contrast one piece of information relative to another, as in the answer to the question from the following example (capital letters indicate focus):

1. Did Carol eat the apple?
2. No, SARAH ate the apple.

Descriptions of prosodic focus in several languages have shown that the highlighted constituent bears a recognizable intonational contour (see Di Cristo, 2000; Morel & Danon-Boileau, 1998; Rossi, 1999; Touati, 1989; Touratier, 2000 for instance, for French). Focus also has durational correlates such as lengthening of the focused constituent. These cues (intonational and durational) are in fact well identified by listeners. Quite a number of studies have explored the auditory perception of prosodic contrastive focus in several languages (French: Dahan & Bernard, 1996; English: Baum *et al.*, 1982; Bryan, 1989; Gussenhoven, 1983; Weintraub *et al.*, 1981; Italian: D'Imperio, 2001; Swedish: Brådvik *et al.*, 1991). They have shown that, for all these languages, focus is very well perceived from the auditory modality.

As mentioned above, although prosodic focus typically involves acoustic parameters, several studies have suggested that articulatory – and more specifically visible lip and jaw motion – modifications are also involved (*e.g.* Cho, 2005; De Jong, 1995; Erickson, 2002; Erickson *et al.*, 2000; Harrington *et al.*, 1995; Kelso *et al.*, 1985; Lœvenbruck, 1999, 2000; Summers, 1987; Vatikiotis-Bateson & Kelso, 1993). That these cues exist suggests that prosodic focus should be detectable visually.

Several studies on English, Swedish and reiterant French showed that visual perception of prosodic focus, even though not perfect, is possible (Bernstein *et al.*, 1989; Dohen *et al.*, 2004; Keating *et al.*, 2003; Risberg & Agelfors, 1978; Risberg & Lubker, 1978; Thompson, 1934). Adding the visual modality also improves overall auditory-visual perception of prosodic focus when the acoustic prosodic information is degraded in whispered speech for example (Dohen & Lœvenbruck, In Press). These studies suggest that visual information and, typically, lip dynamics convey crucial prosodic information that can improve lip reading in conversational situations.

In order to examine the possibility of extracting prosodic information from visual lip features, we have used several measurement techniques enabling automatic lip feature extraction. We have chosen to use very accurate measurement methods, which provide detailed precise data but which are unpractical for technical applications. The aim was to identify what the "lip pattern" of prosodic focus consists of, taking into account inter-speaker variability. The findings presented here will provide criteria for automatic prosodic focus detection from lip data in French which can be implemented in automatic lip feature extraction systems and which will complement the segmental information already used in most systems.

MAIN THRUST: EXTRACTION OF PROSODIC INFORMATION FROM LIP FEATURES

Experimental Procedures

Corpora

Two different corpora were used consisting of sentences with a subject-verb-object (S, V, O) structure and CV syllables. Sonorants were favored in order to facilitate F0 tracking. Corpus 1 consisted of 8 sentences and corpus 2 of 13 sentences. Corpus 2 was designed as an improvement of corpus 1 (through the addition of protruded vowels – please see later) after recording a first speaker. Below is an example of one of the sentences used (the reader may refer to appendices 1 & 2 for the detailed corpora).

[Lou]$_S$ [ramena]$_V$ [Manu.]$_O$ ('Lou gave a lift back to Manu.')

Prosodic Focus Elicitation

For all the recordings described below, four focus conditions were elicited: subject-, verb- and object-focus (narrow focus) and a neutral version (broad focus) thereafter respectively referred to as SF, VF, OF and BF. In order to trigger focus in a natural way, the speakers were asked to perform a correction task thereby focusing a phrase which had been mispronounced in an audio prompt. The recording went as follows (where capital letters indicate focus):

Audio prompt: S1: Lou ramena Manu. ('Lou gave a lift back to Manu.')
S2: S1 a dit : Paul ramena Manu ? ('S1 said: Paul gave a lift back to Manu?')
Speaker utters: LOU ramena Manu. ('LOU gave a lift back to Manu.')

The speakers were given no indication on how to produce focus (*e.g.* which syllables to focus, which intonational contour or which articulatory pattern to produce). Two repetitions of each utterance (one sentence spoken in one focus condition) were recorded.

Visual Lip Feature Selection

The typical lip parameters that characterize French vowels are lip opening (/ɛ, ɛ̃, ɔ, ɔ̃, œ, œ̃, ə, a, ɑ̃/ open vs. /i, y, u, e, o, ø/ closed), lip spreading (/i, e, ɛ, ɛ̃, a, ɑ̃/) and lip protrusion /y, ø, œ, œ̃, u, o, ɔ̃/). Together they satisfactorily describe French vowels (Straka, 1965; Carton, 1974). They were thus chosen as the lip features to be extracted from the articulatory data.

Together they satisfactorily describe French vowels (Carton, 1974; Straka, 1965). They were thus chosen as the lip features to be extracted from the articulatory data.

Data Analysis

Preliminary Acoustic Validation

After the recordings, a first step consisted in acoustically validating the data *i.e.* checking whether focus had actually been produced acoustically. On the one hand, we checked that the focused utterances displayed the typical focus intonation as described in Dohen & Lœvenbruck (2004) for example. On the other hand, an informal auditory perception test was conducted in order to check whether focus could be perceived auditorily.

Pre-Shaping of the Lip Features

The area under the curve of variation of the amplitude of each feature over time was automatically detected for each phrase (S, V and O) and then divided by the duration of the phrase. Thus this parameter represents the mean amplitude of the feature considered over the phrase. The procedure is illustrated in Fig. 1. This provides a total of three values per utterance for each feature.

Isolating Supra-Segmental Variations from Segmental Varying Material

Our aim was to be able to isolate and compare lip features reflecting supra-segmental variations (prosody). The problem was that, for the sake of naturalness and reproducibility as well as for studying variability, we used real speech (*vs.* reiterant speech) *i.e.* segmentally varying material. In order to isolate the lip features resulting solely from supra-segmental variations, and not from segmental variations (/a/ is produced with more open lips than /m/, for instance) we adopted a normalization technique. This first consisted in calculating, for each constituent (S, V, O), the mean of the areas for the neutral versions (BF) of the sentence (as described in the Data Analysis section) *i.e.* two values for each constituent (two repetitions of the same utterance consisting of three constituents). Then all the area values corresponding to the same constituent in the same sentence uttered in the different focus conditions (obtained using the method described in the Data Analysis section) – *i.e.* 6 values: 3 focus conditions, 2 repetitions – were divided by this neutral mean. After this normalization, a value of 1 corresponds to no variation of the considered feature when the constituent considered is under focus compared to a BF case, a value above 1 corresponds to an increase and a value below 1 to a decrease.

Figure 1. Illustration of the data pre-shaping: computation of the area under the curve corresponding to each constituent (here shown in red for the verb)

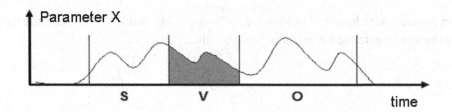

Complementary Durational Measurements

For all the experiments described below, complementary durational measurements were conducted since duration is an important aspect of prosodic focus (see *e.g.* Dohen & Lœvenbruck, 2004: focal syllables are lengthened and sometimes the pre-focus syllable is also lengthened as part of an anticipatory strategy) and can also be detected/processed visually. The durations of all the syllables were computed from acoustic labels assigned using Praat (Boersma & Weenink, 2005) and normalized according to the method described in The Data Analysis section in order to isolate variability due to supra-segmental variations.

Presentation of the Results

The results will all be presented using the same convention. Several graphs (such as those in Fig. 3) will be provided for each speaker, summarizing the results for all the features measured (both durational and lip features). In these graphs, the means of a specific feature over all the utterances produced by the speaker are represented for three types of within utterance locations. The 'foc' item represents the mean of all the data corresponding to all the focused constituents (*i.e.* the focused phrase within the utterance, being either the subject, the verb or the object). The 'pre-foc' item represents the mean of the data corresponding to pre-focus constituents *i.e.* the subject in the case of verb focus or the subject + verb in the case of object focus. The 'post-foc' item represents the mean of all the data corresponding to post-focus constituents *i.e.* the verb + object in the subject focus case and the object in the verb focus case. In this representation, a value above 1 represents an increase compared to the neutral version of the same utterance.

Statistical Analyses

For the sake of clarity and comparability, the same statistical analysis protocol was used for all the analyses described below. After the pre-shaping of the data described above, one value was available for each constituent (S, V, O) for each utterance. The statistical analyses were conducted for all the data corresponding to focus cases (SF, VF and OF) since the normalization procedure (see Data Analysis section) used the neutral case as the basis for normalization.

The first analysis aimed at testing **intra-utterance contrasts** *i.e.* contrasts within the utterance. The question was: *is there a significant difference between the focused constituent and the rest of the utterance?* This led to the analysis of two within-subject factors. The first one was a two-level factor called Congruency. The congruent cases correspond to S and subject focus (S&SF), V and verb focus (V&VF) and O and object focus (O&OF). The incongruent cases correspond to V and O for subject focus (V&SF, O&SF), S and O for verb focus (S&VF, O&VF) and S and V for object focus (S&OF, V&OF). The second within-subject factor was a three-level factor corresponding to Focus Type (SF, VF or OF). For each lip and durational feature, a two-way multivariate analysis of variance (MANOVA; see Howell, 2004) was conducted with the aforementioned within-subject factors (*i.e.* Congruency and Focus Type). The sphericity of the data was tested using Mauchly's sphericity test. When the test was significant we used a Huynh-Feldt correction on the degrees of freedom (the results presented below include these corrections but, for clarity, the "true" numbers of degrees of freedom are in fact reported when the F values are presented).

The second analysis aimed at testing **inter-utterance contrasts** in order to answer the following question: *is there a significant difference between a constituent in the focused version of the utterance and in the neutral version of the utterance?* This was tested using t-tests (Howell, 2004) comparing the values corresponding to a specific constituent in the focused case to 1 (after normalization the neutral case corresponds to 1). The following tests were conducted:

- test 1: comparison of the values corresponding to the focused constituents to 1
- test 2: comparison of the values corresponding to the pre-focus constituents (S in the VF and OF cases and V in the OF case) to 1
- test 3: comparison of the values corresponding to the post-focus constituents (V and O for SF cases and O for VF cases).

The results of all these tests are summarized in tables such as Table 1.

Method 1: Lip Tracking from Video Data

Lip Feature Extraction

A first set of measurements was collected using a lip tracking device designed at the former Institut de la Communication Parlée (now Speech & Cognition Department, GIPSA-lab) (Audouy, 2000; Lallouache, 1991). This device consists in using blue lipstick, a blue marker on the chin and front and profile blue references (front: on the eyeglasses; profile: vertical ruler fixed on the eyeglasses). The speaker is filmed using front and profile cameras (digital; 25 fps). Fig. 2 provides an example of the images recorded.

Figure 2. Lip tracking device: a. (left) example of a recorded image; b. (right) extracted features

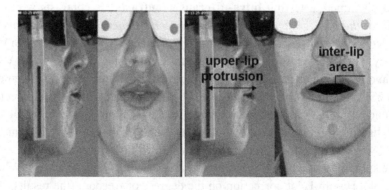

A software program automatically extracts the lip contour from the sequence of digitalized video frames and derives parameters describing inter-lip area (LA) and upper-lip protrusion. Inter-lip area accounts for both lip opening and lip spreading making it possible to study the variations of both these features using one parameter. We analyzed these parameters as well as LA's first derivative using the procedures described in the Data Analysis section.

Recordings

Corpus 1 was recorded for one native speaker of French (speaker A). Due to the fact that these data were recorded for parallel studies as well, the corpus was mainly designed to test lip opening and lip spreading and contained very few protruded vowels. Therefore for speaker A, only inter-lip area was extracted from the video. Corpus 2 was adapted to additionally make lip protrusion analysis possible and was recorded for another native speaker of French (speaker B). Therefore for speaker B, both inter-lip area and upper-lip protrusion were extracted from the video.

Results

The results from the lip feature extraction are provided in Fig. 3 for both speakers. Table 1 provides the results of the statistical analyses conducted using the procedure described in the Data analysis section. A number of articulatory and durational correlates to prosodic focus can be extracted from these measurements for each speaker.

First, for the **intra-utterance comparisons**, Table 1 shows that Congruency has a significant effect for both speakers on duration, inter-lip area, inter-lip area's first derivative (SA only) and upper-lip protrusion (SB only). This means that when a constituent is focused, its duration, inter-lip area, inter-lip area's first derivative (SA only) and upper-lip protrusion (SB only) are significantly greater than those corresponding to the other constituents in the same utterance (intra-utterance contrast). Focus Type has a significant effect on duration (SA only) and inter-lip area (SB only). The effect on duration for speaker A is due to the fact that all the syllables of the utterance were longer when the verb was focused. The effect on inter-lip area for speaker B is due to the fact that this feature was always greater when the verb or the object were focused than when the subject was focused. There is a significant interaction between Congruency and Focus Type for duration for SA only. This is due to the fact that intra-utterance contrasts for duration were much greater for the focused verbs than for the focused subjects and objects. This is an artefact of the corpus for SA, in which there were many occurrences of monosyllabic verbs: when the focused constituent is mono-syllabic, the mean syllabic correlates of focus are increased.

Secondly, for the **inter-utterance comparisons**, Table 1 shows that test 1 is significant for duration, inter-lip area (SA only), inter-lip area's first derivative and upper-lip protrusion (SB only). This shows that overall, when a constituent is focused, it is lengthened and hyper-articulated (larger and "faster" inter-lip area and upper-lip protrusion) compared with the same constituent in a neutral version of the utterance. Fig. 3 illustrates this (values above 1). Test 2 is significant for all features for SA and for duration for SB. For speaker A, lip features were not only enhanced for the focused constituent but also for the pre-focus constituent (see Fig. 3: values above 1). This corresponds to an anticipatory strategy described in Dohen *et al.* (2004). For speaker B, the duration of the pre-focus constituent was significantly reduced compared with the neutral rendition (see Fig. 3: value below 1). Test 3 is significant for

Figure 3. Lip tracking: durational measurements and lip features for speakers A and B: normalized values corresponding to the pre-focus, focus and post-focus sequences (the dark horizontal lines correspond to the neutral case).

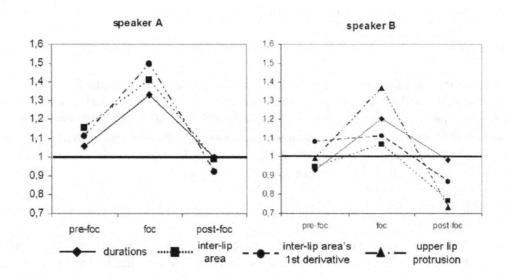

Table 1. Results of the statistical analyses for the lip-tracking data for speakers A and B, using the statistical analysis protocol described in the Data Analysis section. The F values correspond to the F-test statistic. The t-values correspond to the T-test statistic. The p values correspond to the significance level. An effect was considered as significant when p < .01 (bold characters signal significant effects).

		Intra-utterance Contrasts			Inter-utterance Constrasts		
		Congruency	Focus Type	Interaction	Congruency	Focus Type	Interaction
Duration	SA	*F(1,15)=158.9* *p<.001*	*F(2,30)=19.2* *p<.001*	*F(2,30)=13.6* *p<.001*	*t=8.6* *p<.001*	*t=3* *p=.004*	*t=-0.3* *p=.731*
	SB	*F(1,25)=180.7* *p<.001*	*F(2,50)=3.6* *p=.036*	*F(2,50)=2.2* *p=.117*	*t=8.2* *p<.001*	*t=-4.8* *p<.001*	*t=-1.1* *p=.281*
Inter-lip Area (LA)	SA	*F(1,15)=202.2* *p<.001*	*F(2,30)=4.3* *p=.023*	*F(2,30)=3.8* *p=.061*	*t=9.8* *p<.001*	*t=4.3* *p<.001*	*t=-0.8* *p=.447*
	SB	*F(1,25)=53.4* *p<.001*	*F(2,50)=8.6* *p=.001*	*F(2,50)=2.3* *p=.112*	*t=2.3* *p=.026*	*t=-2* *p=.047*	*t=-10.4* *p<.001*
LA's 1st derivative	SA	*F(1,15)=47.5* *p<.001*	*F(2,30)=1.9* *p=.17*		*t=6.6* *p<.001*	*t=2.8* *p=.007*	*t=-2.9* *p=.006*
	SB	-	-	-	*t=3.8* *p<.001*	-	*t=-2.6* *p=.011*
Upper-lip Protrusion	SB	*F(1,25)=19.8* *p<.001*	*F(2,50)=2.7* *p=.076*		*t=3.3* *p=.001*	*t=-0.1* *p=.945*	*t=-6.2* *p<.001*

inter-lip area and upper-lip protrusion for speaker B. This shows that for speaker B, inter-lip area and upper-lip protrusion are decreased on the post-focus constituent compared to the same constituent in the neutral version (see Fig. 3: values below 1).

The strategies of both speakers are summarized below:

- **Speaker A** – focal lengthening; focal increase of lip feature amplitudes (inter-lip area and its first derivative); largest contrast for inter-lip area features.
- **Speaker B** – focal lengthening; focal increase of lip feature amplitudes (inter-lip area and its first derivative and upper-lip protrusion); largest contrast for upper-lip protrusion.

These findings suggest that, for speaker A, values of normalized duration, normalized inter-lip area and its first derivative above 1.2 may characterize a focused constituent. For speaker B, the pattern is a little more complex: the graph suggests that a focused constituent may be detected when all parameters are above 1 for the given constituent and below one for the following constituent. This latter result is in line with the post-focus deaccenting phenomenon that has been described acoustically (see *e.g.*, Dohen & Lœvenbruck, 2004).

Method 2: Optotrak

Recordings

Five native speakers of French (B, C, D, E and F) were recorded using corpus 2 (see Corpora section) and the procedure described in the Prosodic Focus Elicitation section. Speaker B was the same as the speaker B recorded using method 1 (see section describing the lip tracking study). The recordings were

Figure 4. Optotrak measurement device: experimental setup

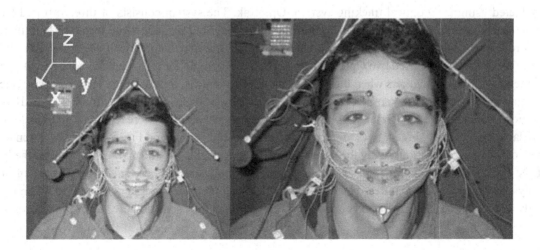

Figure 5. Map of the locations of the IRED diodes referred to as "markers"

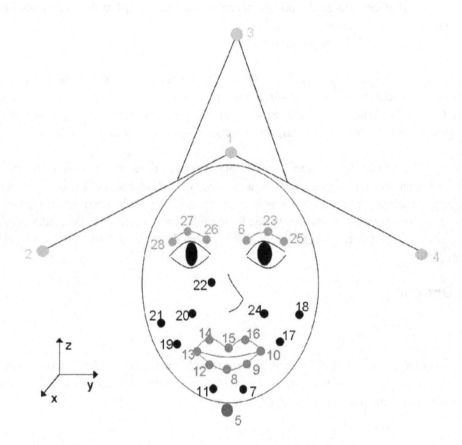

conducted using a 3D optical tracking system: Optotrak. The system consists of three infrared (IR) cameras which track the positions of infrared emitting diodes (IREDs) glued to the speaker's face (thereafter referred to as markers). The 3D coordinates of each IRED were automatically detected over time. For this experiment, we used two Optotraks in order to compensate for missing data, corresponding to momentary hiding of markers when the speaker moves (head turns, for example). Data were corrected for head motion using 4 markers placed on a head rig as shown on Fig. 4 and Fig. 5 (markers 1-4). IRED positions were sampled at 60Hz and low-pass filtered. The acoustic signals were recorded simultaneously and sampled at 22kHz. Fig. 4 gives an idea of the experimental setup and Fig. 5 provides a schematic view of the marker locations. Only the measurements corresponding to the markers located on the lips of the speakers (see Fig. 5: markers 8-10 and 12-16) will be discussed here since the purpose of this analysis was to study lip features. The other facial and head movement markers were used for another study and for the sake of clarity and conciseness, they will not be discussed here. After the recordings, an acoustic validation was conducted using the procedure described in the Data Analysis section. It showed that, from an acoustic point of view, all the speakers had correctly produced focus.

Lip Feature Extraction

Various lip features were computed from the 3D coordinates of the IREDs:

- **Lip opening** was computed as the difference between the z coordinates of the upper and lower middle lip markers (see Fig. 5: markers 8 and 15).
- **Lip spreading** corresponded to the difference between the y coordinates of the two lip corner markers (see Fig. 5: markers 13 and 10).
- **Upper lip protrusion** was assimilated to the x coordinate of the middle upper lip marker (see Fig. 5: marker 15).

In addition, vertical jaw movements (z coordinate of the chin marker, *i.e.* marker 5) were also analyzed but the results will not be discussed here, as they were intended for a different study.

Results

The results for all speakers are provided in Fig. 6 and summarized thereafter. The jaw parameter was collected for a different study. Only results on the lips are reported here. For the sake of clarity, we will only give a general overview of the statistical results in the text. The aim is to put forward trends which are consistent from one speaker to another. The detailed results of the statistical analyses are however provided in Table 2.

First, for the **intra-utterance comparisons**, Table 2 shows that, for all speakers, Congruency has a significant effect on duration, lip opening and upper-lip protrusion and no significant effect on lip spreading (except for SE). This shows that, when a constituent is focused, it is significantly lengthened and hyper-articulated (larger lip opening, greater upper-lip protrusion) compared to the other constituents of the same utterance. There is a significant intra-utterance contrast between the visual lip features corresponding to the focused constituent and the visual lip features corresponding to the other constituents of the utterance. For duration, Focus Type also has a significant effect, illustrating the fact that when the verb is focused, all the syllables of the utterance are lengthened. There is also a significant interaction between congruency and focus type for duration for all speakers. This is due to the fact that, when the verb is focused, the intra-utterance contrast for duration is significantly stronger.

Secondly, for the **inter-utterance comparisons**, Table 2 shows that test 1 is significant for all speakers for duration, lip opening and upper-lip protrusion. This shows that, overall, when a constituent is focused, it is lengthened and hyper-articulated (larger lip opening and greater upper-lip protrusion) compared with the same constituent in a neutral version of the utterance. It is also the case for lip spreading for three of the five speakers. Fig. 6 illustrates this (values above 1). For SC, SD, SE and SF, this corresponds to a significant lengthening of the pre-focus constituent compared to the same constituent in a neutral version of the utterance (see Fig. 6: values above 1). For SB, it corresponds to a significant reduction of the duration of this constituent (see Fig. 6: values below 1). Test 2 is also significant for SC and SD for lip opening (see Fig. 6: values above 1). This corresponds to an increase in lip opening for the pre-focus constituent. These results (for test 2) suggest that some speakers use an anticipatory strategy to signal focus by starting to lengthen and hyper-articulate before focus. Test 3 is significant for SB, SD and SE for lip opening, for SB for lip spreading and for SE and SF for upper-lip protrusion. In all these cases (except for SF for upper-lip protrusion), this corresponds to a decrease on the post-focus constituent compared to the same constituent in the neutral version (see Fig. 6: value below 1). This suggests that, after focus, some speakers tend to shorten and articulate less.

The strategies of all the speakers are summarized below:

- **Speaker B** – focal lengthening; focal increase of lip feature amplitudes (except for lip spreading); post-focus decrease of lip feature amplitudes of all the parameters; largest contrast for protrusion and duration. Since speaker B was recorded using both methods (see section describing the lip tracking study), the results can be compared. It appears that the trends are the same for the two methods with the same ranges except for protrusion. It is difficult to accurately measure lip protrusion, as it is very sensitive to the reference used. This could explain the range difference.
- **Speaker C** – focal lengthening; focal increase of lip feature amplitudes; slight post-focus decrease of lip opening amplitudes; largest contrast for protrusion and duration.

Figure 6. Optotrak: durational measurements and lip features for speakers B to F: normalized values corresponding to the pre-focus, focus and post-focus sequences (the horizontal line corresponds to the neutral case)

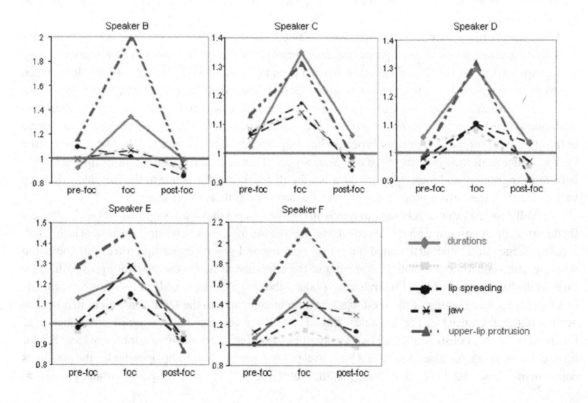

Table 2. Results of the statistical analyses for the Optotrak data for speakers B to F using the statistical analysis protocol described in the Data Analysis section. The F values correspond to the F-test statistic. The t-values correspond to the T-test statistic. The p values correspond to the significance level. An effect was considered as significant when $p < .01$ (bold characters signal significant effects).

		Intra-utterance Contrasts			Inter-utterance Constrasts		
		Congruency	Focus Type	Interaction	Congruency	Focus Type	Interaction
Duration	SB	**$F_{(1,25)}=198.7$ $p<.001$**	**$F_{(2,50)}=15.6$ $p<.001$**	**$F_{(2,50)}=5.6$ $p=.006$**	**$t=-9.8$ $p<.001$**	**$t=-2.8$ $p=.007$**	$t=-0.8$ $p=.402$
	SC	**$F_{(1,25)}=323.9$ $p<.001$**	**$F_{(2,50)}=13.9$ $p<.001$**	**$F_{(2,50)}=6.6$ $p=.003$**	**$t=13.9$ $p<.001$**	**$t=4$ $p<.001$**	**$t=4.3$ $p<.001$**
	SD	**$F_{(1,25)}=109.4$ $p<.001$**	**$F_{(2,50)}=15.5$ $p<.001$**	**$F_{(2,50)}=10.2$ $p<.001$**	**$t=9.5$ $p<.001$**	**$t=3.2$ $p=.003$**	$t=2.2$ $p=.033$
	SE	**$F_{(1,25)}=50$ $p<.001$**	**$F_{(2,50)}=5.8$ $p=.005$**	**$F_{(2,50)}=7.3$ $p=.002$**	**$t=9$ $p<.001$**	**$t=5.3$ $p<.001$**	$t=0.8$ $p=.434$
	SF	**$F_{(1,25)}=239.6$ $p<.001$**	**$F_{(2,50)}=10.7$ $p=.001$**	**$F_{(2,50)}=7.9$ $p=.003$**	**$t=11.7$ $p<.001$**	**$t=3.8$ $p<.001$**	$t=2.1$ $p=.041$
Lip Opening	SB	**$F_{(1,25)}=11.1$ $p<.001$**	**$F_{(2,50)}=11.7$ $p<.001$**	$F_{(2,50)}=0.907$ $p=.41$	**$t=-5.3$ $p<.001$**	$t=-0.1$ $p=.89$	**$t=-10$ $p<.001$**
	SC	**$F_{(1,25)}=149.1$ $p<.001$**	$F_{(2,50)}=0.1$ $p=.880$	-	**$t=10$ $p<.001$**	**$t=6$ $p<.001$**	$t=-2.4$ $p=.02$
	SD	**$F_{(1,25)}=49.2$ $p<.001$**	$F_{(2,50)}=0.6$ $p=.557$	-	**$t=4.2$ $p<.001$**	**$t=3.3$ $p=.002$**	$t=-3.5$ $p=.001$
	SE	**$F_{(1,25)}=111.4$ $p<.001$**	$F_{(2,50)}=2.1$ $p=.137$	-	**$t=9.1$ $p<.001$**	$t=-2.4$ $p=.018$	**$t=-3.7$ $p<.001$**
	SF	**$F_{(1,25)}=97.9$ $p<.001$**	$F_{(2,50)}=0.6$ $p=.562$	-	**$t=7.3$ $p<.001$**	$t=1$ $p=.335$	$t=-1$ $p=.332$
Lip Spreading	SB	$F_{(1,25)}=0.6$ $p=.462$	$F_{(1,725.50)}=2.2$ $p=.134$	-	$t=0.2$ $p=.831$	$t=0.6$ $p=.567$	**$t=-5.7$ $p<.001$**
	SC	**$F_{(1,25)}=11.8$ $p=.002$**	$F_{(2,50)}=3.7$ $p=.033$	$F_{(2,50)}=0.5$ $p=.59$	**$t=3.6$ $p=.001$**	$t=0.7$ $p=.459$	$t=-1.5$ $p=.130$
	SD	$F_{(1,25)}=3.8$ $p=.063$	$F_{(1,421.50)}=1.2$ $p=.298$	-	$t=1.7$ $p=.092$	$t=0.1$ $p=.943$	$t=0.8$ $p=.436$
	SE	**$F_{(1,25)}=47.1$ $p<.001$**	$F_{(2,50)}=4$ $p=.024$	$F_{(2,50)}=1.4$ $p=.250$	**$t=3.5$ $p=.001$**	$t=0.7$ $p=.514$	$t=-2.4$ $p=.021$
	SF	**$F_{(1,25)}=11.6$ $p=.002$**	$F_{(2,50)}=3.7$ $p=.033$	$F_{(2,50)}=1.6$ $p=.218$	**$t=3.6$ $p=.001$**	$t=-0.6$ $p=.585$	$t=1.5$ $p=.139$
Upper-lip protrusion	SB	**$F_{(1,25)}=72$ $p<.001$**	**$F_{(2,50)}=10.5$ $p<.001$**	**$F_{(2,50)}=7.8$ $p<.001$**	**$t=8.3$ $p<.001$**	$t=2.7$ $p=.01$	$t=-2$ $p=.048$
	SC	**$F_{(1,25)}=38.2$ $p<.001$**	**$F_{(2,50)}=7.4$ $p<.001$**	$F_{(2,50)}=0.5$ $p=.628$	**$t=6.5$ $p<.001$**	$t=1.9$ $p=.065$	$t=-0.3$ $p=.803$
	SD	**$F_{(1,25)}=5.5$ $p<.001$**	$F_{(2,50)}=3.2$ $p=.05$	$F_{(2,50)}=0.5$ $p=.592$	**$t=4$ $p<.001$**	$t=0.6$ $p=.574$	$t=-2.5$ $p=.014$
	SE	**$F_{(1,25)}=5.7$ $p<.001$**	$F_{(2,50)}=0.2$ $p=.860$	-	**$t=5.1$ $p<.001$**	$t=2$ $p=.046$	**$t=-2.5$ $p=.002$**
	SF	**$F_{(1,25)}=17$ $p<.001$**	$F_{(2,50)}=6.1$ $p=.099$	-	**$t=5.7$ $p<.001$**	$t=2.7$ $p=.011$	**$t=3.2$ $p=.002$**

- **Speaker D** – focal lengthening; focal increase of lip feature amplitudes (except lip spreading); post-focus decrease of lip opening and protrusion amplitudes; largest contrast for protrusion; smallest contrast for lip spreading.
- **Speaker E** – focal lengthening; focal increase of lip feature amplitudes; post-focus decrease of lip feature amplitudes; largest contrast for protrusion; smallest contrast for lip opening and spreading.
- **Speaker F** – focal lengthening; focal increase of lip feature amplitudes; largest contrast for protrusion; smallest contrast for lip opening.

The results suggest that when the normalized values of duration, lip opening, lip spreading and upper-lip protrusion are above 1 for a given constituent and decrease for the following constituent, the first constituent might bear focus. Furthermore, when the normalized values are only slightly above 1 for a given constituent, the fact that the values for the next constituent are below one is a further indication that the first constituent was focused.

CONCLUSION: LIP FEATURE CRITERIA FOR THE DETECTION OF PROSODIC FOCUS

The results described above suggest that it is possible to extract information from lip features about an important phenomenon in conversational situations, namely prosodic focus. One of the main conclusions that can be drawn is the fact that focus affects the lip features of the whole utterance and not only that of the specific focused constituent. Another important observation is that there is inter-speaker variability. However, after examining the productions of six different speakers, two main lip feature patterns can be extracted corresponding to prosodic focus production:

Figure 7. Schematic representation of a. (left) the absolute contrast pattern and b. (right) the differential contrast pattern

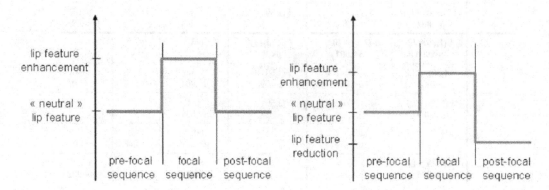

- **Absolute contrast pattern:** the focused constituent is lengthened and the features describing lip shape (inter-lip area, lip opening, lip spreading, upper-lip protrusion) are increased to a large extent. The peak velocities of the evolution of these features over time are also increased. This pattern is illustrated in Fig. 7.a.
- **Differential contrast pattern:** in this case, the focal constituent is also lengthened and the features describing lip shape are also increased but to a smaller extent. Additionally, the lip features corresponding to the post-focus sequence are decreased. An important contrast is thus created inside the utterance: the focal increase is not made very strong but is reinforced by the post-focus decrease. Fig. 7.b illustrates this pattern.

Therefore although inter-speaker variability exists, consistent strategies can be described. Furthermore, the differential contrast strategy seems to be the most used (4 speakers out of 6). This strategy seems the most economical in terms of articulatory effort while preserving a good contrast within the utterance and allowing correct focus detection. These production strategies provide good criteria for focus detection. An absolute contrast or a differential contrast on a given constituent in the utterance seem to be a good criterion for detecting the presence of focus.

We found that whatever the pattern observed, the lip feature with the highest variations under focus was upper-lip protrusion. This is consistent with the finding that lip protrusion is the most visible lip feature (Benoît *et al.*, 1994).

We note also that the results obtained with the second method are consistent with those found with the first method. Inter-lip area was used in the first method, where internal lip contour was easily derivable from video data. Lip opening + lip spreading were used in the second method, where the positions of specific markers were easily obtainable and could provide these distances. The consistency in the results suggest that any of these two parameter sets (inter-lip area or lip spreading + lip opening) can be used to detect prosodic focus.

These findings therefore enabled us to sketch a model for the production of visual features corresponding to prosodic focus in French obtained with very accurate and detailed measurement techniques. This model covers the different strategies used by different speakers. The consistency in the findings using two different measurement methods suggests that other lip feature extraction techniques could be used to automatically detect prosodic focus. The proposed model could now be used on visual data extracted using other (more practical) methods that extract lip parameters such as lip protrusion and lip opening or inter-lip area.

FUTURE RESEARCH DIRECTIONS: VISUAL SPEECH RECOGNITION

The two studies described in this chapter suggest that it is possible to extract prosodic information from lip information. The measurements and analyses described enabled us to design a model characterizing lip features typically associated with prosodic focus in French. The lip features concerned are vertical lip opening, horizontal lip spreading and upper-lip protrusion. Inter-lip area is a feature which combines lip opening and lip spreading and can be used instead. What this model mainly shows is that prosodic focus results in a marked enhancement of the lip features corresponding to the focused constituent compared to that of the other constituents of the same utterance. These findings can potentially be used for the detection of prosodic focus in automatic visual speech recognition in the following way: the contrast criteria described above can be applied to the pattern of lip features automatically extracted from the utterance.

In the studies described here, we used two lip feature extraction devices which cannot easily be used for commercial applications because of heavy and sophisticated setups, both from the equipment and the speaker point of view. We used these devices because of their very good accuracy, since precision was important to establish a reliable model. We used two different devices in order to evaluate many different lip parameters and test whether the observations were the same from one device to another. However, now that the model is established, it seems feasible to use other more "portable" lip feature extraction devices which could potentially be integrated into practical applications. We suggest that crucial prosodic information, that might improve lip reading in conversational situations, can potentially be detected using our model.

ACKNOWLEDGMENTS

We thank Guillaume Rolland for designing corpus 1 and recording speaker A. For the lip tracking data, we thank Christophe Savariaux and Alain Arnal for their technical help. For the optotrak recordings, we thank Ishi-san, Guillaume Vignali and the ATR Research Institute (Japan) for their help. We are grateful to all the speakers who participated. We also thank Jean-Luc Schwartz for his comments on our work, as well as three anonymous reviewers who provided very helpful comments on a previous version of this chapter.

REFERENCES

Audouy, M. (2000). *Traitement d'images vidéo pour la capture des mouvements labiaux*. Unpublished engineering master's thesis, Institut National Polytechnique de Grenoble, France.

Bartels, C., & Kingston, J. (1994). Salient Pitch Cues in the Perception of Contrastive Focus. In P. Bosch & R. Van Der Sandt (Eds.), *Focus & Natural Language Processing, Proceedings of Journal of Semantics Conference on Focus, IBM Working Papers, TR-80* (pp. 94-106).

Baum, S. R., Kelsch Daniloff, J., Daniloff, R., & Lewis, J. (1982). Sentence Comprehension by Broca's aphasics: effects of some suprasegmental variables. *Brain and Language, 17,* 261-271.

Benoît, C., Mohamadi, T., & Kandel, S. (1994). Effects of phonetic context on audio-visual intelligibility of French. *Journal of Speech and Hearing Research, 37,* 1195-1203.

Bernstein, L. E., Eberhardt, S. P., & Demorest, M. E. (1989). Single-channel vibrotactile supplements to visual perception of intonation and stress. *The Journal of the Acoustical Society of America, 85*(1), 397-405.

Birch, S., & Clifton, Jr. C. (1995). Focus, accent, and argument structure: effects on language comprehension. *Language and speech, 38,* 365-391.

Boersma, P., & Weenink, D. (2005). PRAAT: Doing phonetics by computer (version 4.3) [Computer program]. Retrieved from http://www.praat.org.

Brådvik, B., Dravins, C., Holtås, S., Rosén, I., Ryding, E., & Ingvar, D. (1991). Disturbances of Speech Prosody Following Right Hemisphere Infarcts. *Acta Neurologica Scandinavica, 84,* 114-126.

Bryan, K. (1989). Language Prosody and the Right Hemisphere. *Aphasiology, 3,* 285-299.

Carton, F. (1974). *Introduction à la phonétique du français.* Paris: Bordas.

Cho, T. (2005). Prosodic strengthening and featural enhancement: Evidence from acoustic and articulatory realizations of /a,i/ in English. *The Journal of the Acoustical Society of America, 117*(6), 3867-3878.

De Jong, K. (1995). The supraglottal articulation of prominence in English: Linguistic stress as localized hyperarticulation. *The Journal of the Acoustical Society of America, 97*(1), 491-504.

Di Cristo, A. (2000). Vers une modélisation de l'accentuation du français (deuxième partie). *Journal of French Language Studies, 10,* 27-44.

Dahan, D., & Bernard, J.-M. (1996). Interspeaker Variability in Emphatic Accent Production in French. *Language and Speech, 39*(4), 341-374.

D'Imperio, M. (2001). Focus and Tonal Structure in Neapolitan Italian. *Speech Communication, 33*(4), 339-356.

Dohen, M., & Lœvenbruck, H. (2004). Pre-focal Rephrasing, Focal Enhancement and Post-focal Deaccentuation in French. In *Proceedings of ICSLP 2004* (pp. 1313-1316).

Dohen, M., Loevenbruck, H., Cathiard, M.-A., & Schwartz, J.-L. (2004). Visual perception of contrastive focus in reiterant French speech. *Speech Communication, 44,* 155-172.

Dohen, M., & Lœvenbruck, H. (In Press). Interaction of audition and vision for the perception of prosodic contrastive focus. *Language and Speech.*

Erickson, D., Maekawa, K., Hashi, M., & Dang, J. (2000). Some articulatory and acoustic changes associated with emphasis in spoken English. In *Proceedings of ICSLP 2000, 3,* 247-250.

Erickson, D. (2002). Articulation of Extreme Formant Patterns for Emphasized Vowels. *Phonetica, 59,* 134-149.

Gussenhoven, C. (1983). Testing the Reality of Focus Domains. *Language and Speech, 26*(1), 61-80.

Gussenhoven, C. (1984). *On the grammar and semantic of sentence accents.* Dordrecht: Foris.

Halliday, M. A. K. (1967). *Intonation and Grammar in British English.* The Hague: Mouton.

Harrington, J., Fletcher, J., & Roberts, C. (1995). Coarticulation and the accented/unaccented distinction: evidence from jaw movement data. *Journal of Phonetics, 23,* 305-322.

Howell, D. C. (2004). *Fundamental statistics for the behavioral sciences (5th edition).* Belmont, CA: Brooks/Cole.

Keating, P., Baroni, M., Mattys, S., Scarborough, R., Alwan, A., Auer, E. T., & Bernstein, L. E. (2003). Optical Phonetics and Visual Perception of Lexical and Phrasal Stress in English. In *Proceedings of ICPhS 2003* (pp. 2071-2074).

Kelso, J. A. S., Vatikiotis-Bateson, E., Saltzman, E., & Kay, B. A. (1985). A qualitative dynamic analysis of reiterant speech production: phase portraits, kinematics, and dynamic modeling. *The Journal of the Acoustical Society of America, 77*(1), 266-280.

Ladd, R. D. (1996). *Intonational phonology.* Cambridge studies in Linguistics.

Lallouache, M.-T. (1991). *Un poste Visage-Parole couleur. Acquisition et traitement automatique des contours de lèvres.* Unpublished doctoral dissertation, Institut National Polytechnique de Grenoble, France.

Lœvenbruck, H. (1999). An investigation of articulatory correlates of the Accentual Phrase in French. In *Proceedings of the 14th ICPhS, 1,* 667-670.

Lœvenbruck, H. (2000). Effets articulatoires de l'emphase contrastive sur la Phrase Accentuelle en français. In *Actes des XXIIIes Journées d'Etude de la Parole JEP 2000* (pp. 165-168).

Morel, M.-A., & Danon-Boileau, L. (1998). *Grammaire de l'intonation. L'exemple du français oral.* Paris-Gap: Ophrys, Bibliothèque de Faits de Langues.

Nølke, H. (1994). *Linguistique modulaire : de la forme au sens.* Louvain-Paris: Peeters.

Pagel, V. (1999). *De l'utilisation d'informations acoustiques suprasegmentales en reconnaissance de la parole continue.* Unpublished doctoral dissertation, Université Henri Poincaré - Nancy 1, France.

Pierrehumbert, J., & Hirshberg, J. (1990). The meaning of intonational contours in discourse. In P. Cohen, J. Morgan, M. Pollack (Eds.), *Intentions in Communication* (pp. 271-311). Cambridge, MA: The MIT Press.

Risberg, A., & Agelfors, E. (1978). On the identification of intonation contours by hearing impaired listeners. *Speech Transmission Laboratory Quarterly Progress Report and Status Report, 19*(2-3), 51-61.

Risberg, A., & Lubker, J. (1978). Prosody and speechreading. *Speech Transmission Laboratory Quarterly Progress Report and Status Report, 19*(4), 1-16.

Rossi, M. (1999). La focalisation. In *L'intonation, le système du français: description et modélisation* (Chap. II-6, pp. 116-128). Ophrys.

Selkirk, E. O. (1984). The grammar of intonation. In E. O. Selkirk (Ed.), *Phonology and syntax: the relation between sound and structure* (pp. 197-296). The MIT Press.

Straka, G. (1965). *Album phonétique.* Québec: Les Presses de l'Université de Laval.

Summers, W. V. (1987). Effects of stress and final-consonant voicing on vowel production: Articulatory and acoustic analyses. *The Journal of the Acoustical Society of America, 82*(3), 847-863.

Thompson, D. M. (1934). On the detection of emphasis in spoken sentences by means of visual, tactual, and visual-tactual cues. *The Journal of General Psychology, 11,* 160-172.

Touati, P. (1987). Structures prosodiques du suédois et du français. *Lund Working Papers, 21,* Lund University Press.

Touati, P. (1989). De la prosodie française du dialogue. Rapport du projet KIPROS. *Working Papers, Lund University, 35*, 203-214.

Touratier, C. (2000). *La sémantique*. Paris: Armand Collin.

Vatikiotis-Bateson, E., & Kelso, J. A. S. (1993). Rhythm type and articulatory dynamics in English, French and Japanese. *Journal of Phonetics, 21*, 231-265.

Waibel, A. (1988). *Prosody and speech recognition*. San Francisco, CA: Morgan Kaufmann Publishers Inc..

Weintraub, S., Mesulam, M.-M., & Krahmer, L. (1981). Disturbances in Prosody: A Right-hemisphere Contribution to Language. *Archives of Neurology, 38*, 742-744.

Yousfi, A., & Meziane, A. (2006). The Centisecond Two Levels Hidden Semi Markov Model (CTLHSMM). *International Symposium on Parallel Computing in Electrical Engineering* (pp. 101-104).

ADDITIONAL READING

Abry, C., & Boë, L.-J., (1986). Laws for Lips. *Speech Communication, 5*, 97-104.

Abry, C., Boë, L.-J., Corsi, P., Descout, R., Gentil, M., & Graillot, P. (1980). *Labialité et phonétique. Données fondamentales et études expérimentales sur la géométrie et la motricité labiales*. Grenoble: Publications de l'Université des Langues et Lettres de Grenoble.

Baum, S. R., & Pell, M. D. (1999). The neural bases of prosody: insights from lesion studies and neuroimaging. *Aphasiology, 13*(8).

Beckman, M. E. (1986). *Stress and Non Stress Accent*. Dordrecht: Foris.

Bolinger, D. (1989). *Intonation and its uses. Melody in grammar and discourse*. CA: Stanford University Press.

Collier, R., & 't Hart, J. (1975). The role of intonation in speech perception. In A. Cohen & S. G. Noteboom (Eds.), *Structure and Process in Speech Perception* (pp. 107-123). Berlin: Springer Verlag.

Cruttenden, A. (1986). *Intonation*. Cambridge: Cambridge University Press.

Cutler, A. (1984). Stress and accent in language production and understanding. In D. Gibbon, H. Richter (Eds.), *Intonation accent and rhythm: studies in discourse phonology* (pp. 77-90). Berlin: de Gruyter.

Cutler, A., Dahan, D., & van Donsellar, W. (1997). Prosody in the comprehension of spoken language: a literature review. *Language and speech, 40*(2), 141-201.

Delatttre, P. (1967). La nuance de sens par l'intonation. *French Review, 41*(3), 326-339.

Dohen, M. (2005). *Deixis prosodique multisensorielle : production et perception audiovisuelle de la focalisation contrastive en français*. Unpublished doctoral dissertation, Institut National Polytechnique de Grenoble, France.

Firth, J. R. (1948). Sound and prosodies. *Transactions of the Philological Society*, 127-152.

Fónagy, I. (1981). Fonction prédictive de l'intonation. In P. Léon, M. Rossi (Eds.), *Problèmes de prosodie II, Expérimentations, modèles et fonctions* (pp. 113-120).

Jun, S.-A., & Fougeron, C. (2000). A Phonological Model of French Intonation. In A. Botinis (Ed.), *Intonation: Analysis, modelling and technology* (pp. 209-242). Dordrecht: Kluwer Academic Publishers.

Hirst, D., & Di Cristo, A. (1998). *Intonation systems: a survey of twenty languages.* Cambridge University Press.

House, D., Bruce, G., Ericksson, L., & Lacerda, F. (1990). Recognition of prosodic categories in Swedish: Rule implementation. *Working Papers, Lund University, 34*, 62-66.

Lehiste, I. (1970). *Suprasegmentals.* Cambridge, MA: MIT Press.

Mandel, D. R., Jusczyk, P. W., & Kemler Nelson, D. G. (1994). Does sentential prosody help infants organize and remember speech information? *Cognition, 53*(2), 155-180.

Monrad-Krohn, G. H. (1947). Dysprosody or altered "melody of language". *Brain, 70*, 405-415.

Searle, J. R. (1969). *Speech acts.* Cambridge: Cambridge University Press.

Shattuck-Hufnagel, S., & Turk, A. E. (1996). A prosody tutorial for investigators of auditory sentence processing. *Journal of Psycholinguistic Research, 25*(2), 193-247.

Tabain, M. (2003). Effects of prosodic boundary on /aC/ sequences: Articulatory results. *The Journal of the Acoustical Society of America, 113*(5), 2834-2849.

Terken, J. (1993). Issues in the perception of prosody. In *Prosody-1993*, 228-233.

Truss, L. (2003). *Eats, shoots and leaves. The zero tolerance approach to punctuation.* London: Profile Books Ltd.

Vaissière, J. (1989). The use of prosodic parameters in automatic speech recognition. In H. Niemann, M. Lang, G. Sagerer (Eds.), *Recent advances in speech understanding and dialog systems.* Nato Asi Series, Springer Verlag.

Welby, P. (2003). French intonational rises and their role in speech seg mentation. In *Proceedings of Eurospeech: The 8th Annual Conference on Speech Communication and Technology* (pp. 2125–2128).

APPENDIX 1 – CORPUS AV1

The number next to S/V/O is the number of syllables of the constituent.

(s1) [Jean]$_{S1}$ [veut ménager]$_{V4}$ [nos jolis nouveaux navets]$_{O7}$
'Jean wants to spare our fine new turnips.'

(s2) [Romain]$_{S2}$ [ranima]$_{V3}$ [la jolie maman]$_{O5}$
'Romain revived the good-looking mother.'

(s3) [Mélanie]$_{S3}$ [vit]$_{V1}$ [les mauvais loups malheureux]$_{O7}$
'Mélanie saw the unhappy bad wolves.'

(s4) [Véroniqua]$_{S4}$ [mangeait]$_{V2}$ [les mauvais melons]$_{O5}$
'Véroniqua was eating the bad melons.'

(s5) [Les mauvais loups]$_{S4}$ [mangeront]$_{V3}$ [Jean]$_{O1}$
'The bad wolves will eat Jean.'

(s6) [Mon mari]$_{S3}$ [veut ranimer]$_{V4}$ [Romain]$_{O2}$
'My husband wants to revive Romain.'

(s7) [Les loups]$_{S2}$ [suivaient]$_{V2}$ [Marilou]$_{O3}$
'The wolves were following Marilou.'

(s8) [Le beau marin]$_{S4}$ [vit]$_{V1}$ [Véroniqua]$_{O4}$
'The good-looking sailor saw Véroniqua.'

APPENDIX 2 – CORPUS AV2

The four first sentences of corpus AV2 are (s2), (s4), (s6) and (s7) from corpus AV1. The nine other sentences are given below (the number next to S/V/O is the number of syllables of the constituent).

(s9) [La nounou]$_{S3}$ [mariera]$_{V3}$ [Li]$_{O1}$
'The nanny will marry Li.'

(s10) [La lama lent]$_{S4}$ [lu]$_{V1}$ [Marinella]$_{O4}$
'The slow lama read Marinella.'

(s11) [Marinella]$_{S4}$ [va laminer]$_{V4}$ [Numu]$_{O2}$
'Marinella will laminate Numu.'

(s12) [Lou]$_{S1}$ [mima]$_{V2}$ [le lama]$_{O3}$
'Lou mimed the lama.'

(s13) [Le nominé]$_{S4}$ [lu]$_{V1}$ [les longs mots.]$_{O3}$
'The nominee read the long words.'

(s14) [La nounou]$_{S3}$ [vit]$_{V1}$ [Lou]$_{O1}$
'The nanny saw Lou.'

(s15) [Les loups]$_{S2}$ [mimaient]$_{V2}$ [Marilou]$_{O3}$
'The wolves mimed Marilou.'

(s16) [Lou]$_{S1}$ [ramena]$_{V3}$ [Manu]$_{O2}$
    'Lou gave a lift back to Manu.'
(s17) [Li]$_{S1}$ [ralluma]$_{V3}$ [les moulinets]$_{O4}$
    'Li lit the wheels again.'

Chapter XV
Visual Speech Perception, Optical Phonetics, and Synthetic Speech

Lynne E. Bernstein
House Ear Institute, Los Angeles, USA

Jintao Jiang
House Ear Institute, Los Angeles, USA

ABSTRACT

The information in optical speech signals is phonetically impoverished compared to the information in acoustic speech signals that are presented under good listening conditions. But high lipreading scores among prelingually deaf adults inform us that optical speech signals are in fact rich in phonetic information. Hearing lipreaders are not as accurate as deaf lipreaders, but they too demonstrate perception of detailed optical phonetic information. This chapter briefly sketches the historical context of and impediments to knowledge about optical phonetics and visual speech perception (lipreading). The authors review findings on deaf and hearing lipreaders. Then we review recent results on relationships between optical speech signals and visual speech perception. We extend the discussion of these relationships to the development of visual speech synthesis. We advocate for a close relationship between visual speech perception research and development of synthetic visible speech.

INTRODUCTION

Modern research on auditory speech perception was initiated towards the middle of the twentieth century. A primary item on its agenda was to discover relationships between acoustic phonetic cues in speech signals and their perceptual effects, with particular attention to the cues in consonant and vowel segments. The research could not have proceeded successfully without contemporaneous developments in acoustic signal analysis and speech synthesis. Today, much is known about acoustic phonetic structure (Stevens, 1998), acoustic speech synthesis by rule and/or by concatenation methods (Klatt, 1987; van Santen, Sproat, Olive, & Hirschberg, 1997), auditory perception of acoustic phonetic cues (for reviews see Pisoni & Remez, 2005), and neural bases of auditory speech processing (Scott & Johnsrude, 2003). Notwithstanding ongoing current research, our knowledge about optical phonetic signals, visual speech perception, and visual speech synthesis remains behind the comparable work involving acoustic speech signals.

In this chapter, we first review some long-standing impediments to knowledge about the visual aspects of speech. One important impediment has been the view that visible speech is not actually very informative on its own. We review perceptual studies that contradict that view. Those studies have revealed much about visual phonetic perception. We then discuss recent findings on relations between optical phonetic signals and phonetic perception. We argue that the link between phonetic signals and phonetic perception should be exploited in developing a visual speech synthesizer. In the last section of this chapter, we report an approach that we have taken to exploit the link.

IMPEDIMENTS TO KNOWLEDGE ABOUT OPTICAL PHONETICS AND VISUAL SPEECH PERCEPTION

One impediment to knowledge about visible speech is the presupposition that, "A relatively small proportion of the information in speech is visually available" (Kuhl & Meltzoff, 1988, p. 240). We would not be surprised if researchers were not drawn to study a signal with little intrinsic information value: The impoverished visual speech stimulus might not deserve the same rigorous approach as that which has been applied to the acoustic speech signal. Indeed, in general, visible speech signals afford inherently fewer phonetic cues than audible signals, particularly, when listening conditions are favorable. Many of the activities of the vocal tract (Catford, 1977) that contribute to the acoustic speech signal (Stevens, 1998) are hidden from view. Paradoxically, the listener has greater access to vocal tract shape and activity than does the viewer, because the acoustic waveform is affected by all of the vocal tract settings.

For example, the hidden actions of the velum are critical to the control of nasality (e.g., the distinction between /b/ with the velum raised versus /m/ with the velum lowered). The hidden actions of the glottis contribute to voicing distinctions (e.g., in pre-vocalic /b/, for which glottal vibration is initiated earlier, versus /p/). The degree to which the tongue causes air flow restriction is only partly visible and affects manner of articulation (e.g., glide consonants, such as /w/, have less restricted air flow versus stop consonants, such as /b/). The position and shape of the tongue are also responsible for the different vowels (Catford, 1977). Nevertheless, research has shown that the talking face is a rich source for phonetic information.

Another apparent impediment to acquiring knowledge about visible speech was an early conclusion from studies on lipreading in children. Lipreading research, carried out almost throughout the twentieth century, was important in the context of hearing loss and deaf education (for a review of early lipreading/speechreading research see Jeffers & Barley, 1971). The research had as one of its goals to improve the education of deaf children, because prior to modern hearing aids and cochlear implants, lipreading skill was viewed to be critical in determining a deaf child's educational success. However, researchers concluded that lipreading was a skill more determined by inborn talent than by education. Summerfield (1991), reflecting on the literature, concluded that, "Indeed, it is to be lamented that excellence in lipreading is not related to the need to perform well, because in formal laboratory tests ..., the best totally deaf and hearing-impaired subjects often perform only as well as the best subjects with normal hearing" (p. 123). Perhaps, less enthusiasm can be generated for research on a skill that is hardwired at birth than one that can be affected by training or practice. However, below, we present results that show experience is a critical factor in lipreading skill.

Another impediment to knowledge was early theorizing that speech perception is special, and that its specialness is tied to the auditory perceptual modality (Liberman, 1982). Early auditory speech perception researchers noted the remarkable rate with which acoustic speech signals are encoded and decoded, rates far faster than can be processed by humans listening to arbitrary combinations of non-speech sounds, such as tones (Liberman, 1982). The researchers also noted the non-invariance of speech signals across different phonetic contexts. Co-articulation, the overlapping gestures of vowel and consonant productions in running speech, is now known to be greatly responsible for the remarkable acoustic phonetic processing rates. While researchers focused their energies almost exclusively on trying to understand such attributes of acoustic speech signals and adopted the view that the specialness of speech is tied to the auditory modality, the optical speech signal received no attention in most research programs. This impediment was substantially lowered by results on audiovisual speech perception, as suggested below. Although the talking face blocks the view of speech articulation in the vocal tract, the external talking face and glimpses into the mouth are rich sources of phonetic information. Reliance on visible speech by deaf individuals has helped to disclose the extent of phonetic information in the signal, as well as the ability to gain a high level of perceptual accuracy. Notably, the specialness of auditory speech perception has had to yield to evidence about visual and audiovisual speech perception (Liberman & Mattingly, 1985).

An initial research study on audiovisual speech perception was carried out by Sumby and Pollack (1954). Speech in various levels of acoustic noise was presented with and without view of the talker. The study results showed that being able to see the talker functionally improved the signal-to-noise (SNR) of the acoustic speech signal, although not as much as is sometimes cited.[1] That is, the study showed that functionally important phonetic information is available through visual perception. Although the study is now viewed as seminal, in fact, it did not inspire much additional research in the decades immediately following its publication.

The single research study that most inspired the shift towards accepting visible speech as a stimulus worthy of theory and empirical study was reported in 1976 by McGurk and McDonald. Their findings became known as the "McGurk effect." They discovered that a visual stimulus such as "ga" paired with an auditory stimulus "ba" could induce the percept "da," thus demonstrating that what was heard could be influenced by what was seen. This finding was appreciated by many in the speech perception research community, and subsequently, many researchers incorporated the visible aspect of spoken language in their theories and research programs (e.g., Liberman & Mattingly, 1985; Massaro, 1987; Summerfield, 1987). Nevertheless, the focus of research is frequently audiovisual phenomena and not visible speech. In the balance of this chapter, we focus on visual speech perception and optical phonetic signals per se.

VISUAL SPEECH PERCEPTION

Historically, some of the applied research involving visual speech perception undertaken in the early 1980s was a side-effect of the first surgical insertion of cochlear implants, which directly stimulate the auditory nerve in order to ameliorate profound hearing loss (for reviews see Zeng, Popper, & Fay, 2004). The early cochlear implants provided a very impoverished speech stimulus, and users of the devices had to rely on integration of their electrical hearing with lipreading.

An issue debated at the time was the ethics of cochlear implantations in young children (Lane, 1995). As the early cochlear implants were not exceptionally effective, and their long-term effects were in question, some researchers sought to develop less invasive technological approaches to aiding lipreading. Many studies were undertaken to determine whether a vibrotactile device could serve the same purpose as a cochlear implant (for reviews see Summers, 1992). Some of the research involved adults whose lipreading with and without a vibrotactile device was compared (e.g., Auer, Bernstein, & Coulter, 1998; Bernstein, Demorest, Coulter, & O'Connell, 1991; Eberhardt, Bernstein, Demorest, & Goldstein, 1990; Waldstein & Boothroyd, 1995). This research led the first author (LEB) of this chapter to studies of prelingually deaf adults at Gallaudet University (GU), a university whose undergraduate student qualifications included hearing loss. While studying the use of vibrotactile devices to enhance lipreading, a population of deaf adults was revealed whose lipreading performance appeared to far surpass reports in the literature (Conrad, 1977; Kuhl & Meltzoff, 1988; Summerfield, 1991). This led to a large normative study of lipreading.

Visual Speech Perception (Lipreading) in Deaf and Hearing Adults

In order to determine the range of lipreading abilities in deaf and hearing populations, Bernstein, Demorest, and Tucker (2000) carried out a visual speech perception study with 96 hearing undergraduates and 72 undergraduates with hearing loss at GU. To qualify for the study, the GU students were required to have English as a first language and to have sensorineural hearing impairments greater than 60 dB HL average in the better ear across the frequencies .5, 1, and 2 kHz. In the participant sample, 71% had profound hearing impairments (90 dB HL or greater, better pure tone average), and 62.5% had hearing impairment by 6 months of age. We refer to all the students with hearing loss from this sample as *deaf*.

Design of the Study

The lipreading test materials were video recorded nonsense syllables, isolated words, and isolated sentences (Bernstein & Eberhardt, 1986a, 1986b). The nonsense syllables were of the form consonant-vowel (CV), each with one of the 22 initial consonants of English followed by the vowel /a/. Each syllable was spoken by a male and a female talker. Participants labeled CV syllables in a 22-alternative forced-choice perceptual identification task. The monosyllabic word stimuli were spoken by the male talker. Sentences were spoken by the male and female talkers.

The participants were tested on isolated words using an open-set word identification paradigm, for which the task was to type all the words or parts of words that were perceived. The sentences that were tested were lists of the CID Everyday Sentences (Davis & Silverman, 1970) and another more difficult set of sentences (Bernstein & Eberhardt, 1986a, 1986b). The sentences were tested in an open-set identification paradigm.

Results of the Study

Results were analyzed in terms of (1) phonemes correct in nonsense syllables, (2) whole words and phonemes correct for isolated monosyllabic words, and (3) whole words and phonemes correct for sentences. A sequence comparator (Bernstein, Demorest, & Eberhardt, 1994) was used to align the open-set sentence responses with the stimuli and extract the correct and incorrect phonemes. The phonemes correct in sentences were also submitted to an information analysis (phoneme substitution uncertainty).

Deaf undergraduates' mean performance levels exceeded those of the hearing students on every measure (statistically significant). The upper quartiles of the deaf students' scores were used to estimate the achievable upper extremes of perceptual accuracy. The proportion nonsense syllables correct upper quartile range for the deaf participants was .35 to .50. The comparable range for the hearing participants was .33 to .46. This demonstrated moderate phoneme identification accuracy for even the best deaf and hearing lipreaders.

The proportion phonemes correct in monosyllabic words in the upper quartiles was .59 to .73 for deaf participants and .47 to .58 for hearing participants. This demonstrated the sizeable lipreading advantage among the deaf lipreaders. But it also showed that hearing lipreaders can perceive good levels of the visible phonetic information in speech. Notably, the monosyllabic words were all ones that rhyme with multiple words, rendering the stimuli potentially highly confusable.

Generally, the upper quartiles of words correct and phonemes correct scores for the sentence stimuli demonstrated extreme differences between the deaf and hearing participants. For example, the deaf participants' upper quartile scores on CID sentences (female talker), scored in terms of phonemes correct were .73 to .88, in contrast with hearing participants' upper quartile scores of .44 to .69. To be noted, however, although the most able deaf lipreaders surpassed the most able hearing lipreaders, the performance levels of the latter indicated good perception of the information in the visible speech stimulus. Also, both groups included very poor lipreaders.

Other results showed that the transmitted information (Wang & Bilger, 1973) for nonsense syllable identification was systematically higher for deaf than for hearing participants. That is, phoneme errors by deaf adults were far more systematic than by hearing adults. Also, an analysis of the phoneme substitution uncertainty in sentence responses showed that uncertainty was always higher in the hearing group. That is, when deaf participants made errors in sentences, their errors were more systematic than the errors of hearing participants.

Finally, phoneme identification and monosyllabic word identification were both correlated with individual participants' scores on the sentence lipreading materials. Regression analyses showed, however, that the best predictors of sentence scores were the group membership (deaf or hearing) and the isolated monosyllabic word scores. The multiple R, ranged between .88 and .90. As was pointed out in Bernstein et al. (2000), these results do not mean that phonetic perception of nonsense syllables is not reliable for predicting sentence lipreading. Rather, word identification measures accounted for the same statistical variance as nonsense syllable scores and additional variance not accounted for by the nonsense syllable scores.

Implications

A question addressed with these results was whether high levels of visual speech perception skill are associated with prelingual deafness (i.e., deafness before the age of 2-3 years), a question thought already to have been answered in the negative (Mogford, 1987; Rönnberg, 1995; Summerfield, 1991). Examination of the deaf participants who contributed scores in the upper quartile of the distributions identified four individuals who had profound, congenital hearing impairments. Each had audiometric pure tone thresholds that exceeded 100 dB HL. They could not identify words by listening under conditions of amplification. These individuals are existence proofs for the acquisition of speech perception at a high level of accuracy without auditory experience. That is, visible speech had been the basis for their acquiring a spoken language and for very accurate visual speech perception.

In order to equate visual and auditory speech perception, Bernstein et al. (2000) compared the results of their study with the auditory speech perception performance curve reported in Miller, Heise, and Lichten (1951) for five-word sentences presented in a range of signal-to-noise (SNR) conditions. Across all of the sentence sets, the range of lipreading scores for the upper quartile deaf participants was approximately equal to the acoustic SNRs of -4 dB to +5 dB. That is, visual speech perception in highly skilled deaf lipreaders is similar in accuracy to auditory speech perception under somewhat difficult to somewhat favorable listening conditions.

Using the same metrics from Miller et al. (1951), the scores for the hearing participants in the upper quartile were characterized as similar to performance in the acoustic range of -8 dB to 0 dB SNR. That is, lipreading in the most skilled hearing lipreaders is similar in accuracy to auditory speech perception under difficult to somewhat difficult listening conditions.

Follow-Up Studies

Subsequent studies have sought to confirm the reliability of the Bernstein et al. (2000) findings. One question was whether the deaf participants were simply more comfortable at lipreading, and therefore, outperformed the hearing participants. A study with good deaf and hearing lipreaders, in which both were given extensive practice, showed small improvements in both groups but reliable advantages on the part of the deaf participants (Bernstein, Auer, & Tucker, 2001).

In the literature, a study of deaf British English lipreaders also showed a lipreading advantage for deaf adults (Mohammed et al., 2005). A Swedish study did so also for one deaf adult (Andersson & Lidestam, 2005).

Recently, Auer and Bernstein (2007) examined lipreading screening scores in a new sample of 112 deaf and 220 hearing adults. They confirmed that lipreading accuracy was highest in the deaf population. An analysis of effect size (Cohen's d)(Cohen, 1988) and the 95% confidence interval for the difference in the lipreading ability of deaf and hearing participants showed an effect size of 1.69, suggesting that the average prelingually deaf lipreader would score above 95% of hearing lipreaders. On the basis of Cohen's rule of thumb, the three studies—Auer and Bernstein (2007), Bernstein et al. (2000), and Mohammed et al. (2005)—support the conclusion that prelingual deafness has a large effect on lipreading ability. That is, the necessity to rely on visible phonetic information coupled with profound hearing loss results in higher levels of skill.

Importantly, all of these studies (Andersson & Lidestam, 2005; Auer & Bernstein, 2007; Bernstein, Demorest, & Tucker, 2000; Mohammed, Campbell, MacSweeney, Milne, Hansen, & Coleman, 2005) are evidence that the optical speech signal affords phonetic information roughly comparable to the acoustic phonetic information available under SNR conditions centered on 0 dB.

One important implication of these studies is that, if a researcher is interested in estimating and/or synthesizing the phonetic information in visual speech stimuli, subjects who are excellent lipreaders should be recruited in studies. Random sampling of hearing lipreaders could easily result in low estimates of the information in visible speech stimuli, because many hearing lipreaders are not very sensitive to the information in visible speech stimuli. In our research, we regularly screen lipreaders so that we can sensitively relate our perceptual data to the caliber of our perceivers and the caliber of our stimuli.

Contributions of the Lexicon to the Intelligibility of Visual Speech

An important part of the explanation for the success of visible speech has come from other studies on the contribution of the lexicon to accurate lipreading. The distribution of phoneme patterns in the words of the English language reduces the ambiguities of visible spoken words (Auer, 2002; Auer & Bernstein, 1997; Iverson, Bernstein, & Auer, 1998; MacEachern, 2000; Mattys, Bernstein, & Auer, 2002). Accurate identification of words can be achieved without access to complete phonetic information, because various potentially ambiguous alternative phoneme patterns are simply not words in the language (see Auer, this volume). In addition, the semantic context of sentences likely contributes to disambiguating words in running speech. Good lipreaders can identify similar alternative words, when the alternatives are limited by the context (Bernstein, 2006).

Summary

The contemporary literature on lipreading shows that the visible aspect of spoken language is phonetically impoverished relative to audible speech that is heard under good listening conditions. But there are individuals with normal hearing and with profound hearing loss who obtain relatively high levels of phonetic information from visual speech stimuli. The lipreading advantage among prelingually deaf adults shows that life-long reliance on visible speech, coupled with deafness, can enhance lipreading skill. The performance levels of deaf lipreaders can provide an upper boundary estimate for the availability of visible phonetic information. The performance levels of hearing lipreaders are not as high but also show the availability and perception of visible phonetic information.

RELATIONSHIP OF THE OPTICAL SIGNALS TO VISUAL SPEECH PERCEPTION

We suggested above that research on auditory speech perception, acoustic phonetic signal analysis, and acoustic speech synthesis have proceeded synergistically. Less synergy has occurred in the comparable domain of visible speech. In particular, relatively little is known about the optical phonetic signal in relationship to its perceptual effects. Visual speech synthesis has generally not been used to study phonetic perception (c.f., Benoit, Guiard-Marigny, Le Goff, & Adjoudani, 1996; Walden, Montgomery, & Prosek, 1987), and visual speech synthesis is currently based on limited knowledge of optical phonetics.

Very frequently, researchers who use visual speech stimuli in audiovisual experiments record natural talkers and describe their stimuli in terms of factors such as the recording conditions, the gender and language of the talker, and the linguistic content of the speech. In contrast acoustic speech can be precisely described in terms of formant frequencies, fundamental frequencies, formant bandwidths, etc., while comparable technical descriptions are not used for specifying visible speech stimuli. Only a few studies have attempted to relate optical speech measures directly to visual speech perception. Quantitative measures have been selected mostly at the level of facial features, such as lip opening height/width.

We do not attempt here to review all the existing research involving measures of visible speech. Two early quantitative studies examined vowels (Jackson, Montgomery, & Binnie, 1976; Montgomery & Jackson, 1983). Jackson et al. (1976) measured the horizontal lip-spreading, lip-rounding, and lip-opening area for a set of 15 vowels spoken by four female talkers. Perceivers rated the similarities among pairs of vowel stimuli. Correlations were modest between the physical measures and the component positions in perceptual space of the vowel. Subsequently, Montgomery and Jackson (1983) conducted additional analyses with 10 of the vowels. They obtained a perceptual space with dimensions labeled as "lip spreading/rounding" and "tongue height." Direct measures of lip height, lip width, lip aperture area, acoustic duration, and visual duration were made on the vowels. Physical stimulus difference scores computed between pairs of stimuli were used as perception predictors in multiple regression models. Variance accounted for by the regression models ranged between 24% and 68% as a function of the talker, and the significant variables in the models differed across talkers. The large differences in variance accounted for across talkers suggest that the direct measures of the stimuli failed to capture adequately the representations that perceivers used to recognize the vowels. A serious pitfall in directly correlating signal measures with perceptual measures (e.g., choosing a few face features) is that there are potentially infinitely many physical measures that could be perceptually relevant. How can the correct ones be efficiently discovered? Furthermore, direct correlations do not take into account how the perceptual system warps the input signal.

These issues are not unique to the perception of visible speech. They extend to any complex perceptual stimulus. Shepard and Chipman (1970) considered the problem of establishing the isomorphism between physical stimuli and internal (perceptual or neural) representations. They noted that internal representations are unlikely to be structurally isomorphic with stimuli in the sense that the internal representation of a square is not likely to be square. In order to approach the problem of establishing relationships between complex physical stimuli and internal/perceptual/neural representations, they argued that an "isomorphism should be sought – not in the first-order relation between (a) an individual object, and (b) its corresponding internal representation – but in the second-order relation between (a) the relations among alternative external objects, and (b) the relations among their corresponding internal representations. Thus, although the internal representation for a square need not itself be square, it should (whatever it is) at least have a closer functional relation to the internal representation for a rectangle than to that, say, for a green flash or the taste of a persimmon" (p. 2). That is, in the absence of a theoretically (or empirically) motivated list of optical phonetic cues, the researcher would be advised first to seek isomorphism between physical dissimilarities and perceptual dissimilarities.

Quantified Second-Order Isomorphism between Signals and Perception

Jiang et al. (2007) adopted this approach in a study of relationships between perception of phonemes in video recorded nonsense syllables and three-dimensional (3-D) optical data obtained by recording positions of retro-reflectors (recorded simultaneously with the video) (see Figure 1). In the Jiang-et-al study, subjects visually identified the 23 initial consonants of English in consonant-vowel (CV) nonsense syllables. Each consonant was followed by the vowels /a/, /i/, or /u/. Four talkers (two males: M1 and M2; two females: F1 and F2) who varied in visual intelligibility produced two tokens of each of the nonsense syllables. In all, there were 522 stimuli. Six participants performed a 23-alternative forced choice perceptual identification task. They identified each stimulus 10 times.

Talkers differed significantly in the information they produced. The perceptual results showed differences in perceptual identification accuracy across the talkers, across the vowels, and across the individual perceivers. The consonants followed by the vowel /a/ were more accurately identified than the ones followed by the vowels /i/ and/u/, which did not differ.

Given the high level of variation across talkers, perceivers, vowel contexts, and also the individual consonants, the identification data were considered a challenging set for attempting to relate perception to the optical signals. Following the logic of the argument concerning the search for second-order isomorphism, the perceptual data were transformed into perceptual spaces via multidimensional scaling (Kruskal & Wish, 1978). Then Euclidean distances were computed between all pairs of phonemes in perceptual space. That is, the perceptual dissimilarity of the nonsense syllables was quantified in terms of their Euclidean distances in multidimensional space.

The next step was to obtain physical distance estimates for the 3-D optical recordings that had been made simultaneously with the video recordings of the nonsense syllables. The method involved analysis of 17 retro-reflector markers on the talker's face (see Jiang et al., 2007 for a complete description). The 3-D data over a 280-msec window were analyzed. Euclidean distances were computed first marker by marker (i.e., channel by channel) and then across frames. This resulted in the physical distances with 51 dimensions/channels (17 retro-reflectors in 3-D space) and 253 phoneme pairs (all of the pairs among

Figure 1. Placement of optical face retro-reflectors

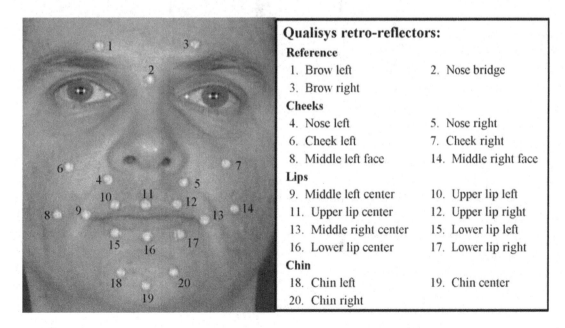

23 consonants). In order to establish relationships between Euclidean distances in perceptual space and multidimensional distances in optical space, least-squares linear estimation was applied (Kailath, Sayed, & Hassibi, 2000). The least squares estimation solutions provided a set of optimal weights (scalars) for transforming the physical measures into perceptual space. Half the perceptual data were used for the estimations, and half were subsequently used for evaluating the correlations between perception and the perceptually weighted distances: The second-order isomorphism between perceptual dissimilarities and optical dissimilarities was operationalized by linearly warping the physical dimensions and then comparing the physical dissimilarities to the perceptual dissimilarities.

A very robust second-order isomorphic relationship was obtained using the scaled dissimilarities among the sparse 3-D optical point representations of visible speech and the perceptual dissimilarities among the video recorded consonants (see Figure 2). The variance accounted for in the perceptual dissimilarity measures by the physical dissimilarities ranged between 36% and 72% across talkers and vowels (see Jiang, Auer, Alwan, Keating, & Bernstein, 2007, for details). In other words, the visual perceptual structure was preserved in the sparse 3-dimensional optical data.

The mean Pearson correlations between perceptual and physical dissimilarities across vowels with the complete set of face points were .76, .68, .81, and .75 for the four talkers. When the correlations were performed on the whole versus subparts of the face, they were .75 for the whole face, .64 for the lips, .53 for the chin, and .46 for the cheeks. When the data were subdivided as a function of vowel, the

Figure 2. Scatterplots of weighted physical distances versus perceptual distances (modeled with 6-D multidimensional scaling; x-axis) for data pooled across all participants with each vowel (/a /, /i/, /u/) and talker (M1, M2, F1, F2). Adapted from Jiang et al. (2007) with additional data.

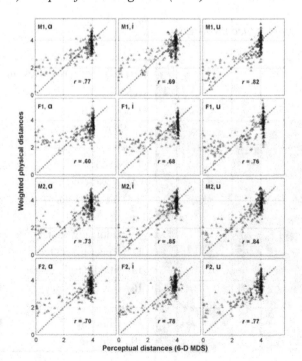

mean Pearson correlations were .70 for syllables with /a/, .75 for syllables with /i/, and .80 for syllables with /u/.

Summary

Second-order isomorphism between perceptual dissimilarities and physical signal dissimilarities resulted in good-to-high levels of correlations across a very large data set of nonsense syllables. An implication of the Jiang et al. (2007) study is that synthetic speech should preserve second-order isomorphism. That is, the dissimilarity relationships in perception based on natural video speech should be represented in synthetic video speech. In the final section of this chapter, we discuss an approach to research on visual speech synthesis that followed from the demonstration of second-order isomorphism.

Second-Order Isomorphism in Development of Synthetic Video Speech

Computer speech facial animation research was initiated in the early 1970s and has steadily expanded in scope and activity. An automated optical speech synthesizer could potentially allow for generating new, spontaneous, and quantitatively controlled speech materials for commercial, research, and clinical applications. Our interest in a synthesized talker is primarily for perceptual and neural research, and for clinical or educational applications. A synthetic talker would allow precise control over stimulus attributes, a fundamental requirement for human perception and neural research.

Currently, talking face animations are available, but their speech information remains inadequate for our purposes. Perhaps, this is because optical speech synthesis has not taken full advantage of the approach that greatly benefited development of acoustic speech synthesis for research. Acoustic speech synthesis was developed in the context of numerous careful acoustic measurements and perceptual experiments that were carried out over many years (Klatt, 1987). For example, early work on acoustic speech perception employed the pattern playback device, which synthesized a schematic representation of the speech signal (Cooper, Delattre, Liberman, Borst, & Gerstman, 1952). This device was critical, for example, in discovering relationships between auditory segmental perception and formant frequencies.

The development of optical speech synthesis would benefit from being an iterative process, with efficient perceptual testing providing detailed quantitative results for synthesis refinement. The synthesizer we envision would be capable of preserving the phonetically relevant differences among spoken consonants and vowels. Our goal is to be able to generate stimuli that can be lipread accurately without auditory cues. This specification is more demanding than merely improving the intelligibility of acoustic speech in noise. Fairly gross visual information appears adequate for improving detection of acoustic speech signals (cf., Bernstein, Auer, & Takayanagi, 2004; Grant & Seitz, 2000). For example, auditory intelligibility for speech in noise can be improved by viewing a synthetic talker's head motion (Munhall, Jones, Callan, Kuratate, & Vatikiotis-Bateson, 2004), and detection of speech in noise can be assisted by a non-speech visual object, such as a rectangle (Bernstein, Auer, & Takayanagi, 2004).

Current evaluation methods for visual speech synthesizers are generally not designed for evaluation of fine phonetic detail needed for visual-only lipreading but instead for evaluation of the general appearance of naturalness, the boost in intelligibility obtained under noisy audiovisual conditions, and/or identification within broad viseme classes (Benoit, Guiard-Marigny, Le Goff, & Adjoudani, 1996; Ma, Cole, Pellom, Ward, & Wise, 2006; Massaro, 1998).

There are challenges to perceptual testing of synthetic speech because of its natural phonetic impoverishment. A method is needed that obtains useful responses to stimuli for which open-set identification typically produces errors. We sought to apply an approach informed by the second-order isomorphism concept introduced above. The similarity structure for optical synthesis was compared against that for natural visible speech. Establishing a similarity structure requires errorful responses. Subsequently, for those pairs of stimuli whose perceptual similarities are different from the computed or predicted similarities, a pair-wise tuning of the synthesizer can be performed.

A methodological advantage in seeking second-order isomorphism in the stimulus-response data is that well-defined computational procedures exist for representations in terms of similarities/dissimilarities. Furthermore, such an approach makes possible the use of prior knowledge on visual speech perception, including distance metrics (Bernstein, Demorest, & Eberhardt, 1994). Results in the section above showed that the relatively sparse 3-D representations of the physical stimuli were effective in accounting for the similarity structure of visual speech perception, suggesting that quantitative adjustments in synthesis parameters that perturb similarity should have direct effects on perception. The evaluation method suggested below should provide an objective and systematic incorporation of human perceptual responses into the synthesis development cycle and contribute to knowledge in psychophysics in visual speech perception.

Visual Speech Synthesis

A variety of approaches have been actualized for visual speech synthesis (Bailly, 2002; Parke & Waters, 1996), falling roughly into three categories, wireframe, muscle-based, and image-based. Furthermore, a visual speech synthesizer can be driven with rule-based, concatenative, acoustics-driven, or direct-physical-measures-driven methods (Bailly, 2002). In wireframe models, the surface geometry of the face is defined by a set of 3-D polygonal meshes. The model is controlled by moving the vertices of the mesh, using simple geometric operations such as rotation or translation. Muscle models use polygonal meshes simulating muscle activities that are directly controlled by muscle activations. These muscle activations could be simulated from physical models or recorded using biomechanical measures (Lucero & Munhall, 1999). Image-based methods reproduce speech movements by morphing and interpolating existing speech images. Muscle models could produce very natural speech, were the required control characteristics well understood. Wireframe models have received more attention and are generally preferred due to their computational advantages. That is, wireframe models allow precise control over individual face points or regions.

Recently, a wireframe face animation model was realized for studying visual speech perception and developing realistic visible phonetic stimuli. We focused on studying the perceptual effects of synthetic speech driven directly from 3-D optical recordings. The model incorporates a mesh of 3-D polygons that define the head and its parts (Xue, Borgstrom, Jiang, Bernstein, & Alwan, 2006). The original 3-D face model was obtained from www.digimation.com. This model was later edited (addition, deletion, and modification of some vertices, polygons, and textures) to have 1915 vertices and 1944 polygons. These polygons were separated into different regions for different textures: teeth, lips, hair, eyebrows, pupil, iris, etc. Additionally, these polygons were divided into different groups based on their motion characteristics, non-moving and moving groups. The moving groups included several sub-regions (e.g., upper lip, lower lip, chin, etc.). An algorithmic layer allows the mesh to be deformed for performing facial actions, as well as preventing errors (such as incursion of the lower lip into the volume of the upper lip).

To drive the face animation model, face motion was captured with a Qualisys™ optical motion capture system using three infrared emitting-receiving cameras and 33 optical retro-reflectors (see Figures 1 and 3). Video was recorded simultaneously with a production quality Sony digital camera and video recorder. An experienced American-English talker with relatively high visual intelligibility spoke the stimuli out loud inside a sound-treated booth. Reconstructed 3-D motion data were processed to remove head and eyebrow motion, recover missing data, remove noise, normalize the head-size, and smooth the motion.

Optical trajectories were registered onto key points on the face model, and these key points were used to deform the rest of the face vertices with modified radial basis functions (Xue, Borgstrom, Jiang, Bernstein, & Alwan, 2006). Radial basis functions have been shown to be effective in deforming the local motion of non-key points (points without data) in relationship to key points (recorded points) in visual speech synthesis (Ma, Cole, Pellom, Ward, & Wise, 2006). Specifically, a radial basis function is used to define the displacement of a vertex based on its distance from the key point and the displacement of the key point. For the current synthesizer, Gaussian radial basis functions were used (Xue, Borgstrom, Jiang, Bernstein, & Alwan, 2006). Texture was then re-mapped onto the deformed face that is then rendered and animated with appropriate lighting and background color using the openGL graphics application-programming interface. The synthetic face was scaled and shifted to have the same position and size as the natural face (see Figure 3).

Perceptual Evaluation of the Visual Speech Synthesizer

A recent perceptual study (Jiang, Aronoff, & Bernstein, 2008) used a discrimination task in order to operationalize the concept of second-order isomorphism. Words, instead of phonemes or consonant-vowel syllables, were used, because approximating contextual information (coarticulation) is a critical

Figure 3. Synthesis: (a) face motions tracked using 33 retro-reflectors; (b) reconstructed and smoothed motion trajectories compensated for head and eyebrow motion and missing data; (c) motion data normalized and registered to key face points; and (d) whole face deformed frame-by-frame using key face points

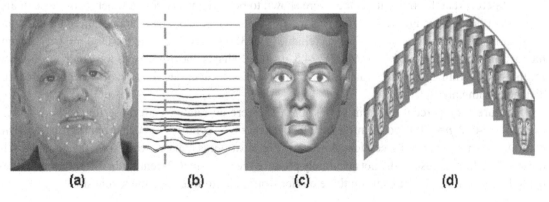

(a)   (b)   (c)   (d)

aspect of visual speech synthesis (Massaro, 1998). Thirty-two words were selected and for each one, four words were chosen that varied in perceptual distance at four levels—*same, near, medium,* and *far* in perceptual distance from each of the initially selected words. The distances were computed using segmental perceptual data (Auer & Bernstein, 1997).

In the experiment, eight participants with normal hearing with above-average lipreading ability (Auer & Bernstein, 2007) were presented with word pairs in a same-different (AX) discrimination task. The task was to view a pair of words and label them as *same* or *different* in terms of their lexical identity. The word pairs comprised either two natural video tokens (AXV) or one synthetic token paired with one natural video token (AXS). For AXV, the *same* pairs comprised different tokens of the same words; for AXS, the *same* pairs comprised the synthetic stimulus and the natural video token that was recorded along with the 3-D optical recording. The *different* pairs comprised the 32 words and the associated *near, medium,* and *far* words. So word pairs for which one token was natural and the other synthetic but both with the same lexical identity would be labeled *same.* Likewise natural speech with different tokens of the same word was to be labeled *same. Same* and *different* pairs were pseudo-randomly ordered during the discrimination task. All tokens were presented without audio.

The experiment was designed to produce several types of results. If the predicted perceptual dissimilarity relationships were obtained with the natural (video-video) word pairs, the use of segmental measures to predict word-level dissimilarity would be validated. If the predicted dissimilarity relationships were also obtained with video-synthetic word pairs, the sparse 3-D optical data would be shown to preserve dissimilarity relationships at the word level. Deviations from the natural dissimilarity structure would point to areas for improvement in the synthesis. Subsequent research could focus on manipulation of the sparse 3-D data so as to achieve more accurate dissimilarity relationships as evaluated using the discrimination paradigm. For those word pairs whose perceptual dissimilarities were different from the predicted dissimilarities, a pair-wise tuning on the synthesizer could be performed.

In order to perform accurately in the condition in which discrimination of words involved viewing first the synthetic video and then the natural video, participants would need to be able to extract the relevant phonetic information from the stimuli that varied greatly on other dimensions, including naturalness and facial details. Importantly, the natural video showed tongue motion when the talker's mouth was open, and the synthetic video did not have a tongue model. A two-way [Dissimilarity (*same, near, medium, far*) x Media (*synthetic, natural*)] repeated measures ANOVA was conducted based on the percentage of different responses with regard to word pairs. Overall, the results were as predicted. The main effect of dissimilarity was significant [$F(1.38,42.68) = 287.3, p < .001$; Huynh-Feldt adjustment used to correct for the violation of the sphericity assumption]: Word pairs predicted to differ across a range of perceptual dissimilarity values were shown to be discriminated as a function of those quantified dissimilarities (see Figure 4a). This was true for video-video word pairs and for the synthetic-video word pairs. The main effect of Media was reliable [$F(1,31)=6.2, p < .02$], and the Dissimilarity x Media interaction was significant [$F(2.07,64.07)=24.8, p < .001$]. That is, the differences were more pronounced for the video-synthetic pairs, because participants were very accurate for *far* and *medium* perceptual distances with natural stimuli.

In Figure 4(b), percent different scores for AXS were correlated with those for AXV [$R^2 = .78$, $F(1,126) = 446.2, p = .000$], confirming the effectiveness of the synthetic speech in approximating visual natural speech in terms of perception. However, several stimulus pairs were far from the diagonal. This implies that the synthesizer did not accurately produce the relevant differentiating information for these pairs. In the future, we can focus on these outlier word pairs to fine-tune the synthesizer.

Figure 4. (a) Boxplots of percent different responses for the words analyses. The five bars in each boxplot indicate the 4th quartile (upper whisker), the 3rd quartile (box top), median (thick), the 2nd quartile (box bottom), and the 1st quartile (lower whisker). Outlier trials are also plotted. (b) Percent different scores for AXS were plotted against those for AXV

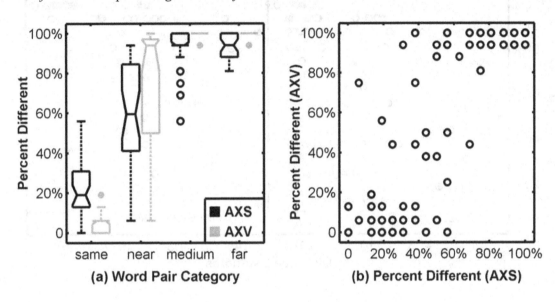

To apply prior results in visual speech perception, proportion different scores for *near, medium,* or *far* pairs in AXS and AXV were submitted to linear regression analyses using as the predictors the pre-computed natural log-transformed dissimilarity measures (Jiang, Aronoff, & Bernstein, 2008). The analysis demonstrated that the dissimilarity scores accounted for a significant portion of the variance in the percent different responses for AXS [$R^2 = .53$, $F(1,94) = 107.0$, $p < .001$] and for AXV [$R^2 = .31$, $F(1,94) = 44.0$, $p < .001$] (Figure 5). Some pairs (e.g., *needs-case, best-space,* and *sent-tax*) were far from the regression line for AXS. However, these pairs were close to the regression line for AXV. This implies that the synthesizer did not accurately produce the relevant differentiating information for words in these pairs. Modeling the tongue and teeth should improve the visual speech synthesizer. We can focus on the phonetic details that are not modeled adequately to fine-tune the synthesizer. In addition, discrimination can be used with perceivers of varying lipreading ability to improve the phonetic details of a visual speech synthesizer. Expert deaf lipreaders can be expected to be more sensitive to deficiencies in the phonetic detail and also more sensitive to subtle information.

CONCLUSIONS

In this chapter, we reviewed some history of and impediments to knowledge about the visual aspects of speech. We reviewed perceptual studies that quantify the information content in visible speech,

Figure 5. Percent different scores for each word pair in AXS (left) and AXV (right) were plotted against distance estimates that were pre-computed using the perception-based cost matrix

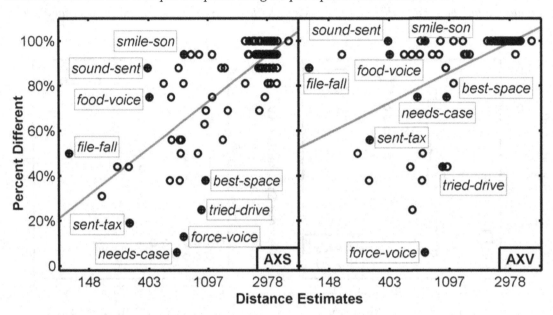

demonstrating that visible speech is a rich detailed source of phonetic information. We discussed recent findings on relations between optical phonetic signals and phonetic perception. Those findings demonstrate second-order isomorphism between optical signals and visual perception. We argued that the link between phonetic signals and phonetic perception can be exploited in developing a visual speech synthesizer. We reported on an approach that we have taken to exploit that link. We suggest that the goal for visual speech synthesis be synthesizers that produce visually intelligible speech that can be lipread. In order to do this, the perceptually relevant phonetic details in visible speech must be synthesized. Because current knowledge is limited concerning how to quantify the relationship between optical quantities *per se* and visual perception, we advocate an approach that uses the second-order isomorphism of perceptual dissimilarities in relation to optical dissimilarities.

FUTURE RESEARCH DIRECTIONS

The perceptual study of synthetic visual speech stimuli demonstrated that relatively sparse 3-D representations of face motion can be used to synthesize visual speech that perceptually approximates visual natural speech. We suggest that synthesizer development and psychophysics can mutually benefit each other when the goals are aligned. Our goal is to develop a synthesizer that affords information that approximates that which is available when a natural intelligible individual produces speech for lipreading.

In order to realize this goal, a necessary synthesizer enhancement is the addition of a visible tongue. Research on lipreading natural speech stimuli shows that glimpses into the mouth provide important information that must be related to the posture and motions of the tongue. Using the same methods reported here, we plan to show enhanced performance with our more accurate, enhanced synthesizer. That synthesizer will in turn afford better stimuli for experiments on perception and its neural underpinnings.

ACKNOWLEDGMENTS

This chapter was written with support of the National Science Foundation (IIS0312434, Bernstein, PI) and the National Institutes of Health (DC008583).

REFERENCES

Andersson, U., & Lidestam, B. (2005). Bottom-up driven speechreading in a speechreading expert: The case of AA (JK023). *Ear and Hearing, 26*(2), 214-224.

Auer, E. T., Jr. (2002). The influence of the lexicon on speech read word recognition: Contrasting segmental and lexical distinctiveness. *Psychonomic Bulletin & Review, 9*(2), 341-347.

Auer, E. T., Jr., & Bernstein, L. E. (1997). Speechreading and the structure of the lexicon: Computationally modeling the effects of reduced phonetic distinctiveness on lexical uniqueness. *Journal of the Acoustical Society of America, 102*(6), 3704-3710.

Auer, E. T., Jr., & Bernstein, L. E. (2007). Enhanced visual speech perception in individuals with early onset hearing impairment. *Journal of Speech, Hearing, and Language Research, 50*(5), 1157-1165.

Auer, E. T., Jr., Bernstein, L. E., & Coulter, D. C. (1998). Temporal and spatio-temporal vibrotactile displays for voice fundamental frequency: An initial evaluation of a new vibrotactile speech perception aid with normal-hearing and hearing-impaired individuals. *Journal of the Acoustical Society of America, 104*(4), 2477-2489.

Bailly, G. (2002, September). *Audiovisual speech synthesis. From ground truth to models.* Paper presented at the ICSLP 2002, Denver, CO.

Benoit, C., Guiard-Marigny, T., Le Goff, B., & Adjoudani, A. (1996). Which components of the face do humans and machines best speechread? In D. Stork & M. Hennecke (Eds.), *Speechreading by Humans and Machines, 150*, 315-328. Berlin: Springer-Verlag.

Bernstein, L. E. (2006). Visual speech perception. In Vatikiotis-Bateson, E., Bailly, G. & Perrier, P. (Eds.), *Audio-Visual Speech Processing*. Cambridge: MIT.

Bernstein, L. E., Auer, E. T., Jr., & Takayanagi, S. (2004). Auditory speech detection in noise enhanced by lipreading. *Speech Communication, 44*(1-4), 5-18.

Bernstein, L. E., Auer, E. T., Jr., & Tucker, P. E. (2001). Enhanced speechreading in deaf adults: Can short-term training/practice close the gap for hearing adults? *Journal of Speech, Language, and Hearing Research, 44*(1), 5-18.

Bernstein, L. E., Demorest, M. E., Coulter, D. C., & O'Connell, M. P. (1991). Lipreading sentences with vibrotactile vocoders: Performance of normal-hearing and hearing-impaired subjects. *Journal of the Acoustical Society of America, 90*(6), 2971-2984.

Bernstein, L. E., Demorest, M. E., & Eberhardt, S. P. (1994). A computational approach to analyzing sentential speech perception: Phoneme-to-phoneme stimulus-response alignment. *Journal of the Acoustical Society of America, 95*(6), 3617-3622.

Bernstein, L. E., Demorest, M. E., & Tucker, P. E. (2000). Speech perception without hearing. *Perception & Psychophysics, 62*(2), 233-252.

Bernstein, L. E., & Eberhardt, S. P. (1986a). Johns Hopkins Lipreading Corpus I-II: Disc 1 [Laser Videodisc]. Baltimore, MD: Johns Hopkins University.

Bernstein, L. E., & Eberhardt, S. P. (1986b). Johns Hopkins Lipreading Corpus III-IV: Disc 2 [Laser videodisk]. Baltimore MD: Johns Hopkins University.

Catford, J. C. (1977). *Fundamental Problems in Phonetics*. Bloomington, IN: Indiana University.

Cohen, J. (1988). *StatisticalPower Aanalysis for the Behavioral Sciences* (2nd ed.). Hillsdale, NJ: Erlbaum.

Conrad, R. (1977). Lip-reading by deaf and hearing children. *The British Journal of Educational Psychology, 47*(1), 60-65.

Cooper, F. S., Delattre, P. C., Liberman, A. M., Borst, J. M., & Gerstman, L. J. (1952). Some experiments on the perception of synthetic speech sounds. *Journal of the Acoustical Society of America, 24*, 597-606.

Davis, H., & Silverman, S. R. (1970). *Hearing and Deafness*. New York: Holt, Rinehart, & Winston.

Eberhardt, S. P., Bernstein, L. E., Demorest, M. E., & Goldstein, M. H., Jr. (1990). Speechreading sentences with single-channel vibrotactile presentation of voice fundamental frequency. *Journal of the Acoustical Society of America, 88*(3), 1274-1285.

Grant, K. W., & Seitz, P. F. (2000). The use of visible speech cues for improving auditory detection of spoken sentences. *Journal of the Acoustical Society of America, 108*(3 Pt 1), 1197-1208.

Iverson, P., Bernstein, L. E., & Auer, E. T., Jr. (1998). Modeling the interaction of phonemic intelligibility and lexical structure in audiovisual word recognition. *Speech Communication, 26*(1-2), 45-63.

Jackson, P. L., Montgomery, A. A., & Binnie, C. A. (1976). Perceptual dimensions underlying vowel lipreading performance. *Journal of Speech and Hearing Research, 19*(4), 796-812.

Jeffers, J., & Barley, M. (1971). *Speechreading (Lipreading)*. Springfield, IL: Charles C. Thomas.

Jiang, J., Aronoff, J., & Bernstein, L. E. (2008, March - April). Development of a visual speech synthesizer via second-order isomorphism. Paper presented at the 2008 IEEE Conference on Acoustics, Speech, and Signal Processing, Las Vegas, Nevada.

Jiang, J., Auer, E. T., Jr., Alwan, A., Keating, P. A., & Bernstein, L. E. (2007). Similarity structure in visual speech perception and optical phonetics. *Perception & Psychophysics, 69*(7), 1070-1083.

Kailath, T., Sayed, A. H., & Hassibi, B. (2000). *Linear Estimation*. Upper Saddle River, NJ: Prentice Hall.

Klatt, D. H. (1987). Review of text-to-speech conversion for English. *Journal of the Acoustical Society of America, 82*(3), 737-793.

Kruskal, J. B., & Wish, M. (1978). *Multidimensional Scaling*. Beverly Hills, CA: Sage.

Kuhl, P. K., & Meltzoff, A. N. (1988). Speech as an intermodal object of perception. In A. Yonas (Ed.), *Perceptual Development in Infancy* (Vol. The Minnesota Symposia on Child Psychology, 20, pp. 235-266). Hillsdale, NJ: Lawrence Erlbaum Associates, Inc.

Lane, H. (1995). Letter to the Editor. *The American Journal of Otology, 16*(3), 393-399.

Liberman, A. M. (1982). On finding that speech is special. *American Psychologist, 37*(2), 148-167.

Liberman, A. M., & Mattingly, I. G. (1985). The motor theory of speech perception revised. *Cognition, 21*(1), 1-36.

Lucero, J. C., & Munhall, K. G. (1999). A model of facial biomechanics for speech production. *Journal of the Acoustical Society of America, 106*(5), 2834-2842.

Ma, J., Cole, R., Pellom, B., Ward, W., & Wise, B. (2006). Accurate visible speech synthesis based on concatenating variable length motion capture data. *IEEE Transactions on Visualization & Computer Graphics, 12*(2), 266-276.

MacEachern, E. (2000). On the visual distinctiveness of words in the English lexicon. *Journal of Phonetics, 28*(3), 367-376.

Massaro, D. W. (1987). *Speech Perception by Ear and Eye: A Paradigm for Psychological Inquiry*. Hillsdale, NJ: Lawrence Erlbaum Associates, Inc.

Massaro, D. W. (1998). *Perceiving Talking Faces: From Speech Perception to a Behavioral Principle*. Cambridge, MA: MIT Press.

Mattys, S. L., Bernstein, L. E., & Auer, E. T., Jr. (2002). Stimulus-based lexical distinctiveness as a general word-recognition mechanism. *Perception & Psychophysics, 64*(4), 667-679.

McGurk, H., & MacDonald, J. (1976). Hearing lips and seeing voices. *Nature, 264*(5588), 746-748.

Miller, G. A., Heise, G. A., & Lichten, W. (1951). The intelligibility of speech as a function of the context of test materials. *Journal of Experimental Psychology: Human Perception and Performance, 41*(5), 329-335.

Mogford, K. (1987). Lip-reading in the prelingually deaf. In B. Dodd & R. Campbell (Eds.), *Hearing by Eye: The Psychology of Lip-reading* (pp. 191-211). Hillsdale, NJ: Lawrence Erlbaum Associates, Inc.

Mohammed, T., Campbell, R., MacSweeney, M., Milne, E., Hansen, P., & Coleman, M. (2005). Speechreading skill and visual movement sensitivity are related in deaf speechreaders. *Perception, 34*(2), 205-216.

Montgomery, A. A., & Jackson, P. L. (1983). Physical characteristics of the lips underlying vowel lip-reading performance. *Journal of the Acoustical Society of America, 73*(6), 2134-2144.

Munhall, K. G., Jones, J. A., Callan, D. E., Kuratate, T., & Vatikiotis-Bateson, E. (2004). Visual prosody and speech intelligibility: Head movement improves auditory speech perception. *Psychological Science, 15*(2), 133-137.

Parke, F. I., & Waters, K. (1996). *Computer Facial Animation*. Natick, MA: A.K. Peters, Ltd.

Pisoni, D. B., & Remez, R. E. (2005). *The Handbook of Speech Perception*. Malden, MA: Blackwell.

Rönnberg, J. (1995). Perceptual compensation in the deaf and blind: Myth or reality? In R. A. Dixon & L. Bäckman (Eds.), *Compensating for Psychological Deficits and Declines* (pp. 251-274). Mahwah, NJ: Lawrence Erlbaum Associates, Inc.

Scott, S. K., & Johnsrude, I. S. (2003). The neuroanatomical and functional organization of speech perception. *Trends in Neurosciences, 26*(2), 100-107.

Shepard, R. N., & Chipman, S. (1970). Second-order isomorphism of internal representations: Shapes of states. *Cognitive Psychology, 1*, 1-17.

Stevens, K. N. (1998). *Acoustic Phonetics*. Cambridge, MA: MIT Press.

Sumby, W. H., & Pollack, I. (1954). Visual contribution to speech intelligibility in noise. *Journal of the Acoustical Society of America, 26*(2), 212-215.

Summerfield, Q. (1987). Some preliminaries to a comprehensive account of audio-visual speech perception. In B. Dodd & R. Campbell (Eds.), *Hearing by Eye: The Psychology of Lip-Reading* (pp. 3-52). London: Lawrence Erlbaum Associates, Inc.

Summerfield, Q. (1991). Visual perception of phonetic gestures. In I. G. Mattingly & M. Studdert-Kennedy (Eds.), *Modularity and the Motor Theory of Speech Perception* (pp. 117-137). Hillsdale, NJ: Lawrence Erlbaum Associates, Inc.

Summers, I. R. (1992). *Tactile Aids for the HearingImpaired*. London: Whurr.

van Santen, J. P. H., Sproat, R., Olive, J. P., & Hirschberg, J. (1997). *Progress in Speech Synthesis*. NY: Springer-Verlag.

Walden, B. E., Montgomery, A. A., & Prosek, R. A. (1987). Perception of synthetic visual consonant-vowel articulations. *Journal of Speech and Hearing Research, 30*(3), 418-424.

Waldstein, R. S., & Boothroyd, A. (1995). Comparison of two multichannel tactile devices as supplements to speechreading in a postlingually deafened adult. *Ear and Hearing, 16*(2), 198-208.

Wang, M. D., & Bilger, R. C. (1973). Consonant confusions in noise: A study of perceptual features. *Journal of the Acoustical Society of America, 54*(5), 1248-1266.

Xue, J., Borgstrom, J., Jiang, J., Bernstein, L. E., & Alwan, A. (2006, July). *Acoustically-driven talking face synthesis using dynamic Bayesian networks.* Paper presented at the Proceedings of IEEE International Conference on Multimedia & Expo (ICME). Toronto, Ontario, Canada.

Zeng, F.-G., Popper, A. N., & Fay, R. R. (2004). *Cochlear Implants: Auditory Prostheses and Electrical Hearing.* NY: Springer.

ADDITIONAL READINGS

Auer, E. T., Jr., Bernstein, L. E., & Coulter, D. C. (1998). Temporal and spatio-temporal vibrotactile displays for voice fundamental frequency: An initial evaluation of a new vibrotactile speech perception aid with normal-hearing and hearing-impaired individuals. *Journal of the Acoustical Society of America, 104*(4), 2477-2489.

Benguerel, A. P., & Pichora-Fuller, M. K. (1982). Coarticulation effects in lipreading. *Journal of Speech and Hearing Research, 25*(4), 600-607.

Bernstein, L. E., Auer, E. T., Jr., & Tucker, P. E. (2000). Can speechreading of sentences be improved by short-term training/practice? Results from deaf and hearing adults trained with speechreading alone and with a vibrotactile speech aid. *Journal of Speech, Language, and Hearing Research, 44*, 5-18.

Bernstein, L. E., Eberhardt, S. P., & Demorest, M. E. (1989). Single-channel vibrotactile supplements to visual perception of intonation and stress. *Journal of the Acoustical Society of America, 85*(1), 397-405.

Bregler, C., Covell, M., & Slaney, M. (1997). Video rewrite: Visual speech synthesis from video. Paper presented at the AVSP, Rhodes, Greece.

Buhmann, M. D. (2003). *Radial basis functions: Theory and implementations.* New York: Cambridge University Press.

Choe, Y. (2002, August). Second order isomorphism: A reinterpretation and its implications in brain and cognitive sciences. In W. D. Gray & C. D. Schunn (Eds.), *Paper presented at the 24th Annual Conference of the Cognitive Science Society*, Fairfax, VA.

Cohen, M. M., & Massaro, D. W. (1993). Modeling coarticulation in synthetic visual speech. In N. M. Thalmann & D. Thalmann (Eds.), *Models and Techniques in Computer Animation* (pp. 141-155). Tokyo, Japan: Springer-Verlag.

Cole, R., Van Vuuren, S., Pellom, B., Hacioglu, K., Ma, J.Y., Movellan, J., Schwartz, S., Wade-Stein, D., Ward, W., & Yan, J. (2003). Perceptive Animated Interfaces: First steps toward a new paradigm for human-computer interaction. *Proceedings of the IEEE, 91*(9), 1391-1405.

Cosatto, E., Ostermann, J., Graf, H. P., & Schroeter, J. (2003). Lifelike talking faces for interactive services. *Proceedings of the IEEE, 91*(9), 1406-1429.

Edelman, S. (1998). Representation is representation of similarities. *Behavior & Brain Sciences, 21*,

449-498.

Engwall, O. (2003). Combining MRI, EMA & EPG measurements in a three-dimensional tongue model. *Speech Communication, 41*, 303-329.

Erber, N. P., & de Filippo, C. L. (1978). Voice/mouth synthesis and tactual/visual perception of /pa, ba, ma/. *Journal of the Acoustical Society of America, 64*(4), 1015-1019.

Erber, N. P., & McMahan, D. A. (1976). Effects of sentence context on recognition of words through lipreading by deaf children. *Journal of Speech and Hearing Research, 19*(1), 112-119.

Ezzat, T.,& Poggio, T. (2000). Visual speech synthesis by morphing visemes. *International Journal of Computer Vision, 38*(1), 45-57.

Fisher, C. G. (1968). Confusions among visually perceived consonants. *Journal of Speech and Hearing Research, 11*, 796-804.

Grant, K. W., Walden, B. E., & Seitz, P. F. (1998). Auditory-visual speech recognition by hearing-impaired subjects: Consonant recognition, sentence recognition, and auditory-visual integration. *Journal of the Acoustical Society of America, 103*(5 Pt 1), 2677-2690.

King, S. A., & Parent, R. E. (2001). A 3D parametric tongue model for animated speech. *Journal of Visualization & Computer Animation, 12*(3), 107-115.

King, S. A., & Parent, R. E. (2005). Creating speech-synchronized animation. *IEEE Transactions on Visualization & Computer Graphics, 11*(3), 341-352.

Montgomery, A. A., Walden, B. E., Schwartz, D. M., & Prosek, R. A. (1984). Training auditory-visual speech reception in adults with moderate sensorineural hearing loss. *Ear and Hearing, 5*(1), 30-36.

Munhall, K. G., & Vatikiotis-Bateson, E. (1998). The moving face during speech communication. In R. Campbell, B. Dodd & D. Burnham (Eds.), *Hearing by eye II: Advances in the psychology of speechreading and auditory-visual speech* (pp. 123-139). East Sussex, UK: Psychology Press.

Munhall, K. G., Kroos, C., Jozan, G., & Vatikiotis-Bateson, E. (2004). Spatial frequency requirements for audiovisual speech perception. *Perception and Psychophysics, 66*(4), 574-583.

Narayanan, S., Nayak, K.S., Lee, S., Sethy, A., & Byrd, D. (2004). An approach to real-time magnetic resonance imaging for speech production. *Journal of the Acoustical Society of America, 115*(5), 1771–1776.

Owens, E., & Blazek, B. (1985). Visemes observed by hearing-impaired and normal hearing adult viewers. *Journal of Speech and Hearing Research, 28*, 381-393.

Thomas, S. M., & Jordan, T. R. (2002). Determining the influence of Gaussian blurring on inversion effects with talking faces. *Perception and Psychophysics, 64*(6), 932-944.

Thomas, S. M., & Jordan, T. R. (2004). Contributions of oral and extraoral facial movement to visual and audiovisual speech perception. *Journal of Experimental Psychology: Human Perception and Performance, 20*(5), 873-888.

Waldstein, R. S., & Boothroyd, A. (1995). Comparison of two multichannel tactile devices as supplements to speechreading in a postlingually deafened adult. *Ear and Hearing, 16*(2), 198-208.

Yehia, H., Rubin, P., & Vatikiotis-Bateson, E. (1998). Quantitative association of vocal-tract and facial behavior. *Speech Communication, 26*(1-2), 23-43.

ENDNOTE

[1] The careful reader can note in Sumby and Pollack (1954) that beyond approximately -12 dB SNR, the curve showing the enhancement obtained with visible speech is essentially flat. This suggests that beyond -12 dB SNR, the performance levels are essentially due to the visual signal alone. Thus, citing the enhancement obtained with visible speech as greater than -12 dB SNR is misleading.

Section IV
Visual Speaker Recognition

Chapter XVI
Multimodal Speaker Identification Using Discriminative Lip Motion Features

H. Ertan Çetingül
John Hopkins University, USA

Engin Erzin
Koç University, Turkey

Yücel Yemez
Koç University, Turkey

A. Murat Tekalp
Koç University, Turkey

ABSTRACT

This chapter presents a multimodal speaker identification system that integrates audio, lip texture, and lip motion modalities, and the authors propose to use the "explicit" lip motion information that best represent the modality for the given problem. The work is presented in two stages: First, they consider several lip motion feature candidates such as dense motion features on the lip region, motion features on the outer lip contour, and lip shape features. Meanwhile, the authors introduce their main contribution, which is a novel two-stage, spatial-temporal discrimination analysis framework designed to obtain the best lip motion features. For speaker identification, the best lip motion features result in the highest discrimination among speakers. Next, they investigate the benefits of the inclusion of the best lip motion features for multimodal recognition. Audio, lip texture, and lip motion modalities are fused by the reliability weighted summation (RWS) decision rule, and hidden Markov model (HMM)-based modeling is performed for both unimodal and multimodal recognition. Experimental results indicate that discriminative grid-based lip motion features are proved to be more valuable and provide additional performance gains in speaker identification.

INTRODUCTION

Audio is probably the most natural modality to recognize the speech content and a valuable source to identify a speaker. However, especially under noisy conditions, audio-only speaker/speech recognition systems are far from being perfect. Video also contains important biometric information such as face/lip appearance, lip shape, and lip movement that is correlated with audio. Due to this correlation, it is natural to expect that speech content can be partially revealed through lip reading; and lip movement patterns also contain information about the identity of a speaker. Nevertheless, performance problems are also observed in video-only speaker/speech recognition systems, where poor picture quality, changes in pose and lighting conditions, and varying facial expressions may have detrimental effects (Turk & Pentland, 1991; Zhang, 1997). Hence robust solutions should employ multiple modalities, i.e., audio and various lip modalities, in a unified scheme.

Indeed in speaker/speech recognition, state-of-the art systems employ both audio and lip information in a unified framework (see Chen (2001) and references therein). However, most of the audio-visual biometric systems combine a simple visual modality with a sophisticated audio modality. Systems employing enhanced visual information are quite limited due to several reasons. On one hand, lip feature extraction and tracking are complex tasks, as it has been shown by few studies in the literature (see Çetingül (2006b) and references therein). On the other hand, the exploitation of this cue has been limited to the use of three alternative representations for lip information: i) *lip texture*, ii) *lip shape (geometry)*, and iii) *lip motion* features. The first represents the lip movement implicitly along with appearance information that might sometimes carry useful discrimination information; but in some other cases the appearance may degrade the recognition performance since it is sensitive to acquisition conditions. The second, i.e., lip shape, usually requires tracking the lip contour and fitting contour model parameters and/or computing geometric features such as horizontal/vertical openings, contour perimeter, lip area, etc. This option seems as the most powerful one to model the lip movement, especially for lip reading, since it is easier to match mouth openings-closings with the corresponding phonemes. However, lip tracking and contour fitting are challenging tasks since contour tracking algorithms are sensitive to lighting conditions and image quality. The last option is the use of explicit lip motion, which are potentially easy to compute and robust to lighting variations.

Following the generation of different audio-visual modalities, the design of a multimodal recognition system requires addressing three basic issues: i) *which modalities to fuse*, ii) *how to represent each modality with a discriminative and low-dimensional set of features*, and iii) *how to fuse existing modalities*. For the first issue, speech content and voice can be interpreted as two different though correlated information existing in audio signals. Likewise, video signal can be split into different modalities, such as face/lip texture, lip geometry, and lip motion. The second issue, feature selection, also includes modeling of the classifiers through which each class is represented with a statistical model or a representative feature set. Curse of dimensionality, computational efficiency, robustness, invariance and discrimination capability are the most important criteria in the selection of the feature set and the recognition methodology for each modality. For the final issue, modality fusion, there exist different strategies: in the *early integration*, modalities are fused at data or feature level, whereas in the *late integration*, decisions (or scores) resulting from each expert are combined to give the final conclusion. Multimodal decision fusion can also be viewed from a broader perspective as a way of combining classifiers, where the main motivation is to compensate possible misclassification errors of a certain classifier with other available classifiers and to end up with a more reliable overall decision. A comprehensive survey and discussion on classifier combination techniques can be found in Kittler (1998).

Nevertheless, the success of a recognition system eventually depends on how efficiently the extracted lip information is represented in a relatively low-dimensional feature vector. For speech recognition, the general approach has been to extract the principal components of the lip movement in order to establish a one-to-one correspondence between phonemes of speech and visemes of lip shape. For the speaker identification problem, however, the use of lip motion requires more sophisticated processing, which has not been addressed in the literature. The main reason for this is that the principal components of the lip movement are not usually sufficient to well discriminate the biometric properties of a speaker. High frequency or non-principal components of the motion should also be valuable especially when

Figure 1. Multimodal recognition system

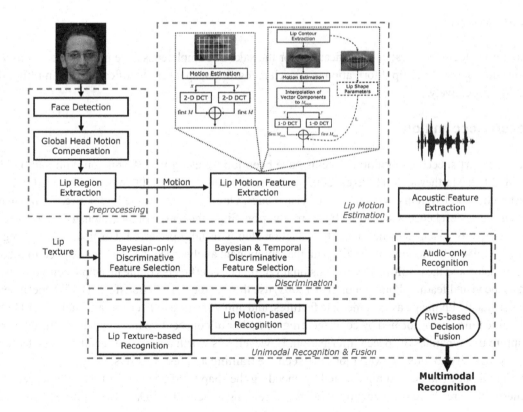

the objective is to model the characteristic lip movements of an individual rather than what is uttered. In order words, discrimination among speakers should be emphasized and selected features should minimize the recognition error rather than the reconstruction error. Although numerous methods have been proposed for the integration of the lip modalities to speaker identification solutions, there is no framework in the literature to optimally select the most discriminative lip motion features.

Hence the objectives of our work are to develop a framework for the determination and usage of the best, i.e., the most discriminative lip motion features, and to build a multimodal system that fuses these motion features with audio and/or and lip texture for speaker identification. Figure 1 depicts the multimodal recognition system with the feature extraction and analysis stages. There are several issues addressed in this chapter to build such a multimodal recognition system:

- *Accurate lip motion estimation:* In order to obtain pure, i.e. accurate, lip motion information, elimination of natural head motion during the speaking act is a must.
- *Feature extraction:* Several lip feature candidates are considered to investigate whether the explicit lip motion, instead of or in addition to lip texture and/or shape, is useful.
- *Discriminative feature selection:* A spatial-temporal discrimination analysis framework is needed to select the most discriminative lip motion features.
- *Modality fusion:* The task is to intelligently fuse the audio-visual modalities in such a way that the most reliable modality has the largest effect on the overall decision.
- *Recognition:* We consider a probabilistic framework such as HMMs for speaker identification.

PRIOR WORK

Although we focus on speaker identification, for the sake of completeness, we present the prior work by considering the use of lip information in speech recognition, speaker identification, and multimodal systems, respectively.

Speech Recognition

State-of-the-art speech recognition systems have been jointly using lip information with audio (Chibelushi, 2002; Matthews, 2002; Perez, 2005; Potamianos, 2003; Zhang, 2002a) since the need to build robust recognition systems urges the use of visual cues. One such a cue is the lip texture, i.e. intensity, which is the easiest hence widely used lip representation. Since the length of the (intensity) image vector is the number of pixels, a dimensionality reduction step is usually preferred. For instance, in Bregler & Konig (1994) and Tomlinson (1996), principal component analysis (PCA) has been applied to reduce the dimension and the resulting low-dimensional vector, i.e., coefficients of the principal components, is used as the visual feature. Potamianos et al. (2003) use the discrete cosine transform (DCT) coefficients of the grayscale lip image as intermediate features, and apply the linear discriminant analysis (LDA) to the final feature vector formed by concatenating a number of consecutive intermediate feature vectors to capture the dynamics of speech information. However, it is worth noting that the lip texture features are very sensitive to intensity variations between the training and test data sets.

Visual lip cue can be also represented by encoding the shape and geometry of the mouth area. The geometric features have been employed in speech reading (Chen, 2001; Da Silveira, 2003; Foo, 2004;

Kaynak, 2004; Wang, 2004b; Zhang, 2002a), since it is easier to match mouth openings-closings with the corresponding phonemes. Deformable templates (Chen, 2001; Foo, 2004), active shape models (ASMs) (Lucey, 2000; Matthews, 2002; Perez, 2005; Wang, 2004b), and active contours (Aleksic, 2002; Wakasugi, 2004) have been used to obtain different geometric lip features; however, they all suffer from complex feature extraction and training procedures. In Chen (2001), Gaussian mixture models (GMMs) are used to model both the lip and the non-lip region, and lip tracking is performed by deformable templates. A number of horizontal and vertical distances representing the lip openings are then selected as features. Kaynak et al. (2004) also use horizontal/vertical distances along with the orientation angle to represent the lip shape. In fact, most of the techniques in the speech reading literature utilize a combination of lip texture and primitive geometric lip features. In Dupont & Luettin (2000), the lip feature vector is formed by concatenating the Karhunen-Loève transformed inner-outer lip contour points with the texture information which is represented in a similar way as in the *eigenlip* technique (Bregler & Konig, 1994). In Matthews (2002), the geometric information extracted by the active shape models is used along with the gray-level appearance features and they are fused with audio for speech recognition. Perez et al. (2005) utilize a set of geometric features extracted by the ASMs together with the DCT coefficients of the intensity information.

There is only a limited amount of work in which explicit lip motion information is used for speech reading. Aleksic et al. (2002) use gradient vector flow (GVF) snakes to extract outer lip contour, and calculate the lip movement at ten predefined points by point-wise coordinates difference. They then reduce the feature dimension by PCA, and use the lip features together with other facial animation features. However, the selection of the best lip motion features, i.e. the ones that contribute the most to the recognition, has not been addressed within a principled framework, and still remains an open problem.

Speaker Identification

For speaker identification, unlike speech recognition, lip information has been only employed in a few works. In Erzin (2004) and Fox (2004), the DCT coefficients of the grayscale lip images are considered as the lip features. It is relatively easy to obtain this feature, but it again suffers from illumination variation between the training and test data sets. Lip geometry is used in Broun (2002), where lip segmentation is carried out by forming an accumulated difference image and considering moving parts of that image. Then a number of predefined horizontal and vertical distances are taken as geometric lip features. Mok et al. (2004) find the outer lip contour by the ASMs, and form a feature vector using both the model parameters and some additional distances representing the lip shape. In the audio-visual fusion system presented in Wark & Sridharan (2001), the lip contour is first tracked, and each contour pixel is associated with the chromatic features that constitute the initial feature vector. The dimension of the feature vector is then reduced via PCA followed by LDA. However, the initial step of PCA reduction filters out some useful discriminative information valuable to biometric speaker identification, and temporal correlations in lip motion are not taken into account in discrimination analysis. The lip feature vector proposed in Jourlin (1997) for speaker verification is composed of lip geometry parameters concatenated with intensity values along the lip contour. The feature dimension is then reduced by PCA with no discrimination analysis at all. In the speaker identification literature, there are only two reported works employing explicit lip motion as lip features. In Froba (2000), following the computation of the optical flow between two consecutive lip frames, the power spectrum of the 3-D motion field is calculated and used as lip motion features. In Frischholz & Dieckmann (2000), the lip motion is represented by a full set of the DCT coefficients of the dense optical flow vectors computed within rectangular lip frames and it is fused with face texture and acoustic features for multimodal speaker identification. However no discrimination analysis is performed and no specific attention is paid to optimize the unimodal performance of the lip motion modality. In our recent studies (Çetingül, 2004; Çetingül, 2005, Çetingül, 2006b), we observed that speaker identification systems can benefit from discriminative lip motion feature extraction.

Multimodal Solutions

When more than one modality is available, the fusion of information from different modalities can reduce the overall uncertainty and increase the robustness of a classification system. As mentioned before, in the *early integration*, the modalities are fused at data/feature level, whereas in the *late integration*, the decisions from each expert are combined to give the final decision. The speaker recognition schemes proposed in Brunelli & Falavigna (1995), Frischholz & Dieckmann (2000), Jourlin (1997), Sanderson & Paliwal (2003), and Wark & Sridharan (2001) are basically opinion fusion techniques that combine multiple expert decisions through adaptive or non-adaptive weighted summation of scores, whereas in Chaudhari (2003) and Civanlar & Chen (1996), fusion is carried out at feature level by concatenating the individual feature vectors so as to exploit the temporal correlations between audio and video signals. In audio-visual speech recognition, Bregler & Konig (1994) concatenate audio and lip data, while in Zhang (2000), unimodal recognition rates are combined. Furthermore, recent works show the success of multi-stream HMMs in speech recognition (Dupont & Luettin, 2000; Perez, 2005; Potamianos, 2003; Zhang, 2002a). In our recent studies (Çetingül, 2006a), we also observed an improvement in recognition performance due to modality fusion.

RECOGNITION: THEORY AND FORMULATION

Recognition task can be formulated as either verification or identification problem. The latter can be further classified as open-set or closed-set identification. In the closed-set identification problem, a reject scenario is not defined hence an unknown observation is classified as belonging to one of the R registered pattern classes. In the open-set problem, given the observation from an unknown pattern, the objective is to find whether it belongs to a pattern class registered in the database or not; the system identifies the pattern if there is a match and rejects otherwise. Hence, the problem can be thought of as an $R+1$ class identification problem including a reject class. Open-set identification has a variety of applications such as the authorized access control for computer and communication systems, where a registered user can log onto the system with her/his personalized profile and access rights. In this work, we formulate the speaker recognition problem in an open-set identification framework, which is a more challenging and realistic way of addressing the problem as compared to closed-set speaker identification and verification. Note that verification is a special case of the general open-set identification problem. From this point, we interchangeably use the phrases "recognition" and "identification" to avoid any confusion.

The speaker identification problem can further be classified as text-dependent or text-independent. In the text-independent case, identification is performed over a content free utterance of the speakers, whereas in the text-dependent case, each speaker is expected to utter a personalized secret phrase for the identification task. The hidden Markov models (HMMs) are known to be effective to model the temporal behavior of speech signals, and thus are widely used for both audio-based speaker identification and speech recognition applications. In particular, the state-of-the-art speaker identification systems use HMMs for text-dependent case and Gaussian mixture models (GMMs) for text-independent case (Reynolds, 1995). HMM-based techniques are preferred in text-dependent scenarios since they can successfully exploit the temporal correlations of a speech signal. Since lip motion is strongly coupled with audio utterance, HMMs can also be employed for the temporal characterization of visual features.

In this work we address the speaker identification problem under text-dependent scenario as an open-set identification problem. Our publicly available database, MVGL-AVD (Erzin, 2004; MVGL, 2008), consists of audio-visual data collected from a population of 50 speakers. We use word-level continuous-density HMM structures for the temporal characterization of the lip features. Each speaker in the database is modeled using a separate HMM that is trained over some repetitions of the lip motion streams of the corresponding class. In the recognition process, given a test feature set, each HMM structure associated with a speaker produces a likelihood. A "world" HMM model representing the impostor class is also trained over the whole training data of the population. The log-ratios of the speaker likelihoods to the world class likelihood result in a stream of log-likelihood ratios that are used to identify or reject a speaker. In the following subsections, we provide the formulation details of the speaker identification problem, and give the basics of building multimodal recognition systems.

Speaker Identification

The speaker identification problem is often formalized by using a probabilistic approach: Given a feature vector f representing the sample data of an unknown individual, compute the a posteriori probability $P(\lambda_r \mid f)$ for each class λ_r, $r = 1, 2,..., R$, i.e. for each speaker's model. The sample feature vector is then assigned to the class λ^* that maximizes the *a posteriori* probability:

$$\lambda^* = \arg\max_{\{\lambda_r\}_{r=1}^R} P(\lambda_r \mid f).$$

(1)

In practice, it is usually difficult to compute $P(\lambda_r \mid f)$; hence one can rewrite it in terms of the class conditional probabilities using the Bayes' rule, i.e.,

$$P(\lambda_r \mid f) = \frac{P(f \mid \lambda_r)P(\lambda_r)}{P(f)}.$$

(2)

Due to the class independence of $P(f)$ and assuming equally likely class distribution, i.e. $P(\lambda_r) = 1/R$ the expression in (1) is equivalent to

$$\lambda^* = \arg\max_{\{\lambda_r\}_{r=1}^R} P(f \mid \lambda_r).$$

(3)

Computation of the class conditional probabilities needs a prior modeling step through which the probability density function of the feature vectors is estimated for each class by using available training data.

In the open-set identification problem, an imposter class λ_{R+1} is introduced as the $(R+1)$-th class. A common and effective approach to model the impostor class is to use a universal background model, which is estimated by using all available training data regardless of which class they belong to. We then employ the following formulation, which includes a reject strategy through the definition of the likelihood ratio

$$\bar{\rho} \triangleq \log \frac{P(f \mid \lambda_r)}{P(f \mid \lambda_{R+1})} = \log P(f \mid \lambda_r) - \log P(f \mid \lambda_{R+1}).$$

(4)

The decision strategy of the open-set identification is implemented in two steps. First, one determines the most likely class by

$$\lambda' = \arg\max_{\{\lambda_r\}_{r=1}^R} \bar{\rho}(\lambda_r),$$

(5)

and then

$$\begin{aligned} &\text{if } \bar{\rho}(\lambda') \geq \tau \quad \text{accept;} \\ &\text{otherwise} \quad \text{reject,} \end{aligned}$$

(6)

τ being the optimal threshold, which is experimentally determined to achieve the desired equal error rate.

The performance of a speaker identification system is often measured using the equal error rate (EER) figure. The EER is calculated as the operating point at which false accept rate (FAR) equals false reject rate (FRR). In the open-set identification, the false accept and false reject rates can be defined as,

$$\text{FAR} = 100 \times \frac{F_A}{C_c + C_i} \quad \text{and} \quad \text{FRR} = 100 \times \frac{F_R}{C_c},$$

(7)

where F_A and F_R are the number of false accepts and rejects, and C_c and C_i are the total number of trials for the true and imposter clients in the testing, respectively.

Multimodal Recognition Framework

In this subsection, we present the basics of the decision fusion along with the estimation of the reliabilities of the modalities for the reliability weighted summation rule.

Multimodal Decision Fusion

Suppose that H different classifiers, which are employing maximum likelihood (ML) solution using the class conditional probabilities $P(f_h \mid \lambda_r)$, are available for each of the H modalities $\{f_h\}_{h=1}^{H}$, and for each of the R classes $\{\lambda_r\}_{r=1}^{R}$. Equivalently, each classifier, say the h-th classifier, produces a set of R log-likelihood values $\rho_h(\lambda_r) \triangleq \log P(f_h \mid \lambda_r)$, $r = 1, 2, ..., R$. The problem then reduces to compute a single set of joint log-likelihood values $\rho(\lambda_1), \rho(\lambda_2), ..., \rho(\lambda_R)$ for these H modalities. In the Bayesian framework, assuming that $f_1, f_2, ..., f_H$ are statistically independent, the joint log-likelihood is given by the sum of the individual log-likelihoods:

$$\rho(\lambda_r) = \log\left[P(f_1 \mid \lambda_r) \times P(f_2 \mid \lambda_r) \times ... \times P(f_H \mid \lambda_r) \right] = \sum_{h=1}^{H} \rho_h(\lambda_r),$$

(8)

which is equivalent to the *product rule* in Kittler (1998). In practice, there are a couple of problems with the optimality of this rule. First, "partial" decisions of different classifiers may be correlated. Second, due to modeling errors and/or measurement noise, the estimated distribution model of the training features, i.e., $P(f_h \mid \lambda_r)$, may not always comply with the actual distribution of the test features. As a result, the log-likelihood values coming from separate classifiers should each be considered as an opinion or likelihood score rather than a probabilistic value. The statistics and the numerical range of these likelihood scores mostly vary from one classifier to another, and thus using sigmoid and variance normalization as described in Erzin (2005), they are normalized into [0,1] interval before the fusion.

In order to cope with the above problems, various approximation approaches have been proposed in the literature as alternatives to the product rule, i.e., the sum rule in log domain, such as *max rule, min rule* and *reliability weighted summation*. In fact, the most generic way of computing the joint ratios (or scores) can be expressed as a weighted summation:

$$\rho(\lambda_r) = \sum_{h=1}^{H} \omega_h \rho_h(\lambda_r), \ r = 1, 2, ..., R,$$

(9)

where ω_h denotes the weighting coefficient for the h-th modality such that

$$\sum_{h} \omega_h = 1.$$

Then, the fusion problem becomes finding the optimal weight coefficients. Note that when $\omega_h = 1/H$, $\forall h \in \{1, 2, ..., H\}$, the expression in (9) is equivalent to the product rule. Since the ω_h values can be regarded as the reliability values of the classifiers, we referred to this combination method as the reliability weighted summation (RWS) rule in Erzin (2005). The reliability values ω_h can be set to some fixed values using some a priori knowledge about the performance of each classifier or they can be adaptively estimated for each decision instant via various methods such as those in Erzin (2005), Sanderson & Paliwal (2003), and Wark & Sridharan (2001). Among them, we favor the one proposed in Erzin (2005), since it is better suited to the open-set speaker identification by assessing both accept and reject decisions of a classifier, and it can be easily defined for the closed-set identification.

Reliability Estimation for the RWS Rule

The RWS rule combines the likelihood ratio values of the H modalities using their reliability values ω_h. The reliability value ω_h of the h-th modality is estimated based on the difference of the likelihood ratios of the best two candidate classes λ' and λ'', that is, $\Delta_h = \rho_h(\lambda') - \rho_h(\lambda'')$. In the absence of a reject class, which is for closed-set identification, the likelihood difference of the best two candidates, Δ_h, can be used as the reliability value. However, in the presence of a reject class, one would expect a high likelihood ratio $\rho_h(\lambda')$ and a high Δ_h value for true accept decisions, and a low likelihood ratio $\rho_h(\lambda')$ and a low Δ_h value for true reject decisions. Hence, a normalized reliability measure ω_h can be estimated by,

$$\omega_h = \frac{1}{\sum_i \gamma_i} \gamma_h, \tag{10}$$

where

$$\gamma_h = \begin{cases} \Delta_h & \text{for closed-set identification,} \\ (e^{(\rho_h(\lambda')+\Delta_h)}-1) + (e^{(\kappa-\rho_h(\lambda')-\Delta_h)}-1) & \text{for open-set identification.} \end{cases} \tag{11}$$

The first and second terms for open-set identification in γ_h are associated with the true accept and true reject, respectively. The symbol κ stands for an experimentally determined factor to reach the best compromise between accept and reject scenarios. The κ value is set to 0.65 as it is found to be optimal for open-set speaker identification task in Erzin (2005). The value of the factor sets some bias to weight true accept decisions slightly more than true reject decisions, which is expected from the nature of the product rule that normally favors true accepts.

EXTRACTION OF LIP MOTION FEATURES

The lip motion feature extraction and analysis system is depicted in Figure 2. It consists of a preprocessing module, a lip motion estimation module, a Bayesian discrimination module, and a temporal discrimination module.

Preprocessing

The purpose of the preprocessing module is to eliminate natural head motion during the speaking act to obtain pure lip movement. For this purpose, each frame of each talking face is aligned with the first frame using a 2-D parametric motion estimator. For every two consecutive frames, global head motion parameters are calculated using hierarchical Gaussian image pyramids and the 12-parameter quadratic motion model specified in Odobez & Bouthemy (1995). The frames are successively warped using the calculated parameters. Thus by only hand-labeling the mid-point of the lip region in the first frame, we automatically extract the lip region in the whole sequence.

Figure 2. Feature extraction system with two-stage discrimination analysis

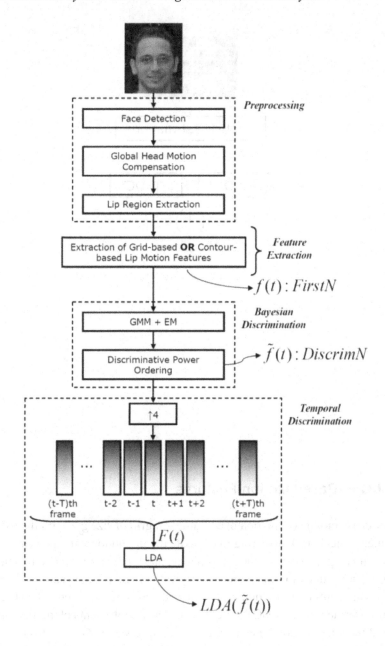

The quadratic transform provides an exact description of the 3-D rotation, translation and scaling of an object with a parabolic surface under parallel projection (Yemez, 2000). Hence, it is successful in modeling rigid motion of the head between consecutive frames, where the movement is not very abrupt.

Figure 3. Extraction of grid-based lip motion features

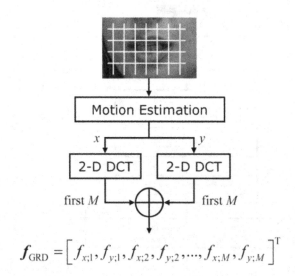

$$f_{\mathrm{GRD}} = \left[f_{x;1}, f_{y;1}, f_{x;2}, f_{y;2}, ..., f_{x;M}, f_{y;M} \right]^{\mathrm{T}}$$

Extraction of Grid-Based Motion Features

We first consider dense motion estimation over a uniform grid of size $g_x \times g_y$ on the extracted lip region image. We use hierarchical block matching to estimate the lip motion with quarter-pel accuracy by interpolating the original lip image using the 6-tap Wiener and bilinear filters specified in H.264/MPEG-4 AVC (Puri, 2004). The motion estimation procedure yields two matrices V_x and V_y of size $g_x \times g_y$, containing the x- and y- components of the motion vectors at grid points, respectively. Then the motion matrices are separately transformed via 2-D DCT. The first M DCT coefficients along the zig-zag scan order, both for x and y directions, are combined to form the feature vector f of dimension $2M$ as depicted in Figure 3. This feature vector representing the dense grid motion is denoted by f_{GRD}.

Transforming the motion data into the DCT domain has two advantages. First, it serves as a tool to reduce the feature dimension by filtering out the high frequency components of the motion signal. These high frequency components are mostly due to noise and irrelevant to our analysis since it is unnatural to have very abrupt motion changes between neighboring pixels of the lip region, where the motion signal is expected to have some smoothness. Second, DCT decorrelates the feature vector so that the discriminative power of each feature component can be independently analyzed.

Extraction of Contour-Based Motion Features

Outer Lip Contour Extraction

The accuracy and robustness of the lip contour extraction method are crucial for a recognition system that uses lip shape information. There exist many techniques in the literature, which attempt to solve the lip segmentation/tracking problem (Aleksic, 2002; Eveno, 2004; Leung, 2004; Nefian, 2002; Sadeghi, 2002; Wakasugi, 2004; Wang, 2004a; Zhang, 2002b). The performance of these techniques usually depends on acquisition specifications such as image quality, resolution, head pose and illumination conditions. In region-based lip segmentation techniques, color information is often used as an important cue to differentiate the "lip" pixels from those of the skin. In order to achieve this, the state-of-the-art techniques use Markov random fields (Zhang, 2002b), linear discriminant analysis (Nefian, 2002), adaptive Gaussian mixture models (Sadeghi, 2002) or fuzzy clustering methods as in Leung (2004) and Wang (2004a). There are also a number of boundary-based techniques to represent and extract the lip contour, such as splines, active shape models, snakes, and parametric models, which use color gradient and/or edge information. The ASMs (Luettin, 1996; Wang, 2004b) impose prior information about possible lip movements to avoid unrealistic lip models; however they require a large training set of registered lip images that are acquired under predefined face orientation and lighting. Classical active contours (Wakasugi, 2004) and their extensions suffer from complex parameter tuning and inability to perfectly fit to certain characteristic lip parts such as Cupid's bow.

In order to extract the outer lip contour, we employ the quasi-automatic technique proposed in Eveno (2004). The technique is based on six designated key points detected on the lip contour. The

Figure 4. Extraction of the outer lip contour: (a) *The 6 key points and parametric models fitted on the outer contour,* (b) *The 8 lip shape features,* (c) *Extracted outer lip contours*

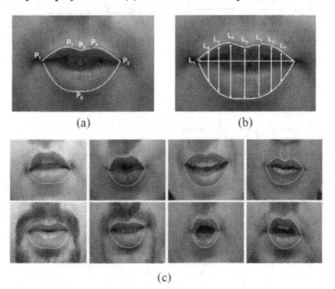

(a)   (b)

(c)

manual selection of a point above the mouth serves as the initialization of a snake-like algorithm. This step locates the points $\{P_2, P_3, P_4\}$ on the upper lip boundary and computes two line segments between them. Pseudo-hue gradient information is then used to locate the other points $\{P_1, P_5, P_6\}$. Least-squares optimization is used to fit four cubic polynomials using five of the key points as junctions. All the key points are then tracked in consecutive frames and the curve fitting steps are repeated. Figure 4(a) shows the 6 key points and the fitted parametric model on a sample lip image; whereas Figure 4(c) displays examples of the lip contours extracted from various lip images of our database.

Contour-Based Motion Features

In the contour-based lip motion representation, the motion vectors computed on the pixels along the extracted lip contour are taken into account. In this case, the two sequences of x and y motion compo-

Figure 5. Extraction of the contour-based motion features and the lip shape [dashed lines show the optional path for feature level fusion of the lip shape and contour-based lip motion]

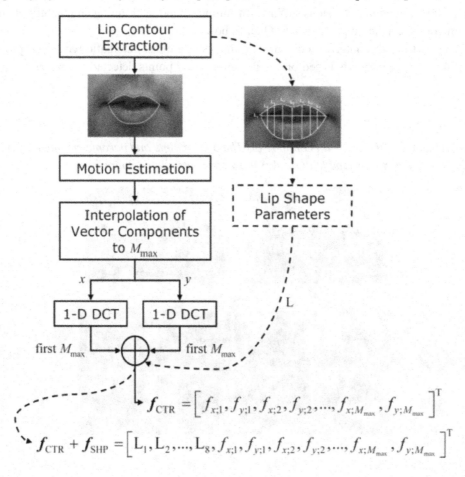

nents on the contour pixels are separately transformed using 1-D DCT. It is worth noting that the length of the resulting sequence of motion components on each direction may vary from one frame to another according to varying lip shape. In order to obtain a feature vector of fixed length in each frame, before computing 1-D DCT, the length of the sequence is normalized to a fixed number using linear interpolation. This number, M_{max}, is the maximum number of contour points achieved in any lip frame of all available sequences. The DCT coefficients computed separately for x and y directions are concatenated to form the feature vector denoted by f_{CTR}. Figure 5 depicts this feature extraction procedure.

Lip Shape Features

The contour-based lip motion feature vector f_{CTR} can further be fused with the lip shape features to improve the representation. We denote the lip shape feature vector by f_{SHP}. Recall that we parameterize the lip shape with four cubic polynomial and two line segments. Polynomial segments can be specified by sampling four points on each whereas a pair of end-points is sufficient to represent a line segment. Since the lip contour is composed of these 6 segments articulated at their end-points, a minimum number of 14 points are necessary to uniquely represent the parameterized lip shape, which corresponds to a feature vector of 28 point coordinates in x and y directions. These points should be appropriately sampled on the lip contour. In order to assure translation and rotation invariance, we represent the lip shape in terms of horizontal and vertical distances between the sampled points. A possible such feature vector is composed of 8 simple parameters: the maximum horizontal distance, L_1, and the 7 vertical distances from the Cupid's bow and from the equidistant upper lip points to the lower lip boundary $\{L_i\}_{i=2}^{8}$ depicted in Figure 4(b). The vertical lines are selected to be perpendicular to the line joining the two corners of the lip. The concatenation of lip shape parameters with contour-based motion information is illustrated in Figure 5.

DISCRIMINATIVE FEATURE SELECTION

There are various subspace representation techniques that can be used for the reduction of dimensionality of the feature vectors in recognition systems. The linear discriminant analysis (LDA) is a well-known dimensionality reduction and feature extraction method to achieve discrimination among multiple classes (Chibelushi, 1993; Potamianos, 2003; Wark, 1998). In this work, we propose a novel approach for reducing feature dimension, where we select the most discriminative lip motion features in two successive stages, i.e., the Bayesian and temporal discrimination stages. In the Bayesian discrimination stage, we use a probabilistic measure that maximizes the ratio of intra-class and inter-class probabilities. The temporal stage uses the LDA. The details of these stages are discussed in the following subsections.

Bayesian Discriminative Feature Selection

Let f_k denote the k-th component of a feature vector f. Given an observation f_k, the maximum a posteriori (MAP) estimator selects the class λ_i with the maximum posterior probability $P(\lambda_i | f_k)$, which can be written in terms of class conditional probability distributions, i.e.,

$$P(\lambda_i \mid f_k) = \frac{P(f_k \mid \lambda_i)P(\lambda_i)}{P(f_k)}$$

$$= \frac{P(f_k \mid \lambda_i)P(\lambda_i)}{P(f_k \mid \lambda_i)P(\lambda_i) + \sum_{j \neq i} P(f_k \mid \lambda_j)P(\lambda_j)}$$

$$= \left(1 + \frac{\sum_{j \neq i} P(f_k \mid \lambda_j)P(\lambda_j)}{P(f_k \mid \lambda_i)P(\lambda_i)}\right)^{-1}.$$

(12)

The MAP estimator becomes the maximum mutual information estimator (MMIE) (Huang, 2001) by maximizing the ratio $\sigma(\lambda_i \mid f_k)$, which is defined as

$$\sigma(\lambda_i \mid f_k) \triangleq \log\left(\frac{P(f_k \mid \lambda_i)P(\lambda_i)}{\sum_{j \neq i} P(f_k \mid \lambda_j)P(\lambda_j)}\right).$$

(13)

This can be interpreted as the ratio of intra-class and inter-class probabilities, and when maximized, it can serve as a measure of discrimination between class λ_i and all other classes for the corresponding feature component f_k.

When the class conditional probability distributions are available for any K-dimensional feature vector $[f_1, f_2, ..., f_K]^T$, and if the components are statistically independent, one can compute the *discriminative power* of the independent feature f_k^i that belongs to class λ_i using $\sigma(\lambda_i \mid f_k^i)$. The larger the ratio $\sigma(\lambda_i \mid f_k^i)$, the more discriminative is the feature; that is, the class conditional probability for its own class is high and the average of the class conditional probabilities over all other classes is low. The class probability $P(\lambda_i)$ is assumed to be equally likely. The class conditional probability distributions are generally computed over some training data using the expectation-maximization (EM) type algorithms, assuming an underlying probability distribution. Let us refer to this training data as $\{f_k^i\}$, that is a collection of observations of the k-th feature component from the i-th class, which is available for all feature components and for all classes. We propose the following discrimination measure, $d(f_k)$, to estimate the discriminative power of each feature f_k:

$$d(f_k) = \sum_i \frac{1}{Z} \sum_{z=0}^{Z-1} \sigma(\lambda_i \mid f_k^i(z)),$$

(14)

where Z is the number of observations in each class λ_i.

Discriminative Feature Ranking

The proposed discrimination measure, when computed for each independent feature, creates an ordering $\{f_{k_n}\}$ among the components of the feature vector such that

$$d(f_{k_1}) \geq d(f_{k_2}) \geq ... \geq d(f_{k_K}).$$

(15)

This ordering can be used to select the most N discriminative features, or similarly to eliminate the least $K-N$ discriminative features from the full set of features. Then the reduced discriminative feature vector can be written as,

$$\tilde{\boldsymbol{f}}^{N} \triangleq \left[f_{k_1}, f_{k_2}, ..., f_{k_N} \right]^{\mathrm{T}}.$$

(16)

This selection strategy makes sense whenever the joint discrimination measure of any two features is less than the sum of their individual discriminative powers. A sufficient condition for this is to have statistically independent features. In this case, the proposed ordering is a valid ordering with respect to feature discriminative power.

We considered two alternative feature vectors $\boldsymbol{f}_{\mathrm{GRD}}$ and $\boldsymbol{f}_{\mathrm{CTR}}$ to represent the lip motion. Both involve the DCT coefficients of the motion vectors computed either on a 2-D rectangular grid covering the lip region or along the 1-D lip boundary pixels. Under the Gaussian distribution assumption, the DCT transformation decorrelates the observation vectors so that each feature approximately becomes independent from the rest of the features. After applying the DCT, traditionally, the low indexed N coefficients, which we refer as *FirstN*, are used as the representative features since they yield the best reconstruction for the original observations. Following the notation introduced in this section, this feature vector can be expressed as $\boldsymbol{f}^{N} = [f_{1}, f_{2}, ..., f_{N}]^{\mathrm{T}}$. The discriminative set of features, $\tilde{\boldsymbol{f}}^{N}$, will be referred to as *DiscrimN*. Note that they are selected according to the discriminative power ordering. The class conditional probability distribution of each transform domain coefficient is estimated so that the discrimination measure for each coefficient can be calculated using (14). The Gaussian mixture models (GMMs) are used to represent the class conditional probability density functions. For GMM estimation, the expectation-maximization (EM) algorithm is employed using diagonal covariance matrices, since feature components are assumed to be independent of each other.

Total Discrimination Measure

The proposed discrimination analysis also offers a means to assess and compare the expected identification performances of different lip feature sets. Note that the measure $\mathrm{d}(f)$ is an estimate of the discrimination power of each component in the feature vector. Thus, the discriminative power of the N selected features, i.e., the reduced feature vector, can be estimated by the total discrimination measure, $\mathrm{D}_{N}(f)$, which is defined as

$$\mathrm{D}_{N}(f) \triangleq \sum_{n=1}^{N} \mathrm{d}(f_{k_n}).$$

(17)

Note that the Bayesian discrimination analysis cannot be applied to the lip shape vector $\boldsymbol{f}_{\mathrm{SHP}}$ since the lip shape parameters are not, in general, statistically independent of each other.

Temporal Discriminative Feature Selection Using the LDA

The Bayesian MMIE-based discriminative feature selection does not model and exploit the temporal correlations between successive lip frames. Following the work of Potamianos et al. (2003), we use the LDA for temporal discrimination analysis, where we successively concatenate the Bayesian-reduced lip feature vectors through a window of fixed duration so as to capture dynamic visual speech information, and obtain a new sequence of higher dimensional feature vectors. Then, each of these feature vectors is projected to a lower dimensional discriminative feature space using the LDA (see Figure 2).

The LDA maps a given high dimensional feature vector to a subspace of reduced dimension that best describes the discrimination among classes. This is achieved using two statistical measures, the within-class scatter matrix S_w and the between-class scatter matrix S_b (Martinez & Kak, 2001). The goal is to maximize the between-class scattering while minimizing the within-class variations. Hence, the LDA seeks for a projection matrix W which maximizes the function $E(W) = \det(W^T S_b W)/\det(W^T S_w W)$ provided that S_w is nonsingular. The function $E(W)$ is maximized when the column vectors of the projection matrix W are the eigenvectors of $S_w^{-1} S_b$. The LDA has two important limitations: i) The matrix $S_w^{-1} S_b$ has nonzero eigenvalues at most one less than the total number of classes, which puts an upper bound on the reduced dimension, and ii) At least $K+R$ training samples are needed to guarantee the existence of the inverse matrix S_w^{-1}, where K denotes the initial feature vector dimension. Thus, the common practice is, prior to LDA, to use an intermediate dimension reduction technique such as PCA that does not involve a discrimination analysis. This intermediate reduction is also preferable to reduce the computational complexity of the LDA analysis. In this regard, the Bayesian MMIE-based analysis can also serve as an intermediate dimension reduction method that selects a discriminative set of features from a larger set of the DCT coefficients including some non-principal, i.e., minor, feature components at each time instant.

As shown in Figure 2, the MMIE-based discrimination analysis results in a feature vector $\tilde{f}(t)$ for each time instant t. Prior to concatenation within a window, the feature vector $\tilde{f}(t)$ is linearly interpolated in time by some factor whose value depends on the frame rate. In the interpolated temporal domain, each feature vector at time instant t is concatenated with the previous and the next T feature vectors to form a new higher dimensional feature vector denoted by $F(t)$:

$$F(t) = \left[\tilde{f}(t-T); \tilde{f}(t-T+1);...; \tilde{f}(t);...; \tilde{f}(t+T-1); \tilde{f}(t+T) \right].$$

(18)

The LDA is then performed on this concatenated vector of dimension $(2T+1)N\times1$. The dimension of the resulting discriminative feature space is bounded above by $R-1$, that is one less than the total number of classes. Figure 2 illustrates the formation of the final feature vector, that we denote by LDA ($\tilde{f}(t)$), via the spatial-temporal discrimination analysis.

EXPERIMENTAL RESULTS

Speaker identification experiments are conducted using the MVGL-AVD database (Erzin, 2004; MVGL, 2008), which contains audio-visual data collected from a population of 50 speakers, i.e., $R = 50$. The

Figure 6. Selected sample images from the MVGL-AVD database

visual data set has video frames of size 720×576 pixels at a rate of 15 fps, each containing the frontal view of a speaker's head. Figure 6 shows images of selected subjects from the MVGL-AVD database.

We consider two distinct scenarios, each represented with a different data set: the *secret phrase* (D_s) and the *public phrase* (D_p) data sets. In the secret phrase scenario, each subject utters ten repetitions of her/his name and surname. A set of impostor data is also collected with each subject in the population uttering five different names from the population. In the public phrase scenario, each subject utters ten repetitions of a fixed digit password "348-572".

In the experiments, an initial lip region of size 128×80 is first segmented from each video frame, following the registration of successive face regions by head motion compensation. For grid-based motion analysis, a rectangular grid of size $g_x \times g_y = 64 \times 40$ is used for each lip segment. Following motion estimation and 2-D DCT, a feature vector of length $2M$ is obtained by interlacing M features from x and y directions, respectively, where $M = 50$. Then the *FirstN* features, f_{GRD}^N, are extracted by eliminating some high-indexed DCT coefficients to obtain a vector of size N, where $N \leq 2M$. For contour-based motion analysis, we follow a similar procedure. First, we extract the lip contour in each frame. Following motion estimation and 1-D DCT on the lip contour pixel locations, a feature vector of size $2M$, is obtained, where M is set to 50, i.e., the same number as in grid-based motion analysis. The low-indexed DCT coefficients then provide us with the contour-based *FirstN* features, i.e. f_{CTR}^N. The third lip feature representation is obtained by concatenating the contour-based motion features with the 8 lip shape parameters, that is $f_{CTR}^N + f_{SHP}$. After feature extraction, we employ two-stage discrimination framework; f^N and $\tilde{f}^N$ stand for the *FirstN* and *DiscrimN* features respectively, whereas LDA(f^N) and LDA($\tilde{f}^N$) denote the features obtained by applying the temporal LDA using $T = 6$ as the temporal window parameter. We then perform unimodal recognition using HMM-based probabilistic modeling.

For multimodal implementation, we consider audio, lip texture and lip motion as different modalities. The audio is represented with the mel-frequency cepstral coefficients (MFCCs), as they yield good discrimination of speech signal. The audio stream is processed over 10 msec frames centered on 25 msec Hamming window for 16 kHz sampled audio signal. Each analysis frame is first multiplied with a Hamming window and transformed to frequency domain using fast Fourier transform (FFT). Mel-scaled triangular filter bank energies are calculated over the square magnitude of the spectrum and represented in logarithmic scale. The resulting MFCC features are derived using the DCT over log-scaled filter bank energies (Rabiner & Juang, 1993). The audio feature vector f_A is formed as a collection of MFCC vector along with the first and second Δ-MFCCs. Second, the features for the lip texture modality are 2-D DCT coefficients of the luminance component of a rectangular region of interest around the lip. Following the DCT, we perform the Bayesian feature selection and form the feature vector, f_{L_t}, by concatenating the 50 most discriminative features. The features for the lip motion modality, f_{L_m}, are first determined by analyzing the unimodal recognition performance, and selected to be the most successful ones. We finally perform multimodal recognition with HMM-based framework by fusing modalities with RWS rule.

The audio recordings are perturbed with varying levels of additive noise during the testing sessions to simulate adverse environmental conditions. The additive acoustic noise is picked to be a mixture of office and babble noise. Abbreviations for the modalities and the fusion techniques are given in Table 1.

We first address the secret and public phrase scenarios in speaker identification, respectively and for each scenario we provide the performances of the three lip motion feature representations, f_{GRD}^N, f_{CTR}^N, and $f_{CTR}^N + f_{SHP}$. We also show the recognition results of the discriminative lip motion features, $\tilde{f}^N$ and LDA($\tilde{f}^N$), as well as the performance of the multimodal systems for each scenario.

Table 1. Abbreviations for the modalities and the fusion techniques

A	**Audio modality**
L_t	**Lip texture modality**
L_m	**Lip motion modality**
$\odot$	**Product Rule**
$\oplus$	**RWS Rule**

Speaker Identification: Secret Phrase Scenario

In the secret phrase scenario, the D_s database is partitioned into two disjoint sets, D_{s_1} and D_{s_2}, each having five repetitions from each subject in the database. The subsets D_{s_1} and D_{s_2} are used for training and testing respectively. Since there are 50 subjects and five repetitions for each true and imposter client tests, the total number of trials for the true accepts and true rejects is $C_c = C_i = 250$.

Figure 7. Speaker identification under secret phrase (NAME) scenario: EER results for grid-based motion f_{GRD}^N, contour-based motion f_{CTR}^N, and contour-based motion with shape $f_{CTR}^N + f_{SHP}$

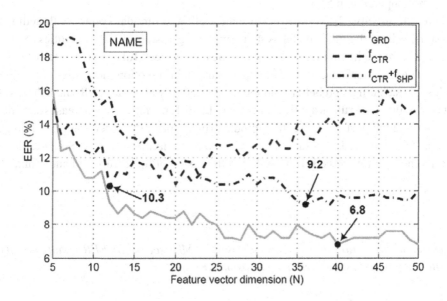

Figure 8. Speaker identification under secret phrase (NAME) scenario: EER results for f_{GRD}^N (FirstN), f_{GRD}^N (DiscrimN), and $LDA(f_{GRD}^N)$ features with varying vector dimension N

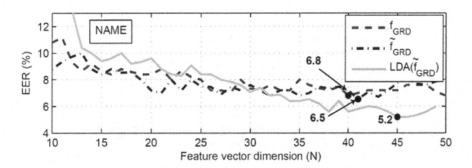

The three lip motion feature representations, f_{GRD}^{N}, f_{CTR}^{N}, and $f_{CTR}^{N} + f_{SHP}$, are tested on the data-base. Figure 7 displays the EER performances with varying feature dimension N. We observe that the grid-based motion features, f_{GRD}^{N}, achieve 6.8% EER, and outperform the contour-based features, f_{CTR}^{N}. We also observe that the addition of lip shape features to the contour-based features, i.e., $f_{CTR}^{N} + f_{SHP}$ results in additional performance gain.

In order to test the effect of the discrimination analysis, we take the most successful lip motion features, i.e., grid-based features f_{GRD}^{N}, and perform the two-stage discrimination. Figure 8 plots the performances of the grid-based *FirstN* features, *DiscrimN* features and *DiscrimN* features with LDA at varying dimensions (10 to 50) for the secret phrase scenario. We observe that: i) *DiscrimN* achieves better performance (6.5% compared to 6.8%) by selecting a discriminative subset of coefficients, which are not necessarily the principal components, ii) As the feature vector dimension N increases, the performance saturates, iii) The use of the LDA in addition to Bayesian discrimination brings additional EER gain (5.2% compared to 6.5%).

We also present, in Table 2, the EER performance of the unimodal system with audio, lip texture or lip motion as well as the multimodal system employing fusion of the modalities. Notice that the unimodal system with the lip motion (L_m) employs the most successful features in terms of recognition (LDA(f_{GRD}^{N})). The EER performances of the lip texture and lip motion modalities are 5.6% and 5.2%, which are close to each other and better than the audio modality at 15 dB SNR and below. When either the product rule or the RWS rule is applied for fusion, the EER performance increases significantly. The RWS rule is observed to perform better than product rule, especially under noisy conditions. The best EER performance is achieved with the fusion of all three modalities at 15 dB SNR and below. Above 15 dB SNR, the best performance is achieved with the fusion of lip texture and audio modalities.

Table 2. Speaker identification under secret phrase (NAME) scenario: EER results at varying noise levels for different modalities and multimodal fusion structures

Source modality	EER (%)						
	Noise level (db SNR)						
	Clean	25	20	15	10	7	5
A	1	1.6	2.4	5.34	14.8	25.4	31.47
L_t	5.6	-	-	-	-	-	-
L_m	5.2	-	-	-	-	-	-
$L_m \odot A$	2.6	3.2	3.6	4.4	7.2	17.47	22.8
$L_m \oplus A$	0.8	1.2	1.8	3.2	5.6	13.6	19.2
$L_t \odot A$	0.4	0.4	0.8	2	4.4	11.2	15.87
$L_t \oplus A$	1	0.8	1	1.8	3	6.8	9.6
$L_m \odot L_t \odot A$	1.6	1.4	1.4	1.4	1.74	3.6	4.4
$L_m \oplus L_t \oplus A$	1.2	1.2	1.2	1.2	1.4	3.2	3.2

Speaker Identification: Public Phrase Scenario

In the public phrase scenario, the $\boldsymbol{D}_p$ database is partitioned into two disjoint sets, $\boldsymbol{D}_{p_1}$ and $\boldsymbol{D}_{p_2}$, each having five repetitions of the same 6-digit number from each subject in the database. The subsets $\boldsymbol{D}_{p_1}$ and $\boldsymbol{D}_{p_2}$ are respectively used for training and testing. Note that, in the public phrase scenario, no imposter recordings are performed since every subject utters the same 6-digit number. The imposter clients are

Figure 9. Speaker identification under public phrase (DIGIT) scenario: EER results for grid-based motion $\boldsymbol{f}_{\mathrm{GRD}}^{N}$, contour-based motion $\boldsymbol{f}_{\mathrm{CTR}}^{N}$, and contour-based motion with shape $\boldsymbol{f}_{\mathrm{CTR}}^{N} + \boldsymbol{f}_{\mathrm{SHP}}$

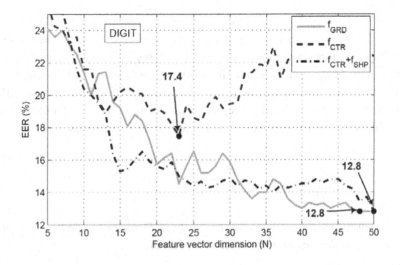

Figure 10. Speaker identification under public phrase (DIGIT) scenario: EER results for $\boldsymbol{f}_{\mathrm{GRD}}^{N}$ (FirstN), $\boldsymbol{f}_{\mathrm{GRD}}^{N}$ (DiscrimN), and $\mathrm{LDA}(\boldsymbol{f}_{\mathrm{GRD}}^{N})$ features with varying vector dimension N

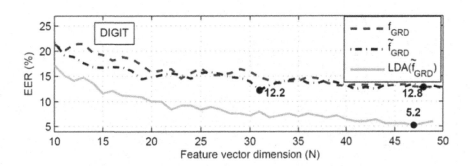

generated by the *leave-one-out* scheme, where each subject becomes the imposter of the remaining R–1 subjects in the population. Having $R = 50$ subjects and five testing repetitions, the resulting total number of trials for the true accepts and true rejects (imposters) becomes respectively $C_c = 250$ and $C_i = 250$.

Figure 9 displays the EER performances for different lip motion representations with varying feature dimension N. We observe that the grid-based motion features, f_{GRD}^N, and the contour-based motion with shape features, $f_{CTR}^N + f_{SHP}$, achieve the same minimum 12.8% EER, and outperform the contour-based only features f_{CTR}^N. Note that the EER performance of speaker identification under the secret phrase scenario is significantly better than that of the public phrase scenario. This is expected since in the secret phrase scenario each speaker in the database utters a different person-specific phrase, making the identification task easier.

Figure 10 plots the performances of the grid-based *FirstN* features, *DiscrimN* features and *DiscrimN* features with LDA at varying dimensions (10 to 50) for the public phrase scenario. Similar to the secret phrase scenario, we observe that *DiscrimN* achieves better performance than *FirstN* with EER of 12.2%, and the LDA in addition to Bayesian discrimination significantly improves the recognition performance from 12.2% to 5.2%.

Table 3 presents the EER performance of the unimodal system with audio, lip texture or lip motion as well as the multimodal system employing fusion of the modalities. Notice that the unimodal system with the lip motion (L_m) employs the most successful features in terms of recognition (LDA(f_{GRD}^N)). The EER performances of the lip texture and lip motion modalities are 1.74% and 5.2%. Since every subject utters the same password in the public phrase scenario, the audio modality suffers and the lip texture modality benefits with respect to the secret phrase scenario. When either the product rule or the RWS rule is applied for fusion, the EER performance significantly increases. The RWS rule is observed

Table 3. Speaker identification under public phrase (DIGIT) scenario: EER results at varying noise levels for different modalities and multimodal fusion structures

Source modality	EER (%)						
	Noise level (db SNR)						
	Clean	25	20	15	10	7	5
A	2.4	3.4	6.93	12.2	24.88	33.12	37.1
L_t	1.74	-	-	-	-	-	-
L_m	5.2	-	-	-	-	-	-
$L_m \odot A$	2.4	2.4	2.4	4	10.4	18	23.2
$L_m \oplus A$	2.4	2.4	2.4	4	10	16.8	22
$L_t \odot A$	0.4	0.4	0.4	1.4	6.8	14	18.4
$L_t \oplus A$	0.4	0.4	0.4	0.8	4	10	13.8
$L_m \odot L_t \odot A$	0.8	0.8	1.2	1.2	2.6	4.2	5.2
$L_m \oplus L_t \oplus A$	0.4	0.4	0.6	0.8	2.4	3.8	5.2

to perform better than product rule at all SNR conditions. The best EER performance is achieved with the fusion of all three modalities at all SNR levels.

CONCLUSIONS

Biometric person identification technologies focus on voice, face, iris and retina scans, signature strokes, fingerprint, palm print, and hand geometry as distinguishing source of personal information. However, state-of-the-art audio-visual speech recognition systems usually employ two critical sources: Speech signal and lip information. The lip motion information, which is highly correlated with the speech signal, has been extensively utilized in speech recognition. Despite the general belief that the lip motion possesses valuable biometric information, there have been few studies investigating this modality in speaker identification. More specifically, almost all of the existing systems employ the lip texture and/or geometry to model the lip motion. The use of the explicit lip motion, which is in fact what is meant by the lip information, is relatively rare. This has been the first issue in the speech/speaker recognition literature that motivates us to investigate the lip motion modality. The second point open to debate is the optimal feature representation for the lip motion information. Determination of the best lip motion features has been the primary objective of this work. By obtaining the best lip motion features, i.e., the most discriminative features among classes, it is possible to maximize the unimodal recognition performance. However, no matter how successful the modality is, robustness has always been an issue for unimodal systems. More reliable and robust recognition systems should be built by fusing individual modalities. This directs us towards integrating visual features with audio, which would provide more information about the identity of the speaker.

Taking the outlined issues into account, we present a multimodal recognition system that integrates audio with several lip modalities. We propose to use explicit lip motion information that best represents the lip dynamics for speaker identification. First, we eliminate the corruptive effect of head motion during natural speaking act to obtain pure lip articulation. A comparative study between several lip motion features including the grid-based dense motion features and the contour-based lip motion features is performed. Firstly we compute the grid-based motion features within a bounding box around the lip region and thus, take the motion of the non-lip, i.e. skin region into account. Secondly we calculate the contour-based motion features on the outer lip contour and discard the effect to the surrounding area. In addition to the explicit motion features on the outer contour, simple lip shape features are also extracted and concatenated with the contour-based motion features to see the contribution of geometric lip information.

In our experiments, we show that the grid-based dense lip motion features are superior and more robust compared to the contour-based lip motion features. This shows the importance of the skin region even if some erroneous vectors show up. Recall that before applying the two-stage discrimination analysis, we first transform the motion data into DCT domain. This transformation has two advantages: First, it serves as a tool to reduce the feature dimension by filtering out the high frequency components of the motion signal. These high frequency components are mostly due to noise and irrelevant to our analysis since it is unnatural to have very abrupt motion changes between neighboring pixels of the lip region where the motion signal is expected to have some smoothness. Second, DCT decorrelates the feature vector so that the discriminative power of each feature component can be independently analyzed.

For optimal lip motion feature representation, we introduce a novel two-stage discrimination analysis technique that involves the spatial Bayesian feature selection and the temporal LDA. The experimental results reveal that the Bayesian discrimination analysis improves the performance. It is interesting to see that after spatial Bayesian discrimination, a small set of DCT features that possess more discriminative power is formed regardless of their energy or coefficient index. The Bayesian discriminative feature selection also serves as an intermediate dimensionality reduction step prior to the temporal LDA, by successfully selecting the lip features that are tailored for the specific problem. The temporal LDA is beneficial especially under the public phrase scenario. The LDA maps a given high dimensional feature vector to a subspace of reduced dimension that best describes the discrimination among classes. We achieve high discrimination among classes, i.e., different speakers, using the LDA.

Apart from the efforts to maximize the unimodal performance of the explicit lip motion modality, we have fused the lip motion features with audio and lip texture to build a reliable and robust system that is able to cope with the real-life problems. The audio features are composed of the MFCCs along with the first and second derivatives whereas the lip texture features are the 2-D DCT coefficients of the grayscale lip images. Since the reliability of each independent source of information (audio, lip texture, and lip motion) may vary under different acoustic and lighting conditions, our multimodal decision fusion strategy significantly improves the overall performance. The RWS decision fusion rule with the given reliability measures provides improved results than the product rule as it introduces a priori information on the modality reliability. It is worth noting that a successful system is built for speaker identification without using the face modality, which is usually considered as indispensable in this problem.

FUTURE RESEARCH DIRECTIONS

In any recognition problem, if one can extract the best, possibly the most sophisticated, features achievable from available data, then it is possible to attain good recognition performance even with simple classifiers. Hence the proposed two-stage spatial-temporal discrimination analysis framework, although structurally complex, is vital in extracting the best motion-based features for speaker identification. Furthermore, having obtained low-dimensional representations for any modality will reduce computational complexity.

In speaker identification, in addition to working in the motion-based feature space, one should not ignore the appearance information, which is indispensable in building robust systems in biometrics and security/surveillance. Another detail worth mentioning is the multimodal fusion. When using modalities such as face/lip appearance, lip shape, lip articulation, etc., feature-level fusion is usually infeasible since it is not trivial to merge different feature spaces. Thus decision fusion schemes that rely on the unified decisions of different classifiers, i.e., experts, should be the way to integrate several modalities.

There are further issues to be addressed: The lip region should be detected in a fully automatic way to allow real-time implementations. There exist a number of ways to detect and segment the lip region however they usually suffer from affine pose changes. The main concern behind the lip segmentation problem is to extract the lip from the mouth image. When lip motion analysis is the primary issue, the lip images should be registered and carefully extracted using a static reference point, for instance the center point in the image. Otherwise, the lip motion analysis cannot be carried out correctly.

Another point worth mentioning is the extraction of 3-D visual features, which needs to employ stereo cameras to acquire 3-D data. Aside from generating similar recognition frameworks, this will provide a way to learn facial motion parameters for 3-D animations and realistic synthesis. A different perspective to synthesize lip articulation is to assume that lip features are the measurements of a linear dynamical system, and system parameters are identified to perform recognition and synthesis. Furthermore, correlation between audio and lip articulation should be solved so as to realize accurate audio-visual synchronization.

We have already mentioned that biometric person identification technologies mostly focus on voice, face, iris and retina scans, signature strokes, fingerprint, palm print, and hand geometry, whereas gait is effective in surveillance applications. In particular, for speaker identification from talking faces, sources such as face appearance and iris can be integrated to build more robust multimodal implementations. Future research directions to improve recognition systems include refining the statistical methods for the underlying biometric and measurement system, developing systems to code and store biometric data, and using sources of information for multi-biometric systems. The reader is referred to the additional materials to investigate the aforementioned research directions.

ACKNOWLEDGMENTS

This work has been supported by *The Scientific and Technical Research Council of Turkey* (TUBI-TAK) under the project EEEAG-101E026 and by *The European FP6 Network of Excellence SIMILAR* (http://www.similar.cc).

REFERENCES

Aleksic, P. S., Williams, J. J., Wu, Z., & Katsaggelos, A. K. (2002). Audio-visual speech recognition using MPEG-4 compliant visual features, *EURASIP Journal on Applied Signal Processing, Special Issue on Joint Audio-Visual Speech Processing, 2002(11)*, 1213-1227.

Bregler, C., & Konig, Y. (1994). "Eigenlips" for robust speech recognition. *Proceedings of the 1994 IEEE International Conference on Acoustics, Speech, and Signal Processing (ICASSP'94), 2*, 669-672.

Broun, C. C., Zhang, X., Mersereau, R. M., & Clements, M. (2002). Automatic speechreading with application to speaker verification. *Proceedings of the IEEE International Conference on Acoustics, Speech, and Signal Processing (ICASSP'02), 1*, 685-688.

Brunelli, R., & Falavigna, D. (1995). Person identification using multiple cues. *IEEE Transactions on Pattern Analysis and Machine Intelligence, 17(10)*, 955-966.

Çetingül, H. E., Yemez, Y., Erzin, E., & Tekalp, A. M. (2004). Discriminative lip-motion features for biometric speaker identification. *Proceedings of the IEEE International Conference on Image Processing (ICIP'04), 3*, 2023-2026.

Çetingül, H. E., Yemez, Y., Erzin, E., & Tekalp, A. M. (2005). Robust lip motion features for speaker identification. *Proceedings of the IEEE International Conference on Acoustics, Speech, and Signal Processing (ICASSP'05), 1*, 509-512.

Çetingül, H. E., Erzin, E., Yemez, Y., & Tekalp, A. M. (2006a). Multimodal speaker/speech recognition using lip motion, lip texture and audio. *Signal Processing, Special Section: Multimodal Human-Computer Interfaces, 86(12),* 3549-3558.

Çetingül, H. E., Yemez, Y., Erzin, E., & Tekalp, A. M. (2006b). Discriminative analysis of lip motion features for speaker identification and speech-reading. *IEEE Transactions on Image Processing, 15(10),* 2879-2891.

Chaudhari, U. V., Ramaswamy, G. N., Potamianos, G., & Neti, C. (2003). Information fusion and decision cascading for audio-visual speaker recognition based on time-varying stream reliability prediction. *Proceedings of the International Conference on Multimedia & Expo (ICME'03), 3,* 9-12.

Chen, T. (2001). Audiovisual speech processing. *IEEE Signal Processing Magazine, 18(1),* 9-21.

Chibelushi, C. C., Mason, J. S., & Deravi, F. (1993). Integration of acoustic and visual speech for speaker recognition. *Proceedings of the 3rd European Conference on Speech Communication and Technology (EUROSPEECH'93),* 157-160.

Chibelushi, C., Deravi, F., & Mason, J. (2002). A review of speech-based bimodal recognition. *IEEE Transactions on Multimedia, 4(1),* 23-37.

Civanlar, M. R., & Chen, T. (1996). Password-free network security through joint use of audio and video. *Proceedings of the SPIE Photonic, 2915,* 120-125.

Da Silveira, L. G., Facon, J., & Borges, D. L. (2003). Visual speech recognition: a solution from feature extraction to words classification. *Proceedings of the XVI Brazilian Symposium on Computer Graphics and Image Processing (SIBGRAPI'03),* 399-405.

Dupont S., & Luettin, J. (2000). Audio-visual speech modeling for continuous speech recognition. *IEEE Transactions on Multimedia, 2(3),* 141-151.

Erzin, E., Yemez, Y., & Tekalp, A. M. (2004). Joint audio-video processing for robust biometric speaker identification in car. In H. Abut, J. H. L. Hansen, K. Takeda (Ed.), *DSP for in-vehicle and mobile systems* (pp. 237-256). Springer.

Erzin, E., Yemez, Y., & Tekalp, A. M. (2005). Multimodal speaker identification using an adaptive classifier cascade based on modality reliability. *IEEE Transactions on Multimedia, 7(5),* 840-852.

Eveno, N., Caplier, A., & Coulon, P.-Y. (2004). Accurate and quasi-automatic lip tracking. *IEEE Transactions on Circuits and Systems for Video Technology, 14(5),* 706-715.

Foo, S. W., Lian, Y., & Dong, L. (2004). Recognition of visual speech elements using adaptively boosted hidden Markov models. *IEEE Transactions on Circuits and Systems for Video Technology, 14(5),* 693-705.

Fox, N. A., & Reilly, R. B. (2004). Robust multi-modal person identification with tolerance of facial expression. *Proceedings of the IEEE International Conference on Systems, Man, and Cybernetics, 1,* 580-585.

Frischholz, R. W., & Dieckmann, U. (2000). BioID: A multimodal biometric identification system. *IEEE Computer, 33(2),* 64-68.

Froba, B., Rothe, C., & Kublbeck, C., (2000). Evaluation of sensor calibration in a biometric person recognition framework based on sensor fusion. *Proceedings of the 4th IEEE International Conference on Automatic Face and Gesture Recognition*, 512-517.

Huang, X., Acero, A., & Hon, H.-W. (2001). *Spoken language processing: A guide to theory, algorithm, and system development*, Prentice Hall.

Jourlin, P., Luettin, J., Genoud, D., & Wassner, H. (1997). Acoustic-labial speaker verification. *Pattern Recognition Letters, 18(9)*, 853-858.

Kaynak, M. N., Zhi, Q., Cheok, A. D., Sengupta, K., Jian, Z., & Chung, K. C. (2004). Analysis of lip geometric features for audio-visual speech recognition. *IEEE Transactions on Systems, Man and Cybernetics - Part A: Systems and Humans, 34(4)*, 564-570.

Kittler, J., Hatef, M., Duin, R., & Matas, J. (1998). On combining classifiers. *IEEE Transactions on Pattern Analysis and Machine Intelligence, 20(3)*, 226-239.

Leung, S.-H., Wang, S.-L., & Lau, W.-H. (2004). Lip image segmentation using fuzzy clustering incorporating an elliptic shape function. *IEEE Transactions on Image Processing, 13(1)*, 51-62.

Lucey, S., Sridharan, S., & Chandran, V. (2000). Initialized eigenlip estimator for fast lip tracking using linear regression. *Proceedings of the 15th International Conference on Pattern Recognition, 3*, 178-181.

Luettin, J., Thacker, N., & Beet, S. (1996). Statistical lip modeling for visual speech recognition. *Proceedings of the 8th European Signal Processing Conference (EUSIPCO'96)*, 10-13.

Martinez, A. M., & Kak, A. C. (2001). PCA versus LDA. *IEEE Transactions on Pattern Analysis and Machine Intelligence, 23(2)*, 228-233.

Matthews, I., Cootes, T. F., Bangham, J. A., Cox, S., & Harvey, R. (2002). Extraction of visual features for lipreading. *IEEE Transactions on Pattern Analysis and Machine Intelligence, 24(2)*, 198-213.

Mok, L. L., Lau, W. H., Leung, S. H., Wang, S. L., & Yan, H., (2004). Lip features selection with application to person authentication. *Proceedings of the IEEE International Conference on Acoustics, Speech, and Signal Processing (ICASSP'04), 3*, 397-400.

MVGL, Multimedia Vision and Graphics Laboratory, Koç University, http://portal.ku.edu.tr/~mvgl, 2008.

Nefian, A. V., Liang, L., Pi, X., Xiaoxiang, L., Mao, C., & Murphy, K. (2002). A couple HMM for audio-visual speech recognition, *Proceedings of the IEEE International Conference on Acoustics, Speech, and Signal Processing (ICASSP'02), 2*, 2013-2016.

Odobez, J.-M., & Bouthemy, P. (1995). Robust multiresolution estimation of parametric motion models. *Journal of Visual Communication and Image Representation, 6(4)*, 348-365.

Perez, J. F. G., Frangi, A. F., Solano, E. L., & Lukas, K. (2005). Lip reading for robust speech recognition on embedded devices. *Proceedings of the IEEE International Conference on Acoustics, Speech, and Signal Processing (ICASSP'05), 1*, 473-476.

Potamianos, G., Neti, C., Gravier, G., Garg, A., & Senior, A. W. (2003). Recent advances in the automatic recognition of audio-visual speech. *Proceedings of the IEEE, 91(9)*, 1306-1326.

Puri, A., Chen, X., & Luthra, A. (2004). Video coding using the H.264/MPEG-4 AVC compression standard. *Signal Processing: Image Communication, 19(9)*, 793-849.

Rabiner, L., & Juang, B.-H. (1993). *Fundamentals of speech recognition.* Englewood Cliffs, NJ: Prentice-Hall.

Reynolds, D. A. (1995). Speaker identification and verification using Gaussian mixture speaker models. *Speech Communication, 17(1)*, 91-108.

Sadeghi, M., Kittler, J., & Messer, K. (2002). Modelling and segmentation of lip area in face images. *IEE Proceedings of Vision, Image and Signal Processing, 149(3)*, 179-184.

Sanderson, C., & Paliwal, K. K. (2003). Noise compensation in a person verification system using face and multiple speech features. *Pattern Recognition, 36(2)*, 293-302.

Tomlinson, M. J., Russell, M. J., & Brooke, N. M. (1996). Integrating audio and visual information to provide highly robust speech recognition. *Proceedings of the IEEE International Conference on Acoustics, Speech, and Signal Processing (ICASSP'96), 2*, 821-824.

Turk, M., & Pentland, A. (1991). Eigenfaces for recognition. *Journal of Cognitive Neuroscience, 3(1)*, 71-86.

Wakasugi, T., Nishiura, M., & Fukui, K. (2004). Robust lip contour extraction using separability of multi-dimensional distributions. *Proceedings of the 6th IEEE International Conference on Automatic Face and Gesture Recognition*, 415-420.

Wang, S. L., Lau, W. H., Leung, S. H., & Liew, A. W. C. (2004a). Lip segmentation with the presence of beards. *Proceedings of the IEEE International Conference on Acoustics, Speech, and Signal Processing (ICASSP'04), 3*, 529-532.

Wang, S. L., Lau, W. H., Leung, S. H., & Yan, H. (2004b). A real-time automatic lipreading system. *Proceedings of the IEEE International Symposium on Circuits and Systems (ISCAS'04), 2*, 101-104.

Wark, T., Sridharan, S., & Chandran, V. (1998). An approach to statistical lip modeling for speaker identification via chromatic feature extraction. *Proceedings of the IEEE International Conference on Pattern Recognition (ICPR'98), 1*, 123-125.

Wark, T., & Sridharan, S. (2001). Adaptive fusion of speech and lip information for robust speaker identification. *Digital Signal Processing, 11(3)*, 169-186.

Yemez, Y., Sankur, B., & Anarim, E. (2000). A quadratic motion-based object-oriented video codec. *Signal Processing: Image Communication, 15(9)*, 729-766.

Zhang, D. D. (2000). *Automated biometrics: Technologies and systems.* Dordrecht : Kluwer Academic Publishers.

Zhang, J., Yan, Y., & Lades, M. (1997). Face recognition: eigenface, elastic matching, and neural nets. *Proceedings of the IEEE, 85(9)*, 1423-1435.

Zhang, X., Broun, C. C., Mersereau, R. M., & Clements, M. A. (2002a). Automatic speechreading with applications to human-computer interfaces. *EURASIP Journal on Applied Signal Processing, 2002(11)*, 1228-1247.

Zhang, X., Mersereau, R. M., Clements, M. A., & Broun, C. C. (2002b). Visual speech feature extraction for improved speech recognition. *Proceedings of the IEEE International Conference on Acoustics, Speech, and Signal Processing (ICASSP'02), 2*, 1993-1996.

ADDITIONAL READINGS

Aleksic, P. S., Potamianos, G., & Katsaggelos, A. K. (2005). Exploiting visual information in automatic speech processing. In A. Bovik (Ed.), *Handbook of Image and Video Processing* (pp. 1263-1289). Academic Press.

Aleksic, P. S., & Katsaggelos, A. K., (2005). Audio-visual biometrics. *Proceedings of the IEEE, 92(11)*, 2025-2044.

Arsic, I., & Thiran, J.-P. (2006). Mutual information eigenlips for audio-visual speech recognition. *Proceedings of the 14th European Signal Processing Conference (EUSIPCO'06)*, from http://www.eurasip.org/ Proceedings/Eusipco/Eusipco2006/papers/1568982005.pdf.

Bouvier, C., Coulon, P.-Y., & Maldague, X. (2007). Unsupervised lips segmentation based on ROI optimisation and parametric model. *Proceedings of the IEEE International Conference on Image Processing (ICIP'04), 4*, 301-304.

Campbell, J. P., Jr. (1997). Speaker recognition: A tutorial. *Proceedings of the IEEE, 85(9)*, 1437-1462.

Cosatto, E., Ostermann, J., Graf, H. P., & Schroeter, J. (2003). Lifelike talking faces for interactive services. *Proceedings of the IEEE, 91(9)*, 1406-1429.

Çetingül, H. E. (2005). *Discrimination analysis of lip motion features for multimodal speaker identification and speech-reading*. Unpublished master's thesis, Koç University, Istanbul, Turkey.

Çetingül, H. E., Chaudhry, R. A., & Vidal, R. (2007, October). A system theoretic approach to synthesis and classification of lip articulation. *3rd International Workshop on Dynamical Vision*, available at http://vision.jhu.edu/publications.htm

Faraj, M.-I., & Bigun, J. (2007). Synergy of lip-motion and acoustic features in biometric speech and speaker recognition. *IEEE Transactions on Computers, 56(9)*, 1169-1175.

Fox, N. A., Gross, G., Cohn, J. F., & Reilly, R. B. (2007). Robust biometric person identification using automatic classifier fusion of speech, mouth, and face experts. *IEEE Transactions on Multimedia, 9(4)*, 701-714.

Han, C.-H., & Sohng, K.-I. (2005). DTV lip-sync test using time-indexed audio and video signals without effect on program. *IEEE Transactions on Broadcasting, 51(1)*, 62-68.

Jain, A. K., Chelappa, R., Draper, S. C., Memon, N., Phillips, P. J., & Vetro, A. (2007). Signal processing for biometric systems. *IEEE Signal Processing Magazine, 24(6),* 146-152.

King, S. A., & Parent, R. E. (2005). Creating speech-synchronized animation. *IEEE Transactions on Visualization and Computer Graphics, 11(3)*, 341-352.

Kumar, K., Chen, T., & Stern, R. M. (2007). Profile view lip reading. *Proceedings of the IEEE International Conference on Acoustics, Speech, and Signal Processing, 4*, 429-432.

Nguyen, D., Halupka, D., Aarabi, P., & Sheikholeslami, A. (2006). Real-time face detection and lip feature extraction using field-programmable gate arrays. *IEEE Transactions on Systems, Man, and Cybernetics - Part B: Cybernetics, 36(4)*, 902-912.

Saisan, P., Bissacco, A., Chiuso, A., & Soatto, S. (2004). Modeling and synthesis of facial motion driven by speech. *Proceedings of the 8th European Conference on Computer Vision (ECCV'04)*, 456-467.

Saitoh, T., & Konishi, R. (2006). Word recognition based on two dimensional lip motion trajectory. *Proceedings of the International Symposium on Intelligent Signal Processing and Communications (ISPACS'06)*, 287-290.

Salazar, A., Daza, G. S., Sanchez, L., Prieto, F., Castellanos, G., & Quintero, C. (2006). Feature extraction & lips posture detection oriented to the treatment of CLP children. *Proceedings of the 28th Annual International Conference of the Engineering in Medicine and Biology Society*, 5747-5750.

Sargın, M.E., Yemez, Y., Erzin, E., & Tekalp, A.M. (2007). Audiovisual synchronization and fusion using canonical correlation analysis. *IEEE Transactions on Multimedia, 9(7)*, 1396-1403.

Xie, L., & Liu, Z.-Q. (2007). Realistic mouth-synching for speech-driven talking face using articulatory modeling. *IEEE Transactions on Multimedia, 9(3)*, 500-510.

Chapter XVII
Lip Motion Features for Biometric Person Recognition

Maycel Isaac Faraj
Halmstad University, Sweden

Josef Bigun
Halmstad University, Sweden

ABSTRACT

The present chapter reports on the use of lip motion as a stand alone biometric modality as well as a modality integrated with audio speech for identity recognition using digit recognition as a support. First, the auhtors estimate motion vectors from images of lip movements. The motion is modeled as the distribution of apparent line velocities in the movement of brightness patterns in an image. Then, they construct compact lip-motion features from the regional statistics of the local velocities. These can be used as alone or merged with audio features to recognize identity or the uttered digit. The author's present person recognition results using the XM2VTS database representing the video and audio data of 295 people. Furthermore, we present results on digit recognition when it is used in a text prompted mode to verify the liveness of the user. Such user challenges have the intention to reduce replay attack risks of the audio system.

INTRODUCTION

The performance of multimodal systems using audio and visual information in biometrics is superior to those of the acoustic and visual subsystems (Brunelli and Falavigna (1995)), (Tang and Li (2001)), (Bigun et al. (1997b)), and (Ortega-Garcia et al. (2004)) because these systems have a high potential for delivering noise robust biometric recognition systems compared to the corresponding single modalities. This is the general motivation for why there has been increased interest in multimodal biometric identity recognition. For example in audio based person recognition, phoneme sounds can be acoustically very similar between certain individuals and therefore hard to differentiate. By adding information on lip-motion, the discrimination of identities can be improved.

Speaker recognition using visual information in addition to acoustic features is particularly advantageous for other reasons too. It enables interactive person recognition which can be used to reduce impostor attacks that rely on prerecorded data. Raising antispoofing barriers, known as liveness detection, e.g. to determine if the biometric information being captured is an actual measurement from the live person who is present at the time of capture, for biometric systems is becoming increasingly necessary.

In this chapter extraction of lip-motion features that takes advantage of the spatiotemporal information in an image sequence containing lip-motion is discussed. Motion features are suggested for recognition of human identities and word (digit) recognition which can be used for liveness detection. The discussions include filtering, feature extraction, feature reduction, feature fusion and classification techniques.

Section 2 presents a review of some previous studies relevant to the chapter. The emphasis is on audio-visual systems rather than the massive research body existing in the individual recognition technologies. In particular, lip features suggested previously are discussed in greater detail.

Section 3 presents the theory of three different concepts of motion estimation which is directly relevant to this chapter. The motion estimation techniques based on texture translations and line translations are explicitly contrasted against each other. A further quantification of the speed accuracy of the used motion estimation that assumes moving lines or edges is given. How motion is exploited in other audio-visual recognition studies is also discussed.

In Section 4 we present a discussion on how one can use estimated velocities to produce compact feature vectors for identity recognition and liveness detection by uttered digits. A technique for quantization and dimension reduction is presented to reduce the amount of extracted features. The section also presents the audio and visual features concatenated at the feature level allowing, the integration of different audio and video sampling rates. The visual frames come at one fourth pace of the audio frames do, but contain more data. Yet the final concatenated feature vector must come at the same pace and contain approximately the same amount of data each, to avoid favoring one over the other. The section also presents the performance of visual information as an audio complement feature in speaker recognition and speech recognition using the XM2VTS database. We present a single and multimodal biometric identity recognition system based on the lip-motion features using a Gaussian Mixture Model (GMM) and a Support Vector Machine (SVM) as model builders. Furthermore, we present the experimental test using only one word (digit) to recognize the speaker identity. A discussion on related studies exploiting different techniques for audio-visual recognition is also included.

Section 5 discusses the conclusions of the chapter and presents directions for future work.

REVIEW

In speech recognition, two widely used terms are *phoneme* and *viseme*. The first is the basic linguistic unit and the later is the visually distinguishable speech unit (Luettin (1979)).[1] Whereas the use of *visemes* has been prompted by machine recognition studies, and hence it is in its start stage, the idea of phonemes is old. The science of Phonetics has for example been playing a major role in human language studies. The consonant letters complemented with vocals are approximations of phonemes and the alphabet belongs to greatest inventions of humanity.

Early work from (Petajan (1984)) and (Mase and Pentland (1991)) introduced visual information by the use of lip information as an important aid for speech recognition. (Yamamoto et al. (1998)) proposed visual information semi automatically mapped to lip movements through the aid of sensors put around the mouth to highlight the lips. The experimental results showed that significant performance could be achieved even by only using visual information. (Kittler et al. (1997)) presented a study using geometric features of the lip shapes from model based lip boundary tracking confirming the importance of lip information in identity recognition.

(Luettin et al. (1996)) presented a speaker identification system based only on dynamic visual information from video sequences containing the lip region. The geometrical features of the lips contained information about the shape and intensity information of the lips. The experiments were carried out by 12 speakers uttering digits and were later extended to the M2VTS database (37 speakers) by (Jourlin et al. (1997)). The person identification system based on Hidden Markov Model (HMM) achieved 72.2% using labial information and 100% using merged acoustic and visual features. They achieved good performance with joint systems utilizing a score fusion (late integration) method. They used 14 lip shape parameters, 10 intensity parameters, and the scale as visual features, resulting in a 25 dimensional visual feature vector. The speaker verification system score is computed as a weighted sum of the audio and visual scores.

(Brunelli and Falavigna (1995)) developed a text-independent speaker identification system exploiting acoustical information in combination with visual information from static face images. The system is based on several experts: two acoustic modalities (static and dynamic), containing derived features from short time spectral analysis of the speech signal, and three visual experts containing information from the eyes, nose and mouth. By using weighted function to classify the experts, the system performed well on approximately 90 speakers. Other studies using static visual information in recognition systems are (Tistarelli and Grosso (2000)) utilizing morphological filtering for a facial/eye localization followed by a simple matching algorithm for identity verification, (Duc et al. (1997) and Ben-Yacoub et al. (1999)) using Gabor filter responses on sparse graphs on faces but in the context of an audio-visual speaker verification system, (Sanderson and Paliwal (2004)) using Principal Component Analysis (PCA) for face feature extraction for identity verification and (Hazen et al. (2003)) using visual information from the different components in the face in a speaker identification system.

(Wark and Sridharan (1998)) developed a speaker verification system based on dynamic lip contour features extracted by Linear Discriminant Analysis (LDA) in combination with principal component analysis, yielding favorable results. This study was extended to merge audio-visual information by late integration using mixed densities of Gaussians, (Wark et al. (1999)).

(Dieckmann et al. (1997)), proposed a system using multimodal visual information from a video sequence. The modalities, face, voice and lip movement, were fused utilizing voting and opinion fusion. A minimum of two experts had to agree on the opinion and the combined opinion had to exceed the predefined threshold. Other related work has exploited dynamic visual information for speaker recognition (Frischholz and Dieckmann (2000)) and (Kittler et al. (1997)), and used multimodal information for speaker identification (Bigun et al. (1997a) and Bigun et al. (1997b)).

(Nakamura (2001)) proposed a method based on HMMs to integrate multimodal information considering synchronization and weights for different modalities. He built compound HMMs, each including a large number of states, incorporating states in an audio HMM and a visual HMM for all possible combinations. The system showed improved performance of speech recognition when using multimodal information.

Figure 1. The figure illustrates a block diagram of audio-visual biometric system used for speech and speaker recognition studies of this chapter

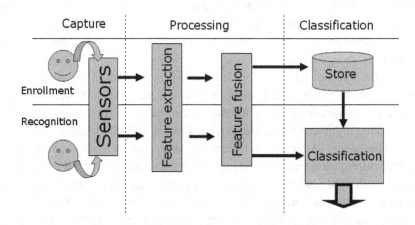

By utilizing the lip contour, such as the contour height, width and area, (Chen 2001)) presented a speech recognition system based on these features with real-time tracking using the multi-stream HMM without automatic weight optimization.

Biometric Recognition Framework

The generic framework describing biometric recognition systems is useful to understand the present work. We describe it in **Fig. 1** and it consists of three main blocks that of capturing, processing (feature extraction and feature fusion) and classification. In the case of offline recognition one does not need to take into account the capturing methods. This chapter falls under the category of processing block, proposing novel methods mainly for visual feature extraction. The classification block, also known as matching, is based on already developed systems such as GMM (using HTK toolkit) and SVM using SVM library. Below, we outline the existing methods used for feature extraction and feature fusion.

Visual Feature Extraction

The main benefit, in speech recognition, of using visual cues is that they are complementary to the acoustic signal: some phonemes that are difficult to understand acoustically in noisy environments can be easier to distinguish visually, and vice versa.

We distinguish two challenges in lip features processing, **Fig. 2**, i) detection of face/mouth/lips and ii) extraction of features. The first problem amounts to finding and tracking a specific facial part (mouth,

Figure 2. The figure illustrates visual feature representation approaches

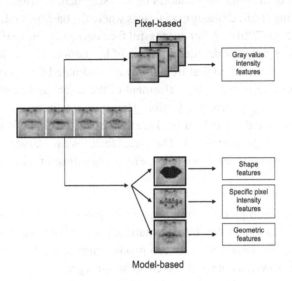

Figure 3. The figure illustrates the stages of information extraction in a biometric recognition system utilizing lip features. The video stream is first processed by a tracking and detection technique and in the second block the lip features are extracted from the tracked object (mouth region, lip contours, lips, etc.)

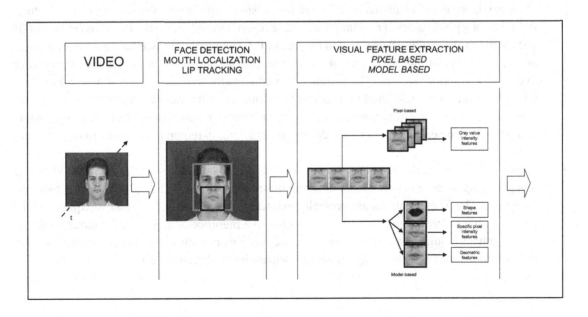

lips, lip contours etc.) whereas the second problem comprises the extraction of the visual information in terms of a small number of informative variables or measurement entities.

Successful mouth tracking is still challenging in cases where the background, head pose and lighting vary greatly, (Iyengar and Neti (2001)). After successful face detection, the region is processed further to obtain lip features. Though not very detailed in terms of lip motion description, even the bounding boxes of lip regions can reveal useful lip features if they are estimated for every frame independently because such rectangles reveal the dynamic evolvement of the height and width (Zhang et al. (2002)) and (Luettin et al. (1996)) during speech production. However, the lip information within the mouth region is most commonly extracted. Visual features are then extracted either from single frames (static) or from a set of consecutive images (dynamic). The visual features can be categorized into two groups: pixel based approaches and model based approaches, **Fig. 3**, regardless of whether they model the static or dynamic information.

- *Pixel based approach*: Each pixel in the image participates into computations of features such as Fourier transform, discrete cosine transformation, optical flow, etc. The features are directly pixel driven without form constraints between pixels which are to be contrasted to for example lip contour models. However, even pixel driven techniques presuppose the extraction of at least a sufficiently narrow region containing the mouth. The extracted lip region is often processed further with normalization techniques in an attempt to improve resilience against disturbances caused by head pose and lighting information. The pixels of the found mouth region can be mapped to a different space for lip features extraction. A popular mapping is projection to an image basis obtained by PCA. Such methods model static information in single image frames explicitly, even though they implicitly can represent the dynamic information between the frames, such as motion. Motion estimation (optical flow) which can capture the lip velocity and acceleration information in each pixel over time is by contrast an approach that explicitly models motion information. (Chan (2001)) presented a combined geometric lip features utilizing the PCA projection. The PCA are determined by a subset of pixels contained within the mouth. (Chiou and Hwang (1997)) on the other hand, presented combination of a number of snake lip contour vectors with PCA features from the color pixel values of a rectangle mouth region of interest. Furthermore, (Neti et al. (2000)) and (Matthews et al. (2001)) uses joined model of PCA techniques for estimating dimensionalities of shape models and appearance vectors. In this chapter we pursue the motion modeling approach to extract lip-motion features. The features are undoubtedly pixel driven, yet it describes but the allowable motions are restricted in direction to conform to what can be expected from a lip-motion. Using the motion estimation technique, requirements for accurate mouth state or lip contour extraction may be eased since a rough detection of the mouth region is sufficient to obtain visual features.
- *Model based approach*: Geometric and shape based methods represent the dynamic visual lip images by lip contour information and shape information of lips (Chan (2001)) and (Chiou and Hwang (1997)). These features are normally extracted from the region-of-interest equipped with a lip tracking preprocessing algorithm. Excluding the preprocessing part (lip contour tracking), these methods require less computation since they only work with a few control points. However, lip contour detection can be computationally demanding and prone to errors.

Next, we will present three mouth region features, proposed by (Jourlin et al. (1997)), (Dieckmann (1997)) and (Liang et al. (2002)) as they represent well the two categories outlined above.

Lip Feature Representation Approaches

Jourlin et al. (1997)

The lip feature extraction proposed by (Luettin et al. (1996)) is model based and assumes that most relevant information is contained in the *shape* (contours) of the speaker's lips.

The approach consists of a combination of lip contour information and the gray level distribution around the mouth area. During speech production the lip shape varies. For each speaker a spatiotemporal model that describes the mouth shape of the speaker and its temporal change is built.

They use a shape model that describes the outer and inner lip contour and a deformable gray level model to describe intensity values around the lip contours. Active shape models are used to locate, track and parameterize the lips over an image sequence. The principal modes of deformation are obtained by performing PCA on a labeled training set. A shape model is then approximated by a linear combination of the first few principal modes of deviation from the average lip curve.

Gray levels representing the intensities perpendicular to the contour at each control point of the model are concatenated to form a *profile* vector. The profile vectors of speakers in a training set are subjected to PCA to capture the profile variation modes. A profile is then represented as a linear combination of deviation modes (PCA basis) from the average gray profiles. The concatenated vectors of all model points represent a profile model for a speaker. PCA is performed on all profiles to obtain the principal modes of the profile variation.

In a lip sequence unseen by the system, the profile model is used to enable tracking whereby the curve parameters (weights, or basis coefficients) corresponding to the curves defined by the tracked control points are subsequently computed. The found contour and profile parameters are used as lip features for speaker recognition.

Dieckmann et al. (1997)

(Dieckmann et al. (1997)) presented a speaker recognition system (SESAM) using lip features that are pixel based. Beside the lip information, facial information from the speaker was added.

Their approach is based on the optical flow analysis using the (Horn and Schunck (1981)) method applied to mouth sequences. The Horn and Schunck method is a differential motion estimation method based on two frame differences. The main difference between Horn and Schunck technique and Lukas and Kanade technique is the weighting function to enforce the spatial continuity of the estimated optical flow. If we set the weighting function to zero we will have the method suggested by Lucas and Kanade, which we will discuss in detail in Section Performance measurement.

The lip movement estimation of the SESAM system calculates a vector field representing the local movement of each two consecutive frames in the video sequence. An averaging is used to reduce the amount of velocity vectors to 16 (one fourth of the original size), representing velocities in 16 sub regions. 3D fast Fourier transforms are applied on the velocity vectors to represent the movement of identifiable points from frame to frame.

Zhang et al. (2002)

Automatic speech reading as well as speaker recognition by visual speech has been studied by (Zhang et al. (2002)). In this pixel based work, the authors suggest a primarily color driven algorithm for automatically locating the equivalents of 3 bounding boxes for the i) mouth region, outer lip contour, inner lip contour. Though this is not part of the features, motion is also modeled but after that the points of the bounding boxes have been identified. The used fusion is a decision fusion consisting of averaging the audio and lip expert scores. The study presents visual feature performance comparisons and confirms that the visual information is highly effective for improving recognition performance over a variety of acoustic noise levels.

Liang et al. (2002)

The technique proposed by (Liang et al. (2002)) is categorized as pixel based because its features are extracted using all pixels without an explicit constraint on the shape of the lips.

The visual observation vector is extracted from the mouth region using basically two algorithms in cascade. The gray pixels in the mouth region are mapped to a 32 dimensional eigenvectors produced from a PCA decomposition of gray value deviations from the average mouth region. This is computed from a set of approximately 200000 mouth region images. Temporally, the feature are up sampled and normalized to match the acoustic sample rate. The visual observation vectors are concatenated and projected on a 13 class linear discriminant space, using Linear Discriminant analysis (LDA). By this the visual features are reduced to a new set of dimension 13.

Other Relevant Studies

PCA has been used by (Luettin et al. (1996)), (Potamianos et al. (1998)) and (Sanderson and Paliwal (2004)) to represent mouth movements in speaker and speech recognition systems. The PCA data projection achieves optimal information compression in the sense of minimum square error between the original vector and its reconstruction based on its projection. The achieved dimension reduction serves to reduce the massive image data. Here, however, it serves an even more important purpose, to prevent the intra class covariance matrix, needed at the next stage (LDA), from being singular. This is because there is typically never enough data to compute a reliable estimation of the intra class covariance matrix for a high dimensional dataset, as is the case in a mouth region image (which has approximately 40000 gray values, and there are a couple of hundreds of frames available per class/person, typically). LDA transform maps the feature space to a new space for improved classification, i.e. features that offer a clear separation between the pattern classes. In image pattern classification, it is common that LDA is applied in a cascade following the PCA projection of a single image frames.

Integration of Audio and Visual Information

Feature fusion is used here fuse different information sources with the ultimate goal of achieving superior recognition results. Fusion techniques are divided into three categories: feature fusion, intermediate fusion and decision fusion, (Sanderson and Paliwal (2004)) and (Aleksic and Katsaggelos (2006)).

- *Feature fusion*: Because it occurs early in the information processing chain leading to the decision, feature fusion can intuitively be perceived as the simplest fusion method as it can be implemented by concatenation. Though used in other fields frequently, there are few studies using feature fusion in audio-visual pattern recognition, (Liang et al. (2002)), essentially because of increased dimension and different data rates and types, causing modeling difficulties if carried out in a straight forward manner. There are even fewer studies reporting results on large, publicly available audio-visual databases. Other studies using feature fusion is (Chaudhari et al. (2003)) and (Fox et al. (2007)).

- *Decision fusion*: Some form of recognition is performed separately for each modality and these results are fused at the decision level. When there are more than 2 machine experts, ranked lists can be utilized (Brunelli and Falavigna (1995)), (Kittler et al. (1997)), (Wark et al. (1999)), (Luettin and Thacker (1997)) and (Chibelushi et al. (2002)). This is relevant even in multiple algorithms or multiple classifier decision making strategies too. The latter strategy has been specifically used here, when we identified people and the digits they uttered, where numerous 2-class SVM are combined to obtain a decision on n-class (persons or digit identities) problems. The majority voting and combined voting are commonly utilized techniques in decision fusion. Majority voting refers to that the final decision is made by taking the (common) decision of most sub classifiers. For ranked lists, each sub classifier provides a ranked list that is combined with other classifiers' lists in the final stage. The method requires less computation but can be more complex to grip and implement because some combinations will not work for some users and an automatic selection and combination rules will be needed.

- *Intermediate fusion*: Information from audio and visual streams is processed during the procedure of mapping from feature space into opinion/decision space. In a decision fusion process this mapping for audio and video streams would run in parallel and without influence on each other. In intermediate fusion HMMs are used often to couple and extend these two processing strands ending in a common decision (Liang et al. (2002)), (Aleksic and Paliwal (2002)), (Chaudhari et al. (2003)), (Bengio (2003)) and (Fox et al. (2007)). Complex intermediate fusion schemes promise to take into account for the different reliability of the two streams dynamically, and even for different temporal sampling rates.

Decision fusion can be complex quickly if it is user adaptive. This is because for large number of classes (users), a large amount of training is needed.

Many biometric systems support multiple experts even within one modality as they apply decision fusion. However, with increased number of machine experts, the complexity of the classifier increases because in addition to training individual experts the training of supervisors will be mandatory as the experts will differ in their recognition skills (performance). Accordingly, it is not self evident that decision fusion will yield a more efficient decision making as compared to feature fusion with increased number of independent experts. Feature fusion might have a higher computational entry cost in terms of implementation because modality specific issues need to be tackled e.g. the audio and video feature rates as well as the amount of data are significantly different between audio and video. On the other hand, feature fusion gives a better opportunity to design an effective synergy between the audio and video signals reducing the need for more complex decision making rules later.

Databases

There exist only few databases suitable for recognition systems using audio-visual information. Databases usually vary in the number of speakers, vocabulary size, number of sessions, scenarios, evaluation measures or protocols. The way of collection of databases can influence the methods or scenarios for which they can be useful. For example, the database could have been collected with a specific scenario in mind whereas the real scenario for which a biometric system needs to be developed could be very different from this scenario. This makes the comparison of different visual features and fusion methods, with respect to the overall performance of a biometric system difficult. Here, we present an overview of some of the datasets that are currently publicly available and have been utilized in several published literatures aiming audio-visual biometric systems.

- M2VTS and XM2VTS database: The M2VTS (Multimodal Verification for Teleservices and Security Applications) database consists of audio and video recording of 37 subjects uttering digits in different occasions, (Pigeon and Vandendorpe (1997)). Because it has a small set of different users the work was extended to 295 subjects (Messer et al. (1999)). The resulting XM2VTS (extended M2VTS) database is actually a different database that offers three fixed phrases, two ten digit sequences and one seven word sentence and a side view images of the subjects. All recordings were performed in a studio in four sessions, separated by a lapse of approximately 6 weeks, during a period of five months. The database is intended for researches in areas related to biometric multimodal recognition systems and have been frequently used in the literature. (Teferi and Bigun (2007)) presented recently the DXM2VTS (Damascened XM2VTS) by replacing the background of the speakers in the XM2VTS database with videos of different real scenes. Furthermore, the merged images are offered with appropriate test protocols and different levels of disturbances including motion blur, (translation, rotation, zooming), and noise (e.g. Gaussian and salt/pepper noise) to measure the performance of biometric systems at different scenarios.
- BANCA database: The BANCA (Biometric Access Control for Networked and e-Commerce Applications) database consists of audio and video recordings of 208 subjects recorded by three different scenarios, (Bailly et al. (2003)). The subjects were recorded while they were saying a random 12 digit number, name, address and date of birth. The BANCA database contains four different language recordings. It is aimed for realistic and challenging conditions for real time applications, though there are very few studies which have published results on it.
- AV-TIMIT: The database consists of 223 subjects, (Sanderson (2002)), and its main properties are continuous phonetically balanced speech, multiple speakers, controlled office environment and high resolution video. Speakers were video recorded while reciting sentences from the TIMIT corpus. Each speaker was asked to read 20 to 21 sentences. The first sentence of each round was identical for all speakers and the rest of the sentences were random for each speaker.

Additional datasets, (Potamianos et al. (2003)), are DAVID, containing 100 speakers uttering digits, the alphabet, syllables and phrases, VALID which consists of 106 speakers recording the same sentences as recorded in the XM2VTS database with some additional environment and acoustical noise, and AVICAR (AV speech corpus in a car environment) which consists of 100 subjects uttering isolated digits, isolated letters and phone numbers inside a car.

Our experiments have been performed on XM2VTS because a large number of biometric recognition studies are based on it using standard protocols. A major reason for its popularity is that it is publicly available and that it contains biometric data of a large number of individuals in several modalities across time, allowing for both impostor and client tests.

Performance Measurement

In general, the performance of a biometric recognition system is evaluated by its error rates at various situations. The performance of identification systems is normally reported in terms of identification error, defined as the probability that the correct match of the unknown person's biometric data is correlated to one of the speaker subjects in the dataset. In practice this translates often to give a list of 10 (or any other practicable number) best matches sorted in resemblance order. Such systems could also be equipped with an option to reject to provide a "10 best" list on various valid grounds, e.g. because data quality is too poor, or the likelihood that the queried identity is in the database of clients is below a preset threshold.

For verification systems, two commonly used error measures are the *false acceptance rate* (FAR)—that is an impostor is accepted—and *false rejection rate* (FRR)—where a client is rejected. These error rates are defined by

$$FAR = IM_A / IM$$
$$FRR = CL_R / CL$$

where IM_A and IM denote the number of accepted impostors and the number of impostor claims and CL_R and CL represent the number of rejected clients and the number of client claims, respectively. FAR and FRR curves of a biometric system decrease, respective increase as a function of the threshold (assuming 0 means the identity claim is false, an impostor, and 1 means it is true, a client). Verification systems also present the performance by choosing a threshold where FAR is equal to FRR, called the equal error rate (EER).

In the Lausanne protocol, (Luettin and Maitre (1998)), the system performance is tested at two levels after the training. Although there is a fully functional system at hand at the end of the training, one has yet to set a threshold to make it operational. The evaluation test presents the performance of the system by plotting FAR and FRR curves for all possible thresholds (in practice a discrete set of thresholds) by using images that the recognition system has not seen during the training (evaluation set). The FAR and FRR in all our experiments are obtained on the evaluation set of the Lausanne protocol. However, a system owner is yet to decide at which point (or points) on the ROC curve the system should be operated, and determine the corresponding threshold. In our publications we reported the (correct) verification rate (VR) which is

$$VR = (1 - (FAR + FRR))$$

to represent the successful or correct decision rate.

MOTION ESTIMATION TECHNIQUES

A fundamental problem in image sequence processing is the measurement of optical flow (or image velocity). The aim is to determine (approximate) the 2D motion field from spatiotemporal patterns of image intensity. The computed measurements of the image sequence are used, here, providing a close approximation to the lip motion in the 2D field.

Several methods for computing optical flow have been proposed (Barron et al. (1992)). Here, we will give an overview of the differential method proposed by (Lucas and Kanade (1981)) and the structure tensor based technique proposed by (Bigun et al. (1991)) in addition to our proposed method. Next we present the motion of two image patches that contain fundamentally different patterns.

Point and Line Motion

We can study motion in image sequences by making assumptions on the contents of the (local) 2D image patches on the move. Although patch types are many and therefore difficult to enlist, two types, the motion of lines and the motion of points, are particularly important for motion estimation. When an image patch consisting of points translates (the dots move in a group) relative to a fixed camera, the image plane of the camera registers continuously images of the motion which can be stacked to generate the 3D volume. The interest in this motion has been uncertain in image analysis community mainly because it is possible to establish automatically by "walking" along a fixed direction (the direction of the parallel bunch of lines in the figure) in the stack of images. Because every point in the original patch can be tracked without ambiguity in the next frame, it is this type of motion that is used to "track" patches and even real objects in image sequences. The (common) direction of the lines generated by the moving dots represents the velocity of the 2D patch in motion, which is known as the *Brightness Constancy Constraint* (BCC).

However, images are also full of other patches (local images) that do not contain points and they too move. A particularly important class of patches is those that contain lines, edges and other patterns that have a common direction patches that possess linear symmetry, (Bigun and Granlund (1988)). When such a patch translates, this motion generates a tilted plane (or several parallel planes if there are parallel lines in the patch. Here the motion does not generate a bunch of lines that can be utilized to establish correspondence between points belonging two different image frames any more. One can track lines between image frames but not the individual points (of the lines) since it is not possible to observe a difference between a line that translates perpendicular to its direction, and the same line when it translates along its direction in addition to the translation it performs in the perpendicular direction[2]. This non uniqueness (at point level) in tracking is generally not desirable in image analysis applications and is therefore called as the aperture problem with emphasis on "problem". When optical flow is computed patches containing directions (linear symmetries) are typically avoided whereas patches containing points (texture) are promoted. There is a BCC assumption even in this scenario but the brightness constancy is now at the line level.

The question is whether the motion of lines, normally not desirable in image sequence analysis, can be useful for lip-motion quantification. This is significant from resource utilization point of view because the moving patches that contain lines outnumber greatly those that contain dots[3] in lip sequences. Before

Figure 4. The figure illustrates a lip sequence for a speaker uttering digits zero to nine. The vertical and horizontal cross section indicates the existing lip movements.

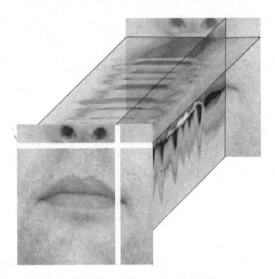

discussing how to proceed to obtain lip-motion, we outline two methods, (Lucas and Kanade (1981)) and (Bigun et al. (1991)) that represent the distinction between point-motion and line-motion well.

Motion Estimation by Differentials

The motion direction of a contour is ambiguous, because the motion component parallel to the line cannot be inferred based on the visual input. This means that a variety of contours of different orientations moving at different speeds can cause identical responses in a motion sensitive neuron in the visual system.

Differential techniques, (Lucas and Kanade (1981)) and (Horn and Schunck (1981)) compute the optical flow from spatial derivatives of the image intensity and the temporal difference between a pair of frames in an image sequence **Fig. 4**. The approach assumes that the studied patch contains points and that the patch undergoes a translational motion, to be precise the image observed a time instant t later is obtainable from the original patch at $t = 0$ by translation, as follows

$$I(\mathbf{x},t) = I(\mathbf{x} - \mathbf{v}t,0) \tag{1}$$

Here I represents the local image with the spatial vector $\mathbf{x}$, and $\mathbf{v} = (v_x, v_y)^{\mathrm{T}}$ is the velocity to be estimated. A differential expression for the brightness change constraint equation can be obtained if the mathematical concept of total differential is utilized. It amounts to that the gray value change of the same point, i.e. the total differential, is nil as represented by the following equation

$$\frac{dI}{dt} = 0$$

(2)

This, when the chain rule of multivariable functions is utilized,

$$\frac{dI}{dt} = \frac{dI}{dx}\frac{dx}{dt} + \frac{dI}{dy}\frac{dy}{dt} + \frac{dI}{dt}\frac{dt}{dt} = 0$$

(3)

yields the desired differential expression for BCC.

$$\nabla_s I(\mathbf{x},t) \cdot \mathbf{v} + I_t(\mathbf{x},t) = 0,$$

(4)

Here, $I_t(\mathbf{x},t)$ denotes the partial time derivative of $I(\mathbf{x}, t)$ and $\nabla_s I(\mathbf{x},t) = (I_x(\mathbf{x},t), I_y(\mathbf{x},t))^T$ is the spatial gradient. The first component of this equation is a projection of the velocity vector on the gradient. If the local patch is a line (violating the underlying assumption of translating points), the velocity components that are parallel to this line will be orthogonal to the gradient (which is orthogonal to the line in the patch) and will produce zero after the projection. This means that any velocity parallel to the line direction will not be recoverable from equation (4), which is another way of telling that there is an aperture problem.

However, as it stands this equation cannot be solved even if the patch contains only points because there is one equation and two unknowns, (v_x, v_y). To obtain the velocity components, the equation is applied to every point in the patch and new equations are obtained for different points, in practice for all points of the patch. Because the patch pattern consists of dots (and not lines) and all dots move with the same translational velocity, the common velocity components can be obtained in the least squares error sense as below.

$$\mathbf{g} = -\,G\mathbf{v}$$

(5)

where **v** is unknown

$$G = \begin{pmatrix} \dfrac{\partial(x_1,y_1,t_0)}{\partial x} & \dfrac{\partial(x_1,y_1,t_0)}{\partial y} \\ \dfrac{\partial(x_2,y_2,t_0)}{\partial x} & \dfrac{\partial(x_2,y_2,t_0)}{\partial y} \\ \vdots & \vdots \\ \dfrac{\partial(x_N,y_N,t_0)}{\partial x} & \dfrac{\partial(x_N,y_N,t_0)}{\partial y} \end{pmatrix}, \quad \begin{pmatrix} \dfrac{\partial(x_1,y_1,t_0)}{\partial t} \\ \dfrac{\partial(x_2,y_2,t_0)}{\partial t} \\ \vdots \\ \dfrac{\partial(x_N,y_N,t_0)}{\partial t} \end{pmatrix}$$

(6)

The equation (6) contains the first order partial derivatives coming from all points in the observed image patch (N in total) and can be estimated by convolutions efficiently. Suggested by (Lucas and Kanade (1981)), this is a linear regression problem for optical flow estimation. The standard solution of such a system of equation is given by mean square estimate, obtained by multiplying the equation with $\mathbf{G}^T$ and solving the 2x2 system of equations for the unknown $\mathbf{v}$

$$\mathbf{G}^T g = -\mathbf{G}^T \mathbf{G} v \tag{7}$$

For a discrete 2D neighborhood $I(x_k, y_k, t_0)$, a unique solution exists if the matrix

$$\mathbf{S} = \mathbf{G}^T \mathbf{G} = \sum_k (\nabla_{s_k} I) \cdot (\nabla_{s_k}^T I) \tag{8}$$

is invertible where

$$(\nabla_{sk} I) = \begin{pmatrix} \dfrac{\partial I(x_k, y_k, t_0)}{\partial x} \\ \dfrac{\partial I(x_k, y_k, t_0)}{\partial y} \end{pmatrix} \tag{9}$$

However, $\mathbf{S}$ is the structure tensor for the 2D discrete image $I(x_k, y_k, t_0)$,

$$\mathbf{S} = K \begin{pmatrix} \left\langle \dfrac{\partial I(x_k, y_k, t_0)}{\partial x} \dfrac{\partial I(x_k, y_k, t_0)}{\partial x} \right\rangle & \left\langle \dfrac{\partial I(x_k, y_k, t_0)}{\partial x} \dfrac{\partial I(x_k, y_k, t_0)}{\partial y} \right\rangle \\ \left\langle \dfrac{\partial I(x_k, y_k, t_0)}{\partial x} \dfrac{\partial I(x_k, y_k, t_0)}{\partial y} \right\rangle & \left\langle \dfrac{\partial I(x_k, y_k, t_0)}{\partial y} \dfrac{\partial I(x_k, y_k, t_0)}{\partial y} \right\rangle \end{pmatrix} \tag{10}$$

with "$<>$" representing the average over the pixels (K is the number of pixels) in the 2D neighborhood. If the structure tensor $\mathbf{S}$ has en eigenvalue that equals to zero (singular $\mathbf{S}$) then no unique velocity can be estimated from the image measurements. This is explained by the fact that then the pattern in the patch consists of lines. The tensor can be singular no matter how many points participate into the regression of velocities, because the 2D pattern can consist of long (possibly parallel) lines. Accordingly, this situation represents the aperture problem. In this case the structure tensor is not invertible, which the method in (Lucas and Kanade (1981)) chooses to avoid by not calculating it. Alternatively the optical flow estimations for such patches are down weighted (Horn and Schunck (1981)) since they otherwise would cause severe discontinuities.

Motion Estimation by the 3D Structure Tensor

This method can estimate both the velocity both in the translating points, and the translating lines scenarios, as it can provide a measure of confidence as to which type of scenario is most likely prevailing in the investigated patch.

Assume that the local intensity function *f* represents the intensity (gray value) of a local image in a 3D spatiotemporal image (continuously stacked patches) and that the local intensity function *f* consists of parallel planes. This corresponds to parallel planes in 3D which is the same as that the energy is concentrated along an axis through the origin in the 3D Fourier transform of *f*. Thus, the problem of finding a representative velocity for the local image corresponds to finding the inclination angle of the parallel planes, which in turn can be solved by fitting an axis through the origin of the local image's Fourier representation (Bigun (2006)). Fitting an axis is classically performed by the minimization problem, in the total *least square error* (LSE) sense. The solution is obtained by an eigenvalue analysis of the 3x3 matrix, also known as the 3D structure tensor of the local intensity function. This 3x3 tensor can, however, be obtained directly in the spatial domain thanks to the conservation of the scalar product between the spatial and Fourier (frequency) domains. It can be written as follows in the spatial domain

$$J = trace(A)I - A \tag{11}$$

with

$$\mathbf{A} = \begin{pmatrix} \iiint \left(\frac{\partial f}{\partial x}\right)^2 & \iiint \left(\frac{\partial f}{\partial x} \cdot \frac{\partial f}{\partial y}\right) & \iiint \left(\frac{\partial f}{\partial x} \cdot \frac{\partial f}{\partial t}\right) \\ \iiint \left(\frac{\partial f}{\partial x} \cdot \frac{\partial f}{\partial y}\right) & \iiint \left(\frac{\partial f}{\partial y}\right)^2 & \iiint \left(\frac{\partial f}{\partial y} \cdot \frac{\partial f}{\partial t}\right) \\ \iiint \left(\frac{\partial f}{\partial x} \cdot \frac{\partial f}{\partial t}\right) & \iiint \left(\frac{\partial f}{\partial y} \cdot \frac{\partial f}{\partial t}\right) & \iiint \left(\frac{\partial f}{\partial t}\right)^2 \end{pmatrix} = \iiint (\nabla f)(\nabla f)^T$$

where

$$\left(\frac{\partial f}{\partial x}\right),$$

$$\left(\frac{\partial f}{\partial y}\right)$$

and

$$\left(\frac{\partial f}{\partial t}\right)$$

correspond to partial derivatives of the image in x, y and t coordinate directions and *trace*($\mathbf{A}$) is the sum of the diagonal elements of $\mathbf{A}$, which also equals to the sum of all eigenvalues of $\mathbf{A}$. The matrix $\mathbf{A}$ can be estimated by a discrete approximation:

$$\mathbf{A} \cong \sum_{j} (\nabla f_j)(\nabla f_j)^T$$

(12)

where (∇f_j) is the gradient at a specific discrete image position j wherewith j running over all positions (in all 3 directions x, y and t in the three dimensional neighborhood). The least square error corresponds to the least eigenvalue of $\mathbf{J}$ with its corresponding eigenvector representing the optimal plane fit. Finding the eigenvector corresponding to the least eigenvalue of $\mathbf{J}$ is the same as finding the eigenvector corresponding to the largest eigenvalue of $\mathbf{A}$. By investigating the errors of the fit (the eigenvalues), an approximation of the quality of the fit to the local image can be estimated along with the plane fit, the normal of which encodes the normal velocity in f.

The gradient image (∇f_j) can be estimated through convolutions with partial derivative filters of three dimensional Gaussians. After that, the above mentioned outer products and the three dimensional smoothing corresponding to the triple integral equation (12) is carried out.

It turns out that even motion of points case reduces to the same eigenvalue problem as above. The difference is that the multiplicity of the smallest eigenvalue is 1 and this smallest eigenvalue is zero, (close to zero in practice) whereas for motion of lines case the multiplicity of the smallest eigenvalue is 2.

Figure 5. The graph shows the geometry used to derive the 2D velocity vector from the 3D normal vector along with the plane generated by a translating line

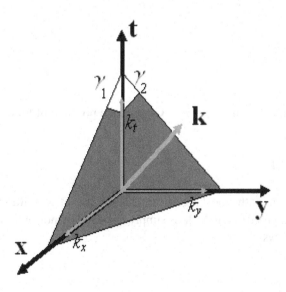

However, this method requires multiple image frames although it simultaneously derives the velocity of moving points and lines. Accordingly, the computations can be excessive for applications that only need line motion features. Assuming that line motion is the most relevant motion type in lip images the computations can instead be carried out in 2D subspaces of the 3D spatiotemporal space. This is described next.

Motion Estimation by Line Translation, *Normal Optical Flow*

Assume that $f(x,y,t)$ is generated by a line translated in its normal direction with a certain velocity. The local image containing a moving line in the xy manifold will generate a plane in the (spatiotemporal) xyt space, **Fig. 5**. The normal of the plane, $\mathbf{k} = (k_x, k_y, k_t)^T$ with $\|\mathbf{k}\| = 1$, is directly related to the observable normal velocity. Thus this velocity is encoded by the orientation of the spatiotemporal plane in the xyt space. Let the normal velocity, $\mathbf{v} = (v_x, v_y)^T$, be encoded as $\mathbf{v} = v\mathbf{a}$ with v as the absolute speed and $\mathbf{a}$ as the direction of the velocity which also represents the normal of the line. Being a normal vector, the length of $\mathbf{a}$ is fixed to 1, i.e. $\|\mathbf{a}\| = 1$. Because the local image f is assumed to consist of a moving line, it can then be expressed as

$$g(\mathbf{a}^T\mathbf{s} - vt), \qquad \mathbf{s} = (x, y)^T \tag{13}$$

for some 1D function $g(\tau)$, where $\mathbf{s}$ represents a spatial point in the image plane and t is the time. Defining now $\widetilde{\mathbf{k}}$ and $\mathbf{r}$ as

$$\widetilde{\mathbf{k}} = (a_x, a_y, -v)^T, \qquad \mathbf{r} = (x, y, t) \tag{14}$$

in equation (13), we have a (linearly symmetric) function f that has iso-curves that are parallel planes i.e.

$$f(x, y, t) = g(\widetilde{\mathbf{k}}^T\mathbf{r})$$

Here $\|\widetilde{\mathbf{k}}\| \neq 1$ because

$$\sqrt{\left(a_x^2 + a_y^2\right)} = 1$$

is required by the definition of $\widetilde{\mathbf{k}}$ (equation (14)). Given f, the problem of finding the best $\mathbf{k}$ fitting the hypothesis

$$f(x, y, t) = g(\mathbf{k}^T\mathbf{r}) \text{ with } \|\mathbf{k}\| = 1$$

in the total LSE sense is given by the most significant eigenvector of $\mathbf{A}$. Calling this vector $\mathbf{k}$, and assuming that it is already computed using $\mathbf{A}$, $\widetilde{\mathbf{k}}$ is simply obtained by normalizing $\mathbf{k}$ with respect to its first two components as follows

$$\widetilde{\mathbf{k}} = \frac{\mathbf{k}}{\sqrt{\left(k_x^2 + k_y^2\right)}} \tag{15}$$

In agreement with the definition of $\widetilde{\mathbf{k}}$, equation (14), we will have $\mathbf{a}$ (2D direction of the velocity in the image plane) and v (the absolute speed in the image plane) as

$$\mathbf{a} = \left(\frac{k_x}{\sqrt{\left(k_x^2 + k_y^2\right)}}, \frac{k_y}{\sqrt{\left(k_x^2 + k_y^2\right)}} \right)^T \tag{16}$$

$$v = -\frac{k_t}{\sqrt{\left(k_x^2 + k_y^2\right)}} \tag{17}$$

Consequently, the velocity or the *normal optical flow* can be obtained by v**a**

$$\mathbf{v} = v\mathbf{a} = \frac{k_t}{k_x^2 + k_y^2} (k_x, k_y)^T = \frac{1}{\left(\frac{k_x}{k_t}\right)^2 + \left(\frac{k_y}{k_t}\right)^2} \left(\frac{k_x}{k_t}, \frac{k_y}{k_t}\right)^T = (v_x, v_y)^T \tag{18}$$

so that the velocity components are given by

$$v_x = \frac{k_x k_t}{k_x^2 + k_y^2} = -\frac{\left(\frac{k_x}{k_t}\right)}{\left(\frac{k_x}{k_t}\right)^2 + \left(\frac{k_y}{k_t}\right)^2} \tag{19}$$

$$v_y = \frac{k_y k_t}{k_x^2 + k_y^2} = -\frac{\left(\frac{k_y}{k_t}\right)}{\left(\frac{k_x}{k_t}\right)^2 + \left(\frac{k_y}{k_t}\right)^2} \tag{20}$$

As discussed above, $\mathbf{k}$ can be estimated by the most significant eigenvector of 3D tensor $\mathbf{A}$, (Bigun et al. (1991)), if computational resources would not be an issue.

Forming the 3D matrix $\mathbf{A}$ via triple integrals and solving for its eigenvectors and eigenvalues may be avoided all together if only normal flow is needed for the application at hand. From equations (18)-

(20), the velocity and direction can be estimated by determining the tilts $\left(k_x / k_t \right)$ and $\left(k_y / k_t \right)$. The tilts can in turn be estimated by local orientation estimation of the intersection of our original motion plane with the *tx* and *ty* planes, (Isaac-Faraj and Bigun (2006)) and (Kollreider et al. (2005)). This 2D orientation estimation can be done by fitting a line to the 2D spectrum in the total least square error sense. This is discussed next.

A local 2D image with ideal local orientation is characterized by the fact that the gray values do not change along one direction. Since the gray values are constant along lines, local orientation is also denoted as linear symmetry orientation. Generally, an image is linearly symmetric if the iso-gray values are represented by parallel hyperplanes. A linearly symmetric 2D image in particular consists of parallel lines in 2D, and has a Fourier transform concentrated along a line through the origin. Detecting linearly symmetric local images is consequently the same as checking the existence of energy concentration along a line in the Fourier domain, which corresponds to the minimization problem of solving the inertia matrix in 2D. By analyzing the local image this time as a 2D image, *f*, the structure tensor can be represented as follows for the *tx* plane:

$$
\begin{pmatrix}
\iint \left(\dfrac{\partial f}{\partial t} \right)^2 & \iint \left(\dfrac{\partial f}{\partial t} \cdot \dfrac{\partial f}{\partial x} \right)^2 \\[2em]
\iint \left(\dfrac{\partial f}{\partial t} \cdot \dfrac{\partial f}{\partial x} \right)^2 & \iint \left(\dfrac{\partial f}{\partial x} \right)^2
\end{pmatrix}
$$

Note that this structure tensor has double integrals as opposed to its 3D counter part in equation (11). Eigenvalue analysis in 2D yields a particularly simple form by using complex numbers (Bigun and Granlund (1987))

$$
I_{20} = (\lambda_{max} - \lambda_{min}) e^{i2\varphi} = \iint \left(\frac{\partial f}{\partial t} + i \frac{\partial f}{\partial x} \right)^2 dx\,dy
$$

(21)

The argument of I_{20}, a complex number in the *t*- and *x*-manifold, represents the double angle of the fitting orientation if linear symmetry exists. In consequence, this provides an approximation of a tilt angle via

$$
\frac{k_y}{k_x} = \tan \left(\frac{1}{2} \arg(I_{20}) \right)
$$

(22)

Using this idea both in the *tx* and *ty* manifolds and labeling the corresponding complex moments as I_{20}^{tx}, and I_{20}^{ty} the two tilt estimations and in turn velocity components are obtained as follows:

$$
\frac{k_x}{k_t} = \tan \gamma_1 = \tan \left(\frac{1}{2} \arg(I_{20}^{tx}) \right) \Rightarrow \tilde{v}_x = \frac{\tan \gamma_1}{\tan^2 \gamma_1 + \tan^2 \gamma_2}
$$

(23)

Figure 6. The figure illustrates the quantization and reduction technique. (Left) Only a limited free degree of the velocity component is allowed, e.g. direction restraints. (Right) The amount of features is reduced by applying 10x10 block wise averaging.

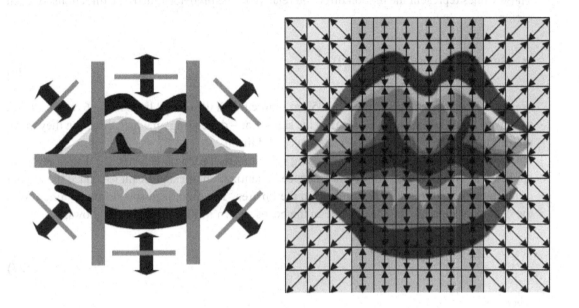

$$\frac{k_y}{k_t} = \tan\gamma_2 = \tan\left(\frac{1}{2}\arg(I_{20}^{ty})\right) \Rightarrow \widetilde{v}_y = \frac{\tan\gamma_2}{\tan^2\gamma_1 + \tan^2\gamma_2}$$

(24)

The *tx* and *ty* manifolds are shown in **Fig. 5** along with the angles γ_1 and γ_2. The I_{20}^{ty} corresponds to equation (21) but applied to the *ty* manifold.

Feature Quantization and Reduction: Lip Motion Features

We need to perform additional processing to extract lip-motion specific and discriminative information for speech and speaker recognition applications. To this end we proceed as follows.

1. In each pixel of the lip region image we have a motion estimation, given by the horizontal and vertical components of the velocity, (v_x, v_y).

$$v = \| \mathbf{v} \| = \sqrt{(v_x^2 + v_y^2)}$$

(25)

2. The image is divided into six regions, which are physically meaningful in the case of lip movements, e.g. mid of upper lip, left of lower lip, etc. The regions are used to quantize the angle of the velocity estimation. The angle α is computed for every pixel and is represented as –1, 0 or 1. These values represent the motion direction relative to the predetermined line directions of each region

$$\alpha = \text{sgn}(\angle \mathbf{v}) = \text{sgn}(\arctan(v_y / v_x)) \tag{26}$$

We only allow 3 orientations (0°, 45°, –45°) as marked with the 6 solid lines in the 6 regions, (**Fig. 6** – left). The 1D scalars at all pixels take the signs + or – depending on which direction they move relative to their expected spatial orientations (solid lines).

3. Due to the large dimension of the data, using velocities, **v** at each pixel is not a realistic option for applications. We found that direction and speed quantization are significant to reduce the impact of noise on the motion information around the lip area. The quantized speeds are obtained from the data by calculating the mean value in the boxes shown in **Fig. 6** – right as follows,[4]

$$g(l,k) = \sum_{p,q} f(Nl + p, Nk + q), \tag{27}$$

where

$$f(p,q) = v(p,q)\alpha(p,q) \tag{28}$$

Here, $(p, q) = 0 \dots (N-1)$, and $(l, k) = 0 \dots (M-1)$, where $N = 10$ and $M = 12$ represent the window size of the boxes and the number of boxes, respectively.

Implementation

The proposed motion estimation technique is a fast and robust alternative to its more time consuming variant discussed earlier. We will present the implementation steps to determine the optical flow components (v_x, v_y), according to the scheme illustrated in **Fig. 7**. The Gaussian filter derivative, known for its separable filters, are represented here by w_z, where z represents an arbitrary axis x, y and t. Given a spatiotemporal image of four $\{f\}$ frames the following steps are performed:

Step 1. The images of the video sequence are cropped to the lip area with size 128x128 pixels and furthermore converted to a grayscale image by $0.21*R + 0.72*G + 0.07*B$.

Step 2. The sequence is extracted and the orthogonal cross sections $\{tx\}$ and $\{ty\}$ are generated from the permuted xyt space.

Step 3. The $\{tx\}$ and $\{ty\}$ space time manifolds are determined by computation of the orientation according to equation (22) and its analogue for $\{ty\}$. For each $\{tx\}$ plane and $\{ty\}$ plane calculate its gradient by filtering with Gaussian derivative filters w_x, w_y and w_t, yielding a set of images with complex values representing the linear symmetry.

Figure 7. The figure illustrates the processing steps to obtain quantized and dimension reduced lip-motion features

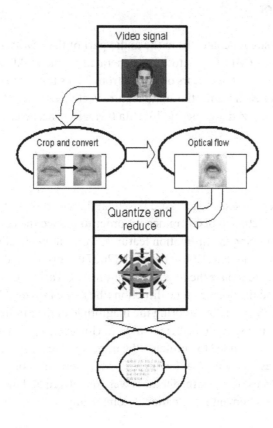

Step 4. Every calculated linear symmetry slice enables us to estimate the normal image velocities in the lip images from equation (23)-(24). In that, only the processing along two planes embedded in the 3D spatiotemporal images is needed.

Step 5. The motion features are quantized and reduced by the mean method.

Using the quantization and reduction the feature vector is represented by 144 dimensions (free variables) instead of the original 128x128x2 = 32768 (free variables) dimensions that describe the motion at all pixels of the mouth region. It is worth noting that the local lip motions are not completely free but must follow physical constraints. It is possible to conclude from related studies and our early published work that the articulation of the lips progresses in a constrained manner during lip movement, i.e. motion in lip image sequences is very symmetrical.

IDENTITY RECOGNITION AND LIVENESS DETECTION BY UTTERED DIGITS

Acoustic Feature Vector

In our experiments, the data stream comes from the audio part of the XM2VTS database and the Mel Frequency Cepstral Coefficient (MFCC) vectors are generated by the Hidden Markov Model Toolkit (HTK) (Young et al. (2000)), where the vectors originate from 25 ms frames (overlapping time periods), streaming out every 10 ms. For each frame, the audio feature vector contains a total of 39 real scalars–12 cepstral coefficients plus normalized log energy, 13 delta (velocity) coefficients, and 13 delta-delta (acceleration) coefficients.

Visual Feature Vector

The image sequences used for our experiments are based on the video part of the XM2VTS database. The video was captured with 720x576 pixel frames. In order to reduce the computational complexity, the image frames, before computing the lip-motion features, were automatically cropped to the lip area (128x128) by the technique presented in (Kollreider et al. (2007)). This method suggest quantized angle features ("quangles") designed to reduce the impact of illumination variation. This is achieved by using both the gradient direction and the double angle direction (the angle provided by the 2D structure tensor, (Bigun and Granlund (1988))), and by ignoring the magnitude of the gradient. Boosting techniques are applied in a quantized feature space to detect the mouth. However, by visual inspection, we verified that the cropping functioned as intended to eliminate the impact of localization errors on the errors that can be attributed to the suggested lip-motion features. Furthermore, the color images are transformed to grayscale. After the motion estimation, the features were quantized and the dimension is reduced to represent the relevant mouth movement information automatically.

Feature Fusion: Association and Concatenation

Images come at 4 times slower pace than the audio features. If a classifier is to model the audio and video information at a certain time, somehow the rates of audio and video features must be equalized while keeping as much information as possible from both. For simplicity, this rate equalization problem is called synchronization, which is a term also used by several audio-video compression studies, here. The vectors will be merged to a single vector because we wanted to develop synergetic (joint) modeling of the data as opposed to merging decisions in a late stage of the classification process.

Synchronization is carried out by first extracting the reduced motion features discussed earlier. This amounts to a 144 feature vector. The lip image is divided into 4 sub quarters so that each sub quarter is represented by 36 scalars of the total 144, **Fig. 8**. Second, each one of the obtained sub quarter feature vectors is concatenated with one of the four audio vectors available at the time support of the lip image (the audio features come at 4 times faster rate than image frames). There are different possibilities to do this concatenation given that the four visual vectors can be associated with 4 audio vectors in different combinatorics. However, it turns out that, the particular order does not impact the recognition performance significantly, (Isaac-Faraj and Bigun (2007)). Even using only one of the lip sub quarter motion features in the mentioned concatenation (i.e. repeating it 4 times) will yield almost as good recognition results. Experimental results on this will be presented in Section Experimental setup and tests.

Figure 8. The figure illustrates the joint audio-video information utilizing only 1 sub quarter of the visual information

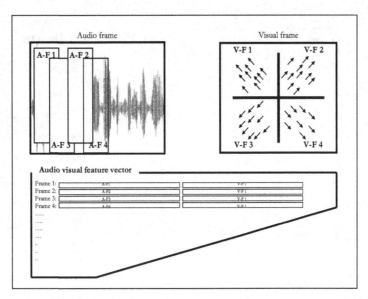

Throughout this work, we assumed that motion in lip images is reasonably symmetric. Because of this and that the motion vectors are both quantized and compactly represented as 1D scalars, we assumed that the order of associating the four visual sub quarters of lips with speech has not a significant impact on the performance. In next section we present experiment where this assumption is tried out. In the experiment we have merged audio visual feature vectors by only using 1 sub quarter of the visual frame and repeating it 4 times, **Fig. 8**.

Experimental Setup and Tests

The XM2VTS Database

In all the experiments, one sequence ("0 1 2 3 4 5 6 7 8 9") was used from the XM2VTS database for every speaker. The database contains 295 speakers (speech with faces) (Messer et al. (1999)). In each

Figure 9. The figure illustrates protocol 1 (left) used for identity recognition and protocol 2 (right) used for digit recognition

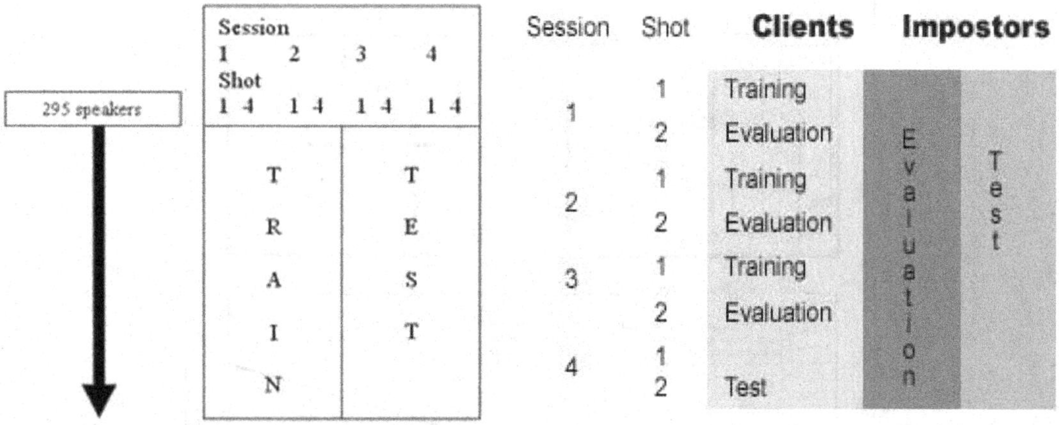

session, the subject is asked to pronounce three sentences when recording the video sequence. Because of the different purposes, one extra protocol is presented for digit recognition in addition to the well known *Lausanne protocol* used for identity recognition. The database needed to be segmented for the digit recognition experiment, which was performed nearly 100% automatically. The "continuous" pronunciation of "0 1 2 3 4 5 6 7 8 9" was divided into single digit subsequences 0 to 9 using the methods presented in (Teferi and Bigun (2007)). Furthermore, the segmentation was manually verified and corrected so as to eliminate the impact of database segmentation errors.

Protocol 1: **Fig. 9**(left), this is the Lausanne protocol (Configuration I) defined by the M2VTS consortium standardizing person recognition experiments conducted on XM2VTS. It splits the database into training, evaluation, and test groups (Luettin and Maitre (1998)). This protocol is used in person verification and person identification experiments below. For the XM2VTS database, the Lausanne protocol is commonly used as a standard protocol for speaker identity experiments. However, no protocol is proposed for speech recognition by the M2VTS consortium which conceived the database.

Protocol 2: **Fig. 9**(right), illustrates this protocol wherein 10 words (digits from zero to nine) are spoken by 295 speakers, each with 8 pronunciations. For the training group, sessions 1 and 2 are used and sessions 3 and 4 are used for the test set. The training samples we used were completely disjoint from the test samples. We used a total of 4 pronunciations for training and another 4 for testing.

Classification: Speaker Verification

Speaker verification is carried out in the following steps and is implemented in the HTK software environment (Young et al. (2000)) and (Veeravalli et al. (2005)).

Step 1. Partition the database for training, evaluation, and testing according to protocol 1.

Step 2. Use single left-to-right state constellation using 5 HMM states and a GMM comprised of 3 Gaussians at each state

Step 3. Perform training process by using Baum-Welch re-estimation. In the training, a model for each client is built. Additionally a world model (average impostor), is also built, λ_w. This world model is common for all clients and is built by aggregating the entire training set specified by the Lausanne protocol.

Step 4. Verify using the Viterbi decoding giving a score L which is obtained as the difference between the client probability and the world probabilities $log(L) = log(P(\mathbf{O}|\ \lambda_i) - log(P(\mathbf{O}|\ \lambda_w))$ given a word sequence $\mathbf{O}$.[5] Here, the score L is compared to a threshold T obtained from the FAR and FRR curves.[6] Using the threshold T, the decision L is made according to the rule: if $L > T$ accept the speaker else reject her/him. The reported verification rates are $1 - (FAR+FRR)$.

Classification: Speaker Identification

The following steps are conducted in our speaker identification system and are implemented by using an SVM:

Step 1. Partition the database for training, evaluation, and testing according to protocol 1.

Step 2. Train the SVM for an utterance so that the classification score, L, is positive for the user and negative for impostors.

    a.   Identify the speaker from a group of speakers

        i.   We construct a classifier for each person in the group to separate the user from other users in the training data. The training data is defined by protocol 1 (Lausanne Protocol).

        ii.   The speaker identity is determined by the classifier that yields the largest score.

Classification: Digit Recognition for Liveness Detection

The following steps are conducted in our digit recognition system for the purpose of liveness detection and are implemented by using an SVM (Chang and Lin (2001)):

Step 1. Partition the database for training, evaluation, and testing according to protocol. Audio-visual feature vectors of dimension 75 (39 audio and 36 video) for each digit utterance were extracted. Each digit had thus several feature vectors coming from the same digit. Furthermore the feature vectors of all speakers of uttering the same digit were given the same digit label to obtain a person independent digit recognizer.

Step 2. We constructed simple SVM classifiers to separate the feature vectors of one digit (75 dimensional each) from those of every other digit pair wise, i.e. we solved a two-class problem 45 times (10 choose 2 combinations). The responses of these classifiers, L_{ij} were binary, i, or j. After the training there were thus a fixed hyperplane associated with each classifier such that one could classify an unknown feature vector (of dimension 75) into one of the two digit labels i or j.

Step 3. The feature vectors of the unknown digit were extracted. We note that the utterance of a digit normally has many feature vectors because the duration of utterances of digits are completely free, i.e. they vary with the digit, the person, as well as the mood of the person, whereas each feature vector has a fixed time support of 25 ms. For each vector we obtained 45 decisions from the SVM classifiers L_{ij}, obtained via training. These responses were digit labels i or j such that they could be used as a vote for one of the 10 digit labels, "Zero", ... , "Nine". A voting was thus carried out involving each feature vector (each casting 45 votes "Zero", ... , "Nine"). The digit label receiving most votes was output as the recognized digit label.

Experimental Results and Discussion

The experiments were performed for speaker verification using GMM (states in an HMM setup within HTK), speaker identification using SVM and digit recognition for liveness detection using SVM. The systems were tested using joint audio-visual and single modalities, respectively. The tests used the XM-2VTS with all 295 subjects uttering the sentence 0 to 9. The protocol 2 setup was introduced for digit recognition because the XM2VTS Lausanne protocol is mainly proposed for identity recognition.

Table 1 shows the results utilizing protocol 1 for the experiments. The verification performance is approximately 77% for a speaker verification system based on only visual information. Speaker verification based on a bimodal system gives approximately 98% correct verification, which is better than the single modality system based on the audio or the visual information.

In this experiment the merged audio-visual feature vectors are presented according to **Fig. 10**. The features are put into HMM system (with GMM at each state) for audio-visual speaker verification. The ROC curves in **Fig. 10** illustrate the audio-visual speaker verification performance for the evaluation set. System 1(red) represents the feature fusion technique by associating four audio features with four different sub quarters of the video (as in the experiments above). The system 2 (blue) uses by contrast the motion features of one of the image sub quarters and repeats it for 4 consecutive audio frames during the concatenation. The blue line across the figure represents the EER line, i.e. its intersections with the ROC curves yield the EER of the corresponding systems.

We can see that using the EER threshold computed on the evaluation set, the verification rates (1 – TER, i.e. equation (2.5)) are 98% and 97% for System 1 and System 2, respectively. The results support our hypothesis, that the lip-motion of an individual is highly symmetric. Accordingly, it would be possible to reduce the video computations with a factor of 4, with little degradation of recognition performance, **Fig. 10**. For demonstration purposes, we have chosen to use all the estimated velocities rather than repeating one sub quarter. However, if done in a real system, this extra computation can be

Table 1. The table presents the results for acoustic, visual, and merged bimodal audio-visual speaker verification systems using protocol 1 in a GMM model

Set / System	Evaluation	Test
Audio	96%	94%
Visual	81%	77%
Audio-Visual	99%	98%

viewed as a way to increase the robustness against noise (including asymmetric lighting, imperfect detection of lip area, etc.) as the feature vectors of the same (repeated) sub quarter contain noise that is more dependent on each other than those using estimations from 4 different sub quarters. It can also occur that for certain individuals the prevailing symmetry is less pronounced and can be discriminative information in identity recognition.

We also used SVM classifiers with a Radial Basis Function (RBF) kernel to perform speaker identification using a single word. The reason for using a single word is that SVM has a tendency to become computationally exhaustive for large feature vectors. The performance obtained using bimodal recognition (100%) compares favorably with the classical single modality recognition system based only on the speech signal (92%) or only on the visual signal (80%).

*Figure 10. The figure illustrates the ROC curve of verification performance for audio visual speaker verification systems using the evaluation set. System 1 represents the feature fusion technique obtained by association of four audio frames with one visual frame(4 sub quarters) and System 2 represents the feature fusion obtained by repeating one sub quarter of lips, **Fig. 8**. The straight line represents the threshold for FA=FR.*

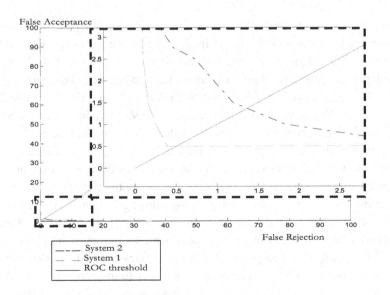

Figure 11. The graph presents multimodal and single modal digit recognition system rates for digits 0 to 9 using protocol 2 in an SVM classifier.

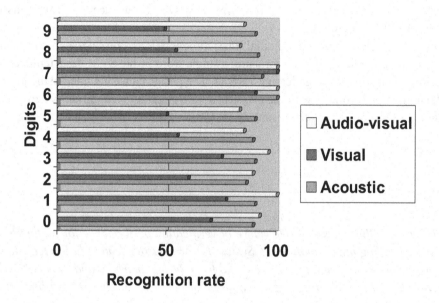

Fig. 11 presents the results for SVM digit recognition for the purpose of liveness detection using protocol 2. Varying between 50-100% for individual digits, the system performed best for digits 1, 6 and 7. The average of the digit recognition over all digits was 68% and 90% for the visual and audio systems in isolation, respectively. Digit recognition using combined audio and video varied between 83% and 100%. The amount of visual information for some of the digits is very little for many people and digit utterances, which is not surprising because the XM2VTS database was collected for identity recognition. As a consequence the speech and the video were recordings of continuous speech without specific emphasis on utterance length or quality. The lack of sufficient visual data for certain digits has negatively influenced the results. However, the uneven results are attributable to the simple SVM classifier we used. The classifier is fast but it does not model the time relationships of the features. A classifier achieving a better and more even digit recognition performance is possible by employing time modeling (at the cost of making the classifier more complex), e.g. HMM or SVM with time modeling. However, it is worth noting that for our main purpose, which is to show that our features are informative in an application targeting digit recognition for liveness assessment, the performance of this classifier is sufficient. This is because we can demand from the user to utter the digits at which the recognizer is good, e.g. any combination of 1, 6 and 7 at any length, when the identity of the person is completely unknown. If the liveness detection is implemented after the identity recognition module, we have then even a possibility to pull out the digits at which the digit recognizer performance is good for the pretended identity and increase the arsenal of digits to be uttered and decrease the length of the sequence to be uttered.

To evaluate our suggested lip features we had to implement audio-visual speech and speaker recognition systems demanding purposive setups of classifier constellations, protocols and databases in addition to implementing compact features, fusing these with appropriate rate conciliation. Each implemented system has a unique difference, in the hope that it will help to evaluate the feature extraction.

Experimental Comparison

We present in this section various audio-visual bi-modal and single modal systems and provide some comparisons related to our work, when possible.

- (Luettin et al. (1996)) developed a visual only speaker identification system using only the lip contour information by extracting *model* and *pixel* based features. These features were extracted by calculating the lip contours and then shape deformations of the contours were modeled temporally by a classifier (HMM). They used the Tulips database, consisting of 12 speakers evaluated by the identification on the speaker models (48 models for each speaker) of the spoken word. The identification system based on HMMs, achieved approximately 73%, 90% and 92% recognition rates when using *shape* based, *pixel* based and joint features. This experiment was extended by (Jourlin et al. (1997)) using the M2VTS database consisting of 37 speakers, utilizing audio-visual information in an identity verification system. The acoustic features were based on the Linear Prediction cepstral coefficients with first and second order derivatives. The visual feature representation was based on the shape and intensity information according to (Luettin et al. (1996)) technique. They utilized HMMs to perform audio only, visual only and audio-visual experiments. The audio-visual score is computed as a weighted sum from the audio and visual classifier. They achieved approximately 97%, approximately72% and approximately 100% verification for audio only, visual only and audio-visual information. The discussed system is comparable to our system except that i) the video features modeled by the classifier were intra frame, and ii) it is a decision fusion system. Comparing the video only experimental results confirm that our features perform better (approximately 6 percentage points) and yet they are complementary because our video features are inter frame based. Their decision fusion has improved the recognition performance by 2 percentage points over the best performing expert (audio) in identification mode and 3% in the verification mode. Our feature fusion has improved the recognition performance by 8 percentage points and 4 percentage points over the best expert (audio) in the (significantly larger) tests corresponding to identification and verification. This indicates that even our feature fusion contributes to performance improvement.
- (Wark and Sridharan (1998)) and (Wark et al. (1999)) presented a system using multi-stream HMMs to develop audio-visual speaker verification and identification systems tested on the M2VTS database. By utilizing decision fusion on the acoustic (based on MFCC) and visual information (based on lip contours and applying PCA and LDA on them), they outperformed the system using only acoustic information. The verification experiments were performed using GMMs on the M2VTS database.
- (Fox et al. (2007)) developed an audio-video person identification system using HMMs as classifier. The experimental tests were performed on the XM2VTS database, using the experts consisting of

acoustic information, dynamic mouth information and static face information. The audio features used are MFCC and their first derivatives. The visual mouth features were derived from pixels to represent the visual information based on the discrete cosine transform. The face features were derived by the PCA technique using the FaceIt software. The 3 experts were fused by a cascade of fusion where expert 1 and 2, decisions were merged in parallel with expert 2 and 3. The resulting two decisions were then merged to yield the final decision. The results highlight the complementary nature of the mouth and face experts under clean and noisy tests.

- (Dieckmann et al. (1997)) and (Frischholz and Dieckmann (2000)) developed a system using three experts acoustic, facial information and lip movements. The acoustic information is based on cepstral coefficients, and facial information is derived to be invariant to rotation and illumination. The optical flow of the lip movement is determined using the traditional method by Horn and Schunk. These three experts are combined by opinion threshold to perform person identification. The experiments were performed on a staff recording of 66 members, achieving best performance approximately 93% when all three modalities were used.

- (Nefian et al. (2002)) demonstrated accurate improvements of speech recognition using audio-visual information. The extracted visual features based on Discrete cosine transform (DCT) and then LDA are combined with acoustic features (MFCC). These features are combined in an intermediate fusion sense, using coupled HMM. The tests were extended by (Liang et al. (2002)), using the XM2VTS database for speech recognition. An extension of visual extraction was also presented based on PCA and LDA and DCT and LDA. They performed in clean SNR environment approximately 99% correct digit recognition using XM2VTS database.

- (Dupont and Luettin (2000)) present a speech recognition system based on bi-modal (audio-visual) information. The visual information is extracted according to (Luettin et al. (1996)) technique by shape and intensity information that generates models for a specific person. The audio information is based on perceptual linear predictive coefficients plus the first derivative and the energy. The features are combined in an intermediate fusion sense, by multi-stream HMMs which were possible by up sampling the visual features, performing approximately 99% correct word recognition.

Other related work using static information are (Brunelli and Falavigna (1995)), (Ben-Yacoub et al. (1999))}, (Sanderson and Paliwal (2004)) and (Hazen et al. (2003)). They developed speaker recognition systems based on audio-visual static information. The visual information was based on static images from the face in combination or without combination of acoustic information. Vector quantization, HMM, GMM and SVM were used to perform different identification and verification tests. In all of these reports decision fusion are used to reconcile the individual decisions.

Applying SVMs to speech recognition can perform better than HMMs (Wan and Carmichael (2005)) in some cases by the use of an appropriate kernel function that can encode temporal information. An SVM will be more accurate than HMMs if the quantity of training data is limited, (Wan and Carmichael (2005)). The latter work exploited the fact that SVMs generalize well to sparse datasets and SVMs were applied on isolated word identification tasks. However, results on small vocabulary tests with sufficient data the accuracy of HMMs and SVMs will asymptote. In this case the HMM is favored because it is more efficient in terms of speed (Wan and Carmichael (2005)). In our case we exploited SVM classifier to limit the scope of the study while obtaining a quick indication on the usefulness of the features, without introducing time variation models for features vectors.

CONCLUSION

Biometric recognition is a popular subject in today's research and has been shown to be an important tool for identity establishment. Using visual information as an adjunct to speech information improves accuracy for not only identity recognition but also speech recognition.

In this chapter, we have described lip-motion features for dynamic lip image sequences to be used in different recognition systems. The technique exploits information from a set of 2D space time signals in the 3D space time image that yields the normal of an optimal motion plane and allows the estimation of velocities. The visual lip features are extracted without iterative algorithms or assuming successful lip contour tracking, which is a computationally efficient alternative to the available lip dynamics estimations. The experimental tests were performed on the XM2VTS database. The database, representing hundreds of thousands of images and hours of speech, was segmented with respect to digit boundaries automatically and verified manually to be able to test the digit recognition systems for the purpose of liveness detection. The addition of visual data to the systems confirms that it is possible to do feature level fusion in such massive data and obtain benefits for biometric recognition systems.

The experimental performance of the proposed biometric systems, yielding approximately 80% video only identification and 100% audio visual identification (for the word 7) of person identities, supports the conclusion that the proposed lip-motion features contain significant information for person authentication. Furthermore, the average digit recognition rate is approximately 70% using only visual information, is suitable for liveness detection system using simple classifier. Our technique for early audio-video feature integration results in an improved speaker verification performance (approximately 98%) and speaker identification performance (approximately 100%), on top of the already high verification rate achievable by speech only.

The results of the digit recognition system are different for the 10 digits. Our examination of the results indicates that once the visual feature extraction is performed on a sufficient amount of visual speech data, the available modeling for recognition tasks is highly successful. Accordingly, the validation in the digit recognition with respect to digits can be explained with the lack of visual data. One obvious consequence is to use lip reading word selectively or by using weights in future designs.

In all cases, no attempt was made to improve the recognition performance by optimizing the classifier. We used what was available to us and in largest diversity of classification constellation, as a significant goal has been to show that the same basic features contained sufficiently rich information for purposes of identity as well as message recognition, regardless what classification method has been used.

Discussion

The system proposed by (Liang et al. (2002)) showing experimental results on XM2VTS database, can not be studied in conjunction with our results in depth primarily because the experimental details of their tests were not mentioned in the publication. The classification/fusion technique they used is an advanced HMM permitting synchronization of the different strands (audio and video) of the data. However, temporal up sampling of video is used to achieve synchronization between the two sampling rates of the audio and video. Their experimental tests report word error rates for a single word/number i.e. 0123456789, since this is the only word that was tested. Because the temporal segmentation of the XM2VTS audio-video was not undertaken in the study, it is not clear how the performance will be affected if the digits are uttered in a different order. Part of this criticism is valid even to our system despite segmentation because a digit's utterance is influenced by the pre and post digit utterances in the continuous speech. However, we argue that this influence is more difficult to "abuse" by a simple classifier (our system) as compared to giving the full content of the pre and post digits to an advanced classifier, (the system of (Liang et al. (2002))). Even though a digit sequence is recognized from always the same 0-9 sequence uttered by different and same speakers at different times, no information on where in the uttered digit sequence the recognized digits are to be found is available in the reported experiments. Accordingly, with which digits there is greatest confusion can not be evaluated.

The work of (Jourlin et al. (1997)) presented a speaker verification system using features originating from the work of (Luettin et al. (1996)). The main difference of this feature set and our features is that their model based features demand more from the pre processing step which both need. Whereas we need initially an approximately correct localization of the mouth region only, they would additional need a correct detection of the lip boundaries. Our results (undertaken on the XM2VTS database which is 9 times larger than what was available to them at the time) suggest that one can obtain the same descriptive information even without precise boundary tracking while achieving as good as, or better recognition performance. Furthermore, we think that using a crude pre processing step has a significant importance for robustness since non satisfaction of higher pre processing demands will manifest a higher risk of system failure in practice.

We reached favorable results for person recognition by feature fusion strategy. In the future one could quantify how much feature fusion has brought as compared to decision fusion. This would require to implement 3 classifiers (1 audio, 1 audio, and 1 for decision fusion) with their corresponding training. We refrained from doing this, because i) the qualitative comparisons with the studies of (Luettin et al. (1996)) and (Jourlin et al. (1997)) indicated that there was a gain in feature fusion, ii) this would be a sub optimal solution from computational, implementation, and maintenance view point (3 classifiers must be trained and maintained as opposed to 1), and iii) we had to limit the scope of our study.

REFERENCES

Roth, K., & Neidig, J. (2007). Title of chapter. In C. Coulson (Ed.), *Title of book that the chapter appears in* (pp. 19-29). Hershey, PA: Information Science Reference.

Aleksic, P., & Katsaggelos, A. (2006). Audio-visual biometrics. *Proceedings of the IEEE 94(11)*, (pp. 2025-2044).

Aleksic, P., Williams, J., Wu, Z., & Katsaggelos, A., (2002). Audio-visual speech recognition using mpeg-4 compliant visual features. *EURASIP J. Appl. Signal Process*, 2002 (1), 1213-1227.

Bailly, E., Bengio, S., Bimbot, F., Hamouz, M., Kittler, J., Mariethoz, J., Matas, J., Messer, K., Popovici, V., Poree, F., Ruiz, B., & Thiran, J. P. (2003). *The banca database and evaluation protocol. In: AVBPA.* (pp. 625-638).

Barron, J., Fleet, D., Beauchemin, S., & Burkitt, T. (1992). Performance of optical ow techniques. *IEEE Comp. S. conference on Computer Vision and Pattern Recognition*, (pp. 236-242).

Ben-Yacoub, S., Abdeljaoued, Y., & Mayoraz, E. (1999). Fusion of face and speech data for person identity verification. *IEEE Trans. on Neural Networks, 10*(5), 1065-1074.

Bengio, S. (2003). Multimodal authentication using asynchronous HMMs. *In: AVBPA03. Springer Berlin Heidelberg*, (pp. 770-777).

Bigun, E., Bigun, J., Duc, B., & Fischer, S., (1997a). Expert conciliation for multi modal person authentication systems by bayesian statistics. In J. Bigun, G. Chollet, and G. Borgefors, (Eds.), *Audio and Video based Person Authentication - AVBPA97 1206*, (pp. 291-300).

Bigun, J. (2006). *Vision with Direction*. Halmstad, Springer, Heidelberg.

Bigun, J., Duc, B., Fischer, S., Makarov, A., & Smeraldi, F. (1997b). Multi modal person authentication. *In H. Wechsler et al., & editor, Nato-Asi advanced study on face recognition*, (pp. 26-50).

Bigun, J., & Granlund, G., (1987). Optimal orientation detection of linear symmetry. *In First International Conference on Computer Vision, ICCV. IEEE Computer Society*, (pp. 433-438).

Bigun, J., Granlund, G., & Wiklund, J. (1991). Multidimensional orientation estimation with applications to texture analysis of optical flow. *IEEE Trans. Pattern Analysis and Machine Intelligence, 13*(8), 775-790.

Brunelli, K., & Falavigna, D., (1995). Person identification using multiple cues. *IEEE Trans. on Pattern Analysis and Machine Intelligence, 17*(10), 955-966.

Chan, M., (2001). Hmm-based audio-visual speech recognition integrating geometric and appearance-based visual features. *IEEE Fourth Workshop on Multimedia Signal Processing*, (pp. 9-14).

Chang, C., & Lin, C., (2001). *Libsvm-a library for support vector machines. software available at www. csie.ntu.edu.tw/ cjlin/libsvm*.

Chaudhari, U., & Ramaswamy, G., & Potamianos, G., & Neti, C., (2003). Information fusion and decision cascading for audio-visual speaker recognition based on time-varying stream reliability prediction. *International Conference on Multimedia and Expo, 2003. ICME '03.* (pp. 9-12).

Chen, T., (2001). Audiovisual speech processing. *IEEE Signal Processing Magazine, 18*(1), 9-21.

Chibelushi, C., Deravi, F., & Mason, J. (2002). A review of speech-based bimodal recognition. *IEEE Trans. on Multimedia, 4*(1), 23-37.

Chiou, G., & Hwang, J.-N., (1997). Lipreading from color video. *IEEE Transactions on Image Processing, 6*(8), 1192-1195.

Dieckmann, U., Plankensteiner, P., & Wagner, T. (1997). Sesam: A biometric person identification system using sensor fusion. *Pattern Recognition Letters, 18*(9), 827-833.

Duc, B., Fischer, S., & Bigun, J. (1997). Face authentication with sparse grid gabor information. *IEEE International Conference Acoustics, Speech, and Signal Processing, 4*(21), 3053-3056.

Dupont, S., & Luettin, J. (2000). Audio-visual speech modelling for continuous speech recognition. *IEEE Trans. on Multimedia, 2*(3), 141-151.

Faraj, M., & Bigun, J. (2007). Audio-visual person authentication using lipmotion from orientation maps. *Pattern Recognition Letters - Advances on Pattern recognition for speech and audio processing, 28*(11), 1368-1382.

Faraj, M. I., & Bigun, J. (2006). Person verification by lip-motion. *Conference on Computer Vision and Pattern Recognition Workshop (CVPRW),* (pp. 37-45).

Fox, N., & Gross, R., & Cohn, J., & Reilly, R. (2007). Robust biometric person identification using automatic classifier fusion of speech, mouth, and face experts. *IEEE Transactions on Multimedia, 9*(4), 701-714.

Frischholz, R., & Dieckmann, U. (2000). Biold: a multimodal biometric identification system. *IEEE Trans. On Computer, 33*(2), 64-68.

Hazen, T. J., & Weinstein, E., & Kabir, R., & Park, A., & Heisele, B. (2003). Multimodal face and speaker identification on a handheld device. *In Proc. Workshop Multimodal User Authentication,* (pp. 113-120).

Horn, B., & Schunck, B. (1981). Determining optical flow. *The journal of Artificial Intelligence, 17*(1), 185-203.

Iyengar, G., & Neti, C. (2001). Detection of faces under shadows and lighting variations. *IEEE FourthWorkshop on Multimedia Signal Processing,* (pp. 15-20).

Jourlin, P., Luettin, J., Genoud, D., & Wassner, H. (1997). Acoustic-labial speaker verification. *Proceedings of the First International Conference on Audio- and Video-Based Biometric Person Authentication, LNCS 1206,* (pp. 319-326).

Kittler, J., Li, Y., Matas, J., & Sanchez, M. (1997). Combining evidence in multimodal personal identity recognition systems. *Proceedings of the First 48 International Conference on Audio- and Video-Based Biometric Person Authentication, LNCS 1206,* (pp. 327-334).

Kollreider, K., Fronthaler, H., & Bigun, J. (2005). Evaluating liveness by face images and the structure tensor. *In AutoID 2005: FourthWorkshop on Automatic Identification Advanced Technologies - IEEE Computer Society,* (pp. 75-80).

Kollreider, K., H. Fronthaler, M. I. F., & Bigun, J. (2007). Real-time face detection and motion analysis with application in liveness assessment. *IEEE Trans on Information Forensics and Security, 2*(3), 548-558.

Liang, L., Liu, X., Zhao, Y., Pi, X., & Nefian, A. (2002). Speaker independent audio-visual continuous speech recognition. *IEEE International Conference on Multimedia and Expo, 2002. ICME '02. Proceedings,* (pp. 26-29).

Lucas, B., & Kanade, T. (1981). An iterative image registration technique with an application to stereo vision. *International Joint Conference on Artificial Intelligence,* (pp. 674-679).

Luettin, J. (1997). *Visual speech and speaker recognition.* Unpublished doctoral dissertation, University of Shefield, U.K.

Luettin, J., & Maitre, G. (1998). *Evaluation protocol for the extended m2vts database (xm2vtsdb).* In: IDIAP Communication 98-054 Technical report R R-21.

Luettin, J., & Thacker, N. (1997). Speechreading using probabilistic models. *Computer Vision and Image Understanding, 65*(2), 163-178.

Luettin, J., Thacker, N., & Beet, S. (1996). Speaker identification by lipreading. *Proceedings of the 4th International Conference on Spoken Language Processing ICSLP 96*, (pp. 62-65).

Mase, K., & Pentland, A. (1991). Automatic lip-reading by opticalflow analysis. *Systems and Computers in Japan, 22*(6), 67-76.

Matthews, I., Potamianos, G., Neti, C., & Luettin, J. (2001). A comparison of model and transform-based visual features for audio-visual lvcsr. *IEEE International Conference on Multimedia and Expo, 2001. ICME 2001*, (pp. 825-828).

Messer, K., Matas, J., Kittler, J., Luettin, J., & Maitre, G. (1999). XM2VTSDB: The extended m2vts database. *In: Audio and Video based Person Authentication- AVBPA99.* (pp. 72-77).

Nakamura, S. (2001). Fusion of audio-visual information for integrated speech processing. *Proceedings Third International Conference on Audio- and Video-Based Biometric Person Authentication: AVBPA 2001 2091*, (pp. 127-149).

Nefian, A., Liang, L., Pi, X., Liu, X., & Murphy, K. (2002). Dynamic Bayesian networks for audio-visual speech recognition. *EURASIP J. Appl. Signal Process*, (1), 1274-1288.

Neti, C., Potamianos, G., Luettin, J., Matthews, I., Glotin, H., Vergyri, D., Mashari, J. S. A., & Zhou, J. (2000). *Audio-visual speech recognition.* Final Workshop 2000 Report. Baltimore, MD: Center for Language and Speech Processing. The Johns Hopkins University.

Ortega-Garcia, J., Bigun, J., Reynolds, D., & Gonzalez-Rodriguez, J. (2004). Authentication gets personal with biometrics. *IEEE Signal Processing Magazine*, (pp. 50-62).

Petajan, E. (1984). Automatic lipreading to enhance speech recognition. *Global Telecommunications Conference.* (pp. 265-272).

Pigeon, S., & Vandendorpe, L. (1997). The m2vts multimodal face database (release 1.00). *In: AVBPA '97: Proceedings of the First International Conference on Audio- and Video-Based Biometric Person Authentication.* (pp. 403-409).

Potamianos, G., Graf, H., & Cosatto, E. (1998). An image transform approach for hmm based automatic lipreading. . *Proceedings International Conference on Image Processing, 1998. ICIP 9.* (pp. 173-177).

Potamianos, G., Neti, C., Gravier, G., Garg, A., & Senior, A. (2003). Recent advances in the automatic recognition of audiovisual speech. *Proceedings of the IEEE, 91*(9), 1306-1326.

Sanderson, C. (2002). The vidTIMIT database (IDIAP communication). *IDIAP Communication 02-06, Martigny, Switzerland.*

Sanderson, C., & Paliwal, K. (2004). Identity verification using speech and face information. *Digital Signal Processing, 14*(5), 449-480.

Tang, X., & Li, X. (2001). Fusion of audio-visual information integrated speech processing. *Third International Conference on Audio- and Video-Based Biometric Person Authentication AVBPA2001, LNCS 2091.* (pp. 127-143).

Teferi, D., & Bigun, J. (2007). Damascening video databases for evaluation of face tracking and recognition - the dxm2vts database. *Pattern Recognition Letters, 28*(15), 2143-2156.

Teferi, D., Faraj, M., & Bigun, J. (2007). Text driven face-video synthesis using gmm and spatial correlation. *The 15th Scandinavian Conference on Image Analysis (SCIA 2007) LNCS 4522*, (pp. 572-580).

Tistarelli, M., & Grosso, E. (2000). Active vision-based face authentication. *IEEE International Conference on Multimedia and Expo, ICME 2001, 4*(18), 299-314.

Veeravalli, A., Pan, W., Adhami, R., & Cox, P. (2005). *A tutorial on using hidden markov models for phoneme recognition.* Proceedings of the Thirty- Seventh Southeastern Symposium on System Theory, SSST 2005.

Wan, V., & Carmichael, J. (2005). Polynomial dynamic time warping kernel support vector machines for dysarthric speech recognition with sparse training data. *Interspeech'2005 – Eurospeech.* (pp. 3321-3324).

Wark, T., & Sridharan, S. (1998). A syntactic approach to automatic lip feature extraction for speaker identification. *IEEE International Conference on Acoustics, Speech and Signal Processing.* (pp. 3693-3696).

Wark, T., Sridharan, S., & Chandran, V. (1999). Robust speaker verification via fusion of speech and lip modalities. *IEEE International Conference on Acoustics, Speech and Signal Processing 1999. ICASSP 99.* (pp. 3061-3064).

Yamamoto, E., Nakamura, S., & Shikano, K. (1998). Lip movement synthesis from speech based on hidden markov models. *Journal of Speech Communication, 26*(1), 105-115.

Young, S., Kershaw, D., Odell, J., Ollason, D., Valtchev, V., & Woodland, P. (2000). *The htk book (for htk version 3.0) Http://htk.eng.cam.ac.uk/docs/docs.shtml.*

Zhang, X., Broun, C., Mersereau, R., & Clements, M. (2002). Automatic speechreading with applications to human-computer interfaces. *EURASIP Journal on Applied Signal Processing, 2002*(11), 1128-1247.

ENDNOTES

[1] Several phonemes can correspond to the same visual configuration. In fact, in most cases, *visemes* are not uniquely associated with a single phoneme.

[2] We assume that the direction of a line is either of the two normals of the line

[3] It is worth noting that there is a patch type whose motion can not be observed at all, the patches consisting of a constant gray value.

[4] 4 pixels width boundary are removed in the lip region.

[5] The output from the Viterbi decoder is logarithmic, and we used this for convenience.

[6] According to Lausanne protocol, the evaluation set is selected to produce client and impostor access scores, thereby to produce FAR and FRR curves. From these certain operation points (thresholds) are selected to be used latter on as thresholds on the test set for recognition.

About the Contributors

Liew, Alan Wee-Chung received his B.Eng. with first class honors in Electrical and Electronic Engineering from the University of Auckland, New Zealand, in 1993, and Ph.D. in Electronic Engineering from the University of Tasmania, Australia, in 1997. He worked as a Research Fellow and later a Senior Research Fellow at the Department of Electronic Engineering at the City University of Hong Kong. From 2004 to 2007, he was with the Department of Computer Science and Engineering, The Chinese University of Hong Kong as an Assistant Professor. In 2007, he joined the School of Information and Communication Technology, Griffith University as a Senior Lecturer. His current research interests include computer vision, medical imaging, pattern recognition and bioinformatics. He serves as a technical reviewer for many international conferences and journals such as IEEE Transactions, IEE proceedings, bioinformatics and computational biology. Dr. Liew is a senior member of the Institute of Electrical and Electronic Engineers (IEEE) since 2005, and his biography is listed in the Marquis Who's Who in the World and Marquis Who's Who in Science and Engineering.

Wang, Shilin received his B.Eng. degree in Electrical and Electronic Engineering from Shanghai Jiaotong University, Shanghai, China in 2001, and his Ph.D. degree in the Department of Computer Engineering and Information Technology, City University of Hong Kong in 2004. Since 2004, he has been with the School of Information Security Engineering, Shanghai Jiaotong University, where he is currently an Assistant Professor. His research interests include image processing and pattern recognition. His biography is listed in Marquis Who's Who in Science and Engineering.

*　　*　　*　　*　　*

Petar S. Aleksic received his B.S. degree in electrical engineering from the Belgrade University, Serbia, in 1999. He received his M.S. degree in electrical engineering from the Department of Electrical and Computer Engineering at Northwestern University in 2001, and his Ph.D. degree in electrical engineering at Northwestern University in 2004. He is currently a member of the Speech Research Group at Google, Inc in New York. His current research interests include audio-visual speech and speaker recognition, speech-to-video synthesis, computer vision, and pattern recognition.

Lynne E. Bernstein is head of the Communication Neuroscience Department at the House Ear Institute, Los Angeles, California, USA. Her research areas are visual speech perception, audiovisual speech perception, and non-speech audiovisual perception. She carries out behavioral, computational, and neuroimaging studies with hearing and prelingually deaf adult participants. An ongoing focus of her research is the perceptual and neural processing of optical phonetic information. She holds an adjunct Professor position in the Psychology Department and in the Neuroscience Graduate Program of the University of Southern California, Los Angeles, and she is an Adjunct Researcher at Gallaudet University, Washington, DC.

Josef Bigun received the MSc and PhD degrees from Linköping University, Sweden, in 1983 and 1988, respectively. In 1988, he joined the Swiss Federal Institute of Technology in Lausanne (EPFL), where he worked until 1998 as an "adjoint scientifique." He was elected as a professor to the Signal Analysis Chair, his current position, at Halmstad University and the Chalmers Institute of Technology, Sweden, in 1998. His professional interests include biometrics, texture analysis, motion analysis, and the understanding of biological processing of audiovisual signals, including human face recognition. He is an elected fellow of the IAPR and the IEEE. He has contributed to the organization of several international conferences as a cochair or track chair, including the initiation of the Audio and Video-Based Biometric Person Authentication (AVBPA) conference series and the organization of several International Conferences on Pattern Recognition (ICPRs) and International Conferences on Image Processing (ICIPs). He has been an editorial member of several journals in the areas of pattern recognition and image understanding.

Christian Bouvier received the M.Sc. degree in electrical engineering from the French Grenoble Institute of Technology (Grenoble) in signal and image processing in 2005. He is currently Ph.D. student at both GIPSA-lab in Grenoble and at Vision and Systems Laboratory of Laval University. His research interests involve facial feature detection and recognition.

Alice Caplier was born in 1968. She graduated from the Ecole Nationale Superieure des Ingenieurs Electriciens de Grenoble (ENSIEG) of the Institut National Polytechnique de Grenoble (INPG), France, in 1991. She obtained her Master's degree in Signal, Image, Speech Processing and Telecommunications in 1992 and her PhD from the INPG in 1995. Since 1997 she is teaching at the Ecole Nationale Superieure d'Electronique et de Radio electricite de Grenoble (ENSERG) of the INPG and is a permanent researcher at GIPSA-lab, Image and Signal Department in Grenoble. Her interest is on human motion analysis and interpretation. More precisely, she is working on the recognition of facial gestures (facial expressions and head motion) and the recognition of human postures.

H. Ertan Çetingül received the B.Sc. degree in Electrical & Electronics Engineering with a minor degree in General Management from Middle East Technical University, Ankara, Turkey, in 2003, and the M.Sc. degree in Electrical & Computer Engineering from Koç University, İstanbul, Turkey, in 2005. He is currently pursuing the Ph.D. degree in Biomedical Engineering at the Johns Hopkins University, Baltimore, MD. His research interests include computer vision, pattern recognition, medical image analysis and biometrics.

Pierre-Yves Coulon received the Ph.D. degree in Automatic Control from the Grenoble Institute of Technology -Grenoble INP-, France, in 1982. He has worked in different areas such as Target Tracking for biological applications and Architectures for Vision Machine. Since 1996, he is a Professor at Grenoble INP and GIPSA-Lab (Grenoble Image Speech Signal Automatic Control Laboratory). His current research interest is image processing and segmentation applied to face components detection and caracterization

Patrice Delmas completed his MEng and PhD degrees at the National Polytechnic Institute, Grenoble, France. He has been with the Department of Computer Science at the University of Auckland since 2001 and currently holds a Senior Lecturer position. His research interests are visual lip mapping, 3D face analysis and synthesis, 2D/3D face recognition, and theoretical and applied stereo-vision.

Marion Dohen received an engineering training in electronics and signal processing and completed a M. Sc. in cognitive sciences in 2002. She completed her PhD in 2005 at former Institut de la Communication Parlée (now Speech and Cognition Department, GIPSA-lab) on the multi-modality of prosodic focus. She then (2005-2006) worked as a post-doc at Advanced Telecommunications Research International, Kyoto on the neural correlates of auditory-visual perception of prosodic focus. She is now assistant professor at the Grenoble Institute of Technology and the Speech and Cognition Department (GIPSA-lab). She teaches signal processing and conducts research on multimodality, articulatory and neural correlates of the production and perception of prosody, interaction between speech and gestures in speech production and perception, and the physical and neural correlates of non-audible speech, in healthy subjects and schizophrenic patients.

Liang Dong received the B.Eng degree in Electronic Engineering from Beijing University of Aeronautics and Astronautics, China, in 1997, the M.Eng degree in Circuit and System from the Second Academy of China Aerospace in 2000, and the Ph.D degree in Electrical and Computer Engineering, National University of Singapore in 2005. From 2004 to 2007, he worked as a research fellow in the Institute for Infocomm Research in Singapore. Currently, he works as a senior scientist in the Healthcare department, Philips Research Asia – Shanghai, China. His research interests include speech recognition, bio-signal processing and sensor networks.

Engin Erzin received his Ph.D. degree, M.Sc. degree, and B.Sc. degree from the Bilkent University, Ankara, Turkey, in 1995, 1992 and 1990, respectively, all in Electrical Engineering. During 1995-1996, he was a postdoctoral fellow in Signal Compression Laboratory, University of California, Santa Barbara, CA. He joined Lucent Technologies in September 1996, and he was with the Consumer Products for one year as a Member of Technical Staff of the Global Wireless Products Group. From 1997 to 2001, he was with the Speech and Audio Technology Group of the Network Wireless Systems. Since January 2001, he is with the Electrical & Electronics Engineering and Computer Engineering Departments of Koç University, İstanbul, Turkey. His research interests include speech signal processing, pattern recognition and adaptive signal processing.

Maycel Isaac Faraj received the BSc and MSc (in 2003) degrees in computer science engineering from Halmstad University, Sweden, and the Licentiate of technology degree in signals and systems from Chalmers University of Technology, Sweden, in 2006. Since 2004, he has been a doctoral student in the Intelligent System Laboratory at Halmstad University. His research interests include biometrics, signal analysis, computer graphics, computer vision, and their applications in human-machine interaction.

Say Wei Foo received the B.Eng. degree in electrical engineering from the University of Newcastle, Australia in 1972, the M.Sc. degree in industrial and systems engineering from the University of Singapore in 1979, and the Ph.D. degree in electrical engineering from Imperial College, University of London in 1983. From 1973 to 1991, he was with the Electronics Division of the Defense Science Organization, Singapore, where he conducted research and carried out development work on communications equipment. From 1992 to 2001, he was the Associate Professor with the Department of Electrical and Computer Engineering, National University of Singapore. Since 2002, he has been with the School of Electrical and Electronic Engineering, Nanyang Technological University. He is a fellow of the ASEAN Academy of Engineering and Technology. His research interests include speech signal processing, audio signal processing and image processing.

Jorge Márquez works as an investigator at the National Autonomous University of Mexico. He is involved with several projects in applied science and engineering. His focus is on modelling and visualisation of boundary and interface related problems in biomedicine and physics.

Alfonso Gastelum holds a Bachelors degree in Physics from the University of Guadalajara and was awarded a Master in Science in Medical Physics from the National Autonomous University of Mexico in 2006. Since 2007 he has been a Doctoral student at the University of Auckland. His research areas are Image Analysis, Computational Biomechanics and 3D data modelling. His current work is focused on the construction of 3D models of human organs for medical applications.

Georgy Gimel'farb graduated from Kiev Polytechnic Institute, Ukraine, and received a PhD degree from the Institute of Cybernetics (Academy of Sciences of Ukraine), and a DSc (Eng) degree from the Higher Certifying Commission of the USSR (Moscow, Russia). After working in the Institute of Cybernetics, Dr. Gimel'farb joined the University of Auckland, New Zealand in 1997. He is currently an Associate Professor of Computer Science. His research is focussed on image analysis, computer vision, and statistical pattern recognition. His main contributions are in the areas of computational stereovision and probabilistic texture modelling and analysis. He has authored or co-authored more than 250 publications including three books, is a member of programme committees for a number of conferences and workshops, and is a track co-chair for the 19th International IAPR Conference on Pattern Recognition (December 2008, Tampa, Florida, USA).

Harold Hill received his training in experimental Psychology at University College London and completed a PhD at the University of Stirling. He has since worked in research both in the UK and at Advanced Telecommunications Research International, Kyoto before recently taking up a teaching post at the University of Wollongong. His research interests revolve around face processing, including the relationship between facial movement and speech. Other interests include birdwatching, wushu and trumpet.

Jason James holds Bachelors degrees in Science and Resource Engineering, and a Master of Science in Computer Science from the University of Auckland. Previous research areas have included mineral resource evaluation, and mine hazard management. Recent research has focused on wide-baseline stereovision, laser scanning technology, and mobile systems integrating GPS and digital imaging.

Jintao Jiang is a senior research engineer in the Communication Neuroscience Department at the House Ear Institute, Los Angeles, California, USA. His research is in the areas of audiovisual speech processing and perception, signal processing, image processing, and speech recognition by humans and machines. He is exploring questions about how humans perceive acoustic speech signals in combination with watching the talker's face and/or their hand gesture cues. He is also using his engineering knowledge to analyze acoustic and optical speech stimuli and to develop artificial talking heads and/or hand gestures (Cued Speech). He is also interested in exploring topics in audiovisual speech using functional magnetic resonance imaging and electrophysiology. He received his Ph.D. degree from the University of California at Los Angeles in 2003.

Aggelos K. Katsaggelos received the Diploma degree in electrical and mechanical engineering from the Aristotelian University of Thessaloniki, Thessaloniki, Greece, in 1979 and the M.S. and Ph.D. degrees both in electrical engineering from the Georgia Institute of Technology, Atlanta, Georgia, in 1981 and 1985, respectively. In 1985 he joined the Department of Electrical Engineering and Computer Science at Northwestern University, Evanston, IL, where he is currently a professor. He is also the Director of the Motorola Center for Seamless Communications and a member of the Academic Affiliate Staff, Department of Medicine, at Evanston Hospital. During the 1986-1987 academic year he was an assistant professor at Polytechnic University, Department of Electrical Engineering and Computer Science, Brooklyn, NY. His current research interests include multimedia signal processing and communications, computer vision, pattern recognition, and DNA signal processing. He is the editor of Digital Image Restoration (Springer-Verlag 1991), co-author of Rate-Distortion Based Video Compression (Kluwer 1997), co-editor of Recovery Techniques for Image and Video Compression and Transmission, (Kluwer 1998), and co-author of Super-Resolution of Images and Video (Morgan & Claypool Publishers 2007) and Joint Source-Channel Video Transmission (Morgan & Claypool Publishers 2007).

Constantine Kotropoulos was born in Kavala, Greece in 1965. He received the Diploma degree with honors in Electrical Engineering in 1988 and the PhD degree in Electrical & Computer Engineering in 1993, both from the Aristotle University of Thessaloniki. He is currently an Associate Professor in the Department of Informatics at the Aristotle University of Thessaloniki. He has co-authored 33 journal papers, 142 conference papers, and contributed 6 chapters to edited books in his areas of expertise. He is co-editor of the book "Nonlinear Model-Based Image/Video Processing and Analysis" (J. Wiley and Sons, 2001). His current research interests include audio, speech, and language processing; signal processing; pattern recognition; multimedia information retrieval; biometric authentication techniques, and human-centered multimodal computer interaction. Prof. Kotropoulos was a scholar of the State Scholarship Foundation of Greece and the Bodossaki Foundation. He is a senior member of the IEEE and a member of EURASIP, IAPR, ISCA, and the Technical Chamber of Greece.

Dinesh Kant Kumar received the B.E. degree in electrical engineering from the Indian Institute of Technology (IIT), Madras, India, in 1982, and the Ph.D. degree from IIT, Delhi, India, in 1990. He has worked in the engineering industry for over ten years in various capacities. Since 1996, he has been an Academic with RMIT University, Melbourne, Australia. His research interests include iterative signal processing, computer vision, and intelligent systems for applications such as biometrics, human computer interface, and helping the disabled.

S.Y. Kung is a Professor at Department of Electrical Engineering in Princeton University. His research areas include VLSI array processors, system modeling and identification, neural networks, wireless communication, sensor array processing, multimedia signal processing, bioinformatics data mining and biometric authentication. He was a founding member of several Technical Committees (TC) of the IEEE Signal Processing Society, and was appointed as the first Associate Editor in VLSI Area (1984) and later the first Associate Editor in Neural Network (1991) for the IEEE Transactions on Signal Processing. He has been a Fellow of IEEE since 1988. He served as a Member of the Board of Governors of the IEEE Signal Processing Society (1989-1991). Since 1990, he has been the Editor-In-Chief of the Journal of VLSI Signal Processing Systems. He was a recipient of IEEE Signal Processing Society's Technical Achievement Award for the contributions on "parallel processing and neural network algorithms for signal processing" (1992); a Distinguished Lecturer of IEEE Signal Processing Society (1994); a recipient of IEEE Signal Processing Society's Best Paper Award for his publication on principal component neural networks (1996); and a recipient of the IEEE Third Millennium Medal (2000). He has authored and co-authored more than 400 technical publications and numerous textbooks including "VLSI and Modern Signal Processing", Prentice-Hall (1985), ``VLSI Array Processors'', Prentice-Hall (1988); ``Digital Neural Networks'', Prentice-Hall (1993) ; ``Principal Component Neural Networks'', John-Wiley (1996); and ``Biometric Authentication: A Machine Learning Approach'', Prentice-Hall (2004).

Lau, Wing-Hong received the B.Sc. and Ph.D. degrees in electrical and electronic engineering from University of Portsmouth in 1985 and 1989, respectively. In 1990, he joined the City University of Hong Kong, where he is currently an Associate Professor in the Department of Electronic Engineering. His current research interests are in the area of digital signal processing, digital audio engineering, visual speech signal processing. Dr. Lau was the recipient of the IEEE Third Millennium Medal. He served as the Chairman of the IEEE Hong Kong Section in 2005. He was the Chairman of the IEEE Hong Kong Joint Chapter on CAS/COM for 1997 and 1998. He was the Financial Chair of the TENCON 2006, and the Registration Co-Chair of the ISCAS 1997 and ICASSP 2003.

Leung, Shu-Hung received his first class honor B.Sc. degree in electronics from the Chinese University of Hong Kong in 1978, and his M.Sc. and Ph.D. degrees, both in electrical engineering, from the University of California at Irvine in 1979 and 1982, respectively. From 1982 to 1987, he was an Assistant Professor with the University of Colorado, Boulder. Since 1987, he has been with the Department of Electronic Engineering at City University of Hong Kong, where he is currently an Associate Head. His current research interest is in digital communications, adaptive modulation, OFDM, and adaptive signal processing. He has served as an organizing committee member for 2003 ICASSP and a number of international conferences and as a reviewer for IEEE Transactions, IEE Proceedings, and Electronics Letters. He is listed in Marquis Who's Who in Science and Engineering and Marquis Who's Who in the World.

Marc Liévin received an Electrical Engineering degree from the National Polytechnic Institute, Grenoble, France, in 1996 and completed his PhD in 2000. While working as a Research Associate in medical imaging at the Caesar research centre in Bonn, Germany, he contributed as software lead to establish a joint venture in 3D visualisation with Sirona. In 2007, he joined Softimage Co., Montréal, Canada, working on non-linear video editing software. His research interests are in the area of video communication with emphasis on real-time, temporal and spatial, image segmentation and filtering.

Haibo Li is a full Professor in Signal Processing in the Department of Applied Physics and Electronics (TFE), Umeå University, Sweden. He received the Technical Doctor degree in Information Theory from Linköping University, Sweden, in 1993. His doctoral thesis dealt with advanced facial image analysis and synthesis techniques for low bit rate video. Dr. Li got the "Nordic Best PhD Thesis Award" in 1994.

In 1997 Dr. Li was awarded the title of "Docent in Image Coding". From 1990 to 1993 he was a teaching assistant of digital video at Linköping University. After graduation Dr. Li joined the technical faculty of Linköping University first as an Assistant Professor and then promoted to an Associate Professor in 1998. During his period at Linköping University he developed advanced image and video compression algorithms, including extremely low bit rate video compression, 3D video transmission, and tele-operation and tele-presence. After joining Umeå University as a full professor in 1999, he is now directing the Digital Media Lab, Umeå Center for Interaction Technology (UCIT), Umeå University, and working on advanced Human, Thing and Information interaction techniques. Prof. Li has been chairing sections at relevant international conferences and was actively involving in MPEG activities in low bit rate video compression. He has contributed to several EU projects, like VIDAS, SCALAR, INTERFACE and MUCHI. He has published more than 100 technical papers including chapters in books and holds six international patents as the first inventor in multimedia area. Prof. Li has supervised several PhD students. He is also active in commercialization of his research works. Four companies have been spun-off from Digital Media Lab and one of them was listed in the London Stock Market, 2005.

Li Liu received the B.S. degree in Biochemistry from Nanjing University, China in 1986, and the degree of technical licentiate in Applied Physics from Linköping University, Sweden, 1994. In 1997 she received her PhD degree in Biophysics from Göteberg University, Sweden. She is an active researcher in the department of Applied Physics and Electronics, Umeå University, Sweden. Dr. Liu was awarded "Wallenbergs Excellent Woman Researcher", by Knut och Alice Wallenbergs Foundation, 1999. Her research interests include tactile video for visually impaired persons, computer assessment of infant pain and e-health.

Hélène Lœvenbruck received an engineering training in electronics, signal processing, and computer science and obtained a M. Sc. in cognitive sciences. After her PhD at former Institut de la Communication Parlée (ICP, now Speech and Cognition Department, GIPSA-lab) on articulatory control, she was assistant lecturer and obtained a second M. Sc. in phonetics. She then spent a post-doctoral year at the Department of Linguistics of the Ohio State University in the United States. She became CNRS Research Associate at ICP in 1998. Her research areas include the neural circuits of deixis (pointing), the acoustic, articulatory and perceptual correlates of prosody, language acquisition and the physical correlates of non-audible speech, in healthy subjects and schizophrenic patients. She was awarded a bronze medal from the CNRS in 2006. She is editor-in-chief of *In Cognito - Cahiers Romans de Sciences Cognitives*, an international quadrilingual journal of Cognitive Science.

Patrick Lucey received his B.Eng (Hons) degree in Electrical Engineering from the University of Southern Queensland, Australia, in 2003 and his PhD degree from the Queensland University of Technology, Brisbane, Australia in 2008. He is currently a Post-Doctoral Research Fellow within the Speech, Audio, Image and Video Technology Laboratory at QUT. In 2006, he was a research intern within the Human Language Technology at IBM T.J. Watson Research Centre in Yorktown Heights in New York, USA. He also was a visiting scholar in the Robotics Institute at Carnegie Mellon University, Pittsburgh, USA in 2007. Also in 2007, his paper on "pose-invariant lipreading" was awarded the best student paper at the "INTERSPEECH" conference. His areas of research include, audio-visual automatic speech recognition, emotion recognition, computer vision, pattern recognition and human-computer-interaction.

Dr. Eric Petajan is the Chief Technology Officer of VectorMAX Corporation, which provides comprehensive solutions for the creation and delivery of natural and synthetic video, via any network, to both PCs and mobile devices. Eric joined VectorMAX from face2face animation, where he was chief scientist and founder. Prior to founding face2face in 2000, as a Lucent Technologies venture, Eric was a distinguished Bell Labs researcher. From 1984-2000, his developments in the areas of facial motion capture, high-definition TV, and interactive graphics systems were widely recognized. Eric was the chairman of the MPEG-4 Face and Body Animation (FBA) group, and was a leader in the development of HDTV technology and standards that led to the formation of the U.S. HDTV Grand Alliance.

Eric received a PhD in electrical engineering in 1984 and an MS in physics from the University of Illinois, where he built the first automatic lip-reading system.

Ioannis Pitas received the Diploma in Electrical Engineering in 1980 and the PhD degree in Electrical Engineering in 1985, both from the Aristotle University of Thessaloniki, Greece. Since 1994 he has been a Professor at the Department of Informatics, University of Thessaloniki, Greece. From 1980 to 1993 he served as Scientific Assistant, Lecturer, Assistant Professor, and Associate Professor in the Department of Electrical and Computer Engineering at the same University.

He has published over 607 papers, contributed in 27 books and authored, co-authored, edited, co-edited 7 books in his areas of interest. The number of citations to his work by third authors is 3600+. His H-index is 30+. Prof. Pitas has co-organized 11 special sessions in conferences, 7 special issues in scientific journals. He is/was editor in 20 journals. He was member of the program committee of more than 165 scientific conferences and workshops. He was reviewer in 51 scientific journals, 150 conferences, 30 R&D funding agencies and 4 publishers. His current interests are in the areas of human centered interfaces, digital image/video processing, multimedia signal processing, emotional intelligence, and computer vision.

Gerasimos Potamianos received his Diploma degree from the National Technical University of Athens, Greece in 1988, and the M.S.E. and Ph.D. degrees in Electrical and Computer Engineering from the Johns Hopkins University, Baltimore, Maryland, in 1990 and 1994, respectively. During 1994-1996 he has been a Postdoctoral Fellow with the Center for Language and Speech Processing, and from 1996 to 1999 a Senior Member of Technical Staff with the Speech and Image Processing Services Laboratory at AT&T Labs-Research. In 1999, he joined the Human Language Technologies department at the IBM T.J. Watson Research Center as a Research Staff Member, where he is currently manager of the Multimodal Conversational Solutions Department. His research interests are multimodal speech processing and human-computer interaction with particular emphasis on audio-visual speech processing, automatic speech recognition, multimedia signal processing and fusion, as well as computer vision for human detection and tracking. He has published over 75 articles and has six patents granted.

Shafiq ur Réhman received his M.S. degree in 2004 from Department of Computer Science, Umeå University, Sweden. Currently he is pursuing his PhD degree in Applied Electronics at Department of Applied Physics and Electronics, Umeå University, Sweden. His research interests are computer vision, multimodal signal processing, interaction technology, vibrotactile coding and related applications.

Derek J. Shiell received his Bachelor of Science degree from the Northwestern University Department of Electrical and Computer Engineering in June 2004. He received his Masters of Science from the

Dept. of Electrical Engineering and Computer Science at Northwestern University in June 2007. He is currently working in the Algorithms Group at Epson Research & Development on facial feature localization and tracking, and face analysis as well other computer vision related projects. He is pursuing his doctorate degree part-time through the Image and Video Processing Laboratory at Northwestern University under Professor Aggelos K. Katsaggelos with emphasis in the fields of audio-visual automatic speech and speaker recognition, audio-visual biometrics, face alignment/tracking, and facial feature extraction. His other research interests include: structure from motion, multimedia processing, and pattern recognition.

Sridha Sridharan has a BSc (Electrical Engineering) degree and obtained a MSc (Communication Engineering) degree from the University of Manchester Institute of Science and Technology (UMIST), UK and a PhD degree in the area of Signal Processing from University of New South Wales, Australia. He is a Senior Member of the Institute of Electrical and Electronic Engineers - IEEE (USA). He is currently with the Queensland University of Technology (QUT) where he is a full Professor in the School of Engineering Systems. Professor Sridharan is the Deputy Director of the Information Security Institute and the Leader of the Research Program in Speech, Audio, Image and Video Technologies at QUT. In 1997, he was the recipient of the Award of Outstanding Academic of QUT in the area of Research and Scholarship. In 2006 he received the QUT Faculty Award for Outstanding Contribution to Research.

Sebastien Stillittano was born in Saint-Martin-d'Heres (France) in 1979 and is graduated from the Grenoble's ENSERG (School of Electronics and Radioelectricity) engineering school since 2002. He is currently a PhD student at the laboratory GIPSA of Grenoble within the Images and Signal Department (DIS) and in collaboration with the start-up VESALIS of Clermont-Ferrand. The laboratory GIPSA works on the automatic facial feature segmentation for multimedia applications for many years and in particular on the outer lip contour extraction. Sebastien's research activities include lip segmentation and tracking, and he is focusing on the inner lip contour in still images and video sequences for lip reading applications.

A. Murat Tekalp received his Ph.D. in Electrical, Computer, and Systems Engineering from Rensselaer Polytechnic Institute (RPI), Troy, NY in 1984. He has been with Eastman Kodak Company, Rochester, NY, from December 1984 to June 1987, and with the University of Rochester, Rochester, NY, from July 1987 to June 2005, where he was promoted to Distinguished University Professor. Since June 2001, he is a Professor at Koç University, İstanbul, Turkey. His research interests are in the area of digital image and video processing, including video compression and streaming, motion-compensated video filtering for high-resolution, video segmentation, object tracking, content-based video analysis and summarization, multi-camera surveillance video processing, and protection of digital content.
Prof. Tekalp is a Fellow of IEEE and a member of Turkish National Academy of Sciences. He received the TUBITAK Science Award (highest scientific award in Turkey) in 2004. At present, he is the Editor-in-Chief of the EURASIP journal Signal Processing: Image Communication published by Elsevier. Prof. Tekalp holds seven US patents. He is a project evaluator and reviewer for the European Commission and European Research Council.

Louis H. Terry received his B.S. from the Department of Electrical Engineering and Computer Science at Northwestern University in Evanston, IL in 2005 and his M.S. degree in 2007 with his thesis entitled "Ergodic Hidden Markov Models for Visual-Only Isolated Digit Recognition." He is currently working towards his doctoral degree under the supervision of Prof. Aggelos K. Katsaggelos in the area of audio-visual signal processing. His research focus is on the contextual modeling of acoustic, visual, and linguistic environments and their effects in the context of audio-visual automatic speech recognition. His research interests also include computer vision, and its applications; general multi-stream information fusion; image and video compression; and stochastic modeling, pattern recognition, and signal analysis in financial and economic contexts.

Hans Weghorn is the head of Mechatronics Department at BA University of Cooperative Education, Stuttgart , Germany. Since 1995, Prof. Weghorn has been working in HCI-related applications and research such as voice control, speech recognition, and efficient use of constraint devices including personalization and location-based services. These activities cover product development and product engineering for consumer applications in industry and investigations with strong fundamental scope in university research. E. g., research on voice control was not only limited to audio capture, but it also covered investigations on bio-signal and video analysis.

Alexander Woodward is a doctoral candidate in the Department of Computer Science at the University of Auckland, New Zealand. He holds Bachelor of Technology and Master of Science degrees from the University of Auckland. His current research centres on the evaluation of stereo reconstruction algorithms applied to human faces and their application in a 3D video scanner system. Alexander is a recipient of the Top Achiever Doctoral Scholarship from the TEC of New Zealand. His previous research has focussed on facial animation, 3D scanner design, and 3D reconstruction algorithms such as binocular and photometric stereo.

Wai Chee Yau received the B. E. degree in electronic engineering from the Multimedia University, Malaysia, in 2004. She has worked as an embedded software engineer at Robert Bosch Malaysia in 2004. Since 2005, she has been a PhD candidate in the School of Electrical and Computer Engineering, RMIT University, Melbourne Australia. Her research interests include image processing, motion analysis, pattern recognition and visual speech recognition.

Yücel Yemez received the B.S. degree from Middle East Technical University, Ankara, Turkey, in 1989, and the M.S. and Ph.D. degrees from Boğaziçi University, Istanbul, Turkey, respectively in 1992 and 1997, all in Electrical Engineering. From 1997 to 2000, he was a postdoctoral researcher in the Image and Signal Processing Department of Télécom Paris (Ecole Nationale Supérieure des Télécommunications). Currently he is an assistant professor of the Computer Engineering Department at Koç University, İstanbul, Turkey. His current research is focused on various fields of computer vision and graphics.

Index